Law in the Schools

WILLIAM D. VALENTE
Villanova University

CHRISTINA M. VALENTE
Villanova University

PEARSON

Merrill
Prentice Hall

Upper Saddle River, New Jersey
Columbus, Ohio

Library of Congress Cataloging-in-Publication Data

Valente, William D.
    Law in the schools / William D. Valente, Christina M. Valente—6th ed.
        p. cm.
    Includes bibliographical references and index.
    ISBN 0-13-114155-4
        1. Educational law and legislation–United States. I. Valente, Christina M. II. Title.
    KF4119.V28 2005
    344.73'07—dc22   2004044516

Vice President and Executive Publisher: Jeffery W. Johnston
Executive Editor: Debra A. Stollenwerk
Editorial Assistant: Mary Morrill
Associate Editor: Ben M. Stephen
Production Editor: Linda Hillis Bayma
Design Coordinator: Diane C. Lorenzo
Cover Designer: Jeff Vanik
Production Manager: Pamela D. Bennett
Director of Marketing: Ann Castel Davis
Marketing Manager: Darcy Betts Prybella
Marketing Coordinator: Tyra Poole

This book was set in Palatino by Carlisle Communications, Ltd. It was printed and bound by R.R. Donnelley & Sons Company. The cover was printed by R.R. Donnelley & Sons Company.

Pearson Education Ltd.   Pearson Education Australia Pty. Limited
Pearson Education Singapore Pte. Ltd.   Pearson Education North Asia Ltd.
Pearson Education Canada, Ltd.   Pearson Educación de Mexico, S.A. de C.V.
Pearson Education—Japan   Pearson Education Malaysia Pte. Ltd.

10 9 8 7 6 5 4 3 2 1
ISBN: 0-13-114155-4

PUBLISHER'S NOTE:
NEW TO THIS EDITION

This new edition contains more than 20 new decisions by the U.S. Supreme Court and more than 14 significant new decisions by the federal Courts of Appeal. For your convenience, each of these has been included and identified in the new Appendix 3, Select Table of Cases. This edition also contains expanded coverage of many topics, including:

- School district liability related to the control, use, and access to school property by students, teachers, and outside groups.
- "Zero tolerance" policies and school security and disciplinary measures, including those limiting school-site speech to reduce school violence, drug trafficking, and sexual abuse.
- Legislation and regulation of charter schools and home schooling as their prevalence grows.
- Government assistance to religiously affiliated schools, including Supreme Court approval of the use of government-employed teachers and government-supplied computers in religious schools.
- Growing use of computer and In]ternet technology in distance learning and the legality of packaged electronic commercial and educational materials in public school classrooms.
- New case law on the Family Educational Rights and Privacy Act (FERPA).
- Student and teacher speech issues and suspicionless searches, including urinalysis.
- School officials' responsibility for parental "Do not resuscitate" orders.
- Rights of students with disabilities under the 1997 IDEA amendments and the impact of the Supreme Court's 1999 decision on the provision of "related services."
- School district or supervisor liability for student-on-student sexual harassment, teacher sexual abuse of students, and student suicides.
- Unresolved divisions among the states on the validity of tuition vouchers.

⌘ PREFACE

This new edition is required by sea changes in statutory and case law that have occurred in the past few years. New legislation and judicial rulings have displaced,
overturned, or substantially altered the law reported in the prior edition. These
changes represent new trends regarding the control and uses of school property,
with correlative changes in the rights and liabilities of school managers, teachers,
students, parents, and community groups. They also herald divergent movements
in school law. On one hand, school authorities have been given broader leeway to
adopt strict security and disciplinary measures and to restrain certain forms of
school-site speech in order to reduce school violence, drug trafficking, and sexual
abuse. To some extent, the expansion of teacher and student liberties following the
"rights" revolution of the 1960s and 1970s has given way to "zero tolerance" policies. On the other hand, school authorities risk expanded liability for infringing on
the civil rights of students and teachers, especially in the areas of sex abuse and of
race, gender, and disability discrimination. The latest Supreme Court opinions on
topics of sexual orientation and the uses of racial criteria for employment or other
benefits are as noteworthy for the new questions they raise as for their guidance on
old questions.

Legislation and regulation for private schools, charter schools, and home
schooling also continue to grow. Courts and legislatures are still attempting to
catch up with issues presented by the rapid growth of charter schools and home
schooling. With regard to religiously affiliated schools, the latest Supreme Court
decisions revise and in some instances reverse older constitutional law regarding
some forms of government assistance to those schools.

The scope of these changes and the need for a fresh study of school laws are
reflected in the cases listed in the Select Table of Cases. There are more than 20 new
decisions by the U.S. Supreme Court and more than 14 significant new decisions
by the federal Courts of Appeal. Some of those appeals are, at this writing, pending review and decision by the Supreme Court.

The use of computer and Internet technology for in-house and distance learning projects raises new problems as well as new opportunities. The *Dawson* case in
Chapter 1 addresses the legality of electronic transmission of combined commercial and educational materials into public schools. The drive to wire all schools for
computerized education may have also influenced the Supreme Court's approval
of state loans of state-purchased computers to religiously affiliated schools.

Chapter 3 traces the latest constitutional rulings on religious speech and activities at public school sites and events by students and community groups. New
materials on employment discrimination in Chapters 5, 6, and 9 include cases that

significantly alter or clarify the law on gender, disability, and age discrimination. Chapter 6 presents cases that delimit constitutional protection for teacher speech and suspicionless teacher searches, including urinalysis testing.

Kindred issues are revised in Chapter 7 with regard to student speech and searches. One first-of-its-kind case explores the enforcement of parental "do not resuscitate" orders, which pit school obligations to aid an afflicted student against the rights of parents to control medical treatment of their children. Chapter 7 also reports the changes wrought by the 1997 IDEA amendments on the rights of students with handicaps and the 1999 Supreme Court decision on the mandatory school provision of "related services" to such students.

Chapter 8 updates the interpretation of overlapping but uncoordinated discrimination statutes. The new lead cases on school district or supervisor liability for student-on-student sexual harassment under Title IX (*Davis*, Chapter 7), for teacher sexual abuse of students (*Doe*, Chapter 8), and for student suicides (*Hasenfus*, Chapter 7) are particularly significant. The *Walker* case in Chapter 8 provides a good review of the untidy state of the law regarding the allowance of alternative remedies for violations of more than one civil rights statute.

Chapter 9 updates the legal status of home education, private schools, and charter schools in the various states, including Supreme Court decisions on the use of government-employed teachers and government-supplied equipment in religious schools and the divisions among the states on the validity of tuition vouchers.

This edition continues the linked themes of prior editions—that law and educational practice interact in response to changing needs, and that educational decisions inevitably involve elements of both educational policy and of law. Accordingly, this text aims to equip educators with the information and insights that will enable them to identify and minimize potential legal problems, and to recognize instances where the unsettled law merits consultation with higher administrative authority or legal counsel.

CHAPTER ORGANIZATION

This edition slightly modifies the topical organization of the preceding edition. The major change involves the reorganization of teacher employment discrimination to an expanded Chapter 6. Otherwise, the topical coverage of each chapter is similar to that of the prior edition. As indicated in the detailed outline at the beginning of each chapter, some section headings have been reworded to provide more concrete specification of covered subjects. We have omitted from the reproduced case opinions the case footnotes and dissenting opinions unless otherwise expressly indicated.

As explained in Chapter 1, we have employed a simplified, nontechnical form of citation for cases cited in the text and footnotes, in order to indicate the essential source and date of each cited case without burdening the reader with the full technical form of case citation. For ease of reference, statutes and cases of major interest are collected in the Appendices, and technical legal terms are explained in the Glossary, which precedes the Index.

ACKNOWLEDGMENTS

In completing this edition, we remain indebted to the many persons, too numerous to list here, who provided indispensable support for prior editions as well as this edition. We are particularly grateful to the following persons for their encouragement and assistance in preparation of this sixth edition. To Dean Mark Sargent of the Villanova University School of Law, and his Associate Deans, Doris Del Tosto Brogan and William James, we owe special thanks for providing invaluable research assistants and facilities at the Villanova law library. Without those resources, the completion of an accurate manuscript would have been substantially delayed. In this regard, our student research assistant, Julie Pfaff, also provided enthusiastic and reliable checks of law sources.

At Merrill/Prentice Hall, our very special thanks go to Debbie Stollenwerk, senior editor; Ben Stephen, associate editor; Linda Bayma, production editor; and Lorretta Palagi, copy editor, for direction and assistance through every stage of this edition's preparation.

Finally, we are grateful to the following reviewers for their criticisms and comments without which we might well have overlooked or given inadequate treatment to significant points of interest: Brian E. Boettcher, Minnesota State University, Mankato; Larry W. Hughes, University of Houston; Louise L. MacKay, East Tennessee State University; Ralph D. Mawdsley, Cleveland State University; and Robert S. Ramsey, Troy State University–Phenix City.

William D. Valente
Christina M. Valente
Villanova University

EDUCATOR LEARNING CENTER: AN INVALUABLE ONLINE RESOURCE

Merrill Education and the Association for Supervision and Curriculum Development (ASCD) invite you to take advantage of a new online resource, one that provides access to the top research and proven strategies associated with ASCD and Merrill— the Educator Learning Center. At **www.EducatorLearningCenter.com** you will find resources that will enhance your students' understanding of course topics and of current educational issues, in addition to being invaluable for further research.

How the Educator Learning Center will Help Your Students Become Better Teachers

With the combined resources of Merrill Education and ASCD, you and your students will find a wealth of tools and materials to better prepare them for the classroom.

Research

- More than 600 articles from the ASCD journal *Educational Leadership* discuss everyday issues faced by practicing teachers.
- A direct link on the site to Research Navigator™ gives students access to many of the leading education journals, as well as extensive content detailing the research process.
- Excerpts from Merrill Education texts give your students insights on important topics of instructional methods, diverse populations, assessment, classroom management, technology, and refining classroom practice.

Classroom Practice

- Hundreds of lesson plans and teaching strategies are categorized by content area and age range.
- Case studies and classroom video footage provide virtual field experience for student reflection.
- Computer simulations and other electronic tools keep your students abreast of today's classrooms and current technologies.

Look into the Value of Educator Learning Center Yourself

A four-month subscription to Educator Learning Center is $25 but is **FREE** when used in conjunction with this text. To obtain free passcodes for your students, simply contact your local Merrill/Prentice Hall sales representative, and your representative will give you a special ISBN to give your bookstore when ordering your textbooks. To preview the value of this website to you and your students, please go to **www.EducatorLearningCenter.com** and click on "Demo."

BRIEF CONTENTS

CHAPTER 1   EDUCATION UNDER THE AMERICAN LEGAL SYSTEM   2

CHAPTER 2   PUBLIC SCHOOLS: PROGRAMS AND SERVICES   39

CHAPTER 3   PUBLIC SCHOOLS: RELIGIOUS CONTROVERSIES   62

CHAPTER 4   TORT LIABILITY UNDER STATE LAW   114

CHAPTER 5   PROFESSIONAL EMPLOYEES: EMPLOYMENT RIGHTS
              AND OBLIGATIONS   154

CHAPTER 6   PROFESSIONAL EMPLOYEES: CIVIL RIGHTS   191

CHAPTER 7   STUDENT RIGHTS AND DISCIPLINE   282

CHAPTER 8   THE PYRAMID OF DISCRIMINATION REMEDIES   386

CHAPTER 9   PRIVATE EDUCATION: ALTERNATIVES TO PUBLIC SCHOOLS 426

APPENDIX 1   SELECTED PROVISIONS—CONSTITUTION OF THE
              UNITED STATES   494

APPENDIX 2   PRINCIPAL FEDERAL LAWS AFFECTING EQUAL OPPORTUNITY
              IN EDUCATION   497

APPENDIX 3   SELECT TABLE OF CASES   500

              GLOSSARY   506

              INDEX   511

☙ CONTENTS

CHAPTER 1   EDUCATION UNDER THE AMERICAN LEGAL SYSTEM   **2**

The Nature of School Law   4
The Relation of Law, Politics, and Education   4
   Contests for Control   4
   School Violence and Crime   5
Legal Interests of Participants   6
   Government Interests   7
      The States   7
      The National Government   7
      Supremacy of Federal Law   8
   Individual Interests   8
      Students and Parents   8
      School Authorities, Teachers, and Staff   8
      Citizen Interests   9
The American Legal System—Structure and Sources of Law   9
   Constitutional Law—The Basic Charter   9
   Statutory Law—The Role of Legislatures   10
   Administrative Law—The Role of Administrators   10
      Scope of Administrative Authority   11
      Legislative Delegation Issues   11
      Administrative Structure of Public Education 12
   Case Law—The Role of Courts   15
      Structure and Jurisdiction of American Courts 16
      Judge-Made Law—Common Law and Equity Law   19
      Access to Court Relief   19
      Court Review of Administrative Decisions   21
   Note on Law References and Citations   23
      Constitutions   24
      Statutes and Regulations   24
      Case Citations   25
      Professional Literature   27
Chapter Discussion Questions   27

Cases
1.1 Dawson v. East Side Union High School District, 34 Cal. Rptr. 2d 108 (1994)   29
1.2 Conover v. Board of Education of Nebo School District, 267 P.2d 768
      (Utah 1954)   33

Endnotes   36

CHAPTER 2   PUBLIC SCHOOLS: PROGRAMS AND SERVICES   **39**

Attendance and Admission   40
    Compulsory Attendance Laws   40
    Admission Standards   42
        Residence   42
        Immunization and Health Requirements   42
        Age Requirements   43
    School Assignments   43
Studies Program   44
    Curriculum   44
        Prescribed Courses and Activities   44
        Textbooks and Reading Materials   45
    Extracurricular Activities   46
        Student Clubs   46
        Interscholastic Athletic Associations   47
    Placement, Grading, Promotion, and Graduation   47
Student Services   48
    School Transportation   48
        Distance Limits   48
        Bus Routes   49
    Fees and Charges   49

Chapter Discussion Questions   49

Cases
2.1 Board of Education v. Pico, 457 U.S. 853 (1982)   51
2.2 Cardiff v. Bismark Public School District, 263 N.W.2d 105 (N.D. 1978)   54

Endnotes   59

CHAPTER 3   PUBLIC SCHOOLS: RELIGIOUS CONTROVERSIES   **62**

Constitutional Constraints on Public School Actions   64
    The Establishment of Religion Clause—Bar to Promoting Religion   65
    The Free Exercise Clause—Bar to Burdening Religion   68
    The Freedom of Speech Clause—Bar to Limiting Speech   68
    Community Uses of School Facilities   69
    State Law Constraints   71
Typical School–Religion Controversies   72
    Prayer, Bible Reading, and Meditation   72
        Classroom Exercises   72
        Nonclassroom Prayer and Religious Activities   73

Religious Art—Holiday Commemorations 76
School Excusals for Religious Purposes 77
Religion-Related Courses and Programs 79
Evolution 79
The Bible as History and Literature 79
Sex Education 79
Course Textbooks and Class Readings 81
Other Religious Objections and Exemptions 82
Flag Salutes 82
Dress and Conduct Requirements 82
Immunization 82
Public School Services to Nonpublic Schools and Students 82
Direct School–Church Dealings 83
Public School Uses of Church Property 83
Church Uses of Public School Property 83

Chapter Discussion Questions 84

Cases
3.1 Good News Club v. Milford Central School, 121 S. Ct. 2093 (2001) 85
3.2 Santa Fe Independent School District v. Jane Doe, 120 S. Ct. 2266 (2000) 91
3.3 Adler v. Duval County School Board, 250 F3d 1330 (11th Cir. 2001) 95
3.4 Lee v. Weisman, 112 S. Ct. 2649 (1992) 98
3.5 Brown v. Hot, Sexy and Safer Productions, Inc., 68 F.3d 525
    (1st Cir. 1995) 101

Endnotes 110

CHAPTER 4   TORT LIABILITY UNDER STATE LAW   114

General Principles of State Tort Law 116
Duty of Care Requirement 117
The Causation Requirement 118
General Defenses 118
Privileged Conduct 119
Victim Fault 119
Written Waivers of Tort Claims 120
School District Vicarious Liability 120
Common Tort Situations 121
Corporal Punishment 121
Constitutionality 121
When Corporal Punishment Is Not Tortious 121
Premises Liability 123
Standard of Care for Premises Safety 123
Examples of Premises Liability 124
Supervision Liability 124
When the Duty of Supervision Arises 124
General vs. Special or Direct Supervision 125

Foreseeable Criminal Conduct 125
Circumstances Affecting Degree of Supervision 125
Defamation (Libel or Slander) 130
Educational Malpractice 131
Limitations on Tort Recovery 132
Governmental Immunity 132
Nuisance Exceptions 133
Governmental vs. Proprietary Functions 134
Discretionary vs. Ministerial Functions 134
Personal Immunity 136
Notice and Time Limits and Dollar Caps 136
Statutes of Limitations 137
Dollar Recovery Limits 137

Chapter Discussion Questions 137

Cases
4.1 Grant v. Lake Oswego School District No. 7, 515 P.2d 947
(Or. App. 1973) 138
4.2 Soper v. Hoben, 195 F.3d 845 (6th Cir. 1999) 140
4.3 Ayala v. Philadelphia Board of Public Education, 305 A.2d 877
(Pa. 1973) 142

Endnotes 145

CHAPTER 5   PROFESSIONAL EMPLOYEES: EMPLOYMENT RIGHTS
AND OBLIGATIONS   154

Statutory and Contract Terms 156
Employment Rights and Duties 156
Employment Eligibility 156
State Certification 156
Personal Conditions 158
Performance Issues 159
School Assignments 159
Implied Duties 160
Evaluations and Ratings 160
Demotions 161
Job Security 162
Nontenured Teachers—Nonrenewal 162
Tenured Teachers 163
Collectively Bargained Contracts 165
Bargaining Units—Union Representation 165
Bargainable Matters 166
Dispute Resolution 168
Suspension and Termination 170
Resignation and Abandonment 170

Reductions in Force (RIF)   171
    Grounds for RIF   171
    Order of Release and Recall   172
Discharge for Cause   172
    Grounds for Discharge   173
    Remedies for Wrongful Discharge   177

Case
5.1 Poole v. Little Valley Central School District, 472 N.Y.S.2d 226 (1984)   178
Endnotes   180

CHAPTER 6   PROFESSIONAL EMPLOYEES: CIVIL RIGHTS   191

Constitutional and Statutory Spheres of National Civil Rights   194
Universal Constitutional Rights   194
    Procedural Rights—Due Process   195
        Parties Entitled to Due Process   195
        Due Process Procedures   196
    Substantive Rights—Due Process   200
        Freedom of Expression   200
        Rights of Privacy   208
    Remedies for Constitutional Violations   212
Topical Civil Rights—Equal Opportunity Laws   212
    Overview—Antidiscrimination Laws   212
        Constitutional Protections—Antidiscrimination   213
        Statutory Protections—Antidiscrimination   214
    Racial and Ethnic Discrimination   215
        Constitutional Protections—Race   215
        Statutory Protections—Race   215
    Gender Discrimination   217
        Constitutional Protections—Gender 217
        Statutory Protections—Gender   218
    Homosexual Discrimination   226
        Constitutional Protections—Homosexual Persons   227
        Statutory Protections—Homosexual Persons   228
    Disability Discrimination   228
        Constitutional Protections—Disability   228
        Statutory Protections—Disability   228
    Age Discrimination   232
        Constitutional Protections—Age   232
        Statutory Protections—Age   232
    Alien Discrimination   234
        Constitutional Protections—Aliens 234
        Statutory Protections—Aliens   235
    Religious Discrimination   235
        Constitutional Protections—Religion 235

Statutory Protections—Religion   235
Language Barriers   236
Constitutional Protections—English Deficiency   236
Statutory Protections—English Deficiency   237
Concurrent Violations of Different Laws   237
Immunity Defenses to Civil Rights Violations   237

Chapter Discussion Questions   238

Cases
6.1 Curtis v. Oklahoma City Public Schools Board of Education,
     147 F.3d 1200 (10th Cir. 1998)   240
6.2 Downs v. Los Angeles Un. School District, 228 F.3d 1003
     (9th Cir. 2000), cert. denied, 121 S. Ct. 1653 (2001)   244
6.3 Lacks v. Ferguson Reorganized School Dist., 147 F3d 719
     (8th Cir. 1998)   248
6.4 O'Connor v. Ortega, 480 U.S. 709 (1987)   251
6.5 Aubrey v. School Board of Lafayette Parish, 148 F.3d 559
     (5th Cir. 1998)   254
6.6 Taxman v. Board of Education, 91 F.3d 1547 (3d Cir. 1996)   256
6.7 Schroeder v. Hamilton School District, 282 F.3d 946 (7th Cir. 2002) 258
6.8 Faragher v. City of Boca Raton, 524 U.S. 775 (1998)   263
6.9 Oncale V. Sundowners Offshore Services, Inc., 118 S. Ct. 998 (1998) 263
6.10 Bibby v. Phila. Coca Cola Bottling Co., 260 F.3d 257 (3d Cir. 2001) 264
6.11 Salmon v. Dade County School Board, 4 F. Supp. 2d 1157
     (S.D. Fla. 1998)   267
6.12 Auerbach v. Board of Educ. of the Harborfields Central School Dist.,
     136 F.3d 104 (2d Cir. 1997)   270

Endnotes   273

CHAPTER 7   STUDENT RIGHTS AND DISCIPLINE   282

Background Note   285
Universal Constitutional Rights   285
Procedural Rights—Due Process   286
Cases Entitled to Due Process   286
What Process Is Due?   287
Substantive Rights—Due Process   291
General Right to Rational Treatment   291
Right to Bodily Security   292
Freedom of Expression   293
Rights of Privacy   301
School Searches   301
Body Searches   307
School Desks and Lockers   308
Informational Privacy   308
Decisional Privacy—Autonomy   311
Liability for Constitutional Violations   312

Topical Civil Rights—Equal Opportunity Laws   312
   Review Note   312
   Racial and National Origin Discrimination   313
      Interdistrict Segregation   313
      Affirmative Action Issues   314
      Discriminatory Conduct   316
      Racial Disparities in Testing and Placement   316
      Linguistically Disadvantaged Minorities   317
      Remedies for Racial Discrimination   318
   Gender Discrimination   319
      Sexual Abuse and Harassment   320
      Disparate Treatment   320
      Sports Programs   321
      Academic Benefits   322
      Remedies for Gender Discrimination   323
   Homosexual Discrimination   323
      Constitutional Protections   323
      Statutory Protections   323
   Children with Disabilities   324
      The IDEA Law   324
      Procedural Requirements   325
      FAPE Requirements   325
      Placement Rules—Mainstreaming   326
      Access to IDEA Benefits by Private School Students   328
      Discipline of Children with Disabilities   328
      Rights of Those with Disabilities Under State Law   329
      Rights of Separated Parents   329
   Alien Children   329
   Poverty Groups   330
   Concurrent Violations of Different Laws   330
   Special Immunity Defenses   330
Rights Under State Law   330

Chapter Discussion Questions   331

Cases
7.1 Hasenfus v. LaJeunesse, 175 F.3d 68 (1st Cir. 1999)   333
7.2 Bethel School District No. 403 v. Fraser, 478 U.S. 675 (1986)   336
7.3 Hazelwood School District v. Kuhlmeier, 484 U.S. 260 (1988)   338
7.4 Gonzales v. McEuen, 435 F. Supp. 460 (1977)   341
7.5 Jones v. State, 64 S.W.2d 728 (Ark. 2002)   344
7.6 Board of Education v. Earls, 122 S. Ct. 2559 (2002)   348
7.7 U.S. v. Miami University, 294 F.3d 797 (6th Cir. 2002)   353
7.8 Missouri v. Jenkins, 515 U.S. 70 (1995)   355
7.9 Debra P. by Irene P. v. Turlington, 730 F.2d 1405 (11th Cir. 1984)   357
7.10 Davis v. Monroe County Board of Education, 119 S. Ct. 1661 (1999)   360
7.11 ABC School v. Mr. and Mrs. M., 1997 Mass. Super., 97-518, Lexis 43   363
7.12 Hudson Dist. Board of Educ. v. Rowley, 458 U.S. 176 (1982)   366

7.13 Taylor v. Vermont Department of Education, 313 F.3d 768 (2d Cir. 2002)   369

Endnotes   376

CHAPTER 8   THE PYRAMID OF DISCRIMINATION REMEDIES   386

Background Note   388
Remedies for Violation of Constitutional Rights   389
Remedies Under Specific Discrimination Statutes   389
    Federal Aid Statutes   390
        The FERPA Statute   390
        Titles VI and IX   390
        The IDEA Statute   392
    Employment Discrimination Statutes   393
        Title VII   393
        ADA and Rehabilitation Acts   393
        Age Discrimination in Employment Act   393
    Equal Rights Statute (42 U.S.C. § 1981)   394
Remedies Under 42 U.S.C. § 1983   394
    Requisites for § 1983 Relief   395
    School District Defenses   398
        School District Policy or Custom   398
        Causation by Inaction   399
        Special Relationship Claims   400
        School District Immunity Under § 1983   400
    Individual Defenses   400
        Qualified Personal Immunity   401
Recovery of Attorneys' Fees   402
Eleventh Amendment Immunity Defenses   403
    Statutes Abrogating Immunity   406
    Statutes Not Abrogating Immunity   407

Cases
8.1 Gonzaga Univ. v. Doe, 122 S. Ct. 2268 (2002)   408
8.2 Boulahanis v. Board of Regents, 198 F.3d 633 (7th Cir. 1999)   410
8.3 Walker v. District of Columbia, 969 F. Supp. 794 (D. D.C. 1997)   413
8.4 Riddick et al. v. School Board, 238 F.3d 518 (4th Cir. 2000)   416
8.5 Doe v. Board of Educ., 18 F. Supp. 2d 954 (N.D. Ill. 1998)   416
8.6 Board of Trustees v. Garrett, 121 S. Ct. 955 (2001)   419
8.7 Buckhannon Board and Care Home, Inc. v. W. Va. Dept. of Health and
    Human Resources et al., 121 S. Ct. 1835 (2001)   420

Endnotes   422

CHAPTER 9   PRIVATE EDUCATION: ALTERNATIVES TO PUBLIC SCHOOLS   426

Background Note   428
Private Schools: State Regulation and Services   428

Constitutional Constraints on State Regulation   428
State Approval Requirements   430
Teacher Rights and Duties   432
   Individual Contracts   432
   Collectively Bargained Contracts   433
Student Rights and Duties   434
   Contract Rights   434
   Student Discipline   435
Civil Rights: Teachers and Students   435
   Note on Civil Rights in Private Schools   435
   Race and Ethnic Discrimination   436
   Gender Discrimination   437
   Disability Discrimination   437
   Age Discrimination   438
   Religious Considerations   438
   State Antidiscrimination Laws   438
Government Aids to Education in Private Schools   438
   Aid Directed to Religious Schools   440
   Aid Directed to Students and Parents   440
   School Transportation   440
   Instructional Materials and Equipment   441
   Remedial Services   442
   Tuition Assistance and Tax Relief   442
   Aid Directed to Nonreligious Schools   444
Charter Schools   444
   Background Note   444
   Creation and Legal Status   447
      Charter Grant, Renewal, and Revocation   448
   Operational Requirements   448
      Student Admissions   448
      Teacher Qualifications   449
      Curriculum Requirements   449
   Funding of Charter Schools   449
Home Schooling   450
   State Regulation   450
   Participation in Public School Activities   451
Tort Liability in Nonpublic Schools   452
   Topical Tort Situations   452
      Premises Liability   452
      Duties of Supervision   453
      Affirmative Defenses   456
      First Aid   456
      Defamation Liability   456
      Educational Malpractice   456
   Immunity Defenses and Dollar Recovery Limits   456

Cases
9.1 Catholic High School Assn. of Archdiocese of New York v. Culvert,
      753 F.2d 1161 (2nd Cir. 1985)   458
9.2 Geraci v. St. Xavier High School, 3 Ohio Op. 3d 146 (1978)   462
9.3 Agostini v. Felton, 521 U.S. 203 (1997)   465
9.4 Mitchell v. Helms, 530 U.S. 793 (2000)   470
9.5 Zelman v. Simmons-Harris, 122 S. Ct. 2460 (2002)   478
9.6 Hooks v. Clark County School District, 228 F.3d 1036 (9th Cir. 2000) 482
Endnotes   486

APPENDIX 1   SELECTED PROVISIONS—CONSTITUTION OF THE
             UNITED STATES   494

APPENDIX 2   PRINCIPAL FEDERAL LAWS AFFECTING EQUAL OPPORTUNITY
             IN EDUCATION   497

APPENDIX 3   SELECT TABLE OF CASES   500

             GLOSSARY   506

             INDEX   511

Law in the Schools

CHAPTER 1

Education Under the American Legal System

∽ **CHAPTER OUTLINE**

I.   The Nature of School Law
II. The Relation of Law, Politics, and Education
     A. Contests for Control
     B. School Violence and Crime
III. Legal Interests of Participants
     A. Government Interests
         1. The States
         2. The National Government
             a. Supremacy of Federal Law
     B. Individual Interests
         1. Students and Parents
         2. School Authorities, Teachers, and Staff
         3. Citizen Interests
IV. The American Legal System—Structure and Sources of Law
     A. Constitutional Law—The Basic Charter
     B. Statutory Law—The Role of Legislatures
     C. Administrative Law—The Role of Administrators
         1. Scope of Administrative Authority
             a. Expressed and Implied Powers
         2. Legislative Delegation Issues
         3. Administrative Structure of Public Education
             a. State-Level Agencies
             b. Regional Agencies
             c. Local School Districts
             d. Local School Boards
     D. Case Law—The Role of Courts
         1. Structure and Jurisdiction of American Courts
             a. Federal Courts
             b. State Courts
         2. Judge-Made Law—Common Law and Equity Law
         3. Access to Court Relief
             a. Standing Issues—Who Can Sue?
             b. Exhaustion Issues—When May a Party Sue?
         4. Court Review of Administrative Decisions
             a. Remedies for Administrative Errors

  E. Note on Law References and Citations
    1. Constitutions
    2. Statutes and Regulations
    3. Case Citations
      a. United States Supreme Court
      b. Federal Courts of Appeal
      c. Federal District (Trial) Courts
      d. State Appellate Courts
      e. Endnote Symbols
    4. Professional Literature

∞ CHAPTER DISCUSSION QUESTIONS

∞ CASES

1.1 Dawson v. East Side Union High School District, 34 Cal. Rptr. 2d 108 (1994)
1.2 Conover v. Board of Education of Nebo School District, 267 P.2d 768 (Utah 1954)

∞ ENDNOTES

THE NATURE OF SCHOOL LAW

The enterprise we call *education* involves a network of legal relationships between private and public parties who are either providers or beneficiaries of educational services. The providers of education, traditionally dominated by public and private schools, now include licensed home schools and charter schools, which have distinctive legal features and are the subjects of new, rapidly growing state laws.

The laws that regulate the different sources of education, which are for convenience called "school law", are not a a discrete branch of law, like constitutional law, enacted law, regulatory law, and the law of contracts and torts. Rather, so-called "school law" is the collection of those established branches of law that bear particularly on the rights and obligations of all parties (administrators, teachers, parents, students, taxpayers, and civil libertarians) who interact with each other on educational issues. As with all law, school law has fairly settled, static elements and newly developing elements that address new questions or clarify or modify prior law. Law is, therefore, truly a "work in progress" at every government level (federal, state, and local) which seeks to address new educational needs. The dictum of Justice Oliver Wendell Holmes that the life of the law has not been logic, but experience, reflects the ongoing historical element of lawmaking, but it is too simple as a guide to law study. Law is not merely a heap of happenstance reactions cast up by the demands of new experience. It is significantly shaped and rationalized by legal institutions that make up the American legal system. Knowledge of the structure and workings of that system is essential to learning about school law. We benefit, therefore, by beginning our study of school law with a review of the components of the American legal system and of the legal interests and rights of educators and persons who are governed by that system.

The approaches to law study are as varied as the purposes of such studies. Some law studies focus on abstract principles of jurisprudence, or on legal or political theory, or on the utilitarian efficiency or deficiencies of particular laws, or on the legal means of harmonizing and adjusting competing public and private individual interests in a particular enterprise. While none of these perspectives is totally divorced from the others, this book approaches the study of law as a system intended to resolve conflicts and problems that arise in the school setting. The stress on the human dimensions as to what educational practices are fair and efficient directly confronts the practical day-to-day problems of all parties concerned with the operations of schools and school programs.

THE RELATION OF LAW, POLITICS, AND EDUCATION

Contests for Control

In our history, the schools have been not only an institution in which to teach . . . but an arena where interest groups fight to preserve their values, or to revise the judgments of history, or to bring about fundamental social change. Given the diversity of American society, it has been impossible to insulate the schools from pressures that result from differences.... [D. Ravitch, Multiculturalism: *E Pluribus Unum,* 56 *The Key Rptr.* 1 (Autumn 1990); *see also* J. Coleman, *The Struggle for Control of Education and Social Policy* 64 (1970).]

Supreme Court Justice Jackson prophetically anticipated disputes over control of the widening range of public school policies and practices in the landmark flag salute case. He there captured the control problem in one sentence:

As government pressure towards unity becomes greater, so strife becomes more bitter as to whose unity it shall be. [*W. Va. Board of Educ. v. Barnette,* 319 U.S. 624, 641 (1943)]

Courts decide who does or should control children's education under laws that acknowledge the varied interests of governments, parents, students, teachers, churches, taxpayers, and private civic organizations. All have acknowledged interests, but the extent to which any of those interests is empowered by law to influence or control a particular educational decision requires special analysis of those interests. Control issues are sharply highlighted by political and legal initiatives to improve the quality of education, including stricter student testing and achievement standards, stricter teacher certification standards, heavier sanctions for teacher or student misconduct, and better security arrangements to prevent violent assaults against the school community and school property.

School Violence and Crime

The unprecedented escalation of school-site violence raises control problems that far outrun the bounds of traditional school discipline. The criminal culture of drug trafficking, thefts, physical assaults, possession of lethal weapons, and student harassment and intimidation that has spread into the schools has stiffened the resolve of legislatures, courts, and school authorities to adopt far stricter restraints on personal conduct than were previously deemed acceptable. For instance, the tide of law changes during the 1960s and 1970s that expanded student rights and protections against penalties for unruly speech and warrantless school searches has reversed course in the last decade, bringing a new balance between legal authority of school managers and the scope of student rights. These significant changes will be seen in the new cases that appear in the following chapters, cases that largely confined or reversed the law found in earlier editions of school law texts. The following statements of two respected jurists sum up these changes:

The administration of the public schools in this country in the current climate of rancid identity politics, pervasive challenges to authority and mounting litigiousness is an undertaking at once daunting and thankless. We judges should not make it even more daunting by injecting our social and educational values. . . . [Judge Richard Posner, concurring, in *Schroeder v. Hamilton School District,* 282 F.3d 946 (7th Cir. 2002)]

[W]e must make as certain as possible that we do not permit criminality to begin with juveniles in schools. We do not have police officers in our classrooms. We do not have parents in our classrooms. Therefore we must give to teachers and principals all the tools they reasonably need to preserve order in classrooms and school grounds. [Judge Stanley Mosk, formerly of Supreme Court of California, Foreword, *School Safety Legal Anthology* (Pepperdine University Press 1985) prepared by the National School Safety Center in cooperation with the U.S. Dept. of Justice, U.S. Dept. of Education, and Pepperdine University.]

Newly enacted state laws on school safety are noted in the endnotes.[1] The National Center for Education Statistics reported that more than half of U.S. public schools reported experiencing at least one crime incident during the 1996–97, school year, and 1 in 10 schools reported at least one serious violent crime during that school year. [See *Violence and Discipline Problems in U.S. Public Schools: 1996–97* (1998)] A West Virginia statute that authorized student expulsion from public schools for weapons possession for up to one year was recently challenged under the West Virginia constitution, but upheld.[2] As will be seen in Chapters 6 and 7, school authorities need to relearn the law in light of the latest decisions that alter the contours of civil rights in public schools and that undercut much of the case law that prevailed in prior decades.

Although some courts may uphold school zero tolerance policies against possession of weapons or illegal drugs and may sustain preemptive bans against intimidating speech or "gang" activity in troubled schools, the legality of new disciplinary regimes has not been fully tested. Such regimes must still be crafted to minimize the risks of infringing constitutionally guaranteed freedoms of speech, association, and privacy when tightening discipline of students, teachers, and other members of the school community.

The changes in school law have been so rapid, and often so radical, that the authors have decided in this text to favor, where feasible, the report of law changes in the quoted words of the court and case decisions. Use of those official, quoted pronouncements avoids any oversimplification of the degree and complexity of recent law changes and any concern that the authors' narrative summaries of those decisions might include some personal hyperbole rather than firm law changes.

LEGAL INTERESTS OF PARTICIPANTS

As indicated above, the legal authority to control various school functions involves counterbalancing interests of government agencies and school supervisors and interests of private parties who participate in and are affected by school managers. Where the control of a particular school function or the legality of a particular school decision is challenged as unlawful, courts must assess the respective legal claims of school administrators, school employees, parents, students, or special-purpose organizations. Without a recognized legal interest in the disputed question, a party will not even have "standing" to raise a legal claim. But even with such an interest, the legal question often comes down to the question of which party has the more weighty recognized interest. All school disputes, therefore, must be decided by reference to the respective legal interests of the opposed parties.

Government Interests

The States

State constitutions mandate the creation of state public education systems, and state legislatures carry out that mandate by enacting the laws that establish and fund the structure and administration of public schools. They further the state constitutional goal by enacting compulsory school attendance laws pursuant to their inherent police powers to enact laws for the general welfare. Public education is, therefore, *primarily*, but *not exclusively*, the province of state law.

The National Government

Although the national Constitution makes no mention of education in enumerating the powers of the federal government, the national government nevertheless exercises significant influence and jurisdiction over many school operations by congressional enactments and administrative regulations that are justified as advancing legitimate federal interests. The major federal law sources that support federal jurisdiction regarding education are the federal Constitutional provisions that protect civil liberties [U.S. Const., Amend. XIV] and the powers the Constitution assigns to the Congress and the federal government to regulate interstate and foreign commerce, to provide for the national defense, to spend for the general welfare, and to conduct foreign affairs [U.S. Const., Art. I]. For example, the Bill of Rights and the Fourteenth Amendment protect persons against infringement of their constitutional liberties by public school authorities, and they further authorize enforcement of those rights by the array of federal antidiscrimination laws, which are reviewed in Chapters 6, 7, and 8. The congressional power to regulate Interstate Commerce includes the power to prohibit practices that "affect" interstate commerce, however indirectly, and thus supports enactment of the employment discrimination laws that are reviewed in Chapters 6 and 8. The federal interests in conducting foreign affairs and maintaining national defense and the armed forces support federal spending to promote school courses in foreign language studies and the sciences in order to equip federal officials to conduct international relations efficiently and to improve national security and the military services. Finally, the national spending power supports federal subsidies to the schools to support broad national interests. That power includes the power to impose federal conditions and regulations regarding the states' uses of federal funds. State violation of federal funding conditions is ground for federal government recapture of the amount of funds so misused, and states may not defeat the recapture of those funds on a claim that imposition of liability on the state would interfere with state sovereignty.[3]

Supremacy of Federal Law.   The impact of federal laws on state educational policies and practices is magnified by the Supremacy Clause of the national Constitution under which federal law subordinates and displaces state law whenever federal law comes into conflict with state laws. That clause reads:

> This Constitution, and the laws of the United States which shall be made in pursuance thereof; and all treaties made . . . under the authority of the United States, shall be the *supreme law of the land; and the judges in every state shall be bound thereby, anything in the Constitution or laws of any state to the contrary notwithstanding.* U.S. Const., Art. VI, § 2) (Emphasis added)

Individual Interests

Students and Parents

Students and parents possess recognized interests, both as beneficiaries of school services and as citizens. Those interests affect a wide range of school activities. Parents have a constitutional civil right to control the upbringing of their children and to resist laws or decisions that infringe on that right. For example, while states may compel parents to satisfy state compulsory education requirements for their children, they may not force parents to send their children to public schools if the child receives alternative, state-qualified schooling. Public schools may also be compelled to exempt an enrolled student from a public school activity in circumstances where that activity would violate the child's religion and is not shown to be essential to meet a compelling state interest. Parent–school conflicts are commonplace in public and private education, and illustrations of those conflicts will appear in the following chapters.

School Authorities, Teachers, and Staff

The professional, employment, and civil rights interests that school administrators, supervisors, teachers, and other employees possess in the conduct of school affairs require perennial clarification and adjustment under the wide range of special laws that are discussed in every succeeding chapter.

Citizen Interests

The interests of citizens as voters and taxpayers and of civic organizations regarding particular school policies or activities may also trigger legal disputes or claims regarding certain school decisions or programs.

THE AMERICAN LEGAL SYSTEM—STRUCTURE AND SOURCES OF LAW

The interests discussed above find expression both in the laws of the nation and of the states. The respective authority of those laws is best seen in terms of the structure and law sources of each government. As a republic, the United States consists of coexisting state and federal governments, one for the nation as a whole, and one for each of the 50 constituent states, with each having its own government structure and laws. The legal powers of each government are expressed by the term "jurisdiction", which denotes law-based *authority,* as opposed to an assertion of raw power that has no valid legal foundation. As noted above, where federal jurisdiction exists, federal law governs the nation, even where it conflicts with state law. In most cases, however, federal and state laws operate harmoniously and concurrently. Where state jurisdiction exists, it governs only its own state.

Each government has four general sources and ranks of law: its constitution, its legislative enactments (statutes), its administrative regulations and decisions (administrative law), and the decisions of its courts (case law). These are described more fully below.

Constitutional law ranks highest and supersedes any inconsistent statute or administrative law, while statutes and court decisions in turn rank higher than administrative law. The source of law will, therefore, dictate its legal force with reference to other applicable laws. For example, a school administrator must be satisfied that even if his desired action is authorized by one level of law, say, a school board resolution, it must not violate a higher level of law, say, a school statute. Nor can school officials rely on a statute that has been found to violate the U.S. Constitution. This interplay of different levels of law will be illustrated by many familiar school experiences that are reported in later chapters.

Constitutional Law—The Basic Charter

Constitutions are basic written government charters that are adopted or ratified by the entire electorate. Because they are intended to establish the structure and powers of government that will endure indefinitely until amended, constitutions are broadly worded to cover unforeseen as well as known or anticipated future conditions. They are seldom amended, if only because the legislative and electoral requirements for adoption of a constitutional amendment are politically difficult to achieve. As explained in the next chapter, when the validity of school actions is challenged on constitutional grounds, courts must interpret and decide the proper meaning and application of constitutional provisions, some of which, such as the "due process" clause, are open ended and nonspecific. In the process of resolving contested constitutional readings, courts may be said to create law by supplying a binding version of the U.S. Constitution.

Statutory Law—The Role of Legislatures

The authority to enact statutes, which is vested by constitutions in elected legislative bodies, is continuous and cannot be exhausted by any current or prior legislature. Statutes are therefore subject to legislative change at any time. This feature of legislative control distinguishes constitutional law from statutory law. "The legislature, having tried one plan, is not precluded from trying another. It . . . may change its plans as often as it deems necessary or expedient." [*State v. Haworth*, 23 N.E. 946, 948 (Ind. 1890)]

Most statutes that directly relate to public schools are statutes compiled in official state school codes, and they are summarized in unofficial publications by government education departments and by education organizations. As with constitutions, courts are called on to supply the authoritative interpretation of statutes where their meaning or application is contested.

Since state constitutions vest control of public schools in the state legislature, and not in local school districts, local school boards lack the authority to ignore or disobey state legislative directives unless their state constitution directly confers independent powers in the district. This remains true notwithstanding fervent beliefs that the local community, and not distant state agencies, should exercise local control over its schools. For this reason, state legislatures can, unless barred by the state constitution, (1) create, alter, and abolish school districts and school boards; (2) remove incumbent school board members and abolish their offices; (3) prescribe school calendars and curricula; (4) determine the sources and procedures for providing school revenues and expenditures; (5) fix the appointment, term, and qualifications of teachers; (6) fix admission policies for local schools; and (7) impose penalties for noncompliance with state regulations.

Administrative Law—The Role of Administrators

When school officials make decisions and adopt rules and regulations that are legally authorized, they are making law in the sense that those actions have the force of law. That body of administrative actions is known as *Administrative Law*. However, such officials and administrators have only those express or implied powers which are granted to them by state statutes or the state constitution. Administrative law is, therefore, to be distinguished from acts that exceed the bounds of the actor's legally conferred authority. Such acts are called *ultra vires,* meaning "beyond their powers." *Ultra vires* acts generally occur in one of two ways. The first arises where the challenged action exceeds the scope of the powers conferred by law. The second, more complex, objection arises where the statute itself is invalid so that the acting administrative official or board is acting beyond its legal scope of authority. In either case, courts will overturn *ultra vires* administrative acts as being legally void or voidable.[4]

Scope of Administrative Authority

The scope of administrative authority is normally determined by the terms of an enabling statute. For example, a school board attempt to empower the teachers' union to determine how negotiated employment benefits should be allocated among its members was held void as unauthorized by the law.[5] And a statute that authorized a commission to supervise creation of independent school districts was held not to include authority for the commission to order one district to annex territory of another district.[6] Recent battles between community and central school boards over hiring authority essentially have involved statutory interpretation to determine their respective scope of authority.[7]

Expressed and Implied Powers.   The interpretation of the scope of authority conferred by a statute is not limited to powers expressly mentioned in the law. Administrative authority may also be implied from the law as authority that is reasonably necessary or incidental to carrying out the expressly conferred powers. Courts tend to sustain a generous scope of implied administrative powers, and many assumptions of implied power by school authorities go unchallenged. Even so, courts will not imply a power that contradicts or is inconsistent with an express administrative duty or with the manifest intent of state enactments. Thus a school board could not claim implied power to determine tenure policy or to delimit areas of tenure when those subjects are fixed directly by tenure statutes.[8] Nor could a board claim implied authority to lease a building for school purposes on the basis of its express authority to construct school buildings.[9] A legislature can always settle implied power questions by enacting laws that expressly grant or deny a disputed power.[10]

Legislative Delegation Issues

State legislatures sometimes elect to control certain school functions directly by statute, e.g., by laws that set the terms for school budgets, school board membership, attendance requirements, and school calendars. But they more commonly delegate to state and local officials the authority to decide whether, when, and how to carry out school functions.[11] The legal doctrines that limit such delegations of authority are deceptively simple in form, but vague in fact.

A state legislature may not transfer or delegate to anyone the authority to enact laws, because that authority is vested exclusively in the elected state legislature by the state constitution and is therefore nondelegable. The legislature may, however, delegate *administrative* authority to carry out properly enunciated statutory policies. In sum, a delegation of *lawmaking power* is unconstitutional and void, but a delegation of *administrative power* is constitutional and valid. These limits on delegation of authority apply only to transfers of authority that require an exercise of *discretion*. They do not apply to authority to authorize others to carry out a ministerial act, such as an order to a teacher to enforce an attendance policy that the school board has adopted.[12]

Courts will uphold a delegation of power to administrators if they find that the delegating statute contains guidelines that are *reasonably adequate* to indicate the "will" of the legislature.[13] Courts generally consider broadly worded guidelines sufficiently adequate to render the delegation one of *administrative* and not of lawmaking power. They may, however, require more precise guidelines where a challenged delegation affects important civil rights or empowers school authorities to impose substantial individual penalties.

The foregoing principles that limit delegations by a legislature also govern redelegation or subdelegation of that authority from higher to lower levels of school administration. Unless the delegating statute contemplates redelegation, the original authorized administrative body cannot transfer its discretion to others. Redelegation issues are commonly raised in challenges to school hiring decisions. For example, a school board's attempt to transfer its hiring discretion to a supervisor was held to be an unauthorized redelegation so that the supervisor's hiring decision was unlawful and void.[14]

Administrative Structure of Public Education

Most states have a three-tier structure of school administration, namely, state, regional (intermediate), and local agencies. A minority of states employ a two-echelon (state and local) structure, while Hawaii has a single statewide administration.[15] The organization of these agencies varies from state to state.[16] The more prominent types of organization found in most states are indicated by the following summary.

State-Level Agencies.   Central state agencies typically include the following offices: a state Department of Education; a state Board of Education, which may contain divisions for specialized services such as research, administration, finance, teacher certification, and instructional services; and a Chief State School Officer, who often acts as the executive head of state education departments[17] and is variously designated a *Commissioner, Superintendent,* or *Secretary of Education.* State Boards of Education develop policies and regulations on topics such as school district organization, school closings, reductions of professional staff, and state-level review of appeals from local boards. These agencies also perform regulatory functions relating to their assigned tasks.[18]

Regional Agencies.   Mid-tier regional entities provide state-mandated special services (such as special education and transportation) to school districts in their territory. They may be authorized to conduct or coordinate nonmandated programs that their local districts elect to sponsor. A number of states have replaced older mid-tier agencies, such as county boards of education, with entities called *intermediate units,* whose jurisdiction may span more than one county.

Local School Districts.   School districts, acting through their school boards, are the front-line managers of public schools. State legislatures may create different classes of school districts that have different powers and duties, and may subject certain school districts to local municipal control. Such districts are "dependent" districts, while those that are free of control by a municipal government are called "independent" districts.

In addition to their powers to operate schools, local districts have certain corporate powers, such as the right to sue and be sued, make contracts, hold property, and receive grants from private sources as well as from governments.

School administrators must observe the laws that govern their particular school district. They may not ignore or violate state laws that require their school district to reorganize, unless those laws are voided as unconstitutional. Local challenges to school district reorganization laws commonly allege that the state has unconstitutionally taken local property without compensation or has unconstitutionally impaired the affected district's contracts. But altering school district boundaries, assets, and obligations is not "taking" anything from the district because public school property is not district property but state property.[19] Contract impairment claims by school districts are equally rejected because courts have overwhelmingly found that, as creatures of their parent state, local districts do not have any legal right or power to sue the state. Only district creditors may complain of their contract impairment if a reorganization law diverts assets of the prior district that were pledged to secure payment of the creditor's debt. But if, as is more common, the creditor never bargained for or received a pledge of property to secure his claim, there is no impairment of the district's promise to pay the debt, if the debtor district continues to exist or if the surviving reorganized district succeeds to the prior district's contract obligations.[20] State legislatures may elect to avoid the burdens or windfalls that reorganized districts may suffer by including provisions for adjustments of district assets and obligations in the reorganization laws.[21]

Local School Boards.   Because their powers and duties are derived from school statutes, school boards must observe the methods of operation that are prescribed by law and may not adopt alternative methods. For instance, a local board may not extend the term of a teacher contract beyong the term limit that is fixed by statute.[22]

State law provisions also govern the composition, selection, term, and qualifications for school board office, e.g., age, residency, noncriminal history, the absence of prohibited kinships to district personnel, and avoidance of conflicts of interest.[23] State legislatures may not, however, adopt terms that violate constitutional rights, such as denying employment to persons because of their political party affiliation.[24]

As a general rule, a school board can only make official decisions at an official board meeting that is duly convened in accordance with law.[25] As previously noted, board members may not redelegate their discretion to other persons, and a board authorization to a school superintendent to determine whom to hire was accordingly voided as *ultra vires*.[26] State laws usually require that school boards take official actions at meetings that are convened pursuant to proper public notice, attended by a required quorum of board members, and open to the public. These formal meeting requisites may be suspended and excused by a court of equity where a school board unjustly seeks to avoid a just obligation based on its own failure to comply with the law, as where the board sought to void a teacher appointment after it misled the teacher into believing that the board had officially approved the teacher's contract at a properly convened meeting.[27]

Notice of official board meetings must be given to each board member as well as the public, and must afford a reasonable opportunity for notified parties to prepare for and attend the meeting. The consequences of notice defaults vary from state to state—from nullifying action taken at the meeting, to imposing only personal penalties against offending board members. Nor may board members waive the meeting notice requirement by an (unlawful) agreement to have some board members act for all board members. School boards may set their meetings at any reasonable time or place, but meetings set at unreasonable distances from the district may be invalid.[28] Courts may excuse notice defaults in special circumstances, e.g., where an emergency requires immediate board action before notice could be effected, or where notice would serve no purpose because the non-notified board member is so ill or so distant that she could not respond or attend the meeting in any event.[29]

A majority of board members must be present to constitute a necessary quorum for an official meeting, but a state legislature may vary the quorum requirement for specified board actions, such as requiring a higher than majority quorum or a supermajority affirmative vote of the entire board for certain board actions, e.g., dismissal of a tenured teacher or adoption of school district budgets.[30] The legal effect of a present member's withdrawal from a meeting or abstaining from voting will depend on the circumstances of that withdrawal and the language of the governing state statute. For example, full withdrawal from the meeting place may destroy the required quorum, while merely leaving the board table may not be considered a withdrawal. The failure to vote may, depending on the state law, be taken as agreement with the majority, or may be treated as either approving or disapproving a measure, depending on the subject of the vote. But on subjects requiring a specified number of affirmative votes, abstention has the same effect as a negative vote.[31]

A variety of state laws that aim to guarantee public access to official doings as well as to board meetings are variously titled as *open meeting, sunshine, freedom of information,* and *public records laws.*[32] Open meeting laws generally allow closed board meetings for specified, excepted subjects and permit nondisclosure of certain confidential material in order not to prejudice important public or individual interests. Such exceptions usually include board deliberations on the conduct or review of ongoing labor negotiations, district plans to acquire property, and board discussion of accusations that are being investigated and which could cause irreparable harm to an individual's reputation.[33] The case law is very mixed on questions whether open meeting laws govern private board meetings so as to entitle members of the public to attend those meetings and to inspect records of those meetings.[34] Board members may generally meet unofficially and informally as long as they defer official discussion and decision on school matters to a later open meeting. Courts are not agreed, however, on whether a board may, after discussing a nonexcepted subject at a closed (executive) session, act on it without further discussion or deliberation at a later official open meeting. For examples of the state law variations on these questions, see the endnote.[35]

Whether particular school records qualify as "public records" that must be made open to public inspection and copying (at reasonable times and places on payment of reasonable copying costs) depends on the definition of a "public record" that is contained in a governing statute. Some statutes even apply to unofficial board records, such as school files (if not privileged as confidential), payroll records, and even the names of job applicants.[36]

The *Conover* opinion at the end of this chapter (Case 1.2) illustrates the diverse conclusions that different state courts have drawn from their records statutes on the question when notes of a board meeting become official board minutes that are subject to public inspection. Whether or not they are deemed "public records," however, board minutes remain subject to timely board correction and clarification.[37] In one state, the minutes of an executive board session were held subject to public inspection even though the law of that state did not require the board to make or preserve such minutes.[38] With regard to student records, however, the law of many states has been effectively modified and superseded by the federal student records statute, which is discussed in Chapter 7.

Case Law—The Role of Courts

As the last stop in any legal dispute, the courts have the last say on the meaning and effect of contested laws. They have, in addition, created their own laws regarding legal procedures as well as substantive rights that are not written in the positive law of constitutions, statutes, and administrative regulations. To state a few obvious examples, courts:

- Create the law that is known as the common law and equity law.
- Create the rules for allowing or disallowing court consideration of a petition for relief.

- Determine what conflicting evidence and testimony to accept or reject, and when presented evidence is sufficient to support a particular claim.
- Determine whether a school administrator's exercise of authority is lawful, *ultra vires*, or an abuse of discretion.
- Determine what process is due or required for different types of school hearings or decisions.

The considerable powers of judges to determine facts, define the issues, interpret the law, and influence case outcomes is well illustrated by the *Dawson* case, which appears at the end of this chapter as Case 1.1, and by the contrasting treatment that the judges of the First and Eighth Circuit Courts of Appeal gave to the issues in the *Brown* case (which appears at the end of Chapter 3 as Case 3.5) and in the *Lacks* case (which appears at the end of Chapter 6 as Case 6.3).

Structure and Jurisdiction of American Courts

The following discussion considers only courts of general jurisdiction. It does not cover specialized courts, such as courts that deal with the military, international commerce, or patents, which are of little relevance to school law.

The federal and state courts are distinct in their structure and jurisdiction. The legal effect of each court's decision is determined by its *subject matter* jurisdiction, by its *territorial* jurisdiction, and by its relation to a higher appeals court within the same system.

Subject matter jurisdiction refers to topics or questions that a court can decide. For example, federal courts have primary *subject matter jurisdiction* on federal law questions, while state courts have primary *subject matter jurisdiction* on state law issues. While courts in either system may decide issues of either federal and state law, state courts must follow federal court rulings on questions of federal law (when available), and federal courts must follow the rulings of a governing state court on questions of state law (when available). Where the federal and state laws or decisions are in conflict on the same question, the federal law and federal court decisions control by reason of the above-discussed Supremacy Clause of the national Constitution.[39]

Territorial jurisdiction refers to the geographic area that is assigned for a particular court's functions and in which its decisions take effect. Therefore, parties and courts that are outside the territorial jurisdiction of a particular court are not bound to follow its decisions or views of the law.

The rank and authority of a decision by a court that has subject matter and territorial jurisdiction for that case are further determined by the level of its judicial authority with respect to the level of authority exercised by other courts in the same system. Thus, an appellate court decision will displace an inconsistent trial court decision on the same question.

It is therefore essential to observe the foregoing elements of a court's jurisdiction to determine the legal effect of that court's decision.

FIGURE 1.1   The Federal
Court System

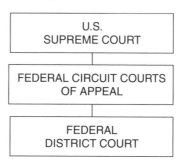

Federal Courts.   As indicated in Figure 1.1, the federal court system has a three-level structure: trial courts, which are called *District Courts;* intermediate courts of appeal, which are called *Circuit Courts of Appeal;* and the high court of final appeal, the United States Supreme Court.

The District Courts (about 92 in number) hear and decide suits arising within their assigned local district territory. The Circuit Courts of Appeal (13 in number) hear appeals from decisions of the District Courts within their respective circuits, as indicated in Figure 1.2. The limited territorial jurisdiction of these courts explains why the decisions of one district or circuit court are often in conflict with similar cases from their counterparts in other federal district or circuit courts.

Only the Supreme Court of the United States has the nationwide, federal-question jurisdiction that binds all courts of the nation, federal and state, on federal law questions. Only the Supreme Court can resolve lower court conflicts on federal law questions. That fact explains why Supreme Court decisions command special attention, especially with respect to the entire field of teacher and student rights under the Constitution and under the array of federal civil rights statutes that are reviewed in subsequent chapters. However, the Supreme Court can only review a tiny percentage of the many school cases that request its review, so that many important school law decisions by the respective Circuit Courts of Appeal are not reviewed by the Supreme Court, often for long time periods, with the result that the decisions of each Circuit Court remain the binding law within its territory, even though its decisions are in conflict with those of other Circuit Courts. In the absence of a Supreme Court resolution, therefore, school administrators and other affected persons must be particularly attentive to decisions of the particular Circuit Court that covers their place of work. Many examples of significant geographic variations on important school law questions that result from circuit court conflicts will be seen in Chapters 3, 6, 7, 8, and 9.

State Courts.   The structure of state courts also consists of three tiers in most states, with trial courts at the base, followed by midlevel appellate courts, and then a state high court of final appeal. In most states, trial courts operate

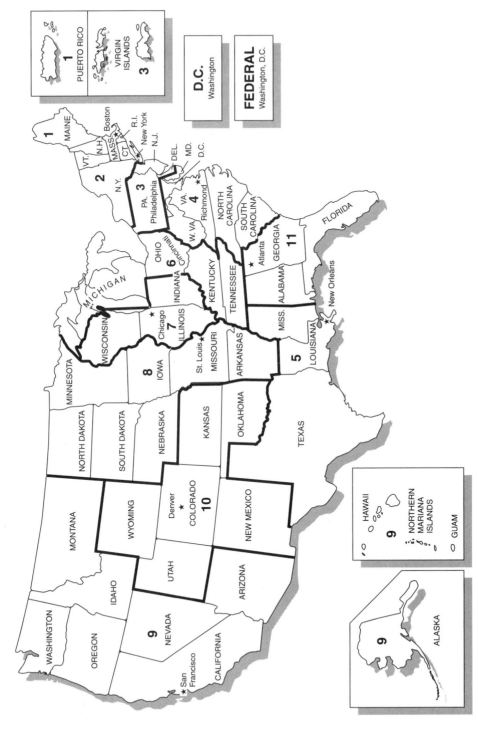

FIGURE 1.2 The Thirteen Federal Judicial Circuits
See 28 U.S.C.A. § 41

within the bounds of established counties, while the intermediate and high courts of appeal take cases from all parts of the state, though they may assign different kinds of cases to each level for initial consideration. Decisions from the highest state court may be appealed to the United States Supreme Court, but as explained above, the Supreme Court decides whether or not to entertain such appeals.

Judge-Made Law—Common Law and Equity Law

The courts have, over time, by their own decisions, created two categories of law that are known as the *common law* and *equity law*. The common law was built, case by case, from legal principles that courts derived initially from established community values and customs and later from their practice of following prior case decisions under a doctrine called *stare decisis* (meaning "let the [past] decision stand") whereby courts felt obliged to follow prior case precedents. The law of contracts, property, and torts originated from and, in many respects still rests on, common law principles.

When the common law courts, petrified through rigid adherence to case precedents, proved inadequate to provide fair and just outcomes in certain situations, royal officials created a separate system of equity courts to provide relief that was not provided by the common law. Equity courts looked less to precedents than to broader principles of justice, and fashioned a separate body of equity doctrines and remedies that became the law of equity. Court decrees to enjoin (order) wrongdoers to desist from harmful conduct as well as to undo past harms are a prominent feature of equity law, and the direct court enforcement of those orders, by subjecting disobedient parties to fines or imprisonment (for contempt of court), are also hallmarks of equity jurisprudence. For example, the court injunction continues to this day to have a crucial impact in labor disputes and in cases of unlawful discrimination. The inherent equity power of courts to provide relief exists in federal as well as state court. As the Supreme Court wrote in a desegregation case:

> The essence of a court's equity power lies in its inherent capacity to adjust remedies in a feasible and practical way to eliminate the conditions or redress the injuries caused by unlawful action. Equitable remedies must be flexible if these underlying principles are to be enforced with fairness and precision. [*Freeman v. Pitts*, 112 S. Ct. 1430, 1444 (1992)]

The common law and equity courts were merged and unified as part of court reform in most states, but the law produced by those courts is preserved as distinct branches of law in all courts.

Access to Court Relief

Courts have fashioned a body of legal standards and principles that a party must meet in order to obtain court relief. Sometimes referred to as the law of "judicial review", these principles determine whether and when parties will be permitted to bring a particular suit. Unless a right to sue and be heard by courts is explicitly created by statute, therefore, courts determine whom they will hear and whose complaint they will review and decide. The law on judicial review, which is fairly extensive and technical, cannot be fully covered here, but two doctrines of special import for school cases are worthy of note, namely, *standing to sue* (which determines *who* can sue) and the *exhaustion* requirement (which determines *when* a party can sue).

Standing Issues—Who Can Sue?   In order to be heard by a court, a party must establish "standing to sue", which requires that a party has suffered a concrete injury-in-fact (as distinguished from an abstract, ethical, or philosophical grievance) from the school practice which the party seeks to challenge. In brief, the suing party must have a personal stake in the subject of the suit and must seek a form of relief that the court is competent to provide. Standing to sue doctrine is concerned only with the required interest of the party bringing suit. It is not concerned with the substantive question whether the sued party has acted illegally. A citizen who has suffered no real or threatened injury to his or her personal right cannot pursue the matter in court, even though the challenged action is manifestly unlawful with regard to other parties. For example, taxpayers have standing to sue on matters regarding the levy or expenditure of taxes which affect their legal obligation to pay taxes, but taxpayers do not have standing to appeal an alleged unlawful suspension of students with whom they have no parental or custodial relationship.[40]

Exhaustion Issues—When May a Party Sue?   Courts generally require that a party with standing first "exhaust" all available avenues of administrative hearing and appeal before the courts will consider a case that challenges an administrative decision.[41] The exhaustion doctrine is intended to encourage efficient settlement of disputes by administrative tribunals and to allow administrative officials to rectify administrative errors by barring premature appeals to courts and, failing such resolution, by providing courts with an adequate record of administrative findings and conclusions that the court is asked to review. [*Weinberger v. Salfi*, 422 U.S. 749, 756–66 (1975)] These reasons for requiring exhaustion of administrative remedies were well summarized by the First Circuit Court of Appeals:

> [E]xhaustion enables the education agency to develop a factual record, to apply its expertise to the problem, to exercise its discretion, and to correct its own mistakes, and is credited with promoting accuracy, efficiency, agency autonomy, and judicial economy. [*Frazier v. Fairhaven School Committee*, 276 F.3d 52, at 59 (1st Cir. 2002)]

Courts recognize certain established exceptions to the exhaustion requirement. Exhaustion is not required where a legislature affirmatively grants a right to institute suit to challenge an administrative decision without recourse to administrative proceedings, and where the exhaustion requirement would not serve its purpose but would frustrate effective judicial relief. For instance, courts do not require administrative exhaustion when the dispute involves only a question of law that an administrative remedy could not effectively correct, or where the administrative agency lacks the authority to provide appropriate relief, or where pursuit of administrative relief would be futile because of intransigent administrative refusal or failure to provide legally required hearings or information, or where the delays incident to pursuit of administrative relief would themselves irreparably defeat or jeopardize the complainant's rights.[42] Thus, exhaustion was not required when administrative hearings on a student's exclusion from a school program could not be completed before that demanded program would expire, or where a school district's repeated failure to provide a required due process hearing for a child with a disability frustrated any prospect of adequate administrative relief.[43] The strongest exceptions to the exhaustion rule are made when delays associated with administrative hearings jeopardize important civil rights, such as freedom of speech.[44] Other important applications of the exhaustion barrier are noted in later chapters.

Court Review of Administrative Decisions

In reviewing challenged administrative decisions, courts do not usually reconsider the entire case, but limit their review to the specific issues that were properly raised by the complainant, and only on the basis of the written record of the administrative proceedings.[45] The fact that a court will not consider questions that were not properly raised with or considered by the administrative tribunal explains why court decisions often ignore important law arguments that could have been, but were not, properly submitted, and why a number of court decisions are sometimes needed to settle all aspects of a particular school problem.

The three principal grounds for judicial reversal of a challenged administrative action or decision are:

1. That it was based on an erroneous interpretation of the law,
2. That it was not supported by substantial factual evidence, or
3. That the author of the the challenged action abused its discretion in taking that action.

For questions of law objections, i.e., where facts are not disputed, courts need only identify and apply the governing law. Thus a board's failure to follow required procedures or its misinterpretation of pertinent law is clear ground for reversal.[46] Where the record of evidence on important facts is conflicting, courts generally look only to the administrative record to decide whether it contains substantial evidence to support administrative findings. In such limited reviews, courts decide not whether they would have viewed the evidence differently than the administrative tribunal, but only whether the administrative record presented "such relevant evidence as a reasonable mind might accept as adequate to support a conclusion."[47]

Similarly, when determining whether administrators abused their discretion, courts only consider the reasonableness of the administrators' judgment, not whether they would have independently arrived at the same judgment.[48] Administrative decisions enjoy a rebuttable presumption of correctness, so that challengers have the burden of demonstrating administrative error in seeking a reversal of administrative decision. In deciding whether a challenged action was rational or arbitrary, courts give greater deference to administrative educational judgments, for which educators are presumptively the primary experts (such as decisions regarding curriculum development),[49] than to judgments that involve legal standards for which judges are the primary experts (such as due process procedures).[50]

Remedies for Administrative Errors.   Past administrative errors can always be cured by timely corrective administrative action, such as providing timely new hearings where past hearings lacked legality. Where timely correction is not taken, courts have also devised several doctrines to excuse or minimize the disruptions of school operations that would take place were the court to overturn unlawful administrative actions.

The *harmless error* doctrine allows courts to treat some errors as harmless and therefore as insufficient ground to invalidate administrative action. With regard to administrative failure to follow statutory procedures, the courts adopted a distinction between *mandatory* and *directory* statutory requirements under which a failure to observe the requirements of a *directory* (merely a helpful but not indispensable) provision may be excused, whereas a failure to follow the requirements of a *mandatory* (meaning a strict obligation) provision would require reversal of the challenged action. While the mandatory/directory classification hinges in theory on legislative intent (whether the provision in question should be taken as mandatory or only as directory), the courts candidly acknowledge that their treatment of a violated provision as mandatory or directory is substantially result oriented and influenced by the practical consequence of overturning the challenged government action.

Generally speaking, the gravity of the error, the magnitude of public cost involved in redoing the statutory process, and the presence or absence of official fault or bad faith are factors that materially affect court decisions. Thus in suits that seek to overturn elections because of some statutory default, courts tend to uphold the election on a finding that the alleged violation involved only directory statutory duties, unless the statutory violation seriously affected the election outcome.[51]

Another judicial doctrine that permits officials retroactively to validate settled arrangements involves a process called *ratification*. The ratification doctrine allows an authorized official, board, or agency retroactively to adopt and approve a past action that could have been, but was not, properly adopted. The technical requisites for effective ratification are complex, but, subject to limited exceptions, the essential requisites for effective ratification are as follows:

1. Ratification can only be effected by a party that is legally authorized to take the action to be ratified.
2. Ratification must follow the same legal formalities as were required by law when the ratified action was initially attempted.
3. Ratification cannot be achieved by accident or in ignorance. The ratifier must specifically intend to affirm the past action with full knowledge of all material facts.
4. Ratification can only be made of the entire past action; it cannot be made for only a part of it.
5. Ratification cannot occur if it results in fraud or unfair consequences to third parties.
6. Ratification can only be made for the actions of parties who purported to act on behalf of the ratifying authority. It cannot cover actions of a party who did not have authority to act as an agent or servant of the ratifier.[52]

Ratification normally requires affirmative administrative action, but in limited circumstances a court may infer a ratification from board inaction, for instance, where a school board silently accepted the benefits of a defectively executed contract.[53] Since the application of the ratification doctrine may require special legal analysis of the relevant facts and circumstances regarding a particular measure, legal counsel should be sought in serious cases.

Note on Law References and Citations

To enable each reader to determine the date and court source of a cited case, and thus to ascertain if that case covers the territory of their particular school and school district (their state or federal circuit), the legal profession and law publishers have developed uniform systems of legal citations which provide that information in convenient capsule form. This information is of special import to educators and administrators who relocate from one state to another, and from one federal circuit region to another. The reader may thus determine from a citation, when, where, and by whom a discussed statute, regulation, or decision was promulgated, and its territorial reach, i.e., whether it is nationwide (Acts of Congress and the U.S. Supreme Court) or regional (decisions of a designated federal circuits or districts) or only statewide or local (cases from state courts or county courts).

The citations used in this book are directed primarily to reports that cover law sources, namely, constitutions, statutes, regulations, and court decisions, but they do include unofficial publications and articles on topics of particular interest to the schools, such as case collections in *Annotations* that are published in *American Law Reports* and in other law journals. The citation references in this text are necessarily selective in their coverage and technical detail, and they do not include all the details of official citation systems. Anyone interested in that exercise may purchase the *Bluebook, A Uniform System of Citation* (17th edition), which is published by the Harvard Law Review Association, 1511 Massachussetts Avenue, Cambridge, Massachusetts 02138.

The following examples illustrate the use of the citation forms in this text.

Constitutions

The citation—U.S. Const., Art. I, § 8, [2]—refers to clause 2 of Section 8 of Article I of the United States Constitution. The citation—U.S. Const., Amend. XIV, § 2 [5]—refers to clause 5 of Section 2 of the Fourteenth Amendment. A roman numeral identifies the particular Article or Amendment, and the following § sign and Arabic numeral indicate the section number within the article being cited. The final bracketed number, e.g., [2], identifies the particular Clause of the Section that is being invoked.

The citation format for state constitutions varies from state to state, but most states employ citations whose initials identify the cited state and whose Articles, Sections, and Clauses are similar to those used for the U.S. Constitution.

Statutes and Regulations

Official statutory citations sometimes include two separate references. The first is a technical, somewhat cumbersome reference to the particular year and session of federal or state legislature that enacted the law. The second is a simplified reference to an official compilation of laws, usually in a multi-volume code whose name, volume, and reference numbers indicate where that statute is to be found. Where code compilations are used, this book uses only the second simplified code citation form, namely, the relevant code name, volume, and page or section that contains the cited statute. Sometimes this citation is preceded by the statute's familiar popular name or by an acronym for that name, e.g., Family Educational Rights and Privacy Act or FERPA.

Generally speaking, the same code name, volume, and page or section number form is used for published administrative regulations of various agencies of the federal and state governments.

Federal statutes are conveniently compiled in the *United States Code.* Thus the citation form "42 U.S.C. § 1983" indicates that the cited law appears in Volume 42 of that code, at § 1983 of that volume. This code does not contain some of the very old federal statutes, but those statutes are not of material interest for this text.

The states also compile and publish their statutes in published state codes, which are labeled and cited in similar manner as the federal code, i.e., by reference to the state code volume and volume section for each law. The titles of state codes, however, are not uniform. Some state codes carry the name or abbreviated name of the state, while others use the name of an official or unofficial compiler. The covered state will however, will be evident from the citation reference to each state code.

Case Citations

Court decisions are published in and cited to official and unofficial case reports, which typically include only cases from an identified court or court level. Thus, one reporter system covers trial courts, while others cover appellate courts. These reporters are generally published in consecutively numbered volumes that are part of a successively numbered series of volumes. For example, decisions of the federal circuit courts appear in a series of the *Federal Reporter* that are marked as F., F.2d, F.3d, and F.4th.

The typical case citation contains the name of the case, which is followed by the volume number of the case reporter that contains it, and is followed by the page number of the reporter where the case is to be found and by the year when the case was decided. For example, *Santa Fe Ind. School Dist. v. Doe*, 530 U.S. 290 (2000) indicates that the *Santa Fe* case is published in volume 530, page 290, of the *United States Reports* and that the case was decided in the year 2000. Because the reporter title "U.S." includes only decisions of the United States Supreme Court, the citation confirms that the case was decided by that Court.

For court decisions that have not or will not be published in a case reporter, the citations usually include reference to the docket number of the court that decided the case along with its name and date of decision. Copies of such cases can often be obtained, for a fee, from the Clerk of the Court whose records contain the unpublished opinion.

United States Supreme Court.   As noted above, the "U.S." reporter is the official reporter for the Supreme Court, but its decisions are also published in unofficial reporters. For example, *Good News Club v. Milford Central Schooling*, 121 S. Ct. 2093 (2001) indicates that this Supreme Court decision may be found in the *Supreme Court Reporter*. Courts and lawyers typically cite to both official (U.S.) and unofficial reporters. This text uses either form as convenience dictates.

Federal Courts of Appeal.   The opinions of the federal circuit courts, as collected in the *Federal Reporter,* are also cited by case name and by the number and page number of the reporter volume that contains the case, together with the number designation of the deciding federal court of appeal and the year of the decision. For example, the citation "*U.S. v. Miami University*, 294 F.3d 797 (6th Cir. 2002)" indicates that the named case is located in Volume 294 of the third federal reporter (F.3d) at page 797 and that the case was decided by the Sixth Circuit Court of Appeals in the year 2002. The citation *"Debra P. by Irene P. v. Turlington,* 730 F.2d 1405 (11th Cir. 1984)" shows that the named case is located in Volume 730 of the second federal reporter (F.2d) at page 1405, and that the case was decided by the Eleventh Circuit Court of Appeals in the year 1984.

Federal District (Trial) Courts.   District court decisions are collected in the *Federal Supplement Reporter.* Like the *Federal Reporter,* the *Federal Supplement Reporter* volumes are published in a series whose volumes are designated as F. Supp and F. Supp. 2d. District Court cases are cited in the same manner as the Circuit Court cases, with an abbreviation indicating the particular federal district in which the case was decided, along with the case name, reporter volume, page number, and year of decision. For example, the citation *"Axtell v. LaPenna,* 323 F. Supp. 1077 (W. D. Pa. 1971)" indicates that the named case is reported in the first F. Supp. series and was decided by the district court for the Western District of Pennsylvania in 1971, whereas the citation *"Doe v. Board of Educ.,* 18 F. Supp. 2d 954 (N. D. Ill. 1998)" indicates that the named case is reported in the second F. Supp. series and was decided by the district court for the Northern District of Illinois in 1998.

State Appellate Courts.   Decisions of state appeals courts are published in official state reporters and in regional reporters, which collect in the same volumes the appellate decisions from a number of states within a specified region. Official state reporters carry an abbreviation of the state's name, while the names of regional reporters indicate the region containing the states whose case reports they contain, e.g., the *Atlantic Reporter* (A. or A.2d), *Northeast Reporter* (N.E. or N.E.2d), *Northwest Reporter* (N.W. or N.W.2d), *Southern Reporter* (So. or So. 2d), *Southwest Reporter* (S.W., S.W.2d), and *Pacific Reporter* (P. or P.2d). Because of the high volume of cases that issue from New York and California courts, cases from those states are reported in separate "regional" reporters (e.g., N.Y.S. and N.Y.S.2d, Cal. Rptr.).

Regional case citations identify the deciding state. For example, *"Sheff v. O'Neill,* 678 A.2d 1267 (Conn. 1996)" indicates that the case issued from a Connecticut appeals court, while the citation *"Hayes v. Board of Educ.,* 431 N.E.2d (Ill. 1982)"* indicates that the case issued from an Illinois appellate court.

State appellate reporters also have a designation that indicates whether the deciding court was an intermediate or the highest court of appeal for that state. For purposes of this book, however, it is not significant that a cited case was made at either level of appeal. For that reason, the state citations in this text often will not include the added citation reference that distinguishes appeal decisions at the intermediate and final appeal stages.

Endnote Symbols.   The endnote case citations often contain italicized symbols that indicate whether the cited case agrees or conflicts with cases decided in other jurisdictions. The specimens illustrate these uses. *"Accord"* means that the case agrees with the previously cited case. *"Contra"* or *"But see"* indicates a case that takes a contrary or different position from that of a previously cited case. *"Cf."* indicates that the cited case offers a different approach than a preceding case reference. *"Compare . . . with"* invites a comparison of cases that present different treatment of the cited matter.

Professional Literature

In addition to case and statute citations, the endnotes in this text also have citations to government and private professional publications that contain useful summaries of collected cases and data on special topics, which sort out the law by individual states. These are particularly helpful for readers who wish to confine their research to the law of their home state. For example, a case *Annotation* in the *American Law Reports* series, cited as "A.L.R.3d, Annot.–Corporal Punishment in Public Schools" and its pocket parts would indicate the current case law on corporal punishment. The cited journals often provide data that is not contained in cited cases. For example, the reports of research institutes and of government agencies that are cited in Chapter 9 track the rapid growth of new laws in each state on charter schools and home schooling.

Chapter 1 Discussion Questions

Where the answer to a question may be qualified by special circumstances, explain the potential qualification.

1. How do a constitution, a statute, and a school board resolution differ from each other?

2. What is the legal import of the following terms?
   a. Jurisdiction
   b. Standing to sue
   c. Administrative law
   d. *Ultra vires*

3. On what grounds may the federal government regulate public education?

4. Where federal and state laws conflict on a given subject, why does the federal law supersede state law?

5. May a court overturn a school board decision that is neither unconstitutional nor *ultra vires*?

6. Which has ultimate legal control over the disposition and use of public schools: the state or a local school district?

7. Name some important areas of day-to-day school operations that are regulated by state education agencies rather than by local school districts.

8. What legal body has authority to:
   a. Alter or abolish your school district without its consent?
   b. Alter the legal powers of your school board?
   c. Determine public school course requirements and textbook selection?

9. What is legally required to conduct official school board business?

10. May a school board meeting be held outside the school district?

11. How does the common law differ from equity law?

12. Why do courts, rather than legislatures or school administrators, have the final word in school disputes?

❧ C A S E S

Case 1.1

DAWSON v. EAST SIDE UNION HIGH SCHOOL DISTRICT
34 Cal. Rptr. 2d 108 (1994)

> [*Focus Note. Whittle Communications, L.P., a for-profit publisher, developed an educational network and audio-video channel called Channel One to transmit into schools a daily program consisting of 10 minutes of current events and 2 minutes of commercial ads by vendors of teen products. Whittle offered its program and the necessary receiving equipment to schools free of charge, because it relied on profits from the sale to commercial vendors of advertising time on its network. The state Superintendent of Public Instruction opposed use of Channel One in public schools, while the California State Board of Education concluded that the use of Channel One was lawful and within the authority of the local school districts. Following the decision by the school board of the East Side Union High School District to use Channel One for its high school, the superintendent and others brought suit to enjoin that use. The trial court denied the injunction, and the appeals court affirmed that ruling. The following opinion illustrates the importance of administrative law doctrines.]*

BAMATTRE-MANOUKIAN, ASSOCIATE JUSTICE

* * *

The essence of the plaintiffs' position . . . is that it is unlawful in any circumstances for a public school district to contract for use in its classrooms of video programming which contains commercial advertising.

* * *

1. Local Control

* * *

By the terms of the [state constitution] . . . primary authority over public education is vested in the Legislature. . . .

The Legislature has explicitly recognized that "because of economic, geographic, physical, political, educational, and social diversity, specific choices about instructional materials need to be made at the local level" (Ed. Code, § 60002), that it has given school district governing boards "broad powers to establish courses of study. . . . " (id. § 60003).

* * *

It follows that courts should give substantial deference to the decisions of local school districts and boards within the scope of their broad discretion, and should intervene only in clear cases of abuse of discretion.

2. Incidental Noneducational Matters

. . . [E]very activity of a California public school must be focused upon valid educational purposes.. . . Nevertheless it has long been recognized that activities or procedures other than those which can be characterized as purely and universally educational may be deemed suitable to further the purposes of education. . . .

* * *

Under the principles of local control . . . the essentially factual question whether particular noncurricular matters are or are not incidental must be addressed in the first instance to the broad discretion of local school districts and boards, and a court would be justified in disturbing the local decision only upon a clear showing of abuse of the local district's or board's sound discretion.

* * *

. . . [W]e shall conclude that the trial court correctly rejected the plaintiffs' contentions that classroom video advertising can never be deemed incidental to valid education purpose. . . . We shall also conclude that the trial court correctly determined that the "Channel One" advertising . . . could lawfully be used in classrooms only so long as students were not coerced to view it.

1. Could "Channel One's" Advertising Ever Be Incidental?

. . . The school district's implicit determination that "Channel One's" current-events programming served a valid educational purpose is supported by the record and was well within the sound discretion of the school district.

. . . Neither Whittle nor anyone else suggests that the school district could properly have given Whittle carte blanche to display classroom video advertising without limitation as to content or duration. . . .

As thus framed by the parties, the primary issue before us is whether the concededly noncurricular "Channel One" advertising could be deemed incidental to the valid educational purpose of the current-events programming.

* * *

. . . [T]he determination whether the advertising was incidental was to be entrusted in the first instance to the broad discretion of the local school district, and the trial court's only concern . . . would have been whether the district's determination constituted a clear abuse of the district's discretion. . . .

. . . We should point out, however, that our concurrence does not and cannot extend beyond the precise circumstances of record in this case: In another case, a showing of more intrusive commercial content, or of less effective editorial content, might warrant a conclusion that it would be an abuse of discretion for a school district to enter into such a contract. Nor should we be understood to suggest that it would have been a clear abuse of discretion for this (or another) school district to have declined to enter into the Whittle contract. . . . We must emphasize once again that a local school district's discretion to make such determinations is broad and must be judicially respected as such.

. . . [T]he plaintiffs attack neither the abstract concept that public school students may be exposed to noncurricular matter incidental to a valid educational purpose, nor the sufficiency of the factual record. . . . Instead, the plaintiffs argue, that as a matter of law, a school district may never lawfully contract for, or display, classroom video advertising such as "Channel One's." . . . The plaintiffs assert that "[i]t is the advertising scheme itself that is the problem, not the educational resources purchased with the revenue from the advertising." . . .

* * *

We shall agree with the trial court that contracts for classroom video advertising are not illegal as a matter of law.

* * *

Next the plaintiffs propose that "[t]elevision advertising should be treated the same as partisan political campaigning." . . . The plaintiffs' broader principle is too broad to be persuasive, or even useful. . . . The principle could as readily be applied to any element of orthodox school curriculum as to which a difference of opinion could be anticipated. . . .

* * *

The plaintiffs argue that statutes require . . . that "all instructional materials shall be 'accurate, objective, and . . . suited to the needs of pupils' and must 'encourage thrift,'" but that . . . "Channel One's" advertisements "exag[g]erate and glorify consumption by pandering to adolescent desires for popularity, status, glitter, and sexual attractiveness." . . .

* * *

The plaintiffs argue, broadly, that "[t]he advertising scheme embodied by 'Channel One' is inconsistent with each of these statutory purposes and State Board policies."

* * *

We are satisfied that the various statutes and State Board policy statements the plaintiffs cite by no means establish as a matter of law that classroom video advertising will be illegal in all circumstances.

c. "Core Values"
Finally, the plaintiffs assert that "[w]hile this case presents novel and difficult issues, it must ultimately be resolved by reliance upon our core values regarding 'public education.'"

(1) Commercial Advertising
The crux of the plaintiffs' core-values argument appears to be their perception that the motives and methods of commercial advertising are simply and irreconcilably antithetical to the ideals of public education.

* * *

The plaintiffs generalize, broadly . . . but they identify no specific harm to students. . . .
    That Whittle stands to make a great deal of money from "Channel One" has nothing whatsoever to do with whether, from the educational standpoint . . . the "Channel One" advertisements were incidental to a valid educational purpose. . . .

* * *

. . . [T]he plaintiffs do not deny, that student exposure to many forms of advertising has long been tolerated. . . . Vending machines . . . commercial logos on computer equipment and . . . scoreboards . . . assigned reading materials from magazines or newspapers . . . yearbooks, . . . class photographers, brandname . . . food service products. . . .
    The plaintiffs undertake to distinguish these forms of commercialism . . . from "the invasive nature of the televised program known as 'Channel One'" which, in the plaintiffs' view, "clearly crosses the line of appropriateness. . . . "

* * *

2. Must Student Viewing be Voluntary?

We agree . . . that public school students cannot be compelled to watch class-room video advertising. [The court then decided that the school's exemption of students who desired not to watch the program removed the legal difficulty.]

Case 1.1 Review Questions

1. Could the court reasonably have construed the authority of the state board more liberally to arrive at a contrary result?

2. What guidance may administrators who are considering potential educational uses of commercially driven Internet technology draw from the above opinion?

Case 1.2

CONOVER v. BOARD OF EDUCATION OF NEBO SCHOOL DISTRICT
267 P.2d 768 (Utah 1954)

[**Focus Note.** *In deciding what is a "public record" open to public inspection under Utah law, the following opinion surveyed the variations in the treatment of public record statutes by individual states.*]

HENRIOD, JUSTICE.

On Feb. 16, 1953, . . . the State Superintendent of Public Instruction . . . advised the [school board] Clerk that minutes of local board meetings were not official until approved by the board. . . . On Feb. 18, the board held a meeting. . . . The Clerk took notes of what transpired, and transcribed them into minutes for board approval and placement in his Journal. On Feb. 19 the plaintiffs asked permission to examine and copy the minutes so transcribed, but the Clerk . . . advised that they would not be available for inspection until the board approved them at its next meeting. . . .

Plaintiffs urge that the notes of the Clerk, or at least the transcribed minutes, prepared for Journal entry, subject only to board approval, were a public writing . . . and should have been open to inspection immediately after preparation, and that preparation immediately should have followed the meeting. Defendants say this might lead to public misinformation and embarrassment . . . because of possible inaccuracies in what they claim were tentative minutes, unofficial until approved and placed in the Journal.

The statutes and cases relating to public writings are divergent as the shading of the spectrum. There appears to be no formula for determining what is or is not a public writing, except by defining the terms, looking at the facts, and relying on court decisions. . . . To hold that a public writing includes the unexpurgated scribbled notes of a Clerk, legible, perhaps, to him alone, would be unreasonable. . . . It would be unreasonable also to hold that any record made by the Clerk short of approval by a board and placement in a Journal, is not a public writing. . . . We hold, therefore, that the Clerk's untranscribed notes reasonably are not classifiable as a public writing under the statute, whereas the transcribed minutes, in final form, but awaiting only approval and placement in the Journal, are a public writing in contemplation of the statute. In so holding, we are aware of those authorities stating that not every memorandum of a public officer is a public record. We believe, however, that the more pertinent cases are found in a long line holding that whenever a written record of a transaction of a public officer in his office is a *convenient and appropriate* mode of discharging the duties of his office, and is kept by him as such, whether required by express provision of law or not, such a record is a public record. To hold that the minutes in this case were not, but the Journal was, a public writing, would attach a magic significance to the word "journal," and might repose in boards a power to act on matters of great public moment without opportunity for public scrutiny.

Here the Clerk did everything he intended to do by way of recording the meeting. Under the statute he could have placed the minutes in the Journal as soon as prepared. The board's policy of having him refrain from doing so until approval was had cannot justify circumvention of a statute requiring him to prepare the minutes, nor the withholding of information from the public for an unreasonable length of time. . . .

The parties here have requested that we address ourselves also to the matter of when the minutes should be available for public inspection. . . . We believe that what is a reasonable time to prepare a record of a public board meeting depends entirely on the facts of each case. If the board action called for the purchase of textbooks advocating communism, the record reasonably should be prepared for public release at once after the meeting, while a resolution to dismiss school on Washington's Birthday perhaps need never be documented. . . . It seems to us that the reasonable time when the record of such meetings should be made available to the public, may vary with the exigencies of the particular case, and the time for preparation and dissemination would be directly proportional to the importance of the action taken.

Both sides concede that the public is entitled to know what happened at school board meetings within a reasonable time. . . . We believe further, that a reasonable time after the meeting for making available the record of actions taken there would be some time *before* any important action was to take place. If available only *after* action taken, such information would have little or no news value. . . .

* * *

There is the further problem as to when *information* of what transpired at the meeting should be made available to the public, quite apart from documentation in a public writing. It would seem that, unless matters were of such a delicate nature or of the type where public policy dictates nondissemination, the meeting itself should be open to the public and press, and information concerning what transpired there should be made available at least in a general way . . . at any time thereafter by him whose duties require its recordation. . . . We . . . hold that although the Clerk's action in refusing permission to inspect his minutes was reasonable for the purpose of obtaining an adjudication of correlative rights and duties, it would be unreasonable in preventing the public and press from obtaining information as to what happened at the meeting.

Case 1.2 Review Questions

1. On what basis did the court make the following decisions?
   a. That untranscribed notes are not public records, but transcribed notes may be.
   b. That transcribed, but unapproved, notes must be made available for inspection within a "reasonable time."
   c. That a "reasonable time" has passed.
   d. That unwritten information on the meeting must be made publicly available.

2. By filling in the gaps left by the written law, did the court make law?

⟋ ENDNOTES

1. Safe school acts have been enacted in California, Connecticut, Georgia, Iowa, Louisiana, Massachusetts, Michigan, Missouri, New York, Pennsylvania, Tennessee, Texas, West Virginia, and Wisconsin. Such laws commonly require schools to adopt and enforce student codes of conduct. See R. C. Cloud, Federal, State, and Local Responses to Public School Violence, 120 *Ed. Law Rep.* 877 (1997).

2. Cathe v. Doddridge County Board of Education, 490 S.E.2d 340 (W. Va. 1997).

3. Bell v. New Jersey and Pennsylvania, 461 U.S. 773(1983).

4. Brandon Valley Indep. School Dist. v. Minnehaha County Board of Educ., 181 N.W.2d 96 (S.D. 1970).

5. Chatham Assn. of Educators v. Board of Pub. Educ., 204 S.E.2d 138 (Ga. 1974).

6. State *ex rel.* Dix v. Board of Educ., 578 P.2d 692 (Kan. 1978); Elk Point Indep. School Dist. v. State Comm'n. of Elementary and Secondary Educ., 187 N.W.2d 666 (S.D. 1971).

7. *The N.Y. Times,* Section B, p. 1 (12–24–96); Section A, p. 1 (12–23–96).

8. Haschke v. School Dist., 167 N.W.2d 79 (Neb. 1969). *See also* Elroy Kendall Witton Schools v. Coop. Educ. Service Agency Dist. 12, 302 N.W.2d 89 (Wis. 1981).

9. Bower v. Arizona State School for the Deaf and the Blind, 704 P.2d 809 (Ariz. 1984); Baer v. Nyquist, 357 N.Y.S. 442 (1974).

10. *See, e.g.,* Carter v. Allen, 250 N.E.2d 30 (N.Y. 1969), where a subsequent statute negated a previously implied power.

11. Floyd v. Waiters, 133 F.3d 786 (11th Cir. 1998); Lockhart v. Cedar Rapids Community School Dist., 577 N.W.2d 845 (Iowa 1998); Packer v. Board of Educ. of Town of Thomaston, 717 A.2d 117 (Conn. 1998).

12. Boyd v. Mary E. Dill School Dist., 631 P.2d 577 (Ariz. 1981).

13. Where state constitutions directly delegate specified powers to a named agency or source, the state legislature cannot alter that arrangement. City of Eastlake v. Forest City Enterprises, Inc., 426 U.S. 668 (1976).

14. Jacob v. Fremont R-1 School Dist., 697 P.2d 414 (Colo. 1984); Boyce v. Alexis I. duPont School Dist., 341 F. Supp. 678 (D. Del. 1972).

15. Survey of the State Administrative Structures in Pa. Dept. of Educ., PREP Rep. No. 23 (1971), at 3, 4.

16. *See, e.g.,* U.S. Dept. of Health, Education, and Welfare, State Departments of Education, State Boards of Education, and Chief State School Officers, DHEW Pub. No. (OE) 73–07400 (1973).

17. *E.g.,* Pordum v. State, 492 N.Y.S.2d 204 (1985).

18. National Institute of Education, U.S. Department of Health, Education, and Welfare, A Study of State Legal Standards for the Provision of Public Education (1979).

19. Moses Lake School Dist. No. 161 v. Big Bend Community College, 503 P.2d 86 (1972); New Castle County School Dist. v. State, 424 A.2d 15 (Del. 1980).

20. The fuzzy scope of the contracts clause is discussed in U.S. Trust Co. of New York v. New Jersey, 431 U.S. 1 (1977); Camardo v. Board of Educ. of City School Dist., 434 N.Y.S.2d 514 (1980). *See also* Michigan Educ. Assn v. North Dearborn Heights School Dist., 425 N.W.2d 503 (Mich. 1988).

21. School Dist. No. 47 of Hall County v. School Dist. of City of Grand Island, 186 N.W.2d 485 (Neb. 1971).

22. Wecherly v. Board of Educ., 202 N.W.2d 777 (Mich. 1972); Nethercutt v. Pulaski County Special School Dist., 475 S.W.2d 517 (Ark. 1972). Savino v. Bradford Central School Dist. Board of Educ., 429 N.Y.S.2d 108 (1980).

23. *Age requirements:* Human Rights Party v. Secretary of State, 370 F. Supp. 921 (E.D. Mich. 1973). *Residency requirements:* Brown v. Patterson, 609 S.W.2d 287 (Tex. 1980). *Family relationships:* Rosenstock v. Scaringe, 357 N.E.2d 347 (N.Y. 1976). The laws on board conflicts of interest, plural job holding, and nepotism vary greatly from state to state. Annot., *Teacher as a Member of School Board,* 70 A.L.R. 3d 1188 (1976).

Re ouster of board member for nepotism, see Cross v. Comm. *ex rel.* Cowan, 795 S.W.2d 65 (Ky. 1990). *Re incompatible dual positions, see* Cranston Teachers Alliance Local No. 1704 v. Miele, 495 A.2d 233 (R.I. 1985).

24. Socialist Workers Party v. Hardy, 607 F.2d 704 (5th Cir. 1977); Communist Party of Indiana v. Whitcomb, 414 U.S. 441 (1974).

25. State v. Cons. School Dist., 281 S.W.2d 511 (Mo. 1955); School Board v. Goodson, 335 So. 2d 308 (Fla. 1976); Konovalchik v. School Comm. of Salem, 226 N.E.2d 222 (Mass. 1967) (voiding teacher hire for lack of school board approval in official meeting). *Ministerial delegation upheld:* Whalen v. Minn. Special School Dist., 245 N.W.2d 440 (Minn. 1976); Dugan v. Bollman, 502 P.2d 113 (Colo. 1972).

26. Big Sandy School Dist. v. Carroll, 433 P.2d 325 (Colo. 1967); Nuxabee County School Bd. v. Cannon, 485 So. 2d 302 (Miss. 1986); Board of Educ. of Baltimore County v. County of Ballard, 507 A.2d 192 (Md. 1986).

27. Mullen v. Board of School Directors of DuBois Area School District, 259 A.2d 877 (Pa. 1969).

28. Quast v. Knudson, 150 N.W.2d 199 (Minn. 1967).

29. *Appropriate notice:* Mead School Dist. v. Mead Educ. Assn, 530 P.2d 302 (Wash. 1975). *Reasonable opportunity to attend:* Rhea v. School Board, 636 So. 2d 1383 (Fla. 1994); News & Observer Pub. v. Interim Board of Educ., 223 S.E.2d 580 (N.C. 1976). *Penalties for notice defaults*: Rhea v. School Board, 636 So. 2d 1383 (Fla. 1994). *Emergency exception*: Cons. School Dist. of Glidden v. Griffin, 206 N.W. 86 (Iowa 1925).

30. Endeavor-Oxford Union Free H.S. Dist. v. Walters, 72 N.W.2d 535 (Wis. 1955); Jacob v. Board of Regents, 365 A.2d 430 (R.I. 1976); Wesley v. Board of Educ., 403 S.W.2d 28 (Ky. 1966).

31. *Effect of withdrawal:* State v. Vanosdal, 31 N.E. 79 (Ind. 1892). *Failure to vote*: Edwards v. Mettler, 129 N.W.2d 805 (Minn. 1964); Bunsen v. County Board of School Trustees, 198 N.E.2d 735 (Ill. 1964). *See also* Oldham v. Drummond Board of Educ., 542 P.2d 1309 (Okla. 1975).

32. Rathman v. Board of Directors of Davenport Community School Dist., 580 N.W.2d 773 (Iowa 1998).

33. *See, e.g., re student discipline:* Hanten v. School Dist. of Riverview Gardens, 13 F. Supp. 2d 971 (E.D. Mo. 1998); Davis v. Churchill County School Bd., 616 F. Supp. 1310 (D. Nev. 1985); Racine Union School Dist. v. Thompson, 321 N.W.2d 334 (Wis. 1982). *Re labor negotiations:* Bassett v. Braddock, 262 So. 2d 425 (Fla. 1972). *Re potential land purchase:* Collinsville Comm. Unit School Dist. No. 10 v. White, 283 N.E.2d 718 (Ill. 1972). *Re employment matters:* McCown v. Patagonia Union School Dist., 629 P.2d 94 (Ariz. 1981). *Re teacher discharge:* School Dist. for City of Royal Oak v. Schulman, 243 N.W.2d 673 (Mich. 1976).

34. *Disapproved closed meetings:* Marxsen v. Board of Directors, 591 A.2d 867 (Me. 1991); Ridenour v. Board of Educ., City of Dearborn, 314 N.W.2d 760 (Mich. 1981); Orford Teachers Assn v. Watson, 427 A. 2d 21 (N.H. 1981).

35. *Compare* Bagby v. School Dist. No. 1, 528 P.2d 1299 (Colo. 1974); Reeves v. Orleans Parish School Bd., 281 So. 2d 719 (La. 1973); *with* Board of Educ. v. State Board of Educ., 443 P.2d 502 (N.M. 1968). Some courts nullify board actions, while others refuse to do so on the view that nullification of board actions would entail unreasonable public costs or harm to third parties who relied on those actions. White v. Battaglia, 434 N.Y.S.2d 537 (1980); Matter of Order Declaring Annexation, 637 P.2d 1270 (Okla. 1981); Toyah Indep. School Dist. v. Pecos-Barstow Indep. School Dist., 466 S.W.2d 377 (Tex. 1971); Dobrovolny v. Reinhardt, 173 N.W.2d 837 (Iowa 1970). In several states, courts limit the remedy for open meeting violations to individual penalties on individual board members, such as fines, suspension, loss of school board office, or monetary liability to injured parties. Griswold v. Mt. Diablo Unified School Dist., 134 Cal. Rptr. 3 (1976); Channel 10 Inc. v. Independent School District, 215 N.W.2d 817 (Minn. 1974).

36. Atty. Gen. v. School Comm. of Northampton, 375 N.E.2d 1188 (Mass. 1978) (names of appointive candidates); Mans v. Lebanon School Bd., 290 A.2d 866 (N.H. 1972) (payroll records).

37. Haight v. Board of Educ., 329 N.E.2d 442 (Ill. 1975).

38. Orford Teachers Assn v. Watson, 427 A.2d 21 (N.H. 1981).

39. Erie R. Co. v. Tompkins, 204 U.S. 64 (1938).

40. Brandon v. Ashworth, 955 P.2d 233 (Okla. 1998); Fort Wayne Educ. Assn. v. Indiana Dept. of Educ., 692 N.E.2d 902 (Ind. 1998). For standing to sue on federal questions, *see* Flast v. Cohen, 392 U.S. 83 (1968).

41. *See* Kincel v. Supt. of Marion County Schools, 499 S.E.2d 862 (W.Va. 1997); Assn. for Community Living v. Romer, 992 F.2d 1040 (10th Cir. 1993); Honig v. Doe, 484 U.S. 305 (1988).

42. *Question of law:* Matthews v. Barrios-Paoli, 676 N.Y.S.2d 757 (1998). *Futility of administrative hearing:* Meehan v. Pachogue-Medoford School, 29 F. Supp. 2d 129 (E.D.N.Y. 1998); Grove City College v. Bell, 465 U.S. 555 (1984). *Harmful delays:* Middough v. Board of Trustees, 119 Cal. Rptr. 826 (1975); Hickey v. Board of School Directors, 328 A.2d 549 (Pa. 1975).

43. Indiana H.S. Athletic Assn. v. Blanche, 329 N.E.2d 66 (Ind. 1975); Meehan, *supra.*

44. LaCroix v. Board of Educ., 505 A.2d 1233 (Conn. 1984); Hayes v. Cape Henlopen School Dist., 341 F. Supp. 823 (D. Del. 1972).

45. Antwerp v. Board of Educ. for Liverpool Central School Dist., 668 N.Y.S.2d 737 (1998).

46. McKelvey v. Colonial School Dist., 348 A.2d 445 (Pa. 1975); Hill v. Dayton School Dist., 517 P.2d 223 (Wash. 1974).

47. Tarbox v. Greensburgh Central School Dist., 375 N.Y.S.2d 610 (1975); Sherefield v. Sheridan County School Dist., 544 P.2d 870 (Wyo. 1976). *See also* Wilson v. Board of Educ., 411 S.W.2d 551 (Tex. 1974).

48. Wolf v. Cuyahoga Falls City School Board of Educ., 556 N.E.2d 511 (Ohio 1990); MidValley Taxpayers v. MidValley School, 416 A.2d 590 (Pa. 1980).

49. State of Mo. v. Schoenlaub, 507 S.W.2d 354 (Mo. 1974); Older v. Board of Educ., 266 N.E.2d 812 (N.Y. 1971).

50. Smith v. Siders, 183 S.E.2d 433 (W. Va. 1971). See discussion of procedural due process in Chapter 6.

51. Butsche v. Coon Rapids Comm. School Dist., 255 N.W.2d 337 (Iowa 1977); Little v. Alto Indep. School Dist., 513 S.W.2d 626 (Tex. 1974) (school bond election).

52. American Law Institute, Restatement of the Law, Agency 2d, §§ 82 –104. (1) Comeaux v. School Employees Retirement Sys., 241 So. 2d 298 (La. 1970) (board could not ratify an *ultra vires* contract). (2) Grippo v. Dunmore School Board, 365 A.2d 678 (Pa. 1976).

53. Sabin v. La. State Board of Educ., 289 So. 2d 554 (La. 1974) (holding board to have ratified lease by conduct other than express words).

CHAPTER 2

Public Schools: Programs and Services

∞ **CHAPTER OUTLINE**
I. Attendance and Admission
    A. Compulsory Attendance Laws
    B. Admission Standards
        1. Residence
        2. Immunization and Health Requirements
        3. Age Requirements
    C. School Assignments
II. Studies Program
    A. Curriculum
        1. Prescribed Courses and Activities
        2. Textbooks and Reading Materials
    B. Extracurricular Activities
        1. Student Clubs
        2. Interscholastic Athletic Associations
    C. Placement, Grading, Promotion, and Graduation
III. Student Services
    A. School Transportation
        1. Distance Limits
        2. Bus Routes
    B. Fees and Charges

∞ **CHAPTER DISCUSSION QUESTIONS**

∞ **CASES**
2.1 Board of Education v. Pico, 457 U.S. 853 (1982)
2.2 Cardiff v. Bismark Public School District, 263 N.W.2d 105 (N.D. 1978)

∞ **ENDNOTES**

This chapter deals with the laws governing the basic elements and programs of public school education, namely, laws governing student attendance and admissions, required and optional studies, student services, and student fees, other than tuition. The separate laws governing those elements for charter schools, private schools, and home schooling are treated in Chapter 9.

ATTENDANCE AND ADMISSION

In pursuing their educational mission, states have enacted compulsory education laws (also called compulsory attendance laws) that direct parents to have their children *attend* a state-approved school or education program. With separate laws directed at local public school authorities, the state prescribes the conditions under which children are to be admitted to a particular school or to a particular grade level of a school. These laws raise a number of questions regarding their intended scope and required or allowed exceptions. Together, they involve the interacting rights and obligations of parents on the one hand, and the authority and discretion of school administrators on the other. Yet the issues raised by each type of statute are treated as separate topics for decision by the courts.

Compulsory Attendance Laws

Children of specified ages must attend public schools if they do not receive alternative state-approved education. State laws typically exempt certain classes of children from compelled attendance, such as emancipated youngsters (i.e., those who are married or self-supporting beyond a certain age), youngsters of working age who must work to provide essential family support, and children whose disabilities render them incapable of benefiting from normal schooling.

Exemption from compulsory attendance on religious grounds has been constitutionally required if two conditions are met; first, that continued school attendance would place a "substantial" (not merely inconvenient or distasteful) burden on essential religious beliefs and practices and, second, that the state cannot demonstrate a compelling interest to require continued schooling, notwithstanding religious objections. The lead Supreme Court decision on this issue involved Amish children whose parents claimed that their attendance at school beyond the eighth grade would violate their rights under the Free Exercise Clause of the First Amendment (which is more thoroughly reviewed in Chapter 3). In *Wisconsin v. Yoder*, 406 U.S. 205 (1972), the Court ruled that the state attendance law could not be constitutionally enforced against the parents or their children because the state did not show that the Amish children required further schooling in order to lead self-sufficient, responsible lives within the Amish farming community. The Court made clear, however, that philosophical or cultural objections, as distinguished from religious objections, would not qualify for constitutional exemption. Claims of religious exemption have been denied in most cases because the petitioners did not establish to the courts' satisfaction that compulsory schooling would coerce them to act against basic religious tenets or obligations.[1] Native American objections that public schools do not adequately teach about Indian culture and heritage or that the school's hair length regulation conflicted with Native American religious tradition were found insufficient to require constitutional exemption.[2]

Narrower exemptions from participation in a specific school activity, such as flag salute and pledge of allegiance exercises, have also been allowed for students and teachers whose constitutional freedom of expression overrode the school's interest in fostering patriotism. Parents who object to a particular school exercise may not totally withdraw the child from the school, but may demand excusal of their child from the constitutionally offensive practice.

Protection of children from grave risks of harm is a recognized ground to excuse attendance at an assigned school,[3] but a parent seeking such excusal must establish that the alleged danger is sufficiently grave and that the school authorities are unable or unwilling to provide adequate protection from it. Judicial appraisals of these factors will vary with the environment of each case and also with the perception of the deciding judge. Evidence of extortion, threats, and physical assault by students was held sufficient to excuse student nonattendance at a school in one case, while evidence of violent student assaults with sharp instruments was insufficient to excuse such attendance in another case that arose in the same state.[4] Similar variations in court judgments appeared in New York, where one court found child mistreatment insufficient ground for excusal, while another court upheld a parent's unilateral removal of a child from a dangerous school, even though she used a false address in order to have her child admitted to another school.[5] The early unsafe school cases do not provide much guidance for balancing child safety and orderly school administration in the contemporary culture in which violence has become endemic to many schools and where increased school security arrangements have proven inadequate to control it.

Similar safety problems are presented when a school's location, rather than internal school disorder, puts students who walk to the school in danger. Here also a court may, on a finding of sufficient danger, exempt the child from attending that school.[6] Statutes that directly regulate school assignments and affect school transfer disputes are discussed in the following "School Assignments" section.

Compulsory education laws may be enforced by prosecution of parents for child neglect, by court removal of a child from their custody, or by actions against truant children, including placement of truants in custodial schools.[7] Where severe penalties are sought against parents, state prosecutors must prove the charge by "clear and convincing evidence."[8]

Admission Standards

To receive tuition-free admission to a public school, children must meet state-specified conditions in terms of age, residence, immunization, and other conditions that school authorities may reasonably impose.[9]

Residence

The requirement that a child of school age reside within the school district in order to attend one of the district's schools has been upheld against constitutional challenges.[10] In most states, school districts may admit nonresidents under legally specified conditions, notably that parents or other custodians pay to the admitting district a specified charge, as calculated under a specified formula to determine the district's cost of educating the nonresident child.

To establish local residency, the child must live within the district and have a bona fide intention to live there indefinitely. Legally emancipated minors have their own residence, but an unemancipated minor is presumed to reside with his or her parents or with a legal custodian when parents are divorced, separated, or away.[11] This presumption does not apply to children whose parents have died or abandoned them.[12] For example, legal custody by a child's grandparents was recognized when the addresses of the child's father and mother were unknown. On petitions to award custody of a child to nonparents, courts consider the best interests of the child and the good faith, character, and competence of the petitioning parties.[13] But where a child remained with a natural parent and not with the legally appointed guardian, the child was deemed to reside with the parent.[14]

Homeless children are subject to special federal and state laws that address their unique circumstances and guarantee their public education. The federal Homeless Assistance Act of 1987 defines a homeless person as one who lacks a regular nighttime residence or whose residence is a temporary living accommodation. It directs that each state adopt a plan for the education of homeless children within its borders, including adequate rules and records to ensure that those children are afforded transportation and other school services.[15]

Immunization and Health Requirements

The right to a tuition-free public education under state law may be qualified by health and safety reasons. A strong state interest in protecting school populations from communicable diseases is sufficient to compel immunization of students and to override objections that the practice violates constitutional rights, even religiously grounded rights.[16] However, a state may, as a matter of policy, exempt religious objectors from such immunizations, and many states have done so.

The compelling state interest in preventing the spread of seriously harmful diseases also justifies exclusion of children with communicable diseases. The HIV virus was initially thought to present such a risk and to justify exclusion of infected students and teachers from schools, but courts have since ruled that the risk of transmitting the virus is so limited that it does not justify exclusion of infected individuals.[17]

Age Requirements

Where the minimum age for admitting students to a school is set directly by law, school authorities must enforce it. When the applicable state law grants local school authorities the discretion to waive the minimum age requirement and to admit younger children, local decisions to deny early admission may still be challenged and overruled if a court finds the decision to be arbitrary and an abuse of administrative discretion.[18]

School Assignments

As with admissions, state law determines whether student transfers between schools within a district are prohibited, or whether local authorities have discretion to allow such transfers.[19] Here also courts will not overturn school decisions unless they involve an abuse of discretion or an error of law.[20] Where a musically talented student was reassigned from a school that offered music studies to one that provided none, the court overturned the reassignment as an abuse of discretion.[21]

In making initial school assignments, administrators may subordinate the interests of the assigned student to the needs of the total school population, particularly where limited resources confine school choices.[22] As previously noted, however, weighty considerations of child safety may outweigh otherwise valid fiscal or administrative considerations.

Where school closings necessitate reassignment of students from the closed school, they may be governed by special provisions of school closing statutes.[23] Such closings raise the question whether other forms of reorganization, such as consolidation of classes from different schools, are to be considered and governed by the school closing statute. For example, a partial grade elimination was not deemed to be a closing under North Dakota's statute.[24]

School assignments are also controlled by antidiscrimination principles of constitutional law and civil rights statutes, as such laws supersede state assignment statutes, e.g., where such assignments create or perpetuate racial segregation. The panoply of discrimination laws are reviewed in Chapters 6, 7, and 8.

STUDIES PROGRAM

The classification of school programs affects their administration. For example, laws and regulations on school curriculum may be read narrowly to govern only courses given regularly for credit, or they may be read broadly to govern extracurricular activities and a broad range of life experiences. The following discussion illustrates the range of choices to be made on specific school services.

Curriculum

Curricular arrangements may have different objectives, i.e., "return to basics", "multicultural" studies, or some combination of traditional and progressive themes of education. Educators may, therefore, differ in structuring their school curricula and course offerings beyond those mandated by state law. The general parameters of control over curriculum are summarized in the following, somewhat dated, report.

> In all states the local district must offer a curriculum that the state prescribes. . . . In about half the states the local district must offer the curriculum prescribed by the state. . . . Even in those states where districts retain some discretion, course offerings must still be chosen within state guidelines. . . . For example, all schools must offer courses in American history and government. . . . In addition, the choice of the district is often limited by state board guidelines regulating the number, content or quality of the courses. Some states provide that a district must offer a specified number of courses. . . . Sanctions for noncompliance would include . . . loss of state aid. . . . The local district selects its curriculum offerings on the basis of the . . . authority delegated by the State. [National Institute for Education, A Study of State Legal Standards for the Provision of Public Education (1974), at 28]

Subject to the foregoing constraints, school administrators have broad authority to expand or modify their curricula. Physical education, health inspection, medical treatment, career training, and counseling are now accepted parts of a school's mission.

Prescribed Courses and Activities

Efforts to promote or suppress particular instructional content, teaching methods, or various school programs inevitably involve conflicting interests and values of some parents, school administrators, teachers, churches, and special-interest groups, and thereby invite challenges to the authority to control such programs.

District residents cannot force local school boards to add or delete particular courses unless a state legislature directly empowers them to do so, or unless a challenged course is unlawful under state law, as *ultra vires* the school district's authority, or is unconstitutional for all purposes. Absent such grounds, school officials may eliminate or reduce courses and services not mandated by state law. Conflicts are particularly acute over subjects previously consigned to private or family initiative, such as courses and services dealing with sexual relations, pregnancy, contraception, abortion, homosexuality, and AIDS. These lively topics are discussed in further detail in later chapters.

Disputes over a parental request to choose a child's course of study have been largely limited to the issue whether the school's refusal of such a request amounts to an abuse of discretion. Nor may students demand that a school offer courses or services that are available at other schools.[25] Relief can be had, however, where school authorities unreasonably disregard the welfare of a student.[26] Kindergarten programs are mandated in some states and left to local district option in others. Where the standards for first-grade admission are set by state law, school districts may not alter them by adding other requirements.[27]

Unusual graduation requirements have been challenged under administrative law and under constitutional law. A court sustained the validity of a school requirement that students perform community service in order to graduate and rejected the student argument that compelled community service abridged student liberty and subjected students to involuntary servitude.[28]

Unlike compulsory nonclassroom services, assigned classroom readings present broader and more varied constitutional problems, as discussed next.

Textbooks and Reading Materials

The law on textbook selection varies from state to state. In some states local districts must select class texts from a state-approved list. In others, the local districts may adopt supplementary texts that are not on the state list. In a few states, state agencies provide recommended book lists that do not bind local district discretion to select other course books.

Complaints are perennially raised against the use of particular books, on charges that they ignore or disparage particular racial, ethnic, gender, religious, or political groups or undermine social morality, patriotism, or religious beliefs. Religious objections to book content are considered in greater detail in Chapter 3. To prevail on such complaints, challengers face—and often cannot meet—a high burden of proving that the book contents irremediably injure the challengers. "[D]eference to local control . . . is a recognition of the varying wants and needs of the Nation's diverse and varied communities, each with its unique character, standards and sense of social importance of a variety of values."[29]

Attempts to overturn book selections or removals have been notably unsuccessful.[30] In *Board of Education v. Pico*, reported at the end of this chapter as Case 2.1, the Supreme Court provided some guidance on school board authority to remove books from a high school library over the constitutional objections of teachers, parents, and students. Seven of the nine Justices wrote separate opinions that expressed at least three different constitutional viewpoints. Even so, the majority of Justices agreed on the following points:

- School boards could constitutionally select course books based on their educational judgment without being limited by the desires or opinions of parents, teachers, or students.
- School board decisions on classroom texts are less open to challenge than decisions regarding library books for optional student use.
- School boards could constitutionally undertake to "inculcate" community values by removal of materials that they in good faith consider to be "educationally" unsuitable.

The *Pico* opinions sent the case back to the lower courts to consider the central question without providing much guidance on how to answer it, i.e., how to determine whether the board's reason for removing the books was "educational" (and therefore constitutional) or "political" (and therefore unconstitutional). Later courts interpreted *Pico* to support school board authority to ban, as educationally unsuitable for high school students, Chaucer's *Miller's Tale* and Aristophanes' *Lysistrata*,[31] and to overrule teacher selections of supplemental classroom readings.[32]

Board control over teacher reading assignments and the distribution of noninstructional literature on school property raise related First Amendment issues, which are discussed in Chapters 6 and 7.

Laws that are directed to accommodate students with physical, intellectual, and emotional disabilities require special education programs. Those laws are reviewed in Chapter 7.

Extracurricular Activities

Public schools are expressly required to conduct specified nonacademic activities in many states. In addition, local districts have implied power to sponsor extracurricular activities that reasonably relate to the school's educational goals. The scope of that implied power remains a potential question as to what activities are reasonably related to proper school goals.

Student Clubs

Schools may prohibit "secret" or "oath bound" clubs or clubs that exclude students based on the vote of existing members. The school's educational interests in discouraging undemocratic practices has been held to outweigh student First Amendment freedom of association.[33]

Interscholastic Athletic Associations

School board membership in and submission to associations that regulate school and student conduct in interscholastic contests, both academic and non-curricular, have survived the challenge in most states that such membership involved an unlawful redelegation of school board authority.[34]

Association rules and decisions are subject to reversal for abuse of discretion,[35] but they have generally been upheld as reasonable. Rules to suspend or disqualify students or schools from interscholastic competition for talent raiding, school jumping, residency violations, redshirting, extramural training with outside teams, and student exclusion from interscholastic competition for academic deficiency or misconduct have survived legal challenge.[36] A suspension of a school from association competition was upheld even though the suspension prevented the school from honoring its game contracts with other schools.[37]

As agents of member schools, athletic associations are engaged in "state action". They may not discriminate on the basis of race, gender, or marriage, or among schools, and they must afford due process in disciplinary proceedings that affect student rights.[38] However, in the view of most courts, a student's interest in participating in school athletics does not rise to the level of a constitutional "right" and does not require the highest level of constitutional due process.[39] Association rules that bar coed competitions raise issues of gender discrimination, which are reviewed more fully in Chapter 7. Association rules that exclude or impose different burdens on nonpublic schools or their students have, however, been upheld as having a reasonable basis.[40]

Placement, Grading, Promotion, and Graduation

Class placement, grading, and promotion are generally left to local control. Students have no inherent right to promotion, and courts are disinclined to interfere with school placement policies or decisions.[41] For example, a board's demand that a child register for kindergarten before taking a test for advanced placement was upheld.[42] Courts will, however, strike down decisions that discriminate between new students admitted to higher grades on the basis of age, while requiring other students of like age to pass tests for like advancement.[43] Courts are inclined to uphold school decisions to refuse to advance a bright child to a higher grade.

> Certainly, the court may not hold as arbitrary or capricious the respondent's determination that chronologically determined physical, social, and emotional maturity are vital and proper factors to be considered. . . . [*Ackerman v. Rubin*, 231 N.Y.S.2d 112, 114 (1962)]

Courts are inclined to overturn academic penalties, such as adverse placements, grade reductions, or denials of promotion, as unreasonable when used to punish students for nonacademic misconduct, but academic penalties have been sustained in some circumstances.[44]

Promotion requirements are generally set by local authorities, but a growing number of states have imposed minimum achievement or competency requirements for the award of a standard high school diploma. Unless found to be unfair or discriminatory, these requirements have withstood legal challenge.[45] In some states, students must pass a prescribed exit examination, while in others, local boards have the option to set achievement conditions or prescribe their own tests for graduation.[46]

A student who satisfies the academic requirements for graduation cannot be denied a diploma for nonacademic misconduct or defaults, such as failure to pay school fees.[47] Courts have even overturned denials of diploma for academic infractions where that sanction was deemed unreasonable and excessive.[48] A graduating student's right to participate in graduation ceremonies presents a different question, but there also courts have disagreed on the question whether exclusion from the graduation exercise for disciplinary reasons was reasonable or an abuse of discretion.[49]

STUDENT SERVICES

School Transportation

Courts have refused to imply school board authority to provide school transportation services, but nearly all states have statutes that mandate or authorize school transportation.[50] States may constitutionally prescribe different transportation for different classes of schools or students, so long as the classifications are deemed reasonable.[51] Unless mandated by state law, local boards may refuse to provide school transportation service provided they do so in a nondiscriminatory manner.[52] Parents may not demand transportation to a district school other than the student's assigned school, or to a school outside the district,[53] unless state law expressly requires it, such as laws enacted for students who have specified disabilities.[54]

Distance Limits

Minimum student home-to-school distances for school busing service are generally set by local school boards. A board's refusal to provide transportation for a small number of poor students from an inaccessible part of the district was overruled as an abuse of discretion,[55] but safety factors may also justify board denial of busing services, e.g., to areas where the roads are unsafe.[56] Excessive meticulousness in measuring distances in order to deny transportation may also be overturned as capricious, for instance, where the minimum distance was measured to a student's driveway curbside (disqualified) rather than to his home (qualified).[57]

Bus Routes

A school board may not require pupils to walk unreasonable distances from their homes when setting bus route pickup or discharge points. Here also state laws require accommodation of students who lack safe walking paths or encounter hazardous crossings. School payments to parents for privately provided school transportation, in lieu of school bus service, has not been widely litigated, but the practice was upheld where roads were unsafe for use by school buses.[58]

Fees and Charges

As school fees proliferate to cover school materials or services, their legality has been increasingly challenged, primarily on the ground that they violate state laws that provide for a "free" public education. State education statutes that do not clearly address the fee questions may be read broadly as entitling students to receive all public school materials and services at no charge, or narrowly as entitling students only to free materials and services that are essential or reasonably required for an adequate "education". The state-to-state variations on public school fees may arise from differences in the interpretation of the education articles of state constitutions and of state laws on the meaning of a "free" public education. Courts in different states may also disagree as to what school materials or activities are properly part of such an education.[59] The mixed case law of different states is noted in the endnote[60] and in the *Cardiff* case, which appears at the end of this chapter as Case 2.2.

Similar variations exist on activity fees. The Supreme Court of California, after ruling that the state constitution prohibited assessment of any extracurricular activity fee, later held that school transportation fees were permissible under California law.[61] The law with regard to fees for summer school classes, adult courses, or other programs outside the normal school year, may also invite different readings of state laws that pertain to such programs.

Chapter 2 Discussion Questions

Where the answer to a question may be qualified by special circumstances, explain the potential qualification.

1. Do state agencies, local school boards, or both generally regulate the following functions?
    a. School attendance zones and school assignments
    b. Extracurricular programs
    c. Grading, promotion, and graduation
    d. School transportation

2. Name the principal grounds on which a school district may deny a child admission to public schools.

3. What are the general requirements to establish a legal residence at a particular location?

4. On what grounds may parents challenge or overturn school assignment of their children to a particular class activity? Explain.

5. When, if ever, may a parent resist immunization of a child against contagious diseases?

6. In the absence of a busing statute, may a school district provide school transportation to its students?

7. What laws determine whether or not a school district may charge student fees for:
   a.   Course textbooks?
   b.   Admission to participate in extracurricular activities?
   c.   Gym suits?

Case 2.1

BOARD OF EDUCATION v. PICO
457 U.S. 853 (1982)

> [**Focus Note.** *Suit to challenge school board removal of nine books from school libraries. The Second Circuit Court of Appeals ordered a trial to determine whether the board was acting from unconstitutional motives in removing the books. The Supreme Court by a 5–4 vote affirmed that order, but the Justices could not agree on the constitutional basis for the decision.]*

JUSTICE BRENNAN announced the judgment of the court [in an opinion not signed or joined by a majority of the nine Justices].

We emphasize at the outset the limited nature of the . . . question presented. . . . . . . For as this case is presented to us, it does not involve textbooks, or indeed any books that Island Trees students would be required to read. Respondents do not seek . . . to impose limitations upon their school board's discretion to prescribe the curricula of the Island Trees schools. . . . [T]he only books at issue in this case are *library* books, books that . . . are optional rather than required reading. Our adjudication of the present case thus does not intrude into the classroom, or into the compulsory courses taught there. . . . Rather, the only action challenged in this case is the *removal* from school libraries of books originally placed there by the school authorities. . . . . . .

* * *

We are therefore in full agreement . . . that local school boards must be permitted "to establish and apply their curriculum in such a way as to transmit community values," and that "there is a legitimate and substantial community interest in promoting respect for authority and traditional values be they social, moral, or political."

* * *

Of course, courts should not "intervene in the resolution of conflicts which arise in the daily operation of school systems" unless "basic constitutional values" are "directly and sharply implicate[d] in those conflicts." *Epperson v. Arkansas*, 393 U.S., at 104. But we think that the First Amendment rights of students may be directly and sharply implicated by the removal of books from the shelves of a school library. . . . And we have recognized that "the state may not, consistently with the spirit of the First Amendment, contract the spectrum of available knowledge." . . . In keeping with this principle, we have held that in a variety of contexts "the Constitution protects the right to receive information and ideas. . . . "

This right is an inherent corollary of the rights of free speech and press. . . . . . .

More importantly, the right to receive ideas is a necessary predicate to the *recipient's* meaningful exercise of his own rights of speech, press, and political freedom. . . .

* * *

. . . It appears . . . that use of the Island Trees school libraries is completely voluntary. . . . Their selection of books . . . is entirely a matter of free choice. . . . . . .

* * *

. . . Petitioners rightly possess significant discretion to determine the content of their school libraries. But that discretion may not be exercised in a narrowly partisan or political manner. . . . Thus whether petitioners' removal of books . . . denied respondents their First Amendment rights depends upon the motivation behind petitioners' actions. If petitioners *intended* . . . to deny respondents access to ideas with which petitioners disagreed, and if this intent was the decisive factor in petitioners' decision, then petitioners have exercised their discretion in violation of the Constitution. . . . On the other hand, respondents implicitly concede that an unconstitutional motivation would not be demonstrated if it were shown that petitioners had decided to remove the books at issue because those books were pervasively vulgar. . . . And again, respondents concede that if it were demonstrated that the removal decision was based solely upon the "educational suitability" of the books in question, then their removal would be "perfectly permissible. . . . "

* * *

. . . [I]n brief, we hold that local school boards may not remove books from school library shelves simply because they dislike the ideas contained in those books and seek by their removal to "prescribe what shall be orthodox in politics, nationalism, religion, or other matters of opinion." *West Virginia Board of Education v. Barnette*, 319 U.S., at 642. . . .

Justice Blackmun, concurring in part and concurring in the judgment.

To my mind, this case presents a particularly complex problem. . . . On the one hand, as the dissenting opinions demonstrate . . . the court has acknowledged the importance of the public schools "in the preparation of individuals for participation as citizens, and in the preservation of the values on which our society rests." *Ambach v. Norwick,* 441 U.S. 68, 76 (1979). . . . Because of the essential socializing function of schools, local education officials may attempt "to promote civic virtues," *Ambach v. Norwick,* 441 U.S., at 80. . . .

* * *

In my view, then, the principle involved here is both narrower and more basic than the "right to receive information" . . . I do not suggest that the state has any affirmative obligation to provide students with information or ideas. . . . And I do not believe, as the plurality suggests, that the right at issue here is somehow associated with the peculiar nature of the school library. . . . . . .Certainly, the unique environment of the school places substantial limits on the extent to which official decisions may be restrained by First Amendment values. But that environment also makes it particularly important that some limits be imposed. . . . In starker terms, we must reconcile the schools' "inculcative" function with the First Amendment's bar on "prescriptions of orthodoxy."

In my view, we strike a proper balance here by holding that school officials may not remove books for the *purpose* of restricting access to the political ideas or social perspectives . . . when that action is motivated simply by the officials' disapproval of the ideas involved. . . .

. . . [S]chool officials must be able to choose one book over another, without outside interference, when the first book is deemed more relevant to the curriculum, or better written, or when one of a host of other politically neutral reasons is present. . . . First Amendment principles would allow a school board to refuse to make a book available to students because it contains offensive language . . . or because it is psychologically or intellectually inappropriate for the age group, or even, perhaps, because the ideas it advances are "manifestly inimical to the public welfare." *Pierce v. Society of Sisters,* 268 U.S. 510, 534 (1925). . . .

[Concurring opinion of JUSTICE WHITE *omitted.]*

CHIEF JUSTICE BURGER, *with whom* JUSTICE POWELL, JUSTICE REHNQUIST, *and* JUSTICE O'CONNOR *join, dissenting.*

* * *

I agree with the fundamental proposition that "students do not 'shed their constitutional rights to freedom of speech or expression at the schoolhouse gate.'" . . . Here, however, no restraints of any kind are placed on the students. They are free to read the books in question, which are available at public libraries and bookstores. . . . Despite this absence of any direct external control on the students' ability to express themselves, the plurality suggests that there is a new First Amendment "entitlement" to have access to particular books in a school library. . . .

* * *

In short . . . there is not a hint in the First Amendment, or in any holding of this court, of a "right" to have the government provide continuing access to certain books.

* * *

[Dissenting opinion of JUSTICE POWELL omitted.]
JUSTICE O'CONNOR, *dissenting.*

If the school board can set the curriculum, select teachers, and determine initially what books to purchase for the school library, it surely can decide which books to discontinue or remove from the school library so long as it does not also interfere with the right of students to read the material and to discuss it. As Justice Rehnquist persuasively argues, the plurality's analysis overlooks the fact that in this case the government is acting in its special role as educator.

I do not personally agree with the board's action with respect to some of the books in question here, but it is not the function of the courts to make the decisions that have been properly relegated to the elected members of school boards. . . . I therefore join the Chief Justice's dissent.

[Dissenting opinion of JUSTICE REHNQUIST omitted.]

[The nine books in the high school library were: Slaughterhouse Five, *by Kurt Vonnegut, Jr.;* The Naked Ape, *by Desmond Morris;* Down These Mean Streets, *by Piri Thomas;* Best Short Stories of Negro Writers, *edited by Langston Hughes;* Go Ask Alice, *of anonymous authorship;* Laughing Boy, *by Oliver Lafarge;* Black Boy, *by Richard Wright;* A Hero Ain't Nothin' But a Sandwich, *by Alice Childress; and* Soul on Ice, *by Eldridge Cleaver. The book in the junior high school library was* A Reader for Writers, *edited by Jerome Archer. Still another listed book,* The Fixer, *by Bernard Malamud, was found to be included in the curriculum of a twelfth grade literature course. . . .]*

Case 2.2

CARDIFF v. BISMARK PUBLIC SCHOOL DISTRICT
263 N.W.2d 105 (N.D. 1978)

*[**Focus Note.** School fees. Parents of elementary school children brought suit to overturn school rental fees for required textbooks. In deciding whether the fees violated*

the state constitution, the court surveyed the range of positions taken by sister states.]

SAND, JUSTICE.

* * *

The basic issue . . . is whether or not . . . the North Dakota Constitution . . . prohibits the Legislature from authorizing school districts to charge for textbooks. . . .

To resolve the first issue we must examine and construe the provisions of § 148 of the North Dakota Constitution. . . .

In 1968 this section was amended, as follows:

The legislative assembly shall provide for a uniform system of free public schools throughout the state. . . .

* * *

In 1895 the North Dakota Legislature enacted chapter 109, the title of which provides as follows: "AN ACT to Provide for Free Text Books and School Supplies for the Use of the Pupils in the Public Schools of North Dakota." The body of the Act, however, conditions the free textbooks upon a favorable election by a majority of qualified electors of the district. . . . The title of the Act is misleading when compared to the body of the Act. . . .

From this examination we are left with a firm conviction that the legislative acts referred to do not lend any significant comfort or aid to the resolution of the basic question under consideration. . . . The Journal entries of the constitutional convention are not very helpful in determining the meaning of the language, "free public schools."

* * *

From this brief review it is clear that the framers consistently had in mind a free public school.

A short survey of the constitutional provisions of other states and their case law will shed some light on our question.

Arizona: . . . In *Carpio v. Tucson High School District No. 1 of Pima County,* 111 Ariz. 127, 524 P.2d 948 (1974) . . . the court had under consideration Article XI, § 6 of the Arizona Constitution. The court held that textbooks were not required to be furnished to high school students. However, the court referred to an earlier decision . . . where the court held that these constitutional provisions had been satisfied when the legislature provided for the means of establishing required courses, qualifications of teachers, textbooks to be used in common schools, etc. Considering this statement and the statement in *Carpio* that "textbooks have not been provided free in high schools as they have been in the common schools" leaves the impression that under the constitutional provisions of Arizona textbooks in common schools were provided free of charge.

Colorado: . . . In *Marshall v. School District RE # 3 Morgan County*, 553 P.2d 784 (Colo. 1976), the court held that the school district was not required to furnish books free of charge to all students.

Indiana: . . . In *Chandler v. South Bend Community School Corporation*, 160 Ind. App. 592, 312 N.E.2d 915 (1974), the court held that this constitutional provision did not require textbooks to be provided free, but merely to provide a system of common schools where tuition would be without charge.

Illinois: . . . In *Beck v. Board of Education of Harlem Consolidated School District No. 122*, 63 Ill. 2d 10, 344 N.E.2d 440 (1976), the court held that workbooks, and other educational material, were not textbooks so as to come within the statutory provision of free textbooks, and as such it did not preclude the school board from charging the parents a fee for supplying the students with such material. Earlier, in *Hamer v. Board of Education of School District No. 109*, 47 Ill. 2d 480, 265 N.E.2d 616 (1970), the court was specifically concerned with the constitutional provision and held that under its provisions the school board was not prohibited from purchasing textbooks and renting them to pupils. . . .

Wisconsin: . . . The court in *Board of Education v. Sinclair*, 65 Wis. 2d 179, 222 N.W.2d 143 (1974), held that the schools may charge a fee for the use of textbooks and items of similar nature authorized by statute and that such did not violate the constitutional provision commanding that schools shall be free without charge for tuition for all children. . . .

Idaho: . . . In *Paulson v. Minidoka County School District No. 331*, 93 Idaho 469, 463 P.2d 935 (1970), the court held that school districts could not charge students for textbooks under the state constitutional provision. . . .

Michigan: . . . The Michigan court in *Bond v. Public Schools of Ann Arbor School District*, 383 Mich. 693, 178 N.W.2d 484 (1970), held that the 1963 constitutional provision meant that books and school supplies were an essential part of the system of free public elementary and secondary schools and that the schools should not charge for such items. . . .

Montana: . . . In *Granger v. Cascade County School District No. 1*, 159 Mont. 516, 499 P.2d 780 (1972), the school district, as the school district here, contended that the pertinent language simply meant "tuition-free" as far as required courses were concerned and did not prohibit fees and charges for optional extra-curricular or elective courses and activities. . . . The Montana Supreme Court answered the question in the following manner:

> We believe that the controlling principle or test should be stated in this manner: Is a given course or activity reasonably related to a recognized academic and educational goal of a particular school system? If it is, it constitutes part of the free, public school system commanded by Art. XI, Sec. 1 of the Montana Constitution and additional fees or charges cannot be levied, directly or indirectly, against the student or his parents. If it is not, reasonable fees or charges may be imposed.

The court, however, pointed out that its decision does not apply to supplementary instruction offered by the school district . . . during the summer recess or at special times. . . .

New Mexico: . . . The court, in *Norton v. Board of Education of School District No. 16*, 89 N.M. 470, 553 P.2d 1277 (1976), held that . . . courses required of every student shall be without charge to the student. However, reasonable fees may be charged for elective courses. The court also recognized that the board of education shall define what are required or elective courses in the educational system of New Mexico.

South Dakota: . . . We have found no South Dakota case law on the question of tuition or textbooks.

West Virginia: . . . The court in *Vandevender v. Cassell*, 208 S.E.2d 436 (W. Va. 1974), held that furnishing textbooks free to needy students satisfied the constitutional requirement. But two of the five judges . . . stated that they did not interpret "free" as pertaining only to indigent pupils. . . .

Missouri: . . . The court held in *Concerned Parents v. Caruthersville School District No. 18*, 548 S.W.2d 554 (Mo. 1977), that under this [Missouri] constitutional provision school districts were prohibited from charging registration fees or course fees in connection with courses for which academic credit was given.

Washington: . . . The Supreme Court of the State of Washington, in *Litchman v. Shannon*, 90 Wash. 186, 155 P. 783 (1916), said: "Public schools are usually defined as schools . . . open without charge to the children of all the residents of the town or other district."

. . . From this study we have concluded that the courts have consistently construed the language "without payment of tuition" or . . . such similar language to mean that a school is prohibited from charging a fee for a pupil attending school. This language has also been construed as not prohibiting the charging of fees for textbooks.

However, as to constitutions containing language such as "free public schools" or "free common schools" or similar language, the courts have generally held, with a few exceptions, that this language contemplates furnishing textbooks free of charge, at least to the elementary schools. The exceptions have generally relied upon extrinsic material such as contemporary construction, history, or practices, as well as the language itself. . . .

A comparison of the key constitutional provisions and existing case law of states which entered the Union at the same time and under similar conditions as North Dakota will be very helpful and valuable in determining the intent of the people of North Dakota in adopting § 148 of the North Dakota Constitution. . . .

The key language in the constitutional provisions of the four States are as follows:

Montana: " . . . thorough system of public, free common schools."

South Dakota: " . . . uniform system of public schools wherein tuition shall be without charge."

North Dakota: " . . . uniform system of free public schools throughout the state. . . . "

Washington: " . . . uniform system of public schools. . . . "

We are impressed with the different language employed in the constitutions of the four states . . . Montana, South Dakota, North Dakota, and Washington, which came into the Union at the same time and under the same Enabling Act. . . .

It is significant to note that Montana and North Dakota adopted the "free common schools" and the "free public schools" concept, whereas South Dakota adopted the "public schools wherein tuition shall be without charge" concept, and Washington merely provided for a "uniform system of public schools."

. . . If the framers of the North Dakota Constitution and the people of North Dakota had in mind only to provide public schools without charging tuition they could have, and probably would have, used the language "without payment of tuition" or "wherein tuition shall be without charge," rather than the language "free public schools." The term "free public schools" without any other modification must necessarily mean and include those items which are essential to education.

It is difficult to envision a meaningful educational system without textbooks. . . .

. . . We cannot overlook the fact that attendance at school . . . was compulsory from the very beginning. . . . This lends support to the contention that textbooks were to be included in the phrase "free public schools."

* * *

. . . After a review of the case law and constitutional provisions of other states . . . we have come to the conclusion that the term "free public schools" means and includes textbooks, and not merely "free from tuition." . . . Sections 15–43–07, 15–43–08, 15–43–09, 15–43–10, and 15–43–12, North Dakota Century Code, to the extent that they apply to elementary textbooks, are in conflict with § 148 of the North Dakota Constitution and are therefore invalid and unconstitutional as to elementary school textbooks. . . .

⤎ ENDNOTES

1. State v. Kasubowski, 275 N.W.2d 101 (Wis. 1978) (exemption denied as based on philosophical, not truly religious, grounds).

2. Matter of McMillan, 226 S.E.2d 693 (N.C. 1976); Hatch v. Goerke, 502 F.2d 1189 (10th Cir. 1974).

3. As to unsafe school conditions, *see* Annot., *Conditions at Schools as Excusing or Justifying Nonattendance*, 9 A.L.R. 4th 122 (1981); and cases in next note. As to dangerous travel conditions, *see, e.g., Re* Richards, 7 N.Y.S.2d 722 (1938).

4. *Compare* School Dist. of Pittsburgh v. Zebra, 325 A.2d 330 (Pa. 1974), *with* Comm. *ex rel.* School Dist. v. Ross, 330 A.2d 290 (Pa. 1975).

5. Matter of Baum, 382 N.Y.S.2d 672 (1976); *in re* Foster, 330 N.Y.S.2d 8, 10 (1972).

6. Williams v. Board of Educ., 99 P. 216 (Kan. 1908).

7. *Parental prosecution*: Scoma v. Ill., 391 F. Supp. 452 (N.D. Ill. 1974); Matter of McMillan, 226 S.E.2d 693 (N.C. 1976). *Truancy proceeding: Re* T.V.P., 414 N.E.2d 209 (Ill. 1980).

8. Santosky v. Kramer, 450 U.S. 993 (1982).

9. Hammond v. Marx, 406 F. Supp. 853 (D. Me. 1975) (minimum age requirements for admission to public school upheld); O'Leary v. Wisecup, 364 A.2d 770 (Pa. 1976).

10. Martinez v. Bynum, 461 U.S. 321, 75 L. Ed. 2d 879 (1983).

11. Mathias v. Richland School Dist., 592 A.2d 811 (Pa. 1991); Matter of Montcrieffe, 467 N.Y.S.2d 812 (1983).

12. Sleesman v. State Board of Educ., 753 P.2d 186 (Ariz. 1988). *See also* Simms v. Roosevelt Union Free School Dist., 420 N.Y.S.2d 96 (1976).

13. Sleesman, prior note; University Center, Inc. v. Ann Arbor Pub. Schools, 191 N.W.2d 302 (Mich. 1971).

14. Matter of Proios, 443 N.Y.S.2d 828 (1981); School Dist. No. 3 of Maricopa County v. Dailey, 471 P.2d 736 (Ariz. 1970).

15. 42 U.S.C.A. § 11302. P. First and G. Cooper, *Access to Education by Homeless Children*, 53 Ed.

Law Rep. 757 (1989); Harrison v. Sobol, 705 F. Supp. 870 (S.D. N.Y. 1988).

16. Jacobson v. Cmwlth. of Mass., 197 U.S. 11 (1905); Calandra v. State College Area School Dist., 512 A.2d 809 (Pa. 1986).

17. *See generally* Annot., *AIDS Infections as Affecting Right to Attend Public Schools*, 60 A.L.R. 4th 15 (1988); Hammett, *Protecting Children with AIDS against Arbitrary Exclusion from School*, 74 Cal. L. Rev. 1373 (1986); L. Rothstein, *Children with AIDS*, 12 Nova L. Rev. 1259 (1988); Martinez v. School Board of Hillsborough County, 861 F.2d 1502 (11th Cir. 1988); Doe v. Dolton Elementary School Dist., 694 F. Supp. 440 (N.D. Ill. 1988).

18. *Compare, e.g.,* Zweifel v. Joint Dist. No. 1, Belleville, 251 N.W.2d 822 (Wis. 1977) (sustaining board decision), *with* Blessing v. Mason County Board of Educ., 341 S.E.2d 407 (W. Va. 1985) (overturning decision as abuse of discretion).

19. Board of Educ. v. Oklahoma School Board of Educ., 521 P.2d 390 (Okla. 1974); Board of School Directors v. Dock, 318 A.2d 370 (Pa. 1974).

20. Ramsdell v. N. River School Dist. No. 200, 704 P.2d 606 (1985); Fitzpatrick v. Board of Educ., 578 F.2d 858 (10th Cir. 1978).

21. *In re* Reassignment of Hayes, 135 S.E.2d 645 (N.C. 1964).

22. Bronestine v. Geinsendorfer, 613 S.W.2d 465 (Mo. 1981) (transfer of certain classes to non-neighborhood school); Zoll v. Anker, 414 F. Supp. 1024 (S.D. N.Y. 1976) (shortened school hours).

23. Bartlett v. Board of Trustees, 550 P.2d 416 (Nev. 1976).

24. Choal v. Lyman Ind. School District, 214 N.W.2d 3 (N.D. 1974).

25. *Re course reductions, see* Board of Educ. of Okay Indep. School Dist. v. Carrol, 513 P.2d 872 (Okla. 1973). *Re service reductions, see* Borough v. Governing Bd. of El Segundo Unified School Dist., 173 Cal. Rptr. 729 (1981). *Re elimination of electives, see* Messina v. Sobol, 553 N.Y.S.2d 529 (1990).

26. *In re* Reassignment of Hayes, note 21, *supra.*

27. *See, e.g.,* Morgan v. Board of Educ., 317 N.E.2d 393 (Ill. 1974).

28. Herndon v. Chapel Hill-Carrbora City Board of Educ., 89 F.3d 174 (4th Cir. 1996); Immediato v. Rye Neck School Dist., 73 F.3d 454 (2d Cir. 1996); Stirer v. Bethlehem Area School Distr., 987 F.2d 989 (3rd Cir. 1993).

29. Mercer v. Michigan State Board of Educ., 379 F. Supp. 580, 585 (E.D. Mich.), *aff'd,* 419 U.S. 1081 (1974).

30. *See, e.g.,* Pratt v. Indep. School Dist. No. 831, 670 F.2d 771 (8th Cir. 1982); Zykan v. Warsaw Comm. School Corp., 631 F.2d 1300 (7th Cir. 1980); Sheck v. Baileyville School Comm., 530 F. Supp. 679 (D. Me. 1982); Mozert v. Hawkins County Board of Educ., 827 F.2d 1058 (6th Cir. 1987) (as offensive to Christianity); Williams v. Board of Educ., 388 F. Supp. 93 (S.D. W. Va. 1975) (as offensive to parents' beliefs); Rosenberg v. Board of Educ., 92 N.Y.S.2d 344 (1949) (as offensive to Jews).

31. Virgil v. School Board, 677 F. Supp. 1547(M.D. Fla. 1988).

32. Fisher v. Fairbanks N. Star Borough School, 704 P.2d 213 (Ala. 1985); Case v. Unified School Dist. No. 233, 908 F. Supp. 864 (D. Kan. 1995).

33. Passel v. Ft. Worth Indep. School Dist., 453 S.W.2d 888 (Tex. 1970); Robinson v. Sacramento City Unified School Dist., 53 Cal. Rptr. 781 (1966).

34. *Upheld:* Dennis J. O'Connell H.S. v. Virginia H.S. League, 581 F.2d 81 (4th Cir. 1978) (regulation of literary, debating and athletic competition); ABC League v. Missouri State H.S. Activities Assn., 530 F. Supp. 1033 (E.D. Mo. 1982) (statewide regulation of speech, debate, and music competition as well as athletics). *Contra:* Bunger v. Iowa H.S. Athletic Assn., 197 N.W.2d 555 (Iowa 1972).

35. Crane v. Indiana High School Athletic Assn., 975 F.2d 1315 (7th Cir. 1991) (overturning as abuse of discretion use of school transfer rule to disqualify student moving to reside with a parent).

36. Kirby v. Mich. H.S. Assn., 585 N.W.2d 290 (Mich. 1998); Aldering v. Ohio H.S. Athletic Assn., 779 F.2d 315 (6th Cir. 1985); OSAA v. Stout, 692 P.2d 633 (Or. 1984); E. New York Youth Soccer Assn. v. N.T. State Pub. H.S., 488 N.Y.S.2d 293 (1985). *Suspension for academic failure*: Brands v. Sheldon Comm. School Bd., 671 F. Supp. 627 (N.D. Iowa 1987) (citing supporting cases from 5th, 6th, 8th, and 10th Circuit Courts of Appeal).

37. State v. Judges of the Court of Common Pleas, 181 N.E.2d 261 (Ohio 1962).

38. *State action found:* Arkansas Activities Assn. v. Meyer, 805 S.W.2d 58 (Ark. 1991). *Discrimination prohibited:* Clark v. Arizona Interscholastic Assn., 695 F.2d 1126 (9th Cir. 1982); Dobson v. Arkansas Activities Assn., 469 F. Supp. 394 (E.D. Ark. 1979); Haas v. S. Bend Comm. Corp., 289 N.E.2d 495 (1972) (sex). *See also* Mahan v. Agee, 652 P.2d 765 (Okla. 1982) (age). *Due process:* Duffley v. New Hampshire Interscholastic Athletic Assn., 446 A.2d 462 (N.H. 1982).

39. Bailey v. Truby, 321 S.W.2d 302 (W. Va. 1984); Tenn. Secondary School Athletic Assn. v. Cox, 425 S.W.2D 5097 (Tenn. 1968).

40. Griffin H.S. v. Ill. H.S. Assn., 822 F.2d 671 (7th Cir. 1987); Windsor Park Baptist Church, Inc. v. Arkansas Activities Assn., 658 F.2d 618 (8th Cir. 1981); Walsh v. Louisiana H.S. Athletic Assn., 616 F.2d 152 (5th Cir. 1980); Dennis J. O'Connell H.S. v. Virginia H.S. League, 581 F.2d 81 (4th Cir. 1978); Christian Brothers Institute v. N. New Jersey Int. League, 432 A.2d 26 (N.J. 1981).

41. Arundar v. DeKalb County School Dist., 620 F.2d 493 (5th Cir. 1980); Erik V. v. Causby, 977 F. Supp. 384 (E.D. N.C. 1997); Sandlin v. Johnson, 643 F.2d 1027 (4th Cir. 1981).

42. Frost v. Yerozunis, 385 N.Y.S.2d 181 (1976); Rosenstein v. N. Penn School Dist., 392 A.2d 788 (Pa. 1975).

43. Catlin by Catlin v. Sobol, 569 N.Y.S.2d 353 (1991).

44. *Compare* Jones v. Latexo Indep. School Dist., 499 F. Supp. 223 (E.D. Tex. 1980), *with* Donaldson v. Board of Educ., 424 N.E.2d 737 (Ill. 1981).

45. Brookhart v. Ill. State Board of Educ., 697 F.2d 179 (7th Cir. 1983); Williams v. Austin Ind. School Dist., 796 F. Supp. 251 (W.D. Tex. 1992); Board of Educ. v. Ambach, 436 N.Y.S.2d 564 (1981), *aff'd,* 458 N.Y.S.2d 680 (1982).

46. Brookhart, prior note.

47. *See* Annot., *Student's Right to Compel School Officials to Issue Diploma,* 11 A.L.R. 4th 1182 (1982). Shuman v. Cumberland Valley School Dist. Bd. of Directors, 536 A.2d 490 (Pa. 1988).

48. Ryan v. Board of Educ., 257 P. 945 (Kan. 1927) (overturned denial of diploma for student possession of unauthorized materials during a test); State *ex rel.* Miller v. McLeod, 605 S.W.2d 160 (Mo. 1980) (overturned denial of graduations for one-half credit shortfall).

49. *Compare, e.g.,* Ladsen v. Board of Educ., 323 N.Y.S.2d 545 (1971) (overturning exclusion of student who struck principal), *with* Fowler v. Williamson, 251 S.E.2d 889 (N.C. 1979) (upholding exclusion of student not attired for graduation per the school's regulation).

50. "In almost all states the responsibility for providing pupil transportation rests with the local school districts. However, the districts are almost equally divided between [those] having mandatory and discretionary provisions. . . . Transportation distances vary considerably from state to state. . . . A few states . . . set different distance standards for elementary and secondary schools. . . . A few states require . . . transportation under legislated standards which allow the district a certain amount of discretion. . . . In all states the fixing of school bus routes is left to the local districts, but many state education agencies issue regulations concerning bus routes. . . ." (National Institute of Education, *A Study of State Legal Standards for the Provision of Public Education,* 1974, at 57)

51. Kadrmas v. Dickinson Pub. Schools, 487 U.S. 450 (1988).

52. Plesnicer v. Kovach, 430 N.E.2d 648 (Ill. 1981); Abraham v. Wallenpaupak Area School Dist., 422 A.2d 1201 (Pa. 1980); Shrewsbury v. Board of Educ., 265 S.E.2d 767 (W. Va. 1980).

53. Hatch v. Board of Educ., Ithaca City School Dist., 439 N.Y.S.2d 466 (1981) (transportation denied student attending non-neighborhood schools under open enrollment program).

54. Morrisette v. DeZonia, 217 N.W.2d 377 (Wis. 1974).

55. Manjares v. Newton, 411 P.2d 901 (Cal. 1966).

56. State v. Grand Coulee Dam School Dist., 536 P.2d 614 (Wash. 1975); Randolph v. School Unit 201, 270 N.E.2d 50 (Ill. 1971).

57. Nelson v. Board of Educ., 587 A.2d 1327 (N.J. 1991).

58. State v. Grand Coulee Dam School Dist., note 56, *supra.*

59. *See generally* Annot., *Validity of Public School Fees,* 41 A.L.R. 3d 752 (1972, Supp. 1998). *Re summer school fees, compare* Washington v. Salisbury, 306 S.E.2d 600 (1983) (permitted) *with* Cal. Teachers Assn. v. Board of Educ., 167 Cal. Rptr. 429 (1980) (prohibited). *Re charges for elective courses, compare* Norton v. Board of Educ., 553 P.2d 1277 (N.M. 1976) (permitted), *with* Concerned Parents v. Caruthersville School Dist., 548 S.W.2d 554 (Mo. 1977) (prohibited). *Re use of "related to education" test for such charges, see* Grange v. Cascade School Dist., 499 P.2d 780 (Mont. 1972); Vandevender v. Cassell, 208 S.E.2d 436 (W. Va. 1974).

60. *Re book and supply fees, compare* Marshall v. School Dist., 553 P.2d 784 (Colo. 1976) (upheld); Carpio v. Tucson High School Dist., 524 P.2d 948 (Ariz. 1976) (for elementary school only), *with* Union Free School Dist. v. Jackson, 403 N.Y.S.2d 621 (1978) (disallowed). *Re fees for swim suits and music instruments, compare* Board of Educ. v. Sinclair, 222 N.W.2d 143 (Wis. 1974) (upheld), *with* Grange v. Cascade County School Dist., 499 P.2d 780 (Mont. 1972) (disallowed). *Re fee exemptions for needy students, see* Marshall v. School Dist., *supra;* Chandler v. South Bend Comm. School Corp., 312 N.E.2d 915 (Ind. 1974); Hamer v. Board of Educ., 292 N.E.2d 569 (Ill. 1973).

61. *Compare* Hartzell v. Connell, 679 P.2d 35 (1984) (extracurricular activity fees—overturned) *with* Arcadia Unified School Dist. v. State Dept. of Educ., 825 P.2d 438 (Cal. 1992) (school transportation fee—upheld).

CHAPTER 3

Public Schools: Religious Controversies

☙ **CHAPTER OUTLINE**
I. Constitutional Constraints on Public School Actions
    A. The Establishment of Religion Clause—Bar to Promoting Religion
    B. The Free Exercise Clause—Bar to Burdening Religion
    C. The Freedom of Speech Clause—Bar to Limiting Speech
    D. Community Uses of School Facilities
    E. State Law Constraints
II. Typical School–Religion Controversies
    A. Prayer, Bible Reading, and Meditation
        1. Classroom Exercises
        2. Nonclassroom Prayer and Religious Activities
        3. Religious Art—Holiday Commemorations
        4. School Excusals for Religious Purposes
    B. Religion-Related Courses and Programs
        1. Evolution
        2. The Bible as History and Literature
        3. Sex Education
        4. Course Textbooks and Class Readings
    C. Other Religious Objections and Exemptions
        1. Flag Salutes
        2. Dress and Conduct Requirements
        3. Immunization
    D. Public School Services to Nonpublic Schools and Students
    E. Direct School–Church Dealings
        1. Public School Uses of Church Property
        2. Church Uses of Public School Property

☞ **CHAPTER DISCUSSION QUESTIONS**

☞ **CASES**

3.1 Good News Club v. Milford Central School, 121 S. Ct. 2093 (2001)
3.2 Santa Fe Independent School District v. Jane Doe, 120 S. Ct. 2266 (2000)
3.3 Adler v. Duval County School Board, 250 F.3d 1330 (11th Cir. 2001)
3.4 Lee v. Weisman, 112 S. Ct. 2649 (1992)
3.5 Brown v. Hot, Sexy and Safer Productions, Inc., 68 F.3d 525 (1st Cir. 1995)

☞ **ENDNOTES**

CONSTITUTIONAL CONSTRAINTS ON PUBLIC SCHOOL ACTIONS

The United States Constitution pervasively affects the management of public schools, largely by constraints that prohibit public school policies or practices. This is particularly true for three clauses of the First Amendment, known as the Establishment, Free Exercise, and Freedom of Speech Clauses, all of which figure prominently in religion-related disputes in the public schools. The First Amendment reads as follows:

> Congress shall make no law respecting *an establishment of religion,* or prohibiting *the free exercise thereof; or abridging freedom of speech or of the press;* . . . [U.S. Const., Amend. I] (Emphasis added)

Though this Amendment mentions only the Congress, it now applies to the actions of states and state subdivisions, such as public school districts, by way of the Fourteenth Amendment. [U.S. Const., Amend. XIV] The Fourteenth Amendment was held to "incorporate" the substantive guarantees of the First Amendment in *Cantwell v. Connecticut,* 310 U.S. 296 (1940), an early religious liberty case. Since then, the Supreme Court has repeatedly reaffirmed that holding:

> We have long recognized that the [Fourteenth] Amendment's Due Process Clause . . . guarantees more than fair process. The [Due Process] Clause also includes a substantive component that provides heightened protection against government interference with certain fundamental rights and liberty interests. [*Troxel v. Granville,* 530 U.S. 57, 65 (2000)]

This chapter considers the First Amendment limitations on school policies and practices from the perspective of the managers of public schools at the state and local administrative levels. The effects of the Constitution on particular interests and civil rights of teachers, students, and others are discussed further in Chapters 5, 6, 7, and 8.

As indicated in Chapter 1, once the Supreme Court of the United States decides what the Constitution means and how it operates with regard to the First Amendment clauses, its ruling binds all courts and schools. Its decisions will therefore command special attention and respect in all public schools, and in this text as well.

Some preliminary observations on Supreme Court constitutional interpretation may help the reader to understand why some of its important decisions appear to be choppy and to lack a consistent logical progression from case to case. The first and principal reason is that the Court has not developed a single, overarching doctrine or jurisprudence that governs the application of all three of the above-quoted First Amendment clauses. Rather, it has considered each clause as a separate command, and has developed separate doctrines to test the validity of actions and different remedies for the violation of each one. For example, it is easier to overturn a school action under the Establishment Clause than under the Free Exercise Clause. In order to prevail on an Establishment Clause claim, a party need only show that the challenged action advances or aids religion, whereas to prevail under the Free Exercise Clause, a party must prove that the challenged action "coerces" the complainant to act contrary to the essential tenets of his religion.

> The Establishment Clause, unlike the Free Exercise Clause, does not require a showing of direct governmental compulsions and is violated . . . whether those laws operate directly to coerce nonobserving individuals or not. [*Engel v. Vitale,* 370 U.S. 421 (1962)]

In addition, an Establishment Clause violation voids *in toto* the offensive law or practice, and prohibits continued use of that law or practice. A violation of the Free Exercise Clause, however, does not in most cases void the challenged law or practice *in toto,* but only the application of that law or practice to individuals who are thereby coerced to act contrary to their religion. In sum, exemption rather than nullification suffices as a constitutional remedy for infringement of free exercise of religion.

The divergent law on each Clause presents a second difficulty where both clauses potentially cover the same case, with each Clause supporting a competing constitutional argument. In such situations the courts must decide which Clause should govern.

The third difficulty arises from a human dynamic, namely, the persistent disagreements among the nine Supreme Court Justices on the approach to constitutional interpretation, loosely called strict versus liberal interpretation, and the occasional wavering by "swing" Justices between these approaches, which shifted the balance of many five-to-four Court decisions.

Given the foregoing factors, the constitutional constraints on school management are best understood in terms of specific case treatment of the Establishment, Free Exercise, and Free Speech Clauses.

The Establishment of Religion Clause—Bar to Promoting Religion

The Supreme Court has recognized that the Establishment Clause and the Free Exercise Clause are in some tension with each other and that they would clash if either were pressed to its absolute limit. [*Lemon v. Kurtzman,* 397 U.S. 664, 668–69 (1970)] Taken as an absolute, the Establishment Clause would require denial of all government services or assistance to religiously affiliated entities (hospitals, orphanages, schools), a position which the Court has rejected, e.g., in decisions upholding government employment of chaplains by the armed services and government grants of tax exemptions for church edifices. As further noted later, the Court has also rejected an absolutist reading of the Free Exercise Clause which would bar any government regulation that imposes any burden on one's practice of religion. Courts often avoid pitting one clause against the other by finding that only one of them governs a presented case.

The Supreme Court Justices have often disagreed on what constitutes an "establishment of religion". The general agreement that the Establishment Clause was intended at least to prevent the establishment of an official national religion, thereby avoiding sectarian strife, yields little guidance for contemporary school–religion disputes. Whatever one's view as to what the Court "ought" to decide, one cannot seriously claim that the Supreme Court Justices have achieved a clear consensus on what actions amount to an establishment of religion for all public education purposes. Even the question of what acts involve "religion" remains problematic, as the Supreme Court has carefully declined to venture a constitutional definition of "religion".[1] The real, tough law is thus to be found, not in any of the abstract propositions, but in the case histories where particular constitutional tests are applied or rejected.

As a basis for defining "establishment of religion", the talismanic call for "separation of church and state" is not very helpful. Most cases involve not direct church–state relations, but varied relationships between the states (public schools) and religion in general, and a wide range of personal interests of parents, students, teachers, and taxpayers who have no fixed alignment with a particular church or denomination. Church–state philosophy does not address the narrow question as to what kinds and degrees of government–religion interactions are prohibited or permitted by the Establishment Clause.

Since the Supreme Court initiated the modern development of Establishment Clause interpretation with the 1947 parochial school busing decision, different blocs of Justices have from time to time espoused one or more of the following measures of an Establishment of Religion:

a. The Establishment Clause requires *strict and absolute separation* of state school functions and religion, at least for direct government aids to religious schools. [*Everson v. Board of Education*, 330 U.S.1 (1947)]
b. The Establishment Clause permits government *accommodation of religion,* though it incidentally aids religious interests of students and their parents. [*Zorach v. Clauson*, 343 U.S. 306 (1953)]
c. The Establishment Clause requires that government religion-related programs must serve a *secular (vs. religious) purpose and have a "primary" secular (vs. religious) effect*. [*Lemon v. Kurtzman*, 403 U.S. 602 (1971)]
d. The Establishment Clause only forbids *"excessive entanglement"* of government with religion. [*Agostini v. Felton*, 521 U.S. 203 (1997)]
e. The Establishment Clause requires only that government *does not in fact or appearance endorse religion,* regardless of a law's benefit or burdens to religion. [*Mitchell v. Helms*, 530 U.S. 793, 843 (2000)]
f. The Establishment Clause is satisfied if the government is *"neutral"* to religion. [*Zelman v. Simpson-Harris*, 122 S. Ct. 2460 (2002)]

Each of these cases and tests, as later noted, allow wiggle room for different judgments in their application, so that judges who accept the same test may still disagree on its outcome in a given case. For example, all the Justices in *Everson* expressed a strict church–state-separation/no-aid-to-religion test, but they then fell out on the result, with five Justices deciding that publicly paid bus transportation to parochial schools is a constitutionally valid child-benefit program. But, as with the "wall of separation", the child-benefit theory also produced ragged results, with some cases upholding government aids to students in church-related schools, and others overturning other benefits as aids to religion. The same may be said of other constitutional "tests". The *accommodation* of religion theory has problematic limits. Where the state created a special education district to serve the children of a specific religious community of Orthodox Jews, that action was overturned and held not to be a permissible accommodation of religion.[2] The entanglement test has proven even more elusive:

> Not all entanglements, of course, have the effect of advancing or inhibiting religion. Interaction between churches and state is inevitable . . . and we have always tolerated some level of involvement between the two. Entanglement must be *'excessive'* before it runs afoul of the Establishment Clause. [*Agostini v. Felton*, 521 U.S. 203, 232 (1997)] (Emphasis added)

The *endorsement* test also invites varied readings:

> [What] is crucial is that a government practice not have the effect of communicating a message of government endorsement or disapproval of religion. [*Lynch v. Donnelly*, 465 U.S. 668 (1984)]

> . . . [B]ecause our concern is with the political community writ large, the endorsement inquiry is *not about the perceptions of particular individuals* or saving isolated nonadherents from . . . discomfort. . . . It is for this reason that the reasonable observer in the endorsement inquiry must be deemed aware of the history and context of the community and forum in which the religious [speech takes place]. [*Capitol Square Review and Advisory Bd. v. Pinette*, 515 U.S. 753, 779–80, . . . (1995)] (O'CONNOR, J., concurring) (Emphasis added)

Finally, the oft cited "purpose-effects" *Lemon* test has also commanded wavering support. All of which led Justice O'Connor to disavow strict adherence to any of the mentioned "tests":

> In the end, I would recognize that the Establishment Clause inquiry cannot be distilled into a fixed, per se rule. Thus, "[e]very government practice must be judged in its unique circumstances to determine whether it constitutes an endorsement or disapproval of religion." [*Capitol Square Review and Advisory Board v. Pinette*, 515 U.S. 753, 778 (1995)]

The latest Supreme Court decisions indicate a trend toward favoring the neutrality theme over the separation theme, but those decisions indicate that the votes of the Courts' Justices have been more informed by weighing specific case factors than by any universal "test" of constitutionality.

Later sections in this chapter undertake a more complete review of the Establishment Clause cases in the school context.

The Free Exercise Clause—Bar to Burdening Religion

The Free Exercise Clause prohibits public school authorities from penalizing, discriminating against, or otherwise *unduly* burdening religious belief or practice, unless the state can show a *compelling* government need to do so. The clause does not forbid all laws that place some incidental burdens on the practice of religion. For example, the Supreme Court, in *Wisconsin v. Yoder*, 406 U.S. 205 (1972), ruled that the state could not constitutionally require Amish children to attend school beyond eighth grade, because such attendance violated a basic command of their religion (be not conformed to this world), but the Court carefully limited its ruling to the special case fact that the state did not show a compelling interest or need to force children of the Amish religion and farm culture to attend school beyond eighth grade. It did not overturn the compulsory attendance law of Wisconsin.

Another example that Free Exercise Clause limitations may only require exemption from, but not nullification of, a law is found in the landmark flag salute case, which held that public schools could not compel certain students to participate in classroom flag salute exercises contrary to their religious belief that saluting the flag would be gravely sinful.[3] Nor does the Free Exercise Clause prohibit laws that incidentally place some burden on the practice of religion. [*Employment Division v. Smith*, 110 S. Ct. 1595 (1990)] Nor could Congress reverse Supreme Court decisions by legislation. The Religious Freedom Restoration Act of 1993 attempted to do so, but the Supreme Court overturned that law as interfering with its power to determine what the Constitution permits or prohibits. [*City of Boerne v. Flores*, 117 S. Ct. 2157 (1997)]

Later sections in this chapter provide topical examples of Free Exercise issues that arise in public schools.

The Freedom of Speech Clause—Bar to Limiting Speech

The reference to "speech" in the Constitution and in the following discussion includes written as well as oral expression, and symbolic as well as verbal expression. Freedom of speech claims may intersect with establishment of religion claims, as where school authorities exclude religiously motivated speakers from school-use privileges that are accorded to nonreligious speakers. The resolution of that potential collision is noted in the next section on "Community Uses of School Facilities."

The Free Speech Clause clearly does not bar all school restrictions on school-site speech. For one, it does not prohibit school authorities from suppressing certain unprotected categories of speech, such as obscenity, fighting words, terroristic threats, or defamatory statements, all of which are discussed in Chapters 6 and 7. The scope of constitutional protection of speech depends on the weight and balance of school and private interests in controlling or uttering particular speech. That balancing will vary with the circumstances of uttered expression, i.e., with official rather than private communications, with the age and status of adult and student speakers, and with the general context of such speech.

Official speech, uttered by or on behalf of a school district, is subject to different constitutional treatment than private speech. For example, official school communications that endorse religion violate the Establishment Clause and are not protected speech, whereas like private communications are protected.

> There is a crucial difference between government speech endorsing religion, which the Establishment Clause forbids, and private speech endorsing religion, which the Free Speech and Free Exercise Clauses protect. [*Board of Educ. of Westside Community Schools v. Mergens*, 496 U.S. 226, 250 (1990)]

Under the Free Speech Clause, school communications of official school policy are not subject to the constitutional rule that school authorities may not discriminate between private speakers based on their different viewpoints or ideas. The right of school officials to control school facilities for speech purposes is also expressed in terms of "forum" doctrines which classify school areas or forums as protected or unprotected zones for the exercise of free speech. The classifications of forums as traditional or limited forums or zones of protected speech or as nonpublic forums or zones of unprotected speech are explained in the *Good News* and other cases that are discussed below. The forum doctrines and problems are further discussed in Chapters 6 and 7.

Community Uses of School Facilities

Public school districts are under no legal obligation to open school facilities for outside private uses unless the law of their home state requires them to do so. Absent such a state law, school authorities may reserve school facilities exclusively for school purposes and exclude all outside uses of school facilities. However, when they do permit outside uses under state law authorization, they may not constitutionally deny such access on the basis of the viewpoints which a community group wishes to advance by their proposed use. Such denial would constitute viewpoint discrimination and infringe the freedom of speech of the excluded group.

The major area of dispute involving community uses of school facilities involve exclusion of applicants who propose to use school facilities for programs that express religious viewpoints, short of formal religious worship. Such cases squarely raise conflicting claims under the Establishment Clause by school authorities, and under the Free Speech Clause by religiously motivated speakers. The Supreme Court addressed this problem no less than three times during the past decade, and in each instance it overturned the denials of equal access to religiously motivated groups as unconstitutional infringements of their freedom of speech. In its recent *Good News Club* decision (Case 3.1), the Court summarized its prior holdings [*Lamb's Chapel v. Center Moriches Un. Free School Dist.*, 508 U.S. 384 (1993); *Rosenberger v. Rector and Visitors of the University of Virginia*, 515 U.S. 819 (1995)] as follows:

> In *Lamb's Chapel*, we held that a school district violated the Free Speech Clause of the First Amendment when it excluded a private group from presenting films at the school based solely on the films' discussions of family values from a religious perspective. . . . In *Rosenberger*, a student organization at the University of Virginia was denied funding for printing expenses because its publication, Wide Awake, offered a Christian viewpoint. Just as the Club emphasizes the role of Christianity in students' morals and character, Wide Awake " 'challenge[d] Christians to live, in word and deed, according to the faith they proclaim and . . . encourage[d] students to consider what a personal relationship with Jesus Christ means.' " 515 U.S., at 826. Because the university "select[ed] for disfavored treatment those student journalistic efforts with religious editorial viewpoints," we held that the denial of funding was unconstitutional. . . . Although in *Rosenberger* there was no prohibition on religion as a subject matter, our holding did not rely on this factor.
>
> Instead, we concluded simply that the university's denial of funding to print Wide Awake was viewpoint discrimination, just as the school district's refusal to allow Lamb's Chapel to show its films was viewpoint discrimination.

The *Good News Club* decision significantly extended the *Lamb's Chapel* and *Rosenberger* cases to cover religious community uses of elementary schools, including singing religious songs, memorizing and reciting Bible verses, hearing a Bible lesson, and offering a meeting-closing prayer, under the district's policy of allowing community use of school facilities for the teaching of morals and character. The Court rejected the school's argument that the club's requested use was equivalent to religious instruction or worship that is prohibited by the Establishment Clause, and concluded that the school grant of access would not convey or amount to school sponsorship of the club's religious purposes. The Court's rulings confirmed prior lower court rulings to the same effect.[4] The Ninth Circuit Court of Appeals more recently followed the *Good News* rationale in holding that a public school district created a limited public forum at an elementary school by allowing nonprofit groups to distribute literature of interest to the students, as a community service, and that its exclusion of a nonprofit summer camp operator that wished to distribute its fliers announcing its summer camp amounted to unconstitutional viewpoint discrimination. The court further concluded that the Establishment Clause defense was unavailing because the camp operator's religious motivation, in announcing Bible studies at the camp, did not involve school district sponsorship of the operator's viewpoints.[5]

The fine line between viewpoint discrimination against speech and exclusion of essentially religious subject matter was further highlighted by the Court's additional observations in *Good News* to the effect that its decisions did not forbid exclusion from school facilities of flier content that crossed the line from describing a religious perspective (including courses on Bible studies and perspectives) to direct proselytizing and urging of children to engage directly in religious prayer and observances, and that the school district could exclude specified subject matter from its limited forum, such as commercial, political, or religious material, so long as the exclusion of particular subject matter did not amount to viewpoint discrimination.

It is equally important to note that these acknowledgments do not require school authorities to open schools for public uses unless required to do so by state law. They do not require that school properties be made available to anyone for religious worship. They do not deny that the Establishment Clause forbids school officials to directly sponsor school uses for religious purposes.

The foregoing acknowledgments left in force prior decisions that upheld school confinement of community uses to designated purposes that have a reasonable relationship to educational goals, e.g., for discussion of religious materials, but not for religious instruction, and for presenting community theater, but not for a Bible lecture on the origins of the human race.[7] Limited use classifications can, however, present troublesome questions as to whether the list of permitted uses classifications are "reasonable" or arbitrary. For example, the Second Circuit Court of Appeals held that a request to conduct a Bible seminar was constitutionally denied as not covered by the allowed educational use category.[8] Were the court to allow, as educational, a Bible seminar conducted by a secular institute, say, the Divinity School of Harvard University, rather than by a religious denomination, would that judgment pose a possible discrimination dilemma? Were a court to rely on the different *motives* of Harvard and a denominational educator, would it in effect rely on the speaker's "motive", and if so, would that be constitutionally any different than discriminating against a speaker's "viewpoint", which the Free Speech Clause prohibits?

The above decisions did not address an ancillary question that may surface in the future, i.e., would a school teacher's planned participation in a religiously motivated community use program create an appearance of official school endorsement of the religious viewpoint, or would that teacher's participation still involve a protected exercise of free speech?

The federal Equal Access Act, though limited to student expression on school property during *non-instructional time,* adds statutory support for religiously motivated student speech. That Act is discussed in Chapter 7.

State Law Constraints

The constitutions of some states impose stricter constraints than the federal Constitution. For example, as noted in Chapter 9, the constitutions of some states prohibit state schools from providing some forms of public financial assistance to private schools even though such assistance is permitted by federal law.[9] Thus state constitutions and laws may *forbid* what federal law only *authorizes* but does not *require,* while states may not *forbid* actions that the federal law *requires.* As explained in Chapter 1, the federal law would supersede state law in a federal–state law conflict by reason of the Supremacy Clause of the national Constitution.

For like reason, a state recipient of federal financial assistance must comply with the federal conditions on the use of such aid. If state law prohibits compliance with the federal aid conditions, the state must decline the aid, and if it violates those conditions, federal authorities may cut off further federal subsidies and enforce the return of the amount of federal funds that were improperly expended.[10]

It now remains to consider how the above constitutional principles and issues play out on commonplace topics of school–religion disputes.

TYPICAL SCHOOL–RELIGION CONTROVERSIES

Prayer, Bible Reading, and Meditation

The constitutionality of Bible reading, prayer, or meditation in public schools will depend on the circumstances in which they are conducted.

Classroom Exercises

School-organized *classroom* recitation of verses from the Bible and classroom prayer violate the Establishment Clause because they are considered religious exercises, whether or not they are conducted by teachers or by students, and whether or not they are voluntary or nondenominational.[11] Establishment barriers to classroom religious exercises cannot be overcome by formalistic devices, such as omitting the word "God" from what is essentially a prayer, or by using classroom Bibles that are furnished at private rather than state expense.[12]

The commonplace public school practice of conducting a classroom Pledge of Allegiance exercise, even for *willing* students, was recently challenged by a parent of a student as an unconstitutional violation of the Establishment Clause because the Pledge contains the words "one nation under God". Unlike the *Barnette* flag salute case discussed earlier, in which the Supreme Court held that the state may not constitutionally require a religiously objecting student to participate in the flag salute exercise (by reason of the Free Exercise of Religion and the Freedom of Speech Clauses), the parent in the latest case did not seek to exempt his child, but to bar the practice for all children in all public schools so long as the words "under God" were part of the Pledge. On like argument, he sought a concurrent ruling that the federal statute which added the words "under God" to the Pledge was also unconstitutional. The school authorities defended the Pledge and federal statute as constitutional, and argued further that, in any event, the noncustodial parent plaintiff lacked standing to raise and litigate the constitutional objection.

The Ninth Circuit Court of Appeals originally upheld the parent's standing and invalidated both the school policy and the federal statute, but later issued an amended opinion, which did not speak to the validity of the federal statute. The Supreme Court granted a petition to review the decision, but only on the questions of the parent's standing to bring the suit, and of the validity of the school policy of requiring teachers to conduct classroom recitation of the Pledge by willing students.[13] At this writing the Supreme Court has not rendered its much awaited decision and guidance on the use or modification of the Pledge of Allegiance.

Classroom periods of silence for student meditation, though affording an opportunity for silent prayer, are constitutional if they are neutrally conducted. The Supreme Court struck down an Alabama meditation statute on its finding that the meditation law was enacted for the specific unconstitutional purpose of promoting classroom prayer.[14] The Court there made it clear that moment-of-silence statutes that were religiously neutral in their purpose and administration would be constitutional, even if students freely elected to use the meditation period for prayer or meditation. The lower courts have accordingly upheld laws that permit classroom meditation periods which are not in fact or intent designed to induce classroom prayer.[15]

Nonclassroom Prayer and Religious Activities

The many occasions for prayer or religious discussions outside the classroom, whether on or away from school property, continue to spark objections under the Establishment Clause. Court rulings in these cases are largely confined to the specific circumstances and nature of the challenged activity. For example, the older court rulings that a school commencement inside a church and the lease of a school building for a church baccalaureate service violate the Establishment Clause[16] are no longer seriously contested, but the lower courts remain divided on the constitutionality of other nonclassroom religious activities, such as invocations or prayer at graduation ceremonies, school athletic and social events.

With respect to graduation ceremonies and prayer at extracurricular events, the Supreme Court opinions in *Santa Fe Independent School District v. Jane Doe*, 530 U.S. 290 (2000) (Case 3.2), and *Lee v. Weisman*, 505 U.S. 577 (1992) (Case 3.4), deserve close reading. In *Lee* the Court decided that delivery of a nondenominational invocation at a high school commencement, by a rabbi whom the school authorities invited for that purpose, violated the Establishment Clause though the students were not required to attend the commencement and those who did attend were not required to join in the invocation.

Lower courts, however, have disagreed on the reach of the *Lee* decision to other commencement circumstances.

The Fifth Circuit court issued the following rulings: (a) that *Lee* did not prohibit public schools from giving students the option, on their own initiative and free from direct school control, to have a member of the graduating class deliver a commencement message, with or without a prayer at the student speaker's discretion, so long as the school policy required that any optional student prayer be nonsectarian and nonproselytizing; (b) that school allowance of student-led prayers at school-sponsored sporting events was unconstitutional; and (c) that a school's use of volunteer clergy to conduct a course on "civic virtues and morality", though unattended by religious symbols or by the instructor's religious identification, unconstitutionally aided and entangled religion with government.[17] These case variations may, of course, reflect different perceptions of different judges who sat on the panels that heard each case.

The Eleventh Circuit followed the Fifth Circuit in upholding student-initiated graduation prayer, while the Third Circuit found that such prayers violated the Establishment Clause.[18] The Sixth Circuit Court also delivered mixed conclusions. It held that (a) nonsectarian invocations at college commencements was not barred by the Constitution, but (b) that an opening prayer at a school board meeting that was attended by students was unconstitutional. In contrast, a California federal district court upheld the constitutionality of a school board opening prayer notwithstanding the presence of some students who attended to address the board.[19] The Ninth Circuit Court of Appeals originally upheld a high school policy of allowing merit students to deliver an address at graduation commencement on any topic they chose, including prayers, but it later withdrew that opinion for rehearing on a "standing to sue" question.[20]

In *Santa Fe* (Case 3.2) the Supreme Court considered a question that was not directly addressed in *Lee,* namely, whether student-initiated prayer at a school sports event is government-sponsored prayer and therefore a violation of the Establishment Clause, or private student speech, whose content may not be constitutionally limited by school authorities. The Court decided that the school's policy of allowing a student "statement or invocation" to be broadcast at all varsity football home games to the stadium audience over the public address system violated the Establishment Clause, because the school's *purpose* in adopting its policy was to sponsor the student prayer and therefore was unconstitutional, and also because the school policy expressed a school endorsement of religion. The Court rejected the argument that the school district's policy was content neutral and merely allowed student freedom of speech.

The crucial role of judicial perception of case facts in framing the issues for such cases is highlighted by the contrasting comments of the majority and dissenting Justices in the *Santa Fe* opinion. From the majority opinion:

> It [the school district] reminds us that "there is a crucial difference between government speech endorsing religion, which the Establishment Clause forbids, and

private speech endorsing religion, which the Free Speech and Free Exercise Clauses protect." . . . We certainly agree with that distinction, but we are not persuaded that the pregame invocations should be regarded as "private speech." . . . Whether a government activity violates the Establishment Clause is "in large part a legal question *to be answered on the basis of judicial interpretation of social facts. . . . Every government practice must be judged in its unique circumstances. . . .* (Emphasis added) [*Santa Fe, supra,* 530 U.S., at pp. 302, 315]

From the dissenting opinion:

> The Court so holds despite that [the fact that] any speech that may occur as a result of the election process here would be private, not government, speech. *The elected student, not the government, would choose what to say.* Support for the Court's holding cannot be found in any of our cases. . . . See *Lee, supra,* at 630, n. 8 (SOUTER, J., concurring). ("If the State had chosen its graduation day speakers according to wholly secular criteria, and if one of those speakers (not a state actor) had individually chosen to deliver a religious message, it would be harder to attribute an endorsement of religion to the State".) (Emphasis added) [*Santa Fe, supra,* 530 U.S., at 324, 325]

Santa Fe did not end the argument. The Eleventh Circuit Court of Appeals thereafter upheld a school policy that permitted a high school senior, whom the graduating class elected, to deliver a message of his own choosing at a commencement exercise. The Supreme Court vacated the decision and sent the case back for reconsideration in light of its *Santa Fe* decision. On reconsideration, however, the Eleventh Circuit adhered to its original decision with the following comment:

> Having carefully reviewed the Supreme Court's opinion, . . . we conclude that *Santa Fe* does not alter our previous en banc decision, and accordingly we reinstate that decision. . . . Nevertheless, we take this opportunity to explain why we believe that *Santa Fe* does not alter the outcome of this case. . . . The Court in *Santa Fe* had every opportunity to declare that all religious expression permitted at a public school graduation ceremony violates the Establishment Clause; it did not do so. We could not invalidate Duval County's policy, *on its face,* without taking the very step the Court declined to take. [*Adler v. Duval County School Board,* 250 F.3d 1330, 1332) (11th Cir. 2001)]

The Supreme Court declined the request to review the reinstated decision, and thus let the case stand. [*Adler v. Duval County School Board,* 122 S. Ct. 664 (2001)] The reinstated opinion is reproduced at the end of this chapter as Case 3.3, and it provides fresh illustration of how cases in this controversial area can be limited to their specific circumstances. The significance of case circumstances is indicated by the following hypothetical questions which, though seemingly fantastic, are not far removed from those raised in the cases:

1. Where class presidents, valedictorians, homecoming or prom queens decide whether or not to include a prayer or religious message in their

speeches, must the school authorities take steps to impose an advance prohibition against religious content or require the student to submit the intended speech to school authorities for their review, in order to avoid an establishment of religion objection? Or would such requirements be unconstitutional censorship of student speech?

2. May athletic team members constitutionally form a huddle for silent prayer before beginning a school sports competition or would that action constitute impermissible government endorsement of religion? What if cheerleaders do the same? What if team coaches join the athletes' huddle? Or form their own huddle?

3. Which of the following actions at a school sports event are constitutionally forbidden supports of religion or constitutionally protected freedom of speech? (a) A student spectator stands up and shouts an invitation to all within hearing to join him or her in a prayer for the school team's success. (b) He or she uses a powerful private bullhorn to be heard by half the stadium. (c) An adult nonstudent takes the same actions.

4. May school music directors and student orchestras or choirs use music, classical or otherwise, with religious themes in school studies or performances? One lower court upheld these practices, whereas another held that the formation of a school gospel choir was unconstitutional.[21]

Perhaps the judicial answers to these questions will turn on unarticulated consideration of the degree of religious expression that is tolerable or intolerable, rather than on any fixed classification of conduct as advancing or not advancing a religious message.

Kindred problems arise where students, teachers, or other employees meet outside the classroom during free time for religious discussions, Bible reading, or distribution of religious literature. These problems are discussed in greater detail in Chapters 6 and 7.

Religious Art—Holiday Commemorations

Religious symbols can be seen as expressing historical or cultural themes or as conveying religious messages, or both. The presence of religious symbols and art on government property, including in the courtroom of the United States Supreme Court,[22] has been upheld as constitutional where the courts considered those symbols to serve primarily secular purposes, e.g., as historical references. However, the placement of a plaque containing the Ten Commandments in a public school classroom was held unconstitutional as conveying an impermissible religious message by its explicit reference to God, notwithstanding the role played by those commandments in developing ethical values that are taught in the schools.[23] Displays of school art identified with the person and life of Jesus Christ were similarly held unconstitutional as conveying a Christian religious message.[24]

With respect to holiday displays of religious origin (such as Christmas, Easter, and Hanukkah), the courts have rendered mixed decisions, depending on the details of each display. The Supreme Court has considered crèche and menorah displays on public, but not school, property. It ruled that placement of a crèche at private expense inside the lobby of a county courthouse, unaccompanied by other secular holiday symbols, conveyed government sponsorship of a religious message in violation of the Establishment Clause, but it held that placement of a privately owned 18-foot menorah next to a Christmas tree at the entrance to a city–county building did not convey government sponsorship of a religious message, and thus did not offend the Establishment Clause.[25] The Seventh and Eleventh Circuit Courts of Appeal later ruled that a menorah display *inside* government buildings would not violate the Establishment Clause, but the Third Circuit Court of Appeals took a contrary position.[26] Some lower courts have construed the Supreme Court decisions as permitting school holiday displays, plays, or songs that contain some religious elements, as long as the displays have a secular purpose and effect, and the religious elements do not so dominate the secular holiday symbols as to convey government endorsement of a religious message.[27] The Supreme Court has yet to address these case variations, or to clarify the blurred borders of religious symbols that are significantly or only incidentally religious in nature and impact.

Where students produce and display their art on school property, as part of a school art program, but the religious art of Bible club students is excluded from the art display, the school authorities encounter conflicting First Amendment claims, i.e., that, on one hand, displaying the religious art would violate the constitutional prohibition against government sponsorship or aid to religion, yet on the other the exclusion of that art would amount to unconstitutional content-based censorship of ideas, in violation of student freedom of expression. These opposing claims were discussed earlier in this chapter and must be resolved on the basis of particular case facts. They were avoided where the school authorities established that the refusal to display the religious art was needed to avoid a serious threat of disruption of school order and discipline.[28]

School Excusals for Religious Purposes

School excusal of students from regularly scheduled classes in order to enable them to pursue religious ends has also received different treatment, based on the circumstances of such excusals. The Supreme Court overturned a school program whereby students were *released* from regular classes on parental request in order to attend private religious instruction in another part of the public school building, as an unconstitutional aid to religion.[29] But it thereafter upheld, as a permissible accommodation of religion, school *dismissal* of students at parental request to enable the students to attend religious studies away from the school.[30] Lower courts have followed this distinction between release of students for religious studies inside the school and release of students for religious studies away from the school.[31]

The right of teachers or students to be excused from school attendance in order to observe religious obligations will to some extent depend on the urgency of the school's need to insist on regular attendance and of the counterbalancing individual's need to perform a religious obligation. In striking that balance, courts have overturned school denials of excused absences for religiously compelled observance where such excusal would not create a material operational or educational hardship.[32] Conversely, excusals for compulsory religious observations may be denied where the frequency of absences for weekly religious holidays would defeat the educational program.[33]

A school holiday that coincides with a major Christian holy day (Good Friday) has also received mixed court treatment.[34] One found the action to be an unconstitutional aid to religion, while another found the law to be a constitutional accommodation of religion. The Supreme Court declined to review the latter decision, but such denials of review do not amount to Court approval of the unreviewed decision.

Lower courts have also upheld school rules that prohibit extracurricular school activities during the sabbath periods of various sects, i.e., Friday evenings, Saturdays, and Sunday mornings.[35] One case also upheld a school rule to prohibit public school dances that was adopted in response to vocal community religious opposition to those dances.[36] The cases that uphold administrative decisions that *allow* an accommodation of religion do not imply that the Constitution *requires* schools to reschedule its calendar of events to accommodate a student's religion. For example, a school district could constitutionally reschedule a graduation commencment date in order to avoid a conflict with a Jewish student's Sabbath, but it is not constitutionally required to do so.[37]

Teacher accommodation of religion claims are buttressed by the federal employment discrimination statute (Title VII), which requires employers to provide "reasonable accommodation" of an employee's religion unless such accommodation would cause a significant business hardship for the employer. This law is reviewed in Chapter 6. However, neither the Constitution nor Title VII requires a school district to *subsidize* religious observance by *paid* (rather than unpaid) leave, where such paid leave is not afforded to employees for comparable employee personal needs.[38] A slightly different question is presented where the school district and a teacher union negotiate a contract that includes provision for paid leave for religious observance. The lower courts are in disagreement on the constitutionality of that arrangement.[39]

The denial or withdrawal of academic credits for religiously grounded student defaults may be overturned as an unconstitutional penalty on the practice of religion under the Free Exercise Clause. For example, a court overturned a school's denial of a diploma to a student who could not in religious conscience fulfill a school graduation requirement because it found no compelling state interest to insist on that requirement by that particular student.[40]

Religion-Related Courses and Programs

School courses and services that arguably contradict or advance religious values are also test case targets.

Evolution

Laws prohibiting public instruction of Darwinian evolution theory have been overturned under the Establishment Clause as attempts to advance a religious (fundamentalist) view of human creation.[41] Laws that required equal instruction on "creation science" with Darwinian evolution were also overturned as serving an unconstitutional purpose of advancing a particular religious view on evolution.[42] The argument that instruction only on a materialist version of evolution advances the religion of "secular humanism" also failed, even though one Supreme Court Justice had previously observed, by way of a footnote, that secular humanism is a form of "religion".[43] Finally, a school board requirement that high school science teachers read to their class a disclaimer that evolution lessons "are not intended to influence or dissuade the Biblical version of creation or any other concept" was held unconstitutional by one circuit court as lacking a secular purpose.[44] Could other courts conclude that the purpose of the disclaimer is secular, i.e., to preserve government and school neutrality between secular and religious viewpoints on human creation?

The Bible as History and Literature

In ruling against school-sponsored, classroom recitation of Bible verses without comment, the Supreme Court stressed that the Constitution did not prohibit public schools from teaching *about* religion, and that the Bible could be studied for secular educational purposes, i.e., as a reference source of historical, literary, political, and cultural studies. The question whether Bibles are being used for secular or religious purposes must turn on the case facts. Class discussion of the parables of Jesus as illustrating a method of teaching, and discussion of the biblical account of the rise of the kingdom of Israel were upheld, while study of the prophecies of Daniel, of biblical accounts of worship of the golden calf, and of the fall of Sodom and Gomorrah were held unconstitutional as conveying religious messages.[45]

Sex Education

The expansion of sex-related school courses and services in the wake of the sexual revolution has spurred further constitutional litigation under both religion clauses. Courts have generally upheld such programs as falling within the educational mission of the schools, but the question whether they infringe parental and religious rights has not been directly addressed by the Supreme Court.[46] For Establishment Clause purposes, lower courts held that such courses do not involve government preference of the moral teachings or values of some religious sects, or favor sects that approve those courses over sects that oppose them.[47] As to the parental and free exercise claims, the courts generally found no violation if the challenged course or service was optional and the school exempted students or parents who deemed them religiously offensive.[48] Where the school program does not allow an elective exemption from a religiously offensive sex education program, the free exercise of religion claim is more problematic.

The limits of parental rights to exempt their children from mandatory classes were recently addressed by the Second Circuit Court of Appeals. The court there held, contrary to indications of several Supreme Court precedents, that a parent's constitutional right to control the education of his child was not a "fundamental" right entitling him to excuse his child from seventh-grade mandatory health classes. Applying a rational-basis test for limiting parental rights on school curriculum, the court ruled that the mandatory health curriculum was constitutional and justified limitation of the parental right to oppose it.[49] While the Supreme Court flag salute case ruled that students could not be constitutionally forced to participate in a flag salute or pledge of allegiance exercise against their religious mandates, the issue whether forced participation in sex education courses is like or distinct from the flag salute objection remains largely unaddressed.

The *Brown v. Hot, Sexy and Safer Productions, Inc.* case (Case 3.5) illustrates the tasks that courts face in deciding the nature and validity of school presentations of sex-oriented materials to elementary and high school students. It is not at all clear that courts in other circuits would agree with the *Brown* court's cavalier characterizations of an admittedly bawdy parade of explicit sexual skits, for a continuous 90 minutes, to a captive audience of adolescent students in a mandatory school assembly as just harmless humor. Although the facts in *Brown* are technically different from those of the *Lacks* case (Case 6.3), which upheld the termination of a teacher who insisted on staging lewd and vulgar student class plays, the stark contrast between the perceptions and fact characterizations of the judges in those cases expose these disparate results, and expose the raw power of judges to color case facts and shape legal issues that are critical to case outcomes.

School distribution of condoms, though religiously offensive to some, has generally, but not universally, been upheld on the ground that the complaining parents and their children may decline the service and, hence, are not "coerced" to act contrary to their religion.[50] The contrasting uses of the coercion argument in free exercise and establishment of religion cases in the condom and commencement prayer case (the above-discussed *Lee* case) present a paradox for the ideal of government "neutrality". The Court opinion in *Lee* stressed that the dissident student was subject to subtle "peer pressure" to participate in the commencement invocation. This pressure was considered evidence that the invocation unconstitutionally advanced religion in violation of the Establishment Clause, even though the student could opt not to participate in the invocation or even not to attend the commencement. But in the sex education cases, courts saw no "peer pressure" upon objecting students to participate in religiously offensive courses or programs. "[T]he [First] Amendment does not guarantee that nothing about religion will be taught in the schools, nor that nothing offensive to any religion will be taught in the schools."[51] Since excusal or exemption is curative only for free exercise objections and not for establishment objections, the touchstone of government "neutrality" to religion remains problematic. As one court observed:

> First, the mere fact that certain students are permitted to leave makes the court question whether students are being indoctrinated to religion rather than being taught within the permissible boundaries. If the course is taught within constitutional limits, every student should be required to attend. . . . While permitting non-attendance does not ordinarily raise constitutional questions, it does indicate that a constitutionally questionable course is being taught. . . . If the course is being properly taught within the constitutional limits, there is no reason for nonattendance by any student. [*Vaughn v. Reed*, 313 F. Supp. 431, 433–34 (W.D. W. Va. 1970)]

Course Textbooks and Class Readings

The content of course textbooks, no less than course offerings, raises objections that the books favor or disfavor religion. Text omissions of religious influence in history were held not to convey a government hostility to religion or preference for a materialist view of history.[52] Objection that a book (*Slaughterhouse Five*) was anti-Christian and included derogatory references to Christianity was turned aside because the court did not consider the novel's materials to be antireligious. The court further assumed that teacher neutrality in discussing the book would cure any antireligious potential.[53] The Sixth Circuit Court of Appeals even sustained a school board's refusal to excuse students from required reading of material they deemed antithetical to their religion. It concluded that compelled exposure to religiously objectionable material did not force students to accept or affirm that material and for that reason did not burden their freedom of religion.[54] That holding implicitly rejects the position that a sincerely held religious mandate against reading a particular school text is, like the flag salute objection, entitled to constitutional free exercise protection. Another court avoided the issue by exempting students from required use of religiously offensive material.[55] Textbook controversies are considered in greater detail in Chapters 6 and 7.

Private distribution of religious literature for use in public school classrooms has been held unconstitutional, since such use would inevitably involve school sponsorship and endorsement.[56]

Other Religious Objections and Exemptions

Flag Salutes

As previously noted, the state's substantial interest in fostering patriotism is not sufficiently compelling to coerce students to participate in a flag salute or pledge of allegiance contrary to their religious commands and to override their right to free exercise of religion.[57]

Dress and Conduct Requirements

The recent adoption by some public schools of mandating student use of school uniforms or dress codes was considered and upheld in *Littlefield v. Forney Ind. Sch. Dist.*, 268 F.3d 275 [5th Cir. (2001)], which is reported in Chapter 7. That opinion fairly reveals the issues to be anticipated in like challenges.

With regard to nonclass student activities, the limited case law does not provide sure guides for deciding when a religiously offensive dress requirement (gym or swimming outfits) rises to the level of a sufficiently substantial burden on religion to require constitutional exemption, or when the state's interest in enforcing student compliance with a particular dress requirement is sufficiently compelling to override a legitimate religious objection (e.g., where compliance is required to avoid serious health and safety hazards). The state's interest in maintaining regularity and discipline may not alone justify compulsion of a student to wear a prescribed costume or to engage in a prescribed activity that is deemed sinful under the student's religion.[58]

Immunization

The clear case of a sufficiently compelling state interest to override religious objection is found in statutes that mandate student inoculation against dangerous communicable diseases. Such immunization requirements are uniformly upheld, notwithstanding the plea of religious prohibition,[59] even to the point where the state moves to appoint a guardian to enforce immunizations against the wishes of natural parents: "A person's right to exhibit religious freedom ceases where it . . . transgresses the rights of others."[60] Nevertheless, a number of states have, as a matter of policy, exempted sincere religious objectors from immunization requirements. In such states, school authorities and courts must decide whether a claim of exemption rests on a sincerely held "religious" tenet or only on a broader nonexempt philosophical ground.[61]

Public School Services to Nonpublic Schools and Students

State laws that authorize broad educational programs for the benefit of the general public, such as evening and summer schools, work training courses, and community recreation, do not pose serious religion-relationship problems.

The Establishment Clause ban on state aid to the religious mission of any sect[62] does not bar all public school services to nonpublic schools and their students, including church-related schools, but there are limits to such aid. Those limits require closer study of distinct case lines, which are taken up in Chapter 9. The admission of nonpublic school students to regular public school classes, a practice known as *"dual enrollment"*, presents a hybrid situation. Local boards have no obligation to open regular public school classes to part-time dual enrollment[63] unless state law mandates part-time admissions. In several states "dual enrollment" or "shared time" programs are authorized when those programs are conducted by public school personnel in public schools and in classes jointly attended by students from public and nonpublic schools. These laws were held not to aid religion or violate the Establishment Clause.[64] Where, however, public school courses, though taught by public school personnel, were given in church-school facilities, that practice raised more difficult issues under the Establishment Clause of the federal Constitution and also the state constitutions in Oregon and Montana.[65] The Oregon and Montana state law rulings remain unimpaired, but the issues under the federal Constitution must be reevaluated in light of latest Supreme Court cases on the subject, which are reviewed in Chapter 9.

Direct School–Church Dealings

Public School Uses of Church Property

School districts may lease private property, including church-owned buildings, for public school uses, provided the public school controls and operates the leasehold without religious furnishings or instruction.[66] But leases of parochial school buildings where religious furnishings and religiously garbed teachers were also present were voided under the excessive entanglement test of the Establishment Clause.[67] Courts are reluctant to uphold leases of only part of a church-owned building because of the proximity of religious and secular functions in different parts of the facility. Nevertheless, the use of a Catholic school building for part of the time as a public school and at other times as a Catholic school was upheld where the court found that the school–church contacts were sufficiently minimal to avoid unconstitutional entanglements.[68]

Church Uses of Public School Property

The lease of public school property for a fixed term to a religious organization will be upheld if the lease terms are commercially fair and neutral. Leases of public school and state college properties to a religious organization at reasonable, fair market rentals, when the properties are not being used for public school operations, were upheld as lawful commercial transactions with no implication of religious aid, though the lessee sought the leasehold for its religious purpose.[69] However, leases whose terms favor or discriminate against religious groups will be disapproved.[70]

Citing the *Good News Club* decision (Case 3.1), the Second Circuit Court of Appeals found that the New York City Board of Education could not constitutionally refuse to rent a public school building for religious worship and the teaching of morals and character development, where the school buildings were rented to other groups for teaching of morals and character development, because such refusal would amount to viewpoint discrimination in violation of the applicant's freedom of speech.[71]

Chapter 3 Discussion Questions

Where the answer to a question may be qualified by special circumstances, explain the potential qualification.

1. To what degree do prior court decisions on the interpretation of the religion clauses of the First Amendment control or influence courts in deciding later cases?

2. What are the tests or measures by which courts may decide a religion-related conflict under the Establishment Clause? Under the Free Exercise Clause? Under the Freedom of Speech Clause? In the event of conflicting claims under different clauses, how have the courts reconciled them without suggesting that any one clause should supersede any other clause?

3. Explain what, if any, constitutional differences may be drawn between:
   a. Recitation of classroom prayer and classroom meditation.
   b. In-class student prayer and out-of-class student prayer.
   c. Recitation of Bible verses in school class and recitation of the same verses by outside users of school buildings. (If help is needed, read the *Good News Club* opinion at the end of this chapter.)
   d. Religious activity in public and in nonpublic schools.
   e. State law prohibitions and federal law prohibitions against aid to religion.
   f. Religious objections to mandatory flag salute exercises and mandatory sex education courses.

Case 3.1

GOOD NEWS CLUB v. MILFORD CENTRAL SCHOOL
121 S. Ct. 2093 (2001)

> *[**Focus Note.** The following Supreme Court opinion resolved a conflict among the Circuit Courts of Appeal regarding the operation of the Freedom of Speech and Establishment Clauses of the First Amendment where authorities refused to allow students and their parents to use public school facilities that were open to community uses. The school authorities argued that the Establishment Clause required the exclusion because the intended use was religious.]*

Justice Thomas delivered the opinion of the Court.

This case presents two questions. The first question is whether Milford Central School violated the free speech rights of the Good News Club when it excluded the Club from meeting after hours at the school. The second question is whether any such violation is justified by Milford's concern that permitting the Club's activities would violate the Establishment Clause. We conclude that Milford's restriction violates the Club's free speech rights and that no Establishment Clause concern justifies that violation.

I

The State of New York authorizes local school boards to adopt regulations governing the use of their school facilities. In particular, N.Y. Educ. Law § 414 (McKinney 2000) enumerates several purposes for which local boards may open their schools to public use. In 1992, respondent Milford Central School (Milford) enacted a community use policy adopting seven of § 414's purposes for which its building could be used after school. Two of the stated purposes are relevant here. First, district residents may use the school for "instruction in any branch of education, learning or the arts." Second, the school is available for "social, civic and recreational meetings and entertainment events, and other uses pertaining to the welfare of the community, provided that such uses shall be nonexclusive and shall be opened to the general public."

Stephen and Darleen Fournier reside within Milford's district. . . . Together they are sponsors of the local Good News Club, a private Christian organization for children ages 6 to 12. . . . [T]he Fourniers submitted a request to Dr. Robert McGruder, interim superintendent of the district, in which they sought permission to hold the Club's weekly afterschool meetings in the school cafeteria. . . . The next month, McGruder formally denied the Fourniers' request. . . . According to McGruder, the community use policy, which prohibits use "by any individual or organization for religious purposes," foreclosed the Club's activities. . . .

In response to a letter submitted by the Club's counsel, Milford's attorney requested information to clarify the nature of the Club's activities. The Club sent a set of materials used or distributed at the meetings and the following description of its meeting:

> "The Club opens its session with Ms. Fournier taking attendance. As she calls a child's name, if the child recites a Bible verse the child receives a treat. After attendance, the Club sings songs. . . . Next Club members engage in games that involve, *inter alia*, learning Bible verses. Ms. Fournier then relates a Bible story and explains how it applies to Club members' lives. The Club closes with prayer. Finally, Ms. Fournier distributes treats and the Bible verses for memorization." . . .

McGruder and Milford's attorney reviewed the materials and concluded that "the kinds of activities proposed to be engaged in by the Good News Club were not a discussion of secular subjects such as . . . development of character and development of morals from a religious perspective, but were in fact the equivalent of religious instruction itself." . . . In February 1997, the Milford Board of Education adopted a resolution rejecting the Club's request to use Milford's facilities "for the purpose of conducting religious instruction and Bible study." . . .

In March 1997, petitioners . . . (collectively, the Club), filed an action under 42 U.S.C. § 1983 against Milford. . . . . . .

* * *

In August 1998, the District Court . . . granted Milford's motion for summary judgment. . . .

The Club appealed, and a divided panel of the United State Court of Appeals for the Second Circuit affirmed. . . . Judge Jacobs filed a dissenting opinion. . . .

There is a conflict among the Courts of Appeals on the question whether speech can be excluded from a limited public forum on the basis of the religious nature of the speech. . . . We granted certiorari to resolve this conflict. . . .

The standards that we apply . . . depend on the nature of the forum. . . . If the forum is a traditional or open public forum, the State's restrictions on speech are subject to stricter scrutiny than are restrictions in a limited public forum. . . . When the State establishes a limited public forum, the State is not required to and does not allow persons to engage in every type of speech. The State may be justified "in reserving [its forum] for certain groups or for the discussion of certain topics." *Rosenberger v. Rector and Vis-*

itors of Univ. of Va., 515 U.S. 819, 829 (1995); see also *Lamb's Chapel, supra*, at 392–393. . . . The State's power to restrict speech, however, is not without limits. The restriction must not discriminate against speech on the basis of viewpoint, *Rosenberger, supra*, at 829, and the restriction must be "reasonable in light of the purpose served by the forum," *Cornelius v. NAACP Legal Defense & Ed. Fund, Inc.*, 473 U.S. 788, 806 (1985).

. . . In *Lamb's Chapel*, we held that a school district violated the Free Speech Clause of the First Amendment when it excluded a private group from presenting films at the school based solely on the films' discussions of family values from a religious perspective. Likewise, in *Rosenberger*, we held that a university's refusal to fund a student publication because the publication addressed issues from a religious perspective violated the Free Speech Clause. Concluding that Milford's exclusion of the Good News Club based on its religious nature is indistinguishable from the exclusions in these cases, we hold that the exclusion constitutes viewpoint discrimination. . . .

. . . Milford interprets its policy to permit discussions of subjects such as child rearing, and of "the development of character and morals from a religious perspective." . . . For example, this policy would allow someone to use Aesop's Fables to teach children moral values. Additionally, a group could sponsor a debate on whether there should be a constitutional amendment to permit prayer in public schools, and the Boy Scouts could meet "to influence a boy's character, development and spiritual growth." In short, any group that "promote[s] the moral and character development of children" is eligible to use the school building.

. . . [I]t is clear that the Club teaches morals and character development to children. For example, no one disputes that the Club instructs children to overcome feelings of jealousy, to treat others well regardless of how they treat the children, and to be obedient, even if it does so in a nonsecular way. Nonetheless, because Milford found the Club's activities to be religious in nature—"the equivalent of religious instruction itself"—it excluded the Club from use of its facilities.

Applying Lamb's Chapel, we find it quite clear that Milford engaged in viewpoint discrimination when it excluded the Club from the afterschool forum. . . .

Like the church in *Lamb's Chapel*, the Club seeks to address a subject otherwise permitted under the rule, the teaching of morals and character, from a religious standpoint. Certainly, one could have characterized the film presentations in *Lamb's Chapel* as a religious use. . . . . . . The only apparent difference between the activity of Lamb's Chapel and the activities of the Good News Club is that the Club chooses to teach moral lessons from a Christian perspective through live storytelling and prayer, whereas Lamb's Chapel taught lessons through films. This distinction is inconsequential. Both modes of speech use a religious viewpoint. Thus, the exclusion of the

Good News Club's activities, like the exclusion of Lamb's Chapel's films, constitutes unconstitutional viewpoint discrimination.

Our opinion in *Rosenberger* also is dispositive. In *Rosenberger,* a student organization at the University of Virginia was denied funding for printing expenses because its publication, Wide Awake, offered a Christian viewpoint. Just as the Club emphasizes the role of Christianity in students' morals and character, Wide Awake "'challenge[d] Christians to live, in word and deed, according to the faith they proclaim and . . . encourage[d] students to consider what a personal relationship with Jesus Christ means.'" 515 U.S., at 826. Because the university "select[ed] for disfavored treatment those student journalistic efforts with religious editorial viewpoints," we held that the denial of funding was unconstitutional. . . . Given the obvious religious content of Wide Awake, we cannot say that the Club's activities are any more "religious" or deserve any less First Amendment protection than did the publication of Wide Awake in *Rosenberger.*

Despite our holdings in *Lamb's Chapel* and *Rosenberger,* the Court of Appeals, like Milford, believed that its characterization of the Club's activities as religious in nature warranted treating the Club's activities as different in kind from the other activities permitted by the school. The "Christian viewpoint" is unique, according to the court, because it contains an "additional layer" that other kinds of viewpoints do not. That is, the Club "is focused on teaching children how to cultivate their relationship with God through Jesus Christ," which it characterized as "quintessentially religious." With these observations, the court concluded that, because the Club's activities "fall outside the bounds of pure 'moral and character development,'" the exclusion did not constitute viewpoint discrimination.

We disagree that something that is "quintessentially religious" or "decidedly religious in nature" cannot also be characterized properly as the teaching of morals and character development from a particular viewpoint. . . . What matters for purposes of the Free Speech Clause is that we can see no logical difference in kind between the invocation of Christianity by the Club and the invocation of teamwork, loyalty, or patriotism by other associations to provide a foundation for their lessons. . . . According to the Court of Appeals, reliance on Christian principles taints moral and character instruction in a way that other foundations . . . do not. We, however, have never reached such a conclusion. Instead, we reaffirm our holdings in *Lamb's Chapel* and *Rosenberger* that speech discussing otherwise permissible subjects cannot be excluded from a limited public forum on the ground that the subject is discussed from a religious viewpoint. Thus, we conclude that Milford's exclusion of the Club from use of the school, pursuant to its community use policy, constitutes impermissible viewpoint discrimination.

Milford argues that, even if its restriction constitutes viewpoint discrimination, its interest in not violating the Establishment Clause outweighs the Club's interest in gaining equal access to the school's facilities. In other words, . . . its restriction was required to avoid violating the Establishment Clause. We disagree.

* * *

We rejected Establishment Clause defenses similar to Milford's in two previous free speech cases, *Lamb's Chapel* and *Widmar*. In particular, in *Lamb's Chapel*, we explained that "[t]he showing of th[e] film series would not have been during school hours, would not have been sponsored by the school, and would have been open to the public, not just to church members." 508 U.S., at 395, 113 S. Ct. 2141. Accordingly, we found that "there would have been no realistic danger that the community would think that the District was endorsing religion or any particular creed." *Ibid.* Likewise, in *Widmar*, . . . this Court concluded that there was no Establishment Clause problem. 454 U.S., at 272–273, and n. 13. . . .

* * *

Milford attempts to distinguish *Lamb's Chapel* and *Widmar* by emphasizing that Milford's policy involves elementary school children. According to Milford, children will perceive that the school is endorsing the Club and will feel coercive pressure to participate, because the Club's activities take place on school grounds, even though they occur during nonschool hours. This argument is unpersuasive. . . . Milford's implication that granting access to the Club would do damage to the neutrality principle defies logic. For the "guarantee of neutrality is respected, not offended, when the government, following neutral criteria and evenhanded policies, extends benefits to recipients whose ideologies and viewpoints, including religious ones, are broad and diverse." *Rosenberger, supra,* at 839. . . .

Second, to the extent we consider whether the community would feel coercive pressure to engage in the Club's activities, . . . the relevant community would be the parents, not the elementary school children. It is the parents who choose whether their children will attend the Good News Club meetings. Because the children cannot attend without their parents' permission, they cannot be coerced into engaging in the Good News Club's religious activities. . . .

Third, . . . we have never extended our Establishment Clause jurisprudence to foreclose private religious conduct during nonschool hours merely because it takes place on school premises where elementary school children may be present.

None of the cases discussed by Milford persuades us that our Establishment Clause jurisprudence has gone this far. . . .

Equally unsupportive is *Edwards v. Aguillard*, 482 U.S. 578 . . . (1987), in which we held that a Louisiana law that proscribed the teaching of evolution as part of the public school curriculum, unless accompanied by a lesson on creationism, violated the Establishment Clause. . . . *Edwards* involved the content of the curriculum taught by state teachers *during the schoolday* to children required to attend. Obviously, when individuals who are not schoolteachers are giving lessons after school to children permitted to attend only with parental consent, the concerns expressed in *Edwards* are not present.

Fourth, . . . the facts of this case simply do not support Milford's conclusion. . . . The meetings were held in a combined high school resource room and middle school special education room, not in an elementary school classroom. The instructors are not schoolteachers. And the children in the group are not all the same age as in the normal classroom setting. . . . In sum, these circumstances simply do not support the theory that small children would perceive endorsement here.

* * *

. . . We decline to employ Establishment Clause jurisprudence using a modified heckler's veto, in which a group's religious activity can be proscribed on the basis of what the youngest members of the audience might misperceive. Cf. *Capitol Square Review and Advisory Bd. v. Pinette*, 515 U.S. 753, 779–780, . . . (1995) (O'CONNOR, J., concurring in part and concurring in judgment) ("[B]ecause our concern is with the political community writ large, the endorsement inquiry is *not about the perceptions of particular individuals* or saving isolated nonadherents from . . . discomfort. . . . It is for this reason that the reasonable observer in the endorsement inquiry must be deemed aware of the history and context of the community and forum in which the religious [speech takes place]" (emphasis added)). . . .

. . . Accordingly, we conclude that permitting the Club to meet on the school's premises would not have violated the Establishment Clause.

* * *

The judgment of the Court of Appeals is reversed, and the case is remanded for further proceedings consistent with this opinion.

Case 3.1 Review Question

1. Do you agree with the court's conclusion on the following questions:
   a. Whether the activity of the Good News Club involved protected expression of a "religious" viewpoint and not an exercise of religious worship.
   b. Whether the school decision to exclude the Club was required by the Establishment Clause under the "endorsement" of religion or the "neutrality" test.

Case 3.2

SANTA FE INDEPENDENT SCHOOL DISTRICT v. JANE DOE
120 S. Ct. 2266 (2000)

[**Focus Note.** *The following opinion extended the constitutional ban to student prayer at school varsity football games. Note the court's emphasis on the school district's history of student prayer practices. Further, note that the court findings rested its decision on two grounds, namely, an unconstitutional motive (to aid religion) and an unconstitutional effect (to endorse religion), either of which could alone suffice.]*

JUSTICE STEVENS delivered the opinion of the Court.

Prior to 1995, the Santa Fe High School student who occupied the school's elective office of student council chaplain delivered a prayer over the public address system before each varsity football game for the entire season. This practice . . . was challenged . . . as a violation of the Establishment Clause. . . . While these proceedings were pending . . . the school district adopted a different policy that permits, but does not require, prayer initiated and led by a student at all home games. The District Court entered an order modifying that policy to permit only nonsectarian, nonproselytizing prayer. The Court of Appeals held that . . . the football prayer policy was invalid. . . .

* * *

The August policy, which was titled, Prayer at Football Games, was similar to the July policy for graduations. . . . On August 31, 1995, according to the parties' stipulation, "the district's high school students voted to determine whether a student would deliver prayer at varsity football games. . . . The students chose to allow a student to say a prayer at football games." *Id.* at 65. A week later, . . . they selected a student "to deliver the prayer at varsity football games. . . ." . . .

The final policy (October policy) is essentially the same as the August policy, though it omits the word "prayer" from its title, and refers to "messages" and "statements" as well as "invocations." It is the validity of that policy that is before us.

* * *

The decision of the [5th Circuit] Court of Appeals [in a prior proceeding] . . . announced two rules. In *Jones v. Clear Creek Independent School Dist.*, 977 F.2d 963 (1992), that court held that student-led prayer that was approved by a vote of the students and was nonsectarian and nonproselytizing was permissible at high school graduation ceremonies. On the other hand, in later cases the Fifth Circuit made it clear that the *Clear Creek* rule applied only to high school graduations and that school-encouraged prayer was constitutionally impermissible at school-related sporting events. Thus, in *Doe v. Duncanville Independent School Dist.*, 70 F.3d 402 (1995), it had described a high school graduation as "a significant, once in-a-lifetime event" to be contrasted with athletic events in "a setting that is far less solemn and extraordinary." *Id.* at 406–407.

* * *

We granted the District's petition for certiorari, limited to the following question: Whether petitioner's policy permitting student-led, student-initiated prayer at football games violates the Establishment Clause. . . . We conclude . . . that it does.

* * *

. . . In *Lee v. Weisman*, 505 U.S. 577 . . . (1992), we held that a prayer delivered by a rabbi at a middle school graduation ceremony violated that Clause. Although this case involves student prayer at a different type of school function, our analysis is properly guided by the principles that we endorsed in *Lee*.

* * *

In this case the District first argues that this principle is inapplicable . . . because the messages are private student speech, not public speech. It reminds us that "there is a crucial difference between *government speech* endorsing religion, which the Establishment Clause forbids, and *private speech* endorsing religion, which the Free Speech and Free Exercise Clauses protect." *Board of Ed. of Westside Community Schools (Dist. 66) v. Mergens*, 496 U.S. 226, 250 . . . (1990). . . . We certainly agree with that distinction, but we are not persuaded that the pregame invocations should be regarded as "private speech."

These invocations are authorized by a government policy and take place on government property at government-sponsored school-related events. Of course, not every message delivered under such circumstances is the government's own. We have held, for example, that an individual's contribution to a government-created forum was not government speech. See *Rosenberger v. Rector and Visitors of Univ. of Va.*, 515 U.S. 819 . . . (1995). Although the District relies heavily on *Rosenberger* and similar cases involving such forums, it is clear that the pregame ceremony is not the type of forum discussed in those cases. . . .

Granting only one student access to the stage at a time does not, of course, necessarily preclude a finding that a school has created a limited public forum. Here, however, Santa Fe's student election system ensures that only those messages deemed "appropriate" under the District's policy may be delivered. That is, the majoritarian process implemented by the District guarantees, by definition, that minority candidates will never prevail and that their views will be effectively silenced.

Recently, in *Board of Regents of Univ. of Wis. System v. Southworth*, 529 U.S. (2000), we explained why student elections that determine, by majority vote, which expressive activities shall receive or not receive school benefits are constitutionally problematic:

> The whole theory of viewpoint neutrality is that minority views are treated with the same respect as are majority views. Access to a public forum, for instance, does not depend upon majoritarian consent. That principle is controlling here.

Like the student referendum for funding in *Southworth,* this student election does nothing to protect minority views. . . . . . . [T]he District's elections are insufficient safeguards of diverse student speech.

* * *

. . . Moreover, the District has failed to divorce itself from the religious content in the invocations. It has not succeeded in doing so, either by claiming that its policy is "'one of neutrality rather than endorsement'" or by characterizing the individual student as the "circuit-breaker" in the process. . . . [T]he realities of the situation plainly reveal that its policy involves both perceived and actual endorsement of religion. In this case . . . the "degree of school involvement" makes it clear that the pregame prayers bear "the imprint of the State and thus put school-age children who objected in an untenable position."

. . . Even though the particular words used by the speaker are not determined by those votes, the policy mandates that the "statement or invocation" be "consistent with the goals and purposes of this policy," which are "to solemnize the event, to promote good sportsmanship and student safety, and to establish the appropriate environment for the competition." *Ibid.*

In addition to involving the school in the selection of the speaker, the policy, by its terms, invites and encourages religious messages. . . . The policy itself states that the purpose of the message is "to solemnize the event." . . . Thus, the expressed purposes of the policy encourage the selection of a religious message. . . .

The actual or perceived endorsement of the message, moreover, is established by factors beyond just the text of the policy. Once the student speaker is selected and the message composed, the invocation is then delivered to a large audience assembled as part of a regularly scheduled, school-sponsored function conducted on school property. The message is broadcast over the school's public address system. . . . . . .

In this context the members of the listening audience must perceive the pregame message as a public expression of the views of the majority of the student body delivered with the approval of the school administration. . . . . . . [A]n objective Santa Fe High School student will unquestionably perceive the inevitable pregame prayer as stamped with her school's seal of approval.

* * *

Most striking to us is the evolution of the current policy. . . . This history indicates that the District intended to preserve the practice of prayer before football games. . . .

* * *

The District further argues that attendance at the commencement ceremonies at issue in *Lee* "differs dramatically" from attendance at high school football games, which it contends "are of no more than passing interest to many students" and are "decidedly extracurricular," thus dissipating any coercion. . . .

There are some students, however, such as cheerleaders, members of the band, and, of course, the team members themselves, for whom seasonal commitments mandate their attendance, sometimes for class credit.

. . . Undoubtedly, the games are not important to some students. . . . For many others, however, the choice between whether to attend these games or to risk facing a personally offensive religious ritual is in no practical sense an easy one. The Constitution, moreover, demands that the school may not force this difficult choice upon these students. . . .

Even if we regard every high school student's decision to attend a home football game as purely voluntary, we are nevertheless persuaded that the delivery of a pregame prayer has the improper effect of coercing those present to participate in an act of religious worship. . . . . . .

The Religion Clauses of the First Amendment prevent the government from making any law respecting the establishment of religion or prohibiting the free exercise thereof. By no means do these commands impose a prohibition on all religious activity in our public schools. See, e.g., *Lamb's Chapel v. Center Moriches Union Free School Dist.*, 508 U.S. 384, 395 (1993); *Board of Ed. of Westside Community Schools (Dist. 66) v. Mergens*, 496 U.S. 226 (1990); *Wallace v. Jaffree*, 472 U.S. 38, 59 (1985). . . . Thus, nothing in the Constitution . . . prohibits any public school student from voluntarily praying at any time before, during, or after the school day. But the religious liberty protected by the Constitution is abridged when the State affirmatively sponsors the particular religious practice of prayer.

* * *

The District, nevertheless, asks us to pretend that we do not recognize what every Santa Fe High School student understands clearly—that this policy is about prayer. . . . We refuse to turn a blind eye to the context in which this policy arose, and that context quells any doubt that this policy was implemented with the purpose of endorsing school prayer.

Therefore, the simple enactment of this policy, with the purpose and perception of school endorsement of student prayer, was a constitutional violation. . . .

The judgment of the Court of Appeals is, accordingly, affirmed.

It is so ordered.

[CHIEF JUSTICE REHNQUIST, joined by JUSTICE SCALIA and JUSTICE THOMAS dissented]

Case 3.3

ADLER v. DUVAL COUNTY SCHOOL BOARD
250 F.3d 1330 (11th Cir. 2001)

MARCUS, CIRCUIT JUDGE:

On March 15, 2000, this Court ruled that Duval County's facially-neutral policy permitting high school seniors to vote upon the delivery by a student of a message entirely of that student's choosing as part of graduation ceremonies did not violate the Establishment Clause. . . . Plaintiffs thereafter petitioned the Supreme Court for certiorari. Meanwhile, on June 19, 2000, the Supreme Court rendered its decision in *Santa Fe Independent School District v. Doe*, 530 U.S. 290 (2000), which invalidated a Texas school board's policy permitting students to vote upon the delivery of a "statement or invocation," subject to officials' approval, at each home high school football game. On October 2, 2000, the Court vacated our decision and remanded it for further consideration in light of *Santa Fe*. . . . [W]e proceeded to rehear the case en banc.

Having carefully reviewed the Supreme Court's opinion, . . . we conclude that *Santa Fe* does not alter our previous en banc decision, and accordingly we reinstate that decision. . . . Nevertheless, we take this opportunity to explain why we believe that *Santa Fe* does not alter the outcome of this case. Simply put, after (as before) *Santa Fe*, it is impossible to say that the Duval County policy *on its face* violates the Establishment Clause without effectively banning *all* religious speech at school graduations, no matter how private the message or how divorced the content of the message may be from any state review, let alone censorship. *Santa Fe* does not go that far, and we are not prepared to take such a step. . . . The Duval County policy provides in relevant part:

> "1. The use of a brief opening and/or closing message, not to exceed two minutes, at high school graduation exercises shall rest within the discretion of the graduating senior class;
> 2. The opening and/or closing message shall be given by a student volunteer, in the graduating senior class, chosen by the graduating senior class as a whole;
> 3. If the graduating senior class chooses to use an opening and/or closing message, the content of that message shall be prepared by the student volunteer and shall not be monitored or otherwise reviewed by Duval County School Board, its officers or employees;
>
> The purpose of these guidelines is to allow students to direct their own graduation message *without monitoring or review by school officials*." 206 F.3d at 1072 (Emphasis added).

We defined the issue then before us as "whether the Duval County school system's policy of permitting a graduating student, elected by her class, to deliver an unrestricted message of her choice at the beginning and/or closing of graduation ceremonies is facially violative of the Establishment Clause." *Id.* at 1073. Analyzing this policy under the Supreme Court's opinions in *Lee v. Weisman*, 505 U.S. 577, . . . (1992) and *Lemon v. Kurtzman*, 403 U.S. 602 . . . (1971), we concluded that the policy did not violate the Establishment Clause on its face.

. . . [O]ur *Lee* analysis turned on several key facts. First, we emphasized that under Duval County's policy school officials have no power to direct that a message (let alone a religious message) be delivered at graduation ceremonies, or control in any way the content of any message actually to be delivered. . . . Second, we rejected the argument that the state's role in providing a vehicle for a graduation message by itself transformed the student's private speech into state-sponsored speech. We accepted the assumption that the school board "exerted overwhelming control over the graduation ceremony," but stressed that the board "did not have control over the elements which are most crucial in the Establishment Clause calculus: the selection of the messenger, the content of the message, or most basically, the decision whether or not there would be a message in the first place." *Id.* at 1080.

We likewise rejected the argument that Duval County's policy would have the impermissible effect of coercing unwilling listeners to participate in a state-sponsored religious exercise. As we explained:

> [N]either the Duval County schools nor the graduating senior classes even decide if a religious prayer or message will be delivered, let alone "require" or "coerce" the student audience to participate in any privately-crafted message. While schools may make private religious speech their own by endorsing it, schools do not endorse all speech that they do not censor. We cannot assume . . . that Duval County seniors will interpret the school's failure to censor a private student message for religious content as an endorsement of that message—particularly where the students are expressly informed as part of the election process that they may select a speaker who alone will craft any message. . . . No religious result is preordained. *Id.* at 1084. . . . We closed our prior en banc opinion by defining our holding narrowly, stating that Duval County's policy of "permitting graduating students to decide through a vote whether to have an unrestricted student graduation message at the beginning and/or closing of graduation ceremonies does not *facially* violate the Establishment Clause." *Id.* at 1091 (emphasis added).

Three months after we issued our prior en banc opinion, the Supreme Court decided *Santa Fe.* . . . Because the facts of *Santa Fe* are fundamentally different in many crucial respects from the facts of this case, they are worth presenting in some detail.

* * *

In *Santa Fe* itself the Supreme Court reiterated just how case-specific Establishment Clause analysis must be under its precedent. As the Court explained:

"Every government practice must be judged in its unique circumstances. . . ." 120 S. Ct. at 2282 (citation omitted). We spoke similarly in our prior en banc opinion. . . .

The Court in *Santa Fe* did not attempt to sweep with a broad brush; rather, it found based on the facts then before it. . . . The facts of this case are fundamentally different, and in our view require exactly the same result today as they did at the time of our prior opinion. . . .

First, the Duval County policy does not contain any restriction on the identity of the student speaker or the content of the message that might be delivered. . . . ". . . The purpose of these guidelines is to allow students to direct their own graduation message *without monitoring or review by school officials.*" 206 F.3d at 1072 (quoting policy) (emphasis added). This is in sharp contrast to the Santa Fe policy, under which any message was subject to content regulation by the state. . . . . . .

* * *

. . . These important facts demonstrate why *Santa Fe* is distinguishable from this case, and more particularly why the speech at issue here—unlike the speech contemplated by the Santa Fe policy—cannot reasonably be described as state-sponsored. These key facts also help illustrate why the speech permitted by Duval County cannot reasonably be described as state "coercion" of religion.

* * *

The Duval County policy, unlike the Santa Fe policy, does not subject the issue of prayer to an up-or-down vote; students do *not* vote on whether prayer, or its equivalent, should be included in graduation ceremonies. Rather, students vote on two questions that do not expressly or inherently concern prayer: (1) whether to permit a student "message" during the ceremony, and (2) if so, which student is to deliver the message. *Santa Fe* does not remotely state or suggest that the term "message" connotes prayer. . . . . . .

Although it is possible that under Duval County's policy the student body may select a speaker who then chooses *on his or her own* to deliver a religious message, that result is not preordained, and more to the point would not reflect a "majority" vote to impose religion on unwilling listeners. Rather, it would reflect the uncensored and wholly unreviewable decision of a single student speaker. It cannot seriously be argued that Duval County's policy ensures that persons with "minority" views will *never* prevail in the student electoral process, whether we define "minority" . . . as persons opposed to student-selected speech at graduation, persons opposed to the delivery of religious messages generally, or persons opposed to the delivery of a religious message that does not coincide with their chosen faith. . . .

* * *

The Supreme Court did not rule that an election process itself is always incompatible with the Establishment Clause. Nor did it rule that a student elected to speak to the student body is necessarily a state-sponsored speaker. . . .

Second, the Court did not rule that, simply because the speech at issue is "authorized by a government policy and took place on government property at a government-sponsored school-related event," it always constitutes state-sponsored speech. On the contrary, the Court expressly acknowledged that "not every message delivered under such circumstances is the government's own." *Santa Fe*, 120 S. Ct. at 2275. . . . . . .

* * *

The Court in *Santa Fe* had every opportunity to declare that all religious expression permitted at a public school graduation ceremony violates the Establishment Clause; it did not do so. We could not invalidate Duval County's policy, *on its face*, without taking the very step the Court declined to take. . . .
OPINION AND JUDGMENT REINSTATED.

Case 3.4

LEE v. WEISMAN
112 S. Ct. 2649 (1992)

> [**Focus Note.** *Lee, a high school principal, invited a rabbi to offer a nondenominational invocation at the school's graduation commencement where student attendance was optional. A graduating student and her father unsuccessfully sued to block the invocation. After the commencement, which she attended, they pressed their suit to the Supreme Court, which ruled, 5–4, that the invocation violated the Establishment Clause.*]

Justice Kennedy delivered the opinion of the Court.

* * *

This case does not require us to revisit the difficult questions dividing us in recent cases. . . . . . . We can decide the case without reconsidering the general constitutional framework by which public schools' efforts to accommodate religion are measured. . . . The government involvement with religious activity in this case is pervasive, to the point of creating a state-sponsored and state-directed religious exercise in a public school. . . .

* * *

. . . The degree of school involvement here made it clear that the graduation prayers bore the imprint of the State and thus put school-age children who objected in an untenable position. . . . . . . It is argued . . . that prayer at a high school graduation does nothing more than offer a choice. By the time they are seniors, high school students no doubt have been required to attend classes and assemblies and to complete assignments exposing them to ideas they find distasteful or immoral or absurd or all of these. Against this background, students may consider it an odd measure of justice . . . to be denied a brief, formal prayer ceremony that the school offers in return. This argument cannot prevail, however.

* * *

It is of little comfort to a dissenter, then, to be told that for her the act of standing or remaining in silence signifies mere respect, rather than participation. . . . We do not address whether that choice is acceptable if the affected citizens are mature adults. . . . Research in psychology supports the common assumption that adolescents are often susceptible to pressure from their peers towards conformity. . . . . . .

* * *

Inherent differences between the public school system and a session of a State Legislature distinguish this case from *Marsh v. Chambers,* 463 U.S. 783 (1983) [which upheld invocations at the opening of a state legislature]. . . .
        . . . We do not hold that every state action implicating religion is invalid if one or a few citizens find it offensive. People may take offense at all manner of religious messages, but offense alone does not in every case show a violation. . . . But . . . the conformity required of the student in this case was too high an exaction to withstand the test of the Establishment Clause. . . .

* * *

JUSTICE SCALIA, with whom the CHIEF JUSTICE, JUSTICE WHITE, and JUSTICE THOMAS join, dissenting.

Three Terms ago, I joined an opinion recognizing that the Establishment Clause must be construed in light of the "[g]overnment policies of accommodation, acknowledgement, and support for religion [that] are an accepted part of our political and cultural heritage." . . . It said that "[a] test for implementing the protections of the Establishment Clause that, if applied with consistency, would invalidate longstanding traditions cannot be a proper reading of the Clause." [quoting Kennedy J. concurring opinion in *Allegheny County v. Greater Pittsburgh ACLU*, 492 U.S. 573, 657, 670 (1989)]

In holding that the Establishment Clause prohibits invocations and benedictions at public-school graduation ceremonies, the Court . . . lays waste a tradition that is as old as public-school graduation ceremonies themselves. . .

* * *

From our Nation's origin, prayer has been a prominent part of governmental ceremonies and proclamations. The Declaration of Independence . . . "appeal[ed] to the Supreme Judge of the world. . . ." . . . In his first inaugural address, after swearing his oath of office on a Bible, George Washington deliberately made a prayer a part of his first official act as President:

* * *

. . . Thomas Jefferson . . . prayed in his first inaugural address. . . . In his second inaugural address, Jefferson acknowledged his need for divine guidance and invited his audience to join his prayer. . . .

* * *

Most recently, President Bush . . . asked those attending his inauguration to bow their heads, and made a prayer his first official act as President. . . .

Our national celebration of Thanksgiving likewise dates back to President Washington. . . .

* * *

. . . And this Court's own sessions have opened with the invocation "God save the United States and this Honorable Court" . . . .

. . . According to the Court, students at graduation who want to avoid the fact or appearance of participation, . . . are *psychologically* obligated by "public pressure, as well as peer pressure . . . to stand as a group or, at least, maintain respectful silence" during those prayers. . . . This assertion—*the very linchpin of the Court's opinion*—is almost as intriguing for what it does not say as for what it says. It does not say, for example, that students are psychologically coerced to bow their heads . . . pay attention to the prayers, utter "Amen," or in fact pray. . . . It claims only that students are psychologically coerced "to stand . . . *or*, at least, maintain respectful silence." . . .

* * *

. . . Since the Court does not dispute that students . . . at graduation ceremonies retain . . . the free will to sit . . . there is absolutely no basis for the Court's decision. . . .

* * *

... Many graduating seniors, of course, are old enough to vote. Why, then, does the Court treat them as though they were first-graders? ...

* * *

Our religion-clause jurisprudence has become bedeviled (so to speak) by reliance on formulaic abstractions that are not derived from, but positively conflict with, our long-accepted constitutional traditions. Foremost among these has been the so-called *Lemon* test. . . . The Court today demonstrates the irrelevance of *Lemon* by essentially ignoring it. . . . Unfortunately, however, the Court has replaced *Lemon* with its psycho-coercion test. . . .

. . . Given the odd basis for the Court's decision, invocations and benedictions will be able to be given at public-school graduations next June. . . . All that is seemingly needed is an announcement, or perhaps a written insertion to the effect that, while all are asked to rise for the invocation and benediction, none is compelled to join in them, nor will be assumed, by rising, to have done so. . . . . . .

Case 3.4 Review Questions

1. Does the majority opinion rest primarily on the finding of coercive peer pressure to conform or on a finding of school sponsorship and endorsement of religion?

2. If an invocation creates material peer pressure, can any future graduation prayers be validated, as the dissent suggests, by school announcement that students are free to leave, sit, or ignore the invocation?

3. In future graduations, can a school disclaim that it is not endorsing, but only accommodating student expression, including religious expression, and thus avoid the endorsement objection?

4. Does the court's acceptance of the peer pressure argument for a single event in this establishment case square with ignoring the rejection of peer pressure objections in free exercise cases involving sex education?

Case 3.5

BROWN v. HOT, SEXY AND SAFER PRODUCTIONS, INC.
68 F.3d 525 (1st Cir. 1995)

> [***Focus Note.*** *Public high school students and their parents sued the school district, school officials and supervisors, and the school's contractor, Hot, Sexy and Safer Productions, Inc., which made a presentation, intended to promote AIDS*

awareness, to a high school assembly. The following facts were accepted as true by the court: The Hot, Sexy presentation was made to a high school assembly which the students were required to attend, and consisted of a series of explicit sexual skits which ran continuously for one-and-a-half hours, throughout which time the defendant school superiors who were in attendance as observers took no responsive action to the manner or content of the presentation. Further, the responsible school superiors, prior to the presentation, failed to follow the official written school district policy which required that they give advance notice of the program to the students' parents as to the nature of the Hot, Sexy presentation and advise the parents of their right to withhold their children from attending the Hot Sexy presentation. One may also infer that the defendant school superiors failed, either when making their contract with Hot Sexy or at any time thereafter, to specify or inquire into the nature of the program to be presented by Hot Sexy.

The following opinion indicates the legal risks posed for school administrators by controversial school presentations, and the power of the deciding judges to shape those risks by fact characterizations and framing of the legal issues. The review questions that follow the opinion expand on these important factors.]

TORRUELLA, CHIEF JUDGE.

* * *

. . . The plaintiffs' complaint alleges the following facts, which we take as true for purposes of this appeal. On April 8, 1992, Mesiti and Silva attended a mandatory, school-wide assembly at Chelmsford High School. Both students were fifteen years old at the time. The assembly consisted of a ninety-minute presentation characterized by the defendants as an AIDS awareness program (the "Program"). The Program was staged by defendant Suzi Landolphi ("Landolphi"), contracting through defendant Hot, Sexy, and Safer, Inc., a corporation wholly owned by Landolphi.

Plaintiffs allege that Landolphi gave sexually explicit monologues and participated in sexually suggestive skits with several minors chosen from the audience. Specifically, the complaint alleges that Landolphi: 1) told the students that they were going to have a "group sexual experience, with audience participation"; 2) used profane, lewd, and lascivious language to describe body parts and excretory functions; 3) advocated and approved oral sex, masturbation, homosexual sexual activity, and condom use during promiscuous premarital sex; 4) simulated masturbation; 5) characterized the loose pants worn by one minor as "erection wear"; 6) referred to being in "deep sh—" after anal sex; 7) had a male minor lick an oversized condom with her, after which she had a female minor pull it over the male minor's entire head and blow it up; 8) encouraged a male minor to display his "orgasm face" with her for the camera; 9) informed a male minor that he was not having enough orgasms; 10) closely inspected a minor and told him he had a "nice butt"; and 11) made eighteen references to orgasms, six references to male genitals, and eight references to female genitals.

Plaintiffs maintain that the sexually explicit nature of Landolphi's speech and behavior humiliated and intimidated Mesiti and Silva. Moreover, many students copied Landolphi's routines and generally displayed overtly sexual behavior in the weeks following the Program, allegedly exacerbating the minors' harassment. The complaint does not allege that either of the minor plaintiffs actually participated in any of the skits, or were the direct objects of any of Landolphi's comments.

* * *

The complaint names eight co-defendants along with Hot, Sexy, and Safer, and Landolphi, alleging that each played some role in planning, sponsoring, producing, and compelling the minor plaintiffs' attendance at the Program. . . .

* * *

. . . All the defendants were physically present during the Program.

A school policy adopted by the School Committee required "[p]ositive subscription, with written parental permission" as a prerequisite to "instruction in human sexuality." The plaintiffs allege, however, that the parents were not given advance notice of the content of the Program or an opportunity to excuse their children from attendance at the assembly.

* * *

The plaintiffs seek . . . relief, alleging that the school sponsored program deprived the minor plaintiffs of: (1) their privacy rights under the First and Fourteenth Amendments; (2) their substantive due process rights under the First and Fourteenth Amendments; (3) their procedural due process rights under the Fourteenth Amendment; and (4) their First Amendment rights under the Free Exercise Clause (in conjunction with a deprivation of the parent plaintiffs' right to direct and control the upbringing of their children). Plaintiffs also allege that the Program created a sexually hostile educational environment in violation of Title IX of the Education Amendments of 1972. . . .

* * *

I. Privacy Rights and Substantive Due Process

* * *

A. Conscience Shocking Behavior

Plaintiffs' claim that the defendants engaged in conscience shocking behavior when they compelled the minor plaintiffs to attend the Program. The Supreme Court set the standard for analyzing claims of conscience shocking behavior in *Rochin.* . . . Although we have not foreclosed the possibility that words or verbal harassment may constitute "conscious shocking" behavior in violation of substantive due process rights . . . our review of the case law indicates that the threshold for alleging such claims is high and that the facts alleged here do not rise to that level.

* * *

The facts alleged at bar are less severe than those found insufficient in *Souza* and *Pittsley* [police and prosecutor misconduct cases]. The minor teenagers . . . were compelled to attend a sexually explicit AIDS awareness assembly without prior parent approval. While the defendants' failure to provide opt-out procedures may have displayed a certain callousness towards the sensibilities of the minors, their acts do not approach the mean-spirited brutality evinced by the defendants in *Souza* and *Pittsley*. We accordingly hold that the acts alleged here, taken as true, do not constitute conscience shocking and thus fail to state a claim under *Rochin*.

B. Protected Liberty Interests

The Supreme Court has held that the Fourteenth Amendment encompasses a privacy right that protects against significant government intrusions into certain personal decisions. . . .

1. Right to Rear Children

* * *

. . . We need not decide here whether the right to rear one's children is fundamental because we find that, even if it were, the plaintiffs have failed to demonstrate an intrusion of constitutional magnitude on this right.

The *Meyer* and *Pierce* cases, we think, evince the principle that the state cannot prevent parents from choosing a specific educational program. . . . That is, the state does not have the power to "standardize its children". . . . We do not think, however, that this freedom encompasses a fundamental constitutional right to dictate the curriculum at the public school to which they have chosen to send their children. . . . . . . We cannot see that the Constitution imposes such a burden on state educational systems, and accordingly find that the rights of parents as described by *Meyer* and *Pierce* do not encompass a broad-based right to restrict the flow of information in the public schools.

2. Right to be Free from Offensive Speech

The minor plaintiffs maintain that the defendants' conduct violated their privacy right to be free from "exposure to vulgar and offensive language and obnoxiously debasing portrayals of human sexuality." Plaintiffs cite no cases—and we have found none—indicating that such a fundamental privacy right exists. Rather, they attempt to extract the claimed privacy right from the

Supreme Court's First Amendment cases which uphold the state's limited power to regulate or discipline speech to protect minors from offensive or vulgar speech. See *Bethel Sch. Dist. No. 403 v. Fraser,* 478 U.S. 675, 685, . . . (1986) (cited for the proposition that "[a] high school assembly or classroom is no place for a sexually explicit monologue directed towards an unsuspecting audience of teenage students"). . . . We agree with the district court that these cases "do not create a private cause of action against state officials for exposure" to patently offensive language.

II. Procedural Due Process

The plaintiffs' third claim alleges that their procedural due process rights under the Fourteenth Amendment were violated when the defendants compelled the minor plaintiffs to attend the Program without giving the parents advance notice and an opportunity to opt out of attending.

* * *

Defendants concede . . . that the Sex Education Policy confers a liberty interest in freedom from exposure to the content of the Program and in being afforded an opportunity to opt out. They argue, however, that the plaintiffs still fail to state a claim because the violation of the Sex Education Policy was a "random and unauthorized" act within the confines of the Parratt-Hudson doctrine. . . .

* * *

Parratt and Hudson preclude § 1983 claims for the "random and unauthorized" conduct of state officials because the state cannot "anticipate and control [such conduct] in advance." . . .

* * *

The plaintiffs contend that the deprivation cannot be characterized as "random and unauthorized" because the performance was planned well in advance. . . . The deprivation alleged here is not the staging of the Program itself, but rather the defendants' failure to follow the procedures mandated by the Sex Education Policy. . . . Rather, the Sex Education Policy states that "[p]ositive subscription, with parental permission, will be a prerequisite to enrolling," and, accordingly, vested no discretion in school officials. We therefore conclude that the failure to follow the Sex Education Policy was a "random and unauthorized" act within the confines of the Parratt-Hudson doctrine.

III. Free Exercise Clause

Plaintiffs' fourth claim seeks . . . relief, alleging that the defendants' endorsement and encouragement of sexual promiscuity at a mandatory assembly "imping[ed]" on their sincerely held religious values regarding chastity and morality," and thereby violated the Free Exercise Clause of the First Amendment.

In *Employment Div., Oregon Dep't of Human Resources v. Smith*, 494 U.S. 872, . . . (1990), the Supreme Court addressed a free exercise challenge to a facially neutral and generally applicable criminal statute. . . . The Court explained that the First Amendment was not offended by neutral, generally applicable laws, unless burdening religion was the object of the law. . . .

* * *

. . . The plaintiffs do not allege . . . that the compulsory attendance at the Program was anything but a neutral requirement that applied generally to all students. . . .

* * *

IV. Sexual Harassment

The plaintiffs' fifth claim alleges that the defendants engaged in sexual harassment by creating a sexually hostile environment, in violation of Title IX of the Education Amendments of 1972. Title IX provides in relevant part:

> No person in the United States shall, on the basis of sex, be excluded from participation in, be denied the benefits of, or be subjected to discrimination under any education program or activity receiving Federal financial assistance. . . .

Because the relevant case law under Title IX is relatively sparse, we apply Title VII caselaw by analogy. . . .

Title VII, and thus Title IX, "strike at the entire spectrum of disparate treatment of men and women," including conduct having the purpose or effect of . . . creating an intimidating, hostile or offensive environment. *Meritor Sav. Bank, FSB v. Vinson*, 477 U.S. 57, 64–65. . . .

* * *

Title IX is violated "[w]hen the [educational environment] is permeated with 'discriminatory intimidation, ridicule, and insult' that is 'sufficiently severe or pervasive to alter the conditions of the victim's employment and create an abusive . . . environment.'" *Harris*, 510 U.S. at—, 114 S. Ct. at 370 . . . While a court must consider all of the circumstances in determining whether a plaintiff has established that an environment is hostile or abusive, it must be particularly concerned with (1) the frequency of the discriminatory conduct; (2) its severity; (3) whether it is physically threatening or humiliating rather than a mere offensive utterance; and (4) whether it unreasonably interferes with an employee's work performance. See *Harris*, 510 U.S. at—. . . .

* * *

. . . If the conduct is not so severe or pervasive that a reasonable person would find it hostile or abusive, it is beyond Title IX's purview. . . . Thus, the court must consider not only the actual effect of the harassment on the plaintiff, but also the effect such conduct would have on a reasonable person in the plaintiff's position.

Turning to the case at bar, we find that the facts alleged here are insufficient to state a claim for sexual harassment under a hostile environment theory. . . . First, plaintiffs cannot claim that the offensive speech occurred frequently, as they allege only a one-time exposure to the comments.

We also think that the plaintiffs' allegations do not establish that Landolphi's comments were so severe as to create an objectively hostile environment. . . . . . .

Moreover, during his introductory remarks, defendant Gilchrist advised students that the purpose of the Program was to educate them about the dangers of sexual activity. . . . stating:

> We see young people in their twenties who are infected with the AIDS virus. . . . It means they caught the virus when they were in high school, and will be dead before they are thirty years old. . . . And today, we have a very special messenger, who uses probably one of the most effective forms of communication—humor. I want you to listen carefully. Enjoy it, but also remember the message.

Similarly, Landolphi stated in her opening remarks that "[w]e're going to talk about AIDS, but not in the usual way." These prefaces framed the Program in such a way that an objective person would understand that Landolphi's allegedly vulgar sexual commentary was intended to educate the students about the AIDS virus rather than to create a sexually hostile environment.

. . . In this context, while average high school students might have been offended by the graphic sexual discussions alleged here, Landolphi's remarks could not reasonably be considered physically threatening or humiliating so as to create a hostile environment.

Similarly, the plaintiffs' allegations establish that the Program did not significantly alter their educational environment from an objective standpoint. The Program consisted of two ninety-minute sex-education presentations, and although the plaintiffs allege that "coarse jesting, sexual innuendo, and overtly sexual behavior took place for the weeks following the Program," they fail to explain how the coarse jesting and overtly sexual behavior "create[d] an atmosphere so infused with hostility toward members of one sex that [it] alter[ed] the [educational environment] for them." . . . If anything, then, they allege discrimination based upon the basis of viewpoint, rather than on the basis of gender, as required by Title IX. We therefore find that their claim under Title IX fails.

* * *

Case 3.5 Review Questions

1. Did the court fairly characterize the admitted facts as harmless humor? Did it fairly characterize the violation of the official school parent notification policy as an excusable isolated event, in light of the weeks or months it required to plan, order, and discuss the planned presentation before the actual day of presentation? Compare the treatment of sexual vulgarity by the Eighth Circuit Court of Appeal in the *Lacks* case which appears at the end of Chapter 6.

2. Could federal judges from the other 10 federal circuits reasonably disagree with the above opinion on the following questions?
   a. Was the authorization and/or compliant observation of the Sexy program by school authorities sufficient to "shock the conscience" for a constitutional "substantive due process" violation? The above opinion does not make clear whose conscience or value judgments should control. Neither does the general case law. Should the "conscience" monitor be that of the judges? The education profession? The parents? The general community?
   b. Are the police brutality cases cited by the court relevant to the question whether a sex-laden presentation to a captive audience of adolescent students is "conscience shocking"?

3. In characterizing the defendants' conduct as "random and unauthorized" as ground to dismiss the due process claim, did the court fairly ignore the time and effort expended by the administration in planning and contracting for the skit that was ultimately delivered?

   What actions were "random" or "unauthorized"? The decision to have the program? The program planning? The making of the contract with Sexy? The failure to inquire into and review the presentation ultimately devised by Hot Sexy? The failure to notify parents? The passive observation of the presentation throughout the 90-minute succession of lewd skits, without any responsive action to protect the students?

4. The above opinion (Part B) noted that the Fourteenth Amendment encompasses a privacy right that protects against significant government intrusions into certain personal decisions. Does the above opinion comment about parental attempts *to dictate* the school curriculum fairly address this question, or does its distract from the question of parental right *to be exempt from* the Hot Sexy program, as conferred by state law and school policy?

5. Since the court found no foursquare precedent case to cover the Hot, Sexy situation (a common problem in all cases of first impression), was the Supreme Court decision (*Bethel*), which upheld a school's authority to

protect students from unwelcome lewd speech by another student, irrelevant and inapposite as Judge Tortuella's opinion suggests? Put another way, are students more accountable for lewd speeches to school assemblies than are school authorities and school contractors?

6. On the free exercise claim, the court noted that the school written exemption *policy* was "neutral" and therefore constitutional, but does that observation address the question whether the defendant's *conduct* in executing that policy was neutral, rather than a form of "deliberate indifference" that might support a theory of liability? This question should be saved for later consideration after the "deliberate indifference" concept is explained in detail in Chapter 8.

7. On the Title IX claim, could the court have reasonably viewed the Hot, Sexy program as creating a sexually harassing environment? This basis of Title IX liabilities is also discussed in later chapters. For now, it suffices to observe that the test of a Title IX violation is the effect of school actions, not the subjective intent of anyone.

8. The above opinion concluded, "We also think that the plaintiffs' allegations do not establish that Landolphi's comments were so severe as to create an objectively hostile environment." What more should a court require for an objective sexual harassment in a mandatory school assembly, short of physical sexual contact?

   The court referred to comments by Landolphi to the effect that she was only using humor. As noted in past and future chapters, the plea, I was only kidding, does not go very far to avoid liability for debasing sexual language.

∞ ENDNOTES

1. The Supreme Court construed the term *religion* as used in the federal military draft statute very broadly, but has not adopted that statutory definition for First Amendment purposes. United States v. Seeger, 380 U.S. 163, 165–66 (1965).

2. Board of Educ. of Kiryas Joel Village School Dist. v. Grumet, 512 U.S. 687 (1994); Grumet v. Pataki, 675 N.Y.S.2d 662 (N.Y. 1998).

3. W. Va. Board of Educ. v. Barnette, 319 U.S. 624 (1943).

4. *Religious group use:* Peck v. Upshur County Board of Educ., 155 F.3d 274 (4th Cir. 1998); Garnett v. Renton School Dist., 987 F.2d 641 (9th Cir. 1993); Hoppock v. Twin Falls School Dist., 772 F. Supp. 1160 (D. Idaho 1991); Youth Opportunities Unlimited v. Board of Public Educ., School Dist. of Pittsburgh, 769 F. Supp. 1346 (W.D. Pa. 1991)(nonprofit corporation summer religious program).

   Rental of school facility to religious groups: Seas v. School Dist., 811 F. Supp. 183 (E.D. Pa. 1993); Randall v. Pegan, 765 F. Supp. 793 (W.D. N.Y. 1991) (lease of school auditorium); Grace Bible Fellowship, Inc., v. Maine School Administrative Dist., 941 F.2d 45 (1st Cir. 1990) (refusal to rent facility leased to other outside groups).

   Religious fund raiser: Travis v. Owego-Appalachian School Dist., 927 F.2d 688 (2d Cir. 1992).

   Testimonial to Christ: Gregoire v. Centennial School Dist., 907 F.2d 1366 (3d Cir. 1990).

5. Hills v. Scottsdale Un. High School District, 329 F.3d 1044 (9th Cir. 2003).

6. Bronx Household of Faith v. Community School Dist. No. 10, 127 F.3d 207 (2d Cir. 1997). *Cf.* Verbena United Methodist Church v. Chilton County Board of Educ., 765 F. Supp. 704 (M.D. Ala. 1991) (refusal to rent school auditorium for baccalaureate service).

7. Saratoga Bible Training Inst. v. Schuylerville, 18 F. Supp. 2d 178 (N.D. N.Y. 1998).

8. Travis v. Oswego-Appalachin School Dist., 972 F.2d 688 (2d Cir. 1991).

9. *See, e.g.,* Lanner v. Wimmer, 662 F.2d 1349 (10th Cir. 1981); Smith v. Smith, 523 F.2d 121 (4th Cir.

1975); State v. Thompson, 225 N.W.2d 678 (Wis. 1975).

10. Bell v. New Jersey and Pennsylvania, 461 U.S. 773 (1983); Wheeler v. Barrera, 417 U.S. 402 (1974).

11. Engle v. Vitale, 370 U.S. 421 (1962) (school-sponsored prayer); School Dist. of Abington Twp. v. Schempp, 374 U.S. 203 (1963) (recitation of the Lord's prayer and Bible verses). *See also* Roberts v. Madigan, 921 F.2d 1047 (10th Cir. 1991); Walker v. San Francisco Unified School Dist., 761 F. Supp. 1463 (N.D. Cal. 1991); Doe v. Shenandoah County School Bd., 737 F. Supp. 913 (W.D. Va. 1990).

12. *E.g.,* "We thank You for the flowers so sweet; we thank You for the food we eat; we thank You for the birds that sing, we thank You for everything." DeSpain v. DeKalb County Comm. School Dist., 384 F.2d 836 (7th Cir. 1967); *see also* Berger v. Renselaer Central School Corp., 982 F.2d 1160 (7th Cir. 1993).

13. Newdow v. U.S. Congress et al., 292 F. 3d 597 (9th Cir. 2002), *republished as* amended opinion, 328 F. 3d 466 (9th Cir. 2003); *cert granted sub nom.* Elkgrove Un. School Dist., 124 S. Ct. 384 (2003).

14. Wallace v. Jaffree, 473 U.S. 38 (1985).

15. Brown v. Gilmore, 258 F.3d 265 (4th Cir. 2001); DeBord v. Board of Educ., 126 F.3d 1102 (8th Cir. 1997); Bown v. Gwinnett County School District, 112 F.3d 1464 (11th Cir. 1997).

16. Lemke v. Black, 376 F. Supp. 7(E.D. Wis. 1974); *cf.* Bronx v. Household of Faith, note 6, *supra.*

17. (a) Jones v. Clear Creek Indep. School Dist., 977 F.2d 963 (5th Cir. 1992).

   (b) Doe v. Duncanville Ind. School Dist., 70 F.3d 402 (5th Cir. 1995). *See also* Ingebretson v. Jackson Public School Dist., 88 F.3d 274 (5th Cir. 1996).

   (c) Doe v. Beaumont School Dist., 173 F.3d 274 (5th Cir. 1999).

18. Adler v. Duvall County School Board, 206 F.3d 1070 (11th Cir. 2000), reinstated at 250 F.3d 1330 (11th Cir. 2001). *Contra:* ACLU of New Jersey v. Black Horse Pike Regional Board of Educ., 84 F.3d 1471 (3rd Cir. 1996).

19. Chaudhuri v. State of Tenn., 130 F.3d 232 (6th Cir. 1977) (college commencement); Coles v. Cleveland Board of Educ., 171 F.3d 369 (6th Cir. 1999) (board meeting invocation). *Contra:* Bacus v. Palo Verde Un. School Dist.,11 F. Supp. 2d 1192 (C.D. Cal. 1998).

20. Doe v. Madison School Dist., 147 F.3d 832 (9th Cir. 1998), withdrawn 165 F.3d 1265 (1999). The 1998 opinion distinguished an earlier decision of the same circuit because the students in that case were selected for the express purpose of delivering a prayer. Collins v. Chandler Unified School Dist., 644 F.2d 759 (9th Cir. 1981).

21. *Compare* Baumann v. West High School, 132 F.3d 542 (10th Cir. 1997) (rejecting challenge of Jewish choir member to use of Christian music, and choir performance of Christian songs at Christian sites), *with* Sease v. School Dist. of Philadelphia, 811 F. Supp. 183 (E.D. Pa. 1993) (disapproving student-organized gospel choir under supervision of school secretary).

22. Lynch v. Donnelly, 465 U.S. 668, 677 (1984).

23. Stone v. Graham, 449 U.S. 39 (1980). *Compare, e.g.,* Freethought Society v. Chester County, 334 F.3d 247 (3d Cir. 2003) (upholding retention of long placed plaque on county courthouse, as a public secular monument). *See also* Glassroth v. Moore, 335 F.3d 1282 (11th Cir. 2003) (court order to remove placement of Ten Commandment monument in state courthouse).

24. Washagesic v. Bloomingdale Public Schools, 33 F.3d 679 (6th Cir. 1994) (portrait of Jesus Christ); Joki v. Board of Educ., 745 F. Supp. 823 (N.D. N.Y. 1990) (student art of a crucifixion).

25. Allegheny County v. Greater Pittsburgh American Civil Liberties Union, 492 U.S. 473 (1989). *See also* Lynch v. Donnelly, 465 U.S. 668 (1984).

26. Grossbaum v. Indianapolis-Marion County Bldg. Authority, 63 F.3d 581 (7th Cir. 1995); Chabad-Lubavitch of Georgia v. Miller, 5 F.3d 1383 (11th Cir. 1993). *Contra:* American Civil Liberties Union v. Schundler, 104 F.3d 1435 (3d Cir. 1997), which held display of crèche and menorah unconstitutional. *Cf.* Americans United for Separation of Church and State v. Grand Rapids, Mich., 980 F.2d 1538 (6th Cir. 1992) (privately funded 20-foot menorah in public square held not to violate the Establishment Clause).

27. Clever v. Cherry Hill Twp. Board of Educ., 838 F. Supp. 929 (D. N.J. 1993) (classroom calendars depicting religious and other holidays, and classroom displays containing religious symbols). Florey v. Sioux Falls School Dist., 619 F.2d 1311 (8th Cir. 1980) (singing of Christmas carols—allowed).

28. Gernetzke v. Kenosha Un. School Dist., 274 F.3d 464 (7th Cir. 2001).

29. McCollum v. Board of Educ., 333 U.S. 203 (1948).

30. Zorach v. Clauson, 343 U.S. 306 (1952).

31. *E.g.,* Springfield School Dist. v. Dept. of Educ., 397 A.2d 1154 (Pa. 1979).

32. *Student request:* Church of God Worldwide Tex. Region v. Amarillo, 670 F.2d 46 (5th Cir. 1982). *Teacher request:* Niederhuber v. Camden County Vocational Technical School Dist. Board of Educ., 495 F. Supp. 273 (D. N.J. 1980); *aff'd,* 671 F.2d 496 (3d Cir. 1981).

33. Cmwlth. v. Bey, 70 A.2d 693 (Pa. 1953) (Mohammedan Friday Sabbath); *in re* Currence, 248 N.Y.S.2d 251 (1963) (Wednesday and Thursday Sabbath).

34. *Compare* Metzl v. Leininger, 57 F.3d 618 (7th Cir. 1995) (voiding state setting of school holiday on Good Friday), *with* Koenick v. Felton, 190 F.3d 259 (4th Cir. 1999), *cert denied,* 120 S. Ct. 938 (1999) (statute providing school holidays on Good Friday—held constitutional). *See generally* Annot., *Validity of Laws Making Day of Religious Observance a Legal Holiday,* 90 A.L.R. 3d 752 (1979).

35. Student Members of the Playcrafters v. Board of Educ. of the Twp. of Teaneck, 424 A.2d 1192 (N.J. 1981) (school ban on extracurricular activity on religious sabbaths). *See also* Cammack v. Waihee, 932 F.2d 765 (9th Cir. 1991).

36. Clayton v. Place, 884 F.2d 376 (8th Cir. 1989).

37. Smith v. Board of Educ., 708 F.2d 258 (7th Cir. 1983).

38. DiPasquale v. Board of Educ. 457 (W.D. N.Y. 1985).

39. *Compare* California School Employees Assn. v. Sequoia Union H.S. Dist., 136 Cal. Rptr. 594 (1977) (upheld paid holiday), *with* Hunterden Central High School Board of Educ. v. Hunterden Central High School Teachers Assn., 416 A.2d 980 (N.J. 1980) (overturned paid holiday).

40. Spence v. Bailey, 465 F.2d 797, 798–800 (6th Cir. 1972).

41. Epperson v. Arkansas, 393 U.S. 97 (1968).

42. Edwards v. Aguillard, 482 U.S. 578 (1987) (voiding statute requiring teaching of creation science). *See also* McClean v. Ark. Board of Educ., 529 F. Supp. 1255 (E.D. Ark. 1982).

43. "Among religions in this country which do not teach . . . a belief in the existence of God . . . [are] Ethical Culture, Secular Humanism, and others." *See* Torcaso v. Watkins, 376 U.S. 488, 495, at note 11 of the court's opinion (1961). Ploza v. Capistrano Unified School Dist., 782 F. Supp. 1412 (C.D. Cal. 1992); Wright v. Houston Indep. School Dist., 486 F.2d 137 (5th Cir. 1973).

44. Freiler v. Tangipahoa Parish Bd. of Educ., 185 F.3rd 337 (5th Cir. 1999).

45. Wiley v. Franklin, 497 F. Supp. 390 (E.D. Tenn. 1980); Annot., *Bible Distribution or Use in Public Schools,* 111 A.L.R. Fed. 121 (1993; Supp. 1998).

46. See Annot., *Validity of Sex Education Programs in Public Schools,* 82 A.L.R. 3d 570 (1978, Supp. 1998).

47. *See, e.g.,* Citizens for Parental Rights v. San Mateo County Board of Educ., 124 Cal. Rptr. 68 (1975); Smith v. Ricci, 446 A.2d 501 (N.J. 1982).

48. Hopkins v. Board of Educ., 289 A.2d 914 (Conn. 1971); *aff'd,* 305 A.2d 536 (Conn. 1973) (upholding sex education). *But see* Mercer v. Mich. State Board of Educ., 379 F. Supp. 580 (E.D. Mich. 1974) (state law barring birth control instruction, upheld); Hobolth v. Greenway, 218 N.W.2d 98 (Mich. 1974); Medeiros v. Kyosaki, 478 P.2d 314 (Hawaii 1970).

49. Leebaert v. Harrington, 332 F.3d 134 (2d Cir. 2003).

50. *Compare* Curtis v. School Committee, 652 N.E.2d 580 (Mass. 1995) (school program of condom distribution and instruction, upheld as not violating parental rights or student free exercise of religion); *accord:* Parents United for Better Schools, Inc. v. School Dist. of Philadelphia 148 F.3d 260 (3d Cir. 1998). *Contra:* Alfonso v. Fernandez, 606 N.Y.S.2d 259 (1993) (similar program struck down on both constitutional and state law grounds). *See generally* Annot.,

Propriety of Prophylactic Availability Programs, 52 A.L.R. 5th 477 (1997); E. Bjorklun, *Condom Distribution in the Public Schools: Is Parental Consent Required?* 91 Educ. Law Rep. 11 (1994).

51. Williams v. Board of Educ., 388 F. Supp. 93; *aff'd,* 530 F.2d 972 (4th Cir. 1975). *See also* Davis v. Page, 385 F. Supp. 395 (D. N.H. 1974).

52. Smith v. Board of School Commissioners, 827 F.2d 684 (11th Cir. 1987).

53. Todd v. Rochester Comm. Schools, 200 N.W.2d 90 (Mich. 1972).

54. Mozert v. Hawkins County Board of Educ., 827 F.2d 1058 (6th Cir. 1987). *Cf.* Frost v. Hawkins County School Board, 851 F.2d 822 (6th Cir. 1988).

55. Grove v. Mead School Dist., 753 F.2d 1528 (9th Cir. 1985).

56. Berger, note 12, *supra;* Meltzer v. Board of Public Instruction, 548 F.2d 559 (5th Cir. 1977).

57. W. Va. Board of Educ. v. Barnette, 319 U.S. 624 (1943) (student); Russo v. Central School Dist., 469 F.2d 623 (2d Cir. 1972) (teacher). *But see* discussion in Palmer v. Board of Educ., 603 F.2d 1271 (7th Cir. 1979) on circumstances where teacher cannot reject curriculum directive for classroom patriotic exercises, based on her religious grounds.

58. Mitchell v. McCall, 143 So. 2d 629 (Ala. 1962); Hardwick v. Board of School Trustees, 205 P. 49 (Cal. 1921).

59. Jacobson v. Cmwlth. of Massachusetts, 197 U.S. 11 (1905); Calandra v. State College Area School Dist., 512 A.2d 809 (Pa. Cmwlth. 1986) (condition of participation in school athletics); *In re* Clark, 185 N.E.2d 128 (Ohio 1962).

60. Cude v. State, 377 S.W.2d 816, 819 (Ark. 1964).

61. *E.g.,* Mason v. General Brown Cent. School Dist., 851 F.2d 47 (2d Cir. 1988) (Universal Life Church held a system of ethics, not a religion). *Compare* State v. Miday, 140 S.E.2d 325 (N.C. 1965), *with* McCartney v. Austin, 293 N.Y.S.2d 188 (1968).

62. Americans United for Separation of Church & State v. Paire, 348 F. Supp. 506 (D. N.H. 1972); Moore v. Board of Educ., 212 N.E.2d 833 (Ohio 1965); Zellers v. Huff, 236 P.2d 949 (N.M. 1951).

63. Citizens to Advance Public Educ. v. Porter, 237 N.W.2d 232 (Mich. 1976); *in re* Proposal C, 185 N.W.2d 9 (Mich. 1971).

64. Snyder v. Charlotte Public School Dist., 333 N.W.2d 542 (Mich. 1983).

65. Fisher v. Clackamas Cty. School Dist., 507 P.2d 839 (Or. 1973); State v. School Dist. No. 10, 472 P.2d 1013 (Mont. 1970).

66. Brown v. Heller, 273 N.Y.S.2d 713 (1966).

67. Fisher, note 65, *supra*.

68. Thomas v. Schmidt, 397 F. Supp. 203 (D. R.I. 1975). A good analysis of the entanglement issue is contained in Buford v. S.E. DuBois County School Corp., 472 F.2d 890 (7th Cir. 1973).

69. Pratt v. Arizona Board of Regents, 520 P.2d 514 (Ariz. 1974) (lease of state college arena); Cooper v. County School Board, Fla. Sup. Ct. No. 81–3625 (11–2–82) (lease to a Catholic mission).

70. Fairfax Covenant Church v. Fairfax County School Board, 17 F.3d 703 (4th Cir. 1994) (school charging higher rent for religious than for nonreligious users); Resnick v. E. Brunswick Twp. Board of Educ., 343 A.2d 127 (N.J. 1975). Cases are collected in Annot., *Schools—Use for Religious Purposes*, 79 A.L.R. 2d 1148 (1961).

71. Bronx Household of Faith v. Board of Educ. of City of New York, 331 F.3d 342 (2d Cir. 2003).

Tort Liability Under State Law

∽ **CHAPTER OUTLINE**

I. General Principles of State Tort Law
  A. Duty of Care Requirement
  B. The Causation Requirement
  C. General Defenses
    1. Privileged Conduct
    2. Victim Fault
    3. Written Waivers of Tort Claims
    4. School District Vicarious Liability
II. Common Tort Situations
  A. Corporal Punishment
    1. Constitutionality
    2. When Corporal Punishment Is Not Tortious
      a. Purpose of Punishment
      b. Reasonableness of Force
      c. Defensive Use of Force
  B. Premises Liability
    1. Standard of Care for Premises Safety
      a. Invitees
      b. Licensees and Trespassers
      c. Child Trespassers
    2. Examples of Premises Liability
  C. Supervision Liability
    1. When the Duty of Supervision Arises
    2. General vs. Special or Direct Supervision
    3. Foreseeable Criminal Conduct
    4. Circumstances Affecting Degree of Supervision
      a. School Grounds
      b. Classrooms and Corridors
      c. Athletics and Physical Education
      d. Laboratory and Shop Facilities
      e. Student Transportation
      f. Off-Campus Activities
      g. First Aid
      h. Student Suicides and Homicides

      D.   Defamation (Libel or Slander)

      E.   Educational Malpractice

III.   Limitations on Tort Recovery

      A.   Governmental Immunity

          1.   Nuisance Exceptions

          2.   Governmental vs. Proprietary Functions

          3.   Discretionary vs. Ministerial Functions

      B.   Personal Immunity

      C.   Notice and Time Limits and Dollar Caps

          1.   Statutes of Limitations

          2.   Dollar Recovery Limits

∞ CHAPTER DISCUSSION QUESTIONS

∞ CASES

4.1 Grant v. Lake Oswego School District No. 7, 515 P.2d 947 (Or. App. 1973)

4.2 Soper v. Hoben, 195 F.3d 845 (6th Cir. 1999)

4.3 Ayala v. Philadelphia Board of Public Education, 305 A.2d 877 (Pa. 1973)

∞ ENDNOTES

GENERAL PRINCIPLES OF STATE TORT LAW

This chapter deals with traditional tort liability under state law. Under state tort law, a person who causes injury to another through violation of some legal duty has committed a tort and is liable to pay monetary compensation to the injured party.

A *tort* is a civil wrong arising out of a breach of duty that is imposed by law. Torts are not crimes, though some acts that amount to torts are also crimes (for instance, intentional assaults). Only the government can prosecute someone for committing a crime; and criminal guilt must be proven beyond a reasonable doubt.[1] The victim of a tort, on the other hand, may file a civil lawsuit and need only prove fault by a preponderance of evidence—a much easier standard to satisfy. Tort law obligations also differ from contract obligations in that torts arise from duties imposed by law, whereas contract obligations arise from the terms of agreements that parties voluntarily undertake.

Tort law governs school districts, their officers, and their employees. School districts often purchase insurance to help absorb the risk of loss through tort claims. In some states, indemnity statutes reimburse and hold school officers and employees harmless from tort liability they incur in the course of their duties. Nonetheless, even with insurance and indemnity statutes, the risks and burdens of tort litigation provide ample incentive for school districts and their individual servants to minimize tortious conduct.

Tort law, as originally developed in the "common law" (judge-made law) and as later codified to some degree in state statutes, is usually grounded in the concept of *fault*. Schools have no duty to ensure the safety of students and other members of the school community at all times.[2] A school district is not liable for every accidental injury but only for injuries caused intentionally or by negligence of employees and officials.

> . . . [A] school district is not the insurer of complete safety of school children, nor is it strictly liable for any injuries which may occur to them. [*Benton v. School Board of Broward County*, 386 So. 2d 831, 834 (Fla. App. 1980)]

Situations in which the law may impose strict liability for injuries without regard to intent or fault and cases of intentional injury by school personnel are uncommon. They may be noted occasionally, but are not stressed in this text.

The principal questions to be resolved in tort claims are these:

1. Did the sued party have a duty of care under the law to avoid the injury suffered by the claimant?
2. If so, was that duty actually breached?
3. If a breach of duty occurred, was it the proximate (or direct) cause of the injury?
4. If so, is the sued party shielded from liability by a *privilege* or *immunity* conferred by law?

5.   If there is liability, does the law place a dollar limit on the money damages that the claimant may recover?

In resolving these questions, courts and juries must initially determine if the evidence is sufficient to support a finding of negligence, and whether any negligence caused the claimant's injury. Courts have the power to dismiss a case without submitting it to the jury or to reverse a jury verdict that is clearly against the law or the evidence. These fact-finding functions explain why seemingly similar tort cases often result in different outcomes.

Duty of Care Requirement

Whether a duty of care exists in a given situation is a question of law to be decided initially by courts.[3] If such a duty exists, courts permit a jury, under court instructions, to determine whether that duty has been breached. The verdict on this question will often depend on the jury's view of conflicting testimony and evidence.[4]

In the overwhelming majority of states, the duty of care is that care which a reasonable person of ordinary prudence would exercise for the safety of others in like circumstances. In limited instances courts have imposed special duties to protect children.[5] State legislatures can also modify the general "duty of care" standard of liability with statutes that impose higher "special duties" for certain situations, or that limit school liability to cases of willful or wanton misconduct. To determine whether an act was negligent, the courts look at what the sued party should reasonably have foreseen and done under the circumstances. As a great tort justice once put it, "The risk reasonably to be perceived defines the duty to be obeyed." [*Palsgraf v. Long Island R.R. Co.*, 162 N.E. 99, 100 (N.Y. 1928) (Cardozo, J.)] The exact act of negligence that caused the injury need not be foreseeable; it is enough if the act or omission which caused the injury involved a general kind of risk that was foreseeable at the time.

Furthermore, for tort liability to attach, the risk must be reasonably preventable as well as foreseeable. The law does not oblige a party to assume impractical and unreasonable burdens to prevent harm to others. Failure to take *every* precaution against *all* foreseeable injury to another does not *necessarily* constitute actionable negligence. That would amount to making the school an insurer. The existence of compulsory attendance laws does not so restrict a student's freedom of action that schools have an affirmative duty to protect students in all circumstances.[6]

Because there is no fixed measure of due care for the limitless variety of risk relationships in schools, the "reasonable person" standard reflects community norms of reasonable conduct as they evolve from time to time and place to place. Generally speaking, the age, relationship, and physical characteristics of the parties involved, the gravity and probability of danger presented in specific circumstances, and the necessity and utility of the risk-creating conduct must all be weighed to determine the required level of care and reasonable response.

The Causation Requirement

A tort claimant must prove that the defendant's act or omission was the *proximate* cause of the claimant's injury. The defendant's conduct must be a *material* and *substantial* factor in producing the harm, "but for" which the harm would not have occurred. This "but for" test is generally reliable, but not exact. Proximate cause may be found where the same harm would have occurred if either of two concurrent acts were solely involved. The defendant's conduct need not be the immediate, or even the primary, cause of injury, but it must be a necessary link in the chain of events that resulted in injury.

Proximate cause often becomes an issue in tort suits when some intervening act of an unsupervised student or other person was the immediate cause of injury. In such cases, the court or jury must decide whether proper supervision could have prevented or deterred the intervening student conduct that directly caused the injury.[7] When a student was killed in a fight during recess, one court ruled that the jury should decide the question of proximate cause.[8] However, in a case of student misconduct during recess, the court decided that teacher negligence was not the proximate cause of the resultant injury.[9] A teacher and a principal who negligently failed to report the unauthorized absence of a 13-year-old girl, who was later found murdered, were found not to have proximately caused her death because there was no evidence as to how and when the crime occurred to justify any inference that a prompt teacher report would have prevented her death.[10] It would not be wise to conclude that failure to note a student's absence would be similarly treated in other circumstances. These examples show how particular case facts critically affect the finding whether school negligence was a proximate cause of an injury.

General Defenses

Several doctrines prevent a tort victim from recovering money damages even where negligence caused his injury. Some of these were recognized by the common law, and others were later created by legislation. Defenses that can bar recovery of tort damages include the following:

- Privileged conduct,
- Victim fault,
- Waiver of claims,
- Scope of wrongdoer's authority,
- Dollar recovery limitations,
- Notice requirements and time barriers, and
- Immunity shields.

The special defenses of dollar recovery limits, notice and time bars, and party immunity are discussed in a later section titled "Limitations on Tort Recovery."

Privileged Conduct

Conduct that is legally "privileged", i.e., which empowers teachers and administrators to engage in certain conduct, is not, in law, tortious. For example, the use of reasonable force in self-defense or to quell a fight would be privileged conduct, even if it causes injury to a student.

Victim Fault

In some states, students who knowingly assume a risk of injury, or whose own negligence contributes to it, may be denied recovery, in whole or in part, against a person whose negligence caused that injury.[11] The recognition of the defenses of *assumption of risk* and *contributory negligence* varies from state to state. They were originally applied to bar any recovery, regardless of the degree of fault on the part of the claimant and defendant. In recent times, however, an increasing number of states have limited these defenses to reflect the comparative fault of the tort actor and tort victim. In lieu of the contributory negligence defense, many states adopted a doctrine of *comparative negligence*, which does not completely extinguish a wrongdoer's liability, but reduces the recovery to the extent that the tort victim contributed to his own injuries.[12] For instance, if the victim and another person were equally negligent and equally responsible for the victim's injuries, the victim's tort recovery would be reduced by half.

Comparative negligence can only be attributed to persons who are sufficiently mature to recognize the risks that can cause injury. Similarly, the assumption of risk defense applies only where the injured individual could reasonably recognize the assumed danger:

> A child is not held to the same degree of care as an adult. Rather, the test is whether the particular child, considering his age, background, and inherent intelligence, indulged in gross disregard of his own safety in the face of known, understood, and perceived danger. . . . A defense of assumption of risk is, however, narrowly . . . restricted by requirements that a party must have full knowledge and appreciation of the danger, yet voluntarily expose himself to the risks and embrace the known danger. [*Simmons v. Beauregard Parish School Bd.*, 315 So. 2d 883, 888 (La. 1975)]

Teachers should not rely too heavily on these defenses in dealing with students, especially the very young. Consider the following examples: (a) a kindergarten child who wandered off school grounds into a busy street was not contributorily negligent; (b) a student injured by an explosion in preparing a science project did not assume the risk of explosion; (c) a 13-year-old was not contributorily negligent in placing his hand inside a door jamb; but (d) a 17-year-old who ran around a darkened school stage and fell into a hatchway was contributorily negligent; as was (e) a visitor who chose to walk across an unlit portion of open school grounds; and, finally (f) a strong high school student athlete who challenged a coach to a wrestling match assumed the risk of injury.[13] A student's knowing violation of school safety rules may constitute comparative negligence. Juries are often left to determine the extent of a victim's fault. The *Grant* opinion (Case 4.1) illustrates these principles.

Written Waivers of Tort Claims

Schools often request written parental consent for student participation in special activities, such as field trips and athletic competitions. The consent forms state that parents release the school and its employees from all legal responsibility for any injury the child may sustain in the consented activity. These releases may have the psychological effect of deterring parents from bringing tort actions, but their *legal* effect is limited. First, many courts hold that these releases violate public policy and are void.[14] Second, even in states that allow parents to surrender their own tort claim, they may not legally surrender the independent claim of an injured minor child for pain and suffering and for any loss of the child's future earning power.[15] In most cases, minors lack the legal capacity to make binding agreements so their signature on a release form is equally unenforceable.

By definition, a release is an "intentional" abandonment of a "known" right. It can, therefore, be challenged as having been obtained or signed without full disclosure or knowledge of the relevant risks of the school activity. Further, the release may be held ineffective if the signor was not knowledgeable about the rights relinquished by the release. The relatively few reported court cases in this area indicate that school authorities frequently do press the validity of such releases through the courts.[16]

School District Vicarious Liability

A school district is a fictional legal "person" and can only be *vicariously* liable for the torts of its teachers, staff, and officials (referred to as its "servants"). Where the torts of its servant are *legally imputed* to the district, the district may be held liable. This doctrine, called *respondeat superior* ("Let the master answer for the conduct of his servant"), renders the school district liable only for acts of individuals that are within the scope of their authority or employment.[17] The reasoning is that a school district is accountable for conduct that it has the legal authority to control, but not for conduct that is beyond its legal authority to control. Courts and juries must, therefore, decide when a particular act departs so far from an employee's scope of employment or authority that it should be treated as a purely personal act and not that of the school district.[18]

Determining the scope of authority or employment involves difficult factual issues. This is particularly true of willful rather than negligent misconduct acts of its employees. In such cases, courts disagree on whether that miscon-duct should be imputed to the employer school district.[19] Earlier artificial dis-tinctions between active wrongdoing (*misfeasance*) and passive wrongdoing (*nonfeasance*) have done little to harmonize the case conflicts.

COMMON TORT SITUATIONS

Corporal Punishment

Constitutionality

In the case of *Ingraham v. Wright,* 430 U.S. 651 (1977), the Supreme Court held that corporal punishment, where permitted by state law, does not vio-late the federal Constitution. If there are no statutory constraints, school au-thorities may administer corporal punishment without prior notice, hearing, or consent of students or their parents. In its extensive survey of state law variations on corporal punishment, the Court noted that Massa-chusetts and New Jersey generally prohibit disciplinary corporal punish-ment, while California requires parental consent for its use. But even there, the use of bodily force is permitted if required for self-defense or to halt other assaults.

Disciplinary restraints on student movement (e.g., in-school detention during and after school hours) are not considered corporal punishment, and are also privileged if used reasonably.[20]

When Corporal Punishment Is Not Tortious

Corporal punishment is not a tort when authorized and administered in a *privileged* manner. In most states, corporal punishment is privileged only when administered by authorized individuals in a manner that is reasonable as to purpose, method, and degree of force.[21] Many school employees are not privi-leged to use corporal punishment except where force is necessary to preserve the safety of students. A school bus driver was subject to dismissal for admin-istering unauthorized corporal punishment.[22] The so-called *in loco parentis* privilege of teachers "acting in the place of parents" is not equivalent to the broader disciplinary privileges of natural parents.

In states that permit corporal punishment, school boards may still regu-late its use. Many boards limit the grounds for corporal punishment and the manner of its administration. Many districts require the school principal, rather than individual teachers, to determine whether and how corporal pun-ishment should be given. School boards may require the presence of another adult under conditions calculated to avoid unnecessary abuse or embarrass-ment of students.[23] Only rarely have schools and courts allowed corporal pun-ishment for purely instructional purposes.[24]

Purpose of Punishment.   Corporal punishment must serve a reasonable educational purpose. The child or parent has the burden of alleging and showing that the corporal punishment lacked a reasonable purpose (and therefore was not privileged). In close cases juries decide that question. Here also, "reasonableness" reflects local community attitudes, and can therefore vary from region to region. Typical considerations include the nature of the student infraction; the student's past record, age, sex, and mental and physical condition; and the suitability of the instrument and force employed. A student's intent (willful misbehavior vs. carelessness) and the motivation of the disciplinarian (benign vs. vindictive) are also relevant. A parent's objection to punishment does not prevent a school disciplinarian from claiming a defense of privilege, unless state law or school board regulation expressly requires parental consent to use corporal punishment.[25]

Reasonableness of Force.   Deciding how much corporal force may be used calls for caution. A teacher is not liable for injuries caused by normal corporal punishment when she could not reasonably anticipate that it would produce serious injury because of the child's undisclosed, latent medical condition. The fact that punishment produces pain or minor bruises does not automatically demonstrate that excessive force was used. Indeed, the use of increased force may be reasonable when dealing with chronically recalcitrant students.[26] But corporal punishments that produce severe physical injuries (bleeding, deep bruises, sprains, or fractures) are likely to be considered excessive and tortious.[27]

    Courts are more likely to uphold spanking and paddling of healthy students as privileged,[28] but courts have disapproved of the use of certain instruments, such as cattle prods or broken paddles, regardless of the degree of force employed, and they have found that excessive force was used (a) when a teacher beat a boy with a broken paddle, resulting in head and body bruises; and (b) when a teacher struck an 8-year-old, puncturing the child's eardrum.[29]

Defensive Use of Force.   It is clear that teachers and employees have the same legal privilege to use reasonable force to defend persons or property as would any other person. In stressful circumstances, a person of ordinary prudence may reasonably act with less detachment and control than he or she would under normal circumstances. The greater the threat of danger, the greater the justification for quick and forceful defensive action. Even the use of a "sneeze gun" to ward off student attack was held reasonable where the accosted teacher thought it necessary to protect herself.[30] The privilege of defense is lost when retaliation against a student assailant becomes vindictive and excessive.[31] In subduing an emotionally upset, mentally retarded student, a teacher was found to have used excessive force and was liable for consequent injuries.[32]

Premises Liability

Tort law imposes a duty of care in maintaining safe premises, but it does not require owners and possessors of land and buildings to keep premises absolutely safe at all times and for all persons. The law considers not only the condition of the premises, but also the purpose for which the injured person was there.

Standard of Care for Premises Safety

Invitees. Persons invited to school premises and school functions are considered *invitees*. Invitees have a right to expect that the premises they visit are reasonably safe, and may recover money damages for injuries caused by negligent failure of school authorities to make the premises reasonably safe.[33] If school authorities take reasonable measures, such as periodic inspections and repairs, victims injured by defects in school property cannot recover.[34] Juries are often left to decide whether the evidence suffices to prove negligence.

Under the principle of *res ipsa loquitur* ("the thing speaks for itself"), a court or jury may infer negligence from clear circumstantial evidence.[35] Courts have found negligence where school personnel actively created the hazard or permitted it to continue after it became known or should have been discovered.[36] School authorities are not generally required to discover and remedy every premises defect that they did not create.[37] However, some states have enacted tort statutes that render districts liable for injuries caused by a "dangerous condition" of school property even though the school district was not negligent in inspecting and maintaining that property.[38]

Licensees and Trespassers. Tort law imposes a lower duty of care due to "trespassers" and "licensees". *Trespassers* are those who unlawfully enter school property, while *licensees* are persons who are allowed entry to the school but who have not been invited there for school purposes. Schools have no general duty to make the premises safe for trespassers or licensees. However, if school authorities learn that licensees or trespassers are on school grounds, they have a limited duty to warn these entrants of known but concealed hazards and to avoid affirmative acts that place them in jeopardy.[39]

Child Trespassers. The usual rule that an owner of property has no duty of care to trespassers does not always apply to children. Potentially dangerous sites or facilities (such as construction sites) that may be expected to attract child trespassers are known as *attractive nuisances*. Some states encourage owners and possessors of land to keep children out of unsafe areas through the attractive nuisance doctrine, which treats child trespassers as if they were invitees. The attractive nuisance doctrine has been applied sparingly to normal school building conditions. School authorities are not obliged to expend great resources to ensure the safety of every child trespasser. For example, a district was held not liable when a 12-year-old used a ladder hanging from the side of a school to climb to the building's roof.[40] But new construction activity and excavations at school sites may fall within the attractive nuisance doctrine.

Examples of Premises Liability

Students have recovered tort damages for injuries resulting from sticky or slippery floors; defective bleachers, handrails, gates, and doors; poorly lighted or darkened passageways; unstable lockers, furniture, equipment, or stacked materials; and unshielded building protrusions.[41] Although school districts are the dominant targets of tort suits for premises liability, school principals and teachers with supervisory duties may also be held personally liable for negligent maintenance of school conditions.[42]

Supervision Liability

Most school-related torts are brought under a claim of negligent supervision. Negligent acts or omissions include the failure to warn students of dangers; failure to report, avoid, and correct unsafe situations; failure to arrange student activities in a safe manner; and failure to aid ill or injured students. Supervision cases raise three basic questions:

1. Was there any duty to supervise students in the circumstances?
2. If so, what kind and degree of supervision would be reasonable under those circumstances?
3. Was the lack of proper supervision a proximate cause of claimed injury?

When the Duty of Supervision Arises

A duty to supervise arises only when a reasonable person would anticipate the need for supervision. But a person who has no duty of supervision and nevertheless volunteers to protect a student is held to the same duty as one who has a legal obligation to do so.[43]

To determine the extent of required supervision, courts consider all relevant factors, such as the nature and location of the activity, the number and ages of the students, and the practicability and expense of providing greater degrees of supervision. The law demands only what is reasonable in light of these factors, unless a "safe school" statute imposes greater responsibility for "dangerous conditions" of school property.[44] While educators share a general obligation for student safety, the level of their respective supervisory duties is largely defined by their position in the school. Generally speaking, prudent supervision has two major aspects: (1) care not to create danger by one's own negligent conduct (such as ordering activities that unreasonably endanger students), and (2) care to avoid perils created by others.

A student injured by fellow students cannot recover for negligent supervision without proof that the acts of fellow students were reasonably foreseeable by school employees.[45]

General vs. Special or Direct Supervision

Teachers cannot observe every movement of every child. Only general supervision, not direct, special supervision, is required where students engage in activities that are not normally dangerous. The *Soper* case (Case 4.2) illustrates this principle. Special supervision is required, however, whenever a school activity poses special dangers, such as instruction for hazardous activity with which students are not familiar or adept.[46] Where a teacher has knowledge of assaultive student behavior, that knowledge triggers a higher duty to protect other students from the assailant.[47] The failure to provide direct supervision on occasions when students are known to engage in rough horseplay may create tort liability.[48]

Foreseeable Criminal Conduct

At one time, under earlier common law, criminal conduct by third parties was thought to be unforeseeable, but more recent school experiences have changed that outlook and have spurred a trend toward holding schools liable for the failure to protect students from criminal conduct that is reasonably foreseeable.[49] Failure to supervise students with known violent tendencies and to warn a substitute teacher about violent students are grounds for holding principals and teachers liable in tort.[50] Student suicide cases present special issues and are discussed below.

Properly published safety rules and procedures may relieve school districts and supervisors of liability for injuries caused by violations of these rules, unless student failure to follow rules was reasonably foreseeable.[51] Whether proper supervision could have prevented one student from injuring another raises the thorny factual issues of causation on which courts and juries often disagree.[52]

Circumstances Affecting Degree of Supervision

Supervisory duties are determined by the nature, time, and place of student activity.

School Grounds. When school is not in session, supervision of school grounds *immediately before or after* classes may be required where students are known to congregate there.[53] Liability for negligent supervision has been imposed for playground injuries sustained shortly before the opening of school, whether caused by regular play, student misconduct, unsafe conditions, or scuffling at school bus pickup points.[54] The school's failure to provide off-hour supervision to prevent snowball fights was held not negligent, especially where school rules prohibit them.[55] But where school authorities knew or should have known that students in the schoolyard were throwing iceballs and attacking isolated children, the district was held liable for failing to take steps to protect injured students.[56]

A stronger case arises where school rules explicitly require such supervision.[57] Absent these circumstances, school authorities are not obliged to supervise dismissed children *indefinitely* before and after school sessions, such as children who remain on school grounds to await private transportation.[58]

When school is in session, there is no general duty to provide special supervision over normal playground activity, and failure to do so is held not to be negligent.[59] Once undertaken, supervision must be adequate under the circumstances. School authorities may be liable for failure to provide an adequate number of supervisors in relation to the number of students to be supervised, *at or away from school*. Some examples of insufficient numbers of supervisors include (a) failure to assign more than one supervisor to the playground; (b) presence of a single supervisor at a field where a child fell from bleachers, 1,000 feet away from the supervisor; (c) assigning one supervisor for several hundred children; and (d) assigning 23 teachers to supervise a heavily attended school carnival.[60]

Classrooms and Corridors.   Classroom absence of the class teacher, during which time a student is injured, is a common ground of tort claim. In such cases, the court and jury must consider whether the teacher's temporary absence was reasonable in light of the purpose and duration of the absence, the distance the teacher was removed from his or her charges, the class makeup, its history of orderly or disorderly conduct, and the student assignments during the teacher's absence.

A teacher who is temporarily distracted or absent from the classroom when an accident occurs is not automatically considered negligent. A kindergarten music teacher who momentarily looked away before a child fell from the piano was not negligent,[61] nor was a teacher who failed to anticipate and prevent a classroom assault while she stood outside the door shepherding children into the room.[62] However, teachers who left a class unsupervised for an extended period, during which time students were injured, were found negligent.[63] Two Louisiana cases indicate the difficulty of predicting how a jury will assess specific circumstances of temporary absence. In one, a teacher was held liable for a brief absence from a normal class; in the other, the teacher of a special education class was absolved of liability when she left the class unattended for a five-minute coffee break.[64] If the absence from class is brief and for school purposes, and if the class has a good behavior record, most courts will not consider such absences to be negligent.[65]

Cases that exonerated teachers for injuries caused by students jostling each other confirm the general view that only prudent, and not prescient, supervision is required in normal circumstances.[66]

When the school is used by outside groups for nonschool activities, the duty of supervision shifts to the outside party, and school personnel are not liable unless they affirmatively assumed a duty of care or negligently created a dangerous condition.[67]

Athletics and Physical Education.   Inadequate supervision of physical education and athletic exercises is typical ground for tort claims. Some examples include dangerous placement of gym equipment, mismatching of contestants, imprudent inducement to perform exercises for which pupils are not physically or psychologically prepared, and placement of different activities in dangerously congested areas.[68] See *Grant v. Lake Oswego School Dist. No. 7* (Case 4.1) at the end of this chapter.

Liability does not necessarily result from any one factor. A football player did not prove negligence simply because he was tackled by a much larger lineman. Nor was the conduct of adjoining games in the same gym unreasonable per se.[69] But instructor violations of school safety rules and provision of faulty safety equipment, such as ill-fitting football helmets, will expose the instructor and the school districts to tort liability.[70]

Instructors are not obliged to head off unknown risks to a student with an unreported, latent medical condition that renders the student abnormally vulnerable to physical activity.[71] For instance, the court found no liability in the case of an unexplained drowning in a supervised swimming pool that could have resulted from an unforeseen or unpreventable medical condition.[72] However, schools have a duty not to aggravate a student's known vulnerable condition. For example, it was negligent to refuse to excuse heat stroke victims from team exercises or to permit careless movement of an injured player by fellow students.[73] Negligence is less likely to be found where mature and properly trained athletes sustain injuries from risks that are inherent in their athletic activities.[74] In such cases, general supervision satisfies the duty of care. But courts found a need for special supervision when an instructor ordered a 7-year-old child to climb a cargo net and failed to monitor wrestling matches.[75] Spectators at school athletic events do not require special supervision.

Laboratory and Shop Facilities.   Due care is commensurate with the hazards presented. For this reason, laboratory and shop instructors are typically held to a higher degree of care in the use of dangerous chemicals or equipment and in the provision of proper safety instructions.[76]

The defenses of contributory or comparative negligence and assumption of risk do not apply to uninformed students who cannot appreciate the risks posed by shop conditions.[77] However, students who removed chemicals from storage without permission to conduct unauthorized experiments were held to be contributorily negligent.[78]

Instructor violations of state safety laws may constitute negligence per se. Failure to secure shop equipment (such as power presses, grinders, saws, and cutting equipment) or to supply effective safety devices (pressure gauges or goggles) may be found to be negligence per se.[79] In the absence of a safety statute, an instructor's failure to establish safety rules in apparently dangerous situations still constitutes negligence, as where the instructor who failed to stop student horseplay in a school shop.[80] Where shop injuries arise from sudden, unauthorized student actions, courts have not found instructors liable. Examples include a case where a student threw a power switch, thereby activating a power tool that was being cleaned, after shop class was over, and another where a student threw nails toward the trash box rather than depositing them into the box as ordered by the instructor.[81]

Student Transportation.   Absent a transportation statute, public schools have no obligation to provide or supervise student transportation between school and home.[82] When school transportation is provided, most courts adopt the general standard of reasonable care for tort cases, so that no liability arises for unavoidable accidents, such as when a bus driver lost control when severely stung by a bee, or instinctively swerved the bus to avoid a snowball.[83] A small minority of state courts adopt a special rule of automatic (i.e., absolute) liability for accidents caused by defective bus equipment that does not meet the requirements of their school bus safety statutes.[84]

Transportation-related torts usually arise from unsafe equipment, negligent bus operation, and negligent supervision of students at bus pickup and discharge points.[85] Typical examples include breakdowns of defective tires and lack of on-board supervision to prevent foreseeable injuries by unruly students.[86] But drivers are not held negligent where student-to-student injury cannot be reasonably anticipated.[87] Cases of negligent bus operation include (a) driving too fast on school grounds, (b) sudden stops and starts, (c) sudden turns at unsafe speed, (d) failing to flash warning lights at crossings, and (e) discharging passengers at unsafe places.[88]

Courts have stressed the need for special caution at bus stops, especially for very young children who can be expected to run alongside a moving bus or dart into traffic. Bus drivers are obliged to caution hasty children about running near the bus and of moving traffic at street crossings.[89] But boarding or deboarding accidents do not automatically prove driver negligence, as where a student is shoved out of a stationary bus or falls or is pushed under a bus.[90]

School authorities are duty bound to establish reasonably safe bus stop points, but they are not obliged to select the safest points, and they are not responsible for injuries at unassigned stops.[91] Unless a statute requires it, school authorities have no general duty to provide safety patrols for student pedestrians. However, if a school employs crossing guards, it will be responsible for negligent failure to deploy them properly.[92] While school is in session, a court may find a duty to supervise student pedestrians, such as when students cross a public highway to reach a particular class.[93]

Off-Campus Activities.   The duty of supervision extends to school-sponsored activities, whether on or away from school property, but no such duty exists for nonsponsored off-campus activities.[94] School club moderators were held liable for failure to supervise a school club initiation ceremony that caused student injury.[95] The degree of required supervision for field trips depends on the nature of the trip. A child injured on a seashore outing after the teacher abandoned supervision to pursue other interests was entitled to have a jury determine if the teacher was negligent,[96] but a teacher who allowed a student to wander out of her presence during a class visit to a museum was held not negligent.[97]

First Aid.   The duty to render first aid to students arises only when the need is apparent,[98] and not when there is no reasonable indication that first aid is needed. There is no duty to provide aid that requires special training, but where teachers volunteered medical assistance to students and caused student injuries by their incompetence, the court held that they could be held liable.[99]

Student Suicides and Homicides.   The recent rise in student suicides and homicides has opened a new front of state tort law, including the following claims: that the school district (and school personnel) negligently failed to take precautionary steps to secure the safety of a student with observable suicidal tendencies, that the district was negligent in failing to warn the suicides' parents of the recognizable suicidal tendencies of their children, and that the school district was negligent in failing to implement a suicide prevention program where the school conditions indicated a need for such a program. The recent cases also advance a nascent federal law claim that the schools' negligence infringed the students' constitutional rights to bodily security. That federal claim is explored in Chapter 8.

The general duty of supervision to preserve student safety includes a duty to protect students with observable suicidal tendencies, and to take reasonable steps to *prevent* vulnerable students from attempting suicide, including warnings to parents.[100] These cases build on the cases which held licensed physicians and psychiatrists liable for failure to warn appropriate persons of their patients' threats to commit suicide (or homicide) notwithstanding the fact that such threats were disclosed in a confidential doctor–patient relationship.[101]

Courts are not in agreement on the proofs that are sufficient to establish that school authorities knew or should have detected a student's suicidal tendencies. They are also divided on the following proximate cause questions: (1) whether the suicide itself should be considered a supervening cause that broke the chain of causation, and (2) in failure to warn claims, how to determine whether that failure was a proximate cause of the student injuries, i.e., whether failure to warn or act was too remote from the student's suicidal act. While most recent cases leave these difficult questions to jury determination,[102] a Wisconsin court recently held that a student's suicide is, as a matter of law, a superceding cause of death, which relieved school officials and teachers of any tort liability. The court made that finding even though (1) officials knew that the student was under enormous pressure and extremely upset about numerous failing grades and removal from the school basketball team, and (2) officials failed to tell the boy's parents of his unexcused absence from school on the day of his suicide, as required by official school policy.[103]

Student suicide cases also raise novel questions on the availability of tort immunity defenses of school districts or teachers. Those immunity issues are considered in the later sections of immunity from suit doctrines.

With regard to third-party assaults on students, recent cases found no reason for school authorities to anticipate stabbings and shootings by outsiders who unlawfully entered the school premises.[104] Those cases can be readily distinguished from foreseeable threats of violence by students. If plaintiffs establish that the school authorities knew or could by prudent action have identified violence-prone students and that they failed to take reasonable measures to control them, a court and jury may well find liability for actionable negligence.[105] The widespread adoption of strict security measures and zero-tolerance policies against carrying weapons to school, in the aftermath of school massacres in several states, is a clear recognition of the school's duty to protect students from such hazards.

Defamation (Libel or Slander)

A leading authority on tort law describes defamation as follows:

> Defamation is made up of the twin torts of libel and slander—the one being, in general, written, while the other in general is oral. . . . In either form, defamation is an invasion of the interests in reputation and good name. . . . Consequently, defamation requires that something be communicated to a third person that may affect that opinion. Derogatory words and insults directed at the plaintiff himself (but not communicated to another person) cannot form the basis for a defamation suit. . . . Defamation is rather that which tends to injure "reputation" in the popular sense, to diminish the esteem, respect, good will or competence in which the plaintiff is held, or to excite adverse, derogatory or unpleasant feelings or opinions against him. [W. Prosser, *Law of Torts* 737, 739 (4th ed.)]

In brief, defamation (libel or slander) is a communication of a false or misleading statement that damages the victim's reputation. It may be committed by direct statement or indirectly by innuendo, and by unprivileged repetition of a defamatory statement authored by others. However, not every unpleasant criticism is defamatory. In a suit for defamation, the plaintiff must prove that the alleged defamatory statement (1) asserts a fact rather than an opinion, (2) is untrue, (3) the speaker knew or had reason to know the statement was false, (4) the statement was communicated to a third party, and (5) it injured the claimant's reputation. If a person did not intend and could not reasonably foresee that the statement would reach anyone other than the subject of the statement, there is no injury to reputation and no liability for defamation. Nor can liability attach if the speaker has no reason to know that the statement is untrue.

Perhaps the most contentious defense is that the statement was one of opinion, rather than fact. There are, in addition, several special defenses to defamation claims. Truth is always an absolute defense since truth, by definition, cannot be defamatory. If the party has a legal right or duty to make statements for the good of the school community that would be defamatory in other contexts, courts find that the potential harm to an individual's reputation is outweighed by the public's need for the information, and that such statements are accordingly *privileged* and nonactionable.[106] This privilege typically involves school hearings or discussions of a teacher's fitness, in which administrators or even parents make adverse comments that relate to official consideration of the teacher's competence, so long as those statements are not known by the speaker to be false.[107] Similar conditional privileges apply to comments made by teachers about students for appropriate school purposes.

Defamatory statements about "public officials" or "public figures" are further privileged and protected by the First Amendment. For a statement about a public figure to be actionable, the speaker must make it with *actual knowledge* that it was false *or* with *reckless disregard* of its truth or falsity. The law thus ensures public debate on matters of public interest by shielding news agencies and others from liability for *negligent* falsehoods about public officials and public figures.[108] Though the case law on public figures is relatively sparse in the school context, it is worth noting that school board members, school superintendents, and principals may be considered public officials or figures in certain circumstances, and may be exposed to defamatory statements that are not actionable unless they are knowingly false or reckless.

Educational Malpractice

The ambiguous phrase "educational malpractice" expresses two related tort claims: (1) failure of school authorities to properly evaluate and place a student, with consequent injury to that student's educational development, and (2) failure to bring a properly placed student up to a satisfactory level of learning achievement. Courts have declined to impose any tort liability for these academic shortfalls because they lack objective standards to measure educational performance and to determine the effect of numerous education-related factors that may be beyond educators' control. However, as the endnote examples illustrate, the cases do not eliminate the possibility of recovering for negligent or wanton misconduct in the testing and evaluation of special student needs.[109] Nor, as noted in Chapter 8, do they preclude federal law claims under federal statutes that mandate special programs for children with special needs, such as children with disabilities.

LIMITATIONS ON TORT RECOVERY

State laws accord special defenses and protections to school districts and their employees, in addition to the above-noted general defenses. These special defenses include (1) immunity from suit, (2) statutory limits on dollar recoveries, (3) statutory time bars to tort suit for failure to give notice of tort claims and for failure to institute suit within statutory time deadlines, and (4) statutory indemnity and payment by school districts of the litigation expenses and judgments entered against their teachers and officials. The scope of these protections varies in some details from state to state.

Unlike the defenses of "privilege" (to inflict corporal punishment, or to make defamatory charges) or of "justification" (use of excessive force in emergency situations), immunity from suit does not derive from the *conduct* of the sued party but from the *function* that party performed at the time of the alleged injury.

The federal law immunity doctrines, which apply to claims under federal law, are discussed in Chapter 8.

Governmental Immunity

For reasons hereafter noted, government entities have different immunities from suit than individuals who act on behalf of those entities. The scope and limits of their respective immunities may be established by a state's courts or by its legislature, which may opt to modify tort immunities. Tort immunity for government entities developed historically in two distinct forms, called *sovereign immunity* and *governmental* immunity. *Sovereign immunity* is based on the principle that the sovereign state cannot be sued without its consent. This immunity generally attaches only to the state government and not to its subdivisions. *Governmental immunity* is based on a policy of shielding government entities from the burdens of tort litigation and tort liability and it attaches to local government entities such as school districts.[110] The distinction between sovereign and governmental immunity is largely mooted in the majority of states, which have by law consented to be sued for torts, thereby waiving sovereign immunity. The distinction remains significant, however, in the few states that retain sovereign immunity and that clothe their school districts with sovereign immunity.[111]

The foregoing immunities do not shield individuals from suit. The separate law on the *personal* immunity of public school teachers and supervisors is considered in a later section.

Most states continue to adopt the broad principles of governmental tort immunity for school districts, even as they continue to refine their allowance of and exceptions from tort immunity for selected tort claims.[112]

School districts may waive their governmental immunity, and in many states, they are deemed to have waived their immunity to the extent that they have liability insurance coverage for the tort claim.[113]

A number of states exclude certain kinds of tort claim from from tort immunity, such as injuries suffered from defective equipment or property conditions, or nuisance conditions, including "attractive nuisances". The variations in tort immunity exceptions that are made by different states are noted in the endnote samples.[114] An extreme instance of variation in the same state appears in an Illinois case which held that a child injured on a defective playground slide could fully recover tort damages if the city owned the playground, but only in certain circumstances if the school district owned the playground, and not at all if a park district owned the site.[115]

Where an injury is caused by equipment that violates safety statutes, courts must decide whether the legislative policy of promoting safety should prevail, by imposing tort liability, or whether the policy of immunizing government entities from exposure to tort suits should prevail. In such cases, many courts favor the safety motivation policy and impose liability on school districts.[116]

The most prominent exceptions to immunity include injuries caused by (1) a "nuisance", (2) school activities that are deemed to be "proprietary" rather than "governmental" in nature, (3) school actions that are deemed "ministerial" rather than "discretionary", or (4) defective conditions of school property or equipment, particularly where the injury results from violation of a school safety statute.

Nuisance Exceptions

Some states favor school district liability for nuisances:[117]

> A municipal corporation has no more right to create and maintain a nuisance than does a private person. To constitute a nuisance . . . the condition must in some way constitute an unlawful invasion of the property rights of others. And it has been said that the invasion . . . must be inherent in the thing or condition itself, beyond that merely from its negligent or improper use. [*Stein v. Highland Park Indep. School Dist.*, 540 S.W.2d 551, 553 (Tex. 1976)]

Under this concept of nuisance, school districts retain immunity for injuries resulting from negligent *uses* of property but not from defective *conditions* of property.[118] Conditions that have been classified as nuisances include (a) a sewage lagoon that pollutes an adjoining dairy farm, (b) a wall that diverts natural surface drainage away from the school onto neighboring land, and (c) a school building's unlawful encroachment of another property, causing students continually to trespass and throw litter on the adjoining property.[119] Many tort statutes have broadened the common law nuisance exception to permit tort recovery for personal injuries resulting from specified property conditions whether or not they fit the common law definition of a nuisance.[120]

Governmental vs. Proprietary Functions

Courts are hopelessly divided on the classification and treatment of particular school functions as being "proprietary" and therefore excepted from the shield of "governmental" immunity, or as being "governmental" and shielded by "governmental" immunity. These case divisions appear not only between different states, but often within the same state. Broadly speaking, activities that are deemed more commercial than educational in nature are deemed proprietary,[121] while more education-related school operations are likely to be considered governmental.[122] Fee-funded operations, such as admission fees for school events, have been held in several states to be proprietary functions subject to tort liability, while nominal school charges for community uses of the school have been held not to render the operation "proprietary" or excepted from tort immunity.[123]

Discretionary vs. Ministerial Functions

Many states limit governmental immunity to acts that are found to be "ministerial," and not "discretionary." Here also the classification of acts as "discretionary" or "ministerial" is a source of continuing uncertainty in case law.[124] In theory, discretionary acts are those that involve the exercise of judgment regarding school policy or planning, while ministerial acts are those that do not require significant exercises of judgment. While the distinction has an abstract logic, it is fuzzy and difficult to apply. The following excerpt illustrates this difficulty.

DOE v. BOARD OF EDUC.
18 F. Supp. 2d 954 (N.D. Ill. 1998)

[**Focus Note.** *High school students sued school district and district administrators and teachers, alleging numerous violations of federal and state tort law rights arising from teacher's sexual activity with them. The following excerpt deals with the state tort claims. The federal rights claims are reported in Chapter 8 as Case 8.5.]*

* * *

STATE CLAIMS

. . . [P]laintiffs allege that *the District* willfully and wantonly hired and retained Vasquez in violation of Illinois common law and the Illinois School Code. . . . In Count VI, plaintiffs allege that the *individual defendants* willfully and wantonly failed to supervise Vasquez, and failed to report Vasquez's conduct in violation of the School Code and the Abused and Neglected Child Reporting Act.... Defendants have moved for summary judgment ... arguing that they are immune from liability under the Local Governmental Employees Tort Immunity Act....

Section 3–108 (a) of the Tort Immunity Act provides: Except as otherwise provided by this Act ... neither a local public entity nor a public employee is liable for an injury caused by a failure to supervise an activity on or the use of any public property.

The section unambiguously grants immunity from liability that would otherwise arise from both negligent and willful and wanton conduct. . . .

Plaintiffs argue that § 3–108 applies only to physical injuries occurring in the use of public property. . . . Plaintiffs are wrong. . . . Accordingly, the court concludes that the section applies to plaintiffs' claims.

Section 2–201 of the Tort Immunity Act provides: . . . [A] public employee serving in a position involving the determination of a policy or the exercise of discretion is not liable for an injury resulting from his act or omission in determining policy when acting in the exercise of such discretion even though abused.

Plaintiffs do not argue that the District's decision to hire Vasquez is not an exercise of discretion covered by the section. Instead, they argue that § 2–201 (and § 3–108) do not apply to allegations of willful and wanton conduct. . . .

This argument was recently rejected by the Illinois Appellate Court in *Henrich v. Libertyville High School*, 289 Ill. App. 3d 809 . . . 683 N.E.2d 135 (2d Dist. 1997). . . . Because the legislature did not express any exceptions to the immunity provided by § 3–108(a), the court refused to read one in. . . .

Finally, plaintiffs argue that defendants' duty to report sexual abuse is a ministerial act, not a discretionary act covered by § 2–201. . . . It is undisputed that defendants are mandated by state law to report suspected sexual abuse. However, the reporter must first determine what constitutes "suspect sexual abuse" within the meaning of the reporting act, and whether such abuse likely occurred. Reaching such a conclusion clearly entails the exercise of a degree of judgment and discretion.

Accordingly, the court concludes that § 2–201 applies to plaintiffs' claims based on failure to report under the Reporting Act.

Compare a recent Idaho case, where the school district and teacher were sued for failing to act on a student's suicidal tendencies, which he recorded in a school class journal. The court first held that the district was immune from liability for its failure to adopt suicide prevention policies because that decision involved a "discretionary" function. However, it also ruled that the district and the teacher were both liable for failure to warn the student's parents of the student's journal, because the decision not to warn the parents was an "operational" decision and not part of an immune discretionary decision.[125]

Personal Immunity

Suits against school board members in their official capacity are treated as suits against the school district itself,[126] but when board members are sued personally as individuals, they, along with school supervisors, teachers, and other "employees" may be entitled to *personal* immunity from tort suits. This immunity differs from governmental immunity. A growing number of state legislatures have extended limited personal immunity to such individuals.[127]

Personal tort immunity is intended to encourage public servants to perform their duties without fear of tort suits,[128] but it is largely confined to actions that involve the use of educational discretion rather than routine workplace conduct. Even school officials who fail to maintain safe premises may be deemed not to be exercising educational discretion, hence are not granted personal tort immunity.[129] Reckless, unauthorized, or unlawful acts are often excepted from tort immunity.[130] A supervisor is normally not liable for the tortious conduct of a subordinate *unless* the supervisor personally fostered that conduct.[131]

A number of states further protect school officials and employees from personal losses by *indemnification* statutes that require school districts to pay for the litigation costs and tort judgments that are suffered by those individuals for actions they took within the scope of their job duties.[132]

Notice and Time Limits and Dollar Caps

Many states impose notice requirements and time deadlines for making tort claims, and also set dollar ceilings on the allowed recovery of tort damages.

Notice of claim statutes aim to ensure government agencies receive timely notice that will enable them to investigate and evaluate the legitimacy of tort claims and to cure defective conditions. Claimants must give timely written notice of their tort claim, usually within three to six months of the injury, in a form specified by the notice statute, and failure to do so will bar suit on that claim.[133] Notice statutes are construed liberally by most courts to allow exemptions for excusable failures to comply with them.[134] For example, notice requirements are satisfied or excused when (1) the defendant was not prejudiced by the lack of statutory notice (having adequate notice from other sources); (2) the claim notice substantially, though not fully, met statutory requirements; (3) the required notice could not be given because of excusable conditions (physical or mental incapacity, minority, or incompetency); or (4) the sued district waived the right to notice.[135]

Statutes of Limitations

Many states have short statutes of limitations for tort lawsuits against government agencies, usually one year from the date of injury. Here also, courts may allow late filing in special circumstances where late filing is excusable.

Dollar Recovery Limits

The statutes of many states set dollar limits for money recoveries for torts, caps that often differ for different types of tort injury. These state-to-state cap variations range from a modest ceiling of several thousand dollars in one state to a ceiling of several hundred thousand dollars in another.[136]

Chapter 4 Discussion Questions

Where the answer to a question may be qualified by special circumstances, explain the potential qualification.

1. What is a tort?
2. What are the limits of school district *respondeat superior* liability for the acts of its employees?
3. What constitutes "negligence" in tort law?
4. Are school district tort obligations and liability coextensive with school teacher tort obligation and liability? Explain.
5. What do the terms *respondeat superior* and *vicarious liability* mean?
6. Are the defenses of tort immunity the same for school districts as for teachers? Explain.
7. Are statutory dollar limits on tort recovery the same for school districts as for teachers? Explain.
8. Explain how juries may play a more crucial role than courts in tort cases.
9. Under state tort law, to what extent are school districts obliged to protect students from physical or sexual abuse? From their own suicidal acts?
10. Under tort law, to what extent are teachers obliged to protect students from physical or sexual abuse? From their own suicidal acts?

   Note: Additional federal law obligations, as discussed in Chapter 8, do not relieve school districts and teachers from obligations under state tort law.

Case 4.1

GRANT v. LAKE OSWEGO SCHOOL DISTRICT NO. 7
515 P.2d 947 (Or. App. 1973)

*[**Focus Note.** Suit by a 12-year-old seventh-grade student against the school district and her physical education teacher for personal injuries sustained when she jumped off a springboard stored in an alcove and struck her head on the low doorway beam.]*

LANGTRY, JUDGE

Plaintiff alleged that defendants were negligent:

1. In placing a springboard under a low ceiling and doorway.
2. In failing to turn the springboard on its side or otherwise make it harmless.
3. In failing to warn the students of the danger of hitting the low ceiling and/or doorway.
4. In failing to supervise the students in the use of dangerous exercise equipment.

Defendants School District and Berke alleged that the plaintiff was contributorily negligent in jumping on the board without permission at a time and place when and where it was not supposed to be used . . . and in failing to maintain a proper [student] lookout. Evidence showed that . . . a class of 17 seventh grade girls was having its first instruction in gymnastics in a school "exercise room" with a high ceiling. . . . Near the end of the class plaintiff and three other girls, on instruction of defendant Toni Berke, dragged the springboard from the middle of the exercise room to an entrance alcove where the springboard was normally stored. The alcove had a low ceiling. . . .

After instructing the girls to move the springboard, defendant Toni Berke turned her attention elsewhere. . . . She was standing in position where she had no view into the entrance alcove. . . . Plaintiff then jumped off the springboard. She felt that she would propel herself into the exercise room. The lighting was good and she was aware of the low clearance of the doorway. She struck her head on the beam above the door and fell, injured. . . . The jury returned a verdict for plaintiff. . . . Upon motion by defendants the trial judge granted judgment notwithstanding the verdict. . . .

* * *

(1) The child was not barred from recovery by contributory negligence as a matter of law. A child may be, under proper evidence, so barred. . . .

> Whether the question of a child's contributory negligence is regarded as one of capacity, standard of care, or compliance with that standard, the courts are in substantial agreement that normally, if not always, a question of fact for the jury is presented, rather than one of law for the court. . . . Annotation, 77 A.L.R. 2d 917, 932 (1961).

This rule appears to apply in Oregon. . . .

* * *

In the case at bar there is no testimony to the effect that plaintiff knowingly embarked on a course of dangerous conduct. Her contributory negligence, if any, was in her failure to appreciate the danger of her act, not in her failure to perceive the source of her danger. She knew the beam was there but jumped anyway, thinking she would miss it. If she should have known this was dangerous and did it anyway, then she would be guilty of negligence. . . . However, the question of what she should have known (absent testimony that she actually knew) is a question that depends upon what a hypothetical child of like age, intelligence, and experience should have known given similar circumstances. From the evidence presented in this case, that this was plaintiff's first experience with the use of a springboard and the apparent absence of in-depth instruction in its use and characteristics, a reasonable jury could have concluded that a similar child would not have appreciated the danger. . . .

. . . Defendant School Board's negligence is predicated on a finding that its servant Toni Berke was negligent. . . .

The evidence presented a conflict as to whether Toni Berke told the girls to "just drag [the springboard] over here" or to put the springboard away and "tip it on its side." . . .

* * *

Here there was sufficient evidence to support a jury finding that the injury suffered was foreseeable. Toni Berke testified that inexperienced students should not use the springboard. The question of plaintiff's experience was as we have noted above a jury question.

Plaintiff's second two specifications of negligence—"(3) in failing to warn the students of the danger of hitting the low ceiling and/or doorway (4) in failing to supervise the students in the use of dangerous exercise equipment"—are also interrelated. Failure to warn can be viewed as a specific instance of failure to supervise.

* * *

However, the facts of this case indicate that it can reasonably be found that proper supervision could have prevented this accident for the teacher would have noticed that the springboard was not being stored properly before plaintiff jumped off and struck her head on the beam. A quick admonition could have prevented her injury.

. . . We have concluded . . . that there was a jury question presented on all four specifications of negligence. This is contrary to the trial court's conclusion. . . . It follows that the ruling below must be reversed and remanded with instructions to reinstate the jury verdict. . . .

Case 4.2

SOPER v. HOBEN
195 F.3d 845 (6th Cir. 1999)

> [**Focus Note.** *Suit by Renee Soper, a 15-year-old mentally impaired child, and her mother, Lina Soper, against school employees, the school district and board, for gross negligence in failing to prevent sexual molestation and rape by male students at the school and on the bus. Renee's mother alleged that she had warned Renee's teacher of prior sexual harassment by the boy who raped Renee.*]

SILER, CIRCUIT JUDGE

Renee is a mentally retarded adopted foster child. Because of her learning disability, Renee attended special education or "educable mentally impaired" ("EMI") classes . . . but also attended certain mainstream classes outside the special education program. . . .

Both Ms. Soper and Renee's [elementary school] teacher, Kathy Rombach, noticed that Renee engaged in frequent hugging of other adults and children while in grade school, a common characteristic of Down's Syndrome children. While the hugging was not sexual in nature, the two women worked to decrease the behavior. In 1993, while Renee was a student at Oxbow Elementary, Boy A (who is one or two years older than Renee and was then a student in defendant Michele Harmala's EMI classroom in the middle school) and Renee left the school boundaries together. Later, Renee told her mother that Boy A had kissed her and said that he could not wait for her to come to junior high. Ms. Soper reported the incident to Rombach and asked her to make sure that someone would keep an eye on Renee and Boy A so as to prevent any further incidents. . . .

At an IEPC [Individualized Educational Planning Committee] meeting in May 1994, before Renee entered Muir Middle School, it was decided that

Renee would continue in the EMI program. Harmala was designated as the teacher responsible for implementing Renee's IEP. The IEPC report lists Renee's cognitive level of functioning at age seven years and six months, although her chronological age was twelve years. At the May meeting, Ms. Soper contends that she discussed Renee's history of sexual abuse by her foster brother as well as the incident with Boy A in elementary school. In response to Ms. Soper's concerns, Ms. Soper submits that Harmala said, "we'll keep an eye on the children. They're well supervised." Harmala denies that Ms. Soper mentioned Boy A to her as a concern or that she assured Ms. Soper that Renee would be supervised at all times while she was in school. . . .

At the initial meeting at the beginning of the 1994 school year, Ms. Soper expressed further concern about Boy A to Harmala. (Rombach also attended this meeting.) At the time, Ms. Soper was aware of Boy A's abusive family background, and told Harmala that she did not want her daughter left alone with Boy A. Harmala denies having heard this. Additionally, Harmala, who had taught Boy A for the two previous years, submits that she never observed any sexually aggressive behavior by Boy A toward other students in the class. . . . When Ms. Soper returned home [from a parent-teacher conference on October 6, 1994], Renee told her that Boy B and Boy C fondled her breasts and vagina at Muir Middle School in the back of the classroom while the teacher was outside in the hallway, that the boys did the same on the school bus, and that Boy A had raped her at school. As to the latter incident, she explained that her teacher allowed Boy A to accompany her to her locker to assist her in getting the door open, and that while Harmala was locking up the classroom for lunchtime, Boy A told her to hide in the back room, and that after the teacher left, he raped her. She reported that all the boys had threatened to beat her up if she told anyone. Boy A alleges that the sexual penetration was consensual and Boy B and Boy C deny any sexual misconduct. . . .

Ms. Soper confronted Harmala and [school principal Christine] Hoben immediately and then reported the incidents to the police. . . . [School officials] prepared a plan for increased supervision of Renee while in school, including an escort. However, Ms. Soper opted to keep Renee at home, as Boys A, B, and C were allowed to continue attending Muir Middle School during the police investigation.

* * *

Negligence and Gross Negligence

Michigan statutory law provides for absolute immunity and governmental immunity from tort liability in certain situations. . . . The relevant statute provides:

(2) [Governmental immunity.] . . . [E]ach officer and employee of a governmental agency . . . and each member of a board . . . shall be immune

from tort liability for injuries to persons . . . while in the course of employment or service . . . or while acting on behalf of a governmental agency if all of the following conditions are met:

* * *

(c) The officer's, employee's, [or] member's . . . conduct does not amount to gross negligence that is the proximate cause of the injury or damage. . . . "[G]ross negligence" means conduct so reckless as to demonstrate a substantial lack of concern for whether an injury results.

* * *

The district court correctly found that as superintendent of the HVPS District, defendant [James] Doyle has absolute immunity. . . .

Defendants Harmala, Hoben, Director of Special Education Robert Shaw, the HVPS [Huron Valley Public School] District, and the HVPS Board.

These defendants are immune from suits for ordinary negligence. . . . However, the Sopers argue that the following actions constitute gross negligence: (1) the failure to have a policy in effect to protect at-risk students like Renee; (2) Harmala's failure to supervise Renee so as to make sure that she was taken from the classroom to the cafeteria; and (3) the failure to place a para-professional in Harmala's classroom. . . .

Plaintiffs argue that because they have alleged "some" improper conduct on the part of defendants, whether it constitutes gross negligence within the meaning of the statute is a factual question to be determined by a jury. . . . [I]f, on the basis of the evidence presented, reasonable minds could not differ [as to whether the defendant's conduct amounted to gross negligence], then the motion for summary judgment should be granted. The district court correctly found that reasonable minds could not find that the failure to have a policy in effect to protect at-risk students and/or the failure to place a para-professional in Harmala's classroom constitutes gross negligence. Additionally, even assuming the Sopers' factual assertions are true regarding Harmala's knowledge and conduct, we agree that reasonable minds could not find that Harmala's conduct constitutes gross negligence.

Case 4.3

AYALA v. PHILADELPHIA BOARD OF PUBLIC EDUCATION
305 A.2d 877 (Pa. 1973)

> [*Focus Note.* Suit by 15-year-old student for injuries suffered in upholstery class when his arm was caught in a shredding machine, necessitating its amputation.]

ROBERTS, JUSTICE.

* * *

Appellants alleged that appellee school district, through its employees, was negligent in failing to supervise the upholstery class, in supplying the machine for use without a proper safety device, in maintaining the machine in a dangerous and defective condition, and in failing to warn the children of the dangerous condition. Appellee, the Philadelphia Board of Public Education, interposed preliminary objections asserting the defense of governmental immunity. These objections were sustained and the Superior Court affirmed in a per curiam order.

* * *

We now hold that the doctrine of governmental immunity . . . is abolished in this Commonwealth. In so doing, we join the ever-increasing number of jurisdictions which have judicially abandoned this antiquated doctrine. [Citing cases from District of Columbia, Indiana, Colorado, Idaho, New Jersey, Rhode Island, Nebraska, Arkansas, Arizona, Kentucky, Michigan, Nevada, Alaska, Minnesota, Wisconsin, California, Illinois, and Florida]

I.

It is generally agreed that the historical roots of the governmental immunity doctrine are found in the English case of *Russell v. Men of Devon*, 2 T.R. 667, 100 Eng. Rep. 359 (1788). . . . There, the court . . . expressed the fear that if suits against such political subdivisions were permitted, there would be "an infinity of actions." . . . Finally, Justice Ashurst . . . observed that it is better that an individual should sustain an injury than that the public should suffer an inconvenience. *Id.*

* * *

Although the English courts abandoned the doctrine . . . this Commonwealth continued to deny recovery. . . . Thus, until the present action, we have retained the archaic and artificial distinction between tortious conduct arising out of the exercise of a proprietary function and tortious conduct arising out of exercise of a governmental function.

II.

Today we conclude that no reasons whatsoever exist for continuing to adhere to the doctrine of governmental immunity. . . .

* * *

. . . Moreover, the distinction between governmental and proprietary functions is probably one of the most unsatisfactory known to the law, for it has caused confusion not only among the various jurisdictions but almost always within each jurisdiction.

* * *

. . . [A]ppellee does not attempt to justify retention of immunity on policy grounds. Rather, it contends that abrogation, if it is to be achieved, should be accomplished by legislative direction rather than by judicial determination.

   . . . [W]e stated in *Flagiello v. Pennsylvania Hospital, supra,* 417, Pa. at 503, 208 A.2d at 202: "[T]he controverted rule of charitable immunity is not the creation of the Legislature. *This Court fashioned it, and, what it put together, it can dismantle* (Emphasis added). . . . Similarly, here, the doctrine of governmental immunity, judicially imposed,may be judicially terminated. . . .

* * *

. . . [T]he order sustaining appellee's preliminary objections is reversed and the record remanded for proceedings consistent with this opinion.

ENDNOTES

1. State v. Hoover, 450 N.E.2d 710 (Ohio 1982) (criminal assault charge against teacher).

2. Brown v. Calhoun County Board of Educ., 432 So. 2d 230 (Ala. 1983) and the following endnotes.

3. Barrett v. Phillips, 223 S.E.2d 918 (N.C. 1976).

4. Dist. of Columbia v. Connelly, 465 A.2d 395 (D.C. Cir. 1983); Tiemann v. Ind. School Dist., 331 N.W.2d 250 (Minn. 1983); Benton v. School Board, 386 So. 2d 831 (Fla.1980).

5. *See* Barth v. Board of Educ., 490 N.E.2d 77 (Ill. 1986) (special duty to protect); Rodriguez v. Inglewood Un. School Dist., 230 Cal. Rptr. 823 (1986) (duty to render school safe from assaults); Phyllis P. v. Superior Court, 228 Cal. Rptr. 776 (Cal. 1986) (duty to notify parents of sexual assaults). *See generally* Annot., *Public Schools—Torts—Student Activity*, 36 A.L.R. 3d 330 (1970).

6. Wyke v. Polk County School Board, 129 F.3d 560 (11th Cir. 1997).

7. Hoyem v. Manhattan Beach City School Dist., 585 P.2d 851 (Cal. 1978) (question whether motorist injury to student was preventable by proper supervision—submitted to jury for decision); State Farm Mut. Ins. Co. v. Pharr, 808 S.W.2d 769 (Ark. 1991); Ehlinger v. Board of Educ., 465 N.Y.S.2d 378 (1983); Dibartolo v. Metropolitan School Dist., 440 N.E.2D 506 (Ind. 1982).

8. Daily v. L.A. Unified School Dist., 470 P.2d 360 (Cal. 1970).

9. Fagan v. Summers, 498 P.2d 1227 (Wyo.1972) (dictum).

10. Levandoski v. Jackson City School Dist., 328 So. 2d 339 (Miss. 1976).

11. Walcott v. Lindenhurst Union Free School Dist., 662 N.Y.S.2d 931 (1997) (assumption of risk in wrestling competition); Berman by Berman v. Phila. Board of Educ., 456 A.2d 545 (Pa. 1983); Hutchison v. Toews, 476 P.2d 811 (Or. 1970) (student use of chemical explosives, without permission, which he knew to be dangerous barred his tort claim); Becker v. Beaverton School Dist., 551 P.2d 498 (Or. 1976) (student violation of school rule).

12. *See* Annots., *Effect of Comparative Negligence in Assumption of Risk*, 16 A.L.R. 4th 700 (1982); *Modern Trends in Contributory Negligence*, 32 A.L.R. 4th 56 (1984). Summerall v. Quachita Parish School, 665 So. 2d 734 (La. 1995).

13. (a) Ballard v. Polly, 387 F. Supp. 895 (D. D.C. 1975); (b) Simmons v. Beauregard Parish School Board, 315 So. 2d 883, 888 (La. 1975). *But see* Kush v. City of Buffalo, 462 N.Y.S.2d 831 (1983) (injuries from unsecured stolen chemicals); (c) Robinson v. City of New York, 377 N.Y.S.2d 576 (1975); (d) Tannenbaum v. Board of Educ., 214 N.E.2d 378 (N.Y. 1966); (e) Shannon v. Addison Trail High School, 339 N.E.2d 372 (Ill. 1972); (f) Kluka v. Livingston Parish School Board, 433 So. 2d 302 (La. 1983).

14. Wagenblast v. Odessa School Dist., 758 P.2d 968 (Wash. 1988) (tort claim not waivable by student); *semble:* Whittington v. Sowela Technical Inst., 438 So. 2d 236 (La. 1983) (adult student).

15. A.L.I. Restatements, Torts Sec. 575.

16. Apicella v. Valley Forge Military Academy, 630 F. Supp. 20 (E.D. Pa. 1985) (parent, but not child, bound by release and waiver); Haynes v. County of Missoula, 517 P.2d 370 (Mont. 1973) (voiding waiver).

17. Gaston v. Becker, 314 N.W.2d 728, 731, 732 (Mich. 1982) (no liability for acts of independent contractors); Hunter v. Board of Educ., 439 A.2d 582, 587 n.8 (Md. 1982) and authorities there cited.

18. Withers v. Charlotte-Mecklenburg Board of Educ., 231 S.E.2d 276 (N.C. 1976) (no board liability for collision of school bus driven by unauthorized student).

19. Annot., *Vicarious Liability for Intentional Assault,* 17 A.L.R. 4th 870 (1982); Kimberly M. v. Los Angeles Un. School Dist., 263 Cal. Rptr. 612 (Cal. App. 1989) (no liability for abuse of authority by teacher molester). *Compare* Galli v. Kirkeby, 248 N.W.2d 149 (Mich. 1977), *with* Adam v. Tatsch, 362 P.2d 984 (N.M. 1961).

20. *See* Small v. Board of Educ., 450 N.Y.S.2d 987 (1982) (grabbing a student's face to get his attention held not corporal punishment); Daniels v. Gordon, 503 S.E.2d 72 (Ga. 1998).

21. Roberts v. Way, 398 F. Supp. 856 (Vt. 1975); Illinois v. DeCaro, 38 N.E.2d 196 (Ill. 1974); Indiana St. Personnel Board v. Jackson, 192 N.E.2d 740 (Ind. 1963).

22. Allen v. LaSalle Parish School Board, 341 So. 2d 73 (La. 1977).

23. Glaser v. Marietta, 351 F. Supp. 555 (W.D. Pa. 1972).

24. For case authorities re: corporal punishment for instructional purposes, *see* Hogenson v. Williams, 542 S.W.2d 456 (Tex. 1976) (helmet slapping by a football coach).

25. Baker v. Owen, 395 F. Supp. 294 (M.D. N.C. 1975).

26. Guillory v. Ortego, 449 So. 2d 182 (La. 1984); Simms v. School Dist. No. 1, 508 P.2d 236 (Or. 1973); Andreozzi v. Rubano, 141 A.2d 639 (Conn. 1958).

27. Commonwealth v. Douglas, 588 A.2d 53 (Pa. 1991) (excessive paddling of seven-year-old boy). People v. Smith, 335 N.E.2d 125 (Ill. 1975) (bleeding nose and swollen eye).

28. Glover v. Jackson, 71 So. 2d 49 (Ala. 1954).

29. (a) Johnson v. Horace Mann Mutual Insurance Co., 241 So. 2d 588 (La. 1970). *See also* Rolando v. School Directors, 358 N.E.2d 945 (Ill. 1976) (cattle prod); (b) Calway v. Williamson, 36 A.2d 377 (Conn. 1944); Tinkham v. Kole, 110 N.W.2d 258 (Iowa 1961).

30. *See* Small, note 20, *supra.*

31. Frank v. Orleans Parish School Board, 195 So. 2d 451 (La. 1967).

32. Williams v. Cotton, 346 So. 2d 1039 (Fla. 1977).

33. Smith v. Broken Arrow Pub. School, 655 P.2d 858 (Okla. 1983) (patron at school supper). *See* Annots., *Public School Premises Liability,* 37 A.L.R. 3d 712, 738 (1971); *Tort Liability of Public Schools . . . for Accidents due to Condition of Buildings and Equipment,* 34 A.L.R. 3d 1166 (1970).

34. Hernandez v. Renville P.S. Dist. No. 654, 542 N.W.2d 671 (Minn. 1996) (fall from safe

playground slide); Narcisse v. Cont'l. Ins. Co., 419 So. 2d 13 (La. 1983) (no duty to install door closures); Kass v. Board of Educ., 193 N.E.2d 643 (N.Y. 1963) (fall from stage screen).

35. Douglas v. Board of Educ., 468 N.E.2d 473 (Ill. 1984); Watts v. Town of Homer, 301 So. 2d 729 (La. 1974) (collapsing slide).

36. *Cf.* Milliken v. City of Lewiston, 580 A.2d 151 (Me. 1990); Giosa v. School Dist. of Phila., 562 A.2d 417 (Pa. 1989) (icy walks); Gurule v. Salt Lake City Board of Educ., 661 P.2d 957 (Utah 1983); Lostumbo v. Board of Educ., 418 A.2d 949 (Conn. 1980); Kingsley v. Ind. Dist. No. 2, 251 N.W.2d 634 (Minn. 1977) (ragged metal locker).

37. Jackson v. Cartwright School Dist., 607 P.2d 975 (Ariz. 1980) (insufficient time to discover fresh hazard); Quigley v. School Dist., 446 P.2d 177 (Or. 1968) (no recovery—fall of recently delivered equipment); Duncan v. Board of Educ., 159 N.Y.S.2d 745 (1955) (broken door check); Dausend v. Board of Educ., 138 N.Y.S.2d 633 (1955) (floor cleanup at reasonable intervals).

38. Constantinescu v. Conejo Valley Unified School Dist., 20 Cal. Rptr. 2d 734 (Cal. 1993) (school pickup area could be held a statutory basis for liability).

39. Brewer v. Ind. School Dist., 848 P.2d 566 (Okla. 1993) (no liability for playground injury); Slovin v. Gauger, 200 A.2d 565 (Del. 1964) (no liability for visitor fall from stage exit).

40. Jackson v. Board of Educ., 441 N.E.2d 120 (Ill. 1982) (attractive nuisance liability). *But see* Yeske v. Avon School, Inc., 470 A.2d 704, 710–11 (Conn. 1984).

41. *E.g.,* Ackler v. Odessa-Montour School Dist., 663 N.Y.S.2d 352 (1997) (gym floor); Tieman v. Indep. School Dist., 331 N.W.2d 259 (Minn. 1983) (gym horse without handles); Bessette v. Enderlin School Dist., 310 N.W.2d 79 (N.D. 1981) (defective slide); Board of Educ. v. Fredericks, 147 S.E.2d 789 (Ga. 1966) (stadium seats); Wiener v. Board of Educ., 369 N.Y.S.2d 207 (1975) (loose handrail); Cappel v. Board of Educ., 337 N.Y.S.2d 836 (1972) (hockey cage).

42. Caltavuturo v. City of Passaic, 307 A.2d 115 (N.J. 1973).

43. Barnes v. Bott, 615 So. 2d 1337 (La. App. 1993); Greene v. City of New York, 566 N.Y.S.2d 40

(1991); Padgett v. School Board, 295 So. 2d 504 (Fla. 1981); Guerreri v. Tyson, 24 A.2d 468 (Pa. 1842).

44. Texas Education Code, Title 2, subtitle G, *Safe Schools* (1996). California "Safe Schools Act of 1990." *See* Constantinescu, note 38, *supra.*

45. Malik v. Greater Johnstown Enlarged School Dist., 669 N.Y.S.2d 729 (1998).

46. *See* Note, *School Liability for Athletic Injuries*, 21 Washburn L.J. 315, 321, note 52 (1982).

47. *See also* Maynard v. Board of Educ., 244 A.2d 622 (N.Y. App. 1997).

48. Titus v. Lindberg, 228 A.2d 65 (N.J. 1967) (schoolyard horseplay before opening of the school).

49. Hill v. Safford Unified School Dist., 952 P.2d 754 (Ariz. App. 1997); Bell v. Board of Educ., 687 N.E.2d 1325 (N.Y. 1997) (liable for injuries of sixth-grader left in park after school trip); Gross v. Family Services, Inc., 716 So. 2d 337 (Fla. App. 1998) (special relationships duty to protect against criminal conduct). *Compare* Dickerson v. City of New York, 684 N.Y.S.2d 584 (N.Y. 1999) (no school duty to protect student shot by school intruder).

50. Garufi v. School Board, 613 So. 2d 1341 (Fla.1993) (violent student assault); Ferraro v. Board of Educ., 221 N.Y.S.2d 279 (1961) (failure to warn substitute teacher of problem student); Korenak v. Curative Work Shop Adult Rehabilitation Center, 237 N.W.2d 43 (Wis. 1976) (student exposed to crime-prone person).

51. Schuyler v. Board of Educ., 205 N.E.2d 311 (N.Y. 1965); Morris v. Ortiz, 437 P.2d 652 (Ariz. 1968). *But see* Hoyem v. Manhattan Beach City School Dist., note 7, *supra.*

52. James v. Gloversville Enlarged School Dist., 548 N.Y.2d 87 (1989). *Compare* Raymond v. Paradise Un. School Dist., 31 Cal. Rptr. 847 (1963) (whether duty existed—held question of law for the court), *with* Fazzolari v. Portland School Dist., 717 P.2d 1210 (Or. 1986) (whether duty existed—held question for the jury). See supervision cases in Annotations, note 5, *supra.*

53. *Ibid.* Broward County School v. Ruiz, 493 So. 2d 560 (Fla. 1985) (cafeteria assault); Constantinescu, note 38, *supra* (pickup area).

54. *Regular play:* Tymkowicz v. San Jose Unified School Dist., 312 P.2d 388 (Cal. 1957)(10-year-old injured before school hours). *Student misconduct:* Titus, note 48, *supra. But see* Sly v. Board of Educ., 516 P.2d 895 (Kans. 1973) (no notice of prior conduct). *Unsafe conditions:* Rice v. School Dist., 248 P. 388 (Wash. 1926) (electric shock from new aerial). *Contra:* Fitzgerald v. Montgomery County Board of Educ., 336 A.2d 795 (Md. 1975) (exposed wire).

55. Lawes v. Board of Educ., 16 N.Y.2d 302 (1965).

56. Cioffi v. Board of Educ., 278 N.Y.S.2d 249 (1967).

57. Tashjian v. N. Colonie Central School Dist., 353 N.Y.S.2d 467 (1975) (permitting third grader to play baseball contrary to school rules); Briscoe v. School Dist., 201 P.2d 697 (Wash. 1949) (permitting football games in playground—against school rules).

58. Lee v. School Dist., 324 N.W.2d 632 (Mich. 1982). *Cf.* Sutton v. Duplessis, 584 So. 2d 363 (La. 1991).

59. *See* Gordon v. Deer Park School Dist., 426 P.2d 824 (Wash. 1967) (student spectator struck by bat).

60. (a) Charronat v. San Francisco Un. School Dist., 133 P.2d 643 (Cal. 1943); (b) Decker v. Dundee Central School Dist., 151 N.E.2d 866 (N.Y. 1958); (c) Gibbons v. Orleans Parish School Board, 391 So. 2d 976 (La. 1980); (d) Beck v. San Francisco Unified School Dist., 37 Cal. Rptr. 471 (1964). *Compare* Glanker v. Rapides Par. School Board, 610 So. 2d 1020 (La. 1992) (three teachers, plus 11 parents, held adequate to supervise 78 kindergarten children).

61. Barbato v. Board of Educ., 182 N.Y.S.2d 875 (1959).

62. Swaitkowski v. Board of Educ., 319 N.Y.S.2d 783 (1971) (teacher brief absence to aid another teacher—held not negligent).

63. Simonetti v. School District of Phila., 454 A.2d 1038 (Pa. 1982) (teacher standing outside classroom door talking to another teacher, held not negligent when student in classroom injured by another student); Collins v. School Board, 471 So. 2d 560 (Fla. 1985) (10 minute teacher absence supported finding of negligence re: student sexual assault); Gonzales v. Mackler, 241 N.Y.S.2d 254 (1963) (half-hour absence from class—mentally retarded

children); *contra:* Jackson v. Chicago Bd. of Educ., 549 N.E.2d 829 (Ill. 1989).

64. *Liable for absence:* Schnell v. Travelers Insurance Co., 260 So. 2d 346 (La. 1972). *Not liable:* Banks v. Terrebone Parish School Board, 339 So. 2d 1295 (La. 1976).

65. James for James v. Charlotte-Mecklenburg Board of Educ., 300 S.E.2d 21 (N.C. 1983).

66. *Cf.* Sutton v. Duplessis, 584 So. 2d 362 (4th Cir. 1991); Lewis v. St. Bernard Parish School Board, 350 So. 2d 1256 (La. 1977).

67. Brand v. Sertoma Club of Springfield, 349 N.E.2d 502 (Ill. 1976) (no liability—injurious activity); Sims v. Etowah City Board of Educ., 337 So. 2d 1310 (Ala. 1976) (liability—defective stands).

68. Benitez v. New York City Board of Educ., 73 N.Y.2d 650 (1989); Summers v. Milwaukee Un. H.S. Dist., 481 P.2d 369 (Or. 1971) (girl with history of falls); Kefesee v. Board of Educ., 23 N.Y.S.2d 300 (1962) (inexperienced girls put into soccer game); Dobbins v. Board of Educ., 335 A.2d 23 (N.J. 1975) (racing over macadam surface).

69. *Adjoining games:* Bauer v. Board of Educ., 140 N.Y.S.2d 167 (1955) (16 three-man teams, on eight adjoining gym areas).

70. Gerrity v. Beatty, 373 N.E.2d 1323(Ill. 1977) (ill-fitted helmet); Armlin v. Board of Educ., 320 N.Y.S.2d 402 (1971) (violation of gym rules).

71. *Unknown medical condition:* Kerby v. Elk Grove Unified School Dist., 36 P.2d 431 (Cal. 1934) (fatal head blow to student with undetected aneurism). *Cf.* Rodriguez v. San Jose Unified School Dist., 322 P.2d 70 (Cal. 1958) (fatal fall of child with cerebral palsy and heart disease whose parent advised school that child could take care of himself).

72. *Unexplained drowning:* Wong v. Waterloo Comm. School Dist., 232 N.W.2d 865 (Iowa 1975) (11-year-old); Stephens v. Shelbyville Central Schools, 318 N.E.2d 590 (Ind. 1974) (14-year-old).

73. *Heat stroke:* Lovitt v. Concord School Dist., 228 N.W.2d 479 (Mich. 1975); Peck v. Board of Educ., 30 N.Y.S.2d 700 (1972). *Negligent movement of injured student:* Welch v. Dunsmuir Jt. Un. H.D. Dist., 326 P.2d 633 (Cal. 1958).

74. Banks v. Terrebonne Parish School Board, 339 So. 2d 1295 (La. 1976) (no liability for absence during gym recess); Seda v. Board of Educ., 152 N.Y.S.2d 356 (1956) (student falling from horizontal bar).

75. Ragnone v. Portland School Dist., 633 P.2d 1287 (Or. 1981); Carabba v. Anacortes School Dist., 435 P.2d 936 (Wash. 1967).

76. Velmer v. Baraga Area Schools, 424 N.W.2d 770 (Mich. 1988) (milling machinery); Bush v. Oscoda Area Schools, 250 N.W.2d 759 (Mich. 1977) (explosion in science experiment). *See* Annot., *Schools—Tort Liability—Shop Training,* 35 A.L.R. 3rd 758 (1971).

77. Lemelle v. State through Board of Secondary and Elementary Educ., 435 So. 2d 1162 (La. 1983) (welding shop); Isard v. Hickory City Board of Educ., 315 S.E.2d 765 (N.C. 1984) (power saw). *Compare* Lorte v. Board of Educ., 395 N.Y.S.2d 262 (1977) (no fault of student—upset bottle of acid), *with* Bottorf v. Waltz, 369 A.2d 332 (Pa. 1976) (where candle mold fell—for jury decision).

78. Hutchison v. Toews, 476 P.2d 811(Or. 1970) (15-year-old); Frace v. Long Beach City High School Dist., 137 P.2d 60 (Cal. 1943) (17-year-old student). *But see* Kush v. City of Buffalo, 59 N.Y.S.2d 831 (1983).

79. Scott v. Indep. School Dist., 256 N.W.2d 485 (Minn. 1977) (failure to enforce safety goggle law); Matteucci v. High School Dist., 281 N.E.2d 383 (Ill. 1972); Ayala v. Philadelphia Pub. Board of Educ., 305 A.2d 877 (Pa. 1973).

80. *Absence of safety rules:* Steffani v. Baker, 387 N.Y.S.2d 355 (1976) (unsupervised car lift); Govel v. Board of Educ., 60 N.E.2d 133 (N.Y. 1944) (shop repair of loaded gun).

81. Meyer v. Board of Educ., 86 A.2d 761 (N.J. 1952); Ressle v. Board of Educ., 395 N.Y.S.2d 263 (1977); Hammond v. Scott, 232 S.E.2d 336 (S.C. 1977); Morris v. Ortiz, 437 P.2d 652 (Ariz. 1968).

82. Plesnicav v. Kovach, 430 N.E.2d 648 (Ill. 1981); Hoyem v. Manhattan Beach County School Dist., 139 Cal. Rptr. 769 (1977); Oglesby v. Seminole City Board of Instruction, 328 So. 2d 515 (Fla. 1976).

83. Schultz v. Cheney School Dist., 371 P.2d 59 (Wash. 1962); Sparrow v. Forsyth County Board

of Educ., 198 S.E.2d 762 (N.C. 1973). *See also* Cooper v. Millwood Ind. School Dist., 887 P.2d 1370 (Okla. 1994); Gardner v. Biggart, 417 S.E.2d 858 (S.C. 1992).

84. *Safety statutes:* Van Gaasbeck v. Webatuck Cent. School Dist., 243 N.E.2d 253 (N.Y. 1967) (bus light signals); State v. Board of County Commiss'rs, 113 A.2d 397 (Md. 1955) (defective emergency door).

85. *See, e.g.*, Annots., *Schools—Transportation*, 23 A.L.R. 5th 1 (1994).

86. *Reason to expect student misconduct:* Cooper v. Millwood, 887 P.2d 1370 (Okla. 1994); Brantly v. Dade County School Board, 493 So. 2d 471 (Fla. 1986); Blair v. Board of Educ., 448 N.Y.S.2d 556 (1982).

87. Garza v. McAllen Indep. School Dist., 613 S.W.2d 526 (Tex. 1981); Arnold v. Hayslett, 655 S.W.2d 941 (Tenn. 1983) (thrusting head out of bus window).

88. (a) Crawford v. Wayne County Board of Educ., 168 S.E.2d 33 (N.C. 1968); (b) Coral Gables v. Patty, 162 So. 2d 530 (Fla. 1964); (c) Croghan v. Hart City Board of Educ., 549 S.W.2d 306 (Ky. 1977); Slade v. New Hanover County Board of Educ., 179 S.E.2d 453 (N.C. 1971); (d) County School Board v. Thomas, 112 S.E.2d 877 (Va. 1960); Van Gaasbeck, note 84, *supra;* and (e) Scott v. Thompson, 363 N.E.2d 295 (Mass. 1977).

89. Anderson v. Ohm, 258 N.W.2d 114 (Minn. 1977); Slade v. New Hanover Board of Educ.,178 S.E.2d 316 (N.C. 1971); Van Gaasbeck, note 84, *supra.*

90. Bailey v. Gallatin County Board of Educ., 383 S.W.2d 63 (Ky. 1964); Norris v. American Casualty Co., 176 So. 2d 677 (La. 1965).

91. *Safe route selection:* Pratt v. Robinson, 360 N.Y.S.2d 349 (1974); Sanderlin v. Cent. School Dist., 487 P.2d 1399 (Or. 1971). *Student use of other stops:* DeCerbo v. Raab, 516 N.Y.S.2d 995 (1987).

92. Barnes v. Bott, 615 So. 2d 1337 (La. 1993).

93. Verbel v. Indep. School Dist., 359 N.W.2d 579 (Minn. 1984); Whorley v. Brewer, 315 So. 2d 511 (Fla. 1975).

94. Coates v. Tacoma School Dist., 347 P.2d 1093 (Wash. 1960).

95. Chappel v. Franklin Pierce School Dist., 426 P.2d 471 (Wash. 1967) (failure to provide substitute for absent instructor).

96. Morris v. Douglas County School, 403 P.2d 775 (Or. 1965); Williamson v. Board of Educ., 375 N.Y.S.2d 221 (1975).

97. Mancha v. Field Museum of Natural History, 283 N.E.2d 899 (Ill. 1972). *See also* Arnold v. Hafling, 474 P.2d 638 (Colo. 1970) (no duty to supervise high school students at mountain camp).

98. *Compare* Declouet v. Orleans Parish School Board, 715 So. 2d 69 (La. 1998) (failure to call ambulance promptly for student suffering severe asthma attack). *Cf.* Peck v. Board of Educ., 319 N.Y.S.2d 919 (1970) (gym student kicked in the head).

99. Applebaum v. Nemon, 678 S.W.2d 533 (Tex. 1984) (no duty); *volunteer negligence:* O'Brien v. Twp. H.S. Dist., 392 N.E.2d 615 (Ill. 1980); Guerrieri v. Tyson, 24 A.2d 468 (Pa. 1942).

100. Annot., *Liability, Student Suicide*, 17 A.L.R. 5th 179 (1994); Brooks v. Logan, 903 P.2d 73 (Idaho 1995); Eisel v. Board of Educ., 97 A.2d 447 (Md. 1991). *See generally Restatement (Second) of Torts*, § 315(1965). *Cf.* Hammond v. Board of Educ., 629 A.2d 223 (Md. 1994) (no liability for student suicide absent official notice of the suicide threat).

101. Snow v. State, 469 N.Y.S.2d 959 (1983); Tarasoff v. Regents, U. of Calif., 551 P.2d 334 (Cal. 1976). McIntosh v. Milano, 403 A.2d 500 (N.J. 1979). For other views, *see* Cole v. Taylor, 301 N.W.2d 766 (Iowa 1981); Durflinger v. Artiles, 673 P.2d 86 (Kan. 1983).

102. Brown v. Board of Educ., 681 A.2d 996 (Conn. 1996); Eisel v. Board of Educ., 597 A.2d 447 (Md. App. 1991). *See also Restatement (Second) of Torts*, § 315 (1965); Eugene C. Bjorklun, *School Liability for Student Suicides*, 106 Ed. Law. Rep. 21 (March 1996).

103. (McMahon v. St. Croix Falls School Dist., 596 N.W.2d 875 (Wis. 1999).

104. Dickerson v. City of New York, 684 N.Y.S.2d 584 (N.Y. 1999) (student stabbing by outsider); Rodrigues v. Englewood School Dist., 230 Cal. Rptr. 823 (1986) (student shooting by outsider). *See also* notes 58 and 59 and related text.

105. Maynard v. Board of Educ., 244 A.2d 622 (N.Y. 1997).

106. Santavicca v. City of Yonkers, 518 N.Y.S.2d 29 (1987) (comments by superintendent—held absolutely privileged); Grostick v. Ellsworth, 404 N.W.2d 685 (Mich. 1987) (superintendent negative comments—held qualifiedly privileged). *Also* Morrison v. Mobile County Board of Educ., 495 So. 2d 1086 (Ala. 1986); Berlin v. Supt. of Pub. Instruction, 448 N.W.2d 764 (Mich. 1989). Annot., *Libel—School Board Members Privilege*, 85 A.L.R. 3d 1137 (1978). Re: report child abuse, *see* Annot., *State Statute Requiring Doctor or Other Person to Report Child Abuse*, 73 A.L.R. 4th 782 (1989).

107. *Ibid. Board members:* Malia v. Monchak, 543 A.2d 184 (Pa. 1988); Freir v. Ind. School Dist., 356 N.W.2d 724 (Minn. 1984); Mancuso v. Oceanside Un. School Dist., 200 Cal. Rptr. 535 (1984). *See* Annot., *Libel and Slander—School Board Members Privilege*, 85 A.L.R. 3d 1137 (1978) and 1996 pkt. part. *Parents:* Martin v. Kearney, 124 Cal. Rptr. 281 (1975); Schulze v. Coykendall, 545 P.2d 392 (Kan. 1976); *but see* Everett v. Cal. Teachers Assn., 25 Cal. Rptr. 120 (1962) (knowingly false statement).

108. New York Times Co. v. Sullivan, 376 U.S. 254 (1964). *Public figures:* Scott v. News-Herald, 496 N.E.2d 699 (Ohio 1986) (school superintendent); Garcia v. Board of Educ., 777 F.2d 1403 (10th Cir. 1985) (board members); Stevens v. Tillman, 855 F.2d 394 (7th Cir. 1988) (school principal). *Not public figures:* Franklin v. Elks Lodge, 97 C.A.3d 915 (1979) (teachers); Jones v. Maness, 648 S.W.2d 629 (Mo. 1983) (students).

109. (1) *Failure to achieve satisfactory educational levels—no cause of action:* Heilbig v. City of New York, 597 N.Y.S.2d 587 (1993); Rich v. Kentucky Country Day, 793 S.W.2d 832 (Ky. 1990); Smith v. Phila. School Dist., 679 F. Supp. 479 (E.D. Pa. 1988). (2) *Failure to properly test, evaluate, and place student—cause of action:* Daniel B. v. Wis. Dept. of Pub. Instruction, 581 F. Supp. 585 (E.D. Wis. 1984); Tubell v. Dade County Pub. Schools, 419 So. 2d 388 (Fla. 1982) (misplacement in special educational program); Doe v. Board of Educ., 453 A.2d 814 (Md. 1982) (misplacement, as brain injured); D.S.W. v. Fairbanks N. Star Borough School Dist., 628 P.2d 554 (Alaska 1981) (misplacement of dyslexic students); Hoffman v. Board of

Educ., 400 N.E.2d 317 (N.Y. 1979) (student misclassified as retarded). *But see contra:* B.M. v. State, 649 P.2d 425 (Mont. 1982) (misclassification of student as mentally retarded). *See generally* Annots.,*Tort Liability Misclassification or Wrongful Placement of Student,* 33 A.L.R. 4th 1166 (1984); *Tort Liability—Educational Malpractice,* 1 A.L.R. 4th 1139 (1980); Note, *Nonliability for Negligence in the Public Schools—Educational Malpractice,* 55 Notre Dame L. Rev. 814 (1980).

110. Davis v. DeKalb County School Dist., 996 F. Supp. 1478 (N.D. Ga. 1998) (state Tort Claims Act did not waive immunity for school districts; therefore, school district could not be held liable for teacher sexual molestation of student).

111. On the differences between state sovereign immunity and school district immunity, *see* Mt. Healthy School Dist. v. Doyle, 429 U.S. 274 (1977). *Denial of state sovereign immunity:* Ohio Valley Contractors v. Board of Educ. of Wetzel County, 293 S.E.2d 437 (W. Va. 1982). *Granting state sovereign immunity:* Hutt v. Etowah County Board of Educ., 454 So. 2d 973 (Ala. 1984).

112. For a good summary of state legislative changes in tort law, *see* J. Martinez, *Contemporary Trends in State Public Tort Law,* 18 McQuillin Municipal Law Report, No. 6, pp. 7–10 (June 2000). On legislative extension of tort immunity to teachers and employees, *see, e.g.,* Bankston v. Pulaski County School Board, 65 S.W.2d 859 (Ark. 1984); McManus v. Anahuac Indep. School Dist., 667 S.W.2d 275 (Tex. 1984); Bodano v. Wayne-Westland Comm. School, 318 N.W.2d 613 (Mich. 1982); Daniels v. Gordon, 503 S.E.2d 72 (Ga. 1998) (official immunity extended to school employees); S.W. v. Spring Lake Park School Dist., 580 N.W.2d 19 (Minn. 1998).

113. Alter v. City of Newton, 617 N.E.2d 656 (Mass. 1993). *Waiver by taking out insurance:* Durham City Board of Educ. v. Nat'l Union Fire Ins. Co., 426 S.E.2d 451 (N.C. 1993); Crowell v. School Dist., 805 P.2d 522 (Mont. 1991); School Board of Orange County v. Coffey, 524 So. 2d 1052 (Fla. 1988); Vendrell v. School Dist., 360 P.2d 282 (Or. 1971). *Contra:* Dugger v. Sprouse, 364 S.E.2d 275 (Ga. 1988); Nelson v. House, 402 N.W.2d 639 (Minn. 1987); Bartley v. Special School Dist., 649 S.W.2d 864 (Mo. 1983); Bernhard v. Kerrville Indep. School Dist., 547 S.W.2d 685 (Tex. 1977).

114. See generally, Annot., *Schools—Torts—Sovereign Immunity*, 33 A.L.R. 3d 703 (1970) and 1996 pkt part. *Defective property conditions*: Wilson v. Ridgway Area School Dist., 596 A.2d 1161 (Pa. 1991); Bonamico v. City of Middletown, 706 A.2d 1386, *on remand*, 713 A.2d 1291 (Conn. 1998); Edmonson v. Brooks County Board of Educ., 423 S.E.2d (Ga. 1992). *See also* McGeregor v. Middletown School Dist., 190 A.3d 923 (N.Y. 1993) (statutory exceptions to immunity); Edmonson v. Brooks County Bd. of Educ., 423 S.E.2d (Ga. 1992). *Contra:* Goben v. School Dist. of St. Joseph, 848 S.W.2d 20 (Mo. 1992). *Attractive nuisance conditions*: Brewer v. Ind. School Dist., 848 P.2d 566 (Okla. 1993).

115. Bankenship v. Peoria Park Dist., 647 N.E.2d 287 (Ill. 1994); Harvey v. Clyde Park Dist., 203 N.E.2d 573, 577 (Ill. 1964).

116. *Cf.* Scott v. Indep. School Dist., 256 N.W.2d 485 (Minn. 1977).

117. Grames v. King, 332 N.W.2d 615 (Mich. 1983); Stein v. Highland Park Indep. School Dist., 540 S.W.2d 551 (Tex. 1976); Kreiner v. Turkey Valley Comm. School Dist., 212 N.W.2d 526 (Iowa 1973). *Contra:* Kellam v. Board of Educ., 117 S.E.2d 96 (Va. 1960).

118. Sly v. Board of Educ., 516 P.2d 895 (Kan. 1973) (negligent supervision—held not a nuisance).

119. (a) Kreiner, note 117, *supra*; (b) Sturges v. School Dist., 33 Pa. D. & C. 525 (1938); (c) Stein, note 117, *supra*.

120. *E.g.,* Everhart v. Board of Educ., 310 N.W.2d 338 (Mich. 1981); Canon-McMillan School Dist. v. Bioni, 555 A.2d 901 (Pa. 1989).

121. *See, e.g.,* Ross v. Consumer Power Co., 363 N.W.2d 641 (Mich. 1984); Marilyn S. v. City of New York, 521 N.Y.S.2d 485 (1987); Matthews v. Elder; 400 So. 2d 251 (La. 1981).

122. Lovitt v. Concord School Dist., 228 N.W.2d 479 (Mich. 1975) (school games); Rennie v. Belleview School Dist., 521 S.W.2d 423 (Mo. 1975); Coleman v. Beaumont Indep. School Dist., 496 S.W.2d 245 (Tex. 1973) (playground maintenance).

123. Sawaya v. Tuscon H.S. Dist., 281 P.2d 105 (Ariz. 1955) (lease of school stadium to another school district). *Contra:* Watson v. School Dist., 36 N.W.2d 195 (Mich. 1949).

124. *Compare, e.g.,* Doe v. Park Center High School, 592 N.W.2d 131 (Minn. 1999) (execution of policy is discretionary, not ministerial), *with* Burns v. Board of Educ., 638 A.2d 1 (Conn. 1994) (discretionary immunity superseded).

125. Brooks v. Logan, 903 P.2d 73 (Idaho 1995).

126. Scott, note 116, *supra*.

127. Barr v. Bernhard, 562 S.W.2d 844 (Tex. 1978); Morrison v. Comm. Anita School Dist., 358 N.E.2d 389 (Ill. 1976); Baird v. Hosmer, 347 N.E.2d 533 (Ohio 1976) (citing numerous authorities from other states); Lovitt v. Concord School Dist., 228 N.W.2d 479 (Mich. 1975); Caldwell v. Griffin Spalding County Board of Educ., 503 S.E.2d 43 (Ga. 1998) (negligent supervision of student safety held to be a discretionary function, and immune from tort suit).

128. *See* Annot., *Student Injury—Teacher Liability*, 34 A.L.R. 4th 228, 234–46 (1984); Moore v. Port Arthur Ind. School Dist., 751 F. Supp. 671 (E.D. Tex. 1990); Vitale v. Lentine, 358 N.W.2d 2 (Mich. 1984).

129. *Failure to maintain safe premises:* Elgin v. Dist. of Columbia, 337 F.2d 152 (D.C. Cir. 1964); Whitt v. Reed, 239 S.W.2d 489 (Ky. 1951). *Violation of tenure law:* Babb v. Moore, 374 S.W.2d 516 (Ky. 1964); Bronaugh v. Murray, 172 S.W.2d 591 (Ky. 1951).

130. Holman v. Wheeler, 677 P.2d 645 (Okla. 1983); Board of Trustees v. Holso, 584 P.2d 1009 (Wyo. 1978).

131. Wood v. Board of Educ., 412 S.W.2d 877 (Ky. 1967); Annots., *Personal Liability of Public School Teacher*, 34 A.L.R. 4th 228 (1984); *Personal Liability of Public School Executive or Administrative Officer*, 34 A.L.R. 4th 272 (1985).

132. Annot., *Indemnification of Public Officer or Employee*, 71 A.L.R. 3d 90 (1976).

133. *See, e.g.,* Baldi v. Mt. Sinai School Dist., 679 N.Y.S.2d 89 (1998); Doe v. Town of Blandford, 525 N.E.2d 403 (Mass. 1988); Professional Detail Service, Inc. v. Board of Educ., 479 N.Y.S.2d 40 (1984); Faucher v. Auburn, 465 A.2d 1120 (Me. 1983).

134. SENA School Bus Co. v. Board of Educ., 677 P.2d 639 (N.M. 1984); Brown v. Portland

School Dist., 617 P.2d 665 (Or. 1980). Some state courts found short-notice statutes to be unconstitutional. Hunter v. N. Mason H.S., 539 P.2d 845 (Wash. 1974); Friedman v. Farmington Twp. School Dist., 198 N.W.2d 785 (Mich. 1972); Turner v. Staggs, 510 P.2d 879 (Nev. 1973).

135. State law variations are noted in Annots.: *Tort Claims against Public Entity—Notice*, 53 A.L.R. 5th 689 (1997); *Incapacity . . . as Affecting Notice of Claim . . .* , 44 A.L.R. 3d 1108 (1976) and 1996 pkt part; *Minority as Affecting Notice of Claim Requirement*, 58 A.L.R. 4th 402 (1987). *Waiver of notice requirement:* Flandera v. Jamesville-Dewitt Cent. Schools, 369 N.Y.S.2d 920 (1975). *Excuse for incapacity:* Draper v. City of Los Angeles, 276 Cal. Rptr. 864 (1990); Welsh v. Berne-Knox-Westerlo Central School Dist., 479 N.Y.S.2d 567 (1984) (minor). *Excuse for substantial compliance:* Oliber v. Sioux City Comm. School Dist., 389 N.W.2d 665 (Iowa

1986); Urban v. Waterford-Halfmoon Unified Free School, 483 N.Y.S.2d 462 (1984); Lucas v. Indep. School Dist., 674 P.2d 1131 (Okla. 1983). *But see* Scarborough v. Granite School Dist., 531 P.2d 480 (Utah 1975). *Excuse where no prejudice from delay:* Murray v. LeRoy Cent. School Dist., 491 N.E. 2d 1100 (N.Y. 1985); Shope Enterprises Inc. v. Kent School Dist., 702 P.2d 499 (Wash. 1985). *Excuse where notice received from other sources:* Friedman v. Syosset Central School Dist., 545 N.Y.S.2d 814 (1989). *Other good cause:* Valiquette v. City School Dist., 391 N.Y.S. 2d 23 (1977).

136. *See, e.g.,* Turrentine v. Brokhaven Miss. School Dist., 794 F. Supp. 620 (S.D. Miss. 1992) (dollar cap for school bus accident—upheld); Annot., *Tort Action Against Government Unit, Limits on Recoverable Damages*, 43 A.L.R. 4th 19 (1986); Doe v. Board of Educ., 453 A.2d 814, 822 (Md. 1982); *cf.* Thompson v. Sanford, 603 S.W.2d 932 (Ark. 1984); Packard v. Joint School Dist., 661 P.2d 770 (Idaho 1983).

CHAPTER 5

Professional Employees: Employment Rights and Obligations

∞ **CHAPTER OUTLINE**

I. Statutory and Contract Terms
II. Employment Rights and Duties
   A. Employment Eligibility
      1. State Certification
         a. Decertification
      2. Personal Conditions
         a. Residency
         b. Health
         c. Citizenship and Loyalty
         d. Conflicts of Interest
   B. Performance Issues
      1. School Assignments
      2. Implied Duties
      3. Evaluations and Ratings
      4. Demotions
   C. Job Security
      1. Nontenured Teachers—Nonrenewal
      2. Tenured Teachers
         a. Required Service Period
         b. Scope of Tenure
         c. Tenure by Official Errors
   D. Collectively Bargained Contracts
      1. Bargaining Units—Union Representation
      2. Bargainable Matters
         a. Union Fees and Privileges
         b. School Statute—Labor Law Conflicts
      3. Dispute Resolution
         a. Mediation and Arbitration
         b. Strikes
         c. Strike Sanctions

III. Suspension and Termination
   A. Resignation and Abandonment
   B. Reductions in Force (RIF)
      1. Grounds for RIF
      2. Order of Release and Recall
   C. Discharge for Cause
      1. Grounds for Discharge
         a. Incompetence
         b. Incapacity
         c. Insubordination
         d. Unprofessional Conduct
         e. Immorality
      2. Remedies for Wrongful Discharge

∽ **CASE**
5.1 Poole v. Little Valley Central School District, 472 N.Y.S.2d 226 (1984)

∽ **ENDNOTES**

STATUTORY AND CONTRACT TERMS

In this chapter we consider the employment rights and professional obligations of teachers and other school professional employees under state law. The rights of teachers under federal law, to be free from employment discrimination and from infringement of their civil rights as citizens, will be covered in Chapter 6.

Under state law, public school employee rights and obligations are grounded in contracts, including individually negotiated contracts, collectively bargained union contracts, and statutory provisions, which are by law made a part of school contracts. With regard to teacher employment, the laws of each state have many parallels, but there are also some important state-to-state variations. For example, school nurses are classified and treated as professional employees in Pennsylvania, but not in Texas.[1] Furthermore, legal classifications of teaching positions (e.g., as substitute, temporary, probationary, or tenured) affect many employment rights, so that differently classified teachers receive different compensation and job security protections, even though they perform substantially the same work. Finally, the courts of each state independently interpret those laws, which also produce some variations of like provisions. For example, where a teacher was given the position of temporary principal at a principal's salary scale, the court had to decide whether his claim for overtime pay in that temporary position was governed by the law fixing the compensation of principals or by his regular teacher contract.[2] The following sections outline the dominant patterns of state laws on teacher rights and duties. However, in view of the variations of law in different states, and of their continual revisions by state legislatures, the following general review must be read in that light.

EMPLOYMENT RIGHTS AND DUTIES

Employment Eligibility

School districts may set job qualifications for teaching positions over and above the minimums prescribed by state law, provided that the added requirements are reasonable and consistent with state law. Individual school district employment decisions must also be consistent with the district's own general employment practices; if they are not, they are subject to reversal as arbitrary abuses of administrative discretion.[3]

State Certification

To be eligible for employment as a teacher or school professional, a person must have credentials that are specified by state law, usually in the form of a state certificate.[4] Where an uncertified person performs work for which certification is required, the courts of different states have been divided on the question whether a school board may pay the uncertified person for work actually done.[5]

Certification standards and records are administered by central state agencies in most states, but a state legislature may vest that authority in local school districts. Local school boards may not, however, waive certification requirements unless so authorized by law.[6] Certification laws have been influenced by two countermovements. On one hand, dissatisfaction with student achievement outcomes has spurred movements to adopt stricter certification requirements for new teachers, and to require recertification of employed teachers. On the other hand, actual or anticipated shortages of teachers have produced a movement toward relaxing traditional education training requisites for teacher certification.[7] The following excerpts indicate current trends in state certification laws:

> . . . [S]chool districts rely on teacher credentials, such as state certification, or teacher tests to determine the qualifications of a candidate.
>
> From 1987–88 to 1993–94, increasing percentages of public school districts required passage of state tests of basic skills and subject knowledge in the teacher hiring process, although teacher credentials were the most widely used criteria at each survey point.
>
> . . .
>
> In 1993–94, state tests were relied upon more frequently than the NTE in the South and Midwest; in the Northeast, this pattern was reversed.
>
> . . . [T]he NTE was the most frequently used teacher assessment in the Northeast, with half of all districts requiring passage of the national exam. Following the NTE, similar percentages of Northeastern districts relied on state tests of basic skills and subject knowledge. . . . In the West, districts most frequently required passage of state tests of basic skills. . . . Across all four regions, district-level tests were required less frequently than national and state tests. [Issue Brief, *Credentials and Tests in Teacher Hiring: What Do Districts Require?* (February 1997)]

A 1998 report from The National Center for Education Statistics found the following:

> More than 90% of the teachers were fully certified in their main teaching field, and the percentage of teachers teaching out of their field ranged from 4 to 10%. [http://www.nces.ed.gov/pubsinfo]

On the other hand, a recent report of a study by The Education Trust stated, *inter alia:*

- • Only 29 states require teacher candidates to pass tests in subjects they wish to teach; and eligibility examinations are "insultingly easy" to pass.
- • States whose school districts face severe teacher shortages may hesitate to require more rigorous testing for fear of intensifying the shortage.

- Some states, notably California, are being sued and accused of discrimination because their teacher tests result in disproportionate failure rates of minority group candidates. [News Article, *Study Says States Don't Require a Lot from Teacher*, The Philadelphia Inquirer, p. A13 (5–28–99); *see also* Lines, *Teacher Competency Testing*, 23 Ed. Law 811, 827 (1985)]

The subjects or areas covered by a teacher's certificate limit the holder's eligibility to teach given subjects. A teacher certified for foreign language instruction may not be hired to teach English, nor can a teacher claim seniority rights to a position for which that teacher lacks certification. Nor may a teacher avoid assignment to a position that is covered by his or her certificate, unless that assignment violates the teacher's contract rights.

Some states require that certificates be registered with the employing school district *before* an employment contract is made or before commencement of work. The penalty for noncompliance varies with state law, from dismissal without pay, to surrender of employment rights for the period preceding proper filing, to excusal without penalty if the court finds that the filing default is harmless error.[8] Courts may also extend filing deadlines in special circumstances, e.g., for emergencies or bureaucratic delays.[9]

Certification tests that result in disproportionate failures of a particular racial or other minority group have been challenged as discriminatory or unfair, but as noted in Chapter 6 those challenges have been largely rejected, absent clear proof of intentional discrimination in test content or administration.

Decertification.   In proceedings to withdraw a teacher's certificate, the teacher has a constitutional right to due process hearings because a teaching certificate is considered to be a species of constitutionally protected property. Grounds for decertification are specified by statutes (e.g., grave misconduct, disabling mental illness, or drug addiction). In some states such grounds must be shown to be job related. The decision as to what conduct or conditions are job related or sufficiently affect job performance is made by courts on the basis of the facts of each case.[10]

Decertification statutes are distinct from and operate independently of teacher dismissal statutes. For example, a school board may dismiss a teacher whose position is abolished or decline to renew a probationary teacher contract, but it may not for those reasons decertify the teacher.[11]

Personal Conditions

Residency.   Unless forbidden by state law, school boards may require their teachers and other employees to reside within the employing district.[12] A minority of states prohibit local boards from imposing in-district residence for teacher employment.

Health.   Boards may suspend or dismiss an employee whose condition impairs teaching performance or poses a danger to others at school.[13] Teachers may in appropriate circumstances be required to submit to a wide range of physical and medical testing, from common vision and hearing tests, to tests for communicable diseases, addiction, or mental illness. As explained in Chapter 6, an employee may challenge medical examinations as being unreliable, or unduly intrusive upon personal privacy, especially where the examination involves extraction and testing of body fluids or other body-invasive procedures.[14]

Citizenship and Loyalty. Citizenship preconditions to public school employment have been challenged as unconstitutional with mixed results. For the reasons set forth in Chapter 6, the Supreme Court held that school districts may constitutionally deny teaching posts to noncitizens.[15] That decision does not speak to the eligibility of noncitizens to work in nonteaching, nonconfidential positions. The requirement that teachers take a loyalty oath has withstood constitutional challenge provided the oath is limited to disavowal of subversive *action*, as opposed to advocacy of revolutionary *ideas*. The oath must be limited to a vow to uphold constitutional government against attempts to overthrow it by force or violence. A teacher who refuses to take a lawfully worded oath may, therefore, be denied public school employment.[16] The constitutional right to express ideas, however unpopular, does not include a right to refuse to cooperate in a school investigation of subversive action by others in the school community, so that a recalcitrant teacher was held to be constitutionally terminated for his refusal to cooperate.[17]

Conflicts of Interest. Persons whose interests conflict with official or work duties, whether financial, political, or familial, may be disqualified from holding public school office or employment. However, statutory definitions of a disqualifying conflict of interest (i.e., with regard to the nature, magnitude, duration, and penalty for prohibited conflicts) vary widely from state to state, as do court decisions under those statutes. A sampling of these variations is presented in the endnote.[18]

The major disfavored conflicts involve (1) nepotism (i.e., favoritism of close relatives by blood or marriage), (2) holding outside employment or office, and (3) interests in outside organizations that do business with the school district.

Performance Issues

School Assignments

Teachers do not have a free-standing affirmative right to be assigned to a particular school or class,[19] independently of their contract agreements.[20] A school board need not grant a due process hearing to a teacher who objects to a disciplinary school assignment, since, as explained in Chapter 6, there is no constitutional right to teach at a particular school.[21] A different question is presented where a teacher claims that his or her assignment violates a civil right that is guaranteed by the Constitution or by a specific employment discrimination statute. In such cases, the issue is not one of the right of school authorities to determine school assignments, but whether in making such an assignment the school has violated a teacher's civil right.

To overturn a placement decision, therefore, a teacher must prove that the decision is based on an error of law, an abuse of administrative discretion, or a violation of a civil right. School boards and officials may not violate their own official assignment rules. Nor may they make transfers for an unlawful reason, such as the desire to avoid contract salary obligations.[22] Nor may a board make an assignment for the unconstitutional purpose of retaliating against a teacher's constitutional freedom of speech, such as engaging in outside political activity or in offering criticisms of school policy at a school-sponsored public forum.[23] Chapter 6 provides more detailed examples of civil rights which public school authorities must respect in making employment decisions.

Implied Duties

Arguments over assigned job duties that are not expressly specified in a contract raise the question whether those duties are as a matter of law properly implied as part of the teacher's contract. Courts will not imply a duty that is contrary to law or to an express contract provision. In the absence of such conflict, courts have implied teacher duties to perform noninstructional tasks that are reasonably incidental to performance of the teacher's position, such as supervision of study halls, cafeterias, and school-sponsored events (social or athletic) or attendance at open house and teacher workshops.[24] Courts can disagree on the judgment of what duties are reasonable incidental to teaching positions. Some have overturned, as unreasonable, demands that the teacher undertake work not related to their particular positions, such as supervision of after-school bowling that is not school sponsored, or the coaching of sports by a mathematics teacher,[25] while a different court found that an assignment of a physical education teacher to do coaching work was reasonable.[26] The availability of school volunteers or hired assistants to conduct nonacademic work does not of itself prevent a finding of a teacher-implied duty to perform those same tasks.[27]

Arguments over the scope of implied duties have diminished with the increased specification in union-bargained contracts of duties which may not be implied but which must be negotiated.

Evaluations and Ratings

Teacher evaluations and rating systems significantly affect teacher career opportunities, such as selection for particular school or class assignments, contract renewals, tenure eligibility, order of layoff, and disciplinary actions.[28] In most states, the law authorizes state education agencies to establish rating systems, but state laws vary greatly on such questions as whether such systems are mandatory or advisory, whether they vest local school boards with discretionary choices of alternative rating systems, and how rating regulation is shared between central state and local education agencies. Rating categories range from almost meaninglessly vague "satisfactory" or "unsatisfactory" grades, to detailed scoring systems that include separate ratings on many different aspects of teacher performance.

Because of potentially severe consequences of an adverse teacher rating, courts tend to insist on strict compliance with rating procedures, and will overturn ratings that do not comply with them. They retain the power in special cases to excuse a faulty rating as a harmless error, where the rating process does not materially prejudice the rights of the rated teacher.[29] Where state law or union-bargained agreements provide for a teacher right to a hearing on contested ratings, school authorities have the burden of proof in such hearings to support the adverse rating.[30] If a union contract requires that rating challenges be submitted to arbitration, the teacher's status quo is preserved during such arbitration. The administrative and expense burdens of arbitrating a challenged teacher rating may deter school districts from supporting a challenged teacher rating through the arbitration process.

Demotions

Though teachers have no affirmative right to a particular school assignment, they may challenge a change of assignments as an unlawful "demotion". The law does not treat every disadvantageous transfer as a demotion.[31] Demotions are presumptively valid,[32] so that an aggrieved teacher has the burden of proving, first, that the transfer in question amounted to a demotion, and second, that the demotion was unlawful in the circumstances.

The legal definition of a "demotion" is provided by state law. In some states a demotion occurs only if the transfer results in reduced compensation; in other states a demotion occurs if a transfer results in a loss of professional rank, reputation, or prestige, as well as in compensation; while in still other states, a demotion occurs only when the transfer produces a change in the teacher's certification or tenure area.[33] Where diminished professional prestige is ground for objection, the teacher may prevail by showing adverse community reactions or a loss of professional reputation or responsibility (namely, from principal to classroom teacher).[34]

Under the law of some states, a teacher can demand a notice and hearing procedure to challenge a proposed change as a demotion. Courts decide whether those procedures must be strictly followed or whether a faulty procedure may be excused as harmless error.[35] However, a teacher who fails to make timely demand for statutory demotion procedures may be held to waive those protections and be barred from further challenging the alleged demotion.[36] Acceptance of a new assignment pending a hearing on an alleged demotion was not deemed to waive the teacher's challenge, and even a resignation in protest of the challenged reassignment was held not to waive the right to contest the demotion at a demanded hearing.[37] Whether indirect notice of an intended transfer satisfies the demotion procedure will also depend on the particular case circumstances. For example, one court held that a well-publicized board resolution to eliminate a teaching position satisfied the legal notice requirement for a demotional transfer, but other forms of indirect notice may not be considered fair or sufficient in law.[38]

Demotions may be lawfully made in appropriate circumstances for disciplinary reasons[39] as well as nondisciplinary reasons. While nondisciplinary transfers may effect a challengeable demotion, transfers necessitated by staff reductions are not challengeable where no comparable position for the transferred teacher survives the staff reduction. However, where a senior or tenured teacher has a priority right to claim an available position to which another is assigned, exclusion from that position provides an independent ground to resist the transfer to the lower position.

In special circumstances, a state law ban against a demotional transfer may be suspended if it is superseded by higher federal law, such as a court decree to undo unconstitutional school staff segregation to achieve better racial balance of school teaching staffs.[40]

Job Security

The job security rights of tenured and nontenured teachers are subject to separate provisions of school statutes and teacher contracts.

Nontenured Teachers—Nonrenewal

Probationary teachers with renewable annual contracts may acquire tenure by completion of the prescribed period of satisfactory service. But teachers hired for limited time or purpose, such as emergency, temporary, or substitute teachers, are not eligible to acquire tenure. Until probationers gain tenure, school boards may decline to renew their contracts at the expiration of their current contracts. Unless board discretion is expressly constrained by statute or by teacher contracts, school boards are not required to give any particular form of notice, hearing, or a statement of reasons for the nonrenewal.[41] Nevertheless, school boards are not given unbridled discretion in making nonrenewal decisions, and a court may overturn a nonrenewal decision for abuse of discretion.[42]

In most states, the law requires school boards to notify probationers in writing before a specified calendar deadline of the district's intention not to renew the current contract.[43] Failure to provide required timely notice of nonrenewal normally entitles the teacher to a renewal contract. The required details of nonrenewal notices vary with each state's law and with each school district's teacher contract.

The right to receive a statement of the board's reasons for nonrenewal and some additional protections (such as the right to appeal nonrenewal decisions to a higher agency or court and a preservation of probationer rights of recall to newly opened positions) have been added to the probationer's job security rights by law in a number of states and by union agreements.[44]

Union-bargained nonrenewal procedures must be followed even where they are stricter than those provided by statute. Minor nonrenewal notice defaults are strictly enforced by courts in some states, but excused as harmless error in other states.[45] Teachers may not willfully frustrate timely delivery of a notice and then seek to defeat it as legally defective.[46] A board may, of course, cure a notice default by a timely substitute notice. As with other challenges to administrative action, probationers seeking to overturn nonrenewals must prove that the board committed an error of law or abuse of discretion.

As explained in the next chapter, nontenured teachers, unlike tenured teachers, do not have a constitutional *property* interest in retaining their positions, and most states have not accorded such a *property* interest in probationary employment.[47] Nevertheless, probationers may constitutionally challenge a nonrenewal decision if that decision were made to punish the probationer for exercising a personal constitutional *right* such as promoting unionization of teachers.[48] In such cases, the challenger has the burden of proving that the nonrenewal was made for an unconstitutional purpose of retaliation.[49] The range of rights protected from school employer retaliation are covered in Chapter 6.

Where a probationer is terminated *before* the expiration of the existing contract period, the termination is governed by the general law of contracts, and not by the law on renewals of expired contracts. Contracts may be terminated before expiration by either party to the contract[50] if the other party committed a material breach of contract. In claiming a breach by a probationer, therefore, school authorities would have to establish that the teacher breached material duties under the employment contract.

Tenured Teachers

The central value of tenure is job security through contract continuation. One author well described tenure as "the right of employment for a continuing or indefinite period of time, subject to removal only for a cause prescribed by . . . law."[51] Tenure status and rights can only be created by state legislation. Tenure is not created by commmon law or by constitutional law, though tenure rights, once vested, are protected by constitutional law. As a creature of state legislatures, tenure laws may be altered by subsequent legislatures.[52]

In most states, tenure vests only on probationer completion of the designated period of continuous satisfactory service. Temporary or substitute teachers are not generally eligible for tenure, regardless of their length of service.[53] Where tenure is confined to teaching positions, nonteaching service may be excluded in calculating tenure credit or seniority rank.[54]

The positions eligible for tenure are fixed by state law.[55] Some states extend separate tenure to administrative positions while others accord like tenure to teaching positions and to supervisory positions, such as school principals and supervisors. In such states, a tenured teacher with greater service seniority may have a priority of retention right over a school principal.[56] Vested tenure rights are considered a "property" interest that are entitled to constitutional due process protection. However, tenure statutes often provide even greater procedural protections than constitutional due process.

Tenure rights may be suspended or terminated only for grounds specified in tenure statutes, such as position abolitions, staff reductions, or for "cause", i.e., an incumbent's misconduct that justifies dismissal from school employment. Because tenure status carries a presumption of fitness for continued employment, school authorities must establish and prove the pertinent statutory grounds for a layoff, suspension, or discharge of a tenured teacher.

Required Service Period.   The required period of satisfactory service to acquire tenure, usually three years, may not be waived, ignored, or modified by school officials.[57] The service period usually begins with commencement of service, not date of hire.[58] Discontinuous part-time teaching does not generally qualify for tenure service credit, unless state legislation allows such credit. The laws of New York and Oklahoma allowed part-time service credit toward tenure in some nonprobationary positions, but the laws of Alaska and Louisiana did not.[59] In several states, service credit accrues only if the teacher devoted at least half of work time to the area or subject for which tenure is sought.[60] A teacher who breaks continuous service by resignation or voluntary (not maternity) leave may be held to forfeit service credit,[61] but federal and state laws on gender discrimination and maternity rights prohibit most forms of maternity leave from being treated as a break in employment service.

The portability of earned service credit in one school district toward tenure service credit in another district within the same state also depends on the particulars of state law. Some states permit such transfer of service credit and others prohibit it.[62] For teachers who are reassigned by reason of school reorganizations and consolidations, the portability of service credit may also be governed by special statutes governing such changes.

Whether acquired tenure status in one district is portable to another district will also depend on the peculiarities of each state's law.[63]

Scope of Tenure.   In Pennsylvania, a teacher's tenure extends to all positions for which the teacher is certified, regardless of teaching lack of service in positions covered by the certificate, while other states limit tenure to the area of actual teaching service.[64] New York's complex system of tenure by area rather than by subjects actually taught must be left to fuller study elsewhere, but under that system, courts must determine which positions fall within a recognized tenure area.[65]

Tenure by Official Errors.   Where official error or misconduct contributes to a denial of tenure, courts of equity may order that tenure be granted, but such extraordinary relief lies wholly within a court's discretion.[66] A school board that failed to complete removal proceedings prior to expiration of the teacher's probationary period was enjoined from denying tenure.[67] However, where a board revoked preliminary approval for tenure following the probationer's arrest and consequent inability to complete his current contract, the court upheld the denial of tenure.[68] Where a board failed to give legally required notices of intention not to reemploy a probationer for the final year of required service for tenure, some courts ordered that tenure be granted, while others upheld denials of tenure and limited the remedy to recovery of money damages or another year of employment.[69]

Collectively Bargained Contracts

Prior to 1959 when a state enacted the first public employee labor statute, there was little law governing teacher collective bargaining. Neither the common law nor the National Labor Relations Board conferred collective bargaining rights upon public school teachers. While teachers always had a constitutional right to form and join labor organizations,[70] that right did not include a right to compel school districts to bargain collectively with such associations. In the absence of a state labor statute covering teachers, therefore, school districts could refuse to engage in collective bargaining. Since 1959, however, practically every state has enacted public employee labor relations laws to require school districts to bargain collectively with their teachers on specified working terms and conditions. The massive, continually changing law on teacher collective bargaining must be left to specialized texts, but the following overview sketches the major bargaining issues that affect teachers.

State labor statutes have not adopted a common model for teacher bargaining.[71] In many instances state legislatures made no attempt to dovetail the operations of the new labor statutes with the older laws that also affect teacher employment, thus leaving to the courts the task of harmonizing the labor relations statutes with the employment provisions of school codes and individual teacher contracts.

The principal topics of interest that are addressed by teacher labor relations laws relate to the size and composition of the school employee group that is to be represented as a single bargaining unit, the selection and certification of the association (hereafter union), that is entitled to bargain on behalf of each bargaining unit, the subjects that must or may be bargained between the employer district and teacher union, and the means of resolving disputes regarding the negotiation process and the administration of executed union contracts.

Bargaining Units—Union Representation

Labor statutes prescribe the rules to determine the size and composition of employees who may lawfully be grouped into a single "bargaining unit". The determination of a bargaining unit affects the interests of unions as well since different unions often compete to represent the same employees. The dominant legal standards for approving a proposed bargaining unit are economy and efficiency. For example, the total number of bargaining units with which the district employer will bargain should be minimized, on one hand, but placement of employees with different bargaining interests and priorities in the same unit should be avoided to avert conflicts in bargaining their divergent interests.[72] For example, the separation of professional and nonprofessional employees into separate bargaining units may clarify bargaining priorities and avoid tensions between their respective pay demands, but in very small school districts that separation may be impractical and therefore not required.[73] State labor boards generally decide whether a disputed bargaining unit is the "appropriate bargaining unit" for a particular school district under legislated guidelines, but the law in some states requires that specified employee groups, such as supervisors, security personnel, or confidential secretaries be placed in separate exclusive bargaining units.[74]

State labor boards also determine and certify which union organization is entitled to act as the "bargaining representative" of that unit. In most states, the officially certified union representative becomes the *exclusive* bargaining agent for all members of the bargaining unit, including those who do not wish to be so represented.[75] The Supreme Court ruled that laws granting exclusive representation rights do not infringe the dissident employees' constitutional freedom on the ground that the state's strong interest in promoting effective labor relations through exclusive unit representation outweighed and therefore justified the burden on the dissidents' freedom of association.[76]

Bargainable Matters

Once representation issues are settled, the parties must agree on the topics to be negotiated, and failing that, submit the disagreement to legal authority for resolution. The duty of a school district to bargain collectively on any given subject will depend on the law of its home state, i.e., whether the employment term or condition in question is a subject of *mandatory* bargaining on which a school district must negotiate; or a subject of *permissive* bargaining on which a school district may, but is not legally required to, negotiate; or a subject which is not negotiable but is reserved exclusively to school district control as part of its *management rights*, so that, at most, a school board may be required to "meet and discuss" such subjects but retains unilateral authority to decide their disposition.

The treatment of these bargainability questions varies widely from state to state.[77] For example, some states treat a particular subject as one of *mandatory* bargaining while other states treat it as one of *permissive* bargaining or of *management rights*. In some states the law itself specifies topics that fall within these categories; while in others, the law only prescribes broad criteria which state labor boards and courts are to use in deciding the scope of bargaining on a particular topic.[78] For example, a law may specify that tenure rights, pension rights, or budget items are nonbargainable topics of managerial rights.

A wide path has been cut around "managerial rights" in a number of states by court decisions that distinguish between inability to bargain on the *substance* of managerial rights and the ability to bargain on the *impacts* of managerial decisions on the employees' working terms and conditions.[79] For example, in Connecticut, a government employer was required to negotiate the impact of a decision to institute a smoke-free workplace policy, and in New York a school district could not impose a non-negotiated smoking ban in empty buses because the labor law was held to require bargaining on secondary impacts, even though a state smoke-free environment statute authorized the ban.[80] Similar ingenuity appeared in a holding that while class size was not mandatorily bargainable, teacher workloads affected by class size were bargainable.[81] Most courts favor a balancing approach to decide whether exclusive school board control over a given subject outweighs or is outweighed by employee interests in that subject.[82]

The case-by-case approach to determine bargaining subjects has produced varied results. For example, state authorities are divided on the bargainability of class size,[83] and on the setting of working hours and length of the school day.[84] In Wisconsin, the school calendar was considered bargainable with a dictum hint that curriculum matters were not bargainable.[85] Legislatures can, of course, override court interpretations, as did the Nevada legislature which enacted laws to exclude from mandatory bargaining such items as class size, school calendar, workload, and teacher selection.[86] A sampling of other negotiation items that receive diverse treatment in different states appears in the endnote.[87]

"Permissive" bargaining has been upheld where the law neither mandates nor prohibits it,[88] provided a court does not consider it to be contrary to public policy. The case trend to favor permissive bargaining on any subject not "explicitly and definitely prohibited by statute" is particularly clear in the industrialized states.[89]

Union Fees and Privileges.   A majority of states authorize union representatives to bargain for certain union rights and privileges, such as employer collection of union dues or fees by payroll deductions. Here also variations in state laws are considerable.[90] The Supreme Court upheld the constitutionality of such bargaining, but it limited union assessment of fees for nonunion employees to amounts that are reasonably related to union representation activities.[91] In a minority of states "right to work" laws restrict payroll collections of union dues and service fees.[92]

Bargaining for use of school facilities for union representation purposes and for denial of like privileges to uncertified unions was upheld as justified by the state interest in promoting effective labor relations through exclusive dealing with the certified union.[93]

School Statute—Labor Law Conflicts.   There is no universal rule for reconciling overlapping provisions of labor and education statutes. In Connecticut and Ohio, a bargained agreement "shall prevail" over any conflicting law or regulation, but in Massachusetts, prior school laws were held to prevail over later inconsistent labor laws.[94] Courts may read their labor laws narrowly to restrict the scope of bargaining, while others read education statutes broadly to reinforce their application to doubtful situations,[95] especially where the education statute affords greater teacher protections than bargained agreements or labor arbitration (e.g., on dismissal, maternity leave, superannuation benefits, layoff, and seniority credit).[96] Nor would courts permit a bargained procedure to allow "back door" grant of tenure or union control over distribution of negotiated wage benefits.[97] Labor agreements may lawfully affect layoffs in ways not contemplated by school statutes, but courts will not allow such agreements to diminish rights accorded teachers under tenure statutes.[98]

Dispute Resolution

Labor statutes generally prescribe the means by which parties may resolve four different kinds of labor disputes, namely, *representation disputes,* which involve contests between unions for appointment and certification as a unit's exclusive bargaining representatives; *interest disputes,* which involve disagreements on contract negotiation questions; *grievance disputes,* which involve disputes on the interpretation and performance obligations under an existing union contract; and *labor stoppages (lockouts, strikes)* following an impasse in contract negotiations.

Mediation and Arbitration.   In mediation, a designated third party attempts to bring negotiating parties into agreement, but mediation, unlike arbitration, relies only on persuasion. Some states require that mediation efforts be exhausted before either party can terminate bargaining and resort to other measures. Arbitration involves submission of dispute questions to an arbitrator or panel of arbitrators. There are distinct uses of arbitration, known as *Interest Arbitration* and *Grievance Arbitration. Grievance Arbitration* is used to resolve performance dispute issues under a current contract, i.e., regarding the respective contract duties of employer and employees, or fact disputes regarding allegations of performance defaults. *Interest Arbitration* is used to resolve disputes that arise in the course of contract negotiations. A number of states make *Grievance Arbitration* mandatory while making *Interest Arbitration* optional at the will of the parties,[99] except for security personnel (guards and safety employees), for whom interest arbitration is usually made compulsory.

Where the scope of grievance arbitration is not made clear by law or contract provisions, many states follow the rule that its scope is to be determined by the "essence" of the entire outstanding labor agreement, including the negotiating background as well as contract language.[100] However, where the labor agreement subjects particular matters of disputes to an alternative settlement procedure, grievance arbitration may be foreclosed.[101]

The decisions of arbitrators are presumptively valid and upheld as long as they are rationally related to and derived from the parties' agreement,[102] but courts will overturn awards that are contrary to law or to the terms of arbitration.[103] The cases are mixed on the forms of relief that an arbitrator may order. One case overturned an arbitrator's orders to renew a teacher's contract while another upheld arbitrator authority to award monetary recovery for the same grievance.[104] Courts may, but are disinclined to, sustain arbitration orders that require the grant of tenure, even to an improperly dismissed teacher.[105]

Union contracts usually provide that a filing of a grievance effects a "stay" or freeze of the status quo. This prevents disciplinary measures against a teacher, unless the school district can persuade a court to lift that stay.[106]

Interest Arbitration issues parallel bargaining issues, i.e., what matters are arbitrable and whether arbitration is binding or advisory. As with bargaining, the arbitrability of various issues varies from state to state. If a disputed matter involves a managerial right, it cannot be a subject of arbitration.[107] In several states interest arbitration is also banned on particular subjects, such as position elimination, board examination of teachers' files, teacher evaluation, leaves of absence, teacher nonrenewal, and teacher discharge for cause.[108] Other illustrations of state divisions on the arbitrability of particular topics appear in the endnotes.[109] Where the scope of interest arbitration is not made clear by law, many courts favor the rules that any subject not excluded by law is arbitrable.

Strikes. Strikes against government agencies were unlawful at common law and must, therefore, be authorized by legislation.[110] In a growing number of states, the labor statutes give teachers a limited right to strike under specified conditions.[111] The statutory definition of a "strike" can be very broad to include any concerted action, such as failing to report for work; work stoppage or slowdown; or absence in whole or in part from the full, faithful, and proper performance of employment duties for the purpose of inducing, influencing, or coercing a change in the conditions, compensation, or other rights, privileges, or obligations of employment. Some forms of concerted action, such as slowdowns, "going by the book" (refusing to perform duties not specified in written contracts), and massive sick call-ins, are used occasionally as a negotiation weapon, but they carry the risk of being adjudged as unlawful stoppages.[112]

Picketing to support teacher bargaining demands may be lawful or unlawful, depending on its form and purpose. Purely *informational* picketing is constitutionally protected *speech*, but picketing that trespasses or blockades others, or incites an illegal stoppage, is not.[113]

The purposes, timing, and duration of teacher strikes are confined by law. For example, strikes may not be permitted to protest performance grievances or alleged unfair labor practices, or to support organization drives or strikes by other organized labor groups. The laws in most states permit strikes only after the parties have arrived at a negotiation impasse and have exhausted mandatory statutory procedures to break the impasse. They further typically authorize courts to terminate a legally commenced strike where the strike poses a danger to public health, safety, or public welfare.[114] Public inconvenience is not alone a sufficient ground to enjoin a strike, and the degree of danger that justifies strike injunctions is left to court determination.[115] Courts may refuse to enjoin even an admittedly harmful strike if they conclude that the public interest in achieving labor settlement is of greater importance than the resumption of school service.[116]

Strike Sanctions.   The penalties for violating a court strike injunction include monetary fines or imprisonment for contempt of court, as well as statutory fines and penalties.[117] In addition to these labor law sanctions, a school district may have grounds to discharge employees who persist in supporting an unlawful strike, namely, termination for unauthorized absence from work, insubordination, or a finding of teacher abandonment of the district employment position.[118]

SUSPENSION AND TERMINATION

The grounds for suspending or terminating employment by school districts, whether those grounds are based on alleged voluntary employee acts such as by resignation or abandonment of a position or on unilateral district decision, by nonrenewal of probationer contracts, or by layoffs, suspensions, or discharge for cause, are specified and governed by statute and case decisions. The following sections consider the conditions for dismissal under each of these grounds, except for district nonrenewal of probationer contracts, which was reviewed in a prior section.

Resignation and Abandonment

Voluntary resignation or abandonment of position forfeits all employment rights, including tenure.[119] It is imperative, therefore, that teachers know what acts by them may qualify as a binding resignation or abandonment of their position, lest they unwittingly sever their employment. Unless a statute requires specific formalities to effect a resignation,[120] any statement or act that manifests an intent to abandon a position may have the effect of a resignation. Unusual unexcused absence from work, acceptance of another full-time job, or rejection of tendered work assignments can manifest an intention to resign or abandon a position.[121] Other examples of conduct manifesting an intent to resign appear in the endnotes.[122] The question whether absence of illegally striking teachers conveys an intent to abandon their position has drawn contrary responses from different state courts.[123]

An agreement or statement of resignation must be made knowingly and voluntarily, and school authorities may not seize on equivocal statements to claim a resignation. An objection to a new assignment or calling in sick was not of itself sufficient to qualify as a resignation.[124] A resignation must be accepted as tendered, and any material change of its terms by the recipient may invalidate the acceptance.[125] Resignations obtained by coercion or undue influence, or if made under excusable mistake of material facts, are legally void,[126] but resignations submitted to avoid adverse board charges or as part of a settlement agreement are not deemed coercive.[127]

A generally worded resignation may surrender all employment with the school district,[128] but a resignation that referred only to a subordinate position was held not to surrender rights to the other positions.[129] In some states, courts held that written resignations become final and irrevocable only when formally accepted by the school board, so that a teacher could withdraw a resignation before board acceptance, but courts in other states found resignations to be effective and irrevocable on proper delivery, without further need for board acceptance.[130]

Reductions in Force (RIF)

RIF statutes authorize school boards to reduce school staff in special, specified circumstances by dismissal of teachers and administrators. RIF dismissals are not subject to the rules that govern non-RIF dismissals, such as dismissals of tenured teachers or nonrenewal of probationers in circumstances not governed by the RIF statute.[131] The most common grounds for conducting a reduction in force are the existence of school district fiscal shortfalls, declining enrollments, and substantial reorganizations or consolidation of schools within a district or school districts. RIF dismissals in no way impugn the reputation or employment history of the affected teachers.

The major legal issues in contested RIFs were crisply summarized as follows: "when to RIF, whom to RIF, and how to RIF,"[132] i.e., whether statutory grounds exist to conduct a RIF; whether the RIF was properly implemented; and whether the legally required order of teacher retention, reassignment, and dismissal was observed. Because RIF statutes vary in significant details the governing statute must be reviewed in each case. The following discussion outlines major considerations that are common to most RIFs.

Grounds for RIF

RIFs may only be undertaken for purposes listed in the RIF statute.[133] In some cases, fiscal shortfalls, though an important factor, do not alone suffice to justify

a RIF process.[134] Courts have overturned position abolitions in fiscally distressed districts where abolished positions were deemed necessary to carry out
state-mandated duties or to maintain quality education.[135]

The determination whether necessary conditions exist to justify a RIF lies
initially with a school board so that challengers have the burden of proving
that the board's decision was not justified either in law or under the proven
facts.[136] For example board decisions may be overturned if nominally abolished positions were not truly eliminated, but only retitled.[137] On the other
hand, redistribution of the duties of an eliminated position to a different surviving position is lawful.[138]

Order of Release and Recall

Under a RIF, the order of teacher retention, release, and later recall follows the
order of teacher rank, with priority of retention normally given to qualified
tenured teachers over qualified nontenured teachers,[139] followed by seniority
preferences among qualified teachers within the same rank.[140] Tenured teachers on leave retain their priority rank, and probationers may be released to
make way for returning tenured teachers.[141] The calculation of seniority service,
which significantly affects a teacher's retention or dismissal, invites recurrent
legal challenges. School boards may be required to give seniority service credit
for military, maternity, or approved leaves under federal and state law,[142] while
such credit may not be allowed for other types of leave (e.g., leaves without
pay).[143] Furthermore, seniority rank that is forfeited by resignation, discharge
for cause, or retirement may not be revived by subsequent reemployment.[144]

The law does not require a school district to retain unneeded teachers.[145] In
school district mergers, seniority rankings of the merged staff will depend on the
governing reorganization statute. Some courts read their law to credit teacher
service in either of the consolidated systems,[146] while the staffing of a newly created regional school was left to the discretion of the board of the new school under a statute that created the new school without mention of earned seniority.[147]

The law in many states requires school boards to realign the positions that
survive a RIF in order to ensure fair assignment of teachers who qualify for the
surviving positions, especially with reference to their seniority and position
classifications. However, court decisions regarding a "reasonable" realignment
are very checkered, both in their view of the facts in each case and of the criteria of a "reasonable" realignment.[148]

Discharge for Cause

Unlike nonrenewals and RIF dismissals, teachers of all ranks may be discharged at any time, with termination of all employment rights with the employer district, for "just cause" as that phrase is defined by school statutes.
The statutory grounds and procedures for "just cause" dismissals are
mandatory, i.e., teachers may not be discharged unless those grounds are es-

tablished in hearings if the charged teachers request them. Board failure to follow statutory procedures will void a discharge, regardless of the teacher's alleged misconduct. Union agreements may add protective procedures in just cause proceedings, but they cannot reduce the requirements set by school statutes. Discharges for alleged cause that do not meet the statutory minima will be overturned.[149] Indeed, a wrongful discharge could constitute a breach of contract, rendering the district liable not only to reinstate the employee with compensation for back wages and lost fringe benefits, but in some case also for monetary damages for injury to the teacher's reputation.[150]

Grounds for Discharge

The statutory grounds for discharge encompass a broad range of acts or omissions. The principal grounds for a just cause discharge are *incompetency, incapacity, insubordination, unprofessional conduct, neglect of duty, immorality, intemperance,* and *sufficient cause,* with some states adding *disloyalty, intemperance, cruelty, willful misconduct, good and sufficient cause, evident unfitness,* and *neglect of duty.*[151] These broad standards have withstood court challenges that they violate constitutional due process in that they do not give fair notice of conduct that is subject to the discharge sanction.[152]

Practically every one of the above-listed grounds for discharge embraces the core idea of "fitness" to be a teacher, but that touchstone is also subject to disagreement among state courts as to whether their law intended to cover only conduct that affects a teacher's ability to perform essential teaching duties, or whether it intended to authorize discharge for conduct that undermines a teacher's ability to serve as a role model for students, however competent his performance of teaching duties. As will appear most clearly in the following discussion of "immorality", the case variations are even broader in different states and regions that reflect different social mores and attitudes regarding the gravity of particular misconduct.[153] In view of the mixed law on the scope of "just cause" grounds for discharge in sister states, the following discussion provides only an illustrative framework in which individual state courts apply their respective state school statutes.

School boards have the burden of proving grounds for teacher discipline, including discharge, by substantial evidence.[154] Discharge statutes *authorize,* but generally do not *command,* school boards to impose the strongest penalty of discharge for teacher misconduct, hence school boards retain the discretion to impose lesser penalties. Courts may also overturn a discharge which they consider to be unreasonable and excessive in the circumstances.[155]

A discharge statute or union agreement may also require school boards to afford an errant teacher an opportunity for "remediation" (i.e., rehabilitation) *before* any final action is taken to discharge the teacher. But the question remains whether the alleged misconduct is in fact "remediable". Only if it is, must remediation be attempted.[156]

Incompetence.   This broad ground is sufficiently expansive to encompass most other specified grounds for discharge. It may embrace performance deficiency, or personal incapacity or character defect,[157] and may cover the following conditions:

1.   Physical or mental incapacity,
2.   Lack of knowledge or inability to impart knowledge,
3.   Failure to adapt to new teaching methods,
4.   Physical mistreatment of students,
5.   Violation of school rules,
6.   Violation of duties to superiors or coworkers,
7.   Lack of cooperation,
8.   Persistent negligence,
9.   Failure to maintain discipline, or
10. Personal misconduct, in or out of school.[158]

Isolated incidents of incompetence may be sufficiently serious to sustain discharge, but incompetence charges usually involve a pattern of behavior.

Incapacity.   Serious physical, mental, or emotional illness or disability of an indefinite duration is generally grounds for discharge,[159] but discharge for accommodatable disability has been foreclosed by the Americans with Disabilities Act, which is discussed in Chapters 6 and 8.

Insubordination.   Insubordination commonly involves a series of acts, but a single incident, if sufficiently serious, may support discharge. Courts look to the gravity and persistence of insubordination in deciding whether discharge is warranted.[160] Examples of insubordination include unauthorized absence from work, encouraging student disobedience or disrespect, violation of corporal punishment regulations, and untoward criticism of school superiors.[161] Teacher initiation of a federal narcotics investigation without the knowledge or approval of superiors, and teacher failure to report suspicious student conduct were held to support discharge for insubordination.[162] Innocent mistakes are not insubordinate, as where a teacher who was late the first day of the school term due to her registration for graduate studies at a nearby university,[163] but a school principal who left students unsupervised to register for summer programs was held insubordinate.[164]

Unprofessional Conduct.   Like "conduct unbecoming a teacher", this standard potentially includes the use of offensive language, abuse of corporal punishment, threats and insults to fellow teachers, taking time off without permission, and shoplifting.[165] Other examples are use of classroom time to promote partisan political causes, distributing poems that herald the joys of marijuana, encouraging students to ignore family morals, improper sexual contacts, and fomenting teacher disloyalty.[166] As with other grounds, court appraisals of conduct range from strict to indulgent. One court held that a teacher who fought with a rowdy student and a teacher who had private consensual sexual relations with a former student could not be dismissed for unprofessional conduct.[167] But a teacher who dressed and undressed a publicly exposed mannequin in a lewd and suggestive manner was dischargeable for unprofessional conduct.[168]

Immorality.   The courts continue to declare that public schools have "a legitimate and substantial interest in promoting . . . traditional values, be they social, moral, or political." [*Board of Educ. v. Pico*, 457 U.S. 853, 864 (1982)] But, as with the cases of unprofessional conduct charges, the kinds of conduct that justify teacher discipline or discharge are far from uniform and continue to change as community standards change. In addition to considering shifting moral standards and expectations engendered by the sexual revolution, courts must also consider whether ongoing changes in the law of civil rights (which are reviewed in Chapter 6) also limit the kinds of conduct that are punishable under school statutes. Their findings and judgments involve two pivotal questions:

1.   What kind and degree of alleged misconduct amounts *in law* to "immorality"?

The answers to this question reflect in part the social attitudes of a given state or region and in part the influence of contemporary trends in civil rights law.

2.   When conduct is admittedly immoral in law, is that conduct sufficiently serious or persistent to justify the extreme penalty of discharge from public school employment?

The answers to this question depend on the deciding court's criterion of teacher fitness (role model and/or classroom performance and community support) and the weight courts will give to extenuating circumstances, e.g., whether the misconduct occurs at or away from school, whether it involves students or adult school staff, whether it gained public notoriety,[169] and whether it adversely affected school–community relationships, as well as intramural school relationships.[170] Given these variations, the best guidance is to be found in the case decisions of the home state or region which deal directly with those circumstances and charges. The dominant grounds for immorality charges are those relating to dishonesty, drug abuse, and sexual misconduct.

Dishonesty may justify discharge,[171] but only if a court decides that the particular offense is sufficiently grave to warrant discharge. Misappropriation of school funds sustained discharge, while negligent mishandling of funds did not.[172] Regional variations appear in drug abuse cases. Private possession of marijuana was grounds for discharge in Florida and Illinois, but not in West Virginia and California.[173] Acquittal of a criminal charge does not preclude school discharge of a teacher on the same evidence.[174]

Charges of teacher sexual misconduct pose special problems for school administrators. On one hand, they risk criticism and potential liability for failure promptly to investigate and protect alleged victims of sexual misconduct. On the other hand, they face criticism for failure to deal fairly with accused teachers. The determination whether particular sexual allegations amount to punishable "immorality" will depend upon the nature and context of the alleged conduct, i.e., whether it involves a student, adult school employee, or outsiders and whether it is a matter of private or public notice.[175]

Teacher sexual abuse of students has supported stricter disciplinary action. For example, two courts recently upheld school board discharge of tenured teachers for sexual abuse of students though their misconduct occurred 16 and 24 years prior to its disclosure to the school board.[176] The courts found no unfairness or denial of due process since the boards acted promptly upon being notified of that misconduct by the students who suffered that abuse. A recent Missouri case sustained teacher discharge although the school district could not prove actual sexual contact between a teacher and student. In that case, a private detective hired by the parents of a 14-year-old eighth-grade student observed her enter and remain at the home of a probationary teacher-coach until nearly midnight and reported his observations to the police. The police went to the probationer's residence to inquire of the child, but the teacher denied them entry, and when asked if he had contact with her, he admitted that he had spoken to her by phone. The police left, but kept the house under observation, and shortly thereafter caught the girl leaving the property by the back alley. The court upheld his discharge for immorality, and rejected the teacher's argument that the student's presence in his home was insufficient to prove immoral conduct.[177]

The treatment of sexual misconduct under teacher discharge statutes varies with case circumstances and community attitudes. Some cases upheld teacher discharge in the following circumstances: public discussion of "swinger" conduct, publicized request for homosexual marriage license, publicized sex change surgery, posing nude for a magazine, and lewd gestures with mannequin in public view.[178] With regard to extramarital cohabitation and pregnancy, one case line disfavors teacher discharge unless there is clear factual proof that such conditions adversely affect job performance.[179] Episodic adultery, though publicly known, was held insufficient cause for discharge where the general community supported the adulterous teacher.[180]

The discharge of homosexual teachers (male and female) for "immorality" is no longer solely a matter of interpreting what homosexual manifestations constitute immmorality under a state school statute. Courts must now consider if and how the latest Supreme Court decision [*Lawrence v. Garner*, 123 S. Ct. 2472 (2003)] limits the operation of such laws. In *Lawrence*, the Court held that a state may not constitutionally forbid or punish adults for engaging in private, consensual homosexual acts in a home, on the finding that such persons have a constitutional "liberty" to do so, and that the state had no rational basis to interfere with that conduct. The *Lawrence* opinion raises, but does not address, the broader question: May state laws constitutionally authorize discharge of public school employees for homosexual conduct, and if so, in what circumstances? The *Lawrence* opinion contains the following hedging language that may limit the scope of its declared homosexual liberty:

> The present case does not involve minors. It does not involve persons who may be injured or coerced or who are situated in relationships where consent might not be refused. It does not involve public conduct or prostitution. It does not involve whether government must give formal recognition to any relationship that homosexual persons seek to enter. [123 S. Ct. at p. 2484]

Whether or how the *Lawrence* decision will apply to homosexual conduct or relationships in varied school circumstances remains open to question and future court settlement. The potential influence of the *Lawrence* case with regard to teacher and student civil rights is revisited in Chapters 6 and 7.

Teacher use of vulgar language may be a ground for discharge in some states, but as with the immorality ground, courts do not view all instances of vulgarity as a sufficient "cause" for discharging a teacher. One court overturned the discharge of a teacher whose grossly vulgar letter addressed to a former student was read by the addressee's mother, on its reasoning that the letter might not have been so offensive to the son as it was to his mother.[181] Another court reinstated a teacher who failed to halt a school presentation that included profane, obscene, distasteful, and inappropriate language because it found extenuating circumstances in the failure of school authorities to interrupt the program, the improbability of a repetition, and the lack of proof of adverse impact on teaching ability.[182] But, as seen in the contrary holdings on like vulgarity in the *Lacks* case (Case 6.3 in Chapter 6) and the *Bethel* case (Case 7.2 in Chapter 7), judicial appraisals of cause for discharge change with time and place.

Remedies for Wrongful Discharge

Wrongfully discharged teachers may recover lost back wages and fringe benefits, less any substitute earnings they made or reasonably could have made following the breach.[183] The general duty of wrongfully dismissed teachers to mitigate damages does not require them to take inferior employment or incur unreasonable burdens, such as pursuing work in a distant region.[184] The school board has the burden of proving that the teacher failed to mitigate damages.[185] Where monetary damages alone cannot adequately compensate for a contract breach, i.e., where the breach resulted in loss of tenure or other important status, courts may order reinstatement to the prior position and status.

Case 5.1

POOLE v. LITTLE VALLEY CENTRAL SCHOOL DISTRICT
472 N.Y.S.2d 226 (1984)

[*Focus Note. Following a statutory hearing and termination on misconduct charges, teacher Poole and his union representative filed a grievance and requested arbitration on his discharge. The question before the court was whether the teacher was entitled to arbitration following the statutory hearing.*]

JOSEPH P. KUSZYNSKI, JUSTICE

* * *

Petitioner [School District] contends also that the respondents no longer have any recourse to the Agreement's grievance procedure, no matter how broad the contract definition may be of a grievance. . . .

* * *

The 1977 amendment changed the effect of Section 3020. . . . Previously a [hearing] Panel's determination served only as a recommendation to the Board of Education. Now the amendment makes such determinations binding upon a school district.

* * *

The rationale advanced by [prior cases] . . . favoring an arbitral review no longer has any application after 1977, when by legislative fiat only two (2) methods are available to a chastised teacher for a review of the adverse determination of charges. . . . Once the issues have been submitted to such a hearing, the binding aspects of the panel's determination upon the School District have stripped the School District of any discretion to agree to a submission of the controversy to any processing under the grievance procedures of the [Labor] Agreement. . . .

    The amendment to . . . the Education Law changed the three way option previously available to a disciplined teacher. . . . Here, respondent Poole, having invoked the panoply of the statutorily provided hearing forum . . . under the Education Law, is bound to a review of its determination only by the two statutorily provided for avenues, an appeal to the State Commission of Education or the Courts. . . . *Abramovich v. Board of Education,* 46 N.Y.2d 450, 414 N.Y.S.2d 109, 386 N.E.2d 1076 (1979), cited by respondents, concerns itself with arbitration absent any 3020–a Education Law Panel determination. Clearly, once a 3020–a Education Law Panel has been convened and has decided charges . . . the recommended penalty is binding upon a school district barring any claim of irregularity. It follows then, that a school district cannot agree to a resubmission of the same issues . . . , which would be tantamount to a retrial of the issues, to an arbitral processing as a grievance. . . .

The arbitration is permanently stayed and the motion to compel arbitration is denied in its entirety.

∽ ENDNOTES

1. Dodd v. Meno, 857 S.W.2d 575 (Tex. App. 1993).

2. Taggart v. Board of Directors of Cannon-MacMillan Jt. School Sys., 185 A.2d 332 (Pa. 1962).

3. Heifner v. Board of Educ., 335 N.E.2d 600 (Ill. 1975).

4. Hunt v. Sanders, 554 N.E.2d 285 (Ill. 1990); Green Bay Ed. Assn. v. State Dept., 453 N.W.2d 915 (Wis. 1990).

5. *Compare* Luz v. School Comm. of Lowell, 313 N.E.2d 925 (Mass. 1974), *with* Sorenson v. School Dist. No. 28, 418 P.2d 1004 (Wyo. 1966).

6. *Requirement not waivable by local board:* Bradford Cent. School Dist. v. Ambach, 436 N.E. 2d 1256 (N.Y. 1982). *Statutory exception for emergencies:* Bradford Cent. School Dist. v. Ambach, 436 N.E. 2d 1256 (N.Y. 1982).

7. *See, e.g.*, State v. Project Principle, Inc., 724 S.W.2d 387 (Tex. 1987); Texas State Teachers Assn. v. State, 711 S.W.2d 421 (Tex. 1987). *But see* Allen v. Alabama State Board of Educ., 816 F.2d 575 (11th Cir. 1987).

8. *Discharge:* Luz v. School Comm. of Lowell, 313 N.E.2d 925 (Mass. 1974). *Contra:* Bates v. Hinds, 324 F. Supp. 528 (D.C. Tex. 1971). *Nonforfeiture of pay for work prior to proper filing:* Mass v. Board of Educ., 394 P.2d 579 (Cal. 1964). *No forfeiture for harmless default:* Woodrum v. Rolling Hills Board of Educ., 421 N.E.2d 859 (Ohio 1981).

9. Board of Educ. of Taos v. Singleton, 712 P.2d 1384 (N.M. 1985); Altoona Area Vo-Tech. School v. Pollard, 520 A.2d 99 (Pa. 1987).

10. A teacher convicted for marijuana possession was held fit in Comings v. State Board of Educ., 100 Cal. Rptr. 73 (1972), *but* not in Walton v. Turlington, 444 So. 2d 1082 (Fla. 1984).

11. Bloomburg-Dubin v. Board of Educ., 43 N.Y.S.2d 956 (1981). *Position abolition:* Steele v. Board of Educ. of City of N.Y., 354 N.E.2d 807 (N.Y. 1976). *Nonrenewal:* Ambrose v. Comm. School Board, 367 N.Y.S.2d 550 (1975).

12. *See* cases in Anno., *Validity, Construction, and Effect of Municipal Residency Requirements for Teachers, Principals, and Other School Employees,* A.L.R. 4th 272 (1990). *Residency upheld:* McClellan v. Paris Public Schools, 742 S.W.2d 907 (Ark. 1988); Wardwell v. Board of Educ., 529 F.2d 625 (6th Cir. 1976). *Grandfather exemption upheld:* Pittsburgh Fed'n of Teachers v. Aaron, 417 F. Supp. 94 (W.D. Pa. 1976).

13. Daury v. Smith, 842 F.2d 9 (1st Cir. 1988); Garrett v. Los Angeles County Unified School Dist., 172 Cal. Rptr. 170 (1981).

14. *See generally* J.D. Weeks, *Public Employee Drug Testing,* 20 The Urban Lawyer 445 (1988).

15. Ambach v. Norwick, 441 U.S. 68 (1979); Sugarman v. Dougall, 413 U.S. 634 (1973).

16. Cole v. Richardson, 405 U.S. 676 (1972); Connell v. Higginbotham, 403 U.S. 207 (1971) (oath upheld).

17. Beilan v. Board of Public Educ., 357 U.S. 399 (1958).

18. *Nepotism:* Chapman v. Gorman, 839 S.W.2d 232 (Ky. 1992). *See also* Annot., *Nepotism in Public Service,* 11 A.L.R. 4th 826 (1982). Some states permit employment of close relatives of a board member provided that member takes no part in the employment decision, while some states only ban such employment for "first hirings." Schere v. Rock Hill Local School Dist. Board of Educ., 597 N.E.2d 525 (Ohio 1990). Some states permit relatives to serve on the same school board: Hinek v. Bowman Public School Dist. No.1, 232 N.W.2d 72 (N.D. 1975).

   The cases are divided on the following questions:—Whether teacher spouses may work in the same school. *Cf.* Waters v. Gaston County, 57 F.3d 422 (4th Cir. 1995); Solomon v. Quinones, 531 N.Y.S.2d 349 (1988).

   —Whether a board member may concurrently hold another public office. Craighead County Board of Educ. v. Henry, 748 S.W.2d 132 (Ark. 1988) (school nurse and guidance counselor allowed to hold elective municipal office); Schulman v. O'Reilly-Lando, 545 A.2d 241 (N.J. 1988); Cmwlth. v. Tekavec, 319 A.2d 1 (Pa. 1975) (intermediate unit supervisor was not disqualified from election to school board); Gretick v. Jeffrey, 465 N.E.2d 412 (Ohio 1984) (school principal could act as county commissioner); Jenkins v. Bishop, 589 P.2d 770 (Utah 1978) (school administrator serving in state legislature). *But see contra:* LoBusco v. Dunn, 502 N.Y.S.2d 200 (1986) (employee barred from board office); Contesi v. Atty. Gen., 416 N.W.2d 410 (Mich. App. 1987); Cranston Teachers Alliance Local No. 1704 v. Miele, 495 A.2d 233 (R.I. 1985) (rehabilitation specialist barred from service on school committee); Town of Cheshire v. McKenney, 438 A.2d 88 (Conn. 1980) (teacher barred from office on town council). Under "resign to run" statutes, a person seeking election to public office may not retain public school employment. Yonts v. Comm. *ex rel.* Armstrong, 700 S.W.2d 407 (Ky. 1985) and authorities there reviewed.

19. Malynn v. Morgan Hill Unified School Dist., 187 Cal. Rptr. 303 (1982); Glanville v. Hickory County Reorganized School, 637 S.W.2d 328 (Mo. 1982); Maupin v. Indep. School Dist., 632 P.2d 396 (Okla. 1981).

20. *See, e.g.,* Lavender v. McDowell County Board of Educ., 327 S.E.2d 691 (W. Va. 1984); Silavent v. Buckeye Cent. Local School Dist. Board of Educ., 500 N.E.2d 315 (Ohio 1985).

21. *Disciplinary transfers:* Brough v. Board of Educ., 463 P.2d 567 (Utah 1970) (disobeyed order to attend a workshop).
    Hearing rights: Wheeler v. School Dist. No. 20, 535 P.2d 206 (Colo. 1975); State v. Berger, 314 So. 2d 700 (Ala. 1975).

22. Kotan v. School Dist. No. 110C, 509 P.2d 452 (Or. 1973).

23. Givhan v. Western Line Consol. School Dist., 439 U.S. 410 (1979); Calhoun v. Cassady, 534 S.W.2d 806 (Ky. 1976).

24. Blair v. Robstown Indep. School Dist., 556 F.2d 1331 (5th Cir. 1977) (high school football game); Fox v. Board of Educ., 236 S.E.2d 243 (W. Va. 1977) (parent conference).

25. Pease v. Millcreek Twp. School Dist., 195 A.2d 104 (Pa. 1963); Parrish v. Moss, 106 N.Y.S.2d 577 (1951).

26. Lockhart v. Board of Educ., 735 P.2d 913 (Colo. 1986).

27. Dist. 300 Educ. Assn. v. Board of Educ., 334 N.E.2d 165 (Ill. 1975).

28. Banks v. Comm. School Board No. 29, 364 N.Y.S.3d 379 (1975) (nonrenewal for unsatisfactory rating).

29. Tyler v. Jefferson City-DuBoise Area Voc. Tec., 359 A.2d 761 (Pa. 1976) (failure to rate); Morse v. Wozniak, 398 F. Supp. 597 (E.D. Mich. 1975) (failure to give proper notice); Longarzo v. Anker, 578 F.2d 469 (2d Cir. 1978) (noncompliance with district bylaws). *Compare* Smith v. Board of School Directors, 328 A.2d 883 (Pa. 1974) (harmless error).

30. Gunter v. Board of Trustees of Pocatello School Dist., 854 P.2d 253 (Id. 1993).

31. Ala. State Tenure Comm'n v. Shelby County Board of Educ., 474 So. 2d 723 (Ala. 1985).

32. Kaczmarcik v. Carbondale Area School Dist., 625 A.2d 126 (Pa. 1993).

33. *Re* loss of pay or prestige, *compare,* Ellis-Adams v. Whitfield County Board of Educ., 356 S.E.2d 219 (Ga. 1987); Kenaston v. School Admin. Dist. No. 40, 317 A.2d 7 (Me. 1974).
    Re loss of pay only, *see* Glanville v. Hickory County Reorganized School Dist., 637 S.W.2d 328 (Mo. 1982). *Re* loss of certification or tenure, King v. Board of Educ., 447 S.E.2d 667 (Ga. 1994); Preuss v. Board of Educ., 667 S.W.2d 391 (Ky. 1984).

34. *Ibid;* Glennon v. School Committee of Boston, 378 N.E.2d 1372 (Mass. 1978).

35. Hatcher v. Board of Public Educ., 809 F.2d 1546 (11th Cir. 1987); White v. Banks, 614 S.W.2d 331 (Tenn. 1981); Candelari v. Board of Educ., 428 A.2d 331 (Conn. 1980).

36. Williams v. Cody, 545 P.2d 905 (Or. 1976); Clark v. Mt. Greylock Regional High School Dist., 336 N.E.2d 750 (Mass. 1975).

37. Board of School Directors v. Pittinger, 305 A.2d 382 (Pa. 1973); Calhoun v. Cassady, 534 S.W.2d 806 (Ky. 1976).

38. *Compare* Clark, note 36, *supra* (publicized board resolutions satisfied notice obligation).

39. *Disciplinary demotions:* Harris v. School Dist., 624 A.2d 784 (Pa. 1993).

40. Lee v. Macon County Board of Educ., 463 F.2d 1174 (5th Cir. 1972); Singleton v. Jackson Mun. Sep. School Dist., 425 F.2d 1211 (5th Cir. 1970).

41. *Compare* Durant v. Ind. School Dist., 990 F.2d 560 (10th Cir. 1993) (hearing not required), *with* English v. Central Educ. Agency, 866 S.W.2d 73 (Tex. 1993); Tucker v. Board of Educ., 624 N.E.2d 643 (N.Y. 1993) (hearings required by statute).

    On differences among states and federal circuits, *see* Marxsen v. Board of Directors, 591 A.2d 867 (Me. 1991); Irving v. School Dist., 813 P.2d 417 (Mont. 1991).

42. Cronacher v. Scribner, 369 N.Y.S.2d 780 (1975).

43. Giangreco v. Mulless, 939 P.2d 596 (N.M. 1997). *But* board delay of nonrenewal notice to afford teacher opportunity to convince board to renew did not void nonrenewal. Carl v. S. San Antonio Indep. School Dist., 561 S.W.2d 560 (Tex. 1978). For authorities on nonrenewal notices in 41 states, *see* Annot., *Sufficiency of Notice*, 52 A.L.R. 4th 283 (1987) and pkt part.

44. *Advance statement or hearing:* Gibson v. Board of Educ. of Jackson County, 805 S.W.2d 673 (Ky. 1991) (statutory entitlement to statement of reasons); Kruse v. Board of Directors, 231 N.W.2d 626 (Iowa 1975).

45. *Formal failures not excused:* Bently v. School District, 586 306 (Neb. 1998) (notice from superintendent, due from the board). *See also* Rhoads v. Board of Trustees (WL432161); Sills v. Ala. State Tenure Comm'n., 718 So. 2d 1145 (Ala. 1998) (timely mailing, not received by statutory deadline). *Defect excused as harmless error:* Joanou v. Board of Educ., 345 A.2d 46 (Conn. 1974).

46. Conte v. School Committee, 356 N.E.2d 261 (Mass. 1976).

47. Roth v. Board of Regents, 408 U.S. 564 (1972); Perry v. Sindermann, 408 U.S. 593 (1972).

48. Givhan v. Western Line Cons. School Dist., 439 U.S. 410 (1979); Hanover Twp. Fed'n. of Teachers v. Hanover Comm., 318 F. Supp. 757 (D. Ind. 1970).

49. Mt. Healthy City Board of Educ. v. Doyle, 429 U.S. 274 (1977).

50. Wertz v. St. Cloud Unified School District, 542 P.2d 339 (Kan. 1975).

51. Bolmeier, *School in the Legal Structure* 192 (1973).

52. Alexander v. Delano Jt. Unified High School, 188 Cal. Rptr. 705, 708–9 (1983).

53. Buckner v. School Board, 718 So. 2d 862 (Fla. 1998); Welk v. Iowa City Comm. School Dist., 470 N.W.2d 57 (Iowa 1991).

54. Sadler v. Board of Educ., 851 S.W.2d 707 (Mo. 1993).

55. *See, e.g.,* Wrightgorman v. Board of Educ., 491 A.2d 644 (N.J. 1985) (custodians covered); State *ex rel.* Haak v. Board of Educ., 367 N.W.2d 461 (Minn. 1985) (some supervisory positions covered); Roberts v. Comm. School Board, 486 N.E.2d 818 (N.Y. 1985) (some substitute service covered).

56. Jefferson v. Compton Unified School Dist., 17 Cal. Rptr. 2d 474 (Cal. 1993).

    States with separate tenure for administrators: Wooten v. Alabama Tenure Comm'n., 421 So. 2d 1288 (Ala. 1982); Paqua v. LaForche Paris School Board, 408 So. 2d 438 (La. 1981).

    States where administrators hold tenure as teachers: Snipes v. McAndrew, 313 S.E.2d 294 (S.C. 1984); Waltz v. Board of Educ., 329 N.W.2d 131 (S.D. 1983); Fuller v. N. Kansas City School Dist., 629 S.W.2d 404 (Mo. 1982).

57. Halsey v. Board of Educ. of Garrett County, 331 A.2d 306 Md. (1975); *cf.* City Univ. v. Board of Higher Educ., 330 N.Y.S.2d 688 (1972).

58. Kletzkin v. Board of Educ., 642 A.2d 993 (N.J. 1994).

59. Dist v. Lollar, 547 P.2d 1324 (Okla. 1976); People v. Kapp, 389 N.Y.S.2d 645(1976)(kindergarten teacher on half-day sessions). *But see* Fairbanks N. Star School v. NEA-Alaska, 817 P.2d 923 (Alaska 1991); Thompson v. E. Baton Rouge Parish School Board, 303 So. 2d 855 (La. 1974); Dial v. Lathrop R-11 School Dist., 871 S.W.2d 444 (Mo. 1994).

60. Copella v. Board of Educ., 367 A.2d 444 (N.J. 1976); Rhee v. Allegheny Intermediate Unit No. 3, 315 A.2d 644 (Pa. 1974); *cf.* Stang v. Indep. School Dist., 256 N.W.2d 82 (Minn. 1977).

61. *Voluntary leave:* Solomon v. School Committee of Boston, 478 N.E.2d 137 (Mass. 1985). *Compare* Matthews v. School Committee of Bedford, 494 N.E.2d 38 (Mass. 1986). *Resignation:* Williams v. Lafayette Parish School Board, 533 So. 2d 1359 (La. 1988).

62. *Prohibited:* Britt v. Red Mesa Unified School Dist., 748 P.2d 1202 (Ariz. 1987); Nagy v. Board of Educ., 500 P.2d 987 (Colo. 1972).

Permitted: cf. Oak Harbor School Dist. v. Oak Harbor Educ. Assn., 545 P.2d 1197 (Wash. 1976) (seniority determined by total service in the state); Harbe v. Hazelwood School Dist., 532 S.W.2d 848 (Mo. 1975).

63. Lee-Warren v. School Board, 403 S.E.2d 691 (Va. 1991) (principalship tenure lost upon removal to another district). Teachers in some federally funded positions were held eligible for tenure credit in Alabama and Massachusetts but not in Louisiana or Delaware. Berry v. Pike County Board of Educ., 545 So. 2d 43 (Ala. 1987); Brophy v. School Comm., 383 N.E.2d 521 (Mass. 1978); Board of Educ. of Newcastle v. Savino, 494 A.2d 1258 (Del. 1985). *See also* Annot., *Teachers Service Period—Computation,* 2 A.L.R. 2d 1033 (1948).

64. *See* Nagy v. Board of Educ., 500 P.2d 987 (Colo. 1972); Coates v. Ambach, 383 N.Y.S.2d 672 (1976); McNamara v. Board of Educ., 389 N.Y.S.2d 682 (1976) (prekindergarten teachers held to be within elementary tenure area).

65. Hicksville Congress of Teachers v. Hicksville Union Free School Dist. Board of Educ., 499 N.Y.S.2d 774 (1986).

66. Loftus v. Board of Educ. Town of Fairfield, 509 A.2d 500 (Conn. 1986); Roberts v. Comm. School Board, 486 N.E.2d 818 (N.Y. 1985).

67. Elisofon v. Board of Educ., 379 N.Y.S.2d 145 (1976); *but cf.* LaBarr v. Board of Educ., 425 F. Supp. 219 (D. N.Y. 1977).

68. Williams v. Board of Public Instruction, 311 So. 2d 812 (Fla. 1975).

69. *Tenure grant ordered:* Board of Educ. of Harrodsburg v. Powell, 792 S.W.2d 376 (Ky. App. 1990); Dav v. Prowers County School District, 725 P.2d 14 (Colo. 1986); *cf.* Wilt v. Flannigan, 294 S.E.2d 189 (W. Va. 1982) (board policy violated).
    Tenure grant denied, but other relief awarded: School Dist. v. Norwood, 644 P.2d 13 (Colo. 1984); LaBorde v. Franklin Parish School Board, 510 F.2d 590 (5th Cir. 1975); Mugavin v. Nyquist, 367 N.Y.S.2d 604 (1975); Snell v. Brothers, 527 S.W.2d 114 (Tenn. 1975).

70. Tex. State Teachers Assn. v. Garland Indep. School Dist., 777 F.2d 1046 (5th Cir. 1985); Saye v. St. Vrain Valley School Dist., 785 F.2d 862 (10th Cir. 1986); Mo. Nat'l Educ. Assn. v. New Madrid County R-1 Enlarged School Dist., 810 F.2d 164 (8th Cir. 1987).

71. *See* U.S. Dept. of Labor, Labor Management Services Admin., Summary of Public Sector Labor Relations Policies (1981); Education Commission of the States, State Education Collective Bargaining Laws, Elementary/Secondary Sector (July 1984).

72. United Teachers Org. v. WERC, 342 N.W.2d 709 (Wis. 1984); School Board of Polk County v. Fla. PERC, 399 So. 2d 520 (Fla. App. 1981); Detroit Board of Educ. v. Local No. 28, 308 N.W.2d 247 (Mich. 1981).

73. Anthony Oto Comm. School Dist. v. Public Employment Relations Board, 404 N.W.2d 140 (Iowa 1987).

74. *Teachers:* The law in some states required all teachers to be in a single unit. Connecticut, Delaware, and Hawaii required separation of professional employees according to certification classes or administrative duties. *See also* Board of Trustees of Speedway v. Ind. Educ. Employee Relations Board, 498 N.E.2d 1006 (Ind. 1986). Pennsylvania law gives teachers the option to include nonprofessionals in their bargaining unit.
    Supervisors: Rhode Island and Wisconsin prohibited union representation of supervisors, but other states allow such representation in a separate unit. Appeal of Manchester Board of School Comm., 523 A.2d 114 (N.H. 1987); Annot., *Who Are Supervisors for Purposes of Bargaining Unit Determination,* 96 A.L.R. 3d 723 (1980) and pkt. part. Other states left the matter to labor boards. Anthony Oto Comm. School Dist., note 74, *supra,* Mo. N.E.A. v. Mo. State Board of Mediation, 695 S.W.2d 894 (Mo. 1985). "Wall-to-wall" bargaining units include all employees (professional and nonprofessional) of a single employer, notwithstanding potential adverse interests. Sandburg Faculty Assn. v. Ill. Educ. Labor Relations Board, 618 N.E.2d 989 (Ill. 1993).

75. Very few states provide for proportional (union members only) representation. Fayette Co. Educ. Assn. v. Hardy, 626 S.W.2d 217 (Ky. 1980); Minnesota State Board of Comm. Colleges v. Knight, 465 U.S. 271 (1984).

76. Lehnert v. Ferris Faculty Association, 111 S. Ct. 1950 (1991).

77. Rogers v. Board of Educ., 2 F.3d 163 (6th Cir. 1993). Annot., *Negotiable Issues in Public Employment*, 84 A.L.R. 3d 242 (1978) and pocket part.

78. Continually changing state legislative actions are reported in specialized labor law periodicals. *See* Government Employee Relations Reporter (Bureau of National Affairs, Special Reports, Labor Relations in Secondary and Elementary Education).

79. *E.g.,* Board of Educ. v. Kansas Dept. of Human Res., 856 P.2d 1343 (Kan. 1993) (appraisal procedures); Ind. School Dist. v. School Service Employees' Union, 503 N.W.2d 104 (Minn. 1993) (effects of outsourcing). *See also* School Board of Seminole County v. Morgan, 582 So. 2d 787 (Fla. 1991); Board of Educ. v. Illinois Educ. Labor Relations Board, 556 N.E.2d 857 (Ill. 1990).

80. Local 1186 v. State Board of Labor Relations, 620 A.2d 766 (Conn. 1993); Newark Valley Central School Dist. v. Public Employment. Relations Board, 632 N.E.2d 443 (N.Y. 1994).

81. W. Irandequoit Teachers Assn. v. Helsby, 35 N.Y.2d 46 (1974); Yorktown Faculty Assn. v. Yorktown Cent. School Dist., 7 N.Y.P.E.R.B. 3030 (1974). *But see* Susq. Valley C. School Dist. v. Susq. Valley Teachers Assn., 358 N.Y.S.2d 235 (1974).

82. Aberdeen Educ. Assn. v. Aberdeen Board of Educ., 215 N.W.2d 837 (S.D. 1974); Sutherland Educ. Assn. v. Sutherland School Dist., 548 P.2d 647 (Or. 1976); Pa. Labor Relations Board v. State College Area School Dist., 337 A.2d 263 (Pa. 1975).

83. *Held bargainable:* W. Hartford Educ. Assn. v. deCourcey, 295 A.2d 536 (Conn. 1972); Hawaii Public Employee Relations Board decision [Govt. Emp. Relations Rptr. E-1 (1972)].

   Held not bargainable: Aberdeen Educ. Assn., prior note; Nat'l Educ. Assn. of Shawnee Mission v. Board of Educ., 512 P.2d 426 (Kans. 1970).

   Where the labor statute is unclear, some courts leave the question of mandatory bargaining to state labor boards. Central City Ed. Assn. v. Illinois Educational Labor Relations Board, 599 N.E.2d 892 (Ill. 1992).

84. W. Hartford Educ. Assn., prior note.

85. School Corp. v. Ind. Educ. Employment Relations Board, 446 N.E.2d 1007 (Ind. 1983); Joint School Dist. No. 8 v. Wis. Employees' Relation Board, 155 N.W.2d 78 (Wis. 1967). *Compare* Hillsborough Classroom Teachers Assn. v. School Board, 423 So. 2d 969 (Fla. 1982), *with* Eastbrook Comm. School Corp. v. Ind. Educ. Empt. Rel'ns. Bd., 466 N.E.2d 1007 (Ind. 1983).

86. Nev. Rev. Stat. § 228.150.

87. The bargainability of promotional and supervisory appointments, teacher evaluations, transfers, tenure, and nonrenewal of contracts receives conflicting treatment in different states.

   Held not bargainable: Board of Educ. v. NEA-Goodland, 785 P.2d 993 (Kan. 1990); Marsh v. St. Vrain School Dist., 644 P.2d 41 (Colo. 1981); Minn. Fed'n of Teachers v. Minn. Spec. School Dist., 258 N.W.2d 802 (Minn. 1977); Newman v. Board of Educ., 325 A.2d 387 (Del. 1974). On teacher evaluation, *compare* Aplington Comm. School Dist. v. Iowa PERB, 408 N.W.2d 495 (Iowa 1986) (bargainable), *with* Wethersfield Board of Educ. v. Conn. State Board of Labor Relations, 519 A.2d 41 (Conn. 1986); Miller v. Board of Educ., 744 P.2d 113 (Kan. 1988) (nonbargainable).

   Held bargainable to some extent: Alton Comm. School Dist. v. E.L.R.B., 567 N.E.2d 671 (Ill. 1991); Board of Educ. of Yonkers City School Dist. v. Yonkers Fed'n of Teachers, 514 N.Y.S.2d 465 (1987); Wright v. Board of Educ., 491 A.2d 644 (N.J. 1985) (tenure rights bargainable within statutory limits).

   Re bargaining on budget reductions and job eliminations, *see* School Comm. of Hanover v. Curry, 325 N.E.2d 282 (Mass. 1975); City of New Rochelle v. New Rochelle Fed'n of Teachers, 4 PERB 3060 (N.Y. 1971). *Contra:* Cent. City Educ. v. Ill. Educ. Labor Relations Board, 557 N.E.2d 418 (Ill. 1990); Barrington School Comm. v. Rhode Island State Labor Relations Board, 388 A.2d 1369 (R.I. 1978).

   Bargainability of "outsourcing" work that might be performed by school employees remains particularly contentious. A California statute authorizing school hiring of private contractors for pupil driver training was upheld, but courts in Pennsylvania, Michigan, and Wisconsin held that outsourcing contracts for bus and food services was subject to mandatory bargaining. *Compare* Ind. School Dist. v. School Serv. Employees Union, 503 N.W 2d 104 (Minn. 1993) (contracting out held not bargainable), *with* Elizabeth Forward School Dist., 624 A.2d 215 (Pa. 1992) (contracting out held bargainable). *But see* Cent. City Educ. v. Ill. Educ. Labor Relations Board, 557 N.E.2d 857 (Ill. 1990); Board of Educ. v. Poughkeepsie P.S. Teachers Assn., 436 N.Y.S.2d 50 (1981); Bay City Educ. Assn. v. Bay City Public Schools, 397 N.W.2d 219 (Mich. 1986); Un. School Dist. v. Wisconsin Empl't Relations Comm'n, 259 N.W.2d 724 (Wis. 1977). *Cf.* Southwestern Vermont Educ. Assn., 396 A.2d 123 (Vt. 1978)(contract for janitorial service during a labor dispute, held an unfair labor practice).

88. Board of Educ. of Yonkers City School Dist. v. Yonkers Fed'n of Teachers, 383 N.E.2d 569 (N.Y. 1976) (no layoff provision, a subject of permissive bargaining). *Contra:* Westtown Educ. Assn. v. Westtown Public School Board of Educ., 337 N.W.2d 533 (Mich. 1983); Fortney v. School Dist. of W. Salem, 321 N.W.2d 225, 230–1 (Wis. 1981).

89. *See, e.g.,* Montgomery County Educ. Assn. Ind. v. Board of Educ., 534 A.2d 980 (Md. 1987); City of Beloit v. WERC and Beloit Educ. Assn., 242 N.W.2d 231 (Wis. 1976).

90. State laws vary on check-off bargaining. A majority of courts upheld grant of check-off privileges to the certified bargaining agent. Schaffer v. Board of Educ., 869 S.W.2d 163 (Mo. App. 1993); San Lorenzo Educ. Assn. v. Wilson, 32 Cal. 3d 841 (1983); Memphis A.F.T. v. Board of Educ., 534 F.2d 699 (6th Cir. 1976). *But see contra:* Board of School Directors v. Wis. Employment Relations Comm'n, 168 N.W.2d 92 (Wis. 1969).

91. Chicago Teachers Union v. Hudson, 475 U.S. 292 (1986); Abood v. Detroit Board of Educ., 431 U.S. 209 (1977); Crommley v. Mich. Educ. Assn., 843 F. Supp. 1147 (Mich. 1994); Grunwald v. San Bernardino City Un. School Dist., 994 F.2d 1370 (9th Cir. 1993); New Jersey Ed. Assn. v. New Jersey Public Empt. Relations Comm., 628 A.2d 789 (N.J. 1993). Where state legislation is silent on union security bargaining, the decision rests with the courts. School Board of Escombia County v. PERB, 350 So. 2d 819 (Fla. 1978) (check-off held a mandatory subject of bargaining); *contra:* Kentucky Educ. Public Affairs Council v. Ky. Registry of Finance, 667 F.2d 1125 (6th Cir. 1982) (check-off without employee consent, held prohibited).

92. *See also* Weissenstein v. Burlington School Comm'rs, 543 A.2d 691 (Vt. 1988).

93. Perry Educ. Assn. v. Perry Local Educ. Assn., 460 U.S. 37 (1983). *Accord:* Davidson v. Community Cons. School Dist., 130 F.3d 265 (7th Cir. 1997).

94. The distinction between subject matter and "effects" bargaining was adopted in Kansas and Minnesota. Board of Ed. v. Kansas Dept. of Human Resources, 856 P.2d 1343 (Kans. 1993); Independent Sch. Dist. v. School Service Employees Union, 503 N.W.2d 104 (Minn. 1993) (effects of contracting out food services must be negotiated). *See also* Brown v. Milton-Union Ex. Vil. Board of Educ., 531 N.E.2d 1297 (Ohio 1988). *But see* Elizabeth Forward School Dist. v. Pa. Labor Relations Board, 624 A.2d 215 (Pa. 1992) (outsourcing work of bargaining unit employees held subject to mandatory bargaining).

95. *Compare* Boston Teacher's Union v. School Comm., 434 N.E.2d 1258, 1266 (Mass. 1982), *with* Niagara Wheatfield Cent. School Dist., 375 N.E.2d 37 (N.Y. 1978).

96. Martel v. Teachers Retirement Board, 479 N.E.2d 191 (Mass. 1985); Johnson v. Nyquist, 361 N.Y.S.2d 531 (1974) (probationer dismissal, contrary to education statutes—held void); Dauphin County Tech. School Educ. Assn. v. School Board, 357 A.2d 721 (Pa. 1976) (dismissal for failure to pay union dues—held void). *Re* layoff and seniority credit, *see* Oak Harbor School Dist. v. Oak Harbor Educ. Assn., 545 P.2d 1197 (Wash. 1976).

97. Chatam Assn. of Educators v. Board of Public Educ., 204 S.E.2d 138 (Ga. 1974) (union distribution of negotiated benefits).

98. McKee v. Board of Educ., 627 A.2d 951 (Conn. App. 1993); Piquard v. Board of Educ., 610 N.E.2d 757 (Ill. 1993).

99. *E.g.,* Board of Educ. v. Chicago Teachers Union, 412 N.E.2d 587 (Ill. 1980). A third form, "final offer" arbitration, is not covered in this text.

100. Kentwood Pub. Schools v. Kent County Educ. Assn., 520 N.W.2d 682 (Mich. 1994); Matter of Clarkstown Cent. School Dist., 558 N.Y.S.2d 704 (1990) (presumption of intent to arbitrate). *Re* the essence test, *see* Mahoning County Board v. Mahoning County TMR Educ. Assn., 500 N.E.2d 872 (Ohio 1986). The arbitrability of a particular procedure may itself be subject

to arbitration. Piercy v. School Board of Washington County, 576 So. 2d 806 (Fla. 1991).

101. Sup. School Comm. v. Portland Teachers Assn., 338 A.2d 155 (Me. 1975); Rylke v. Portage Area School Dist., 341 A.2d 233 (Pa. 1975).

102. Canon School Dist. v. W.E.S. Constn. Co., Inc., 868 P.2d 1014 (Ariz. 1993).

103. Board of Educ. of Rockford School Dist. v. Illinois Educ. Labor Relations Board, 629 N.E.2d 797 (Ill. 1994); Midland Borough School Dist. v. Midland Educ. Assn., 616 A.2d 633 (Pa. 1992).

104. School Comm. of Danvers v. Tyman, 360 N.E.2d 877 (Mass. 1977).

105. Piquard v. Board of Educ., 610 N.E.2d 757 (Ill. 1993).

106. Board of Directors of Starmont Comm. School Dist. v. Banks, 498 N.W.2d 697 (Iowa 1993) (automatic stay); Chester Upland Educ. Assn. v. Pa. Labor Relations Board, 631 A.2d 723 (Pa. Cmwlth. 1993) (court review of stay order).

107. School Comm. of Springfield v. Springfield Admrs. Assn., 628 N.E.2d 33 (Mass. 1994) (appointment of teachers); North Star School Dist. v. North Star Educ. Assn., 625 A.2d 159 (Pa. 1993) (teacher suspension proceedings); Sup. School Comm. v. Portland Teachers Assn., 338 A.2d 155 (Me. 1975) (workday issue—restricted to meet-and-discuss consultation).

108. *Position elimination:* School Comm. of Hanover v. Curry, 325 N.E.2d 282 (Mass. 1975). *Teacher files:* Board of Educ. v. Areman, 363 N.Y.S.2d 437 (1975). *Teacher evaluation:* Proviso Council of W. Suburban Teachers Union v. Board of Educ., 513 N.E.2d 996 (Ill. 1987). *Leaves of absence:* Tucson Unified School Dist. No. 1 v. Tucson Educ. Assn., 747 P.2d 602 (Ariz. 1987). *Teacher nonrenewal:* Newman v. Board of Educ., 325 A.2d 387 (Del. 1975). *Discharge for cause:* Local 8599 United Steelworkers v. Board of Educ., 209 Cal. Rptr. 16 (1984). *See also* Port Huron Area School Dist., 393 N.W.2d 811 (Mich. 1986); Annot., *Statutory Arbitration for Public Employees,* 68 A.L.R. 3d 885 (1976) and pkt. part.

109. *Supervisory disputes: Compare* School Comm. of W. Springfield v. Korbut, 358 N.E.2d 831

(Mass. 1976) (denying arbitrability), *with* Scranton School Board v. Scranton Fed'n of Teachers, 365 A.2d 1339 (Pa. 1976) (enforcing arbitration).

New Jersey courts upheld arbitration on teacher duty changes, but voided arbitration on class schedule changes. Red Bank Board of Educ. v. Warrington 351 A.2d 778 (N.J. 1976); Ridgefield Park Educ. Assn. v. Ridgefield Board of Educ., 393 A.2d 278 (N.J. 1978).

Union agreements on class size and seniority credits were held enforceable in arbitration. Board of Educ. v. Greenburgh Teachers Fed'n, 381 N.Y.S.2d 517 (1976).

Some courts held that boards may agree to arbitrate teacher evaluations. Central Pt. School Dist. v. Emp. Relations Board, 555 P.2d 1269 (Or. 1976); Board of Educ. v. Harrison Assn. of Teachers, 360 N.Y.S.2d 49 (1974); Milberry v. Board of Educ., 345 A.2d 559 (Pa. 1976).

Teacher termination for cause was subject to grievance arbitration in several states where the bargained agreement so provided. Board of Directors v. Merrymeeting Educ. Assn., 354 A.2d 169 (Me. 1976); Board of Educ. v. Niagara Wheatfield Teachers, 388 N.Y.S.2d 459 (1976); Board of Educ. v. Philadelphia Fed'n of Teachers, 346 A.2d 35 (Pa. 1975); Danville Board of School Directors v. Fifield, 315 A.2d 473 (Vt. 1975); Kaleva-Norman Dickson School Dist. No. 6 v. Kaleva-Norman-Dickson School Teachers Assn., 227 S.W.2d 500 (Mich. 1975).

Agreements to arbitrate board promotion decisions, and to arbitrate sabbatical salaries other than those specified in education statutes, were held unenforceable. Board of Educ. v. N. Bergen Educ. Assn., 357 A.2d 302 (N.J. 1976); Cumberland Valley Educ. Assn. v. Cumberland Valley School Dist., 354 A.2d 265 (Pa. 1976).

110. Martin v. Montezuma-Cortez School Dist., 809 P.2d 1010 (Colo. 1990); Jefferson County Board of Educ. v. Jefferson County Educ. Assn., 393 S.E.2d 653 (W. Va. 1990).

111. *See* Annotation, *Right of Public Employees to Engage in Work Stoppage,* 37 A.L.R. 3d 1147, Section 12 (1971; Supp. 1988).

112. *Compare, e.g.,* Rapid City Educ. Assn. v. Rapid City School Dist., 442 N.W.2d 926 (S.D. 1989), *with* N.E.A.-Goodland v. Board of Educ., 775 P.2d 675 (Kan. 1989).

113. City of Rockford v. Local 113, 240 N.E.2d 705 (1968) (speech); Board of Educ. v. Ohio Educ. Assn., 235 N.E.2d 538 (Ohio 1967); Board of Educ. v. Kankakee Fed'n of Teachers, 264 N.E.2d 18 (Ill. 1970) (conduct).

114. Reichley by Wall v. North Penn School Dist., 626 A.2d 123 (Pa. 1993); Joint School Dist. No. 1 v. Wis. Rapids Educ. Assn., 234 N.W.2d 289 (Wis. 1975); Rockwell v. Board of Educ., 226 N.W.2d 596 (Mich. 1976).

115. State v. Del. Educ. Assn., 326 A.2d 868 (Del. 1974).

116. Timberlane Regional School Dist. v. Timberlane Regional Educ. Assn., 317 A.2d 555 (N.H. 1974).

117. *See* Annotation, *Damage Liability of Public Employee Union or Union Officials for Unlawful Work Stoppage,* 84 A.L.R. 3d 336 (1978) and pkt. part.

118. Hortonville Joint School Dist. No. 1 v. Hortonville Educ. Assn., 426 U.S. 481 (1976).

119. The courts of California, Florida, Idaho, Indiana, Kentucky, Louisiana, Nevada, New Jersey, Ohio, and Pennsylvania uphold tenure termination by resignation, notwithstanding later reemployment of the teacher. Annot., *Termination of Teacher Tenure—Resignation,* 9 A.L.R. 4th 729 (1981) and pocket part.

120. Petrella v. Siegel, 537 N.Y.S.2d 124 (1988) (statute requirement that resignation be in writing).

121. Mullen v. Fayetteville-Perry L. School Dist., 557 N.E.2d 1235 (Ohio 1988).

122. Schwartz v. Board of Educ., 358 N.Y.S.2d 49 (1974); Cords v. Window Rock School Dist., No. 8, 526 P.2d 757 (Ariz. 1974) (failure to perform sabbatical leave agreement); Miller v. Noe, 432 S.W.2d 818 (Ky. 1968) (taking unauthorized leave). *Re* formal resignation, *see* Trumansburg Cent. School Dist. v. Chalone, 499 N.Y.S.2d 92 (1982).

123. *E.g.,* Rockwell, note 114, *supra;* Shiffen v. Board of Educ., 206 N.W.2d 250 (Mich. 1973).

124. Babitzke v. Silverton Union High School, 695 P.2d 93 (Or. 1985). *But see* Kearns v. Lower Merion School Dist., 346 A.2d 875 (Pa. 1975) (failure to report for work).

125. Wiljama v. Board of Educ., 213 N.W.2d 830 (Mich. 1975).

126. Gould v. Board of Educ., 616 N.E.2d 142 (N.Y. 1993) (mistaken belief on resignor's tenure rights); Boulder Valley School Dist. v. Price, 805 P.2d 1085 (Colo. 1991)(resignation by teacher in weakened mental condition).

127. Booth v. Argenbright, 731 P.2d 1318 (Mont. 1987); Knee v. School Dist., 676 P.2d 727 (Idaho 1984).

128. Leithliter v. Board of Trustees, 91 Cal. Rptr. 215 (1971).

129. Mohn v. Indep. School Dist., 471 N.W.2d 723 (Minn. 1991) (resignation as a teacher did not surrender status as a principal).

130. *Board acceptance required:* Braught v. Board of Educ., 483 N.E.2d 623 (Ill. 1985)(acceptance indicated by replacement of resigning teacher); Sherman v. Board of Educ., 389 N.Y.S.2d 515 (1976); Hart v. School Board of Wakalla County, 340 So. 2d 121 (Fla. 1976). *Board acceptance not required:* Teague v. Walnut Ridge Schools, 868 S.W.2d 56 (Ark. 1993); Mitchell v. Jackson County Board of Educ., 582 So. 2d 1128 (Ala. 1991); Sinkevich v. School Committee of Raynham, 530 N.E.2d 173 (Mass. 1988); Booth v. Argenbright, 731 P.2d 1318 (Mont. 1987); Warren v. Buncome City Board of Educ. 343 S.E.2d 225 (N.C. 1986).

131. Palone v. Jefferson Parish School Board, 297 So. 2d 208 (La. 1974). Martin v. School Committee of Natick, 480 N.E.2d 625 (Mass. 1985) (hearing not required for RIF dismissal); Dailey v. Board of Educ., 327 N.W.2d 321 (Mich. 1982) (nonrenewal not applicable to RIF); Minn. Assn. Public Schools v. Hanson, 178 N.W.2d 846 (Minn. 1970) (tenure cannot freeze a RIF).

132. *See* Hartmeister and Russo, *Taxing the System When Selecting Teachers for Reduction-in-Force,* 130 Ed. Law Rep. (No. 3) 989 (1999).

133. E. York School Dist. v. Long, 430 A.2d 267 (Pa. 1981).

134. RIFs were not authorized for budgetary shortfalls in Pennsylvania. E. York School Dist. v. Long, 430 A.2d 267 (Pa. 1981).

135. Palone v. Jefferson Parish School Board, 297 So. 2d 208 (La. 1974); Karbach v. Board 430

A.2d 267 (Pa. 1981); Geduldig v. Board of Educ., 351 N.Y.S.2d 167 (1974).

136. Palos Verses Faculty Assn. v. Governing Board, 183 Cal. Rptr. 196 (1982); Dykeman v. Board of Educ., 316 N.W.2d 69 (Neb. 1982); E. Detroit Fed'n of Teachers v. Board of Educ., 223 N.W.2d 9 (Mich. 1974).
   For application of overlapping statutes, *see* Works v. Abrahamson Un. H.S. Dist. Board of Directors, 483 A.2d 258 (Vt. 1984); Gassman v. Governing Board of Rincon Valley School Dist., 128 Cal. Rptr. 273 (1976).

137. DeSimone v. Board of Educ., 612 F. Supp. 1568 (E.D. N.Y. 1985). *See* authorities discussed in Sullivan v. Teague Superintendent of Educ., 424 So. 2d 574 (Ala. 1982).

138. Young v. Board of Educ., 315 N.E.2d 768 (N.Y. 1974); Jordahl v. Ind. School Dist. No. 129, 225 N.W.2d 224 (Minn. 1974).

139. Holmes v. Board of Trustees, 792 P.2d 10 (Mont. 1990); Strand v. Spec. School Dist., 361 N.W.2d 369 (Minn. App. 1984); Coates v. Board of Educ., 662 P.2d 1279 (Kan. 1983). For an exceptional view in declining enrollments, *see* Underwood v. Henry County School Board, 427 S.E.2d 330 (Va. 1993).

140. Walkowski v. Duquesne City School Dist., 644 A.2d 1277 (Pa. Cmwlth. 1994); Jenson v. Jt. Ind. School Dist., 408 N.W.2d 203 (Minn. 1987) (seniority under collective bargaining agreement).

141. McManus v. Indep. School Dist., 321 N.W.2d 891 (Minn. 1982).

142. *Re* military leave, *see* Rochester Area School Board v. Duncan, 528 A.2d 48 (Pa. 1987). *Re* maternity leave, *see* Somon v. School Committee of Boston, 478 N.E.2d 137 (1985). *Re* approved leave, *see* Andresky v. W. Allegheny School Dist., 437 A.2d 1075 (Pa. 1981).

143. Dreyfuss v. Board of Educ., 339 N.Y.S.2d 547 (1972).

144. Triggs v. Berkeley County Board of Educ., 425 S.E.2d 111 (W. Va. 1992).

145. Dilley v. Slippery Rock Area School Dist., 625 A.2d 153 (Pa. 1993).

146. Gill v. Duchess County Board of Coop. Educ. Services, 472 N.Y.S.2d 435 (1984).

147. Beckett v. Roderick, 251 A.2d 427 (Me. 1969).

148. Klein v. Board of Educ., 497 N.W.2d 620 (Minn. 1993). *Compare, e.g.,* Rappold v. Board of Educ., 464 N.Y.S.2d 240 (1983), *with* Dykeman v. Board of Educ., 316 N.W.2d 69 (Neb. 1982). Butler v. Board of Educ., 769 P.2d 651 (Kan. 1989) (no board duty to create sufficient part-time positions in order to retain a tenured teacher). The cases are also mixed on the question whether the board or a complaining teacher has the burden of proving whether a realignment is or is not reasonable. Musorofiti v. Board of Educ., 482 N.E.2d 1226 (N.Y. 1985).

149. *Exclusive statutory grounds:* W. Va. Dept. of Human Services v. Boley, 358 S.E.2d 438 (W. Va. 1987); Schultz v. Board of Educ., 315 N.W.2d 633, 635 (Neb. 1982). *Hearing requirements: See* McMillan v. U.S.D. Preate, 855 P.2d 896 (Kan. 1993); Janke v. Community School Board, 587 N.Y.S. 2d (N.Y. 1992).

150. *See* case authorities in Annots., *Modern Status of Rule That Employer May Discharge At-Will Employee,* 12 A.L.R. 4th 544 (1982); *Damages— Teacher's Wrongful Discharge,* 22 A.L.R. 3d 1047 (1968).

151. Chicago Board of Educ. v. Payne, 430 N.E.2d 310 (Ill. 1981); Wishart v. McDonald, 500 F.2d 1110 (1st Cir. 1974); Denton v. S. Kitsap School Dist., 516 P.2d 1080 (Wash. 1973). Other grounds for discharge include disloyalty, intemperance, cruelty, willful misconduct, good and sufficient cause, evident unfitness, and neglect of duty. Roberts v. Rapides Par. School Board, 617 So. 2d 187 (La. 1993) (neglect of duty); Stansberry v. Argensbright, 738 P.2d 478 (Mont. 1987); Blaine v. Moffat County School Dist., 709 P.2d 96 (Colo. 1985) (drinking with students); Board of School Directors, 353 A.2d 898 (Pa. 1976) (cruelty).

152. Nat'l Gay Task Force v. Board of Educ., 729 F.2d 1270 (10th Cir. 1984). *See generally* Delon and VanZandt, *Statutory Grounds for Dismissal Survive Vagueness Challenges,* 17 West Ed. Rep. 313 (1984).

153. *Compare, e.g.,* Goldin v. Board of Central School Dist. No. 1, 359 N.Y.S.2d 384 (1973) (consensual sexual activity beween teacher and former student—held insufficient for discharge), with Sullivan v. Meade County Indep. School Dist. No. 101, 387 F. Supp. 1237

(D.S.D. 1975), *aff'd,* 530 F.2d 799 (8th Cir. 1976) (teacher discharged for cohabitation with married man). *But see* Board of Educ. v. Jennings, 651 P.2d 1037 (N.M. 1982) (reinstatement of principal discharged for adulterous affair with school secretary).

154. Schulz v. Board of Educ., 315 N.W.2d 633, 637 (Neb. 1983); Board of Educ. of Baltimore County, 507 A.2d 192 (Md. 1986).

155. West v. Tangipahoa Par. School Board, 615 So. 2d 979 (La. 1993) (failure to screen offensive movies for class viewing, held not ground for dismissal in light of teacher's past record).

156. *Re* warning letter procedure, *see* Shepard v. South Harrison R-II School Dist., 718 S.W.2d 195 (Mo. 1986). *Re* remediation, *see* Mott v. Endicotta School Dist. No. 308, 713 P.2d 98 (Wash. 1986); Hanlon v. Board of Educ., 695 S.W.2d 930 (Mo. 1985). *Compare* Board of Educ. v. State Board of Educ., 577 N.E.2d 575 (Ill. 1991) (sexual letters to students—held irremediable); McCullough v. Ill. State Board of Educ., 562 N.E.2d 430 (Ill. 1990) (criminal tax conviction—held irremediable), *with* Board of Educ. of Chicago v. Johnson, 570 N.E.2d 869 (Ill. 1991) (violation of board rule—held remediable).

157. *See* Annot., *Teachers' Incompetency, Inefficiency,* 4 A.L.R. 3d 1090 (1965) and pkt. part.

158. (1) Singleton v. Iberville Parish School Board, 136 So. 2d 809 (La. 1961). (2) Rainwater v. Board of Educ., 645 S.W.2d 172 (Mo. 1983). (3) Jones v. Jefferson Parish School Board, 688 F.2d 837 (5th Cir. 1982). (4) Fender v. School Dist. No. 25, 347 N.E.2d 270 (Ill. 1976). (5) Sutherby v. Gobels Board of Educ., 348 N.W.2d 277 (Mich. 1984). (6) Spano v. School Dist. of Brentwood, 316 A.2d 162 (Pa. 1974) (refusal to consult superiors on curriculum). (7) Pratt v. Ala. State Tenure Comm'n, 394 So. 2d 18 (Ala. 1980). (8) Mortweet v. Ethan Board of Educ., 241 N.W.2d 580 (S.D. 1976) (insensitivity to student needs; reluctance to try new teaching methods); Di Leo v. Greenfield, 541 F.2d 949 (2d Cir. 1976) (neglect of professional duties). (9) Phillips v. Board of Educ., 330 A.2d 151 (Del. 1975). (10) Katz v. Ambach, 472 N.Y.S.2d 492 (1984).

159. Dusanek v. Hannon, 677 F.2d 538 (7th Cir. 1982); Fitzpatrick School Administrative Dist., 465 N.Y.S.2d 240 (1983).

160. *See* Annot., *What Constitutes Insubordination,* 78 A.L.R. 3d 83 (1977) and pocket part. *Defiance of direct orders:* Alinovi v. Worcester School Committee, 777 F.2d 776 (1st Cir. 1985); Weaver v. Board of Educ., 514 N.Y.S.2d 473 (1987). *Violation of school rules:* Simmons v. Vancouver School Dist., 704 P.2d 648 (Wash. 1985); Thompson v. Board of Educ., 688 P.2d 954 (Colo. App. 1983).

161. *Unauthorized absence:* Christopherson v. Spring Valley Elem. School Dist., 413 N.E.2d 199 (Ill. 1980); Anderson v. Indep. School Dist., 292 N.W.2d 562 (Minn. 1980); Willis v. School Dist., 606 S.W.2d 189 (Mo. 1980). *Encouraging disrespect:* Jacker v. School Board, 426 So. 2d 1149 (Fla. App. 1983); Birdwell v. Hazelwood School Dist., 491 F.2d 490 (8th Cir. 1973) (inciting students to "get the R.O.T.C. off campus"). *Disregard of corporal punishment policy:* Burton v. Kirby, 775 S.W.2d 834 (Tex. 1989).

162. Calvin v. Rupp, 334 F. Supp. 358 (N.D. Mo. 1971).

163. Rumora v. Board of Educ., 335 N.E.2d 378 (Ohio 1973).

164. Beverlin v. Board of Educ., 216 S.E.2d 544 (W.Va. 1975); Howell v. Winn Parish School Board, 321 So. 2d 420 (La. 1975).

165. Elvin v. City of Waterville, 573 A.2d 381 (Me. 1990); Roberts v. Santa Cruz Un. School Dist., 778 P.2d 1294 (Ariz. 1989); Myers v. Orleans Parish School Board, 423 So. 2d 1030 (La. 1983); Kurlander v. School Comm., 451 N.E.2d 138 (Mass. 1983).

166. Scott County School Dist. v. Dietrich, 499 N.E.2d 1170 (Ind. 1986); Brubaker v. Board of Educ., 502 F.2d 973 (7th Cir. 1974); Carrao v. Board of Educ., 360 N.E.2d 536 (Ill. 1977).

167. Clayton v. Board of Educ., 375 N.Y.S.2d 169 (1975).

168. Wishart v. McDonald, 500 F.2d 110 (1st Cir. 1974).

169. *E.g.,* Woo v. Putnam County Board of Educ., 504 S.E.2d 644 (W. Va. 1998) (notorious publicity and public uproar on teacher use of marijuana). *See generally* C. Hooker, *Terminating Teachers for Conduct Beyond the Schoolhouse Gate,* 96 Ed. Law Rep. 1 (1995).

170. Stansberry v. Argensbright, 738 P.2d 478 (Mont. 1987); Rogliano v. Fayette City Board of

Educ., 347 S.E.2d 220 (W. Va. 1986). *Compare* Jefferson County School Dist. v. Fair Dismissal Appeals Board, 812 P.2d 1384 (Or. 1991); Schmidt v. Board of Educ., 712 S.E.2d 45, 48 (Mo. 1986).

171. Westley v. Terrebone Parish School Board, 665 F. Supp. 499 (E.D. La. 1987) (outside theft); McBroom v. Board of Educ., 494 N.E.2d 1191 (Ill. 1986) (locker theft); Bolentine v. Ark. State Board of Educ., 684 S.W.2d 246 (Ark. 1985) (school record falsification).

172. Appeal of Flannery, 178 A.2d 751 (Pa. 1963); Beterson v. Stewart, 140 S.E.2d 482 (S.C. 1965).

173. *Dismissal of Teachers—Illegal Drugs,* 47 A.L.R. 3d 754 (1973); Stredonsky v. Sobol, 572 N.Y.S.2d 445 (1991); Ulrich v. State, 555 N.E.2d 172 (Ind. 1990); Sauter v. Mt. Vernon School Dist., 791 P.2d 549 (Wash. 1990). *Compare* Adams v. State Professional Practices Council, 406 So. 2d 1170 (Fla. 1980); Chicago Board of Educ. v. Payne, 430 N.E.2d 310 (Ill. 1981), *with* Rogliano v. Fayette City Board of Educ., 347 S.E.2d 220 (W. Va. 1986).

174. Rado v. Board of Educ., 583 A.2d 102 (Conn. 1990) (phone tampering and eavesdropping).

175. *See* cases collected in Annot., *Dismissal of Teachers—Sexual Conduct,* 78 A.L.R. 3d 19 (1977) and pkt. part.

176. DeMichele v. Greenburch Centennial School Dist., 167 F.3d 784 (2d Cir. 1999); Parker v. Byron Center Board of Educ., 582 N.W.2d 859 (Mich. 1998) (sexual relations with fifth grader). *See also* Fisher v. Ind. School Dist. No. 622, 357 N.W.2d 152 (Minn. 1984).

177. Hamm v. Poplar Bluff R-1 School Dist., 955 S.W.2d 27 (Mo. l997).

178. Pettit v. State Board of Educ., 513 P.2d 889 (Cal. 1973) (public discussion of "swinger" conduct); McConnell v. Anderson, 451 F.2d 193 (8th Cir. 1971) (publicized request for homosexual marriage license); *in re* Grossman, 316 A.2d 39 (N.J. 1974) (publicized sex change surgery); Weissbaum v. Hannon, 439 F. Supp. 873 (N.D. Ill. 1977) (posing nude for a magazine); Wishart v. McDonald, 500 F.2d 1110 (1st Cir. 1974) (public lewd gestures with mannequin); Board of Educ. v. State Board of Educ., 577 N.E.2d 575 (Ill. 1991) (sexual letters to students).

179. Ponton v. Newport News Sch. Bd., 632 F. Supp. 1056 (E.D. Va. 1986); Avery v. Homeoos City Bd. of Educ., 674 F.2d 337 (5th Cir. 1982) (unwed pregnancy, not a per se "cause for discharge").

180. Erb v. Iowa State Board of Pub. Instruction, 216 N.W.2d 339 (Iowa 1974).

181. Jarvella v. Willoughby-Eastlake City School Dist. Board of Educ., 233 N.E.2d 143 (Ohio 1967).

182. de Groat v. Newark Unified School Dist., 133 Cal. Rptr. 225 (1976). *See also* the *Brown* case (Case 3.5 in Chapter 3).

183. Gross v. Board of Educ., 571 N.Y.S.2d 200 (1991); Greater Clark County School Corp. v. Myers, 493 N.E.2d 1267 (Ind. 1986); Annotation, *Damages—Teacher's Wrongful Discharge,* 22 A.L.R. 3d 1047 (1968) and pkt. part.

184. Annotation, prior note, at p. 1051.

185. Ibid., at p. 1052.

CHAPTER 6

Professional Employees: Civil Rights

CHAPTER OUTLINE

I. Constitutional and Statutory Spheres of National Civil Rights
II. Universal Constitutional Rights
    A. Procedural Rights—Due Process
        1. Parties Entitled to Due Process
            a. Liberty Interests
            b. Property Interests
        2. Due Process Procedures
            a. Notice and Hearing
            b. Prehearing Terminations and Suspensions
            c. Impartial Tribunal
            d. Right to Cross-Examine and Challenge Adverse Evidence
            e. Right to Counsel
            f. Hearing Record and Appeal
            g. Waiver or Cure of Defective Procedures
    B. Substantive Rights—Due Process
        1. Freedom of Expression
            a. Categories of Unprotected Expression
            b. Regulation of Time, Place, and Manner of Speech
            c. Public Forum Doctrines
            d. Classes of Protected Speech
            e. Political Speech
             f. Curriculum-Related Speech
            g. Symbolic Expression
            h. Associational Freedom
        2. Rights of Privacy
            a. Spatial Privacy—School Searches
            b. Spatial Privacy—Property Searches
            c. Spatial Privacy—Personal Searches
            d. Informational Privacy
            e. Decisional Privacy—Autonomy
    C. Remedies for Constitutional Violations

III. Topical Civil Rights—Equal Opportunity Laws
    A. Overview—Antidiscrimination Laws
        1. Constitutional Protections—Antidiscrimination
        2. Statutory Protections——Antidiscrimination
    B. Racial and Ethnic Discrimination
        1. Constitutional Protections—Race
        2. Statutory Protections—Race
            a. Title VII
            b. Title VI (Act of 1964) and § 1981 (Act of 1866)
    C. Gender Discrimination
        1. Constitutional Protections—Gender
        2. Statutory Protections—Gender
            a. Title VII
            b. Administrative Discrimination
            c. Sexual Harassment
            d. Same-Sex Harassment
            e. Mixed-Motive Decisions
            f. Wage Discrimination
            g. Equal Pay Act (EPA)
            h. Title IX
    D. Homosexual Discrimination
        1. Constitutional Protections—Homosexual Persons
        2. Statutory Protections—Homosexual Persons
    E. Disability Discrimination
        1. Constitutional Protections—Disability
        2. Statutory Protections—Disability
            a. What Is a "Disability" Under the ADA?
            b. "Reasonable Accommodation" Requirements
    F. Age Discrimination
        1. Constitutional Protections—Age
        2. Statutory Protections—Age
    G. Alien Discrimination
        1. Constitutional Protections—Aliens

     2. Statutory Protections—Aliens
  H. Religious Discrimination
     1. Constitutional Protections—Religion
     2. Statutory Protections—Religion
   I. Language Barriers
     1. Constitutional Protections—English Deficiency
     2. Statutory Protections—English Deficiency
   J. Concurrent Violations of Different Laws
  K. Immunity Defenses to Civil Rights Violations

CHAPTER DISCUSSION QUESTIONS

CASES

6.1 Curtis v. Oklahoma City Public Schools Board of Education, 147 F.3d 1200 (10th Cir. 1998)

6.2 Downs v. Los Angeles Un. School District, 228 F.3d 1003 (9th Cir. 2000), *cert. denied*, 121 S. Ct. 1653 (2001)

6.3 Lacks v. Ferguson Reorganized School Dist., 147 F.3d 719 (8th Cir. 1998)

6.4 O'Connor v. Ortega, 480 U.S. 709 (1987)

6.5 Aubrey v. School Board of Lafayette Parish, 148 F.3d 559 (5th Cir. 1998)

6.6 Taxman v. Board of Education, 91 F.3d 1547 (3d Cir. 1996)

6.7 Schroeder v. Hamilton School District, 282 F.3d 946 (7th Cir. 2002)

6.8 Faragher v. City of Boca Raton, 524 U.S. 775 (1998)

6.9 Oncale v. Sundowners Offshore Services, Inc., 118 S. Ct. 998 (1998)

6.10 Bibby v. Phila. Coca Cola Bottling Co., 260 F.3d 257 (3d Cir. 2001)

6.11 Salmon v. Dade County School Board, 4 F. Supp. 2d 1157 (S.D. Fla. 1998)

6.12 Auerbach v. Board of Educ. of the Harborfields Central School Dist., 136 F.3d 104 (2d Cir. 1997)

ENDNOTES

CONSTITUTIONAL AND STATUTORY SPHERES OF NATIONAL CIVIL RIGHTS

Chapter 5 dealt with employment rights and duties of public school teachers and other employees, largely under state school laws (e.g., those pertaining to teacher certification, ratings, nonrenewal, demotion, and tenure).

This chapter deals with nationwide civil rights under federal law. The universe of federal civil rights consists of two related but doctrinally distinct spheres of law: (1) the federal Constitution and (2) federal equal opportunity statutes. Both spheres include universal civil rights which are accorded to all persons, and special topical rights which are accorded only to identified classes of persons who are the object of special legal protection based on identified traits, e.g., race, gender, disability, alien status. In addition, state constitutions and special statutes also protect civil rights, in some instances to a greater degree than federal law (e.g., those dealing with teacher due process rights in discharge and disciplinary proceedings).[1] The state constitutions and laws are too varied to permit a fair summary of them in this text,[2] and interested parties must consult the laws of their home states to obtain a full picture of their civil rights and obligations.

Part II of this chapter deals with universal constitutional rights, largely under the Due Process Clause of the Fourteenth Amendment. Part III covers constitutional protections against discrimination, largely under the Equal Protection Clause of the Fourteenth Amendment, together with major federal antidiscrimination statutes which create rights and remedies beyond those afforded by the Constitution.

UNIVERSAL CONSTITUTIONAL RIGHTS

The Fourteenth Amendment, the principal source of constitutional civil rights, reads:

> **No State** shall make or enforce any law which shall abridge the privileges or immunities of citizens . . . ; nor shall any **state** deprive any **person** of life, **liberty** or property without **due process** of law; nor deny to any person . . . the **equal protection of the laws**. (Emphasis added)

The bold words, as construed by the Supreme Court, define and limit constitutional rights. Their significance will be seen shortly, but by way of preview, their impact may be summarized as follows. *First,* the key words "No State shall" speak only to "state action", i.e., acts attributable to the state or its subdivisions, such as public school districts. It does not speak to or govern the acts of individuals, even when their conduct is attributable to the state. *Second,* the Due Process and Equal Protection Clauses incorporate not only the guarantees enumerated in other parts of the Constitution, most notably freedom of religion, of assembly, of speech, and of the press (via the First Amendment), and freedom from unreasonable government searches (via the Fourth Amendment), but also rights considered to be *fundamental* to *liberty*, including certain parental and familial rights, and certain rights of privacy, even though those rights are not mentioned anywhere in the Constitution. *Third*, the words *"due process"* include *procedural* as well as *substantive* rights, resulting in separate categories of constitutional due process.

Procedural Rights—Due Process

A school decision that is made without required due process procedures is invalid even though that decision would have been lawful had due process been afforded. Obviously not every disputed school decision or person affected by a school decision is entitled to constitutional procedures, nor does the Constitution require the same procedures for every school decision where due process is required. Were the law so rigid, school operations would be paralyzed. The core questions, therefore, are twofold, namely, when is a party entitled to constitutional (as distinguished from statutory) due process procedures on a challenged school decision; and, where required, what procedures are sufficient to satisfy the constitutional standards of due process on specific school decisions?

Parties Entitled to Due Process

Only a party who has a constitutionally recognized *liberty* or *property interest* in the questioned school decision may claim a constitutional right to procedural due process. It should be emphasized that the interests that command *due process* protection are not required for constitutional rights of *equal protection* under the Equal Protection Clause.[3] Further, as hereafter noted, the nature and elements of a *liberty* interest are not the same as those of a *property* interest.

Liberty Interests.   Liberty interests are grounded in the Constitution. An obvious example is one's interest in exercising freedom of speech, so that a decision allegedly infringing that right must be made in accord with due process. A less obvious instance is a teacher's liberty to pursue his occupation, which may be destroyed by a decision that injures his reputation. To command due process, a school decision must not only involve a potential liberty interest, it must *infringe it*. A school report that has only a minimal effect on a teacher's reputation does not injure the teacher's liberty interest in reputation. For example, courts have found no injury to a liberty interest from school statements regarding (a) poor work habits; (b) noncooperation; (c) tardiness, absence, and failure to maintain discipline; (d) unsatisfactory work performance; and (e) aggressive behavior.[4] Furthermore, derogatory findings against a teacher were held not sufficiently stigmatizing as to require due process hearings where (a) the charges were undisclosed to the public, or (b) were undisputed or admitted by the teacher, or (c) involved a supervisor's personal opinion but not an official finding. Even where a board member opined to a nonofficial that "We need to get rid of that SOB",[5] that statement, albeit evidence of personal bias, was held not to place an *official* stigma injury on the teacher's reputation. On like reasoning, a district's failure to provide a public explanation for suspending and not renewing a teacher was found not to rise to the level of stigmatizing the teacher's reputation where the district did not publicize its actions or its reasons for those actions.[6] On the other hand, contested charges of dishonesty, emotional instability, and insubordination sufficiently affect an interest in professional reputation to require due process hearings.[7] In sum, the question whether a court will find that a liberty interest has been injured will depend on the context and effect of school actions in each case.

Property Interests.   Unlike liberty interests, property interests are not derived from the Constitution, but from state law.

> Property interests . . . are not created by the Constitution. Rather they are created and their dimensions are defined by existing rules and understandings that stem from an independent source such as state law, rules or regulations. . . . [*Board of Regents v. Roth*, 408 U.S. 564, 577 (1972)]

Tenure and certification rights that are created by state statutes are recognized species of property interests; hence, tenure and certification status cannot be withdrawn without constitutional due process at a minimum, although that minimum is often met by higher procedural protections.[8] Where state law does not vest rights to a particular school position, e.g., as a principal, the holder may not claim a constitutional property interest in continuation of employment in that position.[9] As seen in the teacher nonrenewal cases in Chapter 5 and in the *Curtis* case (Case 6.1 at the end of the chapter), many school positions do not involve a property interest and thus do not qualify for constitutional due process. In exceptional circumstances, a court may find a property interest founded upon unwritten custom, but most courts have refused to find a custom-based property interest.[10]

Due Process Procedures

Once due process is required, the question arises: What process is due? To that question, there is no uniform answer, only a formula.

> The very nature of due process negates any concept of inflexible procedures universally applicable to every imaginable situation. [*Goss v. Lopez*, 419 U.S., at 578 (1975)]

> Due process . . . is not a technical conception with a fixed content unrelated to time, place and circumstances. . . . [*Ingraham v. Wright*, 430 U.S. 651, 675 (1977)]

The Supreme Court in the *Goss* case ruled that due process does not require the same procedures that are used by courts or the same procedures for all school decisions. Rather, the core element of constitutional due process is *fair treatment,* which requires "some kind of hearing" to afford a teacher the opportunity to be notified of and respond to proposed changes or charges. In exigent cases, due process may be satisfied by a postponed hearing, e.g., where a teacher is removed without a hearing on credible allegations of serious misconduct that could threaten school stability or safety. In such cases, however, a fair hearing must be afforded the affected teacher with reasonable promptness following his or her removal.[11]

Unless waived by the affected party, due process requires at a minimum the first three of the following elements:

1.   Reasonable *notice* of the charges or subject of the hearing, which allows a fair *opportunity to prepare* for the hearing,
2.   A *reasonably prompt hearing,* and
3.   An *impartial tribunal* to hear and decide the charges.

Where required by law or fairness, due process may also require one or more of the following additional procedures:

4.   The right to present *evidence* and to *confront* adverse witnesses and evidence,
5.   The right to be represented by legal *counsel,*
6.   The right to an *official record* of the proceeding, and
7.   The right to *appeal* the hearing decisions to higher authority.

What procedures are required beyond the minimum of notice and hearing depend, in the words of the Supreme Court, on the following factors:

> First, the private interest that will be affected . . . ; second, the risk of erroneous deprivation of such interest . . . and the probable value, if any, of additional or substitute procedural safeguards; and, finally, the [public] interests, including the functions involved and the fiscal or administrative burdens that the additional or substitute procedural requirements would entail. [*Mathews v. Eldridge,* 424 U.S. 319, 335 (1976)]

Thus, the need for progressively greater hearing formalities will depend on the need for them to protect the individual's interest, on one hand, and the fiscal and operational burdens that additional procedures would impose on the school administration, on the other. Concrete guidance for applying these factors to specific case circumstances can only be gathered from prior court decisions.[12]

Notice and Hearing.   When process is due, a hearing must be provided unless it is waived or would be pointless, e.g., where the pertinent facts are not disputed and the school board has no discretion but to take legally prescribed action on those facts.[13] If the timing and location of hearings are unfairly set, e.g., within hours after the notice of hearing is delivered, the hearing and resulting teacher discharge are void and subject to reversal.[14] A hearing notice must contain sufficient information to enable the addressee to ascertain and respond to the charges. While school authorities need not provide minute specification of all evidence on a charge, a notice that is unreasonably vague on the charge, or a school board denial of teacher access to essential evidence will nullify the proceedings.[15] Another example of an unfair hearing arose where new charges that potentially supported additional penalties were added at the hearing, but had not been mentioned in a prior notice. Those additions were held to require a new notice and hearing, even though the additional charges were based on the same conduct that led to the prior charges.[16]

The fair notice principle has also been expressed by the void for vagueness doctrine, which invalidates statutes and regulations that do not contain sufficient information to enable persons of ordinary intelligence to ascertain whether their conduct is prohibited and will be punishable.[17]

Prehearing Terminations and Suspensions.   The normal requirement that notice and hearing be afforded *before* adverse action is taken against a teacher may be excused where overriding needs of school safety and security justify immediate action, so long as a hearing is set as promptly as practical thereafter.[18] Where prehearing action is contested, courts must decide whether the alleged threats to school interests were sufficiently grave or imminent to justify action before a hearing.[19] Absent such exigencies, courts have nullified prehearing actions that caused irreparable damage to an employee's reputation and employment prospects.[20]

Impartial Tribunal.   Hearings by biased officials or tribunals are by definition unfair and unconstitutional. However, the constitutional standard of an impartial tribunal is much looser for school decisions than for court decisions. School boards and their members are presumed to be impartial, and the burden of establishing bias by a hearing panel rests with the party alleging such bias. The presumption of impartiality may be rebutted by evidence of malice, fixed prejudgment, or conflict of interest on the part of a hearing officer or board members, but the burden of proving such bias can be fairly heavy. The Supreme Court upheld a school board discharge of a teacher for participating in an illegal strike, even though the board was involved in heated labor negotiations that led to the strike. The Court concluded that the board members' participation in the labor negotiations did not involve their personal or financial interests so as to engender personal bias on their part.[21] In like vein, prehearing board investigations or public statements regarding a teacher's personal conduct or performance do not alone void later board hearings without proof that board members were not open to fresh consideration of the charges on the basis of evidence presented at the later hearing.[22] Conversely, if a teacher satisfies a court that a board member or hearing officer irrevocably prejudged a case, a later hearing will not restore board impartiality or validate its decision.[23] A court had little difficulty in overturning a disciplinary hearing against a teacher where a participating board member was previously involved in a fight with the teacher.[24] In some circumstances, a court may conclude that even the appearance of personal bias denies due process. When a board member's wife testified against a school principal in a demotion hearing and was present during board deliberations and vote on the principal's demotion, the court voided the proceedings.[25] Other common grounds for destroying impartiality include hearings where the same person acts as both judge and witness against the teacher, or as both hearing prosecutor and legal counsel to the deciding tribunal.[26] The importance of specific case circumstances is seen in decisions which held that the participation of school solicitors as prosecutors in school board hearings may not destroy the board's impartiality where the solicitor did not counsel the board in its deliberations.[27]

Right to Cross-Examine and Challenge Adverse Evidence. The right to cross-examine adverse witnesses, a fixed requisite in court hearings, does not extend to all school administrative hearings. In many cases, the charges and affected interests are not sufficiently weighty to require full dress cross-examination. For example, in the above quoted *Goss* case, the Court held that cross-examination was not required for a summary disciplinary hearing on a minor student infraction.

There is no clear pattern of court opinions on the question when teacher interests are sufficiently weighty to require cross-examination or to prohibit the use of hearsay evidence that cannot be cross-examined.[28] Some examples of situations that required allowance of cross-examination of witnesses include board failure to disclose information essential to a defense, or exclusion of a party from a hearing where evidence adverse to that party is being offered, or where the board previously refused a request to produce a material witness (examining doctor).[29]

Right to Counsel. The right to have one's lawyer attend and conduct cross-examination of witnesses will also depend on a court's decision whether the assistance of legal counsel is fairly needed.

> The requirement of counsel as an ingredient of fairness is a function of all of the other aspects of the hearing. Where the proceeding is non-criminal in nature, where the hearing is investigative and not adversarial and the government does not proceed through counsel, where the individual concerned is mature and educated, where his knowledge of the events . . . should enable him to develop the facts adequately through available sources, and where the other aspects of the hearing taken as a whole are fair, due process does not require representation by counsel. [*Wasson v. Trowbridge*, 383 F.2d 807 (2d Cir. 1967)]

Hearing Record and Appeal. The right to a written or electronic record of a particular proceeding is strongest where the teacher interests are substantial and where the law provides for a right to appeal the hearing decision to a higher tribunal.[30] In such cases, courts may require that an adequate hearing record be prepared and available in order to ensure fair and informed review by the appellate tribunal.[31]

Waiver or Cure of Defective Procedures.   A party may expressly or by conduct waive objections to all or some due process defaults, if the waiver is made freely and knowingly. Any lawful waiver forecloses the right to complain later of defects covered by that waiver.[32]

Where due process was denied or defective, school authorities may cure the error by timely provision of proper substitute procedures, provided such substituted procedures do not unfairly burden or prejudice the affected party's defense.[33]

Substantive Rights—Due Process

The substantive rights protected by the Due Process Clause include those enumerated in the Constitution (e.g., freedoms of speech, association, and religion, and freedom from unreasonable searches), as well as unenumerated fundamental rights (e.g., rights to bodily security, autonomy on decisions regarding familial relations and reproduction, and the right to be free from irrational official restraints or punishments). These rights are noted in the *Curtis* and *Lacks* opinions (Cases 6.1 and 6.3, respectively). Laws and regulations whose purpose or means of enforcement have no rational relationship to a legitimate state interest are, therefore, unconstitutional. Laws are, however, presumed to be rational so that a party challenging a law or regulation as irrational has the burden of demonstrating that it lacks a rational foundation.[34] Such challenges are relatively uncommon and usually unsuccessful.

Freedom of Expression

The First Amendment protection of free speech rights against unwarranted school suppression or penalties is neither simple nor straightforward because the scope of "freedom of speech" varies with the context and content of speech. Several different doctrines and standards control the scope of free speech. First, certain *categories* of expression are denied any constitutional protection. Second, *government* speech that expresses official policies is not subject to the same constitutional constraints as *private* speech. Third, *forum* doctrines determine the *free speech zones* where expression is or is not protected by the First Amendment. Fourth, the measure of constitutional protection of private speech differs for speech that is deemed to involve a matter of *public concern* as opposed to speech that is deemed to involve a matter of *personal concern.*

In addition to these factors, courts particularly disfavor "prior restraints" that forbid expression on a particular subject, as contrasted with punishment of speech after it has been uttered. To justify a prior restraint, school authorities must establish clear proof of an overriding school interest.[35] Courts have voided as an unconstitutional prior restraint a school prohibition of teacher comment to the press that was intended to avoid partisan tensions or to maintain confidentiality of school desegregation plans.[36] A school's "don't ask, don't tell" policy for homosexuals was also overturned as a basis for denial of contract renewal to a lesbian volleyball coach.[37]

Forced expression also violates freedom of speech. In upholding a teacher's right to decline to salute the flag in school exercises one court observed that "[T]he right to remain silent . . . is as much a part of First Amendment protections as the right to speak out in the face of an illegitimate demand for silence." [*Russo v. Central School Dist. No. 1*, 469 F.2d 623, 634 (2d Cir. 1972)] However, where a teacher refuses not only to salute the flag, but also to conduct a required classroom pledge of allegiance exercise, the courts must decide whether her right of expression or her classroom duty should prevail in the balance. Some courts solved that problem by allowing teachers to have a student or other person conduct the exercise while respectfully standing aside, on the reasoning that the teacher's expressive silence did not disrupt or undermine the school's program.[38]

To prevail on a retaliation claim, the employee must show not only that the alleged speech was protected speech, but that the alleged retaliatory action was intended to penalize that speech. Such cases raise mixed-motive issues as to whether the challenged school decision was substantially motivated by official disapproval of that speech, and whether the school authorities would have made the same decision independently of the claimant's speech.[39] Thus, where a teacher claimed that the school board had retaliated against her for exposing wrongdoing in her department by abolishing her position and dismissing her, the court refused to overturn her dismissal because she did not prove that her reports of wrongdoings were a substantial or motivating factor behind the decision to dismiss her.[40] Similarly, where a teacher sued school officials charging that they retaliated against her for actively supporting a fellow teacher in a labor grievance proceeding, by subjecting her to extra weekly meetings with a supervisor under a Corrective Action (Professional Development) Plan, the court dismissed her claim as not supported by evidence that the contested action was substantially motivated by a desire to penalize her speech activities.[41]

Categories of Unprotected Expression.   The First Amendment does not protect defamatory statements (subject to special exceptions for the public press), obscene expression, "fighting words", and speech that is classified as a "true threat" to others. These categories are not of major concern to school teachers and employees although they have taken on increased importance for violent student speech, as discussed in Chapter 7. The law discussed there provides adequate references for the relatively few occasions where teacher expression falls within the above categories.

Regulation of Time, Place, and Manner of Speech.   While school authorities may not prohibit all personal speech on school premises, they may reserve certain times and places exclusively for school-related uses and deny access to them for personal speech, provided that such regulations do not selectively exclude only particular speakers, speech content, or viewpoints. The clearest examples are cases that penalize students and teachers for using class sessions for personal expression unrelated to class studies.[42]

Public Forum Doctrines.   "Forum" doctrines also determine whether particular school locations or programs qualify as free speech zones, and when school officials may constitutionally limit access to school facilities or programs for private speech purposes. The forum limits of protected speech were well summarized in the following case:

> In a traditional public forum, such as a park or sidewalks, restrictions on speech are subject to strict scrutiny and regulations must be "narrowly drawn to achieve a compelling state interest. . . . All remaining property is nonpublic fora." *DiLoreto v. Downey Unified School Dist. Bd. of Educ.*, 196 F.3d 958, 965 (9th Cir. 1999). The government may, however, create a "limited public forum" by intentionally opening a nonpublic forum to certain groups or topics. *Id.* In such a case, restrictions are permissible if they are viewpoint neutral and reasonable in light of the purposes served by the forum. *Id.; see also Rosenberger v. Rector & Visitors of the Univ. of Virginia*, 555 U.S. 819, 829, . . . (1995). [*Hills v. Scottsdale Unified School Dist.*, 329 F.3d 1044, 1049 (9th Cir. 2003)]

For clear examples as to when forum doctrines allow or prohibit school authorities to deny freedom of speech at particular school sites or activities, see the *Good News Club* case (Case 3.1 in Chapter 3) and the *Downs* case in this chapter (Case 6.2). Forum doctrines do not generally constrain normal workaday school-site speech of teachers and students. They do, however, significantly affect rights of access to school facilities by outsiders or by persons who wish to contest official school policies. Since, as noted above, school facilities and programs are not traditional public forums, school officials may reasonably control access to them by designating certain facilities as nonpublic or as limited public forums, so long as they do not exclude parties solely because of their particular viewpoints.

Classes of Protected Speech.   The measure of constitutional speech protection varies for different categories. School communications of official policies constitute *government speech*, which is not subject to the same constitutional constraints as private speech:

> We hold that when the school district speaks through bulletin boards that are not "free speech zones," but instead are vehicles for conveying a message from the school district, the school district may formulate that message *without the constraint of viewpoint neutrality.* Here, LAUSD, an arm of local government, is firmly policing the boundaries of its own message. As such, LAUSD did not violate Downs's First Amendment free speech rights. (Emphasis added) [*Downs v. Los Angeles Un. School Dist.,* 228 F.3d 1003 (9th Cir. 2000)]

With respect to school regulation of purely *private* speech, the Supreme Court has classified speech for constitutional purposes in two distinct classes, and adopted different standards of protection for each class, namely, speech on matters of *public concern* and speech on matters of *personal concern*. For *public concern* speech, the Supreme Court applies the "disruption" test, which it formulated in the *Pickering* case and which is discussed below, while for *personal concern* speech, it applies the looser "reasonableness" test, which it formulated in the *Connick* case, also discussed below. In speaking out on a matter of *public concern*, teachers may not be penalized unless their speech imminently threatens or actually *disrupts or interferes* with school operations. But in expressing a matter of *personal concern*, teachers may be punished if school authorities reasonably believe that the speech, though not disruptive, would undermine the efficient operation of the school.

The Court rationalized these distinct tests as follows:

> [T]he State has interests as an employer in regulating the speech of its employees that differ significantly from those it possesses in connection with regulation of speech of the citizenry in general. The problem in any case is to arrive at a balance between the interests of the teacher, as a citizen, in commenting upon matters of public concern and the interest of the State, as an employer, in promoting the efficiency of the public services it performs through its employees. [*Pickering v. Board of Educ.,* 391 U.S. 563, 568 (1968)]

> We hold only that when a public employee speaks not as a citizen upon matters of public concern, but instead as an employee upon matters only of personal interest, absent the most unusual circumstances, a federal court is not the appropriate forum in which to review the wisdom of a personnel decision. . . . [*Connick v. Myers,* 461 U.S. 138, 147 (1983)]

> Whether an employee's speech addresses a matter of public concern must be determined by the content, form, and context of a given statement as revealed by the whole record. . . . Because of the enormous variety of fact situations in which critical statements . . . may be thought . . . to furnish grounds for dismissal, we do not deem it either appropriate or feasible to lay down a general standard against which all such statements may be judged. . . . . . . Although such particularized

> balancing is difficult, the courts must reach the most appropriate possible balance
> of the competing interests. . . . [*Connick v. Myers, supra,* at p. 150]

In the *Pickering* case, the Court overturned school dismissal of a teacher for writing a letter to a newspaper during a school election campaign that criticized the school board's management of school revenues and its allocation of school resources. The Court later extended its protection of public concern speech to oral, face-to-face criticisms by a teacher to her principal regarding the school's racial policies because, in the Court's view, her expression involved a matter of public concern and her private encounter with her principal could not reasonably be deemed to undermine the efficient operation of the school.[43]

An important exception to the stricter protection of public concern speech is made for persons holding policy-making responsibilities. Such an employee has no constitutional right publicly to contradict or oppose the official policy of the employer school or school district, even though that policy is obviously a matter of public concern. Courts accordingly upheld a school principal's demotion for speaking out against his school district's efforts to secure legislative financial aid for districts that served disadvantaged children.[44]

The importance of classifying speech is also illustrated by the *Connick* case, in which the Court upheld dismissal of an assistant district attorney for circulating within the district attorney's office her criticism of the office operations. The Court rejected her claim that her speech involved a matter of public concern and not a personal employment grievance. Another court upheld discipline of a schoolteacher for giving a public speech that her supervisor reasonably believed (albeit mistakenly) undermined the efficiency of school operations.[45]

The application of the foregoing tests to a particular case has a critical impact inasmuch as the school's burden of proving that public concern speech threatens actual or imminent disruption of school functions is significantly more difficult to meet than is the school's burden of proving that school authorities had reasonable grounds to believe that private concern speech would reduce the efficiency of school operations. Put another way, a teacher's right to communicate his or her views as a citizen on a school matter of *public concern* outweighs school interests in harmonious relations absent proof that the speech is disruptive, whereas a teacher's freedom to speak on a matter of *personal concern* does not outweigh that school interest.

The difficulty of predicting which of the public concern/private speech classifications may govern a given case is illustrated by the following case samples. The Supreme Court Justices split 5–4 on the question whether (a) a police station comment by a police department clerk to a fellow employee that she wished an attempt to assassinate President Reagan would succeed qualified as speech on a matter of public concern and (b) whether that speech was disruptive or protected from disciplinary punishment.[46] A teacher who questioned the accuracy of school attendance records was also held to have spoken on a matter of public concern, but the court found that her speech was nevertheless disruptive of school working relationships and therefore punishable under the *Pickering* test. But another court held that a teacher statement that school authorities misrepresented student scores on standardized achievement tests was not disruptive and therefore was protected from punishment.[47] While one court applied the *Connick* test to uphold teacher discharge for criticizing superiors,[48] another court viewed a teacher's remark at a union meeting that the board was attempting to buy off teachers with small concessions as speech on a matter of public, not personal, concern and therefore not constitutionally punishable.

The environment of critical speech is an important factor.[49] Orderly criticisms of school policies at a school-sponsored public forum and in scholarly journals are protected expression. A teacher's remarks at a public school board meeting which impugned his superintendent as a liar were constitutionally punishable.[50] Similarly, a teacher who helped distribute a pamphlet containing false accusations against a school principal was punishable though she did not author the pamphlet, while a teacher who encouraged students to print an underground newspaper, without instigating its particular content, was not found to be disruptive.[51] Clearer examples of disruptive speech are found in activities that threaten personal safety and security at school.[52]

Political Speech. Among topics of expression, political speech, being of public concern, commands the strongest constitutional protection. Teacher wearing of an armband to school, to express an antiwar position, was held to be nondisruptive speech and constitutionally protected from school control. But a teacher who left the school in order to join an antiwar rally could not claim protection from school punishment because that expressive action was disruptive.[53] A teacher request for permission to sponsor a political symposium was not so threatening as to justify a school penalty, but the use of class time to promote union activity or to organize civil rights groups was constitutionally punishable.[54] A teacher's false denial that he made certain statements was not constitutionally protected and could be punished by discharge.[55]

The constitutional protection of political speech does not extend to partisan political campaigning. In contrast to the wearing of a passive antiwar armband, school site wearing of political campaign buttons during instructional time is not constitutionally protected. A teacher who desired to wear a campaign button to oppose a California initiative to adopt a voucher system of financing elementary and secondary education unsuccessfully challenged the state law that prohibited public school districts from sponsoring or subsidizing distribution of partisan political materials. The court noted, however, that the ban might not be constitutional if applied to noninstructional settings.[56]

Curriculum-Related Speech. School punishment of teachers for use of unauthorized class materials or exercises also tests the limits of speech protection. Teacher efforts to organize and develop instructional materials and methods, however admirable, should not be mistaken for a constitutional right to do so independently of school control. Most cases have upheld punishment of teachers for curricular practices that violated school directives,[57] and most cases that reversed such punishments rested on grounds other than freedom of speech, such as unfair or arbitrary penalties.[58] The Supreme Court statements in the *Pico* decision, reported in Chapter 2, and in the following college labor case warn against facile assumptions that there is a *constitutional right* of academic freedom that limits school authority to control expression regarding the school curriculum.

> Appellees [teachers] have no constitutional right to force the government to listen to their views . . . . The academic setting . . . does not alter this conclusion. To be sure there is a strong . . . tradition of faculty participation in school governance. . . . *But this Court has never recognized a constitutional right of faculty to participate in policymaking in academic institutions.* (Emphasis added) [*Minn. State Bd. of Comm'y Colleges v. Knight*, 485 U.S. 271, 283, 287 (1985)]

The *Lacks* case (Case 6.3) rejected the teacher's claim of academic leeway to make classroom assignments beyond the scope of school-approved curriculum. Courts have also denied constitutional shelter to extemporaneous classroom discussions of sex topics, and even to a teacher's decision to discipline an 11-year-old girl for using a vulgar word during school recess by having her write the vulgar word 1,000 times.[59]

The difficulty of importing the higher education model of academic freedom into public schools is manifest in three decisions by the First Circuit Court of Appeals.[60] The court, groping for a constitutional foothold for academic freedom for public school teachers, began by preliminarily enjoining discharge of a high school English teacher for refusing to obey a school order that he discontinue classroom discussion of an offensive epithet following his assigned class reading that explored its uses. One year later the same court refused to stop a university from closing down a campus art exhibit by one of its professors, though the university previously authorized the exhibit, because the court found that the vulgar art captions would be exposed to women and children passing through the campus.[61] In the third case, the court skirted the constitutional question while reversing a teacher discharge for making a transitory reference to a vulgar word for sexual intercourse during a class discussion of taboo words, but it did so on the unrelated ground that the school regulation against the practice was unconstitutionally vague. While insisting that it "in no way" regretted its prior decisions, the First Circuit nevertheless signaled a retreat by stating: "We confess that we are not of one mind as to whether the plaintiff's conduct fell within the protection of the First Amendment."[62] To which remark, the neighboring Second Circuit Court of Appeals commented: "While the First Circuit has indicated that it does not 'regret' its decision in *Keefe v. Geanakos, supra*, its enthusiasm for intrusion into academic issues seems to be lessening."[63] Perhaps the trend against a free-standing constitutional academic freedom reflects a general shift in sentiment away from expanded personal liberties toward greater official control of public school discipline. The foregoing cases do not cover the full range of questions on teacher classroom autonomy, but they do caution against confusing policy arguments with constitutional rights.

Symbolic Expression.   Nonverbal acts, e.g., armbands, political buttons, picketing, and flag burning may qualify as expression covered by the First Amendment. However, courts do not give like weight to all types of symbolic expression, tending to give greater protection to symbolic political expression than to symbolic expression in the choice of one's appearance and dress. The limited case law on the right to control one's appearance varies by region.

With regard to choice of appearance, the more recent cases tend to follow the guideline which the Supreme Court adopted for hair regulation of policemen.[64] That guideline treated choice of hair style more as a generalized substantive liberty that is subject to reasonable regulation, than as an elemental freedom of expression for which official control would require a stronger government need. "Thus the question is not . . . whether the State can establish a genuine public need for the specific regulation. . . . The constitutional issue . . . is whether the petitioner's [employer's] determination . . . is so irrational that it may be branded 'arbitrary,' and therefore a deprivation of respondent's 'liberty' interest in freedom to choose his own hair style."[65] Under this approach, appearance regulations are *prima facie* valid with the burden on challengers to show that they lack a rational basis. Where appearance regulations do not afford teachers fair notice or warning that certain attire or grooming is prohibited and subject to disciplinary penalties, those regulations may be overturned on due process grounds.[66]

Liberty interests in choice of dress may also be limited by or subordinated to school interests. Courts upheld nonrenewal of a teacher who refused to lengthen her miniskirt, and sustained male dress code requirements of jackets and ties.[67] Prohibitions of religious garb or symbols while at school have not been extensively tested, but the Supreme Court dismissed an appeal seeking to overturn an Oregon statute that prohibited religious garb in public schools. While not a formal ruling, that action suggests that a legislature may constitutionally ban or limit teacher religious garb in public schools, assuming the details of the ban are not unreasonable or unduly vague.[68] A federal court also upheld a state law prohibiting religious garb against a challenge that it violated the antidiscrimination provisions and religious accommodation requirements of Title VII of the federal Civil Rights Act.[69]

The wearing of small pins, bracelets, or insignia containing religious symbols has not been seriously challenged by test litigation. Such symbols may command greater protection than overtly religious habits or obtrusive sectarian symbols in assessing the relative weight of the school and personal interests.[70]

Associational Freedom.   Closely related to freedom of expression is the constitutional right of individuals to associate and to express themselves through associations, be they political, social, labor related, or familial. School decisions that favor or disfavor teachers solely because of their affiliation with a particular political party are classic examples of unconstitutional abridgement.[71] The right of association includes teacher rights to belong to a religious order, to marry a civil rights activist, and to opt to send a child to a private, rather than to a public, school. School board denial of employment opportunities or benefits to teachers for electing such associations have been overturned as unconstitutional penalties against the exercise of freedom of association.[72] A board's refusal to renew a teacher's contract because she was living with a person she intended to marry was overturned as an infringement of a constitutional right of intimate association.[73] That decision is indirectly fortified by the latest Supreme Court decision which, on a different due process liberty ground, held that states could not punish private, consensual homosexual conduct. See the discussion of *Lawrence v. Garner*, 123 S. Ct. 2472 (2003), later in this chapter.

As with speech, rights of association may be limited by overriding school interests. Group expression that diverts a teacher from assigned teaching duties[74] or incites disharmony and disruption of school working relationships is not constitutionally protected.[75]

Rights of Privacy

The Constitution protects three distinct areas of privacy, namely:

> *Spatial privacy—school searches,* such as protection from unreasonable government search of persons and places;
>
> *Informational privacy,* such as protection from compelled disclosure of certain types of personal information; and
>
> *Decisional privacy,* such as protection from government interference with certain personal decisions.

Each of the above species of privacy has a separate history and doctrinal foundation. Spatial privacy is expressly governed by the Fourth Amendment, whereas decisional and informational privacy rest on unenumerated rights under less developed law.

Spatial Privacy—School Searches.   The Fourth Amendment guarantees persons "the right . . . to be secure in their persons, houses, papers and effects against *unreasonable* searches and seizures" (Emphasis added) The following discussion deals only with the law of "searches" as it applies to schools, and does not cover the more technical and complex law of "seizures", except to note that evidence seized as a result of an unconstitutional search may be suppressed in court proceedings, but that some courts have allowed such evidence to be used in school disciplinary proceedings.[76] Evidence issues aside, the potential of personal liability for infringing a person's constitutional right to be free from unlawful searches, as discussed in Chapter 8, is a powerful reason for caution in undertaking a public school search.

The Fourth Amendment applies only to parties who have a "reasonable expectation of privacy" in the subject of the search. The validity of school searches therefore turns on two questions: Who has a reasonable expectation of privacy in given materials, and if a person has a sufficient privacy interest, what legal standards determine whether a challenged search is "reasonable"or unconstitutional?

The following situations typically do not support a reasonable expectation of privacy and are not, therefore, subject to Fourth Amendment search limitations: searches that are made with the consent of the affected party[77]; searches of contraband material that the owner or possessor left "in plain view" of passersby; emergency searches undertaken to avoid a serious threat of harm; searches of property in school custody that are made to identify, inventory, and preserve property whose owners are unknown, confined, arrested, or otherwise disabled; searches of abandoned property; and in appropriate circumstances routine inspection searches for the preservation and maintenance of public school property.

A party who consents to a search, who leaves material exposed to "plain view", or who knows or should know that school authorities reserve the right to make routine inspections of school-owned enclosures or materials that are subject to normal supervisory oversight obviously lacks a reasonable privacy expectation. Even videotaping of a teacher's classroom by school supervisors has been found not to violate any expectation of privacy.[78]

Spatial Privacy—Property Searches. The lead Supreme Court decision on search rights of public employees provides a direct analog for public school searches. *O'Connor v. Ortega* (Case 6.4) held that a warrantless search by state hospital administrators of a physician's workplace office, desk, and files could be constitutionally made without individualized suspicion of illegal activity by the physician, if found to be reasonable under the circumstances. While the Court acknowledged that the affected physician had some expectation of privacy in those enclosures, it ruled that his privacy expectation was reduced by the nature of his workplace, stating: "We hold, therefore, that public employer intrusions on the constitutionally protected privacy interests of government employees for non-investigatory, work-related purposes, as well as for investigations of work-related misconduct, should be judged by the standard of reasonableness under all the circumstances." In holding that the same "reasonableness" test applied to both *investigatory* and *noninvestigatory* searches, and that searches of government-owned enclosures could be made without individualized suspicion of a law violation, for purposes of enforcing employer *regulations,* this decision cut away important limitations of earlier law. It also dispensed with any lingering argument that school authorities would need "probable cause" to suspect criminal activity, like a policeman, in order to undertake a search.

O'Connor confirmed the importance of circumstances in assessing the employee's expectations of privacy in desks and files, noting that such expectations may be reduced or destroyed where the searched places or enclosures are subject to continual entry or inspection by fellow employees or supervisors.[79] A court later applied these standards to reject a teacher claim that school authorities violated his Fourth Amendment rights by searching his former desk, file cabinet, tests, quizzes, and educational materials following his dismissal (and conviction) for sexual misconduct with a student. Since the teacher failed to clean out his desk and files, and the school had legal claim to the searched property, the court found that the teacher had no reasonable expectation of privacy in any of the contents.[80]

The use of advanced technology to probe and identify contents of enclosed containers raises new, untested questions. The Supreme Court recently ruled that police use of a sensing device outside a house to detect and measure heat waves emanating through the house exterior walls, in order to detect thermal evidence of marijuana processing inside the house, constituted an unconstitutional search because the police had not established probable cause to suspect criminal activity or obtained a court warrant to conduct the search.[81] While police search cases do not govern school administrative searches, the decision does raise the question whether school use of other external means to detect contraband in school enclosures may also qualify as a search for Fourth Amendment purposes. For example, school authorities have used trained dogs to sniff and detect drugs or explosives in school desks, file cabinets, or lockers.

Spatial Privacy—Personal Searches.   The bounds of privacy expectations at school are being narrowed as concerns over school safety in the face of school violence, drug activities, and sexual abuse increase the pressure to intensify school property searches. Routine, nonintrusive medical examinations do not involve a constitutional expectation of privacy and are not subject to Fourth Amendment restrictions, but intrusive medical examinations or tests that are not part of routine medical checkups implicate privacy expectations, much as do searches for materials hidden in or on a person's body, clothing, or personal effects.

The *Aubrey* opinion (Case 6.5) upheld suspicionless drug testing of a school custodian, while another case upheld suspicionless drug testing (by urinalysis) of applicants for teaching positions and of employed teachers and principals who applied for a transfer or promotion.[82] Those cases extended to teacher searches the safety-sensitive position rationale under which the Supreme Court upheld suspicionless drug testing of trainmen and federal customs agents, and under which the Court later invoked the danger prevention justification to uphold searches of all high school student athletes in a drug-ridden school, though the authorities lacked individualized suspicion of drug use by most of the searched students. The student search cases are discussed in Chapter 7.

The safety-sensitive rationale has uncharted potential to modify prior law, which condemned mandatory urinalysis and blood testing of school employees unless those tests were required by state health laws, or unless school authorities could show an individualized "reasonable" suspicion that the tested individual's condition threatened work performance or well-being of others[83] and that the school's need for medical information could not be met by less intrusive means than the challenged test.[84] The choice between the older case approach based on specified school needs,[85] and the broader approach based on a classification of certain school positions as "safety sensitive" remains to be clarified in future cases.

With respect to teacher drug use, a federal appeals court recently upheld discharge of a teacher for refusing to take a drug test after marijuana was found in her car during a police drug sweep.[86] The court was able to rely on the police discovery to justify the testing demand as based on a reasonable suspicion that the teacher had violated the school's drug policy.

The Constitution requires that a search be reasonable in *scope*, as well as in purpose. Intrusive medical examinations may also be challenged on due process grounds that they are unfair, unreliable or inaccurate, whether in the method of collecting, preserving, or transporting tested specimens, or in the diagnostic procedures to evaluate the tested specimens. These objections were addressed and analyzed by the Supreme Court and other courts in student urinalysis cases. These cases, which are reviewed in Chapter 7, should also be read for their impact on teacher searches.

Informational Privacy. The law regarding the types of personal information that qualify for constitutional protection is relatively new and undeveloped.

> Virtually every governmental action interferes with personal privacy to some degree. . . . Inferring very broad "constitutional" rights where the Constitution itself does not express them is an activity not appropriate to the judiciary. . . . . . . [We] conclude that the Constitution does not encompass a general right to nondisclosure of private information. . . . Our opinion does not mean that we attach little significance to the right of privacy, or that there is no constitutional right to nondisclosure of private information. . . . Our opinion simply holds that not all rights of privacy or interests in nondisclosure of private information are of constitutional dimension. . . . [*J.P. v. DeSanti,* 653 F.2d 1080, 1090–1091 (6th Cir. 1981)]

Public records statutes provide some legislative benchmarks for setting the limits of public and private interests in particular records, but they vary from state to state. Where statutes open school records to public inspection, courts are likely to reject claims of informational privacy, even as to teacher personnel files.[87] Conversely, courts are likely to enforce statutes or union-bargained contracts that shield items of personal information from public disclosure. Where state laws entrust to administrators the task of judging whether a teacher's privacy interest in personal information should outweigh or be subordinated to public needs for its disclosure, courts are likely to defer to administrative judgments.[88] Since the law of each state on employee records varies, one must look to the relevant law of the governing state.[89]

As with searches, the balance between an individual's recognized privacy claim and various public disclosure interests that might outweigh and subordinate that privacy interest (e.g., to ensure employee fitness or school safety) will depend on case circumstances.[90]

Decisional Privacy—Autonomy.   Certain decisions, such as decisions regarding marriage, reproduction, and certain family relationships, have been treated by courts as involving a constitutional "liberty", with the result that laws and regulations that infringe those rights have been overturned as unconstitutional. The decided cases do not cover the full range of personal decisions that might qualify for decisional privacy protection. A recent Supreme Court decision, *Lawrence v. Texas*, 123 S. Ct. 2472 (2003), recognized a constitutional right of adults to engage in private, consensual, homosexual conduct, but whether that decision reaches school-site or school-related conduct is open to further clarification. Its possible implications are discussed in a later section that deals with homosexual orientation and conduct.

Various state statutes prohibit government interference with specified personal decisions, but their selective coverages do not indicate a general pattern of decisional privacy rights.[91]

Remedies for Constitutional Violations

The Constitution does not specify remedies for its violation. Unless a statute authorizes "legal relief" of monetary damages for a constitutional violation, courts can only employ their equity powers to order "equitable relief", namely, to enjoin the violation and to order affirmative actions (other than money damages) in order to rectify the constitutional injury. To provide monetary relief for injury to constitutional rights, Congress enacted the general remedial statute (42 U.S.C. § 1983), which creates a species of tort liability for deprivation of federal rights and authorizes monetary recoveries for violation of those rights. The peculiar features and operation of that statute require separate study and are reviewed in Chapter 8. As explained there and in the following part, the remedies for constitutional injuries are not coextensive with those remedies that are specified by individual antidiscrimination statutes.

TOPICAL CIVIL RIGHTS—EQUAL OPPORTUNITY LAWS

Overview—Antidiscrimination Laws

Protections against discrimination are found both in the Constitution and in an assortment of antidiscrimination statutes whose varied subjects and provisions do not form any common pattern for different types of discrimination.

Constitutional Protections—Antidiscrimination

The Equal Protection Clause of the Fourteenth Amendment prohibits the states and their subdivisions, including school districts, from denying the equal protection of the laws to any person, especially to one with certain class traits, e.g., race, gender, alienage, disability, age, or sexual orientation. However, the level of constitutional protection varies with these different subjects.

Because the Fourteenth Amendment only protects persons from *de jure* (i.e., "state action") discrimination, and not from *de facto* (i.e., by private) discrimination, the Constitution alone subjects only school districts to suit for constitutional violations. It does not subject their officers or employees to such suits unless a federal statute independently creates personal liability on their part.

De jure discrimination occurs in two ways, namely, by laws, regulations, and official directives which create discriminatory *legal classifications,* and by *discriminatory conduct* that is attributable to the school district and that is animated by hostility to an individual because of class trait. Classifications that are irrational or invidiously discriminatory are unconstitutional, whether or not they were created innocently or with intent to discriminate; but *conduct* that has a discriminatory effect is unconstitutional only if the conduct was *intended* to achieve that effect.

All laws discriminate insofar as they classify and assign different benefits and obligations to different citizen groups. The Supreme Court has, accordingly, established the standards to determine what legal classifications are valid or void under the Constitution. In doing so, the Court adopted different standards of equal protection for different group traits.

> The . . . promise that no person shall be denied the equal protection of the laws must coexist with the practical necessity that most legislation classifies . . . with resulting disadvantages to various groups of persons. . . . We have attempted to reconcile the principle with the reality by stating that, if a law neither burdens a fundamental right nor targets a *suspect* class, we will uphold the legislative classification so long as it bears a rational relation to some legitimate end. (Emphasis added) [*Romer v. Evans,* 116 S. Ct. 1620 (1996)]

Labeling a classification as suspect or nonsuspect thus has crucial constitutional consequences. A nonsuspect classification is presumptively constitutional, with the burden placed on the challenger to prove that the classification lacks a rational basis. A suspect or quasi-suspect classification is presumptively unconstitutional, casting upon the defender the burden of showing that the classification is not only rational but is also *necessary* to serve a *compelling* state interest; or in the case of a quasi-suspect classification (gender), an *important* state interest. Courts decide, largely on the basis of historical experience, which of these three equal protection tests (rational, strict scrutiny, quasi-strict scrutiny) apply to a particular societal class. Awareness of these different equal protection standards is, therefore, essential to apprehend the constitutional protections for different subjects of discrimination.

Statutory Protections—Antidiscrimination

To supplement the constitutional protections, successive Congresses enacted a series of antidiscrimination statutes, beginning with the civil war reconstruction laws and continuing through the major civil rights statutes of the 1960s to the present. These enactments, unfortunately, do not present or reflect a common framework of discrimination principles so that their respective provisions do not operate in a dovetailed or coordinated fashion. Each antidiscrimination statute must, therefore, be analyzed separately to determine its peculiar coverage and remedies for discrimination, especially where the same conduct gives rise to suits under several statutes. For example, a black, female teacher, 55 years of age, with a disability might bring suit under several statutes as well as under the Constitution, alleging discrimination against her race, sex, disability, and/or age. Or a white, male teacher who is paid less than a white female teacher might sue for gender wage discrimination under two employment discrimination statutes (Title VII and the Equal Pay Act) as well as for gender-based denial of equal protection.

The essential goal of discrimination statutes is to provide remedies for specific harms in specified circumstances, rather than to create general positive rights. An individual who is personally offended by discrimination but who has not suffered a tangible discrimination injury has no right to relief under them.[92]

The statutes of principal interest to public school employees are predominantly concerned with employment discrimination and for convenience are here listed by their popular names and acronyms.

> Equal Pay Act of 1964 (EPA)
>
> Title VI (of the Civil Rights Act of 1964)
>
> Title VII (of the Civil Rights Act of 1964)
>
> Title IX (of the Education Amendments of 1972)
>
> The ADA (Americans with Disabilities Act of 1990)
>
> The ADEA (Age Discrimination in Employment Act of 1967)
>
> § 1981 (Civil Rights Act of 1866, codified as 42 U.S.C. § 1981)
>
> § 1983 (Civil Rights Act of 1871 and 1874, codified as 42 U.S.C. § 1983)

The core provisions of these and related laws (e.g., the Rehabilitation Act of 1973) are collected in Appendix 2 at the end of this book.

All but three of the above statutes (the Acts of 1866, Title VI and IX) apply only to discrimination in employment. Of the listed laws, only Title VII covers more than a single class of discrimination, e.g., race, gender, disability, age, and religion. Titles VI (race) and IX (gender) are also limited to cover only discrimination in school activities that receive federal financial assistance.

Each of the listed statutes sets its own standard of prohibited discrimination, its own set of allowed exceptions and defenses, and its own prescribed remedies for its violation,[93] except for the § 1983 statute, which provides remedies for violations of any federal civil right. The peculiar requisites for recovery under the § 1983 law and its interaction with other civil rights laws are reviewed in Chapter 8.

The following sections discuss the operation of each of the above-listed laws with respect to specific classes of discrimination.

Racial and Ethnic Discrimination

As used in this text, the terms *race* and *racial* refer to traits of ethnicity or national origin as well as of color. The words *ethnic* and *national origin* are used interchangeably, unless otherwise stated.

Constitutional Protections—Race

The lead school segregation cases[94] which outlawed segregation of public schools by race and which overturned racial segregation of public school staffs and students launched the modern development of equal protection doctrines. Government actors or entities may not engage in racial discrimination even when acting as trustees of a private trust which limited admission to the trust-created school to "white male orphans".[95]

The equal protection ban of racial discrimination applies to all races. Courts have therefore overturned race-based laws or invidious treatments that disfavor Caucasians[96] or that displace white employees to make way for new or less senior minority race employees.[97] As explained in Chapter 7, racial preferences are constitutional only as a remedy to undo past constitutional injuries. The legality of using racial criteria for affirmative action programs is discussed in the following section and revisited in Chapter 7.

Suits that challenge teacher certification tests as racially discriminatory usually allege both constitutional and statutory grounds, as do suits challenging the validity of affirmative action programs. These challenges will be discussed together in the next section.

Statutory Protections—Race

Titles VI and VII of the Civil Rights Act of 1964 are the principal laws on racial and ethnic discrimination in public school employment.

Title VII. This law is the most widely litigated statute on employment discrimination. It governs employers of 15 or more employees, a minimum that is easily met in public school districts. It prohibits *employment discrimination* by employers and unions based upon an individual's *race, color, religion, sex,* or *national origin.* It exempts from its prohibitions employment decisions that are based on bona fide seniority or merit systems, bona fide job qualifications, or business necessity. Title VII applies to all aspects of employment, from hiring to discharge, with reference to "*. . . compensation, terms, conditions,* or *privileges of employment*" including actions that "*limit, segregate, or classify . . . employees . . . in any way which would deprive . . . any individual of employment opportunities. . . .*" Like equal protection doctrine, Title VII prohibits discrimination against all races. In the *Taxman* case (Case 6.6), the court overturned a public school affirmative action policy and appointment whereby a black teacher's race became the *sole* factor in deciding whether she or an equally qualified white female teacher with equal seniority should be appointed to the only open teaching position that remained following a school reduction in force. In another case, the same court overturned an affirmative action hiring preference of a black applicant over an equally qualified white applicant, also as a violation of Title VII.[98]

The limits of permissible racial preferences to overcome historical discrimination remain fuzzy under both the Constitution and Title VII. The developing case law has not produced a bright line test to cover all contexts of "affirmative action".

The recent Supreme Court decision on the constitutionality of college and law school affirmative action programs for student admissions, which is discussed in Chapter 7, did not discuss the legality of school affirmative action hiring programs. In discussing the permissibility of considering race in hiring or promotions, other cases have employed a number of factors, such as whether the program involves flexible goals or closed quotas; whether racial factors totally exclude an employment opportunity or benefit to members of the nonpreferred race or sex; whether the duration of the program is reasonable in terms of time limits or of stated goals; and whether the number of affected positions is reasonable or excessive.[99]

Title VII provides various forms of relief for victims of employment discrimination. In addition to court injunctions to terminate a discriminatory practice and to appoint or reinstate the discrimination victim to the position he could have achieved but for the violation, Title VII authorizes victim recovery of back pay and employment benefits for the period of the discrimination. Addditional relief under the broader § 1983 statute is discussed in Chapter 8.

Title VI (Act of 1964) and § 1981 (Act of 1866).   Title VI prohibits discrimination on account of *race, color,* or *national origin* only with respect to the benefits of "*any program or activity receiving Federal financial assistance.*"[100] (Emphasis added) Consequently, this Title does not authorize a suit against a city and city planning board for alleged discrimination in activities that did not receive federal financial assistance.[101] Nor does Title VI authorize suit by parties who are not beneficiaries of a federally aided activity.[102]

The issues raised by Title VI cases are more factual than doctrinal. For example, courts must decide whether the circumstances of each case of race-based teasing, ridicule or hostile remarks are sufficiently oppressive to materially interfere with the victim's ability to participate in and benefit from a federally aided school program; whether the defending school district did or did not have fair notice or opportunity to respond to alleged discriminatory conduct by its employees; and, assuming it had such notice, whether its response to rectify the discrimination was reasonable and sufficient to negate a finding of purposeful discrimination by the district.[103] The importance of case context is illustrated by the following examples. One court found that a school board decision to pass over a white candidate and instead appoint a black candidate because of his racial identification with a predominantly black student body was a legitimate, nondiscriminatory hiring consideration.[104] But other courts overturned reassignment of white and Latino coaches to make way for a black candidate to coach a predominantly black team, and overturned as discriminatory the appointment of a white teacher over a black candidate, although the district asserted that the white teacher was better able to identify with a predominantly white student body.[105]

Discrimination challenges to teacher certification tests, license renewals, and promotion decisions present common issues which, for convenience, are discussed in a later section together with challenges by linguistically disadvantaged applicants.

Section 1981 prohibits intentional discrimination against nonwhites with respect to the right "to make and enforce contracts . . . and to the full and equal benefit of all laws . . . as is enjoyed by white citizens". Though not limited to federally aided activities, § 1981 also requires a showing that an employment decision is motivated by and results from *intentional* racial discrimination. Failing such proof a teacher candidate for promotion cannot prevail.[106] The circuit courts are currently split on the question whether § 1981 authorizes a discrimination victim to sue a private individual for relief, as well as a school district.[107]

The availability of monetary recoveries for Titles VI and § 1981 violations (in addition to injunctive relief) is taken up in Chapter 8.

Gender Discrimination

The constitutional and statutory law on gender discrimination closely parallels, but is not identical to, the law on racial discrimination.

Constitutional Protections—Gender

Gender-based legal classifications are constitutionally "quasi-suspect" and fall between the loose rational basis test for nonsuspect classes and the strict scrutiny test for racial classes. "To withstand constitutional challenge

... classifications by gender must serve *important* governmental objectives and must be *substantially related* to achievement of those objectives." [*Craig v. Boren*, 429 U.S. 190, 197 (1976)] "And it must not rely on overbroad generalizations about the different talents, capacities or preferences of males and females." [*United States v. Virginia et al.*, 116 S. Ct. 2264, at p. 2275 (1996)]

These technical shadings of this "midtier" constitutional test is not of great practical import since gender-based laws and policies remain presumptively invalid and will be overturned unless school authorities meet their heavy burden of justifying a gender classification. Absent such proofs, gender segregation of public school employees will be voided as unconstitutional for the same reasons that the Supreme Court overturned gender-segregated military colleges and universities.[108] As with race, equal protection principles are gender neutral and protect both sexes.[109] Gender classifications for teachers and other school employees may be constitutionally justified for certain purposes, such as provision of different or separate lavatory and other facilities that assure sex-specific privacy and needs.

The importance of constitutional protection of pregnant teachers against discrimination has diminished in light of the more expansive protections that are afforded by employment discrimination statutes. Other gender discrimination topics, such as sexual harassment under the Title VII statute, are considered in the next section.

Statutory Protections—Gender

Of the major gender discrimination statutes, Title VII and the Equal Pay Act speak only to employment discrimination, while Title IX speaks only to gender discrimination in federally funded school activities.

Title VII. Title VII prohibits discrimination "because of . . . sex". That phrase covers both school policies that discriminate and discriminatory administration of nondiscriminatory policies, as well as individual acts of sexual harassment that create a "hostile work environment" for the victimized employee.

Administrative Discrimination. Where race or gender factors unrelated to job duties substantially influence employment decisions, the adversely treated person is entitled to Title VII relief.[110] Differential treatment is not discriminatory when based on reasonable business needs, a bona fide employment qualification, or bona fide seniority system. An employer may defeat a discrimination charge by showing that the challenged employment decision was made for a nondiscriminatory reason. Hiring a male rather than a female applicant who had a higher degree because the male applicant could be hired at a lower salary and perform supplemental coaching duties was held lawful.[111] Elimination or change of a disputed position, or denial of a benefit to a candidate who lacked required job skills or had a record of poor job performance is also lawful. Absent such justifications, gender-based changes in employment status or benefits, such as reduction of salary or benefits, loss of supervisory rank or significant responsibilities, and imposition of burdens or disadvantages, have been held to violate Title VII.[112]

Title VII required major changes in employer provision of fringe benefits, particularly in health and retirement plans. The use of gender-based life expectancy tables to calculate retirement contributions, or benefits was held to violate Title VII.[113] The Pregnancy Discrimination Act amended Title VII to require that pregnancy, childbirth, or related medical conditions be treated no less favorably than other medical conditions. However, benefit plan provisions that are unrelated to either sex are not discriminatory, though such plans incidentally produce greater benefits to males or females. For example, plans that provide extra benefits to "heads of households" are valid even though more men than women happen to qualify for "head of household" status.

Sexual Harassment.   Sexual harassing conduct that creates a "hostile work environment" is prohibited by Title VII. Courts initially recognized two kinds of sexual harassment, namely, "quid pro quo" harassment (where the employer or its agent demands sexual favors of an employee under a promise or threat to grant or withhold employment opportunities or benefits) and "non quid pro quo" harassment in which no favors are demanded. In 1998 the Supreme Court undertook to resolve confusion in the case law regarding these forms of sex harassment by formulating new standards of actionable harassment and new defenses that might be made to harassment claims. These new complex standards and defenses are best stated in the Supreme Court opinion that follows. The authors of this text have bolded the essential passages.

FARAGHER v. CITY OF BOCA RATON   CASE 6.8
524 U.S. 775 (1998)

JUSTICE SOUTER delivered the opinion of the Court.

This case calls for identification of the circumstances under which an employer may be held liable under Title VII of the Civil Rights Act of 1964, . . . for the acts of a supervisory employee whose sexual harassment of subordinates has created a hostile work environment amounting to employment discrimination. **We hold that an employer is vicariously liable for actionable discrimination caused by a supervisor, but subject to an affirmative defense looking to the reasonableness of the employer's conduct as well as that of a plaintiff victim.**

* * *

. . . [T]he complaint alleged that Terry and Silverman [supervisors] created a "sexually hostile atmosphere" at the beach by repeatedly subjecting

Faragher and other female lifeguards to "uninvited and offensive touching," by making lewd remarks, and by speaking of women in offensive terms. The complaint contained specific allegations that Terry once said that he would never promote a woman to the rank of lieutenant, and that Silverman had said to Faragher, "Date me or clean the toilets for a year."

* * *

Since our decision in *Meritor,* Courts of Appeals have struggled to derive manageable standards to govern employer liability for hostile environment harassment perpetrated by supervisory employees. While following our admonition to find guidance in the common law of agency, . . . the Courts of Appeals have adopted different approaches. . . .

* * *

. . . We have repeatedly made clear that although the statute mentions specific employment decisions with immediate consequences, the scope of the [Title VII] prohibition "is not limited to 'economic' or 'tangible' discrimination" . . . and that it covers more than "'terms' and 'conditions' in the narrow contractual sense." . . . Thus, in *Meritor* we held that sexual harassment so "severe or pervasive" as to "'alter the conditions of [the victim's] employment and create an abusive working environment'" violates Title VII. 477 U.S., at 67. . . .

In thus holding . . . , we drew upon earlier cases recognizing liability for discriminatory harassment based on race and national origin. . . . So, in *Harris,* we explained that *in order to be actionable . . . a sexually objectionable environment must be both objectively and subjectively offensive, one that a reasonable person would find hostile or abusive,* and one that the victim in fact did perceive to be so. 510 U.S., at 21–22. . . . We directed courts to determine whether an environment is sufficiently hostile or abusive by *"looking at all the circumstances," including the "frequency of the discriminatory conduct; its severity; whether it is physically threatening or humiliating, or a mere offensive utterance;* and whether it unreasonably interferes with an employee's work performance." . . . Most recently, we explained that Title VII does not prohibit "genuine but innocuous differences in the ways men and women routinely interact with members of the same sex and of the opposite sex." . . . A recurring point in these opinions is that *"simple teasing,"* . . . *offhand comments, and isolated incidents (unless extremely serious) will not amount to discriminatory changes in the "terms and conditions of employment."*

These standards for judging hostility are sufficiently demanding to ensure that Title VII does not become a "general civility code." . . . Properly applied, they will filter out complaints attacking "the ordinary tribulations of the workplace, such as the sporadic use of abusive language, gender-related jokes, and occasional teasing." . . . We have made it clear that conduct must be extreme to amount to a change in the terms and conditions of employment, and the Courts of Appeals have heeded this view. . . .

* * *

. . . **[W]e adopt the following holding. . . . An employer is subject to vicarious liability to a victimized employee for an actionable hostile environment created by a supervisor with immediate (or successively higher) authority over the employee.** *When no tangible employment action is taken, a defending employer may raise an affirmative defense* **to liability or damages. . . . The defense comprises two necessary elements: (a) that the employer exercised reasonable care to prevent and correct promptly any sexually harassing behavior, and (b) that the plaintiff employee unreasonably failed to take advantage of any preventive or corrective opportunities provided by the employer or to avoid harm otherwise. While proof that an employer had promulgated an antiharassment policy with complaint procedure is not necessary in every instance as a matter of law, the need for a stated policy suitable to the employment circumstances may appropriately be addressed in any case. . . . And while proof that an employee failed to fulfill the corresponding obligation of reasonable care to avoid harm is not limited to showing an unreasonable failure to use any complaint procedure provided by the employer, a demonstration of such failure will normally suffice to satisfy the employer's burden under the second element of the defense.** *No affirmative defense is available, however, when the supervisor's harassment culminates in a tangible employment action, such as discharge, demotion, or undesirable reassignment.* **. . .**

. . . The District Court found that the degree of hostility in the work environment rose to the actionable level and was attributable to Silverman and Terry. It is undisputed that these supervisors "were granted virtually unchecked authority" over their subordinates. . . . It is also clear that Faragher and her colleagues were "completely isolated from the City's higher management." . . .

While the City would have an opportunity to raise an affirmative defense if there were any serious prospect of its presenting one, it appears from the record that any such avenue is closed.

* * *

The judgment of the Court of Appeals . . . is reversed, and the case is remanded for reinstatement of the judgment of the District Court.

Faragher thus adopted three discrete rules to cover three distinct situations: One for harassments by nonsupervisors; another for harassment by a supervisor "with immediate (or successively higher)" authority over the employee *who makes no tangible adverse employment decision* against the victim; and a third for harassment by such a supervisor who *makes a "tangible, adverse employment decision"* against the victim.

 1. For nonsupervisor harassment, the employer is liable only if it had notice of the harassment and failed to take reasonable steps to stop it.
 2. For supervisor harassment not accompanied by an adverse employment decision against the victim, the employer is liable unless it asserts and proves the affirmative defense that it acted with reasonable promptness and care to prevent or rectify that harassment. This may include a showing that the offended employee failed to report the harassment in timely fashion to enable the employer to take reasonable action to protect the employee, especially where a published employer sex discrimination policy is in place to invite employees to report such harassments.
 3. For sexual harassment by the harassed employee's supervisor, which is accompanied by an adverse employment decision by the supervisor against the victim, the employer is *absolutely liable* and cannot assert any affirmative defense of ignorance or of having acted reasonably to prevent that harassment. While the "tangible employment decision" factor has some flavor of the older "quid pro quo" analysis, it is really different, because it requires action that affects the victim, and not merely a threat of such action.

 In endeavoring to apply the *Faragher* rulings, courts continue to stress the importance of specific workplace history and environment, including the attitudes and reactions of the alleged harasser and victim, and the severity of sexually offensive conduct from both an objective (reasonable man) and subjective (the victim's) standpoint. The same sexual remarks or conduct that might be sufficiently severe to constitute harassment in one workplace might not be so in another. These factors demand judgments on which different courts and juries may disagree. For example, the Ninth Circuit Court of Appeals found that a single incident of unwelcome breast fondling by a supervisor did not establish an actionable hostile working atmosphere where neither the victim nor the employer were aware of the supervisor's past history of sexually harassing others, and the employer responded quickly with corrective action when the incident was reported.[114] But the Seventh Circuit Court held that a jury could find actionable harassment and sex discrimination where the supervisor in a single meeting persistently pressed the plaintiff employee to have oral sex, engage in a sexual "threesome", or have "telephone sex", all of which suggestions she rejected with equal persistence.[115] On the other hand, where the complaining employee invited or was unfazed by the alleged harassment, or where the harassment was not so severe or oppressive as to produce a hostile work environment, a school district could avoid liability for its employee's sexual misconduct. In *Clark County School Dist. v. Breeden*, 121 S. Ct. 1598 (2001), the Court found that joking remarks to the plaintiff by her supervisors in a job promotion interview could not reasonably be considered sufficiently severe to establish an abusive workplace environment in violation of Title VII, though those remarks included bawdy suggestions about her sex life.

In contrast to the *Faragher* finding that the pattern of sexually offensive remarks by plaintiff's supervisors was actionable, some courts found that sexually offensive remarks were insufficient to establish a hostile work environment in other contexts. The Eleventh Circuit Court of Appeals held that a male supervisor's staring at, sniffing, and bumping of a female subordinate over an 11-month period, though surely offensive, was insufficient in the case circumstances to create a hostile working environment.[116] The court there cited decisions from other federal circuits that also found sexually offensive conduct insufficient in the particular case circumstances. In sum, while the *Faragher* decision provided fresh guidelines, it did not simplify the task of applying them to different individuals and workplace circumstances.

Same-Sex Harassment. In *Oncale v. Sundowners Offshore Services, Inc.* (Case 6.9), the Supreme Court recently held that the Title VII harassments "because of sex" may cover harassments between members of the same sex. The male worker on an oil drilling platform there suffered threats of sexual assault (rape), ridicule, and humiliation by his male supervisor and fellow workers, and the court ruled that such conduct could amount to discrimination "because of sex". But the Third Circuit Court of Appeals later held that the *Oncale* case did not require a finding of discrimination "because of sex" when a male employee subjected a fellow male employee to physical assaults, threats, and ridicule because that conduct was not directed against the employee's sex as a man, and therefore was not made "because of sex" within the meaning of Title VII.

> [I]t is clear that "[w]hatever evidentiary route the plaintiff chooses to follow, he or she must always prove that the conduct . . . constituted '*discrimina[tion]* . . . because of . . . sex.'" *Oncale* at 81, 118 S. Ct. 998. . . . Bibby simply failed in this respect. . . . . . . There was no allegation that his alleged harassers were motivated by sexual desire, or that they possessed any hostility to the presence of men in the workplace. . . . Moreover, he did not claim that he was harassed because he failed to comply with societal stereotypes of how men ought to appear or behave or that as a man he was treated differently than female co-workers. His claim was, pure and simple, that he was discriminated against because of his sexual orientation. No reasonable finder of fact could reach the conclusion that he was discriminated against because he was a man. [*Bibby v. Phila. Coca Cola Bottling Co.* (Case 6.10)]

Other circuit courts have held that the Title VII language, "because of sex", does not cover all hostile treatment directed against an employee's sexual orientation, but only where the harassment derives from the victim's failure to conform to stereotyping norms of the employee's sex.[117] Some courts concluded that being perceived as gay by fellow employees does not, alone, amount to harassment because of sex.[118] Until the Supreme Court rules further on these possible variants of discrimination "because of sex", school districts and their employees must look to the case law of their home federal circuit. Other forms of same-sex harassment are further elaborated in the *Bibby* case (Case 6.10) and in the following section on homosexual discrimination.

The foregoing Title VII issues are rendered academic in states which have enacted laws that explicitly prohibit sexual orientation discrimination.

Mixed-Motive Decisions. Prior to the Civil Rights Act of 1999, an employer could avoid liability under Title VII for an employment decision that was made partly for a legitimate reason and partly for an illegitimate reason, by showing that the same decision would have been made nothwithstanding any gender-bias.[119] Congress enacted the Civil Rights Act of 1999 to authorize limited court relief in a mixed-motive case, by way of decrees to prohibit any employee penalty arising from the invalid motivation, and to authorize a court to award attorneys' fees and costs of suit to the victimized employee, but not back pay or other Title VII remedies.[120]

Wage Discrimination. Gender-based wage discrimination is prohibited by both Title VII and by the Equal Pay Act. Where the same discrimination is covered by both laws, however, the discrimination claim and relief is governed exclusively by the EPA.[121]

Equal Pay Act (EPA). The EPA allows four exceptions for payment of different wages to members of the opposite sex, namely, (1) payments made under a seniority system, (2) payments made under a merit system, (3) earnings based on the quality or quantity of production, and (4) a catchall exception for "pay differentials based on any other factors other than sex".[122] Absent these exceptions, an employer may not pay lower wages to either sex for work that require equal skill, effort, responsibility, and similar working conditions.[123]

The catchall exception for pay differentials based on factors "other than sex" invites conflicting readings. For example, three federal Courts of Appeal have read this exception broadly to uphold unequal wage payments to men and women under an employer's good faith salary-retention policy for skilled employees during temporary change of work assignments. Another Court of Appeals held that the "other than sex" exception would not apply unless the employer proved that a special, urgent business need (rather than normal business practice) justified the salary retention policy.[124]

A school district may not pay higher wages to women than to men for like work for the purpose of overcoming historical gender disadvantages unless those disadvantages resulted from discrimination by the district.[125]

What constitutes "equal work" is for courts to decide. Payment of higher wages to the male coach of a boys' team than to the female coach of the girls' team, based on his longer hour workload, would not normally violate the Act. Equal pay based on salary classification alone, notwithstanding different workload hours of persons within the same salary class, may be upheld for some positions. One court denied an equal pay claim by a university female professor whose teaching load was double that of her male professor counterpart.[126] Such cases highlight the importance of the broader Title VII law which, unlike the EPA, may prevent wage anomalies on the independent ground of discrimination in work assignments and in access to higher positions.

The broader argument that the EPA requires equal pay for work of "comparable worth" has not taken hold. If the claimant can show that different pay positions actually cover like work and are a pretext to avoid EPA prohibitions, recovery may be had, without reliance on the "comparable worth" theory.

For EPA violations, the discrimination victim may recover back pay in the amount that he or she should have received, and in cases of malicious or egregious violations, a court may award "liquidated" damages in double the amount of normal EPA recovery.

Title IX.   This Title prohibits a narrow form of sex discrimination, i.e., by exclusion from or denial of benefits *"under any education program or activity receiving Federal financial assistance. . . ."* (Emphasis added) The question whether Title IX covers same-sex discrimination has not been extensively tested but the courts of three circuits (the First, Fifth, and Eighth) recently held that Title IX prohibits same-sex discrimination.[127]

The structure and provisions of the Title IX law closely parallel those of Title VI. These laws have accordingly received parallel constructions by the courts. Both apply only to school districts as recipients of federal aid, and not to their individual officers and employees.[128] School district recipients of federal aid are subject to Title IX liability only for conduct that is caused by official school district policies. Nor are districts subject to Title IX liability under tort doctrines (*respondeat superior*) which were discussed in Chapter 4. School districts are liable for sexual discrimination conduct of their employees only where

> an official of the district who at a minimum has authority to address the alleged discrimination and to institute corrective measures . . . has actual knowledge of discrimination in the recipient's program and fails adequately to respond. We think, moreover, that the response must amount to deliberate indifference to discrimination. . . . The premise in other words is an official decision by the recipient not to remedy the violation. [*Gebser v. Lago Vista Ind. School Dist.,* 118 S. Ct. 1989, 1999 (1998)]

"Deliberate indifference" involves more than supervisor negligence in failing to discover risks of sexual mistreatment or to ascertain an employee's sexual predatory history or tendency, or to adopt better or best policies or practices to preclude sexual harassment.[129] Furthermore, the "deliberate indifference" must be shown to have some causal link to the victim's injury. The "deliberate indifference" standard that *Gebser* adopted for Title IX purposes was borrowed from cases which construed and applied the broader § 1983 statute, which is discussed in Chapter 8.

In the lead Title IX *Davis* case, which is reported at the end of Chapter 7, the Supreme Court explained that in order to be actionable under Title IX, sexual harassment must be sufficiently *severe* to effectively deny or curtail the victim's opportunity to receive the benefits of a federally aided program.[130] That determination requires particularized consideration of specific case facts. One court found that a teacher calling a student a prostitute in class, over a period of several weeks, was not sufficiently severe to show a Title IX violation by the school district.[131]

Claims under Title IX (and implicitly under Title VI) are not governed by the discrimination limits of other statutes. For example, Title IX, unlike Title VII, is not limited to employment discrimination, and it allows proof of discrimination by "deliberate indifference" that is attributable to the school district.[132]

Gender segregation of school staff or students in a federally aided activity would qualify as a Title IX violation as well as a Fourteenth Amendment violation. Title IX discrimination may also be found in disparate treatment of male and female staff, e.g., where females are subjected to harsher penalties for misconduct than their male counterparts.[133] The same is true of disparate allocation of school resources for male and female staff. The lead cases on Title IX gender discrimination involve disparate allocation of school facilities and resources for male and female students. Those authorities are collected in Chapter 7, but their reasoning is equally pertinent to discriminatory allocation of school resources for male and female teachers.

Title IX discrimination victims may obtain equitable relief by way of court orders for reinstatement and restoration of a teacher to a deprived position or benefit. In the lead Supreme Court decision on *student* Title IX rights, which is reported in the next chapter (*Davis*, Case 7.10), the Supreme Court declared: "In *Gebser*, we concluded that a recipient of federal education funds may be liable in damages under Title IX. . . ." Even so, the lower court remains divided on the allowance of punitive damages under Title IX.[134] Title IX does not, however, authorize a claimant to bring a suit to enforce a Title IX regulation which creates an obligation that is not authorized by the statute itself.[135]

The remedies provided by Title IX for its violations are exclusive, and as explained in Chapter 8, preclude recovery of remedies under the § 1983 civil rights statute.

Homosexual Discrimination

For economy of language, the term "homosexual" is here used to refer to both male (homosexual) and female (lesbian) sexual orientation and relationships.

The fairly new and still developing law on homosexual employees has not to date tracked the law on biological gender discrimination.

Constitutional Protections—Homosexual Persons

Homosexual orientation disputes involve several issues. For example, if a school district were to issue an official "don't ask, don't tell" policy about disclosing one's homosexual orientation, a teacher may raise several challenges, i.e., that the policy is allegedly infringing freedom of speech; decisional privacy; and rights of intimate sexual relations. These claims would require the assessment of each constitutional claim and of the educational interest of the school district.

The recent Supreme Court decision [*Lawrence v. Texas*, 123 S. Ct. 2472 (2003)], that adult homosexual persons have a constitutional liberty to engage in private, consensual homosexual conduct in a home, free from state punishment or interference, raises the question whether or how this newly recognized liberty affects the authority of public school administrators to regulate school site speech or advocacy relating to homosexual lifestyles. The same might be said of laws propounded in various states to recognize homosexual unions or marriage. As explained in Chapter 5, the *Lawrence* opinion contains different passages which arguably support an expansive or narrow interpretation of that decision. It remains unclear how that case will affect school regulations of discussion of homosexuality at different grade levels and in different circumstances, and how courts will balance teacher and school interests in those varied circumstances, be they educational or not, and the avoidance of possible disruptive conflicts among different school, parent, and community groups.[136]

The majority opinion in the *Lawrence* case relied exclusively on the Due Process Clause to arrive at its finding of a substantive liberty for private homosexual conduct. It did not invoke or rely on a claim of gender discrimination under the Equal Protection Clause and it left unchanged the prior case law that homosexual orientation or conduct is not a suspect classification and is subject to reasonable state regulation. That silence leaves open the question whether or when school regulation of homosexual expression would be deemed "reasonable" or a violation of a substantive right.

> Discrimination against homosexuals by public entities violates the equal protection clause only if it lacks a rational basis, as it would do if it were motivated by baseless hostility to homosexuals, the motivation that the Supreme Court in *Romer v. Evans*, 517 U.S. 620, 634–35, . . . (1996), attributed to a state constitutional provision that forbade municipalities to enact gay-rights ordinances; or if, though devoid of animus, the discrimination simply bore no rational relation to any permissible state policy. [*Schroeder v. Hamilton School District*, 282 F.3d 946, 957 [(7th Cir. 2002) (Posner J., concurring)]

Statutory Protections—Homosexual Persons

The antidiscrimination laws discussed in the preceding section, particularly Title VII, do not single out homosexual orientation as a separate subject of discrimination. As there explained, Title VII protects homosexuals only for discrimination "because of sex", and not from hostility to sexual orientation itself. The distinction between protected discrimination "because of sex" and unprotected discrimination based only on hostility to sexual orientation, as drawn in the *Bibby* case (Case 6.10), may be rejected in other jurisdictions. The laws of each governing state and the regulations of each governing school district remain particularly important for this topic, and must be carefully checked.

Disability Discrimination

Constitutional Protections—Disability

Disability status does not enjoy heightened protection under the Constitution. The Supreme Court recently ruled that disparate treatment of persons with disabilities need only be rational to satisfy the Equal Protection Clause.[137] The limited special constitutional protections have been buttressed by federal and state statutes that deal directly with disability-based job discrimination.[138]

Statutory Protections—Disability

Of the three major federal statutes affecting disabled persons, the IDEA law applies only to students and is covered in Chapter 7. The Rehabilitation Act of 1973 (hereafter § 504) and the Americans with Disabilities Act (hereafter ADA) also cover teachers. This discussion refers only to those parts of these laws which relate to employment discrimination. A full coverage of the somewhat complex, intertwined provisions of these laws that relate to disability discrimination beyond the employment context must be left to more specialized texts.[139]

Section 504 of the Rehabilitation Act (like Titles VI and IX) reaches employment discrimination only in federally aided school programs, by providing that "no *otherwise qualified individual* shall be denied the benefits of any *federally assisted programs or facilities solely by reason of his handicap*". (Emphasis added)

Title I of the ADA provides that no covered employer or union "shall discriminate against a *qualified individual with a disability [as defined in the Act] because of the disability of such individual*". (Emphasis added) Like Title VII, the ADA prohibits discrimination in all aspects of employment, from hire through discharge.

In most cases, § 504 and Title I of the ADA are enforced in much the same manner as Title VII. Like Title VII, the ADA and § 504 do not prohibit or penalize employer decisions that are justified by bona fide business necessity or by bona fide job qualifications. Both statutes were amended to exclude from their coverage current drug users or alcoholics, unless former addicts or alcoholics successfully completed a program of rehabilitation.

Only school districts, and not their individual officers or employees, are covered by and subject to liability under these laws because the ADA prohibits discrimination only by *employers* and § 504 prohibits discrimination only by *federal aid recipients* (i.e., school district employers).[140]

What Is a Disability Under the ADA?   To obtain ADA protection and remedies, a grievant must show:

1. that he or she has a covered "disability" or "handicap";
2. is "qualified" to perform the sought job or job benefit; and
3. that the job or job benefit was denied "because of" the disability or handicap, and not because of a justified reason.

School districts are, therefore, not liable for denying opportunities to a person with a disability who cannot perform essential job functions, even with reasonable employer accommodation of the disability.[141]

The ADA definition of a covered disability is drawn almost verbatim from the Rehabilitation Act.[142] It defines *disability* as "a physical or mental *impairment that substantially limits one* or more of the *major life activities of such individual*". It separately defines a *qualified individual* as "an individual . . . who, *with or without reasonable accommodation,* can perform the *essential functions* of the employment position that the claimant holds or desires." (Emphasis added) [42 U.S.C. § 12111(8)] Under these provisions, impairments that are correctable by medical aids or treatment do not preclude major life activities and do not qualify for ADA coverage.

After considerable confusion of lower court decisions, the Supreme Court in 2002 clarified the bases for determining whether an impairment substantially limits a major life activity. In *Toyota Motor Mfg., Ky. v. Williams*, 534 U.S. 184 (2002), the Court held that an auto plant employee who suffered from carpal tunnel syndrome and tendonitis, conditions that were severely aggravated by her work requirements (lifting and extending her arms to grip and manipulate car parts on a moving line), was not entitled to employer accommodation on her request to be transferred to a less painful position. The Court found that her impairment did not limit her "major life activities" within the meaning of the ADA. It construed "major life activities" to mean activities that "are of central importance to most people's daily lives," and not activities required for a particular job. Since the employee could do routine household tasks (cooking, cleaning, laundry), personal care tasks (washing, bathing, teeth brushing), and gardening, the Court ruled that she did not suffer a disability that is covered by the ADA, and consequently was not entitled to employer accommodation of her impairment.

Persons with correctable impairments who can engage in a broad class of work other than their present or desired occupation are not deemed to be disabled under the ADA. The Supreme Court ruled that licensed airplane pilots who could find work in a broad class of flying jobs with proper lens correction of their myopia were not disabled under the ADA and could not claim ADA discrimination by a passenger-carrying airline that refused to hire them.[143] For like reasons, the Court held that a bus driver with medically correctable hypertension did not suffer an ADA disability.[144] The Second Circuit Court of Appeals later added a negative dimension to medically correctable conditions in holding that a long-distance truck carrier could lawfully refuse to hire an applicant to drive large 18-wheelers over long distances because the applicant's prescribed medication had the side effects of impairing driving ability and safety. Since the employer's decision turned on the negative effects of medication, rather than on a broad class of truck driver work, the employer could not be said to have discriminated against a major life activity.[145] On the other hand, the Court found that a woman with an incurable HIV condition that disabled her from bearing children (a major life activity) did have an ADA disability that limited a major life activity.[146]

Once a claimant establishes a qualifying disability, employers may still avoid liability by showing that the challenged employment decision was based on business necessity or a good faith job qualification. As with Title VII (as discussed in the preceding text at endnote 110), this defense does not apply where an employee with a disability proves that the employer acted not solely for neutral business reasons, but on the basis of the employee's disability. [*Raytheon Co. v. Hernandez*, 124 S. Ct. 513 (2003)]

> [T]he Act creates an affirmative defense for action . . . "shown to be job related for the position in question and . . . consistent with business necessity." Such a standard may include "a requirement that an individual shall not pose a direct threat to the health or safety of other individuals in the workplace. . . " if the individual cannot perform the job safely with reasonable accommodation,". . . . By regulation the EEOC carries the defense one step further, in allowing an employer to screen out a potential worker with a disability . . . for risks on the job to his own health and safety as well. . . . [*Chevron U.S.A. v. Echazabal*, 122 S. Ct. at 2045, 2049 (2002)]

In the above quoted case the Supreme Court upheld a company's dismissal of an oil refinery worker whose liver condition would be severely aggravated by his inhaling the fumes at the oil refinery plant.

An employer may not, however, rely on abstract presumptions to establish a business need or job qualification. The focus must be on the actual or probable impact of an impairment on job performance or the workplace.

> This inquiry must include: (a) the nature of the risk (how the disease is transmitted), (b) the duration of the risk (how long is the carrier infectious), (c) the severity of the risk (what is the potential harm to third parties), and (c) the probabilities the disease will be transmitted and will cause varying degrees of harm. [*Doe v. Dekalb County School Dist.*, 145 F.3d 1441, 1446 (11th Cir. 1998)]

The Supreme Court overturned a school district's refusal to accept a teacher's return from medical leave, on the bare, untested assumption that her tuberculosis, which was then in remission, would render it unsafe to have her work in the school.[147]

The use of impermissible presumptions does not, however, outlaw school requirements that an applicant or current employee undergo a reasonably limited mental or physical examination to ascertain a person's ability to perform essential job functions. A school district could therefore demand that a teacher submit to a medical examination, where her disruptive behavior was not typical of her long work history.[148]

"Reasonable Accommodation" Requirements. The ADA requires only "reasonable" employer accommodation of a covered disability. No duty to accommodate arises if the employer can show that no reasonable accommodation would render an employee qualified to perform essential job functions, or that the requested accommodation would impose undue hardship on the employer's enterprise.[149] The *Salmon* case (Case 6.11) provides a good analysis of the accommodations required by the ADA, and of the proofs which the parties must produce to show that an accommodation request is or is not reasonable.

In each case, the nature of the presented disability, of the sought position, and of the particular needs of the employing school must all be considered in deciding whether a requested accommodation is reasonable. An impairment that would not seriously impede classroom performance of a teacher in one position might impede performance of a teacher in a different position or of a school security officer. In the *Salmon* case (Case 6.11), the court found that a school counselor's request for a changed hourly work schedule was not "reasonable" because the requested work schedule would defeat the essential utility of her work, but another court found that an hourly work schedule change request was reasonable because the change did not destroy the utility of that employee's work.[150] Other examples of reasonable accommodation requests in particular circumstances include a leave of absence and transfers to other positions.[151]

The developing case law supports the view that the ADA does not require accommodations that entail any of the following changes: undue fiscal or administrative burdens or fundamental alteration of the nature of the requester's job; lowering of performance standards, or creation of new jobs; reallocation of job functions; or reassignment of employees with disabilities to positions already occupied by others.[152] The amount of burden that an employer is required to shoulder in order to accommodate an employee with a disability in reassignment to a different position has not been fully explored. The Supreme Court recently decided (by 5–4 vote) that an employer could lawfully deny a disabled cargo handler's request for transfer because the requested transfer would conflict with seniority rights of other employees. [*U.S. Airways v. Barnette*, 122 U.S. 1516 (2002)] However, the Court avoided a fixed rule that seniority rights always trump ADA accommodation requests, or that ADA claims always trump seniority rights. While an accommodation request that raises a conflict with an established seniority system would *ordinarily* be deemed to create an undue business hardship, an employee with a disability could attempt to disprove the presumed undue business hardship and show special circumstances that would make his request "reasonable" even in light of an established seniority system. That passing observation by the Court is a sure invitation to more lawsuits to probe when the ADA requires departure from the employer's seniority system.

Case circumstances will determine whether a request for assignment to a new or existing vacant position is reasonable or poses an employer hardship.[153]

As with Titles VI and IX, ADA and Rehabilitation Act discrimination victims may sue school districts for injunctive relief, including reinstatement to a deprived position or restoration to a deprived benefit. The allowance of monetary damages for disability discrimination is taken up in Chapter 8.

Age Discrimination

Constitutional Protections—Age

Age, like disability, does not command heightened constitutional protection,[154] so that any rationally age-based school policy or decision would satisfy the Equal Protection Clause of the Constitution.[155]

Statutory Protections—Age

The Age Discrimination in Employment Act of 1967 (hereafter ADEA) is modeled after, and has been interpreted to operate in much the same manner as, Title VII. The ADEA protects only individuals age 40 or over and provides that:

> It shall be unlawful for an employer to fail or refuse to hire or to discharge any individual [defined by ADA as 40 or older] or otherwise discriminate against any

individual with respect to his compensation, terms, conditions, or privileges of employment, because of such individual's age. [29 U.S.C. § 623(a)(1) (1994)]

Employment policies based on age brackets over age 40 are, therefore, unlawful. Like Title VII, ADEA does not prohibit employment decisions based on an individual's inadequate skill and performance, even though the individual's age may contribute to those inadequacies. The individual's condition, rather than his or her age, must justify the employment decision. To prevail in an ADEA claim, teachers must produce evidence that they were qualified for and denied an employment opportunity or benefit because of their age, but the school employer may rebut and defeat the claim by evidence of a legitimate nondiscriminatory reason for the challenged decision. If such rebuttal is made, the burden of proving discrimination shifts back to the employee to show that the district's proffered reason is untrue or a pretext for discrimination.[156] The sufficiency of proofs to show or rebut a claim of pretext remains a question for case-by-case decision.[157]

The ADEA permits good faith employment decisions based on nondiscriminatory criteria, such as bona fide considerations of superior performance or seniority of competing employees, and business necessity. An older person could not claim discrimination because an employment preference is given to a younger worker with superior qualifications; or because a new school assignment increases his or her commuting distance to work; or because the older claimant received an unfavorable, but otherwise justified, performance rating.[158] But as with a disability, age alone may not be used as a proxy to decide performance capability.[159]

Cost and efficiency factors may be found to justify a challenged employment decision, but cost motives alone may also be found insufficient in some circumstances, e.g., where cost considerations were the sole basis for discharging older employees in a school staff reduction, or for changing "continuing" contracts to "annual" contracts.[160] In each case, the courts must decide whether age was the essential basis for the contested action.[161]

Mandatory age retirements are prohibited by the ADEA[162] as well as age-based differentials in wages and in fringe benefits, such as health and retirement plans. Congress expressly amended the ADEA to require that employer expenditures for older workers' retirement plans be no less than those expended for younger workers.[163]

Retirement plans that provide incentives for early retirement have been upheld where the plan conditions and employee options thereunder are truly voluntary, but they have been overturned under the ADEA where they are found to exert a coercive and discriminatory effect on older employees. The use of age brackets that qualify for early retirement incentives has been upheld in some cases and overturned in others, depending on the court's determination that a given incentive plan was fair or discriminatory.[164] The *Auerbach* case (Case 6.12) traces the history and analysis of retirement incentive plans, and the role of courts in assessing their fairness.

Layoff decisions may involve age discrimination. To avoid discrimination challenges to layoffs, employers sometimes offer severance packages in exchange for the employee's written release of any further claim against the employer. Such releases have generally been upheld unless the employee could prove that the releases were not made knowingly or voluntarily.[165]

While ADEA cases normally involve discrimination against older workers, the Supreme Court in 2004 finally settled the question as to whether the ADEA also forbids reverse discrimination against younger workers. It held in effect that the ADEA does not prohibit an employer from favoring an older employee over a younger one because the ADEA was only intended "to protect a relatively older worker from discrimination". The Court accordingly held that the ADEA did not prohibit an employer from discontinuing a retirement plan for younger workers over 40 years of age, while continuing (grandfathering) the same retirement plan for still older workers.[166]

ADEA victims may obtain both equitable relief (injunctions, orders for reinstatement to a deprived position or benefit) and recover money damages. The allowance of monetary recovery beyond that specified in the ADEA is taken up in Chapter 8.

Additional age discrimination rights and remedies have been enacted by a majority of states. Those laws should also be consulted.[167]

Alien Discrimination

Constitutional Protections—Aliens

Aliens are protected from discrimination by the Fourteenth Amendment, but different equal protection tests apply for different classes of aliens. Aliens who have not been lawfully admitted to the United States (hereafter "illegal" aliens) may be denied public employment and public benefits. Lawfully admitted aliens are for many purposes treated as a suspect class, but not for public employment positions that involve a *public function* in which *citizen participation and control* is deemed necessary by courts to maintain the integrity of a public function. In such cases, the government need only show a rational basis to deny such employment to aliens. In adopting this two-tiered system of equal protection, the Supreme Court ruled that public school teaching positions fall within the "public function" exception so that a school district could lawfully refuse to hire as a teacher a lawfully resident alien who declines to seek citizenship of the United States.[168] That ruling leaves the question—what public school positions other than that of teaching fall within the "public function" exception? Put another way, which public school positions are not essential to the school's public education mission, so that school districts may not constitutionally deny employment in those positions to lawfully resident noncitizens, unless it can prove a *compelling* need to do so.

Many school district positions cover a broad range of noninstructional work, and some involve both educational and noneducational duties, e.g., teacher aides, therapy specialists, librarians, nurses, and school secretaries. A school district's job description and classification of a given position will thus be relevant to the treatment of aliens. Periodic changes in job duties and classifications within one district and between different districts may well foreclose any fixed rule for like job categories. These questions have not excited much court attention, but they should inform school hiring policies with regard to noncitizens.

Statutory Protections—Aliens

The major federal antidiscrimination statutes do not cover aliens as a class. Their rights under other statutes will depend on the particulars of those statutes. For example, the Supreme Court recently ruled that illegal alien employees may not recover back pay for an employer's alleged violation of the National Labor Relations Act because that Act would conflict with the nation's immigration laws.[169]

Religious Discrimination

Constitutional Protections—Religion

The principal constitutional protections against religion-based employment discrimination are provided by the Free Exercise and the Free Speech Clauses of the First Amendment, and by the Equal Protection Clause of the Fourteenth Amendment. The operation of those sources to religious issues was reviewed in Chapter 3.

Public school employment practices rarely raise claims of religious discrimination. Free exercise claims arise most commonly from denial of teacher requests to be excused from a scheduled work period in order to observe a religious obligation. As explained in Chapter 3, unless the school authorities can show that refusal of such a request would create a serious operational hardship or is necessary to preserve an overriding school need, that refusal could be held to deny equal protection or abridge free exercise of religion as to preclude disciplinary sanctions against the teacher.[170] The constitutional question has been largely mooted by the religious discrimination provisions of Title VII.

Statutory Protections—Religion

As noted above, Title VII expressly prohibits religious discrimination in school employment. Subject to the defenses of undue hardship or bona fide employment qualifications, job applicants and employees may not be denied access to school employment opportunities or benefits on account of religion.

Title VII further requires that employers grant reasonable accommodation requests regarding employees' religion,[171] a requirement that is also noted in Chapter 3. The Supreme Court provided some guidance for determining the reasonableness of religious accommodation requests in a case where the school board accepted a union contract that limited to three days paid leave for religious holy day observance while authorizing six days of paid leave for other employee purposes. The Court agreed that the case raised an employment discrimination issue under Title VII and sent the case back for review of the school district's leave policies.[172] It noted, however, that Title VII does not require an employer to accommodate religion at all costs and in all circumstances.

The recoveries for Title VII violations are noted in prior sections and in Chapter 8.

Language Barriers

The growth of English-only tests in schools has provoked legal challenges, but the case law remains relatively recent and sparse. Parties may look to guidelines and regulations of the Equal Employment Opportunity Commission, with the reservation that courts do not always sustain EEOC interpretations of the law. Briefly summarized, the EEOC guidelines indicate that school districts may consider English proficiency or deficiency of a job applicant and may establish English-only rules for work where English language skills are required by and tailored to specific job requirements and are needed to promote the safe or efficient operation of the schools. These guidelines recognize that, to be actionable national origin discrimination, work-site harassment or ridicule based on language difficulty must be severe and oppressive, and not merely offensive, much like the Title VII standards that the Supreme Court set forth in the *Faragher* case, reported on page 219.

Constitutional Protections—English Deficiency

Linguistic disadvantage, like age and disability, is not a suspect trait that is entitled to heightened constitutional protection. Persons with limited language training or skills cannot overturn English-only tests or work requirements on the sole ground that such tests have disproportionate adverse impacts upon them. In the absence of proof that the content or administration of the challenged test is irrational, or that test results are traceable to a discriminatory purpose or intent, courts have upheld them.[173] The Ninth Circuit Court of Appeals recently upheld, as constitutional, a voter-approved initiative that required the elimination of bilingual education and its replacement by English-only instruction in California public schools.[174]

Where educational and language deficiencies are shown to result from unconstitutional discrimination, courts may order affirmative action measures, including the use of other-than-English tests to undo the effects of that discrimination.

Statutory Protections—English Deficiency

English-only teacher certification or licensing tests have also been challenged as employment discrimination under Titles VI and VII. Those challenges drew conflicting court responses.[175] The Ninth Circuit Court of Appeals found that a certification test was not discriminatory under Title VII, notwithstanding its adverse impacts on certain minorities, because English proficiency was a valid indicator of basic teacher skills, and thus constituted a reasonable term or condition of employment.

The Supreme Court recently held that Title VI does not prohibit employment practices that are not intentionally adopted to discriminate against a minority, even though those practices may have a disproportionate adverse impact on a minority group. [*Alexander v. Sandoval*, 121 S. Ct. 1511 (2001)].

Lower courts also rejected Title VI claims that the use of English-only state teacher certification tests and English-only state driver licensing tests are discriminatory, notwithstanding their adverse results for language-deficient applicants.[176]

Teachers and others might find some right to accommodation of their language disadvantage in federal or state laws that provide funds for special programs to enable persons to overcome language barriers,[177] but most of those laws are directed to assisting students rather than teachers. For a fuller comment on linguistic barriers, see the section on linguistically disadvantaged students in Chapter 7.

Concurrent Violations of Different Laws

When the same conduct concurrently violates different antidiscrimination statutes and those statutes contain no express direction as to how they should interact with each other, courts must decide whether a claimant is limited exclusively to the relief specified by one of them. The complex issues raised by the different grounds for liability, defense, and remedies that are created by different discrimination statutes are postponed for separate discussion in Chapter 8.

Immunity Defenses to Civil Rights Violations

The allowance of immunity-from-suit defenses for federal rights violations is not governed by state law immunity doctrines, but by a combination of federal constitutional and statutory law, namely, whether the Eleventh Amendment to the Constitution and/or the terms of a governing federal statute grant or abrogate immunity from suit. This body of law provides different immunity defenses for public school districts on one hand, and for school officials and employees, on the other. It is reviewed in Chapter 8.

Chapter 6 Discussion Questions

Where the answer to a question may be qualified by special circumstances, explain the potential qualification.

1. What are the general limits of teacher due process procedural rights under the following?
   a. The Constitution
   b. State education statutes
   c. Union agreements

2. When, if ever, may a teacher be suspended without a prior hearing? Explain.

3. When, if ever, may school authorities lawfully search a teacher's desk without the teacher's consent where there is no reasonable basis to suspect that the searched desk contains evidence of criminal conduct?

4. When, in your opinion, may school authorities lawfully require teachers to submit to random collection and analysis of their urine specimens?

5. What, if any, constitutional difference do courts draw between prior restraints of speech and punishments for uttered speech?

6. What, if any, constitutional difference arises between speech of "personal" concern and speech of "public" concern?

7. How have courts treated teacher claims of "academic freedom" as a shield against school regulation of classroom speech?

8. May school authorities constitutionally dictate teacher class assignments? Explain.

9. When, if ever, may a teacher invoke constitutional protection against school penalty for refusing to conduct a prescribed class assignment that conflicts with her religious beliefs? Her political beliefs?

10. When, if ever, does a teacher have a constitutional right to the following?
    a. To join a union
    b. To join the communist party

      c. To participate in partisan school board election campaigns
      d. To criticize school district policies
      e. To criticize fellow teachers
      f. To criticize the school principal

Case 6.1

CURTIS v. OKLAHOMA CITY PUBLIC SCHOOLS BOARD OF EDUCATION
147 F.3d 1200 (10th Cir. 1998)

[**Focus Note.** *Following his termination for willful neglect of duty and incompetence, and a charge that he misdirected a district advisory committee on school desegregation, Curtis sued the school board alleging that it (1) denied him procedural due process, (2) violated his substantive constitutional right to be free of arbitrary government action, (3) retaliated against him for his exercise of freedom of speech, and (4) engaged in employment discrimination in violation of Title VII.*]

Opinion by MURPHY, CIRCUIT JUDGE.

* * *

The Board continued to operate . . . in substantial conformity with the 1972 court-ordered desegregation plan until 1985, when the Board adopted the Student Reassignment Plan ("SRP"). . . .

Under the SRP, a number of previously desegregated schools were returned to primarily one-race status for the asserted purposes of increasing parental involvement and alleviating greater busing burdens on young black children. . . . . . .

* * *

. . . In 1987, Plaintiff was employed as the Equity/Affirmative Action Officer. . . . Plaintiff's job goals included assisting the School District in achieving equity under the SRP. . . . Plaintiff was to achieve these goals in part by . . . serving as a "communication link" between the Committee, Board, and the Superintendent of the School District. . . .

In early 1989, Sylvia Little became Plaintiff's immediate supervisor. Plaintiff experienced a number of conflicts with Little and began to receive written reprimands and other criticisms . . . from Little. Plaintiff contends the disciplinary actions were retaliatory. . . .

On September 25, 1989, Plaintiff testified at a hearing . . . on behalf of a colleague, Belinda Biscoe, who alleged she had been subjected to harassment and salary discrimination by [Superintendent] Steller. . . .

On November 14, 1989, Plaintiff was placed on a Plan for Improvement ("PFI"), a vehicle to correct his alleged performance deficiencies. Plaintiff asserts this was in retaliation for his testimony at the Biscoe hearing. In January 1990, Plaintiff . . . gave testimony to a grand jury investigating the School District. In March 1990, Plaintiff filed a racial discrimination and harassment charge with the EEOC. . . .

* * *

On December 4, 1989, the Board officially adopted a new charge ("1989 charge"). The . . . 1989 charge stated that the Equity Officer and Committee were appoint[ed] and charge[d] . . . with ensuring that black [students] and students of other racial groups are not adversely affected as a result of the Board's 1985 adoption of a Student Reassignment Plan. . . .

* * *

In September 1990, the Committee issued its report on equity. . . . . . . The report concluded the Dowell schools were generally "worse than" the group of comparison schools. . . .

In a memorandum to the Board . . . Superintendent Steller criticized the report as inconsistent with the Board's 1989 charge. Under the 1989 charge, the Committee was to monitor all sub-districts to determine if students of all racial and ethnic backgrounds were receiving equity. . . . The report also examined a number of different factors than those set out in the 1989 charge. . . . . . . Steller further suggested the Committee was biased and stated that "[t]he timing of this report [was] . . . suspiciously close to the date when the oral arguments [were] to be heard [in the Dowell litigation] by the U.S. Supreme Court [in October 1990]."

* * *

. . . On November 6, Steller notified Plaintiff in writing that he was recommending . . . that Plaintiff be discharged for willful neglect of duty and incompetence. The reasons cited for the discharge recommendation included Plaintiff's alleged failure to guide the Equity Committee . . . consistent with the Board's 1989 charge. . . . . . .

A pretermination hearing . . . was scheduled for January 19, 1991. Plaintiff informed the Board that he would not attend the scheduled hearing. At the scheduled hearing, the Board voted to deny Plaintiff's prior request for a continuance until the EEOC acted and then voted . . . to terminate Plaintiff's employment with the School District.

In July 1992, the EEOC dismissed Plaintiff's discrimination complaint . . . .

* * *

1. Protected Speech Under the First Amendment

* * *

. . . [T]he threshold question is whether the speech may be fairly characterized as constituting speech on a matter of public concern as opposed to speech upon matters of only personal interest. . . .

* * *

2. Public Concern

. . . In determining whether the speech in question addressed a matter of public concern, we consider the "content, form, and context of [the] . . . statement[s], as revealed by the whole record." . . .

"In deciding how to classify particular speech, courts focus on the motive of the speaker and attempt to determine whether the speech was calculated to redress personal grievances or whether it had a broader public purpose." . . .

* * *

This court agrees that Plaintiff's speech, both his pre-charge advocacy and his post-charge guidance, involved a matter of public concern. . . .

3. Pickering Balancing

Having concluded Plaintiff's speech involved a matter of public concern, this court next applies the *Pickering* balancing test to determine whether Plaintiff's interest in commenting on such matters was outweighed by his government employer's interest in restricting the speech. . . .

* * *

After reviewing the record and balancing the interests of Plaintiff and Defendants, this court concludes Plaintiff's pre-charge advocacy was protected. . . .

In addition, Defendants have not identified any actual disruption attributable to Plaintiff's pre-charge advocacy. . . .

We reach a different conclusion, however, with respect to Plaintiff's post-charge guidance. Given the inconsistencies between the Board-approved charge and the Committee's Blueprint . . . Defendants were entitled to consider Plaintiff's post-charge guidance . . . as reflecting negatively upon Plaintiff's competence and willingness to perform his job responsibilities. . . . Further, there is evidence that Plaintiff's post-charge guidance had a detrimental impact on the working relationship between the Board, Plaintiff's Supervisors, and the Equity Committee. . . . Additionally, Plaintiff's failure to guide the Committee consistent with the charge disrupted the Board's effective and efficient functioning. . . . . . . Based on the above factors, this court concludes Defendants' interests outweigh Plaintiff's interests with respect to Plaintiff's post-charge guidance and this speech is therefore not constitutionally protected. . . .

B. Due Process Claims

* * *

Plaintiff asserts the Board's decision to terminate his employment violated substantive due process. "In order to present a claim of denial of 'substantive' due process . . . a liberty or property interest must be present to which the protection of due process can attach." . . . Plaintiff asserts he had a property interest in continued employment. . . . Assuming a protected property interest, " '[s]ubstantive' due process requires only that termination of that interest not be arbitrary, capricious, or without a rational basis." . . . "The Due Process Clause of the Fourteenth Amendment is not a guarantee against incorrect or ill-advised personnel decisions".

* * *

Plaintiff has not established a genuine issue of material fact underlying his substantive due process claim. . . .

. . . The fact that the Board members relied on Steller's evaluation and referenced supporting evidence . . . does not render the Board's decision arbitrary or capricious.

. . . The district court therefore properly granted summary judgment to Defendants on Plaintiff's due process claims.

* * *

. . . In his Title VII claim, Plaintiff asserted Defendants terminated him in retaliation for filing a discrimination complaint with the EEOC. The ultimate question to be decided . . . in a Title VII case is which party's explanation of the employer's motivation it believes. . . . The plaintiff always has the burden of persuading the trier of fact that the defendant intentionally discriminated against the plaintiff. . . .

Our review of the record establishes there was evidence supporting the court's determination of no retaliation. . . . [W]e affirm the district court's ruling on Plaintiff's Title VII claim. . . .

III. Conclusion

The district court did not err in granting Defendants' motions for summary judgment on Plaintiff's due process claims, § 1983 claim, and Title VII claim. . . . The district court did, however, improperly conclude that Plaintiff's pre-charge advocacy . . . concerning the need to focus on the Dowell schools . . . was not protected by the First Amendment. The matter is therefore remanded to the district court for further proceedings consistent with this opinion.

Case 6.2

DOWNS v. LOS ANGELES UN. SCHOOL DISTRICT

228 F.3d 1003 (9th Cir. 2000), cert. denied, 121 S. Ct. 1653 (2001)

> [**Focus Note.** *High school teacher sued his employer district to challenge the re-moval by school superiors of messages he posted on a school bulletin board in op-position to the school's messages on school bulletin boards. In rejecting Downs's claims, the court drew a sharp distinction between control of government speech and control of private speech.*]

TROTT, CIRCUIT JUDGE:

The narrow question we must answer is whether the First Amendment compels a public high school to share the podium with a teacher with an-tagonistic and contrary views *when the school speaks to its own constituents* on the subject of how students should behave towards each other while in school. [emphasis added] The answer to this question clearly is no.

* * *

Factual Background

. . . LAUSD [the District] issued "Memorandum No. 111," titled "Gay and Lesbian Awareness Month," to all schools and offices in the school district. Memorandum No. 111 referred to a . . . formal Board of Education resolution designating June of each year as "a time to focus on gay and lesbian issues." The Memorandum noted that the Board of Education's resolution was passed to support "Educating for Diversity" . . . .

The Memorandum informed the schools and offices that the "Office of Intergroup Relations and the Multicultural Unit, Division of Instruc-tional Services, and the Gay and Lesbian Education Commission" would provide posters and materials in support of Gay and Lesbian Awareness Month.

* * *

Pursuant to Memorandum No. 111 . . . some Leichman High staff members created a bulletin board inside the school building on which faculty and staff could post materials related to Gay and Lesbian Awareness Month. . . . Staff members created a similar board the following year. Materials did not need approval before posting on the Gay and Lesbian Awareness bulletin boards, but were subject to the oversight of the school principal, who had ultimate authority within the school over the content of the boards. . . .

* * *

. . . They included a poster titled "The Civil Rights Movement;" a poster titled "Diversity is Beautiful;" a poster on Name Calling; a poster titled "What is a Family;" a bar/pie chart reflecting Statistics on Hate Crimes; a sheet of paper on "The Rainbow Flag;" a sheet of paper explaining the gay and lesbian symbols; a laminated felt rainbow flag with the Greek letter Lambda; a newspaper article regarding LAUSD Board approval of domestic partner benefits; a Board resolution regarding discrimination; a Los Angeles County Human Relations Commission brochure regarding anti-gay and lesbian bashing; a statement that June is Gay and Lesbian Awareness/Pride month; a sheet of paper identifying famous gays and lesbians in history; a sheet of paper discussing the history of the pink triangle symbol; and a sheet of paper discussing the Lambda symbol. There is no evidence in the record that individuals other than faculty and staff at Leichman High posted these or any other materials on the school's Gay and Lesbian Awareness bulletin boards.

Downs objected to the recognition of Gay and Lesbian Awareness Month at Leichman High. In June of 1997, Downs created his own bulletin board across the hall from his classroom titled "Testing Tolerance." In June of 1998, in response to postings on other Gay and Lesbian Awareness bulletin boards within the school, Downs created a competing bulletin board titled "Redefining the Family." Included among the materials posted by Downs were . . . the following four separate excerpts:

According to lesbian activist Tories Osborn, 60% of Americans hold the belief that homosexuality is immoral. Most mainline religions in America . . . condemn homosexual behavior. . . . Do not defile yourselves in any of these ways because this is how the nations that I am going to drive out before you become defiled. Leviticus 18:22–24.

* * *

Anti-sodomy laws in many states stand to prevent or at least complicate homosexual marriage and adoption. . . .

* * *

. . . [A]fter other faculty members complained, Olmsted and Marino either removed Downs's materials or ordered Downs to remove them himself. . . .

Leading up to the 1997 removal of Downs's materials, Olmsted, Downs, and LAUSD's counsel engaged in both a written and verbal dispute over the bulletin board issue. . . .

* * *

Discussion

* * *

. . . [W]e must decide whether his postings on Leichman High's bulletin boards warranted any First Amendment protection. . . . Premised on our conclusion that the bulletin boards contained only "government speech," we conclude that Downs had no First Amendment right to dictate or to contribute to the content of that speech. Thus, LAUSD did not act unconstitutionally in removing Downs's materials or in ordering that the materials be removed. . . .

A. Whose Speech Was It?

* * *

. . . This case is not controlled by *Hazelwood* or *Planned Parenthood* because it is a case of the government itself speaking. . . . . . . [W]e find it more helpful to focus on who actually was responsible for the speech on Leichman High's Gay and Lesbian Awareness bulletin boards. Only school faculty and staff had access to post materials on these boards. While these faculty and staff members may have received materials from outside organizations, the faculty and staff members alone posted material on the bulletin boards, and at all times their postings were subject to the oversight of the school principals. Although much, if not all, of what Downs posted appeared on the bulletin board directly across the hall from his assigned classroom, the proximity of the board to his classroom detracts in no way from the conclusion that the bulletin board, like all others in Leichman High's halls, were the property and responsibility of Leichman High and LAUSD.

* * *

. . . The important point is that any speech on the bulletin boards was directly traceable to LAUSD and the school board through Olmsted's and Marino's enforcement of . . . school board policy.

Because the school district and the school board were in fact responsible for 1) the recognition of Gay and Lesbian Awareness month and 2) the content of the bulletin boards through school principals' oversight, this case is clearly distinguishable from cases involving student-written articles in a school-sponsored newspaper or an outside organization's advertisements in school-sponsored student newspapers, yearbooks, and athletic programs. . . .

We do not face an example of the government opening up a forum for either unlimited or limited public discussion. Instead, we face an example of the government opening up its own mouth. . . .

B. To What Extent Can the Government Control Its Own Speech?

. . . We conclude that when a public high school is the speaker, its control of its own speech is not subject to the constraints of constitutional safeguards and forum analysis. . . . As applied here, the First Amendment allows

LAUSD to decide that Downs may not speak as its representative. This power is certainly so if his message is one with which the district disagrees.

* * *

An arm of local government—such as a school board—may decide not only to talk about gay and lesbian awareness and tolerance in general, but also to advocate such tolerance if it so decides, and restrict the contrary speech of one of its representatives. . . .

* * *

In addition to inviting a "focus on gay and lesbian issues," Memorandum No. 111 made clear that it was "the District's multicultural and human relations education policy" to "Educat[e] for Diversity," . . . .

. . . In fact, Downs had continuous notice that he was violating district policy. . . .

Were we to invoke the Constitution to protect Downs's ability to make his voice a part of the voice of the government entity he served, Downs would be able to do to the government what the government could not do to Downs: compel it to embrace a viewpoint. . . . Our narrow decision does not conflict with the Supreme Court's plurality decision in *Board of Educ., Island Trees Union Free Sch. Dist. No. 26 v. Pico,* 457 U.S. 853, . . . (1982). . . . In *Pico,* the court made clear at the outset that the respondents in that case did not seek to impose limitations upon their school Board's discretion to prescribe the curricula of the Island Trees schools. . . . Thus, . . . the Court was not faced with a case of "school board speech" or "government speech." . . .

* * *

In order . . . to have the opportunity to speak as the government, the speaker must . . . survive the electoral process. . . . The LAUSD school board is elected . . . , and until its current members are voted out of office, they "speak" for the school district through the policies they adopt. . . .

* * *

Our holding, however, does not prevent Downs from propounding his own opinion on the morality of homosexuality. Subject to any applicable forum analysis, he may do so on the sidewalks, in the parks, through the chatrooms, at his dinner table, and in countless other locations. . . .

Conclusion

We hold that when the school district speaks through bulletin boards that are not "free speech zones," but instead are vehicles for conveying a message from the school district, the school district may formulate that message without the constraint of viewpoint neutrality. . . . Because we determine that

Downs has no First Amendment right to speak for the government, his equal protection claim based upon the deprivation of this asserted right also fails to withstand summary judgment.

The district court's grant of summary judgment in favor of LAUSD is AFFIRMED.

Case 6.2 Review Question

1. Had Downs abandoned the bulletin board, but uttered the same messages to students in school corridors, in the cafeteria or in the school gym during class breaks, might the school authorities discipline him for that speech under the above opinion?

Case 6.3

LACKS v. FERGUSON REORGANIZED SCHOOL DIST.
147 F.3d 719 (8th Cir. 1998)

[***Focus Note***. *Lacks sued to overturn her termination for allowing student use of profanity in her classroom assignments. She claimed that the termination violated her constitutional rights to due process and freedom of speech, and subjected her to racial discrimination in violation of Title VII of the Civil Rights Act. The trial court ordered Lacks's reinstatement with back pay, attorneys' fees and costs, and in addition, the jury returned a verdict in her favor for $500,000 on her constitutional claims and $250,000 on her race discrimination claim. The Court of Appeals reversed the judgment and the jury verdicts on all counts.]*

RICHARD S. ARNOLD, CHIEF JUDGE

* * *

. . . Lacks taught English and journalism classes, and she sponsored the school newspaper. In October 1994, Lacks divided her junior English class into small groups and directed them to write short plays, which were to be performed for the other students in the class and videotaped. The plays written by the students contained profanity, including the repeated uses of the words "fuck," "shit," "ass," "bitch," and "nigger." When the plays were videotaped, these words were used more than 150 times in approximately forty minutes. . . . Lacks later admitted that the plays contained an unusual amount of profanity. . . . . . . Lacks was aware of the content of the plays . . . because she had previously reviewed at least one of the scripts and had attended rehearsals of the plays the day before. . . . On October 10, the students performed their plays and were videotaped at the direction of Lacks. . . .

The following January, as a result of complaints . . . the existence of the videotapes came to the attention of Vernon Mitchell, the principal. . . . Mitchell initiated an inquiry. . . . During the investigation, the administrators learned that . . . Lacks had permitted a student to read aloud in a classroom two of his poems which contained profanity and graphic descriptions of oral sex. . . .

Following the investigation, Dr. Robert Fritz, the district superintendent, formally charged Lacks with "willful or persistent violation of and failure to obey [the school district's] policies" . . . . Fritz . . . recommended her termination. . . . Lacks requested a hearing, and the school board heard testimony from Lacks and fifteen other witnesses over five evenings. . . . . . . On March 23, the board issued a decision which found that Lacks was aware of the school board's policy . . . that she could have chosen teaching methods which prohibited profanity, and that her failure to do so constituted a "willful and persistent practice violative of Board policy. . . ." . . . [T]he school board terminated Lacks's teaching contract.

. . . [T]he District Court held that Lacks did not willfully violate board policy 3043, because she believed that profanity was permitted in the context of creative expression in the classroom. . . .

* * *

. . . After a careful review of the evidence, we hold that the record contains sufficient evidence for the school board to have concluded that Lacks willfully violated board policy.

. . . Lacks defended . . . by arguing that she thought that the board's policy . . . applied only to "student behavior" and not to students' creative assignments. She also argued that her teaching method . . . required her to allow her students creative freedom, which included the use of profanity. . . . Lacks could not say with certainty that she would be able to teach at Berkeley High School if her students were not given the freedom to use profanity in their creative activities. . . .

* * *

The school board also heard testimony from Lacks's principal, Vernon Mitchell, that he told Lacks that profanity was not permitted in the school newspaper. . . . Mitchell testified that he discussed the use of profanity in the newspaper with Lacks "[t]wo or three times." . . . Mitchell also noted that signs posted in Lacks's classroom read "No Profanity." . . .

Lacks claimed that Mitchell never warned her. . . . However . . . assessing the credibility of witnesses is the function of the school board, not the reviewing court. . . . The policy prohibiting profanity was explicit and contained no exceptions. . . . We hold that the board's decision was reasonable and supported by substantial evidence on the record as a whole. The judgment in the plaintiff's favor on this claim must be reversed.

When the jury returned a verdict in favor of Lacks on her First Amendment claim, it provided answers to two interrogatories posed by the District Court's instructions. . . . With respect to the first interrogatory— "Did [Lacks] have reasonable notice that allowing students to use profanity in their creative writing was prohibited?"—the jury answered "no." With respect to the second interrogatory— "Did defendant school district have a legitimate academic interest in prohibiting profanity by students in their creative writing, regardless of any other competing interests?"—the jury also answered "no." . . . We reverse and hold, as a matter of law, that the answer to both of those questions was "yes."

* * *

We also hold, as a matter of law, that the school board had a legitimate academic interest in prohibiting profanity by students in their creative writing. . . .

A flat prohibition on profanity in the classroom is reasonably related to the legitimate pedagogical concern of promoting generally acceptable social standards. . . . Allowing one student to call another a "fucking bitch" and a "whore" in front of the rest of the class, and allowing a student to read aloud a poem that describes sexual encounters in the most graphic detail . . . hardly promotes these shared social standards. We consider the matter too plain for argument.

. . . Therefore, the judgment in the plaintiff's favor on her First Amendment claim is reversed.

. . . The jury found that Lacks had proved . . . that race was a motivating factor in the school board's decision to terminate her. . . . We reverse, and hold as a matter of law that race was not a motivating factor in the school board's decision to terminate Lacks. . . .

. . . Mitchell admitted that when he saw the videotape with the students performing their plays, his reaction was that it was "black students acting a fool and white folks videotaping it." . . . Lacks also elicited testimony from another teacher . . . that in the past Mitchell had displayed signs of hostility toward white teachers . . . because Mitchell believed that some white teachers did not care about the students. . . . And Lacks produced some evidence which arguably showed that Dr. John Wright, an assistant superintendent for personnel, viewed the videotaping incident in racial terms. Lacks is white; Mitchell, Wright, and the students are black.

However, Mitchell and Wright did not make the decision to terminate Lacks; that decision was made by the school board. Lacks responds . . . by arguing that the school board was influenced by the bias of the administrators, and that the board consequently served as the conduit, or "cat's paw," of the racial animus of the school administration. . . . But Lacks produced no evidence that the school board deferred to the opinion or judgment of Mitchell or Wright. . . . . . .

. . . The evidence . . . unequivocally shows that the board made an independent determination. . . . Lacks's "cat's paw" theory must therefore fail.

Lacks offers one piece of evidence which allegedly shows direct racial bias . . . a four-page press release issued by the board after it terminated Lacks's teaching contract. The press release reads in part:

> . . . The video produced in Ms. Lacks' class demonstrates a serious and extreme lack of direction from the teacher. Teachers do not have the right to abdicate their responsibility to set standards under the guise of creativity. The content of the video is a violation of our black community; it is a violation of our white community; it is a violation of the values within our community and it is a violation of the ethical teaching standards. . . .

Lacks argues that the references to "white community" and "black community" provide direct evidence that the board "had race on its mind" when it fired Lacks. . . . That proposition is questionable. . . . Moreover, having race on one's mind is not the same thing as acting because of race. At any rate, the single reference in the school board's press release is not sufficient to sustain the jury verdict on the race discrimination claims. . . .

The judgment of the District Court is reversed, and the cause remanded with directions to dismiss the complaint with prejudice.

Case 6.3 Review Question

1. Note the independent judicial review power of courts to curb judges and runaway juries by:
   a. Overruling fact findings
   b. Reviewing sufficiency of the evidence
   c. Reviewing sufficiency of notice for due process

Case 6.4

O'CONNOR v. ORTEGA
480 U.S. 709 (1987)

*[**Focus Note**. Magno Ortega, Chief of Professional Education at a state hospital, brought suit following his dismissal for improprieties, alleging that the dismissal resulted from an unconstitutional search of his state-supplied office, desk, and files. Justice O'Connor delivered the following opinion for the Court.]*

JUSTICE O' CONNOR . . . *delivered an opinion in which the* CHIEF JUSTICE, JUSTICE WHITE *and* JUSTICE POWELL *join.*

* * *

This suit . . . presents two issues concerning the Fourth Amendment rights of public employees. First . . . whether the respondent . . . had a reasonable expectation of privacy in his office, desk, and file cabinets at his place of work. Second, we must address the appropriate Fourth Amendment standard for a search conducted by a public employer in areas in which a public employee is found to have a reasonable expectation of privacy.

* * *

. . . [W]e have held . . . that the Fourth Amendment governs the conduct of school officials. . . . Searches and seizures by government employers or supervisors of the private property of their employees, therefore, are subject to the restraints of the Fourth Amendment.

    . . . Our cases establish that Dr. Ortega's Fourth Amendment rights are implicated only if the conduct of the Hospital officials . . . infringed an expectation of privacy that society is prepared to consider reasonable. . . .

* * *

Because the reasonableness of an expectation of privacy, . . . is understood to differ according to context, it is essential first to delineate the boundaries of the workplace context. The workplace includes those areas and items that are related to work and are generally within the employer's control. . . . These areas remain part of the workplace context even if the employee has placed personal items in them. . . .

* * *

Public employees' expectations of privacy in their offices, desks, and file cabinets, like similar expectations of employees in the private sector, may be reduced by virtue of actual office practices and procedures, or by legitimate regulation. . . .

    Given the great variety of work environments . . . the question of whether an employee has a reasonable expectation of privacy must be addressed on a case-by-case basis.

* * *

. . . In the case of searches conducted by a public employer, we must balance the invasion of the employee's legitimate expectations of privacy against the government's need for supervision, control, and the efficient operation of the workplace.

* * *

There is surprisingly little case law on the appropriate Fourth Amendment standard of reasonableness for a public employer's work-related search of its employee's offices, desks, or file cabinets. . . .

* * *

The legitimate privacy interests of public employees in the private objects they bring to the workplace may be substantial. Against these privacy interests, however, must be balanced the realities of the workplace, which strongly suggest that a warrant requirement would be unworkable. . . . [E]mployers most frequently need to enter the offices and desks of their employees for legitimate work-related reasons wholly unrelated to illegal conduct. . . . An employer may have need for correspondence, or a file or report available . . . while the employee is away from the office. Or . . . employers may need to safeguard or identify state property or records . . . in connection with a pending investigation into suspected employee misfeasance.

In our view, requiring an employer to obtain a warrant whenever the employer wished to enter an employee's office, desk, or file cabinets for a work-related purpose would seriously disrupt the routine conduct of business and would be unduly burdensome. . . .

* * *

. . . Because the parties in this case have alleged that the search was either a noninvestigatory work-related intrusion or an investigatory search for evidence of suspected work-related employee misfeasance, we undertake to determine the appropriate Fourth Amendment standard of reasonableness only for these two types of employer intrusions. . . .

* * *

. . . [P]ublic employers must be given wide latitude to enter employee offices for work-related, noninvestigatory reasons. We come to a similar conclusion for searches conducted pursuant to an investigation of work-related employee misconduct. . . .

In our view, therefore, a probable cause requirement for searches of the type at issue here would impose intolerable burdens on public employers. . . .

* * *

. . . We hold, therefore, that public employer intrusions on the constitutionally protected privacy interests of government employees for noninvestigatory, work-related purposes, as well as for investigations of work-related misconduct, should be judged by the standard of reasonableness under all the circumstances. . . .

* * *

In the procedural posture of this case, we do not attempt to determine whether the search of Dr. Ortega's office and the seizure of his personal belongings satisfy the standard of reasonableness. . . . No evidentiary hearing was held in this case. . . .

* * *

On remand, therefore, the District Court must determine the justification for the search and seizure, and evaluate the reasonableness of both the inception of the search and its scope.

Case 6.5

AUBREY v. SCHOOL BOARD OF LAFAYETTE PARISH
148 F.3d 559 (5th Cir. 1998)

*[**Focus Note**. Aubrey, an elementary school custodian, brought suit alleging that he was subjected to a random, urinalysis drug test in violation of the Fourth Amendment. The trial court dismissed the case and the following opinion affirmed the dismissal, holding that the school board's need to conduct suspicionless searches of persons in safety-sensitive positions outweighed the privacy interests of Aubrey and other safety-sensitive employees.]*

POLITZ, CHIEF JUDGE.

* * *

As a custodian at the Prairie Elementary School, Aubrey's duties included cleaning . . . bathrooms each day, using various chemicals. . . . He constantly was in the presence of the young students.

In December 1992, the Board adopted an Employee Drug Testing Policy. In August 1993, Aubrey attended an in-service training . . . in which the drug testing policy was distributed and reviewed.

. . . On September 28, 1994, the Board requested that Aubrey and fourteen other employees submit to a urinalysis screening. Aubrey's test indicated the presence of tetrahydrocannabinol, the active chemical in marijuana. As an alternative to termination, the Board required that Aubrey attend a substance abuse program. . . .

Denying that he had used marijuana, Aubrey sought an injunction barring the Board from firing him, or requiring that he continue to attend the substance abuse program. . . .

* * *

. . . [T]he fourth amendment . . . extends to all government searches. . . . This restraint . . . generally bars officials from undertaking a search or seizure absent individualized suspicion. Searches conducted without grounds for suspicion of particular individuals have been upheld, however, in certain limited circumstances. . . .

A program which compels government employees to submit to urinalysis is a search. . . .

* * *

In *Vernonia School District 47J v. Acton,* a policy adopted by a school district to test student athletes was held non-violative of fourth amendment protections. . . .

* * *

. . . The Board contends that the urinalysis was obtained to maintain the safe and efficient operation of its schools . . . and decrease the potential spread of drug use among its students. . . . The Board also asserts that it "has a compelling interest and commitment to eliminate illegal and unauthorized drug use . . . drug users, drug activities, and drug effects from all of its workplaces." The Board has not produced any summary judgment evidence to demonstrate a problem of drug abuse or use in its schools, and although such a showing would be of persuasive value, it is not mandatory. . . . . . . We find the Board's interests to be substantial indeed.

The Board's valid and compelling public interests must be weighed against the intrusion and interference with individual liberty. . . .

First, Aubrey had notice that his position . . . was specifically designated as safety sensitive. . . .

Second, the intrusiveness of the search was minimal. . . . Aubrey produced the sample in privacy. . . . [H]e was not required to disclose any personal medical information, nor was the urinalysis used to determine the presence of anything other than the presence or absence of drugs. . . .

. . . Although the facts in this case differ from Acton [Vernonia] in that the [Vernonia] school was testing student athletes as opposed to employees, the most significant element in both this case and Acton is that "the Policy was undertaken in furtherance of the government's responsibilities, under a public school system, as guardian and tutor of children entrusted to its care." . . .

We therefore conclude and hold that the Board's need to conduct the suspicionless searches pursuant to the drug testing policy outweighs the privacy interests of the employees in an elementary school who interact regularly with students, use hazardous substances, operate potentially dangerous equipment, or otherwise pose any threat or danger to the students.

Case 6.6

TAXMAN v. BOARD OF EDUCATION
91 F.3d 1547 (3d Cir. 1996)

MANSMANN, CIRCUIT JUDGE

In this Title VII matter, we must determine whether the Board of Education of the Township of Piscataway violated that statute when it made race a factor in selecting which of two equally qualified employees to lay off. Specifically, we must decide whether Title VII permits an employer with a racially balanced work force to grant a non-remedial racial preference in order to promote "racial diversity".

It is clear that the language of Title VII is violated when an employer makes an employment decision based upon an employee's race. The Supreme Court determined in *United Steelworkers v. Weber*, 443 U.S. 193 . . . (1979), however, that Title VII's prohibition against racial discrimination is not violated by affirmative action plans which first, "have purposes that mirror those of the statute" and second, do not "unnecessarily trammel the interests of the [non-minority] employees," . . .

We hold that Piscataway's affirmative action policy is unlawful because it fails to satisfy either prong of *Weber*. Given the clear antidiscrimination mandate of Title VII, a non-remedial affirmative action plan, even one with a laudable purpose, cannot pass muster. We will affirm the district court's grant of summary judgment to Sharon Taxman.

* * *

In May, 1989, the Board accepted a recommendation from the Superintendent of Schools to reduce the teaching staff in the Business Department at Piscataway High School by one. At that time, two of the teachers . . . were of equal seniority. . . . One . . . was . . . plaintiff Sharon Taxman, who is White, and the other was Debra Williams, who is Black. . . . Decisions regarding layoffs by New Jersey school boards are highly circumscribed by state law. . . . Thus, local boards lack discretion to choose between employees for layoff, except in the rare instance of a tie in seniority between the two or more employees eligible to fill the last remaining position.

. . . In prior decisions involving the layoff of employees with equal seniority, the Board had broken the tie through "a random process which included drawing numbers out of a container, drawing lots or having a lottery." . . . [N]one of those instances, however, had the employees involved been of different races.

. . . Superintendent of Schools Burton Edelchick recommended to the Board that the affirmative action plan be invoked in order to determine which teacher to retain. Superintendent Edelchick made this recommendation "because he believed Ms. Williams and Ms. Taxman were tied in seniority, were equally qualified, and because Ms. Williams was the only Black teacher in the Business Education Department."

While the Board recognized that it was not bound to apply the affirmative action policy, it made a discretionary decision to invoke the policy to break the tie between Williams and Taxman. As a result, the Board "voted to terminate the employment of Sharon Taxman, effective June 30, 1988. . . ."

* * *

. . . [T]he parties do not dispute that Taxman has established a prima facie case or that the Board's decision to terminate her was based on its affirmative action policy. The dispositive liability issue, therefore, is the validity of the Board's policy under Title VII.

* * *

We see this case as one involving straightforward statutory interpretation. . . . . . . The statute . . . provides that race cannot be a factor in employer decisions. . . . If exceptions to this bar are to be made, they must be made on the basis of what Congress has said. The affirmative action plans at issue in *Weber* and *Johnson* were sustained only because the Supreme Court . . . found a secondary congressional objective in Title VII that had to be accommodated—i.e., the elimination of the effects of past discrimination in the workplace. Here, there is no congressional recognition of diversity as a Title VII objective requiring accommodation.

* * *

. . . Our analysis . . . convinces us that a non-remedial affirmative action plan cannot form the basis for deviating from the antidiscrimination mandate of Title VII.

The Board admits that it did not act to remedy the effects of past employment discrimination. . . . Nor does the Board contend that its action here was directed at remedying any de jure or de facto segregation. . . .

* * *

Finally, we are convinced that the harm imposed upon a nonminority employee by the loss of his or her job is so substantial and the cost so severe that the Board's goal of racial diversity, even if legitimate under Title VII, may not be pursued in this particular fashion. This is especially true where, as here, the nonminority employee is tenured. . . .

* * *

. . . The parties have agreed that the legal analysis required by the state statute is essentially the same as that undertaken in Title VII cases. . . .

. . . Analysis of this case under the NJLAD would, therefore, lead to the same result as that which we have reached under Title VII. Sharon Taxman is entitled to summary judgment on her claim made under the NJLAD.

Case 6.7

SCHROEDER v. HAMILTON SCHOOL DISTRICT
282 F.3d 946 (7th Cir. 2002)

[*Focus Note.* A white male former teacher sued his employer school district and its administrators, claiming that they denied him his constitutional right to equal protection of the law, by failing to protect him from harassment by students, parents and some fellow teachers on account of his sexual orientation. The following opinion highlights several important points:

  1. Whether sexual orientation is entitled to heightened constitutional protection, as are race and gender.
  2. Whether equal protection of harassed teachers or school employees is the same as that provided for school children.
  3. That the constitutional sufficiency of protective action undertaken by a school district . . . depends upon practical considerations, such as the limits and priority needs of school resources.
  4. What the aggrieved party must show to establish that the school district, through its authorized supervisors, fostered or encouraged certain conduct or was "deliberately indifferent" to it.
  5. How the constitutional measure of discrimination differs from discrimination standards of civil rights statutes.]

MANION, CIRCUIT JUDGE

Tommy Schroeder, a school teacher, filed suit against his former employer, the Hamilton [Wisconsin] School District, the school district administrator, and several staff administrators . . . alleging that they violated his right to equal protection by failing to take reasonable measures to prevent students and parents, and occasionally fellow staff members, from harassing him about his homosexuality. The district court granted summary judgment for the defendants. . . . [W]e affirm.

I.

In 1990, . . . Tommy Schroeder began teaching sixth grade at Templeton Middle School . . . . Shortly after arriving at Templeton, Schroeder disclosed his homosexuality to a few of his fellow staff members and, during his second or third year at the school, made the same disclosure at a public meeting. This information eventually spread throughout the Templeton community, and Schroeder began receiving unpleasant inquiries and crude, occasionally cruel, taunts from students regarding his homosexuality.

. . . Schroeder has conceded, however, that none of the individual defendants ever made derogatory comments about him personally or his sexual orientation. He also testified . . . that no teacher or staff member at Templeton ever harassed him on a daily basis. Finally, Schroeder has admitted that he refused to disclose the names of staff members who he claims harassed him on occasion.

Many of the reported student comments and actions, however, were far worse— accusations that he had AIDS; a student calling him a faggot and remarking "How sad there are any gays in the world"; another student physically confronted Schroeder after shouting obscenities at him; catcalls in the hallways that he was a "queer" or a "faggot"; obscenities shouted at him during bus duty; harassing phone calls with students chanting "faggot, faggot, faggot" and other calls where he was asked whether he was a "faggot"; and bathroom graffiti identifying Schroeder as a "faggot," and describing, in the most explicit and vulgar terms, the type of sexual acts they presumed he engaged in with other men. He reported this harassment on several occasions, and the defendants "consequenced" (i.e., a term of art in education circles for student discipline) the students identified with the offensive behavior. Much of the harassment, however, was anonymous, and therefore went unpunished. . . .

Because of the widespread, anonymous nature of the harassment, Schroeder demanded that the defendants conduct "sensitivity training" to condemn discrimination against homosexuals . . . . Instead, Polczynski . . . circulated a memorandum to teachers and other staff noting that students were continuing to use "inappropriate and offensive racial and/or gender-related words or phrases," and that "[i]f you observe or overhear students using inappropriate language or gestures, please consequence them as you feel appropriate. . . ." . . .

Finally, after several requests for a transfer, Schroeder was moved to Lannon Elementary School . . . where he taught first- and second-grade classes. After a year's respite, the taunts resumed. This time, however, they came primarily from adults, presumably the parents of students at Lannon. At the beginning of his second year at Lannon, an anonymous memo was circulated by a parent proclaiming, "Mr. Schroeder openly admitted at a district meeting that he was homosexual. Is that a good role model for our 5-, 6- and 7-year-old children?" Schroeder also claims that he began hearing that certain staff

members and parents were calling him a pedophile and accusing him of sexually abusing small boys. One parent removed his child from Schroeder's class.
. . . Another parent's fear that Schroeder was a pedophile led defendant
Richard Ladd, Lannon's principal, to raise the possibility of "proximity supervision" (i.e., meaning that Schroeder could not be alone with male students).
The tires on Schroeder's car were slashed, and he began receiving anonymous,
harassing phone calls at home (e.g., "Faggot, stay away from our kids"). . . .

In February 1998, Schroeder, who has a protracted history of psychiatric problems, experienced a "mental breakdown." On February 11, 1998,
Schroeder's last day at Lannon, Ladd approached him about complaints that
he had received from some of his students' parents. Schroeder told Ladd
that he did not want to talk about it, and that he was resigning. Later that
day, Schroeder handed Ladd a letter of resignation. . . .

Schroeder contends that the harassment he received . . . coupled with
the defendants' failure to properly address the problem, caused him to have
a nervous breakdown that ultimately resulted in his termination. . . .

* * *

In order to establish an equal protection violation, Schroeder must show that
the defendants: (1) treated him differently from others who were similarly
situated, (2) intentionally treated him differently because of his membership
in the class to which he belonged (i.e., homosexuals), and (3) because homosexuals do not enjoy any heightened protection under the Constitution, . . .
that the discriminatory intent was not rationally related to a legitimate state
interest. . . .

* * *

Schroeder attempts to side-step this analysis completely by inviting us to
"hold explicitly that Title VII analysis/law shall apply . . . where discrimination in employment is the basis for the claimed Equal Protection violation." . . . Title VII does not, however, provide for a private right of action
based on sexual orientation discrimination. . . . [T]o the extent Schroeder
seeks to have this court judicially amend Title VII to provide for such a cause
of action, we decline to do so. . . . Finally, to the extent that Schroeder would
like us to import Title VII employment discrimination standards into our
traditional equal protection analysis, we decline the invitation.

We now turn our attention to Schroeder's . . . argument—that even under a traditional equal protection analysis, the district court's decision must
be reversed. . . . His primary contention is that the defendants failed to address his complaints in the same manner that they handled complaints of harassment based on race or gender. . . .

First, as Schroeder acknowledges, the initial memorandum circulated
by Polczynski was generated in response to the pervasive use of racist
comments and symbols by students . . . . Additionally, the district-
wide staff/teacher training sessions on race discrimination . . . were con-

ducted in the early 1990's when the Hamilton School District began busing black students into its schools from the Milwaukee County Schools. . . . By citing these examples, Schroeder attempts to set up a false dichotomy—i.e., disparity of treatment/protection given to blacks/women as compared with homosexuals. In reality, these examples merely demonstrate the school district's priorities for use of time and resources in favor of its students. . . .

* * *

. . . It is uncontested that Schroeder requested to be removed from bus duty, and that his request was denied . . . . There is nothing in the record, however, indicating that, in denying his request, the school administrators treated Schroeder differently from similarly situated non-homosexual teachers. . . .

* * *

Schroeder cites an incident involving vulgar student-authored bathroom graffiti as additional evidence of differential treatment. While admitting that school administrators identified and punished the offending students, he claims that the school's response . . . deviated from its normal policies and procedures. The district court determined, however, that Schroeder's assertion of differential treatment . . . was supported only by "essentially self-serving assertions" and inadmissible hearsay. . . .

Finally, Schroeder contends that the defendants discriminated against him because the Hamilton School District had policies against race and sex discrimination, but did not have one against sexual orientation discrimination. While this is most certainly true, the lack of such a policy is not evidence that the defendants were deliberately indifferent to his complaints of harassment. . . . Schroeder appears to suggest, however, that the only way the defendants could have prevented the harassment was by requiring all Hamilton School District personnel and students to attend mandatory training sessions on sexual orientation discrimination. There are several problems with this argument.

First of all, it is hardly reasonable to expect a school district to devote a substantial amount of resources to curb the harassment of one teacher . . . . As emphasized in *Equal. Found. of Greater Cincinnati, Inc. v. City of Cincinnati*, 128 F.3d 289, 300–01 (6th Cir. 1997), another decision involving a claim of denial of equal protection on grounds of sexual orientation discrimination, it is not irrational to prioritize protective activities. It is in fact unavoidable. . . . . . .

Schroeder's exhortation to adopt a specific policy requiring students to be sensitive to, or accepting of, homosexuals is especially problematic in an elementary or early middle school . . . setting. What would such a policy say? . . . Unfortunately, there is no simple way of explaining to young students why it is wrong to mock homosexuals without discussing the underlying lifestyle or sexual behavior associated with such a designation.

Schools can, however, teach their students that it is wrong to mock anyone, for any reason. . . .

In this case, the record is clear: When school administrators determined that a student harassed Schroeder . . . the student was punished. . . . This is all that was required of them.

. . . [A] short word about difficult parents. . . . Regardless of the parental attitude . . . school administrators have little or no power to "consequence" the parents of students. . . . Schroeder could have reported the anonymous harassing phone calls . . . to the telephone company, and any threats of physical violence to the police. . . .

. . . Given that the majority of the harassment at issue in this case was anonymous, we are skeptical about whether the defendants could have done much more to prevent the harassment without expending a disproportionate commitment of resources, or fashioning a draconian response. . . .

The question . . . is not whether the defendants did enough. . . . Rather, the only issue is whether the manner in which the defendants handled Schroeder's complaints . . . denied him equal protection under the law. . . .

Schroeder's breakdown and his current psychological condition are unfortunate. To the extent that student and parental harassment of him exacerbated his long history of personal and psychological problems, that is also unfortunate. There is, however, no evidence that the defendants denied him the equal protection of the law.

* * *

AFFIRMED.

Posner, Circuit Judge, concurring.

I write separately to emphasize that our decision would have to be the same even if Schroeder were right that the school administrators' response to his complaints about the harassment . . . was tepid in comparison to their response to signs of racial prejudice, so that they were in a sense . . . "discriminating" in favor of blacks by giving blacks more protection than they were giving this homosexual teacher.

. . . But Schroeder is not black. Blacks are one of the groups that the Supreme Court has decided deserve special protection against discrimination by public entities. (Women too— . . .) *Reese v. Jefferson School District No. 14J,* 208 F.3d 736, 740 (9th Cir. 2000). But Schroeder is no more a woman than he is a black. . . .

Homosexuals have not been accorded the constitutional status of blacks or women. This does not make them constitutional outlaws. *Any* group, or for that matter any individual . . . has a right not to be victimized by an irrational withdrawal of state protection. But the word "irrational" is the key to determining the scope of this principle. Discrimination against homosexuals by public entities violates the equal protection clause only if it lacks a rational basis, as it would do if it were motivated by baseless hostility to homosexuals . . . .

Schroeder has not presented evidence from which a reasonable jury could infer that the defendants . . . were hostile to Schroeder because he was a homosexual. . . .

* * *

. . . So while in hindsight it appears that the defendants could have done more to protect Schroeder from abuse, it is equally important to emphasize that lackluster is not a synonym for invidious or irrational. . . .

Case 6.8

FARAGHER v. CITY OF BOCA RATON
524 U.S. 775 (1998)

Reproduced at p. 219, *Supra.*

Case 6.9

ONCALE v. SUNDOWNERS OFFSHORE SERVICES, INC.
118 S. Ct. 998 (1998)

> Justice Scalia *delivered the opinion of the Court.*

This case presents the question whether workplace harassment can violate Title VII's prohibition against "discriminat[ion] . . . because of . . . sex," . . . when the harasser and the harassed employee are of the same sex.

. . . [W]e must assume the facts to be as alleged by petitioner Joseph Oncale. . . . In late October 1991, Oncale was working for respondent Sundowner Offshore Services on a Chevron U.S.A., Inc., oil platform in the Gulf of Mexico. He was employed as a roustabout on an eight-man crew which included respondents John Lyons, Danny Pippen, and Brandon Johnson. Lyons, the crane operator, and Pippen, the driller, had supervisory authority. . . . On several occasions, Oncale was forcibly subjected to sex-related, humiliating actions against him by Lyons, Pippen and Johnson in the presence of the rest of the crew. Pippen and Lyons also physically assaulted Oncale in a sexual manner, and Lyons threatened him with rape. Oncale's complaints to supervisory personnel produced no remedial action. . . . Oncale eventually quit—asking that his pink slip reflect that he "voluntarily left due to sexual harassment and verbal abuse." . . .

Oncale filed a complaint . . . alleging that he was discriminated against in his employment because of his sex. . . . [T]he district court held that "Mr. Oncale . . . a male, has no cause of action under Title VII. . . . On appeal, a panel of the Fifth Circuit . . . affirmed." . . .

Title VII of the Civil Rights Act of 1964 provides, in relevant part, that "[i]t shall be an unlawful employment practice for an employer . . . to discriminate against any individual with respect to his compensation, terms, conditions, or privileges of employment. . . ." . . .

Title VII's prohibition of discrimination . . . protects men as well as women, ... "Because of the many facets of human motivation, it would be unwise to presume as a matter of law that human beings of one definable group will not discriminate against other members of that group." Castaneda v. Partida. . . . . . . If our precedents leave any doubt on the question, we hold today that nothing in Title VII necessarily bars a claim of discrimination "because of . . . sex" merely because the plaintiff and the defendant or the person charged with acting on behalf of the defendant are of the same sex. . . .

We see no justification in the statutory language or our precedents for a categorical rule excluding same-sex harassment claims from the coverage of Title VII. . . . [A]nd it is ultimately the provisions of our laws rather than the principal concerns of our legislators by which we are governed. Title VII prohibits "discriminat[ion] . . . because of . . . sex". . . . Our holding that this includes sexual harassment must extend to sexual harassment of any kind that meets the statutory requirements.

Respondents . . . contend that recognizing liability for same-sex harassment will transform Title VII into a general civility code for the American workplace. But that risk is no greater for same-sex than for opposite-sex harassment. . . . "The critical issue . . . is whether members of one sex are exposed to disadvantageous terms or conditions of employment to which members of the other sex are not exposed." . . .

* * *

. . . Because we conclude that sex discrimination consisting of same-sex sexual harassment is actionable under Title VII . . . the case is remanded for further proceedings consistent with this opinion.

Case 6.10

BIBBY v. PHILA. COCA COLA BOTTLING CO.
260 F.3d 257 (3d Cir. 2001)

> [***Focus Note.*** *Bibby sued his employer, the Philadelphia Coca-Cola Bottling Company, alleging that he was subjected to same-sex harassment in violation of Title VII. In affirming the summary judgment in favor of the employer, the following opinion drew a distinction between same-sex harassment based on gender hostility and same-sex harassment based on hostility to the victim's homosexual orientation.*]

BARRY, CIRCUIT JUDGE:

* * *

Background

. . . In 1993, Bibby, who is gay, experienced some medical difficulties, including weight loss, breathing problems, and vomiting blood. On August 12, 1993, Bibby was having pains in his stomach and chest when he was found by his supervisor with his eyes closed and a machine for which he was responsible malfunctioning with product being destroyed. He was accused of sleeping on the job. Bibby asked for permission to go to the hospital and was told by the supervisor to "just go." . . . Bibby was hospitalized for several weeks. . . . . . . [A]fter receiving clearance from his treating physician, he met with his supervisors to arrange his return to work. At this meeting, he was told that he would be paid $5,000 and would be given benefits . . . if he resigned. . . . Bibby refused the offer and was terminated but, following arbitration . . . he was reinstated . . . and awarded back pay.

On December 23, 1993, the day he returned to work, Bibby was assaulted . . . by a co-worker, Frank Berthcsi. Berthcsi told Bibby to get out of the locker room, shook his fist in Bibby's face, grabbed Bibby by the shirt collar, and threw him up against the lockers. On January 22, 1995, Berthcsi again came after Bibby. On that day . . . Berthcsi was driving a forklift loaded . . . and he "slammed" the load of pallets under the stairs, blocking Bibby's exit from the platform . . . . Bibby paged a supervisor, and Berthcsi was ordered to remove the pallets. . . . Berthcsi and Bibby then exchanged some angry words, and Berthcsi repeatedly yelled at Bibby that "everybody knows you're gay as a three dollar bill," "everybody knows you're a faggot," . . . . Later that day, Berthcsi called Bibby a "sissy." Bibby filed a complaint with the union and with the employer, and Berthcsi was suspended. . . . Bibby refused the union's request that he withdraw the complaint, and Berthcsi's employment was terminated. The union filed a grievance on behalf of Berthcsi, and he was reinstated subject to the employer's condition that he undergo anger management training.

Bibby claims that supervisors also harassed him by yelling at him, ignoring his reports of problems with machinery, and arbitrarily enforcing rules against him in situations where infractions by other employees would be ignored. He does not assert that there was any sexual component to any of this alleged harassment. Finally, Bibby claims that graffiti of a sexual nature, some bearing his name, was written in the bathrooms. . . . The record does not disclose the contents of any graffiti that allegedly mentioned Bibby's name.

* * *

This appeal presents a single issue: did Bibby present evidence sufficient to support a claim of same-sex sexual harassment under Title VII? The District Court found that Bibby was harassed because of his sexual orientation, not because of his sex, and therefore rejected his sexual harassment claim. . . .

* * *

Until 1998, it was unclear whether and under what circumstances Title VII would apply in a case of sexual harassment where both the harasser and the victim were of the same sex. . . .

In *Oncale v. Sundowner Offshore Services, Inc.*, 523 U.S. 75, . . . (1998), the Supreme Court unanimously held that Title VII does provide a cause of action for same-sex sexual harassment. . . .

The question of how to prove that same-sex harassment is because of sex is not an easy one to answer. . . .

There are several situations in which same-sex harassment can be seen as discrimination because of sex. The first is where there is evidence that the harasser sexually desires the victim. . . . Same-sex harassment might also be found where there is no sexual attraction but where the harasser displays hostility to the presence of a particular sex in the workplace. . . .

Further, although it is less clear, a plaintiff may be able to prove that same-sex harassment was discrimination because of sex by presenting evidence that the harasser's conduct was motivated by a belief that the victim did not conform to the stereotypes of his or her gender. . . .

The gender stereotypes method for proving same-sex sexual harassment is based on *Price Waterhouse v. Hopkins*, 490 U.S. 228 . . . (1989), a case in which the Supreme Court reviewed the sex discrimination claim of a woman who had been denied partnership in an accounting firm at least in part on the basis that she was "macho," "overcompensated for being a woman," needed "a course in charm school," was "masculine," and was "a lady using foul language." . . . A plurality of the Court agreed that "[i]n the specific context of sex stereotyping, an employer who acts on the basis of a belief that a woman cannot be aggressive, or that she must not be, has acted on the basis of gender." . . .

Relying on *Price Waterhouse*, . . . the Seventh Circuit held that where evidence indicated that the harassment of a sixteen-year-old young man was motivated by his co-workers' belief that because he wore an earring he was not sufficiently masculine, there was sufficient evidence to support a finding that the harassment amounted to discrimination because of sex. . . .

Thus, there are at least three ways by which a plaintiff alleging same-sex sexual harassment might demonstrate that the harassment amounted to discrimination. . . . . . .

. . . Bibby simply failed in this respect; indeed, he did not even argue that he was being harassed because he was a man. . . . There was no allegation that his alleged harassers were motivated by sexual desire, or that they possessed any hostility to the presence of men in the workplace or in Bibby's particular job. Moreover, he did not claim that he was harassed because he failed to comply with societal stereotypes of how men ought to appear or behave or that as a man he was treated differently than female co-workers. His claim was, pure and simple, that he was discriminated against because of his sexual orientation. No reasonable finder of fact could reach the conclusion that he was discriminated against because he was a man.

. . . Bibby argues that in reaching this conclusion, we will be placing an extra burden on gay and lesbian plaintiffs . . . by requiring that such plaintiffs prove that their harassers were not motivated by anti-gay animus. Bibby is wrong. Whatever the sexual orientation of a plaintiff . . . that plaintiff is required to demonstrate that the harassment was directed at him or her because of his or her sex. Once such a showing has been made, the sexual orientation of the plaintiff is irrelevant. . . .

Harassment on the basis of sexual orientation has no place in our society. . . . Congress has not yet seen fit, however, to provide protection against such harassment. Because the evidence produced by Bibby . . . indicated only that he was being harassed on the basis of his sexual orientation, rather than because of his sex, the District Court properly determined that there was no cause of action under Title VII.

Conclusion

For the foregoing reasons, we will affirm the judgment of the District Court.

Case 6.11

SALMON v. DADE COUNTY SCHOOL BOARD
4 F. Supp. 2d 1157 (S.D. Fla. 1998)

Order Granting Defendant's Motion for Summary Judgment
GOLD, DISTRICT JUDGE

Zilpha Salmon . . . filed this action . . . alleging that the defendant failed to provide a reasonable accommodation for her disability and . . . denied her an equal chance for promotion. . . .

. . . She is the only guidance counselor at the Eneida Hartner Elementary School which has over one-thousand low-income, socially and emotionally deprived students, ranging in age from five to eleven years old. . . . Counselors and teachers are required to report to school by 8:15 a.m. and remain at school during scheduled working hours, which conclude at 3:20 p.m.

Salmon suffers from a back condition—a permanent partial disability. . . . . . . [S]he is unable to sit or stand for long periods of time and cannot climb stairs. . . . . . . Salmon was frequently tardy and her arrival times were unpredictable.

To accommodate Salmon's disability, the school principal provided her with a special chair and moved her counseling sessions from the second floor to the first. . . . Teachers were instructed to walk their students to Salmon's office so that Salmon would not have to walk long distances. . . . Salmon complained that driving . . . exacerbated her back problems and asked that she be permitted to arrive at work five to twenty-five minutes late on a regular basis in order to stretch and rest her back after the car ride. The principal denied this request, telling Salmon that as the only guidance counselor in a school of 1,200 students she needed to arrive at school on a regular and punctual basis in order to serve the needs of the children. No substitute counselors are available for an absent or late counselor. . . . The principal suggested that Salmon leave home a little earlier . . . to give herself time to stretch and rest her back.

* * *

Salmon filed this lawsuit . . . alleging that it [school board] discriminated against her . . . by refusing to grant her a reasonable accommodation by allowing her to arrive late or transferring her to another school closer to her home. . . .

* * *

. . . In demonstrating a viable claim under the ADA a plaintiff must demonstrate three elements: (1) that she has a disability; (2) that with or without reasonable accommodations she can perform the essential functions of her job; and (3) that she was discriminated against because of her disability. . . . Defendant contends, however, that the plaintiff is not a "qualified individual with a disability." . . . According to the defendant . . . arriving to work on time is an essential element of Salmon's job. . . .

An employee with a disability must be qualified for a job in order to be entitled to the non-discrimination protections guaranteed by the ADA. . . . . . . *Southeastern Community College v. Davis*, 442 U.S. 397, 406 . . . (1979) . . . Therefore, the initial inquiry . . . is whether Salmon was capable of performing the essential functions of her job. If the Court finds that Salmon was unable to perform the essential functions of her job, the Court must then determine whether the plaintiff has demonstrated a genuine issue of material fact regarding her ability to perform those functions with any reasonable accommodation. . . .

. . . The term "essential functions" is defined as the fundamental job duties of a position. . . . For example, a job function may be considered essential because the reason the position exists is to perform that function. . . .

Unlike other jobs that can be performed off site or deferred until a later day, a guidance counselor must counsel students at the school during the hours in which the children are in attendance. . . . When a guidance counselor is absent or tardy, no substitute is available so counseling services are simply not provided. . . . The defendant's position . . . has not been disputed by the plaintiff. . . . [T]he Court must accept the defendant's unrebutted claim that arriving promptly for work is a necessary part of Salmon's position and that plaintiff was unable to meet this essential requirement. . . . As the second step, the Court must determine whether any reasonable accommodation by the employer would enable Salmon to perform her job functions. . . . Reasonable accommodation includes modifications or adjustments to the work environment or the manner in which the position is customarily performed to enable an individual with a disability to perform the essential functions of that position. . . . Reasonable accommodation may include a change in work schedule.

Under the ADA, an employer is not required to provide an accommodation that would require significant difficulty or expense . . . or where it would impose undue financial and administrative burdens, or where it would require a fundamental alteration in the nature of the program. . . . Additionally, the duty to accommodate does not require an employer to lower its performance standards, reallocate essential job functions, create new jobs, or reassign disabled employees to positions that are already occupied. . . . . . .

Plaintiff bears the burden to identify an accommodation that would have allowed her to perform her job. She must also demonstrate that such an accommodation is reasonable. . . .

* * *

. . . The undisputed facts show that Salmon was the only guidance counselor at the school and no substitute counselor was available to fill in for her when she was late. . . . Under these circumstances, permitting the employee to come in late to work is not a reasonable accommodation.

Plaintiff also claims that the School Board failed to accommodate her disability by transferring her to a school which afforded her a shorter commute. But plaintiff's commute to and from work is an activity that is unrelated to and outside of her job. . . . [A]n employer is not required to eliminate those barriers which exist outside the work environment.

* * *

She failed to rebut the School Board's claim that arriving to school on time is an essential element of a counselor's responsibilities at Eneida Hartner Elementary School. . . .

* * *

. . . [T]he Court enters summary judgment in favor of the School Board. . . .

Case 6.12

AUERBACH v. BOARD OF EDUC. OF THE HARBORFIELDS CENTRAL SCHOOL DIST.

136 F.3d 104 (2d Cir. 1997)

> [**Focus Note.** *Public school teachers brought suit under the Age Discrimination in Employment Act to challenge the validity of a collectively bargained early retirement incentive plan. The following opinion traces the shifting legislative history of the ADEA provisions regarding early retirement incentive plans.]*

CARDAMONE, CIRCUIT JUDGE.

We are called upon . . . to determine the validity of an early retirement incentive plan for teachers employed at a Long Island, New York, school district. The critical question is whether the plan discriminates against older teachers in a manner that violates federal law prohibiting discrimination in employment on account of age. . . .

. . . All plaintiffs were or are members of defendant United Teachers of Harborfields (the Union). . . . . . .

The defendant Union and the defendant School District entered into a collective bargaining agreement. . . . It contains a provision entitled "Retirement Incentive Plan/Payment for Unused Sick Leave". . . .

Under the plan's terms, a participating teacher must actually retire at the conclusion of the school year in which he or she first becomes eligible to retire (the optimum year) in order to secure the $12,500 fixed sum payment and the accumulated sick leave payment (together, the retirement incentive benefits). Teachers older than 55, but who have not yet fulfilled the service requirements, must retire in the year they complete the service requirements, regardless of their actual age, to receive the retirement incentive benefits. Conversely, a teacher who has already completed the service requirements by the time he or she reaches age 55 must retire at the conclusion of the school year during which he or she becomes 55 in order to obtain these benefits. Otherwise, the benefits are forever lost.

* * *

Here the eight remaining plaintiffs fulfilled the retirement plan's job service requirements and reached the requisite age of 55 or older. But because they did not retire in the precise year when they first fulfilled the requirements of the plan, they are forever precluded from receiving the retirement incentive benefits. Thus, age is a trigger for the denial of their employee benefits. . . .

Consequently, we think it plain that age, not years of service, is the factor behind the disparate treatment of teachers. . . . Nonetheless, we agree . . . that the retirement plan is a valid early retirement incentive plan under the ADEA as a matter of law. To put our reasoning in proper perspective, a review of ADEA legislative history is helpful.

* * *

Congress enacted the ADEA in 1967. . . . Section 4(f)(2) of the Act, 29 U.S.C. § 623(f)(2), addresses the issue of employee benefit plans, including retirement incentive plans. . . . Thus, § 4(f)(2), as originally enacted, allowed an employer to offer disparate employee benefit plans so long as the plan was not a "subterfuge to evade the purposes" of ADEA. . . .

* * *

. . . Congress amended the ADEA. . . . It added a final clause to § 4(f)(2) requiring that an employee benefit plan be voluntary in order to be valid under the ADEA. . . .

* * *

In 1989, the Supreme Court reconsidered the meaning and scope of § 4(f)(2) in *Ohio Pub. Employees Retirement Sys. v. Betts*, 492 U.S. 158 . . . (1989). . . . According to the Court, § 4(f)(2) provided a broad exemption for employee benefit plans under the ADEA. . . . . . . This interpretation would effectively validate virtually all age-based restrictions in retirement incentive plans . . . absent the requisite showing by an employee that the employer subjectively intended to discriminate. . . .

* * *

Congress . . . quickly responded by amending § 4 (f) (2) in the course of passing the Older Workers' Benefit Protection Act of 1990. . . . That Act changed § 4 (f) (2) to its modern form: . . .

. . . Section 4 (f) (2) (B) (i) governs employee benefits and expressly adopts the "equal benefit or equal cost" principle. . . .

Section 4 (f) (2) (B) (ii) controls early retirement incentive plans and, significantly, contains no such increased cost language. In other words, the "equal benefit or equal cost" rule has no application in the retirement incentive plan context. Thus, § 4 (f) (2) (B) (ii) does not require that an employer provide identical early retirement incentives for employees of different ages or incur the same costs for all employees. Rather, the early retirement incentive plan need only be voluntary and consistent with the ADEA's relevant purpose(s). . . .

* * *

Whether such a plan furthers the purposes of the Act is ultimately an inquiry to be made on a case-by-case basis, taking into account all of the relevant facts and circumstances. . . . A court examining the validity of these plans should consider whether the plan (1) is truly voluntary, (2) is made available for a reasonable period of time, and (3) does not arbitrarily discriminate on the basis of age. . . . For the following reasons, we conclude that the subject retirement plan . . . furthers the purposes of the ADEA.

1. Voluntariness. . . . The present early retirement plan provides older teachers with an uncoerced, free choice. No teacher is required to accept the plan. Moreover, the record shows that neither fraud, threats of imminent layoffs, intimidation nor subtle coercion are present. Instead, teachers receive complete and accurate information regarding the benefits available to them under the plan. Those who elect not to retire in the optimum year continue to teach and receive all of the benefits of the collective bargaining agreement, including annual salary increases. Hence, the plan meets Congress' test of voluntariness.
2. Reasonable Period of Time. . . . Under the plan, qualifying teachers must submit to the School District a letter of resignation no later than January 1 of their final full year of service. This requirement gives teachers approximately four months . . . to reflect and weigh their options. Under these circumstances, the district court correctly held that the retirement plan provides a reasonable amount of time for teachers to consider their options.
3. No Arbitrary Discrimination. . . . The plan grants every teacher the opportunity to receive a $12,500 cash payment and an accumulated sick leave payment once he or she reaches the age of 55 and has served the requisite number of years. Teachers who decline to participate in the plan . . . continue to work as valued employees . . . without any corresponding loss of benefits or job status.

The Harborfields Plan is easily distinguished from the plan considered by the Seventh Circuit in *Karlen v. City Colleges of Chicago*, 837 F.2d 314 (7th Cir. 1988), on which plaintiffs rely. . . .

The *Karlen* plan arbitrarily discriminated on the basis of age. . . . . . . The incentives gradually increased between ages 55 and 64, but dropped off precipitously for those participants who retired after age 64. . . . The employer offered no reason other than age for this downward sliding scale of incentive benefits.

An early retirement incentive plan that withholds or reduces benefits to older retiree plan participants . . . so as to encourage premature departure from employment by older workers conflicts with the ADEA's stated purpose. . . . . . . In contrast, the present plan does not provide for an age-based phase out of a lump sum incentive payment. . . . By offering the same incentives . . . to all plan participants who reach the age of 55, it treats those participants equally, regardless of the actual age at which they retire. . . . Consequently, the subject retirement incentive plan does not arbitrarily discriminate on the basis of age. . . .

* * *

⌘ E N D N O T E S

1. Schmidt v. Indep. School Dist. No. 1, 349 N.W.2d 563 (Minn. 1984); Holland v. Board of Educ., 327 S.E.2d 155 (W. Va. 1985); Turner v. Board of Trustees, 121 Cal. Rptr. 715 (1975).

2. Annot., *Recovery of Damages for Wrongful Discrimination under State and Local Law Civil Rights Provisions,* 85 A.L.R. 3d 351 (1978) and Pocket Part. *Re* waiver of state law procedural rights, *see* Thombleson v. Board of School Trustees, 492 N.E.2d 327 (Ind. 1986); Scotchlas v. Board of School Directors, 496 A.2d 916 (Pa. 1985).

3. Thigpen v. Bibb County Ga. Sheriff Dept., 223 F.3d 1231 (11th Cir. 2000).

4. Dudley v. Augusta School Dept., 23 F. Supp. 2d 85 (D. Me. 1998) (demotion as possible stigmatization of teacher).
   (a) Bristol Va. School Bd. v. Quarles, 366 S.E.2d 82 (Va. 1988); Cogdill v. Comal Indep. School Dist., 630 F. Supp. 47 (W.D. Tex. 1985). ". . . [T]he competence of teachers, and the standards of its measurement are not, without more, matters of constitutional dimensions." *See* Scheelhaase v. Woodbury Central Comm. School Dist., 488 F.2d 237, 244 (8th Cir. 1973).
   (b) Irby v. McGowan, 380 F. Supp. 1024 (S.D. Ala. 1974) (teacher allowed to resign with removal of dismissal charges from her record).
   (c) Cooper v. Curry, 399 F. Supp. 372 (S.D. Miss. 1975).
   (d) Coen v. Boulder Valley School Dist., 402 F. Supp. 1335 (D. Colo. 1975).
   (e) Gray v. Union County Int. Educ. Dist., 520 F.2d 803 (9th Cir. 1975).

5. (a) *Undisclosed charges:* Brandt v. Bd. of Coop. Educ. Services, 845 F.2d 416 (2d Cir. 1988); Buhr v. Buffalo Public School Dist. No. 38, 509 F.2d 1196 (8th Cir. 1974).
   (b) *Undisputed charges:* Codd v. Velger, 429 U.S. 624 (1977); Carpenter v. City of Greenfield School Dist., 358 F. Supp. 220 (E.D. Wis. 1973).
   (c) *Expression of opinion:* Strasburger v. Board of Educ., 143 F.3d 351 (7th Cir. 1998).

6. Lancaster v. Ind. School Dist., 149 F.3d 1228 (10th Cir. 1998).

7. Supan v. Michelsfeld, 468 N.Y.S.2d 384 (1983) (dishonesty); Bomhoff v. White, 526 F. Supp. 488 (D. Ariz. 1981) (instability); Morris v. Board of Educ., 401 F. Supp. 188 (D. Del. 1975) (insubordination); Lombard v. Board of Educ., 502 F.2d 631 (2d Cir. 1974) (emotional instability).

8. Mazurek v. Wolcott Board of Educ., 815 F. Supp. 71 (D. Conn. 1993); McCreery v. Babylon Unified Free School Dist., 827 F. Supp. 136 (E.D. N.Y. 1993); Cotnoir v. U. of Maine System, 35 F.3d 6 (1st Cir. 1994).

9. Crim v. Board of Educ., 147 F.3d 535 (7th Cir. 1998) (superintendent); Bailey v. Floyd County Board of Educ., 106 F.3d 135 (6th Cir. 1997) (Head Start administrator); Board of Educ. v. Harrell, 882 P.2d 511 (N.M. 1994).

10. *Finding of promise of tenure from school customs and practices:* Perry v. Sindermann, 408 U.S. 593 (1972). *Semble:* Soni v. Board of Trustees, 376 F. Supp. 289 (E.D. Tenn. 1974) (implied "entitlement"). *Refusal to find unexpressed property right:* Gregory v. Hunt, 24 F.3d 781 (6th Cir. 1994).

11. Mustafa v. Clark County School Dist., 157 F.3d 1169 (9th Cir. 1998).

12. Bostean Los Angeles Unified School Dist., 73 Cal. Rptr. 2d 253 (Cal. 1998).

13. Coleman v. Reed, 147 F.3d 751 (8th Cir. 1998).

14. Cleveland Board of Educ. v. Loudermill, 470 U.S. 532 (1985); Bates v. Hinds, 334 F. Supp. 528 (N.D. Tex. 1971).

15. Cleveland Board of Educ., note 14, *supra;* Okeson v. Tolley School Dist. No. 25, 766 F.2d 378 (8th Cir. 1985); Brown v. State Board of Educ., 391 So. 2d 866 (S.C. 1990).

16. *Cf.* Montoya v. Sanger Unified School Dist., 502 F. Supp 209 (E.D. Cal. 1980).

17. Board of Trustees v. Landry, 638 N.E.2d 1261 (Ind. 1994).

18. Dixon v. Love, 431 U.S. 105 (1977); Janke v. Comm. School Board, 587 N.Y.S.2d 733 (1992).

19. Gilbert v. Homar, 117 S. Ct. 1807 (1997) (prehearing suspension without pay—held consistent with due process); Andresky v. W. Allegheny School Dist., 437 A.2d 1074 (Pa. 1981).

20. Kirschling v. Lake Forest School Dist., 687 F. Supp. 927 (D. Del. 1988); Huntley v. Comm. School Board of Brooklyn, 543 F.2d 979 (2d Cir. 1976).

21. Hortonville Dist. v. Hortonville Educ. Assn., 426 U.S. 483 (1976). To like effect, *see* Byrd v. Greene County School Dist., 633 So. 2d 1018 (Miss. 1994).

22. Larsen v. Oakland Community School Dist., 416 N.W.2d 89 (Iowa 1987). The law is reviewed in Withrow v. Larkin, 421 U.S. 35 (1975). Penn-Delco School Dist. v. Urso, 382 A.2d 162 (Pa. 1978); Weissman v. Board of Educ., 547 P.2d 1267 (Colo. 1976).

23. *Ex parte* Concuh County Board of Educ., 495 So. 2d 1108 (Ala. 1986); Staton v. Mayes, 552 F.2d 908 (10th Cir. 1977).

24. Kamjathy v. Board of Educ., 348 N.Y.S.2d 28 (1973).

25. Katruska v. Dept. of Educ., 727 A.2d 612 (Pa. 1999).

26. Keith v. Comm. School Dist., 262 N.W.2d 249 (Iowa 1978); English v. Northeast Board of Educ., 348 A.2d 494 (Pa. 1975) (solicitor as hearing officer); Miller v. Board of Educ., 200 N.E.2d 838 (Ill. 1964) (solicitor as prosecutor and counsel to board on admissibility of evidence).

27. Harmon v. Mifflin County School Dist., 651 A.2d 681 (Pa. 1994).

28. On the varied treatment of hearsay evidence, *see* Kinkle v. Garrett-Keyser-Butler School Dist., 567 N.E.2d 1171 (Ind. 1991); Casada v. Booneville School Dist. No. 65, 686 F. Supp. 730 (W.D. Ark. 1988).

29. Brown v. South Carolina Board of Educ., 391 So. 2d 866 (S.C. 1990); Springfield School Dist. v. Shellem, 328 A.2d 535 (Pa. 1974).

30. *See, e.g.,* Tucker v. Board of Educ., 492 A.2d 839 (Conn. 1985) (no universal constitutional right of appeal); Mason v. Thetford School Board, 457 A.2d 647 (Vt. 1982) (no right of appeal). For cases where right of appeal allowed, *see* Racine Unified School Dist. v. Thompson, 321 N.W.2d 334 (Wis. 1982).

31. Smith v. Board of Educ., 484 N.Y.S.2d 602 (1985).

32. *See, generally,* Westley v. Terrebone Parish School Board, 656 F. Supp. 499 (E.D. La. 1987). *General waiver of hearing:* Ferguson v. Board of Trustees, 564 P.2d 971 (Idaho 1977) (intentionally leaving hearing); Cords v. Window Rock School Dist., 526 P.2d 757 (Ariz. 1974) (waiver by abandonment). *Waiver of specific aspect of hearing:* McDonough v. Kelly, 329 F. Supp. 144 (D. N.H. 1971) (right to counsel); Hickey v. Board of School Directors, 328 A.2d 529 (Pa. 1974) (right to produce witnesses); Pyle v. Wash. County School Board, 238 So. 2d 121 (Fla. 1970) (hearing record); Mullally v. Board of Educ., 164 N.W.2d 742 (Mich. 1968) (prior notice); Williams v. Cody, 545 P.2d 905 (Or. 1976) (appeal).

33. Board of Educ. of Charles County v. Crawford, 395 A.2d 835 (Md. 1979); Alexander v. School Dist. No. 17, 248 N.W.2d 335 (Neb. 1976).

34. Strasburger v. Board of Educ., 143 F.3d 351 (7th Cir. 1998).

35. *Unconstitutional rule against teacher communications with school board members:* Knapp v. Whitaker, 757 F.2d 827 (7th Cir. 1985); Anderson v. Central Point School Dist., 746 F.2d 505 (9th Cir. 1984). *Unconstitutional prohibitions against school-site distribution of literature:* Hall v. Board of School Comm'rs., 681 F.2d 965 (5th Cir. 1983).

36. Hall, note 35, *supra*; Davis v. E. Baton Rouge Par. School Board, 78 F.3d 920 (5th Cir. 1996) (order barring news media disclosure of labor strategy meetings—overturned).

37. Westbrook v. Teton County School Dist., 918 F. Supp. 1475 (D. Wyo. 1996); Weaver v. Nebo School Dist., 29 F. Supp. 2d 1279 (S.D. N.Y. 1998).

38. Russo v. Central School Dist., 469 F.2d 623 (2d Cir. 1972).

39. Dudley v. Augusta School Dept., 23 F. Supp. 2d 85 (Me. 1998); Harris v. Shelby County Board of Educ., 99 F.3d 1078 (11th Cir. 1996).

40. Brady v. Houston Independent School Dist., 113 F.3d 1419 (5th Cir. 1997). *See also* Bailey v. Floyd County Board of Educ., 106 F.3d 135 (6th Cir. 1997) (failure to prove termination decision was based on employee's speech).

41. Lybrook v. Members of Framington Mun. School Bd., 232 F.3d 1334 (10th Cir. 2000); *cf.*

Vargas-Hamilton v. Racine Un. School Dist., 272 F.3d 964 (7th Cir. 2001).

42. Ward v. Hickey, 996 F.2d 448 (1st Cir. 1993); Miles v. Denver Public Schools, 944 F.2d 773 (10th Cir. 1991) (sanctions for classroom comments on rumors of sexual misconduct); Pelozo v. Capistrano Unified School Dist., 37 F.3d 517 (9th Cir. 1994) (restriction on teacher discussions of religion during school day).

43. Givhan v. Western Line Cons. School Dist., 439 U.S. 410 (1979).

44. Vargas-Hamilton, note 41, *supra.*

45. Connick v. Myers, 461 U.S. 138 (1983); Waters v. Churchill, 62 U.S.L.W. 4397 (1994).

46. Rankin v. McPherson, 483 U.S. 378 (1987) (5–4 holding that the police department clerk spoke on a matter of public, not private, concern).
    Speech ruled of public concern: Mazurek v. Wolcott Board of Educ., 815 F. Supp. 71 (D. Conn. 1993) (comments on teacher quality); Ratliff v. Wellington Exempted Village Schools Board of Educ., 820 F.2d 792 (6th Cir. 1987) (principal's report to school board on poor school conditions and atmosphere of mistrust); Cox v. Dardanelle Public School Dist., 790 F.2d 668 (8th Cir. 1986) (teacher grievances against principal).
    Speech held to be of personal and not public concern: Callaway v. Hafeman, 832 F.2d 414 (7th Cir. 1987) (sexual harassment complaint—held motivated by personal concern); Day v. S. Park Indep. School Dist., 768 F.2d 696 (5th Cir. 1985) (complaint of principal's evaluation); Roberts v. Van Buren Pub. Schools, 773 F.2d 949 (8th Cir. 1985) (complaints on management of field trips); Saye v. St. Vrain Valley School Dist., 785 F.2d 862 (10th Cir. 1986) (teacher complaints to parents on "aide time").
    For skillful manipulation of public–personal balancing factors, *see* Piver v. Pender County Bd. of Educ., 835 F.2d 1076 (4th Cir. 1987) (teacher advocacy of tenure for fellow teacher and encouraging students to circulate petitions in support of tenure candidate—held justified as training in civic action).

47. *Compare* Brewster v. Board of Educ., 149 F.3d 971 (9th Cir. 1998), *with* Bernheim v. Litt, 79 F.3d 318 (2d Cir. 1996).

48. *Unprotected criticism of superiors:* Kuahns v. School Dist., 123 F.3d 1010 (7th Cir. 1997); Stevenson v. Lower Marion County School Dist. 327 S.E.2d 656 (S. Car. 1985) (incitement against school superiors).

49. Roberts v. Lake Central School Dist., 317 F. Supp. 63 (N.D. Ind. 1970); Gieringer v. Central School Dist., 477 F.2d 1164 (8th Cir. 1973).

50. *Compare* Copp v. Unified School Dist., 882 F.2d 1547 (10th Cir. 1989); Seemuller v. Fairfax County School Board, 878 F.2d 1578 (4th Cir. 1989); Thompson v. Board of Educ. City of Chicago, 711 F. Supp. 394 (N.D. Ill. 1989); Adcock v. Board of Educ., 513 P.2d 900 (Cal. 1973); *with* Jones v. Battles, 315 F. Supp. 601 (D. Conn. 1970).

51. *Compare* Gilbertson v. McAlister, 403 F. Supp. 1 (D. Conn. 1975), *with* Bertot v. School Dist., 522 F.2d 1171 (10th Cir. 1975).

52. Solmitz v. Maine School Admin. Dist. No. 59, 495 A.2d 812 (Me. 1985).

53. *Passive armband:* James v. Board of Educ., 461 F.2d 566 (2nd Cir. 1972). *Leaving school:* Petition of Davenport, 283 A.2d 452 (Vt. 1971).

54. *Protected expression:* Petition of Davenport, prior note. *Unprotected conduct:* Knarr v. Board of School Trustees, 317 F. Supp. 832 (N.D. Ind. 1970). *Cf.* Cooley v. Board of Educ., 327 F. Supp. 454 (E.D. Ark. 1971) (civil rights rally); Johnson v. Branch, 364 F.2d 177 (4th Cir. 1966).

55. Fogarty v. Boles, 121 F.3d 886 (3d Cir. 1997); Jones v. Collins, 132 F.3d 1048 (5th Cir. 1998).

56. California Teachers Assn. v. Governing Board of San Diego Unified School Dist., 53 Cal. Rptr. 2d 474 (1996).

57. Boring v. The Buncombe County Board of Educ., 136 F.3d 364 (4th Cir. 1998) (drama teacher play selection); Board of Educ. of Jefferson County School Dist. R-1 v. Wilder, 960 P.2d 695 (Colo. 1998) (showing controversial film without required school approval). Bradley v. Pittsburgh Board of Educ., 910 F.2d 1171 (3d Cir. 1990) (choice of class management techniques); Kirkland v. Northside Indep. School Dist., 890 F.2d 794 (5th Cir. 1989) (selection of class materials); Milliken v. Board of Directors, 611 P.2d 414 (Wash. 1980) (disapproved teaching method).

See M. Yudof, *The Three Faces of Academic Freedom,* 32 Loyola L. Rev. 831 (1987); E. Bjorklun, *Regulating the Use of Theatrical Movies in the Classroom: Academic Freedom Issues,* 100 Edlaw Rep. 1 (1995); *Symposium on Academic Freedom,* 66 Tex. L. Rev. 1274 (1988); J. Tuner-Egner, *Teacher's Discretion in Selecting Instructinal Materials and Methods,* 53 Educ. L. Rep. 365 (1989).

58. Bradley v. Pittsburgh Board of Educ., 910 F.2d 1172 (3d Cir. 1990) (unfair notice to teacher); Proposed Termination of James Johnson's Teaching Contract, 451 N.W.2d 343 (Minn. 1990) (arbitrary directive).

59. Celestine v. Lafayette Parish School Board, 284 So. 2d 650 (La. 1973). *See also* Moore v. School Board of Gulf County, 364 F. Supp. 355 (N.D. Fla. 1973) (teacher's reference to personal sexual attitudes and to student sexual development); State v. Board of Directors, 111 N.W.2d 198 (Wis. 1961) (teacher discussion of sex in class). *Cf.* Simon v. Jefferson Davis Par. School Board, 289 So. 2d 511 (La. 1974). *Compare* Palo Verde Unified School Dist. v. Hensey, 9 Cal. App. 2d 967 (1970), *with* Lindros v. Governing Board of Torrance Unified School Dist., 9 Cal. 3d 524 (1973).

60. Keefe v. Geanakos, 418 F.2d 359 (1st Cir. 1969); Close v. Lederle, 424 F.2d 988 (1st Cir. 1970); Mailloux v. Kiley, 436 F.2d 565 (1st Cir. 1970).

61. Close, prior note.

62. Mailloux, note 60, *supra.*

63. From endnote 7 of the opinion in President's Council v. Comm. School Board, 457 F.2d 289 (2d Cir. 1972).

64. *Later cases:* Domico v. Rapides Par. School Board, 675 F.2d 100 (5th Cir. 1982); Morrison v. Hamilton County Board of Educ., 494 S.W.2d 770 (Tenn. 1973); Miller v. School Dist. No. 167, 495 F.2d 658 (7th Cir. 1974).
    Earlier cases: See Conard v. Goolsby, 350 F. Supp. 713 (N.D. Miss. 1972); Ball v. Kerriville Indep. School Dist., 529 S.W.2d 792 (Tex. 1975) (refusal to shave beard—held not to be grounds for dismissal).

65. *See* Kelley v. Johnson, 425 U.S. 238, 247–8 (1976).

66. Ramsey v. Hopkins, 320 F. Supp. 477, remanded on other grounds, 447 F.2d 128 (5th Cir. 1970); Lucia v. Duggan, 303 F. Supp. 112 (D.C. Mass. 1969).

67. Ball v. Board of Trustees, 584 F.2d 684 (5th Cir. 1978); Miller v. School Dist. No. 167, 495 F.2d 658 (7th Cir. 1974). *See* cases collected in Annot., *Teacher Dress,* 58 A.L.R. 3d 1227 (1974).

68. Cooper v. Eugene School Dist. No. 4J, 723 P.2d 298 (Or. 1986), *appeal dismissed,* 480 U.S. 942 (1987).

69. United States v. Board of Educ., School Dist. of Philadelphia, 911 F.2d 882 (3d Cir. 1990) (Pa. religious garb statute—upheld).

70. Moore v. Board of Educ., 212 N.E.2d 833 (Ohio 1965); O'Connor v. Hendrich, 77 N.E. 612 (N.Y. 1906). *See* early cases in Annot., *Wearing of Religious Garb by Public School Teachers,* 60 A.L.R. 2d 300 (1958).

71. Rutan v. Republican Party of Ill., 110 S. Ct. 2729 (1990); Branti v. Finkel, 445 U.S. 507 (1980). For the school context, *see, e.g.,* Wichert v. Walter, 606 F. Supp. 1516 (D. N.J. 1985); Piazza v. Aponte Roque, 909 F.2d 35 (1st Cir. 1990) (nonrenewal based on party affiliation).

72. Buford v. Southeast Dubois County School Corp., 472 F.2d 890 (7th Cir. 1972); Rawlings v. Butler, 290 S.W.2d 801 (Ky. 1956); Hysong v. School Dist., 30 A.2d 482 (Pa. 1894). *Cf.* McDaniel v. Patty, 435 U.S. 618 (1978); Randle v. Indianola Sep. School Dist., 373 F. Supp. 766 (N.D. Miss. 1974); Fyfe v. Curlee, 902 F.2d 401 (5th Cir. 1990); Brantley v. Surles, 765 F.2d 478 (5th Cir. 1985); Stough v. Crenshaw County Board of Educ., 744 F.2d 1479 (11th Cir. 1984).

73. Lasota v. Town of Topsfield, 979 F. Supp. 45 (D. Mass. 1997).

74. Opdahl v. Zeeland Pub. School Dist., 512 N.W.2d 444 (N.D. 1994) (associational activities during teacher work time).

75. Raposa v. Meade School Dist., 790 F.2d 1349 (8th Cir. 1986) (teacher transfer for speech that created disharmony in small community).

76. Gordon J. v. Santa Ana Unified School Dist., 208 Cal. Rptr. 657 (Cal. App. 1984); Ross v. Springfield School Dist., 641 P.2d 600, 610 (Or. 1981).

77. *But a teacher union representatives may not consent to a search of a represented teacher:* McDonnell v. Hunter, 809 F.2d 1302, 1310 (8th Cir. 1987) (purported consent in union-bargained contract).

78. MR by RR v. Lincolnwood Board of Educ., 843 F. Supp. 1236 (N.D. Ill. 1994) (videotape of public area); Roberts v. Houston Indep. School Dist., 788 S.W.2d 107 (Tex. 1990) (videotape of classroom).

79. O'Connor v. Ortega, 107 S. Ct. at 1492.

80. Shaul v. Cherry Valley Springfield Cent. School Dist., 218 F. Supp. 2d 266 (N.D. N.Y. 2002).

81. Kyllo v. United States, 121 S. Ct. 2038 (2001).

82. Knox County Educ. Assn. v. Knox County Board of Educ., 158 F.3d 361 (6th Cir. 1998); Aubrey v. School Board of Lafayette Parish, 148 F.3d 559 (5th Cir. 1998); Contra Loder v. Glendale, 28 Cal. App. 4th 796 (1997) (overturned *suspicionless* mandatory urinalysis for employees seeking promotions).

83. *Cf.* Vernonia School Dist. v. Acton, 515 U.S. 646 (1995).

84. *E.g.,* Patchogue-Medford Cong. of Teachers v. Board of Educ., 510 N.E.2d 325 (N.Y. 1987); Schaill by Kross v. Tippecanoe County School Corp., 864 F.2d 1309 (7th Cir. 1988); *Dragnet Drug Testing in Public Schools,* 86 Col. L. Rev. 852 (1986).

85. Jones v. McKenzie, 833 F.2d 335 (D.C. Cir. 1987) (testing of school bus aides upheld against a background of widespread drug abuse).

86. Hearn v. Board of Public Educ., 191 F.3d 1329 (11th Cir. 1999).

87. Teachers Local 59 v. Special School Dist., 512 N.W.2d 107 (Minn. App. 1994); Klein Ind. School Dist. v. Mattox, 830 F.2d 576 (5th Cir. 1987); Brouillet v. Cowles Publishing Co., 791 P.2d 526 (Wash. 1990); Hovet v. Hebron Public School Dist., 419 N.W.2d 189 (N.D. 1988).

88. *Cf.* Whelan v. Roe, 429 U.S. 589 (1977).

89. *See* the state authorities in Robinson v. Merritt, 375 S.W.2d 204 (W. Va. 1988); Annot., *What Constitutes Personal Matters Exempt from Disclosure . . . under State Freedom of Information Act,* 26 A.L.R. 4th 666 (1983).

90. Child Protection Group v. Cline, 350 S.E.2d 541 (W. Va. 1986) (parents granted access to medical records of school bus driver whose actions raised questions of student safety); *cf.* Strong v. Board of Educ. of Uniondale Un. Free School Dist., 902 F.2d 208 (2d Cir. 1990); Daury v. Smith, 842 F.2d 9 (1st Cir. 1988) (teacher refusal to undergo reasonable request for psychiatric examination—not protected as constitutional privacy). *See, generally,* Turkington, *The Emerging Unencumbered Constitutional Right to Informational Privacy,* 10 N. Ill. U. L. Rev. 479 (1990); Note, *The Constitutional Right of Informational Privacy,* 14 Fordham Urban L. Rev. 927 (1986).

91. Ibid.

92. Alexander v. Sandoval, 121 S. Ct. 1511 (2001).

93. Suders v. Easton, 325 F.3d 432 (3d Cir. 2003) and authorities there cited.

94. Brown v. Board of Educ. I, 347 U.S. 483 (1954); Brown v. Board of Educ. II, 349 U.S. 294 (1955). *Segregated teacher and staff assignments:* Bradley v. School Board, 382 U.S. 103 (1965); Rogers v. Paul, 382 U.S. 198 (1965).

95. Pennsylvania v. Board of Trusts, 353 U.S. 230 (1957).

96. Fairbairn v. Board of Educ., 876 F.2d 432 (2d Cir. 1995).

97. Covington v. Beaumont School Dist., 714 F. Supp. 1402 (E.D. Tex. 1989) (displacement of white coaches to employ black coaches—held unconstitutional); Cunico v. Pueblo Pub. School Dist., 693 F. Supp. 954 (D. Colo. 1988) (retention of black administrator over senior white administrator—held unconstitutional). Seniority adjustments that do not cause loss of employment are not here covered. *See* Int'l. Brotherhood of Teamsters v. United States, 431 U.S. 324 (1977).

98. Schurr v. Resorts International Hotel Inc., 196 F.3d 486 (3d Cir. 1999).

99. *Cf.* Johnson v. Transportation Agency, Santa Clara Cty., 480 U.S. 616 (1987).

100. Alexander v. Sandoval, 121 S. Ct. 1411 (2001).

101. Hodges v. Public Bldg. Com'n of Chicago, 873 F. Supp. 128 (N.D. Ill. 1995).

102. Grimes by and through Grimes v. Sobol, 832 F. Supp. 704 (S.D. N.Y. 1993).

103. Smith v. Board of Educ., 365 F.2d 770 (8th Cir. 1966).

104. Council of Supervisory Assns. v. Board of Educ., 245 N.E.2d 204 (N.Y. 1969); Porcelli v. Titus, 431 F.2d 1254 (3d Cir. 1970). *Cf.* Morton v. Mancari, 417 U.S. 535 (1974) (employment preference of Native Americans in U.S. Bureau of Indian Affairs—held constitutional). *But see* Auerbach v. African-American Teachers Assn., 356 F. Supp. 1046 (E.D. N.Y. 1973).

105. Covington v. Beaumont School Dist., 714 F. Supp. 1402 (E.D. Tex. 1989) (black displacement of white and Latino coaches); NAACP v. Allen, 493 F.2d 614 (5th Cir. 1974) (white displacement of black teacher).

106. Reynolds v. School District, 69 F.3d 1523 (10th Cir. 1955)

107. *See, e.g.,* Chapman v. Higbee Co., 319 F.3d 825 (6th Cir. 2003), noting a conflict between the Second and Sixth Circuit courts with the Third and Eighth Circuit courts.

108. United States v. Virginia, 116 S. Ct. 2264 (1996); *cf.* Garrett v. Board of Educ., 775 F. Supp. 1004 (E.D. Mich. 1991) (boys-only high school prohibited under Title IX).

109. Grant v. Bullock County Board of Educ., 895 F. Supp. 1506 (M.D. Ala. 1995); Meritor Sav. Bank v. Vinson, 477 U.S. 57 (1986); United Teachers v. Board of Educ., 712 F.2d 1349 (9th Cir. 1983).

110. Farber v. Massillon Board of Educ., 908 F.2d 65 (6th Cir. 1990); Burns v. Gadsden State Comm. College, 908 F.2d 1512 (11th Cir. 1990).

111. Farber v. Massillon Board of Educ., prior note; McCullar v. Ill. Human Rights Comm'n, 511 N.E.2d 1375 (Ill. 1987) (pay differential for boys' basketball coach and girls' volleyball coach—upheld).

112. Kindred v. Northome/Ind. School Dist., 983 F. Supp. 835 (D. Minn. 1997).

113. Los Angeles v. Manhart, 435 U.S. 702 (1978); Norris v. Arizona Governing Comm., 463 U.S. 1073 (1983); Spirit v. TIAA-CREF, 735 F.2d 23 (2d Cir. 1984).

114. Brooks v. San Mateo, 229 F.3d 917 (9th Cir. 2000).

115. *See, e.g.,* Quantock v. Shared Marketing Services, Inc. 312 F.3d 899 (7th Cir. 2002).

116. Mendoza v. Borden Inc., 195 F.3d 1238 (11th Cir. 1999).

117. *Compare, e.g.,* Hamm v. Weyauwega Milk Products Inc., 332 F.3d 1058 (7th Cir. 2003) (being viewed as gay does not alone amount to harassment because of sex), *with* Price Waterhouse v. Hopkins, 490 U.S. 228 (1989); Azteca Rest. Enter. Inc., 256 F.3d 864 (9th Cir. 2002) (harassment of female based on her nonconformance with stereotyping of females is harassment because of sex).

118. Hamm v. Weyauwega Milk Products Inc., prior note; *cf.* Lauermilch v. Findlay City Schools, 314 F.3d 271 (6th Cir. 2003) (comment that male employee was "too macho", held not to be discrimination based on sex).

119. Price Waterhouse v. Hopkins, 490 U.S. 228, 244 (1989).

120. Desert Palace Inc. v. Costa, 123 S. Ct. 2148 (2003).

121. Taylor v. White, 321 F.3d 710 (8th Cir. 2003).

122. *See* Corning Glass Works v. Brennan, 94 S. Ct. 2223, 2229 (1974).

123. EEOC v. Madison Comm'y Unit School Dist., 818 F.3d 577 (7th Cir. 1987).

124. Taylor v. White, 321 F.3d 710 (8th Cir. 2003); Covington v. So. Illinois Univ., 816 F.2d 317 (7th Cir. 1987); Kouba v. Allstate Ins. Co., 691 F.2d 876–8 (9th Cir. 1982). *Contra*: Glenn v. General Motors Corp., 841 F.2d 1567, 1570 (11th Cir. 1988).

125. Board of Regents v. Dawes, 522 F.2d 380 (8th Cir. 1975).

126. Berry v. Board of Supervisors, 715 F.2d 971 (5th Cir. 1983).

127. *See* Frazier v. Fairhaven School Comm'ee, 276 F.3d 52, 65, 66 (1st Cir. 2002), and authorities there cited.

128. Doe v. Beaumont I.S.D., 8 F. Supp. 2d 596 (E.D. Tex. 1998).

129. Ibid.

130. The *Davis* rulings were anticipated by some federal circuits. Murrell v. School Dist. No. 1, 186 F.3d 1239 (10th Cir. 1999); Smith v. Metropolitan School District Perry Township, 128 F.3d 1014 (7th Cir. 1997).

131. Abeyta v. Chama Ind. School District, 77 F.3d 1253 (10th Cir. 1996).

132. *See also* Kinman v. Omaha Public School Dist., 171 F.3d 607 (8th Cir. 1999); Murrell v. School Dist. No. 1, 186 F.3d 1238 (10th Cir. 1999); Haines v. Metropolitan Gov't of Davidson County, 32 F. Supp. 2d 991 (M.D. Tenn. 1998); H.M. v. Jefferson County Board of Educ., 719 So. 2d 793 (Ala. 1998).

133. *Cf.* Schultzen v. Woodbury Central Comm'y School Dist., 187 F. Supp. 2d 1099 (N.D. Iowa 2002).

134. Ibid. at p. 1101.

135. Jackson v. Birmingham Bd. of Educ., 309 F.3d 1333 (11th Cir. 2002), citing like ruling under Title VI, in Alexander v. Sandoval, 532 U.S. 275 (2001).

136. Meltzer v. New York City Board of Educ., 336 F.3d 185 (2d Cir. 2003), which upheld school district termination of a teacher whose public advocacy for sex between men and boys caused severe disruption of school operations.

137. Board of Trustees, Univ. of Alabama v. Garrett, 121 S. Ct. 955, 964 (2001); New York City Transit Authority v. Beazor, 438 U.S. 904 (1979).

138. *See* Annot., *What Constitutes Handicap under State Legislation*, 892 A.L.R. 4th 26 (1990).

139. The confused interoperation of various parts of the Rehabilitation Act (§ 504), the ADA and Title VI with respect to nonemployment discrimination is noted in Ferguson v. City of Phoenix, 157 F.3d 668 (9th Cir. 1998).

140. *See* Connell v. City of New York, 230 F. Supp. 2d 432 (S.D. N.Y. 2002); Baird v. Rose, 192 F.3d 462 (4th Cir. 1999). *But see* McCachren v. Blacklick Valley School Dist., 217 F. Supp. 2d 594 (W.D. Pa. 2002) (discussing a theoretical basis to hold individuals subject to ADA liability).

141. Sandison v. Mich. High School Athletic Assn., 64 F.3d 1026 (6th Cir. 1995) (exclusion based on age rule did not violate ADA); Urban v. Jefferson County School Dist., 870 F. Supp. 1558 (D. Colo. 1994) (denial of desired placement did not violate Rehabilitation Act); Anonymous v. Bd. of Examiners, 318 N.Y.S.2d 163 (1970) (decertification of drug-addicted teacher).

142. Bragdon v. Abbott, 118 S. Ct. 2196, 2202 (1998).

143. Sutton v. United Air Lines Inc., 119 S. Ct. 2139 (1999).

144. Murphy v. United Parcel Service, 119 S. Ct. 2133 (1999).

145. Equal Employment Opportunity Commission v. J.B. Hunt Transport Inc., 351 F.3d 69 (2d Cir. 2003).

146. Bragdon v. Abbott, 118 S. Ct. 2196 (1998).

147. School Board of Nassau County v. Arline, 480 U.S. 273 (1987) (teacher with tuberculosis, in remission, decided under Rehabilitation Act prior to enactment of the ADA).

148. Sullivan v. River Valley School Dist., 197 F.3d 804 (6th Cir. 1999).

149. Lapid-Laurel LLC v. Zoning Board of Adjustment, 284 F.3d 443 (3d Cir. 2002).

150. *Compare* Jacobsen v. Tillman, 17 F. Supp. 2d 1018 (1998), *with* the *Salmon* case (Case 6.11) at the end of this chapter.

151. *Leave of absence:* Cehrs v. Northeast Ohio Alzheimer's Res. Center, 155 F.3d 775 (6th Cir. 1998). *Transfer to open position:* Jackson v. N.Y. State Division of Labor, 205 F.3d 562 (2d Cir. 2000).

152. *See* Comment, R.D. Wenkart, *Public Employment, Reasonable Accommodation and the ADA*, 133 Ed. Law Rep. 647 (1999). Southeast Comm'y College v. Davis, 422 U.S. 397, at

407–12 (1979); Coleman v. Casey County Bd. of Educ., 510 F. Supp. 301, 303 (Ky. 1980).

153. Request to open position—held reasonable, if qualified; but not request to bump another employee. Smith v. Midland Brake Inc., 180 F.3d 1154 (10th Cir. 1999). *See* McMackins v. Elk Grove, 21 F. Supp. 2d 1202 (E.D. Cal. 1998) and authorities there cited; Gaul v. Lucent Technology, 134 F.3d 596 (3d Cir. 1998).

154. Mass. Bd. of Retirement v. Murgia, 427 U.S. 307 (1976); Frantz v. Whitehall School Dist., 331 A.2d 484 (Pa. 1975); Kennedy v. Comm'y. Un. School Dist., 319 N.E.2d 243 (Ill. 1974); Lewis v. Tucson School Dist., 531 P.2d 199 (Ariz. 1975).

155. Mass. Board of Retirement v. Murgia, prior note; Weisbrod v. Lynn, 383 F. Supp. 933 (D. D.C. 1974), *aff'd,* 420 U.S. 940 (1975).

156. Reeves v. Sanderson, 127 S. Ct. 2097 (2000); Sanchez v. Denver Public Schools, 164 F.3d 527, 531 (10th Cir. 1998); Widoe v. District No. 111 Otoe County School, 147 F.3d 726 (8th Cir. 1998).

157. Reeves, prior note.

158. Wooden v. Board of Educ., 931 F.2d 376 (6th Cir. 1991) (hiring younger more qualified person); Spring v. Sheboygan Area School Dist., 865 F.2d 883 (7th Cir. 1989) (change of school assignment); Phair v. Montgomery County Public Schools, 3 F. Supp. 2d 644 (D. Md. 1997) (unfavorable rating).

159. Hodgson v. First Federal Savings & Loan Assn., 455 F.2d 818 (5th Cir. 1972) (disapproving refusal to hire 47-year-old woman as bank teller).

160. E.E.O.C. v. School Board of Pinellas County, 742 F. Supp. 622 (M.D. Fla. 1990); Geller v. Markham, 635 F.2d 1027 (2d Cir. 1980).

161. E.E.O.C. v. Comm. Unit School Dist., 642 F. Supp. 902 (S.D. Ill. 1986) (reclassification of putative retirees—held discrimination); Trans World Airlines v. Thurston, 105 S. Ct. 613, 621 (1985).

162. Los Angeles v. Manhart, 435 U.S. 702 (1978) (pension benefits); E.E.O.C. v. State of Ill., 69 F.3d 167 (7th Cir. 1995) (mandatory age retirement); E.E.O.C. v. Newport Mesa Un. School Dist., 893 F. Supp. 927 (C.D. Cal. 1995) (age-based salary differentials).

163. Pub. L. 101–521 (1990) [overruling the effect of Pub. Employees Ret. System v. Betts, 492 U.S. 158 (1989)].

164. *Compare, e.g.,* EEOC v. Community Union School Dist., 642 F. Supp. 902 (S.D. Ill. 1986) (reclassification of older employees, overturned as discrimination); Cipriano v. Board of Education, 785 F.2d 51 (2d Cir. 1986) (age bracket challenged as pretext for discrimination), *with* Patterson v. Ind. School Dist., 742 F.2d 465 (8th Cir. 1984) (early retirement plan—upheld).

165. *Cf.* Oubre v. Entergy Operations Inc., 522 U.S. 422 (1998). *See also* 68 U.S.L.W. 2243 (11-2-99).

166. General Dynamics Land Systems, Inc. v. Dennis Cline, U.S. No. 02–1080, S. Ct. (2004) (forthcoming); 72 U.S. Law Week 4168 (2004).

167. *See, e.g.,* Kovarsky & Kovarasky, *Economic, Medical, and Legal Aspects of Age Discrimination Law in Employment.*

168. Ambach v. Norwick, 441 U.S. 68 (1979).

169. Hoffman Plastics Compounds Inc. v. National Labor Relations Board, 122 S. Ct. 1275 (2002).

170. Niederhuber v. Camden County Voc. Tech. School Dist. Bd. of Educ., 495 F. Supp. 273 (D. N.J. 1980); *cf.* Church of God Worldwide v. Amarillo, 511 F. Supp. 613 (N.D. Tex. 1981) (student).

171. Philbrook v. Ansonia Bd. of Educ., 757 F.2d 476 (2d Cir. 1985); EEOC v. Chemisco, Inc., 216 F. Supp. 2d 940 (E.D. Mo. 2002).

172. Ibid.

173. *E.g.,* United States v. Lulac, 793 F.2d 636 (5th Cir. 1986), *citing* Washington v. Davis, 426 U.S. 229 (1976).

174. G. Valeria v. Davis, 307 F.3d 1036 (9th Cir. 2002).

175. *See* Assn. of Mexican-American Educators v. State, 231 F.3d 573 (9th Cir. 2000) and case there cited.

176. Assn. of Mexican-American Educators v. State of California, 231 F.3d 572 (2001) (teacher tests); Valeria, note 174, *supra*.

177. Bilingual education laws were enacted in Alaska, Massachusetts, Michigan, Arizona, Arkansas, California, Colorado, Illinois, Iowa, Maine, New Mexico, New York, Oregon, Pennsylvania, Rhode Island, and Texas, among others.

CHAPTER 7

Student Rights and Discipline

CHAPTER OUTLINE

I.   Background Note
II. Universal Constitutional Rights
     A. Procedural Rights—Due Process
         1. Cases Entitled to Due Process
         2. What Process Is Due?
             a. Notice and Hearing
             b. Impartial Tribunal
             c. Right to Present and Confront Evidence
             d. Right to Counsel
             e. Hearing Record and Appeal
             f. Waiver and Cure of Procedural Defects
             g. Statutory Procedures
     B. Substantive Rights—Due Process
         1. General Right to Rational Treatment
         2. Right to Bodily Security
         3. Freedom of Expression
             a. Unprotected Speech
             b. Offensive Speech
             c. Time, Place, and Manner Regulations
             d. Limits of Protected Speech
             e. Critical Speech
             f. Student Press, Plays, and Literature
             g. Political and Commercial Advertisements
             h. Symbolic Expression: Choice of Dress, Hairstyle, and
                 Appearance
             i. Student Organizations—Freedom of Association
     C. Rights of Privacy
         1. School Searches
         2. Body Searches
         3. School Desks and Lockers
         4. Informational Privacy
         5. Decisional Privacy—Autonomy
     D. Liability for Constitutional Violations

III. Topical Civil Rights—Equal Opportunity Laws
    A. Review Note
    B. Racial and National Origin Discrimination
        1. Interdistrict Segregation
        2. Affirmative Action Issues
        3. Discriminatory Conduct
        4. Racial Disparities in Testing and Placement
        5. Linguistically Disadvantaged Minorities
        6. Remedies for Racial Discrimination
    C. Gender Discrimination
        1. Sexual Abuse and Harassment
        2. Disparate Treatment
        3. Sports Programs
        4. Academic Benefits
        5. Remedies for Gender Discrimination
    D. Homosexual Discrimination
        1. Constitutional Protections
        2. Statutory Protections
    E. Children with Disabilities
        1. The IDEA Law
        2. Procedural Requirements
        3. FAPE Requirements
        4. Placement Rules—Mainstreaming
        5. Access to IDEA Benefits by Private School Students
        6. Discipline of Children with Disabilities
        7. Rights of Those with Disabilities Under State Law
        8. Rights of Separated Parents
    F. Alien Children
    G. Poverty Groups
    H. Concurrent Violations of Different Laws
    I. Special Immunity Defenses
IV. Rights Under State Law

∽ CHAPTER DISCUSSION QUESTIONS

∽ CASES

7.1   Hasenfus v. LaJeunesse, 175 F.3d 68 (1st Cir. 1999)
7.2   Bethel School District No. 403 v. Fraser, 478 U.S. 675 (1986)
7.3   Hazelwood School District v. Kuhlmeier, 484 U.S. 260 (1988)
7.4   Gonzales v. McEuen, 435 F. Supp. 460 (1977)
7.5   Jones v. State, 64 S.W.2d 728 (Ark. 2002)
7.6   Board of Education v. Earls, 122 S. Ct. 2559 (2002)
7.7   U.S. v. Miami University, 294 F.3d 797 (6th Cir. 2002)
7.8   Missouri v. Jenkins, 515 U.S. 70 (1995)
7.9   Debra P. by Irene P. v. Turlington, 730 F.2d 1405 (11th Cir. 1984)
7.10 Davis v. Monroe County Board of Educ., 119 S. Ct. 1661 (1999)
7.11 ABC School v. Mr. and Mrs. M., 1997 Mass. Super., 97-518, Lexis 43
7.12 Hendrick Hudson Dist. Board of Educ. v. Rowley, 458 U.S. 176 (1982)
7.13 Taylor v. Vermont Department of Education, 313 F.3d 768 (2d Cir. 2002)

∽ ENDNOTES

BACKGROUND NOTE

Student rights under state education laws were considered in Chapters 1, 2, and 4. This chapter deals with their rights under federal laws. Most of those laws here were reviewed (with regard to religious controversies and to teacher civil rights) in Chapters 3 and 6. Those chapter materials furnish the essential background for this chapter's review of student rights. This chapter will not repeat those discussions, but will occasionally refer to them so that the reader may refresh his or her recollection, if necessary.

Part II of this chapter focuses on constitutional rights that attach to all students, primarily under the First Amendment (e.g., speech, association, religion), the Fourth Amendment (e.g., searches), and their procedural rights under the Due Process Clause of the Fourteenth Amendment. Part III discusses the civil rights that apply only to students who are subject to particular forms of discrimination (e.g., race, alienage, handicap), primarily under federal anti-discrimination statutes (listed and summarized in Chapter 6 and in Appendix 2 at the end of this book) and under the equal protection provisions of the Fourteenth Amendment.

As explained in Chapter 6, when the same course of events gives rise to multiple claims under the several equal opportunity laws, each law source must be considered separately, because Congress has created different rights and remedies under each of those statutes. As to remedies, for example, a court has inherent equity powers to grant **equitable relief** for any law violation (by way of injunctions and affirmative action orders), but it does not have inherent power to grant **legal relief** of monetary compensation and damages. Only if Congress authorized the grant of legal relief by a statute may a school district be liable to pay monetary damages to a discrimination victim. On this "payoff" of legal relief, therefore, the contents of each civil rights statute becomes crucial.

While most state laws mirror the more intensely litigated federal laws, the laws of some states create civil rights not created by federal law. This chapter does not cover the civil rights laws of individual states, because they are too varied to permit a fair general summary. School staff and administrators must, therefore, look to the laws of their home state and, where necessary, consult legal counsel on them.

As explained in Chapter 6, the sphere of civil rights created by the *Constitution* overlaps with, but differs from, the sphere of civil rights created by *Legislation*. It is necessary, therefore, to consider each sphere separately.

UNIVERSAL CONSTITUTIONAL RIGHTS

Federal constitutional rights include specifically named rights (such as freedoms of religion, speech, press, and assembly, and freedom from unreasonable search) and rights or liberties that are not named in the text of the Constitution (such as the right to bodily security, and to make certain personal decisions without government interference). None of these rights is absolute or unlimited. In the public school environment, courts set the constitutional bounds of student rights, on one hand, and of public school authority, on the other.

Procedural Rights—Due Process

Educational decisions that affect a constitutional student interest must comply with constitutional procedures that satisfy due process (as distinguished from special procedural requirements of particular statutes). School decisions that violate procedural due process may be overturned, even if they would have been valid, had the required procedures been observed. However, since due process is not required for all school decisions, the first question arises: When is a student entitled to constitutional due process? Only if a student is so entitled, do parties encounter the next question: What procedures are constitutionally due that student?

Cases Entitled to Due Process

Due process rights attach only if a school decision or action affects a constitutionally recognized *liberty or property interest,* and then only if that interest is *materially or sufficiently* affected by the decision. As will be seen shortly, most school actions do not implicate a recognized liberty or property interest and, therefore, do not require due process.

Liberty interests are created by and found in the Constitution itself, e.g., an interest in exercising freedom of speech which is being curtailed by a school disciplinary charge. But *property interests* are created by and found in state law:

> . . . [property interests] are not created by the Constitution. Rather they are created and their dimensions are defined by existing rules and understandings that stem from an independent source such as state law—rules or regulations. [*Board of Regents v. Roth,* 408 U.S. 564, 577 (1972)]

For example, a student's entitlement to a public education under state law qualifies as a property interest so that any proceeding that could affect that entitlement (suspension or expulsion) must follow due process requisites. However, where a state law leaves to school authorities the discretion to set grade promotion standards, students have no law entitlement or property interest that entitles them to a due process hearing on grading or promotion. Most courts have also found no student property interest in decisions that affect tangential interests, such as access to an honor society, student office, extracurricular activities, or graduation ceremonies.[1] In exceptional circumstances, a court may stretch the property interest concept to require due process procedures for a decision to bar a uniquely talented athlete from varsity sports and thereby destroy the student's opportunity to obtain valuable college scholarships, and a potential lifetime career in professional sports.[2]

What Process Is Due?

The question of what process is "due" to protect a student's interest is often more complex. None is due to a student who freely and knowingly waives his or her due process rights. Where not waived, the Constitution does not require that the same procedures be used in every case, or that school administrators follow the procedures followed by courts.

> Due process . . . is not a technical conception with a fixed content unrelated to time, place and circumstances. [*Ingraham v. Wright*, 430 U.S. 651, 675 (1977)]

> The very nature of due process negates any concept of inflexible procedures universally applicable to every imaginable situation. [*Goss v. Lopez*, 419 U.S., at 578 (1975)]

The core requirement of due process is *fair treatment*; hence, the quantum of required procedures will vary with the nature and gravity of each case.[3] Depending on the case context, courts also consider which of the following elements are required for a fair hearing, over and above the first three, which are always required:

1. Reasonable *notice* of the charges and subject of the hearing, which will enable the student a fair *opportunity to prepare* for the hearing,
2. A *reasonably prompt hearing* on notified charges,
3. Hearing and decision by an *impartial tribunal*,
4. An opportunity to *present evidence* and to *confront adverse witnesses* at the hearing,
5. An opportunity to be represented by *legal counsel*,
6. A right to demand and obtain an *official record* of the proceeding, and
7. A right to *appeal* the hearing decision to higher authority.

Notice and Hearing.   In *Goss v. Lopez*, 419 U.S. 565 (1975), the Supreme Court overturned a 10-day student suspension for lack of a due process hearing because the suspension affected the student's property interest (in receiving public education) and liberty interest (in avoiding injury to reputation). The Court stressed, however, that though the suspension entitled him to "some kind of hearing", only minimal due process would be required for minor disciplinary cases. It observed that an immediate informal conference between that student and school principal or other superior, with oral advice of the disciplinary charge and an opportunity for the student to respond to the charge, would suffice for short suspensions. However, if a short suspension is a prelude to expulsion for the same conduct, that action was held to require due process.[4] Transfers between schools of comparable quality were recently treated as having the same effect as a short-term suspension and thus subject to some informal process, while transfers to less desirable schools or classes involved stronger student educational interests that required a more formal hearing.[5]

Goss and later cases noted that some forms of student discipline are too minimal to require even an informal hearing. Thus, "... measures such as after-school detention, restriction to classroom during free periods, reprimand or admonition do not per se involve matters rising to the dignity of constitutional magnitude."[6]

Two years after deciding *Goss,* the Supreme Court held that normal corporal punishment may be administered without a due process hearing, because such punishment would not seriously interrupt or affect the student's right to public education, or materially abridge a "liberty" interest in a right to bodily security,[7] or violate the Eighth Amendment prohibition against "cruel and unusual punishment", and that in any event, any benefit of a prior hearing for corporal punishment cases is outweighed by the state's interest in prompt, effective discipline. The fact that state tort law provided an adequate remedy for any unlawful use of force in corporal punishment apparently persuaded the court that its decision did not seriously jeopardize student rights. However, as pointed out in Chapter 8 (*Riddick,* Case 8.4), where a student's constitutional right to bodily security is violated (e.g., by a sexually abusive teacher) the students may recover money damages for violation of that right.

The cases on academic decisions manifest a general reluctance of courts to interfere with educational decisions, so that courts will not require due process hearing for academic decisions[8] unless those decisions result in excessive penalties which themselves affect a student's property or liberty interest.

A student who declined an oral request to give his version of a reported marijuana use incident, was held to have waived his right to a hearing, and therefore could not later complain when the school principal, upon further investigation, suspended him on that charge.[9]

Where fairness requires advance written notice of hearing and charges, the notice must be given in a timely manner and provide sufficient information to afford the student a fair opportunity to prepare a defense, but the amount and detail of required notice information is determined by the nature and complexity of the disciplinary charge.[10] However, as found in the *Bethel* and *Hazelwood* cases (Cases 7.2 and 7.3) at the end of the chapter, students cannot complain of lack of specifics regarding conduct that is obviously wrongful.

Whether due process includes a right to demand an open or a closed hearing also depends on the demands of fairness in each case. Unless a right to an open hearing is granted by state law, fairness may require a closed hearing to protect a person's reputation from unproven charges, but in other circumstances, fairness to the parties may require that the hearing be open to the public.[11]

The fair notice principle also finds expression in the "void for vagueness" doctrine, which nullifies laws and regulations that do not provide sufficient information to inform persons of ordinary intelligence as to what conduct is prohibited and what penalties such conduct will incur. The fair notice element of due process does not require schools to publish in advance narrowly drawn written regulations for every conceivable limitation on student conduct or expression. Courts may disagree on the fairness of notice in varied school environments. The word "misconduct" was held unconstitutionally vague for student discipline in some cases, but not in others. The prohibition against "behavior . . . inimical to the welfare, safety, or morals of other pupils" was held not unduly vague in Colorado, while the failure to specify criteria of "substantial disruption" was deemed fatal in Puerto Rico.[12] Courts are inclined to uphold, as sufficiently clear, terms that are customarily understood, such as *willful disobedience, intentional disruption, student walkouts, boycotts, incorrigible behavior, profanity, excessive absenteeism,* and *vulgarity.*[13] Though weakened by later case trends, some of the stricter cases caution against casual reliance on arguably vague regulations.[14]

Emergency exclusions of a student from school without a prior hearing in order to ensure school safety or stable school operations do not violate due process as long as a hearing is provided as soon as practicable following such exclusions.[15]

Impartial Tribunal.   As reported in Chapter 6, school boards are presumed to be impartial tribunals so that a party alleging board bias has the burden of proving that charge.[16] A party may not attempt to provoke tribunal bias in order to disqualify the tribunal as biased by the party's insults, e.g., by calling board members "fascist pigs".[17] Impartiality was clearly destroyed where a prosecution witness also served as a member of the judging panel. The case law is mixed on the extent to which school board counsel can lawfully participate in school board hearings and deliberations.[18] These cases caution against administrative staff performing potentially inconsistent roles in school board hearings and deliberations. The *Gonzales* decision, which appears at the end of this chapter as Case 7.4, overturned student expulsions because the school board's attorney acted as prosecutor in the proceedings and the school superintendent was present for a significant period (45 minutes) while the board deliberated on whether to expel students. The court opinion noted, however, that board familiarity with the case or prehearing exposure to some evidence that was presented at the hearing would not alone impugn the fairness of the board members or deny the students a fair hearing, and that the combination of investigatory and adjudicatory functions in school administrative hearings is not unfair per se. The bias issue is diminished where state law or board regulations require that disciplinary hearings be conducted by persons other than school board members or officials, and which bar school attorneys from participating in such hearings.

Cases that involve severe charges or penalties would require correspondingly greater due process procedures, such as right to legal counsel and right to cross-examine adverse witnesses.

Right to Present and Confront Evidence.   The right to present evidence is universal, but the right to be notified of adverse evidence and to cross-examine witnesses is not. In the above-mentioned *Goss* case, the Court rejected the suggestion that students have a right of cross-examination or to legal counsel in all student disciplinary hearings. These elements are not required for minor infractions or punishments, but are essential for cases that potentially involve serious penalties, especially where the hearing outcome hinges on the credibility of conflicting witnesses.[19] In such cases courts have held that the board had to disclose adverse evidence and to produce adverse witnesses for cross-examination, unless such failure was excused as a harmless error, as where the testimony of the absent witness could not have affected the hearing outcome.[20] Decisions on the use or exclusion of hearsay evidence thus vary with case circumstances.[21]

> Other courts are divided on the issue of confrontation and cross-examination. Some have held that a hearing incorporating that safeguard must be afforded in school expulsion proceedings. . . . Others have declined to accord that right. . . . In *Dillon v. Pulaski City Special Sch. Dist.* (E.D. Ark.) 468 F. Supp. 54, 58, the court held that a student not permitted to confront and cross-examine teachers or administrators who accused him of wrongdoing was denied due process, but stated in dicta that confrontation and cross-examination of student accusers might be disallowed consistent with due process if reprisals were likely. [*Aguirre v. San Bernadino City Unified School,* 170 Cal. Rptr. 206, 215 (1981)]

Right to Counsel.   Like cross-examination, the right to have one's attorney present and participate in hearings depends on the nature of the hearing.

> Where the proceeding is non-criminal in nature, where the hearing is investigative and not adversarial and the government does not proceed through counsel, where the individual concerned is mature and educated, where his knowledge of the events . . . should enable him to develop the facts adequately through available sources, and where the other aspects of the hearing taken as a whole are fair, due process does not require representation by counsel. . . . [*Wasson v. Trowbridge,* 382 F.2d 807, 812 (2d Cir. 1967)]

No right to counsel was found where the school attorney was not present, or where the hearing was considered advisory and not adversarial.[22] But exclusion of a student's attorney from a hearing on charges of academic cheating that, if proven, would disqualify the student from taking a scholarship examination was held to deny due process.[23]

Hearing Record and Appeal.   Constitutional due process does not include a right to appeal to a higher tribunal from an administrative decision in all cases unless state law confers such a right.[24] Where a right of appeal is conferred by law, some kind of hearing record (stenographic or electronic) may be required,[25] if a court decides that such a record is needed for it fairly to review and decide the case.[26]

Waiver and Cure of Procedural Defects.   Students may waive due process rights expressly or by conduct, such as failure to pursue available procedures. Because waiver requires an *intentional* relinquishment or abandonment of a *known* right or privilege, school authorities should document, where possible, such waivers as having been freely and intelligently made. Procedural deficiencies can also be cured by timely corrective procedures. Finally, errors that do not materially affect the fairness or outcome of the case may, though not formally waived or corrected, still be excused if a court finds those errors to be "harmless".[27]

Statutory Procedures.   Federal or state statutes sometimes require school districts to follow special procedures in addition to those required for constitutional due process. For example, the federal Individuals with Disabilities Education Act, discussed below, prescribes special procedures where parents challenge administrative decisions that affect students with disabilities. State legislatures may also mandate specified procedures for particular school actions, such as those dealing with student placement and assignment, or with student access to extracurricular programs.

Substantive Rights—Due Process

While declaring that students do not leave their constitutional rights at the schoolhouse gate, the Supreme Court added the significant qualification: "[T]he constitutional rights of students in public school are not automatically coextensive with the rights of adults in other settings." [*Bethel School District No. 403 v. Fraser*, 478 U.S. 675, at p. 682 (1986)]

General Right to Rational Treatment

The general right to be free from arbitrary government restraints or punishments, i.e., those that do not rationally serve a valid school *purpose*, or that employ irrational *means* to achieve a proper purpose, limits school authority over students. When a student challenges school actions as infringing this right, courts may differ in their judgment whether the challenged action is or is not "reasonable" in purpose or means of achievement. A threatening outburst by a student occasioned by school bureaucratic shuffles was not deemed so serious as to justify her suspension when she promptly apologized for it, whereas in other circumstances, expulsion of a student who was deemed to pose danger to other students or teachers was held reasonable.[28] Out-of-school misconduct that threatens student welfare, such as sale or use of drugs or alcohol or assaults on other students, may be punished as rationally connected to and justified by proper school interests.[29] Courts have overturned punishments, as not rationally based, where a student was arrested away from school on an unproven charge of drug possession, and where the punished student was in a car with other students that contained alcohol or drugs, without proof he possessed or used those items.[30] A manifest violation of the rational nexus test occurred where the school board expelled a student because his parent assaulted a board member.[31]

As with the due process cases discussed above, courts are reluctant to interfere with educational judgments by overturning academic penalties as unconstitutionally irrational. They have upheld school forfeiture of academic credits or privileges for serious student misconduct,[32] but may always overturn academic penalties on the state law grounds that such decisions are arbitrary and an abuse of discretion or are not authorized by state law (*ultra vires*).[33] Where automatic academic penalties are set by legislative enactments, courts tend to uphold them as reasonable even though the statute makes no allowance for mitigating circumstances.[34]

Right to Bodily Security

The *constitutional* right to security of one's person and body is generally protected from *unprivileged* physical contacts be they sexual or nonsexual in nature. This right does not prohibit physical contacts between school superiors and students which are *privileged*, i.e., where they are justified by a school need to protect persons or property or to maintain school discipline and order, and where the manner and degree of authorized physical force or restraint is reasonable. The constitutional right to bodily security is different from that created by statute law or the common law. While some incidents of abuse of students concurrently give rise to multiple constitutional, statutory, and common law claims of injury to bodily security (see, e.g., the *Doe* case which is reproduced in Chapter 8 as Case 8.5), those sources create different standards of student right and school district liability. The Supreme Court's recent decision that teacher sexual abuse of a student is actionable under the Title IX federal aid statute (see the *Franklin* case, discussed below) indirectly supports the view that sexual abuse of students is a serious invasion of a constitutional civil right.

Some forms of corporal punishment that are valid under the Constitution are prohibited by civil rights statutes, such as Title IX and the IDEA laws, which are discussed later in this chapter, and by the § 1983 law, which is reviewed in Chapter 8. Though some 25 states have enacted laws to prohibit the use of corporal punishment in public schools,[35] the Supreme Court found no general *constitutional* bar to corporal punishment.[36] In that case, the Court did not reach or decide the narrower question whether corporal punishments that is so severe or brutal as to "shock the conscience" would infringe the constitutional right to bodily safety and security. The lower courts are in conflict on the validity of a "shock the conscience" theory of a substantive constitutional right,[37] and further Supreme Court decision is required to resolve that conflict, not only with regard to the validity of the "shock the conscience" rationale, but also on the sticky question of what kinds and degrees of bodily abuse are sufficiently severe to "shock the conscience".

The escalation of sexual abuse of students and of student suicides has engendered still another theory of *constitutional* right, namely, that public schools, as state-created, state-operated institutions with full, though temporary, control and custody of their students, have a *special relationship* and an *affirmative constitutional* "duty to protect" students from those harms. That theory would extend the Supreme Court rulings that states have a constitutional duty to protect inmates of state-operated prisons and mental hospitals, since those inmates are state wards who are unable to protect themselves, unlike free citizens.[38] The special relationship/duty-to-protect argument has special appeal for students and parents because it is much easier to prove a violation of an *affirmative* constitutional school duty-to-protect students, than to prove that a school district was grossly negligent or deliberately indifferent to student perils.

Most lower courts have declined to extend the state prison and mental hospital cases[39] to the school setting, in light of the more recent Supreme Court holding in a case whose facts do not clearly cover the public school setting. The Court there held that a state social service agency did not have a duty to protect an abused child from a fatal beating by his custodial father though it knew that the child was severely abused and battered by his father. [*DeShaney v. Winnebago Co. Dept. of Social Services*, 489 U.S. 189 (1989)] Since the state agency did not have legal custody of the child at the time of his injury, the Court concluded that the agency had no *constitutional* duty to protect him. Students injured at school by school employees while in at least temporary custody of the school may well argue that their public school relationship is more like the situation presented in the prison inmate cases than in the *DeShaney* case. The duty-to-protect argument is, therefore, open to further case development and clarification, not only for public school students, but for children placed by the state in residential schools, orphanages, and foster family care.[40]

The *Hasenfus* case (Case 7.1) contains a good review of the limited case law on school duties to protect vulnerable students, in the context of a student with known or observable suicidal tendencies. The court there rejected the special relationship claim of a formerly raped and depressed child who attempted suicide in an empty school room to which she had been banished by her teacher for misconduct during a school field exercise. The disinclination of courts to extend the special relationship argument to public schools is further evident in a case which found no school duty to protect a special education student who had earlier threatened to kill himself, and did so after being suspended and driven to his home without any notice to the parent.[41] The court nevertheless indicated that such a right to protection might be found in other special circumstances.

Freedom of Expression

Students as well as teachers have First Amendment rights of freedom of speech and press while at school. As noted below, those freedoms are limited by counterbalancing factors of school needs, so that constitutional protections will vary with the form, content, and circumstances of such expression. Moreover, one must determine what categories of speech are constitutionally protected, and what categories are denied any constitutional protection.

Unprotected Speech.   The Constitution provides no protection of speech that is defamatory (other than expressions by the press regarding "public figures"), or "obscene", or that amounts to "fighting words" or "true threats" directed against specific parties. The legal definitions of *defamation* and *obscenity* are no longer of major concern in elementary and secondary schools, since school authorities may, under recent Supreme Court decisions (see Case 7.2), prohibit such expression as part of the school mission to educate children to be truthful and to employ decent language. However, the constitutional criteria to distinguish unprotected "fighting words" and "true threats" from merely offensive language require fresh analysis, as school-site student speech becomes increasingly abrasive, bullying, demeaning, and insulting. The distinction between unprotected "fighting words", and protected offensive speech was best stated as follows:

> "Fighting words" have been defined . . . as "those which by their very utterance inflict injury or tend to incite an immediate breach of the peace." *Chaplinsky v. New Hampshire* . . . [T]he *Chaplinsky* Court alternatively described fighting words as those which "have a direct tendency to cause acts of violence by the person to whom, individually, the remark is addressed." [*Jones v. State*, 64 S.W.2d 728, 734 (Ark. 2002)]

The distinction between unprotected "true threats", and protected student speech (that may nonetheless be violent or intimidating) has been described as follows. True threats (which may or may not trigger a violent reaction in the addressee) involve utterances which a *reasonable person* could view as a serious expression of intent to harm another. The true threat doctrine is derived from a 1969 Supreme Court decision which overturned conviction of a protester for remarks (at a political rally) which threatened President Johnson's life. The Court held such remarks to be protected hyperbolic speech in the circumstances, and not a true threat which would not be constitutionally protected. [*Watts v. United States*, 394 U.S. 705 (1969)]

The *Watts* opinion did not provide very clear guidance to differentiate a true threat from protected robust speech, and the cases on alleged student true threats are recent and few in number. For this reason, the *Jones* opinion (Case 7.5) merits careful study for its review of the different measures of a true threat which courts have developed to determine whether particular speech is constitutionally protected. The *Jones* court held that a student's violent "rap song" whose content threatened a female classmate amounted to a true threat, which was a constitutional ground to adjudicate him as a delinquent. The Eighth Circuit Court of Appeal later upheld school expulsion of a seventh-grade student under the true threat doctrine for composing "two violent, misogynic, obscenity-laden rant expressing a desire to molest, rape, and murder K.G." his classmate, even though that composition was not physically delivered to her.[42] Relying on the *Watts* opinion, the Ninth Circuit Court of Appeals also held that a school district could constitutionally expel a student after he composed and showed to a teacher a poem that was "filled with imagery of violent death and suicide and the shooting of fellow students." The court echoed a now familiar theme:

> [W]e live in a time when school violence is an unfortunate reality that educators must confront on an all too frequent basis. The recent spate of school shootings have put our nation on edge. . . . After Columbine, Thurston, Santee and other school shootings, questions have been asked about how teachers or administrators could have missed telltale "warning signs", why something was not done earlier and what should be done to prevent such tragedies happening again. [*Lavine v. Blaine*, 257 F.3d 981, 987 (9th Cir. 2001)]

The stress on "warning signs" and need "to prevent" harm reflects a growing inclination to uphold school punishment of violent student language.

While the above cases agree that expression must be such that a reasonable person would consider it is a serious threat to cause harm, they are not agreed on whose perception of the alleged threat should govern, the speaker's or the addressee's. As the *Jones* opinion noted, two federal circuit courts (Eighth and Ninth) assess a threat from the view of the threatened person, while one circuit court (First) assesses a threat from the view of the threatening person. This split among the circuits underscores the importance of learning the territorial bounds of one's home federal circuit (see Figure 1.1, in Chapter 1) whose rulings often endure without Supreme Court review for indefinite periods of time.

Offensive Speech.   Offensive or harassing speech that does not provoke a violent response, express a true threat, or threaten school disorder enjoys some constitutional protection. After observing that "there is no categorical 'harassment exception' to the First Amendment free speech clause" one circuit court (the Third) recently struck down school antiharassment policies that prohibited harasssing or offensive expression. In one case, the court voided a school ban which defined harassing speech as including "verbal . . . conduct based on one's actual or perceived race, religion, color, national origin, gender, sexual orientation, disability, or other personal characteristics . . . or creating an inimidating, hostile or offensive environment".[43] In the second case, the court held that a school ban of student garb or possession of written material "that creates ill will or hatred" swept too broadly to prohibit protected speech, though another federal circuit court (the Tenth) had upheld a similar policy in similar circumstances, as constitutionally justified to preserve school order.[44] These case variations illustrate the difficulty of drawing constitutional lines between protected and unprotected harassing speech, and the consequent need to draft speech limiting policies narrowly to avoid including protected speech in the policy ban.

Time, Place, and Manner Regulations.   As explained in Chapter 6, school regulations that reasonably regulate the time, place, and manner of speech for the limited purpose of maintaining orderly use and scheduling of school facilities are not deemed to infringe First Amendment rights. For such regulations, school authorities need only show that the regulations are reasonably related to genuine school "housekeeping" needs. School authorities may, therefore, confine student rallies to reasonably prescribed times and places, and may punish students for using facilities for expressive purposes when those facilities are reasonably reserved for other school uses. The courts are divided on the validity of bans on school-site distributions of nonschool newspapers, though such bans arguably fall under the time, place, and manner exception.[45]

Limits of Protected Speech.   School authorities may not constitutionally suppress expression (oral or written) solely on the basis of its content or viewpoint. In addition, the Equal Access Act, which was reviewed in Chapter 3 with reference to religious speech, was also held to prohibit school authorities from denying to one student group (Gay Straight Alliance) the same access to school facilities which was given to other student groups for noncurriculum-related activities, since disorder was threatened not by the petitioning students but by those opposed to their viewpoints.[46]

Absent unconstitutional motivation to discriminate among ideas or viewpoints, the constitutional justification to constrain student speech will be measured by one of two different tests, depending on the type of speech that is restricted, namely, speech that is deemed be involve a matter of *personal concern*, and speech that is deemed to involve a matter of *pedagogical concern* or which may be viewed as *school-sponsored speech.* In each case, courts decide whether the affected speech is of personal or pedagogical concern.

School authorities may not prohibit or punish speech of personal concern unless they demonstrate that the expression materially does or imminently threatens to interfere with the work of the school. This disruption test originated in the case of *Tinker v. Des Moines Ind. Community School Dist.*[47] which voided a high school ban on student use of antiwar armbands because that expressive conduct was not shown to be disruptive in the affected school. The Court, however, cited with approval other cases which upheld school bans on student use of passive symbols, such as wearing a confederate flag clothing patch or symbols in racially tense schools on findings that such expressive symbols threatened imminent school disorder and disruption.[48]

In one recent case the court faced the novel question whether or how *Tinker* might apply to very young children, specifically whether a school could constitutionally prohibit a nine-year-old third grader from soliciting signatures from her classmates at school for a petition which read, *inter alia,* "We 3d grade kids don't want to go to the circus because they hurt animals." The court held that it could do so, stressing the fact that the age of young and impressionable children, both soliciting and solicited, is a legitimate factor in determining the extent to which the *Tinker* test limits school regulation of student speech at school.[49] The majority opinion declared that "*if* third graders enjoy rights under *Tinker*, those rights will necessarily be very limited." (Emphasis added) This case highlights the nice fact questions that the disruption test raises. The kinds and degrees of physical, psychological, or other distraction that qualify as disruptive of school order or educational purposes or as a sufficient threat to orderly school operations will necessarily depend on specific circumstances, including the age of the affected students. Nor does the law answer the question as to how much weight should be given to the opinions of school authorities of the threatened disorder, especially where opposing parties produce conflicting versions of the school environment.

For speech that is of school pedagogical concern or that carries the suggestion that the school has approved it, the Supreme Court held that school authorities need only have reasonable grounds to conclude that the restricted student speech is educationally inappropriate in order to suppress or punish it. The *Bethel* case (Case 7.2) held that the *Tinker* disruption test does not apply to speech of pedagogical concern, and upheld school discipline of a student for delivering a lewd nominating speech to a mandatory, school-sponsored assembly. The Court later extended the *Bethel* doctrine to school censorship of student articles in a school-sponsored student newspaper in the *Hazelwood* case (Case 7.3). The Court further elaborated the difference between the *Tinker* and the *Bethel* measures of student speech protection:

> [T]he question that we addressed in *Tinker*—is different from the question whether the First Amendment requires a school . . . to promote particular student speech. The former question addresses educators' ability to silence a student's personal expression. . . . The latter question concerns educators' authority over school-sponsored publications, theatrical productions, and other expressive activities that students . . . and members of the public might reasonably perceive to bear the imprimatur of the school. These activities may fairly be characterized as part of the school curriculum, whether or not they occur in a traditional classroom setting. . . . [See *Hazelwood School Dist. v. Kuhlmeier,* 484 U.S. 260, 271 (1988).]

Lower courts must now decide whether contested student expression is governed by the "educationally inappropriate" standard or by the disruption standard—a choice that may invite case conflicts. Judges' perceptions or judgments may differ on what speech is of personal or educational concern, and they may not be equally inclined to defer to the judgment of school authorities as to what is educationally appropriate. For example, the Courts of Appeal of the Third, Eighth, and Eleventh circuits upheld school suppression of class readings, student plays, and publication whose content the school authorities deemed to be educationally inappropriate (e.g., text containing passages deemed inappropriately vulgar, from Chaucer's "A Miller's Tale" and Aristophanes' "Lysistrata"; the play *Pippin;* and of school-site use of off-campus publications), while the Ninth Circuit Court overturned school limitations of student speech as either not involving a matter of pedagogical concern or as not being "reasonable" in the circumstances.[50] In considering whether the stricter *Tinker* test or the deferential *Bethel* test should apply to given speech and its context, school authorities must look to cases whose facts most closely proximate their situation. The following case samplings illustrate these contextual variables.

Critical Speech.   Orderly student criticisms of school policies or practices qualify as protected personal speech, but disruptive messages that incite insubordination or disorder, such as abusive speech to school superiors or speech calling for a student strike or takeover of school buildings, are constitutionally punishable.[51]

Student Press, Plays, and Literature.   The *Bethel* and *Hazelwood* decisions displaced older decisions which overturned school censorship of student publications.[52] *Hazelwood* expressly rejected the suggestion of some older cases that schools authorities must give students advance *written* notice that certain published content, e.g., vulgar speech, is prohibited. "We reject respondent's suggestion that school officials be permitted to exercise prepublication control over school-sponsored publications only pursuant to specific written regulations. . . ." The *Hazelwood* opinion equated school control over school-sponsored plays with school control over school newspapers, thereby adding support to decisions that had upheld school suppression of student plays that were deemed educationally inappropriate.[53]

Freedom of the press generally includes a right of anonymous publication, but for distributions on school grounds, school superiors may constitutionally demand disclosure of the authors of those communications.[54]

Political and Commercial Advertisements.   The case law is mixed on school prohibitions of politically partisan or socially controversial ads in student newspapers, and on the right of student editors to choose which outside advertisements to accept or reject based on their approval or disapproval of the advertisement's message.[55]

School control over student distribution of commercial literature is to be differentiated from the allowance of commercial messages by the school itself.

That distinction is starkly presented in the *Dawson* case, which appears at the end of Chapter 1.

Symbolic Expression: Choice of Dress, Hairstyle, and Appearance. As held in *Tinker*, the First Amendment protects symbolic as well as verbal expression. But where an expressive symbol is bracketed with active conduct (such as flag burning[56] or draft-card burning), the Supreme Court forged a special rule:

> [W]hen speech and non-speech elements are combined in the same course of conduct, a sufficiently important governmental interest in regulating the non-speech element can justify incidental limitation of First Amendment freedoms. [*United States v. O'Brien*, 391 U.S. 367, 376 (1968)]

Application of the above ruling to expression that takes a negative form, i.e., refusing to act or to participate in a school exercise, such as a flag salute or pledge of allegiance, is more complex. Earlier cases overturned laws and regulations that required students to stand or leave the room during flag salute ceremonies,[57] but the expressive right to "opt out" does not extend to the point of interfering with such exercises, e.g., by moving around to disturb the exercise. For like reasons, student boycotts, walkouts, and sit-ins are not constitutionally protected.[58]

Choice of personal appearance implicates a general liberty interest that carries less weight than verbal expression in the balance of student and school interests. Still, appearance and dress regulations must be fairly clear and be reasonably connected to proper school purposes.[59] The recent adoption of mandatory school uniforms or dress codes in some school districts has sparked constitutional challenges that raise the following question: Which of the above-discussed constitutional tests govern school dress regulations, the test announced in the *O'Brien* case, the test announced in the *Tinker* case, or the test announced in the *Bethel* case?

The Fifth Circuit Court of Appeals applied the *O'Brien* test and the *Bethel* test to uphold uniform school dress requirements, and in effect accepted the educational interest standard of constitutionality.[60] Given the hotly debated rationale that school uniform requirements serve important educational and disciplinary values, the application of the educational benefit rationale may vary with the conditions encountered at different schools and at different grade levels.

The Fifth Circuit Court of Appeals later restated its test, to hold that a mandatory uniform policy "will pass constitutional scrutiny if it furthers an important or substantial government interest; if that policy is not motivated to suppress student expression; and if the incidental restriction on student expression is no more than is necessary to facilitate the school's educational interest."[61] Applying that test, the court again upheld the constitutionality of uniform dress requirements, noting that the objecting students retained their choice of dress away from school and could use other media of expression while at school.

The cases on regulations of optional student dress also turn on court findings whether school educational and disciplinary interests justified them. Bans on female student dress in jeans were upheld in Kentucky but overturned in Idaho and New Hampshire, while school bans of tight skirts, pants, or miniskirts were held to be justified in Arkansas.[62] One court upheld a high school ban against attire that featured certain colleges or sports teams on its finding that the attire was emblematic of school gangs that intimidated other students, but another court overturned a like ban where that attire was not shown to be a source of trouble.[63] Another court upheld a dress code provision that barred T-shirts that contained sexually vulgar, though not disruptive, messages, while overturning a different provision of the same dress code that barred garb that contained allegedly harassing messages.[64]

Choice of hair length and style also arguably involves a form of symbolic expression. Hairstyle restrictions to protect and enhance the performance of student participants in extracurricular activities (e.g., for athletes during the playing season) have been upheld as reasonable.[65] The constitutionality of school regulation of the hair length and style of all male students is the subject of conflict among the circuit courts. Five federal circuits upheld them (the Third, Fifth, Sixth, Ninth, and Tenth) and four federal circuits overturned them (the First, Fourth, Seventh, and Eighth).[66] Until the Supreme Court resolves these conflicts, school authorities must observe the prevailing law of their governing federal circuit.

The adoption of different hair and dress restrictions for male and female students has generally withstood challenges as sex discrimination, but several courts overturned them on other grounds under state law.[67] The authority of cases on transsexual and gender identity issues has been clouded by the Supreme Court decision (Lawrence), which overturned the Texas antisodomy criminal law as an interference with a general liberty interest of adults.[68] Only future cases will determine whether or how the reasoning of that case affects school regulation of student expression of a homosexual lifestyle. The cases that predated *Lawrence* are mixed and reflect varied judicial perspectives. One court upheld a school decision to bar a male student from attending a prom dressed in girls' clothing, while another court upheld a male student's right to bring a male date to the school prom.[69]

Student Organizations—Freedom of Association.   The First Amendment protects the right to form and join organizations, but that right may be limited by overriding school interests. For example, school authorities may prohibit secret or separatist school clubs in order to foster tolerance and democratic values; and they may prohibit hazing rituals in order to prevent student injury.[70] They may further demand student school organizations to disclose and file with school superiors their organization's bylaws and officers, in order to maintain proper oversight of school activities.[71]

Rights of Privacy

School Searches

School searches to eliminate drugs, weapons, and other contraband from schools have intensified, as have constitutional challenges to those searches. The Fourth Amendment prohibition against "unreasonable" searches is subject to several important exceptions. It does not protect a student from search where that student has no "reasonable expectation of privacy" in the subject of a search. For example, a student cannot claim a reasonable privacy expectation to contest a search where he or she waived any claim to privacy by voluntarily consenting to the search, or by leaving searched material in "plain view" to outside observation (such as a weapon or drug items left on the seat or dashboard of an automobile in the school parking lot), or has left property unidentified which the school authorities search in order to identify the owner, and to inventory and keep the property in safekeeping.[72] Where a reasonable privacy expectation is recognized, school superiors must have a sufficiently serious need to initiate the search that outweighs the student's privacy interest, e.g., to investigate or prevent a risk of serious harm to persons or property, such as a investigating a report of a bomb threat or of weapons in a school locker. Finally, even if school superiors are constitutionally justified in initiating a search, the scope of the search must also be "reasonable", so that an excessively broad or intrusive search may be overturned as unconstitutional. Students who suffer a violation of their Fourth Amendment right to be free from unreasonable searches may sue to recover monetary damages from violators under the § 1983 law, which is discussed in Chapter 8, subject to the conditions and defenses prescribed by that law.

Search cases often present conflicting versions and evidence on the circumstances of a search. For example, where the school claims that the student consented to a search and the student denies that consent was given or was coerced by threats, the validity of a search will depend on particularized fact findings. One court found valid student consent was given after school authorities threatened to call the police, while another court found no consent for a police search where the student's parent, but not the minor student, agreed to the search.[73] Further, in judging whether a search is "reasonable" in light of competing student's privacy interest and the school's search interests, a court will obviously be influenced by the importance of the affected privacy interest, and will give greater weight to a privacy interest against exposure of a student's body than against exposure of a book bag or pocket contents.

Search law is best understood in terms of the subject of the search and the degree of its intrusiveness, factors which were discussed in the three major Supreme Court decisions on school searches. The first, *New Jersey v. T.L.O.*, 469

U.S. 325 (1985) (hereafter *T.L.O.*), involved a search of a high school freshman's pocketbook by her school principal. The second, *Vernonia Sch. Dist. 47J v. Acton*, 515 U.S. 646 (1995) (hereafter *Vernonia*), involved a school's urinalysis testing requirements for participants in high school athletics at a drug-troubled school. The third, *Board of Education v. Earls*, 122 S. Ct. 2559 (2002) (hereafter *Earls*), involved school district-wide urinalysis testing requirements for students who wished to participate in school extracurricular activities, including academic or social activities as well as school athletics. In each case, the Court upheld the challenged school search as reasonable and constitutional. The critical facts and reasoning of *T.L.O.* and *Vernonia* are traced in the latest Supreme Court decision in *Earls* (Case 7.6) and in the following opinion excerpt of the Eleventh Circuit Court of Appeals.

THOMAS ET AL. v. ROBERTS ET AL.
261 F.3d 1160 (11th Cir. 2001)

*[**Case History.** The following opinion was reconsidered and reinstated by the court on March 10, 2003 [Thomas v. Roberts, 323 F.3d 950 (11th Cir. 2003)]. Thirteen schoolchildren sued their classroom teacher (Tracey Morgan), county police officer (Zannie Billingslea), school principals (Ralph Matthews and R. G. Roberts), the school district, and the county, alleging unconstitutional strip searches by teacher Morgan and officer Billingslea following the disappearance from their classroom of an envelope containing twenty-six dollars which a poor student had brought to class for a school trip. After fruitless searching of classroom trash cans, students' desks, book bags, unshod feet, and turned-out pockets, the police officer, Billingslea, took the boys to the boys' restroom and conducted a partial strip search, and the teacher, Morgan, took the girls to the girls' restroom and conducted a partial strip search. The searches did not turn up the missing envelope.*

The Court of Appeals affirmed the trial court finding that the strip searches were unreasonable and unconstitutional, but it dismissed the case on other (special defense) grounds. The following opinion excerpt deals with the limits of a reasonable search under the first two landmark Supreme Court decisions on student searches. The authors of this text have bolded the opinion language that make significant points.]

Cox, Circuit Judge:

. . . Morgan, who oversaw a class filled with children who were too poor to afford their school lunches, testified that she felt that the missing money presented a serious situation. At this point . . . Officer Zannie Billingslea . . . arrived to teach a class in drug awareness . . . . Morgan informed [assistant principal] Roberts that money was missing . . . and asked that she be allowed to conduct a search to find it. Roberts authorized a search.... ...After speaking with Roberts, Morgan returned to her classroom and began to search for the envelope. ...

... Morgan broke up the boys into groups ... and sent them group by group to the boys' restroom with Billingslea. Several of the boys testified that, once in the restroom, Billingslea pulled his pants and underwear down to his ankles to demonstrate what the children were required to do. Billingslea also informed the boys that if they didn't pull down their pants as directed, they would be suspended from school or taken to jail. All of the boys dropped their pants.... ...Billingslea visually inspected the boy's underwear to ensure that the envelope was not inside.

* * *

...Morgan told all of the girls to line up in the hallway outside the girls' restroom. She then brought the girls into the restroom in groups of two to five students at a time. The students testified that Morgan made them lower their pants and raise their dresses or shirts. Most of the girls were also asked to lift their brassieres and expose their breasts to ensure that the envelope was not hidden under their bras.... There is also testimony that Morgan warned the girls that they could be sent to "juvenile" for not complying. ...

The next day, three sets of parents complained to Principal Ralph Matthews.... ...The School District thereafter launched an investigation.... ...

First, the complaint alleges that Morgan, Roberts, Matthews, Billingslea, the District, and the County deprived the students "of their rights to privacy, to be secure in their persons and to be free from unreasonable searches and seizures...."... The complaint seeks compensatory and punitive damages....

* * *

The constitutional standard for assessing the legality of searches ... was first established by the Supreme Court in *New Jersey v. T.L.O.*, 469 U.S. 325 ... (1985). In *T.L.O.*, a high school vice principal searched the purse of a student who had been caught smoking in violation of a school rule.... Upon opening the purse, the vice principal found a pack of cigarettes. ... He also noticed a package of cigarette rolling papers in the purse, which he knew high school students often used to smoke marijuana. ... Further searching revealed a small amount of marijuana, a pipe, a large quantity of dollar bills, an index card which apparently listed those students who owed her money for drugs, and two letters that further implicated her in drug dealing. ... The vice principal turned the evidence over to the police. ... In a subsequent delinquency proceeding, the student moved to suppress the evidence found in her purse, arguing that the search violated the Fourth Amendment. ...

. . . [T]the Supreme Court first determined that the Fourth Amendment applies to searches of schoolchildren conducted by school officials. . . . After weighing students' legitimate expectations of privacy against school officials' need to maintain a proper educational environment, the Court concluded that it would be improper to "require strict adherence to the requirement that searches be based on probable cause to believe that the subject of the search has violated or is violating the law." . . . Instead, the Court held that the "legality of a search of a student should depend simply on the reasonableness, under all the circumstances, of the search." . . .

The *T.L.O.* Court established a two-pronged test to determine whether a search by school officials is reasonable. First, a court must consider whether the search was justified at its inception. . . . A search will be justified . . . if the school official has "reasonable grounds for suspecting that the search will turn up evidence the student has violated or is violating either the law or the rules of the school." . . . Second, the court must determine whether the scope of the search was reasonably related to the "circumstances which justified the interference. . . ." . . . The scope of a search will be permissible "when the measures adopted are reasonably related to the objectives of the search and not excessively intrusive in light of the age and sex of the student and the nature of the infraction." . . .

This court has yet to apply the *T.L.O.* standard to situations in which school officials require students to remove some of their clothing during a search. We have little trouble in concluding, however, that the strip searches in this case were unconstitutional. . . . **While declining to decide if individualized suspicion was a necessary element of the reasonableness standard in school searches, the [TLO] Court noted that the requirement that officials possess suspicion that a particular student committed an illicit act before searching the student is subject to a very limited exception. . . .**

Given the circumstances of the money's disappearance, Morgan reasonably suspected that a student in her class had taken the envelope. However, Morgan and Billingslea did not possess individualized suspicion that pointed to a specific student or group of students as responsible. . . . [W]e must therefore first ask whether the searches were justified absent individualized suspicion.

The Supreme Court has held that a search may be conducted without individualized suspicion when "the privacy interests implicated by the search are minimal, and . . . an important governmental interest furthered by the intrusion would be placed in jeopardy by a requirement of individualized suspicion." *Skinner v. Ry. Labor Executives' Ass'n.*, 489 U.S. 602, 624, . . . (1989). The Court recently applied this test to school searches in *Vernonia Sch. Dist. 47J v. Acton.*, 515 U.S. 646 . . . (1995). The petitioner school district in *Vernonia* had noticed a trend of drastically increasing drug use by high school students. . . . Especially disturbing . . . was that student athletes were in the vanguard of the burgeoning drug scene. . . .

One of the school district's responses . . . was to establish a mandatory drug testing program for all athletes that required the students to provide urine samples. . . . The plaintiff in *Vernonia* was a seventh grader who wanted to play football but refused to consent to the drug testing regime. . . . [H]e and his parents sued the school district, . . . on the grounds that the drug tests were unreasonable searches. . . .

. . . **Because the searches in *Vernonia*, like the searches in the instant case, were not supported by individualized suspicion, the Court [in *Vernonia*] proceeded to determine if the urine tests fit into the limited exception to the Fourth Amendment's requirement of individualized suspicion.** . . . [T]he Court first determined that student athletes had a reduced expectation of privacy because: (1) high school students generally have lesser expectations of privacy than adult members of the public; and (2) athletes, who "voluntarily subject themselves to a degree of regulation . . . " have concomitantly lower expectations of privacy. . . . The Court thereafter concluded that the character of the intrusion caused by the tests was insignificant because students were permitted to provide the samples without invasive monitoring and the tests revealed a limited amount of information. . . .

Finding the privacy interests and the intrusion implicated by the drug tests to be minimal, the *Vernonia* Court then balanced the interests of the athletes against the school district's interest in avoiding widespread drug use by high school students. . . . The Court therefore concluded that the drug tests were justified absent individualized suspicion. . . .

. . . However, there is no question that schoolchildren retain a legitimate expectation of privacy in their persons, including an expectation that one should be able to avoid the unwanted exposure of one's body, especially one's "private parts." . . . We therefore conclude that the students had an important privacy interest in not being unclothed involuntarily.

. . . Because of the important privacy interest at stake . . . school officials must have possessed a truly important interest that would have otherwise been endangered in order to justify Morgan and Billingslea's actions.

. . . A student's theft of another student's money, . . . could seriously impact a teacher's ability to maintain a safe and effective learning environment. . . . However, there is no reason to believe that the government's interests in maintaining classroom discipline and promoting moral development would have been jeopardized if Morgan and Billingslea were required to possess individualized suspicion before forcing the children to remove their clothing. . . .

This case is unlike *Vernonia*, in which a school district was faced with a seemingly intractable problem of students using dangerous

narcotics. . . . Nor is this a case where, for example, school officials receive information that an unidentified student may be carrying a
weapon or other dangerous article on school property, therefore requiring a generalized search to avoid an immediate threat of physical harm
to students, faculty, or staff. . . . **We therefore conclude that the alleged
theft of twenty-six dollars, while certainly not insignificant in the context of a grade school, does not present such an extreme threat to school
discipline or safety that children may be subject to intrusive strip
searches without individualized suspicion.** Because the strip searches
in this case were conducted without individualized suspicion, they were
not justified at their inception and were thus unreasonable under the
Fourth Amendment.[74]

* * *

[End of Opinion]

As the above opinion indicates, *T.L.O.* or *Vernonia* did not provide a rigid
rule to determine when a search is to be governed by the stricter, individualized
suspicion criteria of *T.L.O.*, or by the more lenient criteria of *Vernonia;* neither did
the Supreme Court's latest opinion in the *Earls* case (Case 7.6). With reference to
T.L.O. one court observed that it made no "attempt to establish clearly the contours of a Fourth Amendment right as applied to the wide variety of possible
school settings . . . " [*Jenkins by Hall v. Talladega City Bd. of Educ.*, 115 F.3d 821, 828
(11th Cir. 1997)] *T.L.O.* did make clear that school authorities may search students for violations of school rules as well as for suspected violations of law. It
did not disturb prior case rulings that a school search may be based on sources
other than school staff, e.g., student or anonymous informers, police officers, or
suspicious student actions, such as furtive movements, presence at suspicious
locations, or flight when approached by school superiors.[75] A court recently held
school authorities had sufficient ground for individualized suspicion to subject
a student to a medical assessment and to removal of his shirt to search for drugs,
where the student arrived at school with dilated pupils and acted unruly.[76]

T.L.O. did not address the question whether searches jointly conducted by
school authorities and police officers are to be governed by the stricter constitutional standards that apply to police searches, and whether evidence uncov-
ered in an unlawful police search could still be used in school disciplinary
proceedings, though such evidence would be inadmissible in a court of law, a
question on which the lower courts disagreed.[77]

Fresh questions are also raised by new sophisticated detection technology. The Supreme Court recently held that police use of a thermal-imaging
device from a street to detect unusual heat waves of marijuana processing
emanating through the exterior house walls amounted to a "search". [*Kyllo v.
United States*, 121 S. Ct. 2038 (2001)] While that surveillance of a home (the ul-

timate citadel of constitutional privacy) by policemen may be distinguished from school uses of like devices to detect the contents of school bags, desks, or lockers, some attorney will surely argue that this decision also governs school searches.

Body Searches

The much weightier student privacy interest in their bodies, as opposed to their personal possessions, has led a number of states, such as California, Iowa, Washington, and Wisconsin, to prohibit strip searches of students.[78] Where not prohibited by state law, the constitutional limits on body searches may still vary with the degree of intrusiveness of individual searches. For example, patting down a student's upper body, canine sniffing, and removal of outer but not under clothing, and the age and sex of searched students arguably implicate different weights of privacy interests to be balanced against the school need to conduct a strip search.

Exploratory canine sniffing of a student's body has been held to be a search,[79] and is viewed differently than canine sniffing of student lockers or bags. Random canine sniffs of students in crime-laden or drug-troubled schools have been upheld as reasonable, but the body sniffing practice continues to be disfavored as unreasonable in the absence of serious school-wide problems or of an "individualized suspicion" that the sniffed student possesses improper material.[80]

As previously noted, ". . . [A] highly intrusive [e.g., strip] search in response to a minor infraction would similarly not comport with the sliding scale [of reasonableness] advocated by the Supreme Court in T.L.O." [*Cornfield v. School District No. 230*, 991 F.2d 1316 (7th Cir. 1993)] Earlier cases applied the *T.L.O.* guidelines both to approve and disapprove student strip searches in varied school settings.[81] In any event, the prevailing school practice of requiring that body searches be conducted only by authorized personnel of the same sex as the searched students should be maintained since cross-sex searches clearly heightened student privacy interests and embarassment, subject always to possible exception for a grave emergency or for medical examination by a doctor or medical specialist.

Urinalysis testing of students, admittedly a search, has not been deemed as intrusive as strip searches which expose the student's body. The latest Supreme Court *Earls* decision (Case 7.6) upheld school-mandated urinalysis testing of students who wished to participate in a wide variety of extracurricular activities, though it was not limited to any specially troubled school or to students under individualized suspicion of school or law violations. That decision is open to conflicting interpretations and should be read directly. School administrators and courts now must judge when *T.L.O.* or *Earls* governs a search. *Earls* may be read narrowly to apply only to school activities that involve potential drug or safety problems.

School Desks and Lockers

The Supreme Court has not directly considered the nature of a student privacy interest, if any, in lockers, desks, or other school-supplied enclosures. However, the Court's decision that upheld a state hospital search of the office, desk, and file cabinet of a physician employee, without suspicion of wrongdoing by the employee (Case 6.4 in Chapter 6), points strongly to like treatment of school searches of student desks and lockers. This is especially true where the school announces to students that school-owned property will be subject to random inspection as part of routine safety and maintenance checks. On parallel reasoning, a court upheld random, suspicionless searches by school chaperones of student hotel accommodations which the school arranged for student use on a school outing, and where the school had announced to the students that such searches would be made.[82]

Informational Privacy

A right to informational privacy regarding intensely personal information has been recognized by a majority of federal courts, but its outer limits remain uncertain.[83] As one court stated, "Our opinion does not mean . . . that there is no constitutional right to nondisclosure of private information. . . . Our opinion simply holds that not all rights of privacy or interests in nondisclosure of private information are of constitutional dimension." [*J.P. v. DeSanti*, 653 F.2d 1080, 1090–1 (6th Cir. 1981)] This privacy right rests upon a concept of liberty that is not enumerated in the Constitution. It is independent of privacy rights that are explicitly created by some statutes, such as the FERPA statute on student records, which is considered below. The right to decisional privacy has also been expanded by some state constitutions and statutes.[84]

Courts have enjoined schools from requiring students to answer questionnaires that inquire of intensely personal information about the students' families.[85] The validity of such inquiries will depend on the kinds of information sought and the school's need or reasons for that information. The right of outside parties to obtain personal student information from the school will also depend on the need for the release or *disclosure* of that information. In setting the constitutional bounds of informational privacy, courts must determine, therefore, when the need for particular student information outweighs the privacy rights of students and their families.

School–parent conflicts have flared on the use of school classroom questionnaires which inquire into the personal attitudes and conduct of students and their families. A recently challenged questionnaire was given to all 1,200 high school students and all 800 sixth and eighth graders of a school district, without notice to or consent by parents. The questionnaire contained 90 detailed questions that, among other things, asked whether the student was gay or bisexual; had engaged in oral or group sex (using and explicitly defining the terms "fellatio" and "cunnilingus"); had AIDS; or had used cocaine or any of a long list of drugs. It generated vociferous parental objections that the survey intruded into family privacy, and provided an almanac for bad behavior.[86] The school authorities issued an apology for not giving parents advance notice and an opportunity to exempt their children from the survey, but they insisted that the questionnaire was relevant to school concerns of student mental health. That experience points up the unresolved limits of soliciting personal student information that parents consider to be their and not the school's province. Even where the school provides advance notice and parental option to withdraw their children from such inquiries, the adequacy of such notices to furnish fairly meaningful information on questionnaire content and use may also trigger legal objections.

The federal Pupil Protection Rights Amendment, Sec. 439, 20 U.S.C.A. Sex. 1232 (h),[87] prohibits the use of privacy-invading questionnaires without parental consent in federally funded school surveys. Under that law, no student may be subjected to a questionnaire that relates to sexual conduct, family relationships, or illegal activities, unless that student's parent, after receipt of required advance written notice of the questionnaire, consents to the child's participation in it. That law does not avoid the issue whether a school's notice to parents is adequate and fair.

State statutes that affect informational privacy also require judicial interpretation, especially state "sunshine" laws that mandate public access to some school records. In the absence of clear legislative direction, records administrators must decide when and how state laws require public access to particular student information in light of other laws that are designed to protect student privacy. Some state law variations are noted in the endnote.[88]

The Family Educational Rights and Privacy Act of 1974 (FERPA) nationalizes the law governing access to student records for all schools that receive federal aid. FERPA does not displace state school records laws or policies that are consistent with it,[89] such as those dealing with the alteration, preservation or destruction of records, except where a request for record inspection or release is outstanding.

FERPA applies only to "educational records" of students who have been admitted to the school. It ensures guardian and student (age 18 or over) control of "personally identifying" information by barring (subject to specified exceptions) school disclosure of such information to third parties without the prior written authorizations for each requested release, by a guardian or by students over 18 years of age. The law further requires each authorization for release and waiver of privacy rights to be specific as to content, recipient, and intended use of the requested information. Upon attaining 18 years of age, a student may revoke any outstanding consents and waivers by his or her parent or legal guardian.

FERPA creates important exceptions for privileged access to student records by specified persons, such as school board members, teachers, doctors, and law enforcement professionals.[90] It does not prohibit school release of statistical *directory* information, such as test data, provided the information is in a form that precludes identification of students who are covered by that data. FERPA entitles parents and students over 18 years of age to inspect, reproduce, and challenge the accuracy of their educational records.

The great variety of student records and of access rights of different parties will require ongoing interpretations as to what qualifies as an "educational record" under FERPA. The Supreme Court decision in *Owasso Ind. School Dist. v. Falvo*, 122 S. Ct. 934 (2002), illustrates the importance of the statutory definition. The parent there challenged the classroom practice of peer grading (by students of each other's tests and assignment papers under the teacher's direction) as an unauthorized release of each child's educational record. The Court held that such peer grading did not create an "educational record" within the meaning of FERPA unless and until the teacher entered or modified the peer-developed grades in the teacher's grade book. The definition of an "educational record" was also pivotal to the claim of a student university newspaper to gain access to a university student's disciplinary record. The U.S. Department of Education argued that the disciplinary record was an "educational record", and obtained an injunction against its release. [*U.S. v. Miami University* (Case 7.7)] That case contains a good discussion of the kinds of records that are covered by FERPA and of the interaction of FERPA with state records statutes.

The respective rights of separated or divorced parents under FERPA regarding educational records and decisions of their child pose novel and complex questions. FERPA authorizes school authorities to presume that a natural parent is entitled to record access and participation unless school authorities receive evidence that the natural parent's right has been revoked by state law, court order, or other legally binding instrument.[91] Where one parent objects to record access by the other parent, a school district may avoid guessing about their respective rights by requiring the objecting parent to produce official documentation, usually a court order, that a parent lacks any rights of access to the student records under state law.[92] The laws of individual states may influence a parent's rights under FERPA.[93] While the courts in a majority of states hold that the decision of the custodial parent will prevail in a child control dispute, the courts of each state must determine how their state laws interact with FERPA, especially where parents have a shared custody arrangement. The *Taylor* case (Case 7.13) provides a good review of the issues raised by FERPA and state family law.

Disclosure of information which is provided in confidence by the student to a confidante, but which is not entered in an "educational record", raises a double-edged problem of confidentiality, i.e., whether that information may be lawfully withheld from school authorities and not entered in school records, or whether withholding that information exposes the confidante and possibly the school district to potential legal penalties under laws that mandate reporting or recording of that information.[94] This dilemma is not fully covered by the general law on privileges of confidentiality, as such laws normally confine the privilege to ministers, doctors, and lawyers.[95] A school confidante of students must, therefore, ascertain whether the law of the home state extends a privilege of confidentiality to a particular communication, however it may be viewed under professional standards of ethical conduct.

Nontherapeutic counseling does not generally create a privileged confidence, and some information, such as that relating to infectious social diseases and child abuse, is generally subject to obligatory reporting by school professionals under state law. Conversely, the law in some states exonerates doctors and treating agencies from obligations to disclose or report certain medical conditions of minors (e.g., pregnancy, venereal disease, and drug-related illnesses) to the students' parents without student consent. In the absence of such specific statutory protections, school employees—especially in allied health professions—may encounter a gap between their legal obligations and their ethical ideals. In serious cases, the safe course is to seek legal advice from school district counsel.

The risks of failing to release or report information are heightened where that information relates to child abuse, suicide, or student threats to injure someone. A life-threatening emergency can suspend even classical doctor–patient privileges of confidentiality, as illustrated by three decisions which held psychotherapists to be legally obligated to take some steps to protect persons whom they knew to be targets of their patient's threats.[96]

Decisional Privacy—Autonomy

The constitutional right to make certain personal decisions free from government interference (such as the right to marry, to beget children, the right to withhold or refuse medical treatment, and most recently, the right to pursue a homosexual lifestyle in private) has been labeled a right of *privacy*. That "privacy" label is misleading since many so-called privacy decisions are in fact publicly disclosed and even become publicly accessible official records. It would be more helpful to think of this right as one of personal *autonomy*.

School authorities may not burden or penalize a parent's or student's decisional autonomy, e.g., by excluding pregnant or married students from normal school benefits or activities unless such exclusions are justified by an overriding interest, such as protection of the student's health or safety.[97] School constraints on pregnant students are also limited by sex discrimination statutes, but those laws also permit measures to protect a pregnant student's health or safety. A school's disciplinary exclusion of a student athlete from school-sponsored athletics because he engaged in sexual conduct with another student while on a school trip was upheld as constitutionally justified and as not infringing the student's decisional privacy.[98]

Where a parent objects to a school policy or decision regarding medical care to be provided a student at school, courts must determine whose decision shall prevail. In such cases, the courts have drawn a distinction between a parent's right to refuse or withhold medical treatment and a parent's right to compel the school to provide medical treatment that is not required by law. In a case of first impression, a Massachussetts court ruled that the parents of a four-year-old child with severe disabilities had a constitutional right to refuse school medical treatment if the child went into cardiac arrest while at school. It accordingly enjoined the school from taking "active measures" to resuscitate the child.[99] That case is reproduced as Case 7.11 at the end of this chapter. However, the court noted that the parental right to prevent the school from providing medical care contrary to their wishes did not include any right to *compel* school authorities to take medical action that is contrary to the school's legal or ethical duties. This important distinction—between a privacy right to refuse or withhold medical treatment and a demand for treatment contrary to law—was also stressed by the Eighth Circuit Court of Appeals in upholding the school's right to refuse the parents' demands that a school nurse administer medicine to their child in dosages that exceeded the recommended daily dosage published in the *Physician's Desk Reference*, even though the child's personal physician had prescribed the increased dosage.[100] The sparsity of case law in the area of contested medical care should caution school staff and administrators to seek legal counsel in doubtful cases.

Where separated parents disagree on their child's medical treatment, a majority of state jurisdictions hold that the decision of the custodial parent will be controlling.[101] Here also, the safe course in unclear cases should be pursuit of legal counsel and, where necessary, of a petition to an appropriate court for its decision.

Liability for Constitutional Violations

As explained in Chapter 6, the Constitution itself does not authorize courts to grant monetary recoveries to a private party who sustains a constitutional injury. Without a statute that authorizes monetary recovery, a court could only grant "equitable relief", i.e., court injunction and affirmative action decrees. To authorize the "legal" relief of monetary recoveries for deprivation of federal rights, Congress enacted the special remedial statute, 42 U.S.C. § 1983 (hereafter § 1983). That law in effect creates a species of constitutional tort, whose peculiar features are discussed in Chapter 8. Section 1983 provides remedies beyond those that are directly provided by some the federal discrimination statutes.

TOPICAL CIVIL RIGHTS—EQUAL OPPORTUNITY LAWS

Review Note

The content and court treatment of the statutes considered here were explained in detail in Chapter 6 (see page 214 and following pages).

Racial and National Origin Discrimination

For the sake of brevity and convenience, the terms "race" or "racial" are here used to include ethnic or national origin traits as well as traits of color, and the words "ethnic" and "national origin" are used interchangeably to denote nationality and cultural traits.

Racial discrimination is prohibited in varying degree by different federal laws, i.e., the Equal Protection Clause of the Constitution, the Civil Rights Acts of 1866 (42 U.S.C. § 1981), and Title VI of the Civil Rights Act of 1964. As explained in Chapter 6, none of these laws are race specific. They protect members of all races.

With regard to the Equal Protection Clause, it is now settled that the Constitution treats government classifications by race as suspect and presumptively unconstitutional, and it prohibits individual acts of intentional discriminatory treatment on account of race. Only if school authorities can establish to a court's satisfaction that such classifications or treatments are required to meet a "compelling" state interest (such as a means of overcoming the effects of past de jure discrimination against a racial group) will such actions be valid.

It is now settled that student racial segregation between or within public schools is constitutionally prohibited. The major areas of continuing constitutional concern are interdistrict racial disparities in the makeup of the student populations in adjoining school districts; the limits of permissible affirmative action programs that are intended to overcome historical racial disadvantages; and challenges to school programs and tests that produce disproportionate adverse results for students of a particular race.

Interdistrict Segregation

Severe disparities between the racial makeup of students in adjoining school districts does not, alone, violate the Constitution. Only if such imbalances result from intentional official discrimination, rather than from private societal actions or population shifts, would such interdistrict imbalances amount to unconstitutional segregation.

> Before the boundaries of separate . . . school districts may be set aside . . . for remedial purposes . . . it must first be shown that there has been a constitutional violation within one district that produces a significant segregative effect in another district. Specifically it must be shown that racially discriminatory acts of the state or local school districts, or of a single school district have been a substantial cause of inter-district segregation. [*Milliken v. Bradley*, 418 U.S. 717 (1974)]

Where a court finds that interdistrict segregation was caused by official action, it may order cross-boundary desegregation as a remedy for the constitutional injury.[102] Individual states may outlaw interdistrict segregation independently of the federal Constitution, either by state legislation or under a state constitution that is interpreted to require cross-district assignments to correct racial imbalances. The Supreme Court of Connecticut recently ruled that the racial and economic isolation of black students in the urban public schools of Hartford deprived those students of a substantially equal educational opportunity, in violation of the *state* constitution's requirement of a sound public education.[103]

Affirmative Action Issues

The constitutional validity of affirmative action programs that are undertaken to remedy unconstitutional *de jure* (government-sourced) segregation is well settled.

> Just as the race of students and teachers must be considered in determining whether a constitutional violation has occurred, so also must race be considered in formulating a remedy. [*N.C. State Board of Educ. v. Swann*, 402 U.S. 43 (1971)]

Affirmative action remedies include reassignment of students to nonsegregated schools, busing to non-neighborhood schools, compensatory education, and provision of educational resources or facilities designed to overcome the adverse effects of past segregation. Courts may revise or suspend their affirmative action orders to meet changing circumstances, and may even prevent or permit otherwise lawful school closures that would defeat desegregation goals.[104]

> In fashioning . . . the decrees, the courts will be guided by equitable principles. Traditionally equity has been guided by a practical flexibility in shaping its remedies and by a facility for adjusting and reconciling public and private needs. [*Brown v. Board of Educ.* (Brown II), 349 U.S. 294 (1955)]

The limits of court jurisdiction to order affirmative actions by school districts and related government agencies were expounded by the Supreme Court in the *Jenkins* case (Case 7.8), which involved one of the longest, ongoing, and most comprehensive affirmative action court orders. In that instructive opinion, the Court set the following limitations on court remedial jurisdiction:

1. A court may not order remedies that go beyond the scope or bounds of a constitutional violation.
2. Court discretion in fashioning desegregation remedies must be "reasonable", and is subject to reversal if their exercise of that discretion is unreasonable or arbitrary.
3. The court jurisdiction to remedy unconstitutional injuries ends when desegregation is achieved to the fullest practical extent.

The *Jenkins* ruling was forecast by earlier Court pronouncements:

> The District Court should address itself to whether the board had complied *in good faith* with the desegregation decree . . . and whether the vestiges of past discrimination had been eliminated *to the extent practicable*. . . . (Emphasis added) [*Pasadena City Board of Educ. v. Spangler*, 427 U.S. 424 (1976)]

> The . . . court should *look . . . to every facet of school operations*—faculty, staff, transportation, extracurricular activities and facilities. (Emphasis added) [*Board of Educ. of Okla. Pub. Schools v. Dowell*, 498 S. Ct. 237, 249, 250 (1991)]

The *Jenkins* opinion authorized lower courts to terminate their desegregation oversight *in stages*. Some courts have, accordingly, ceded back to school districts control over some school functions while retaining jurisdiction and control over other school functions.[105]

Once desegregation jurisdiction terminates, it cannot be revived unless a new *de jure* violation occurs that justifies a new remedy for the new violation.[106] A court may not, therefore, order a previously desegregated school district to undo later racial imbalances that were caused by later *de facto* population shifts and not by government actions.[107]

It is important to note that some compensatory education programs that incidentally benefit a disproportionate number of needful children of a particular race are not constitutionally objectionable, even where they are not part of a desegregation remedy. Where such programs are based strictly on educational need and not on considerations of race, there is no equal protection issue of discrimination. For example, a charter school that served only "at-risk" students was held not to violate equal protection.[108]

Very recent Supreme Court decisions establish the governing principles regarding race-conscious affirmative action preferences where such preferences are not justified as a remedy for *de jure* discrimination. While those decisions involve affirmative action student admissions to state university and do not address public school programs, their essential doctrinal reasoning applies as well to public schools. In essence, the Court held that a race-conscious affirmative action program or preference will be constitutional if it furthers a *compelling* state interest in obtaining the educational benefits of a racially diverse student body *and* if the program is *narrowly tailored* to serve the state's compelling interest. Applying these principles, the Court upheld a state university law school admissions program that used race as but one of many flexible factors to determine student admissions, but it overturned the race-conscious freshman admissions program of the same university, as not being *narrowly tailored* to serve the state's compelling interest.[109] These decisions establish, contrary to some prior lower court decisions, that educational interests may satisfy the "compelling" state interest requirement of equal protection, but they leave open the question whether a particular instance of racial preference does in fact serve a compelling state interest and is in fact sufficiently narrowly drawn to serve that interest.[110]

In unique circumstances, courts may uphold affirmative action on grounds other than the value of educational diversity. When a state university undertook to operate an experimental public school as a research project to improve urban education and used racial criteria to decide whom to admit to its school, the admission policy was upheld as necessary to produce a proper laboratory environment for research to advance the important state interest of improving education in urban schools.[111]

Discriminatory Conduct

When motivated by racial hostility or segregative intent, individual official acts may be overturned on constitutional and statutory grounds, notwithstanding the absence of an official policy or racial classification. Administrative selection of school sites, attendance zones, and school transfer plans that are intended to foster racial separation are unconstitutional,[112] but unlike the case of disfavoring *laws,* administrative decisions are not automatically suspect or presumptively unconstitutional. Alleged invidious *treatment* must be *intentional,* but discriminatory intent may be inferred from the totality of the relevant facts. The courts have not agreed on how unusual or severely disproportionate racial disparity must be in order to support an inference of intent to discriminate. This is particularly true with reference to reliance upon statistical evidence.[113]

> Our cases have not embraced the proposition that a law or other official act . . . is unconstitutional *solely* because it has racially disproportionate impact. [*School Dist. of Omaha v. United States,* 433 U.S. 667, at 668 (1977)]

Title VI of the 1964 Civil Rights Act prohibits recipient schools from discriminating against students on account of race in conducting a *federally aided* school program. Race-based harassment by way of student ridicule, slurs, and epithets against fellow African-American students was held to deprive the harassed students of Title VI federal aid benefits, and to support relief against the school district for failing to stop those harassments.[114] The Title VI harassment cases raise several difficult fact issues, e.g., whether teasing, ridicule, or hostile remarks are sufficiently severe and oppressive to interfere with the victim's ability to receive the benefits of a federally aided program; whether the school district had fair notice and opportunity to make an appropriate response to such harassment; and whether the district's response was sufficient, i.e., reasonable, to disprove any intent on its part to allow such discrimination. Student victims of Title VI violations may (in addition to equitable relief of court orders) sue school districts under the § 1983 remedial statute to recover compensatory damages from the district, but they may not claim or recover punitive or penal damages.[115]

Racial Disparities in Testing and Placement

Test requirements for placement in particular schools or courses that produce very disparate failure or lower grades of a racial group, and its consequent assignment to racially dominant classes or inferior educational programs, have been challenged as discriminatory under the Equal Protection Clause, and as unfairly administered under the Due Process Clause. Such challenges typically allege that the racially disparate results are *prima facie* evidence of discriminatory treatment; that the students were not provided adequate instruction and preparation to enable them to perform satisfactorily in the tests; that the test content was culturally biased and targeted to the backgrounds of the white population; and that the test indicators of student learning are unsound and invalid. The complex fact issues that such cases raise are illustrated by the *Debra P.* case (Case 7.9), which involved challenges to a state-mandated competency test that high school students had to pass in order to receive a high school diploma. As *Debra P.* illustrates, a challenged test may be valid for some purposes, but invalid for others.

There is no single standard to validate tests for different test purposes, i.e., aptitude, educability, ability grouping, remedial deficiencies, and achievement for graduation. Test validity can only be assessed in terms of the test's specific purpose, content, and the background history of the school instruction. The mixed decisions on challenged ability grouping tests, noted in the endnote,[116] confirm the importance of the purposes and circumstances of test administration in determining the validity of each test.

Linguistically Disadvantaged Minorities

The use of English-only tests raises another angle of objection. Recent immigration of foreign speaking individuals has exacerbated the problem of educating children with little or no English language skills. The number of English-deficient children has doubled to 5 million in the last decade while the number of qualified teachers for bilingual or English as a second language has not kept pace.[117] The use of standard English for school instruction or testing has been challenged but not disapproved where the sole objection was the disparate adverse impacts of such instruction on linguistically disadvantaged students.[118] Language remediation statutes provide limited relief.[119] The federal Bilingual Education Act, the Equal Education Opportunities Act (EEOA), and Title VI provide federal fiscal incentives for programs to assist students with limited English language skills, regardless of their racial identity.[120] Under these statutes, school authorities are required to take action to overcome language learning barriers,[121] but the federal laws allow states to determine what is "appropriate action" to remedy language barriers. The Supreme Court originally held that a school district was obligated under Title VI to provide special English instruction for a large community of acutely disadvantaged Chinese-American students. [*Lau v. Nichols*, 414 U.S. 563, 568 (1974)] That decision did not answer several important questions, such as how large the number of disadvantaged students with identified linguistic problems must be, or how severe their linguistic deficiency must be, to require group rather than individualized special language programs; and how much deference should courts give to the educational judgments of states and aided school districts on the proper approach to language remediation—bilingual or English "immersion" instruction—in light of the availability or absence of qualified instructors. The lower court responses to the *Lau* decision and these questions varied with different school circumstances.[122] These problems were largely mooted by the later Supreme Court decision which held that (a) Title VI prohibits only *intentional* discrimination and not unintentional disparate impacts; (b) federal agencies may not, by issuing Title VI regulations, prohibit school practices that produce unintended disparate impacts; and (c) that in any event Title VI does not authorize a private party to bring suit to enforce agency regulations. In that case, the Court ruled that a Latino woman could not bring a Title VI suit to overturn a state English-only driver's license test, notwithstanding its adverse impact on English-deficient applicants:

> [W]e have since rejected *Lau's* interpretation of § 601 as reaching beyond intentional discrimination. . . . It is clear now that the disparate-impact regulations do not simply apply . . . —since they indeed forbid conduct that § 601 permits—and [it is] therefore clear that the private right of action to enforce § 601 does not include a private right of action to enforce these regulations. [*Alexander v. Sandoval*, 121 S. Ct. 1511, 1519 (2001)]

Recent circuit court cases also held that linguistically disadvantaged minorities have no constitutional or statutory right to compel a state to provide foreign language services or tests in order to avoid the disparate impacts of English-only instruction. So long as the state's exclusive use of English is reasonably related to legitimate educational or business needs, there is no constitutional discrimination or violation. In one case, the court upheld a California law that eliminated bilingual education and substituted an English-only (immersion) instruction for children with special language needs, and in the other, the court upheld the state's English-only teacher certification tests as serving a legitimate state interest.[123] While these decisions do not foreclose other challenges to English-only tests, they render such challenges more difficult, especially in light of the failure of the federal Department of Education to challenge such English-only programs under Title VI. Perhaps private litigation to compel instruction in languages other than English has been blunted by ongoing efforts by school districts and linguistic minority groups to develop voluntary programs to assist students whose primary language is other than English.

Remedies for Racial Discrimination

The limits of monetary recoveries allowed by different statutes for racial discrimination are noted in Chapter 6 and in the previous discussions of Title VI. Courts have not allowed recovery of punitive (as against compensatory) damages against school districts unless Congress unequivocally and unambiguously authorized that unusual remedy.

Gender Discrimination

The principal sources on student protection against gender discrimination are found in the constitutional rights of equal protection and of bodily security, and in statutory rights under Title IX of the Education Amendments of 1972.

> In order to satisfy the Equal Protection Clause, The State [school district] must show at least that the [gender] classification served "important governmental objectives and that the discriminatory means employed" are "substantially related to the achievement of those objectives" . . . And it must not rely on overbroad generalizations about the different talents, capacities or preferences of males and females. [*United States v. Virginia*, 116 S. Ct. 2264, at 2275 (1996)]

System-wide sex segregation of public schools is generally prohibited by both the Constitution and Title IX,[124] but the operation of special schools for boys and girls with limited objectives in order to achieve narrow, special, and important educational needs and goals could be upheld in exceptional circumstances. Courts have not, however, embraced the argument that single-sex schools serve sufficiently strong educational interests to justify them in all circumstances.

Title IX also prohibits discriminatory gender classifications and acts of *intentional* sexual discrimination, be they committed against a male or female student, or by a school employee or a student peer.[125] Title IX discrimination includes sexual harassment that stops short of physical sexual abuse. However, it applies only to federally aided programs and therefore only to school district *recipients* of federal aid. Title IX liability does not extend to individual actors.[126] To be actionable under Title IX, the discriminatory treatment must be grounded in a *policy* of the school district itself, whether it arises directly from an official school directive, or indirectly from the misconduct of a person whose conduct is attributable to a school policy or custom. The school district link to individual conduct is easily found where that conduct is authorized by a school policy maker. In the absence of such authorization, the required link of individual misconduct to school policy is more technical and is derived from the peculiar, negative standard of "deliberate indifference" to known sexual discrimination by a school overseer who is officially empowered to respond to and rectify individual acts of sex discrimination. This standard requires that:

> an official of the district who at a minimum has authority to address the alleged discrimination and to institute corrective measures . . . has *actual knowledge* of discrimination in the recipient's program and *fails adequately to respond*. We think, moreover, that the response must *amount to deliberate indifference* to discrimination. . . . The premise in other words is an official decision by the recipient not to

remedy the violation. (Emphasis added) [*Gebser v. Lago Vista Ind. School Dist.*, 118 S. Ct. 1989, 1999 (1998)]

The Supreme Court borrowed this two-pronged "deliberate indifference" test for Title IX from the liability standard it developed under the § 1983 remedial statute. As explained in Chapter 8, this standard requires more than negligence in failing to discover or anticipate individual acts of sexual discrimination, or in failing to screen out or uncover an employee with a sexual predatory history, or in failure to develop more effective safeguards against sexual abuse or harassment of students, other than those adopted by the district.[127]

The identification of the person who has authority to direct school policies or practices is thus critical, because not every supervisor qualifies as a "policy maker."

Finally, the "deliberate indifference" must have a causal link to actual student loss of an educational benefit, raising the same difficult issue that appeared under Title VI (for racial discrimination), namely, that the harassment must be sufficiently *severe* to effectively deprive the victim of the benefit of the federally aided program.[128] To cite a stark example, one court found that a teacher calling a student a prostitute, in class, over a period of several weeks, was found not sufficiently severe to result in a student loss of Title IX benefit in the circumstances of that case.[129]

The foregoing unique requirements of Title IX liability are well summarized in the Supreme Court opinion in the *Davis* case (Case 7.10). That and other recent cases leave no doubt that Title IX rights and defenses have no relation whatever to state tort law principles of negligence and respondeat superior.

Sexual Abuse and Harassment

The constitutional right to bodily security may allow student victims of sexual abuse to recover monetary damages under § 1983.[130] Title IX, however, directly creates a personal right to recover monetary damages. In *Franklin v. Gwinnett County Public Schools*, 112 S. Ct. 1028 (1992), the Supreme Court ruled that Title IX impliedly authorized damage recovery for its violation, independently of any § 1983 claim, for a high school graduate who suffered sexual harassment and molestation by her teacher over a period of two school years, during which the school principal and school authorities received complaints of the offending teacher's conduct but took no corrective action.

Disparate Treatment

Disparate treatment discrimination may be found where schools provide disparate resources for male and female students. Where a challenged program does not violate a constitutional right, Title IX takes on special importance, since its guarantee is not limited to constitutional rights. For example, female athletes who were subjected to harsher penalties than their male athlete counterparts for violations of the same school conduct code could sue for Title IX relief, even if their interest in participating in athletics would not command constitutional protection.[131]

Sports Programs

Disparate treatment claims are particularly contentious in school sports programs. Title IX regulations do not require absolute parity of sports programs for each sex, but only reasonably proportionate opportunities and reasonable allocation of school funds and facilities for male and female students.[132] The perennial question in such cases is purely factual, i.e., whether the school arrangements are reasonably comparable and accommodative of each sex group, either in light of their respective interests and physical ability and in light of administrative and budgetary constraints.[133] As the endnote examples illustrate, the answers to these questions vary with school circumstances.[134]

Title IX regulations allow the use of single-gender teams and competitions where the gender restriction reasonably accommodates the physical and psychological characteristics and competetive skills of each sex, notably in *contact sports*.[135] The regulatory guidelines leave ample room for argument as to which school sports are contact sports, and which noncontact sports are reasonably confined to one sex. For example, parties may disagree on whether boys should be excluded from girls' volleyball or hockey teams,[136] and some courts have insisted that individual student capability rather than gender characteristics should determine access to any school activity, including wrestling teams.[137] Indeed, the New Jersey State Commissioner of Education, after ruling that a high school must permit a girl to try out for the varsity football team, changed course one year later in ruling that a high school need not permit a boy to play on the girls' field hockey team. [*New York Times*, May 22, 1986, at B7]. In identifying the uncertain borderlands of gender differences for different sports, administrators must obviously consider the ages and development of individual students in different grade levels. Even so, school authorities face a Catch-22 situation. If they create single-gender teams, someone may view that as a Title IX violation, but if they permit mixed male–female competition, they run a risk that an injured student will seek damages under state tort law for exposing that student to unreasonable risks of harm. In the few jurisdictions which require that "competent" girls (of sufficient strength and dexterity) be allowed to try out with boys for a contact sport team (football),[138] school authorities must trust to luck as well as the judgment of their coaches in mixing male and female participants in contact sports.

Decisions to eliminate or reduce male sports programs in order to provide equitable sports opportunities for female students have withstood both constitutional and Title IX challenges. The constitutional claim was rejected by one court on the ground that students had no constitutional right to demand any level of sports programming while another court ruled that the government's interest in arranging fair allocation of institutional resources between male and female athletes is sufficiently important to justify the gender-based decision. Both cases found no Title IX violation because the challenged reorganizations were required, rather than forbidden by, the Title IX mandate of reasonably comparable opportunities for both sexes.[139] The *Boulahanis* case in the next chapter (Case 8.2) presents a good survey of cases on sports resource allocation.

Academic Benefits

Scholarship examinations that produce gender disproportionate exclusions or failing grades may also be challenged under Title IX. Exclusion of pregnant students from a school program is subject to like challenges unless the exclusion is reasonably necessary to protect student health or safety.

Exclusions of unmarried pregnant students from a national honor society have raised strenuous discrimination challenges under the Constitution, Title IX, and state laws.[140] The courts are not in full agreement on those challenges. Equal protection rights are clearly violated where school selection committees approve admission of male students known to have engaged in premarital sex while excluding unmarried pregnant females for premarital sexual conduct. The claim that exclusion for pregnancy violates rights of reproductive autonomy, privacy, and association have been notably unsuccessful. But the failure of school authorities to inquire into each male candidate's premarital sexual history, absent some indication or notice to the admission of such a history, is more problematic. In any event, it remains doubtful under the scattered case law that a student's desire for national honor society membership implicates a sufficiently significant constitutional interest to command heightened scrutiny. There remains the possibility that state courts may find in state constitutions and statutes sufficient grounds to protect a student's interest in obtaining honor society membership, but the control of such access by the national honor society may limit state courts remedies.

The limited case law assumes, without extensive discussion, that honor society membership is a benefit covered by Title IX. On one hand, it may be argued that National Honor Society membership (along with its requirements of good character and leadership qualities) is an extramural rather than a school-determined benefit. On the other hand, the nominating discretion accorded to local school administrators by the national society suggests school control of that benefit. If so, courts would still have to decide whether exclusion of a particular (unmarried pregnant) student involves gender discrimination since only females become pregnant, or whether the application of character standards is not reasonable since male sexual activity is largely undiscovered and unpunished.[141]

Remedies for Gender Discrimination

The allowed monetary recoveries for Title IX discrimination are parallel to those allowed under Title VI for racial discrimination.

Homosexual Discrimination

The law on discrimination against students perceived as being homosexuals or lesbians is still largely undeveloped, and, as noted in Chapter 6 with respect to teachers, the emerging law does not offer consistent parallels with the law on biological gender discrimination.

Constitutional Protections

Students may challenge discriminatory school policies or practices directed against homosexual orientation as a violation of equal protection rights. For example, the Ninth Circuit Court of Appeals recently held that a school district could be liable for failing to enforce its own antiharassment policy to protect gay and lesbian students. [*High Tech Gays v. Defense Ind. Sec. Clearance Office*, 895 F.2d 563 (9th Cir. 1990)] The Eleventh Circuit Court held that students had a constitutional right to be free from discrimination based on their perceived sexual orientation. [*Flores v. Morgan Hill Un. School Dist.*, 323 F.3d 950 (11th Cir. 2003)]

The question yet to be decided is whether and in what circumstances school authorities may restrain student conduct that affirmatively espouses homosexual conduct. The recent Supreme Court decision [*Lawrence v. Texas*, 123 S. Ct. 2472 (2003), reported in Chapter 6] that adult homosexual persons have a constitutional right to engage in consensual homosexual conduct in the privacy of their homes does not address the validity of school regulation of public homosexual conduct or expression in the school setting. Since the *Lawrence* majority opinion did not rely on an Equal Protection ground, school authorities may still argue that their regulation of homosexual advocacy is rationally related to legitimate school interests and, therefore, is constitutional.

Statutory Protections

The federal antidiscrimination laws do not single out homosexual orientation as a separate subject of discrimination. As explained in Chapter 6 and in the *Bibby* case (Case 6.10), Title VII only protects homosexuals who suffer discrimination "because of sex", and not because of hostility to their sexual orientation. Whether Title IX will be similarly construed to cover only discrimination "because of sex", and not because of sexual orientation, remains to be seen.

Greater protection against homosexual orientation discrimination is found in the laws of a number of states which expressly forbid harassment of homosexuals as well as other forms of discrimination. Those state laws must also be carefully checked.

Children with Disabilities

The core provisions of the Americans with Disabilities Act of 1990 (hereafter ADA), the Rehabilitation Act of 1973 (hereafter § 504), and the Individuals with Disabilities Education Act of 1990 (hereafter IDEA) are reported in Chapter 6 and are listed in Appendix 2 at the end of this book. The ADA and § 504 essentially impose negative prohibitions against disability-based discrimination, while the IDEA creates an affirmative right (to a state-provided free public education)[142] for a wide class of children with handicaps, from ages 3 to 21.

The IDEA Law

The IDEA definition of a covered "handicap" encompasses a very broad spectrum of physical, mental, emotional, and other learning disabilities (e.g., attention deficit disorders).[143] AIDS conditions are covered,[144] but the point at which a child's HIV or AIDS condition becomes sufficiently disabling to qualify for IDEA benefits is a matter for case-by-case determination. The law mandates that states which accept federal financial assistance for the education of children with handicaps undertake detailed steps to provide those children with a free "appropriate" public education, including education-related services that enable covered students to benefit from the education program. In addition, it mandates regular classroom placement of children with handicaps where they can "reasonably" benefit from the "mainstreaming" placement. The many issues of law, fact, and discretionary judgments that arise in administering the IDEA make it one of the most extensively litigated education statutes.[145] Full treatment of the massive IDEA law must be left to more specialized texts, but the following overview covers the more commonly experienced problems in the administration of the IDEA.

The Supreme Court *Rowley* decision (Case 7.12) set forth the essential duties of state and local education agencies under the IDEA:

- Identify children with educational handicaps;
- Evaluate their individual educational needs;
- Prepare and provide them with an "individualized educational program" (IEP) that is tailored to their particular disability needs;
- Provide them with needed "education-related services";
- Afford parents and children input and due process hearing procedures on the adequacy of the foregoing services.

The required IEPs must be developed jointly by a school committee, which includes the child's teacher and the child's parents or guardian. It must be reviewed at least annually and be revised if necessary to maintain the essentials of a free appropriate public education.

Procedural Requirements

The IDEA specifies due process procedures of notice, hearing, and appeal, which parents as well as school districts are obliged to follow. *Unexcused* failure by parents to follow these procedures will normally foreclose them from seeking further review by a higher administrative tribunal.[146] However, failure to exhaust IDEA procedures may be excused where the school administration frustrates the parent's ability to obtain meaningful administrative review, or where the child's safety or welfare requires immediate action, such as removal of a child from a hazardous school situation.[147] The exhaustion issue received different treatment in suits for IDEA violations that are brought under the § 1983 statute. In § 1983 lawsuits, the courts are in conflict on the question whether the plaintiff must first exhaust IDEA procedures before resorting to a § 1983 suit. That problem is further elaborated in Chapter 8.

FAPE Requirements

The free appropriate public education (FAPE) required by IDEA is left initially to administrative tribunals and ultimately to the courts. The law does not require school districts to achieve fixed levels of student achievement, or to "maximize the potential of each child", or even to provide optimal education to suit a child's particular talents. Rather, it requires "meaningful" access to an education that confers "some educational benefit" consistent with the child's abilities and potential. The *Rowley* decision rejected a fixed FAPE standard since what is "appropriate" for a child with one disability is not "appropriate" for a child with a different disability.[148]

The school district must take measures to preserve achieved FAPE benefits from loss by educational regression and backsliding, including where needed, the provision of special or extended class sessions that go beyond the normal school day, week, or year.[149] An extracurricular IEP component may also be required if the child can benefit educationally from it.[150]

IDEA does not exempt students with disabilities from general requirements for a regular high school diploma. Nor are graduation competency tests deemed discriminatory under the ADA or § 504 statutes unless the student can show that he or she was prevented from passing the test by some discriminatory element in the test makeup or administration.[151]

The need for "related services" as part of the required FAPE remains a chronic point of dispute. Such services may include transportation; developmental, corrective, and other supportive services; health-related, psychological, and counseling services; physical and occupational therapy; recreational programs; or other forms of accommodation.[152] The right to related services depends on specific child needs. In *Rowley* the Court held that Amy Rowley, because she was bright, did not need a sign language interpreter to benefit from her FAPE. On the other hand, the Court later ruled that a school district would have to supply a classroom sign language interpreter to assist a deaf student who needed that service in order to receive a proper FAPE.[153]

Medical services, unlike education-related services, are not required by the IDEA, thus raising the question when is a demanded service "medical" or "educational"? The Supreme Court clarified that issue in *Cedar Rapids Community School Dist. v. Garrett,* 119 S. Ct. 992 (1999), which held that the school district must provide one-on-one assistance throughout the school day to a ventilator-dependent student who required continuous monitoring and treatment, including urinary catheterization, suctioning of the student's tracheotomy, lifting and lowering the student every hour to and from a reclining and upright position, and monitoring the student's ventilator for possible malfunction. The Court found those services to be education related because they were essential to enable the student to receive the educational benefits of a FAPE and, most significantly, because the services could be provided by a competently trained person other than a physician. In sum, related services could include those health-related services that are essential for a child's FAPE, no matter how continuous or costly the services, *provided* that they could be competently performed by someone other than a licensed physician. *Cedar Rapids* extended the Court's prior decision [*Irving Ind. School Dist. v. Tatro,* 468 U.S. 883 (1984)] that required school-site intermittent catheterization (CIC) of a student with a disability.

Placement Rules—Mainstreaming

IDEA "stay put" provisions normally prohibit a change of a child's placement until IDEA administrative proceedings to decide the proper placement are exhausted. Unexcused failure to pursue those procedures is generally ground to deny a court hearing on the placement, but courts have excused parties from the "stay put" mandate where resort to further administrative procedures could seriously delay and jeopardize the education of the affected child.[154]

The required IDEA placement in an "appropriate" educational facility may include placement in a private facility when an appropriate public facility is not available.

A parent may not demand an alternative placement if the school district offers an appropriate placement even though the offered placement is not as good as the placement preferred by the parent. Where school authorities are unable or unwilling to place a child in an appropriate facility, parents who directly arrange an appropriate placement may recover reimbursement of that expense if the placement is "reasonable." This is so, even if the requested placement school or facility is not on the state's approved list.[155] Conversely, if the court finds that a parent made an inappropriate (e.g., unsuitable or inordinately expensive) placement, the parent cannot recover reimbursement or other IDEA relief. In placement reimbursement disputes, courts must consider both the appropriateness and the cost of the placement. The Supreme Court held that the trial court, as a matter of equitable discretion, may deny total reimbursement of an alternative placement if the full cost of that placement is not reasonable. [*Florence County School Dist. v. Carter*, 114 S. Ct. 361, 366 (1993)]

The IDEA requirement that a FAPE be provided in "the least restrictive" educational environment, i.e., a regular school classroom, originally drew conflicting responses from the federal circuit courts on the proper test for mainstreaming a child.[156] The 1997 IDEA amendments changed the original mainstreaming goal from a "preference" ("to the maximum appropriate extent") to a higher "presumption" that mainstreaming should be pursued. Even so, those Amendments did not clarify the unsettled law on the need or kinds of mainstreaming (full or part time) that would be "appropriate" for a particular disabling condition, or on the limits, if any, of the costs that must be incurred to mainstream a child. While the courts have not agreed on a formula to assess the reasonable cost limits of mainstreaming, they have rejected the view that mainstream placements must be made "at all cost."[157] In any event, mainstreaming is not required for a child whose conditions prevent the child from benefiting from a less restricted placement or whose condition unavoidably renders the child disruptive to a regular classroom.[158] Where appropriate, a court may require only part-time mainstreaming to meet particular child's needs.[159]

> For [some] children, mainstreaming does not provide an education designed to meet their unique needs. . . . . . . The Act does not, however, provide any substantive standards for striking the proper balance between its requirement for mainstreaming and its mandate for a free appropriate public education. . . . . . . [W]e decline to adopt the approach that other circuits have taken. . . . . . . [W]e discern a two part test for determining compliance with the mainstreaming requirement. First, we ask whether education in the regular classroom . . . can be achieved satisfactorily. . . . If it cannot . . . we ask, second, whether the school has mainstreamed the child to the maximum extent appropriate. [See *Daniel R.R. v. State Board of Educ.*, 874 F.2d 1036, 1044–5, 1048 (5th Cir. 1989)]

In the absence of further clarification, the appropriateness of requested mainstreaming must be guided by current government regulations and the law of the governing federal circuit.

Access to IDEA Benefits by Private School Students

Where parents elect to enroll a child in a private school, the question whether a school district must provide IDEA special services or benefits at the private school site has not been finally settled. The 1997 IDEA Amendments state that such services "may" (rather than "must") be provided to students with handicaps at private school sites, and that amounts spent for such services equal "a proportionate amount of federal funds made available for such services." The courts have taken different readings of these Amendments. In most federal circuits the courts have held that the amendments permit but do not mandate that special services be provided to children with handicaps at private school sites, and that when such services are so provided, the states and their school districts need only expend for nonpublic school children their proportionate share of federal funds received by the state for that purpose. Under this reading, a district need not pay the full costs of off-site services if the cost exceeds the average cost of like services for all children with disabilities in the state. The varied positions of different federal circuits are indicated in the endnote case references to those federal circuits.[160]

The law on required IDEA services is even less developed for home-schooled children. The Court of Appeals for the Ninth Circuit recently held that a school district could deny IDEA services to home-educated children because the state could confine IDEA services to children in a "school" as defined by the state's standard for a "school". The court accordingly ruled that the denial of IDEA services did not violate the Act or the child's constitutional rights to due process and to equal protection of the law. See *Hooks v. Clark County School District*, 228 F.3d 1036 (9th Cir. 2000), which appears at the end of Chapter 9 (Case 9.6). The *Hooks* decision seems at odds with the requirement that FAPE services must be provided to public school children with disabilities who have been suspended or expelled from a public school. Until the state law interaction with IDEA requirements is clarified by the Supreme Court, interested parties must look to the emerging law in their respective state and federal circuit.

Discipline of Children with Disabilities

Prior to the 1997 IDEA amendments, the permissibility of school punishments for misbehaving students with disabilities was left largely to court determination. The 1997 amendments provided that a child with disabilities could be subjected to discipline but only for conduct that was either within the child's reasonable control or that was not a manifestation of the child's disability, *provided* that the selected form of discipline did not defeat the FAPE purposes of the IDEA.[161] The amendments also removed some previous procedural obstacles,[162] by allowing temporary removal (change of placement) of students to interim alternative settings for up to 45 days for weapons or drug infractions, or upon a showing of likely injury by a child with a disability, whether or not the child's behavior was manifestation of the child's handicap. The amendments resolved some court conflicts by requiring that FAPE services be provided to suspended or expelled public school children.

Rights of Those with Disabilities Under State Law

State laws provide some additional procedural and substantive rights and special benefits for limited classes of handicaps (e.g., for blind or deaf children).[163] The failure to follow procedures that are mandated by state law provides additional ground to overturn school decisions.

Rights of Separated Parents

State laws generally govern the rights of separated and divorced parents relative to the education of their children, but they cannot override conflicting federal law. The question then arises whether there is in fact a conflict between state law governing rights of separated parents and the rights conferred on parents by the IDEA. The *Taylor* case (Case 7.13) took the position that there is no conflict between the IDEA and state law on parental rights, but the opinion also notes that other courts have expressed a different view, and that the question has not been fully addressed or settled in other federal circuits.

   Child custody rights, whether full, temporary, shared, or nonexistent, remain an important factor in determining a parent's right to be involved in IDEA processes and educational decisions.[164] A majority of state courts hold that the decision of the custodial parent will prevail where separated parents cannot agree on a specific educational question.[165] Still, the effect of those decisions on parental claims may vary with the particular IDEA claim of the noncustodial parent, as seen in the split decision of the *Taylor* case (Case 7.13). Where a parent claims sole and exclusive rights in IDEA proceedings, school authorities should seek legal counsel on the state of the law in their home state.

Alien Children

Alien children who lawfully reside within a school district have a constitutional right to receive public education benefits on equal terms with citizen students, even when they were illegally brought to the United States by their parents. In *Plyler v. Doe*,[166] the Supreme Court ruled that a school district could not constitutionally exclude alien children because of their parents' illegal entry, even though the government could constitutionally deny other government benefits to the parents. The Supreme Court later held that a school district could exclude an alien child who was sent to the states by his Mexican parents to reside with a relative in the United States for the explicit purpose of securing a free public education. Since the child was not a bona fide resident of the district, the school district did not discriminate against him in denying admission to its schools.[167]

Poverty Groups

Like age and disability, poverty is not a constitutionally suspect trait, so that constitutional protection for poverty classes is limited to acts of *irrational* or *intentional* government discrimination.[168] Nor is poverty discrimination covered by any major federal antidiscrimination law. More promising relief is afforded by states whose legislatures or courts require additional school funding to overcome educational barriers, largely in poor school districts. State-to-state variations on legislative and court-ordered reforms in school finance are noted in the endnote.[169] Relief from other poverty conditions is left largely to state assistance laws.

Concurrent Violations of Different Laws

When the same conduct concurrently violates different statutes and where the written law provides no express directive on the questions whether a claimant is limited exclusively to the rights and relief specified in one of the relevant statutes, courts must decide the combined effect of those laws.

The following quotation illustrates the principles which courts use to bar redundant claims under different statutes, i.e., where one is deemed to provide an exclusive remedy:

> Although the IDEA plaintiff can assert claims under other statutes, including the ADA and § 504 of the Rehabilitation Act, . . . we agree with the Sixth, Eighth and Tenth Circuits that when an administration decision "is upheld on judicial review under IDEA, principles of issue and claim preclusion may properly be applied to short-circuit redundant claims under other laws. . . ." [*Pace v. Bogalusa City School Board*, 325 F.3d 609, 621 (5th Cir. 2003)]

The preclusion issue is further discussed in Chapter 8.

Special Immunity Defenses

The law on immunity from suit for federal law violations is unique because federal law immunities from suit differ from state law immunities, and different federal immunities are created by different statutes and by the Constitution. Finally, federal law immunities from suit for school districts are not the same for individuals. These federal immunities are sorted out and explained in Chapter 8.

RIGHTS UNDER STATE LAW

As previously noted, the constitutions and statutes of individual states often provide broader procedural and substantive rights, and in some cases more efficient remedies, than federal law. The prior sections noted some instances where state constitutions or statutes place greater restraints on school districts, e.g., prohibitions against corporal punishment and strip searches. Other school searches that are lawful under federal law may still be challenged under stricter state law. For example, the Pennsylvania Supreme Court recently ruled that random urinalysis testing of students in extracurricular activities in the absence of proof of a serious school drug problem or individualized suspicion of tested students violated the Pennsylvania state constitution, notwithstanding the prior decision by the United States Supreme Court in *Board of Education v. Earls* (Case 7.6) on almost identical facts, that the search was lawful under the federal constitution. [*Theodore v. Delaware Valley School District*, 836 A.2d 76 PA. (2003)]

Because the state constitutions and laws vary from state to state, school administrators must observe the laws of their home state as well as federal law.

Chapter 7 Discussion Questions

Where the answer to a question may be qualified by special circumstances, explain the potential qualification.

1. May school authorities or teachers lawfully search for and confiscate items taken to school by a student which they deem to be dangerous, without suspicion that the searched student possesses such items? What if the student disagrees that the item sought and confiscated poses no danger to the school?

2. On what grounds may school districts lawfully interfere with or penalize the following?
   a. Student speech
   b. Student dress
   c. Student hairstyle
   d. Student makeup or jewelry

3. How, in your opinion, should school authorities strike a constitutional balance between student liberty and school interests in requiring students to wear school-approved uniforms?

4. How does the FERPA law limit access to and disclosure of student records? Who determines what is a student record under FERPA?

5. When federal and state laws on student records come into conflict, which law governs? Why?

6. May a school district constitutionally demand that a student perform community service to graduate from high school? See Chapter 2, page 45.

7. Why are student rights not coextensive with those of teachers with respect to the following?
   a. Freedom of expression
   b. Freedom from unreasonable searches

8. On what basis do courts decide whether school policies of random, suspicionless searches of students are reasonable and constitutional?

9. Is canine sniffing for drugs considered a "search"?

10. Under the IDEA when, if ever, may public school authorities refuse to:
    a. Mainstream a child with a handicap?
    b. Decline to provide a "related service"?
    c. Reimburse a parent for placement of a child with a disability in a private school or facility?
    d. Provide a due process hearing on parent objections to a child's educational program?

Case 7.1

HASENFUS v. LAJEUNESSE
175 F.3d 68 (1st Cir. 1999)

> [*Focus Note.* The parents of a 14-year-old female student sued the town, the board of education, the district superintendent, the school principal, and her gym teacher, Carlo Kempton. The student attempted suicide, while alone in an unsupervised locker room to which she had been sent by her gym teacher as punishment for misconduct during a class on the school athletic field. She survived the suicide attempt, but suffered permanent physical impairments. The authors of this text have marked key phrases in the opinion in bold type.]

Boudin, Circuit Judge.

* * *

The complaint describes two other incidents as background to the attempted suicide. One was that Jamie had been raped when she was 13 and later underwent the further trauma of testifying against the rapist. School officials were aware of the rape. Jamie had reported it to the school nurse, Jackie Kempton (wife of the gym teacher, Carlo Kempton), and was later counseled by the school nurse and school guidance counselor. According to the complaint, Carlo Kempton knew or should have known of the rape and should not have sent Jamie "alone and unsupervised away from the area he was monitoring when he knew or should reasonably have known that she was despondent or distressed."

The other background event was that seven other students in the Winthrop Middle School had also attempted suicide in the three months prior to May 1996. Several of those attempts had occurred at school or school events, and Jamie apparently knew or was associated with at least two of those students. . . .

. . . The counts with which we are centrally concerned were based upon section 1983; they charged that specific acts and omissions by defendants acting **under color of state law** deprived Jamie of her Fourteenth Amendment rights, including, inter alia, rights to life and physical safety. . . .

The gist of the wrongful acts . . . were the failure to take a range of preventive actions . . . to cope with the suicide epidemic and, specifically as to

Jamie, three narrower failures or mistakes discussed at the end of this opinion. Carlo Kempton's alleged wrongful acts were reprimanding Jamie in front of her classmates and sending her alone to the locker room. . . .

. . . [W]e take the factual allegations of the complaint as true. . . .

The central question for us . . . **is whether the conduct attributed to the defendants violates the federal Constitution so far as it protects against state action depriving one of life or liberty without due process of law.** . . .

* * *

. . . [T]he principal conduct charged against the defendants—apart from Kempton—was their failure to take measures to cope with the rash of attempted suicides at the school. Under common law, inaction rarely gives rise to liability unless some special duty of care exists. . . . In *DeShaney v. Winnebago County,* . . . the Supreme Court took the same view of substantive due process obligations, holding that **ordinarily a state's failure to intervene to prevent harm to an individual by a private actor is not a constitutional violation.**

The main exceptions to this proposition are incarcerated prisoners or involuntarily committed mental patients. . . . In such cases, failures to act . . . may comprise a due process or other constitutional violation because the state-imposed circumstance of confinement prevents such individuals from helping themselves. Liability then arises under section 1983 if the plaintiff shows that the inaction was malicious or reflected the official's "deliberate indifference" to the welfare of the prisoner or inmate. . . .

The plaintiffs urge that Jamie is similar to the prisoners and patients because school attendance is compulsory and because in some measure the school authorities act in loco parentis. The circuits that have confronted this issue have uniformly rejected this argument. . . . The Hasenfuses' position is especially difficult to accept outright since the Supreme Court has come pretty close to rejecting it in a recent dictum . . . :

> [W]e do not, of course, suggest that public schools as a general matter have such a degree of control over children as to give rise to a constitutional "duty to protect." Vernonia Sch. Dist. v. Acton, 515 U.S. 646, 655 . . . (1995). See also Wyke, 129 F.3d at 569.

Nevertheless, we are loath to conclude . . . that inaction by a school toward a pupil could *never* give rise to a due process violation. From a commonsense vantage, Jamie is not just like a prisoner in custody. . . . But neither is she just like the young child in DeShaney who was at home in his father's custody. . . . For limited purposes and for a portion of the day, students are entrusted by their parents to control and supervision of teachers in situations where—at least as to very young children—they are manifestly unable to look after themselves.

Thus, when Vernonia says that the schools do not "as a general matter" have a constitutional "duty to protect," perhaps in narrow circumstances there might be a "specific" duty. If Jamie had suffered a heart attack in the classroom, and the teacher knew of her peril, could the teacher merely leave her there to die without summoning help? . . .

Yet even if we assume arguendo that in narrow circumstances the Supreme Court might find a due process obligation of the school or school employees to render aid to a student in peril—and Vernonia invites some caution—it would require pungent facts. **The basic due process constraint** . . . where substance . . . is involved, **is against behavior so extreme as to "shock the conscience."** *County of Sacramento v. Lewis*, 523 U.S. 833 . . . (1998). . . . . . . [T]his means conduct that is truly outrageous, uncivilized, and intolerable. *Lewis*, 118 S. Ct. at 1717.

. . . **The few circuit cases** that have found or posited possible liability under a shock-the-conscience rubric . . . have usually **involved egregious facts.** . . . The omissions charged against the school authorities here are not even close to violating this outrageousness standard.

* * *

Attempted suicide by school-age children is no slight matter; but it has no single cause and no infallible solution. . . . Possibly there was school negligence here . . . *but negligence is not a due process violation. Daniels v. Williams*, 474 U.S. 327, 332–33 (1986).

We turn now from the charge of inaction . . . to the claims against Carlo Kempton that do charge him with affirmative acts, specifically, the public reprimand of Jamie and her banishment to the unsupervised locker room. . . . Where a state official acts so as to create or even markedly increase a risk, due process constraints may exist. . . . But once again, the behavior must be conscience-shocking or outrageous. See *Lewis*, 118 S. Ct. at 1717–19.

* * *

. . . [I]t is not alleged that Jamie threatened to kill herself then or at any other time known to Kempton. . . . . . . To say that Kempton acted maliciously to cause harm to Jamie, or otherwise acted in a way that should shock the conscience, is not a remotely plausible interpretation of the facts alleged. . . .

Only one circuit case cited to us has found a triable issue on anything remotely like these facts and its own facts were more aggravated. In *Armijo*, 159 F.3d 1253, school officials sent home a 16-year-old special education student for violent behavior at school. The student had earlier threatened to kill himself and, contrary to school policy, the officials did not notify his parents that he had been sent home, where the student had access to firearms—a fact school officials were alleged to have known. Alone at home, the student shot himself. His parents then sued, alleging inter alia a substantive due process claim, and the case went to the Tenth Circuit. . . .

The Tenth Circuit held that *DeShaney* barred any affirmative duty to protect based on a "custodial relationship" between student and school. *Armijo*, 159 F.3d at 1261–62. But the court also said liability might be based on the school's affirmative act—sending the student home alone—if it increased the danger to the child and also met the "shocks-the-conscience" test. . . . The court said that the latter test might be met if at trial the school officials were also shown to have known that the child in question had previously threatened suicide, was now distraught, was a special education pupil not fully able to care for himself, and had access at home to firearms. . . .

Whether or not one agrees with the Tenth Circuit that such behavior would be conscience-shocking . . . the assumed facts are at least very troubling. . . . . . . If sound, the Tenth Circuit decision is at the outer limit, and does not come close to embracing Kempton's actions.

* * *

In closing, we emphasize again that the due process clause is not a surrogate for local tort law or state statutory and administrative remedies. . . .

Case 7.1 Review Questions

1. The hindsight determination of what is conscience-shocking conduct rests with judges and not juries. Could courts disagree in their hindsight review?

2. Had Jamie been sent to a lab or shop that contained dangerous material or equipment would that conduct be conscience shocking?

Case 7.2

BETHEL SCHOOL DISTRICT NO. 403 v. FRASER
478 U.S. 675 (1986)

[**Focus Note.** *Fraser, a high school student, tested the limits of his freedom of speech by giving a lewd nominating speech for student elective office to a school-organized assembly of some 600 students, notwithstanding warnings from two teachers that the speech was inappropriate and should not be given. The speech was laced with elaborate, graphic, and explicit sexual innuendos. After the speech, the assistant principal orally notified Fraser that his speech was considered a violation of the school rule against disruptive, obscene, and vulgar conduct, and that he would be suspended for two days and disqualified as a candidate for commencement speaker. Fraser and his father sue for injunctive relief and monetary damages alleging violations of Fraser's constitutional right to freedom of speech and to due process. The following Supreme Court opinion rejected those challenges.*]

CHIEF JUSTICE BURGER *delivered the opinion of the Court.*

. . . [A] school counselor observed the reaction of students to the speech. Some students hooted and yelled; some by gestures graphically simulated the sexual activities pointedly alluded to in respondent's speech. Other students appeared to be bewildered and embarrassed. . . . A Bethel High School disciplinary rule prohibiting the use of obscene language in the school provides:

> Conduct which materially and substantially interferes with the educational process is prohibited, including the use of obscene, profane language or gestures.

This Court acknowledged in *Tinker v. Des Moines Independent Community School Dist., supra,* that students do not "shed their constitutional rights to freedom of speech or expression at the schoolhouse gate."

* * *

The marked distinction between the political message . . . in *Tinker* and the sexual content of respondent's speech in this case seems to have been given little weight by the Court of Appeals. . . .

It is against this background that we turn to consider the level of First Amendment protection accorded to Fraser's utterances and actions. . . .

The role and purpose of the American public school system were well described by two historians, who state: "[P]ublic education must prepare pupils for citizenship in the Republic. . . . It must inculcate the habits and manners of civility as values in themselves conducive to happiness and as indispensable to the practice of self-government in the community and the nation." . . .

* * *

. . . It does not follow, however, that simply because the use of an offensive form of expression may not be prohibited to adults . . . the same latitude must be permitted to children in a public school. In *New Jersey v. T.L.O.,* 469 U.S. 325, 340–342 . . . we reaffirmed that the constitutional rights of students in public school are not automatically coextensive with the rights of adults in other settings. . . .

Surely it is a highly appropriate function of public school education to prohibit the use of vulgar and offensive terms in public discourse. . . .

The determination of what manner of speech in the classroom or in school assembly is inappropriate properly rests with the school board.

. . . The schools . . . may determine that the essential lessons of civil, mature conduct cannot be conveyed in a school that tolerates lewd, indecent, or offensive speech and conduct such as that indulged in by this confused boy.

The pervasive sexual innuendo in Fraser's speech was plainly offensive to both teachers and students—indeed to any mature person. By glorifying male sexuality, and in its verbal content, the speech was acutely insulting to teenage girl students.

. . . The speech could well be seriously damaging to its less mature audience, many of whom were only 14 years old and on the threshold of awareness of human sexuality. . . .

* * *

. . . Unlike the sanctions imposed . . . in *Tinker*, the penalties imposed . . . were unrelated to any political viewpoint. The First Amendment does not prevent the school officials from determining that to permit a vulgar and lewd speech . . . would undermine the school's basic educational mission. . . . . . .

Respondent contends that his suspension violated due process because he had no way of knowing that the delivery of the speech in question would subject him to disciplinary sanctions. This argument is wholly without merit. . . . Given the school's need to be able to impose disciplinary sanctions for a wide range of unanticipated conduct disruptive of the educational process, the school disciplinary rules need not be as detailed as a criminal code which imposes criminal sanctions. . . .

Two days' suspension from school does not rise to the level of a penal sanction calling for the full panoply of procedural due process protections. . . . The school disciplinary rule proscribing "obscene" language and the pre-speech admonitions of teachers gave adequate warning to Fraser that his lewd speech could subject him to sanctions.

Case 7.3

HAZELWOOD SCHOOL DISTRICT v. KUHLMEIER
484 U.S. 260 (1988)

[**Focus Note**. In this case, the Supreme Court squarely considered students' rights of freedom of the press in student school publications. The unusual circumstances, namely, deletion of two pages of a high school newspaper by school administrators without consulting the student editors, due to time deadlines to have the paper published before end of school term, raises a question whether the decision may be limited to similar emergency situations.]

JUSTICE WHITE *delivered the opinion of the Court.*

This case concerns the extent to which educators may exercise editorial control over the contents of a high school newspaper produced as part of the school's journalism curriculum.

I

Petitioners are the Hazelwood School District . . . ; various school officials; Robert Eugene Reynolds, the principal of Hazelwood East High School; and Howard Emerson, a teacher in the school district. Respondents are three former Hazelwood East students who were staff members of Spectrum, the school newspaper. . . .

Spectrum was written and edited by the Journalism II class at Hazelwood East. . . .

* * *

The Journalism II course was taught by Robert Stergos. . . . Stergos left Hazelwood East on April 29, 1983, when the May 13 edition of Spectrum was nearing completion, and petitioner Emerson took his place as newspaper adviser. . . .

The practice at Hazelwood East . . . was for the journalism teacher to submit page proofs of each Spectrum issue to Principal Reynolds for his review prior to publication. On May 10, Emerson delivered the proofs of the May 13 edition to Reynolds, who objected to two of the articles. . . . One of the stories described three Hazelwood East students' experiences with pregnancy; the other discussed the impact of divorce on students at the school.

Reynolds was concerned that, although the pregnancy story used false names . . . the pregnant students still might be identifiable from the text. He also believed that the article's references to sexual activity and birth control were inappropriate for some of the younger students at the school. In addition, Reynolds was concerned that a student identified by name in the divorce story had complained that her father "wasn't spending enough time with my mom, my sister and I" prior to the divorce, "was always out of town on business or out late playing cards with the guys," and "always argued about everything" with her mother. . . .

Reynolds believed that the student's parents should have been given an opportunity to respond to these remarks. . . . He was unaware that Emerson had deleted the student's name from the final version of the article.

Reynolds believed that there was no time to make the necessary changes . . . before the scheduled press run and that the newspaper would not appear before the end of the school year if printing were delayed. . . . He concluded that his only options . . . were to publish a four-page newspaper . . . eliminating the two pages on which the offending stories appeared, or to publish no newspaper at all. Accordingly, he directed Emerson to withhold from publication the two pages containing the stories on pregnancy and divorce. He informed his superiors of the decision, and they concurred.

* * *

Students . . . do not "shed their constitutional rights to freedom of speech or expression at the schoolhouse gate." *Tinker.* . . .

We have nonetheless recognized that the First Amendment rights of students . . . "are not automatically coextensive with the rights of adults in other settings" . . . A school need not tolerate student speech that is inconsistent with its "basic educational mission," . . . even though the government could not censor similar speech outside the school. . . .

A

We deal first with the question whether Spectrum may appropriately be characterized as a forum for public expression. . . .
. . . [S]chool facilities may be deemed to be public forums only if school authorities have "by policy or by practice" opened those facilities "for indiscriminate use by the general public," or by some segment of the public, such as student organizations. . . . If the facilities have instead been reserved for other intended purposes, then no public forum has been created, and school officials may impose reasonable restrictions on the speech of students, teachers, and other members of the school community. . . . . . .

* * *

School officials did not deviate in practice from their policy that production of Spectrum was to be part of the educational curriculum and a regular classroom activit[y]. The District Court found that Robert Stergos, the journalism teacher . . . ". . . in fact exercised a great deal of control over *Spectrum.*" . . . For example, Stergos selected the editors . . . scheduled publication dates, decided the number of pages for each issue, assigned story ideas . . . advised students on the development of their stories, reviewed the use of quotations, edited stories, selected and edited the letters to the editor, and dealt with the printing company. Many of these decisions were made without consultation with the Journalism II students.

* * *

The evidence relied upon by the Court of Appeals in finding Spectrum to be a public forum . . . is equivocal at best. . . . In sum, the evidence . . . fails to demonstrate the clear intent to create a public forum. . . .
. . . Instead, they "reserve[d] the forum for its intended purpos[e]," . . . as a supervised learning experience. . . . Accordingly, school officials were entitled to regulate the contents of Spectrum in any reasonable manner. . . . It is this standard, rather than our decision in *Tinker*, that governs this case.
The question whether the First Amendment requires a school to tolerate particular student speech . . . is different from the question whether the First Amendment requires a school to affirmatively promote particular student speech. . . . The latter question concerns educators' authority over school-sponsored publications, theatrical productions, and other expressive activities that students, parents, and members of the public might reasonably perceive to bear the imprimatur of the school. These activities may

fairly be characterized as part of the school curriculum, whether or not they occur in a traditional classroom setting. . . .

Educators are entitled to exercise greater control over this second form of student expression. . . . Hence, a school may in its capacity as publisher of a school newspaper or producer of a school play "disassociate itself," . . . not only from speech that would "substantially interfere with [its] work . . . or impinge upon the rights of other students," . . . but also from speech that is, for example, ungrammatical, poorly written, inadequately researched, biased or prejudiced, vulgar or profane, or unsuitable for immature audiences. A school . . . may refuse to disseminate student speech that does not meet those standards. In addition, a school must be able to take into account the emotional maturity of the intended audience in determining whether to disseminate student speech on potentially sensitive topics. . . .

* * *

. . . [W]e hold that educators do not offend the First Amendment by exercising editorial control over the style and content of student speech in school-sponsored expressive activities so long as their actions are reasonably related to legitimate pedagogical concerns.

. . . It is only when the decision to censor . . . has no valid educational purpose that the First Amendment is so "directly and sharply implicate[d]," as to require judicial intervention to protect students' constitutional rights.

* * *

The judgment of the Court of Appeals for the Eighth Circuit is therefore Reversed.

Case 7.3 Review Question

1. What, if any, guidelines does the above opinion offer for school control of student publications?

Case 7.4

GONZALES v. McEUEN
435 F. Supp. 460 (1977)

> [***Focus Note.*** *This opinion excerpt addresses the questions whether or when school boards and school superiors charged with establishing school discipline can act as impartial tribunals in student disciplinary hearings as a matter of due process.]*

Takasugi, District Judge

* * *

Impartiality of the Board

Plaintiffs strongest and most serious challenge is to the impartiality of the Board. They contend that they were denied their right to an impartial hearing. . . . The basis for this claim is, first, overfamiliarity of the Board with the case; second, the multiple role played by defendants' counsel; and, third, the involvement of the Superintendent of the District, Mr. McEuen, with the Board of Trustees during the hearings.

No one doubts that a student charged with misconduct has a right to an impartial tribunal. . . . There is doubt, however, as to what this means. . . . Bias is presumed to exist, for example, in cases in which the adjudicator has a pecuniary interest in the outcome . . . or in which he has been the target of personal attack or criticism from the person before him. . . . The decision maker may also have such prior involvement with the case so as to acquire a disqualifying bias. . . . The question before the Court is not whether the Board was actually biased, but whether, under the circumstances, there existed probability that the decision maker would be tempted to decide the issues with partiality. . . .

Overfamiliarity

. . . Depositions . . . show that the members of the Board met with school officials prior to the hearings. Plaintiffs contend that this prior involvement . . . deprived plaintiffs of the opportunity for a fair hearing. The court rejects this contention. Exposure to evidence presented in a nonadversary investigative procedure is insufficient in itself to impugn the fairness of the Board members. . . . Nor is a limited combination of investigatory and adjudicatory functions in an administrative body necessarily unfair, absent a showing of other circumstances such as malice or personal interest in the outcome. . . . . . . Some familiarity with the facts . . . does not disqualify a decision maker. *Hortonville Dist. v. Hortonville Ed. Assoc.*, 426 U.S. 482, 491 . . . (1976).

Multiple Roles of Counsel

. . . It is undisputed that attorneys . . . who prosecuted the charges . . . in the expulsion proceedings, also represent the Board members in this action. . . . Counsel for defendants admit that they advised the Board . . . with respect to its obligations regarding these expulsions, but they deny that they advised the Board during the proceedings themselves.

A reading of the transcripts reveals how difficult it was to separate the two roles. . . .

It is the opinion of this court that the confidential relationship between the attorneys for the District and the members of the Board, reinforced by the advisory role played by the attorneys for the Board, created an unacceptable risk of bias. . . .

Involvement of Superintendent McEuen

. . . Superintendent McEuen was present with the Board for approximately forty-five minutes during its deliberations on the issue of expelling these plaintiffs. The plaintiffs contend that their due process rights were violated by this involvement of Mr. McEuen with the Board. This court agrees.

* * *

The court concludes that the process utilized by the Board was fundamentally unfair. . . .

Discussion of Individual Students

. . . Plaintiffs Barrington and Munden were expelled . . . on November 10, 1976. Neither Barrington nor Munden was present; neither was represented by either parent or counsel.

On October 29, 1976, letters had been sent to the parents advising them that the principal was recommending expulsion of the students. . . . The letters contained no notice . . . of the student's right to be present at the hearing, to be represented by counsel, and to present evidence. This was a clear violation of . . . the California Education Code. . . .

. . . The defendants maintain that the notices . . . complied, at least, with *federal* due process. . . . They contend that since a hearing was held and there was notice to the parents of the charges against the students, the requisites of procedural due process were satisfied. The court disagrees. . . .

Goss clearly anticipates that where the student is faced with the severe penalty of expulsion he shall have the right to be represented by and through counsel, to present evidence on his own behalf, and to confront and cross-examine adverse witnesses.

Other courts have held that a hearing incorporating these safeguards must be held before or shortly after a child is suspended for a prolonged or indefinite period. *Black Coalition v. Portland School District No. 1*, 484 F.2d 1040, 1045 (9th Cir. 1973); *Esteban v. Central Missouri State College*, 277 F. Supp. 649 (W.D. Mo. 1967). This court agrees.

. . . Defendants next argue that even if the notice was defective, the court must still determine whether the plaintiffs were given a fair and impartial hearing. Defendants misapprehend the meaning of notice. It is not fair if the student does not know, and is not told, that he has certain rights which he may exercise at the hearing.

* * *

It follows that their expulsions were improper.

* * *

Case 7.4 Review Question

1. The above decision notes that the Supreme Court held that school boards are presumed to be impartial in the *Hortonville* case. On what facts did the above opinion rely to overcome that presumption and find that the school board was not impartial?

_____

Case 7.5

JONES v. STATE
64 S.W.2d 728 (Ark. 2002)

[**Focus Note.** *A male high school student who was adjudicated and sentenced as a delinquent for terroristic threatening of a female classmate appealed his conviction claiming that the rap song he wrote and gave her was protected speech. The following opinion found that the fighting words exception did not apply to the case facts, but sustained the conviction as a "true threat" which does not command First Amendment protection. While the case does not delimit the broader constitutional power of school authorities to prohibit and punish violent screeds that threaten school safety, order, or its educational mission, the case is instructive on the category of threatening speech, and the varied standards that courts use to identify and distinguish hyperbolic speech, which is constitutionally protected, and threatening speech, which is not so protected.*]

ROBERT L. BROWN, JUSTICE.

. . . Jones raises two points on appeal: (1) . . . the State had not proven the requisite mental intent for terroristic threatening; and (2) the rap song involved is protected speech under both the Arkansas and United States Constitutions. . . .

* * *

On February 15, 2001, . . . Jones wrote several notes to Arnold in class and gave them to her. She refused to write back and let him know that she was not going to write notes because she wanted to pay attention in class. Her refusal to respond made Jones mad. . . . After she refused to write back to him, he wrote a rap song and gave it to her:

I hope you remember this day, cuz you'll forever be the cause of my violence and rage,

You steadily rejected me, now I'm angry and full of fucking misery,

You try to be judgmental telling me to act right. Before you take the
speck from my eye, take the fucking board from your eye,

I didn't do nothing to deserve this, and now I'm stressed, and when I'm
stressed, I'm at my best,

I'm a motherfuckin murderer, I slit my mom's throat and killed my sister. You gonna keep being a bitch, and I'm gonna cliche [click],

My hatred and aggression will go towards you, you better run bitch,
cuz I can't control what I do. I'll murder you before you can think
twice, cut you up and use you for decoration to look nice,

I've had it up to here bitch, there's gonna be a 187 on your whole family trik [trick],

Then yo'll be just like me, with no home, no friends, no money,

You'll be deprived of life itself, you wo"t be able to live with yourself,

Then you'll be six feet under, beside your sister, father, and mother,

You'll be in hell, and I'll be in Jail, but I won't give a fuck cuz we all
know I've been there before,

Goodbye forever my good friend. I'll see you on judgement day when
I'm punished for my sin.

. . . While Arnold read the song, Jones was laughing. He asked Arnold
whether she liked the rap lyrics, and she told him that she thought they were
"sick and gross." She further testified that she was frightened and appalled
because: "[H]e knew where I lived, he knew my family, he wrote about my
sister[ ] and my dad, that's written to my family. It was handed to me, and
it was given to me. It was written for me." Jones asked her to give the note
with the rap lyrics back to him, and she refused.

There are two matters of factual dispute. . . . First, although Jones
claimed he told her "Don't take this serious," Arnold denied that he made
the statement. The second factual dispute is whether or not Arnold first
asked to see his writing. In Jones's written statement, he asserted that
Arnold asked to see the note. Arnold denied this in her trial testimony.

Instead of handing the note back to Jones, Arnold asked the teacher if
she could use the restroom. She testified that this interchange with her
teacher occurred within three to five minutes after she read the note. . . . After getting permission to leave the classroom, she went directly to principal
John Wesson's office. Once in the principal's office, she showed him the
note. He called the Fayetteville Police Department and then called Jones to
the office.

Officer David Williams arrived, and Arnold told him that she felt scared because she thought Jones was capable of carrying out the conduct described in the note. According to Officer Williams's trial testimony, Arnold was crying and seemed scared of Jones, positioning herself so that the police officer physically separated the two of them. Jones, on the other hand, told the police officer that he did not believe that "this was a big deal, and he didn't understand why everyone was upset." He volunteered an apology to Arnold. He also gave a statement admitting that he wrote the note. According to Principal Wesson's testimony, he told the principal and Officer Williams that he was "modeling his writing after [rap artist] Eminem." He insisted that he was simply writing "to get his feelings out." In his written statement he said: "I got mad and wrote a letter to express myself. It was a rap and pretty gruesome." Principal Wesson testified that Jones seemed to have no understanding that his writing could frighten or harm another person.

On February 16, 2001, the prosecuting attorney filed a Petition for Adjudication of Delinquency against Jones. The petition alleged that Jones had committed an act of terroristic threatening in violation of Ark. Code Ann. § 5–13–301 (Repl. 1997), a Class D felony. On February 27, 2001, the petition was heard in juvenile court. . . . [T]he defense moved for a directed verdict on the specific ground that the State had failed to prove the requisite intent to terrorize or cause extreme fright. The juvenile judge denied the motion. Defense counsel then presented the testimony of Fayetteville High School student Sarah Stone, who testified about Jones's history of writing rap songs, and next the testimony of Jones himself. . . .

* * *

After closing arguments, the juvenile judge ruled from the bench. She found that the rap lyrics constituted a threat. She noted that Jones was mad at Arnold when he wrote the rap song and that the lyrics were intended to cause Arnold fear. The judge further observed that Arnold knew of Jones's criminal history, and that Arnold had been intensely frightened and upset by the episode. She adjudicated Jones delinquent on the charge of terroristic threatening and sentenced him to 24 months of supervised probation, as well as seven days in a juvenile detention facility. She specifically ordered that Jones have no contact with Arnold or her family. . . . [T]he judge committed Jones to the custody of the Department of Youth Services.

* * *

II. Free Speech Argument

We turn next to Jones's contention that his rap song was protected speech under the Arkansas and U.S. Constitutions. As an initial point, we fail to see where Jones's counsel raised the Arkansas Constitution as an argument before the juvenile judge. . . .

* * *

Turning to his free-speech claim . . . Jones urges that neither the "fighting words" nor the "true threat" exception apply to his case and that his rap song was protected speech. We disagree. . . . The United States Supreme Court . . . noted that its jurisprudence, over the years, has recognized several exceptions to blanket protection for expressive speech. . . .

Two of those categories of unprotected speech are at issue in this case. The first is the well-established "fighting words" doctrine. The second is the "true threat" exception. See *Watts v. United States*, 394 U.S. 705, . . . (2001). . . . "Fighting words" have been defined . . . as "those which by their very utterance inflict injury or tend to incite an immediate breach of the peace." *Chaplinsky v. New Hampshire*. . . . We agree with the State that the fighting-words exception is not applicable to the facts of this case.

The "true threat" doctrine was first announced in the United States Supreme Court case of *Watts v. United States, supra.* In *Watts*, the Court held that the defendant could not be prosecuted for a statement made at a political rally which, when taken literally, threatened President Lyndon Johnson's life. . . . The Court did not set out a test in *Watts* for distinguishing between a true threat and hyperbolic political comment.

Since *Watts*, several federal circuit courts have disagreed on the applicable standards governing the assessment of whether a threat is true and, thus, not protected by the First Amendment. . . .

For example, the First Circuit has held that the appropriate standard is "whether [the defendant] should have reasonably foreseen that the statement he uttered would be taken as a threat by those to whom it is made." *U.S. v. Fulmer*, 108 F.3d 1486, 1491 (1st Cir. 1997). However, the Second Circuit has announced its test that a true threat exists when the language "on its face and in the circumstances in which it is made is so unequivocal, unconditional, immediate, and specific as to the person threatened, as to convey a gravity of purpose and imminent prospect of execution." *United States v. Francis*, 164 F.3d 120, 122–23 (2d Cir. 1999). The Second Circuit has further said: "The test is an objective one, namely, whether 'an ordinary, reasonable recipient who is familiar with the context of the letter would interpret it as a threat of injury.'" *United States v. Malik*, 16 F.3d 45 (2d Cir. 1994) (internal citation omitted).

The Sixth Circuit, on the other hand, has said: "Although it may offend our sensibilities, a—communication objectively indicating a serious expression of an intention to inflict bodily harm cannot constitute a threat unless the communication also is conveyed for the purpose of furthering some goal through the use of intimidation." *United States v. Alkhabaz*, 104 F.3d 1492, 1495 (6th Cir. 1997). The Ninth Circuit has set a slightly different objective test: "[W]hether a reasonable person would foresee that the statement would be interpreted by those to whom the maker communicates the statement as a serious expression of intent to harm or assault." *Bauer v. Sampson*, 261 F.3d 775, 782 (9th Cir. 2001). . . .

The Eighth Circuit has taken a somewhat different approach. . . . Rather . . . the Eighth Circuit has outlined five factors which govern its review of whether a threat is true or hyperbolic. . . .

* * *

. . . In *Doe v. Pulaski County Special Sch. Dist.*, 263 F.3d 833 (8th Cir. 2001) . . . , a panel of the Eighth Circuit ruled the defendant school district's expulsion of a student for writing a threatening rap song to his ex-girlfriend unconstitutional. . . .

* * *

Turning to the case at bar, we observe that this court has never addressed the "true threat" doctrine. . . . In considering the various tests adopted by the circuit courts and various state supreme courts, we conclude that an objective test focusing on how a reasonable person would have taken the statement and using the *Dinwiddie* factors has the most merit. . . .

. . . [W]e conclude that Jones's language constituted a true threat to Arnold. First, there was the reaction of Arnold to the threat. Her reaction to Jones's letter was immediate and unequivocal. . . . She was intensely frightened and upset . . . , and she told the attending police officer that she believed Jones was capable of carrying out the threat because he had a criminal record and knew where her family lived.

Secondly, the threat made was not conditional. . . . Thirdly, Jones communicated the threat directly to Arnold by handing the note to her. . . . Viewing these factors together, we conclude that a reasonable person in Arnold's position would have taken the rap song as a true threat.

* * *

We affirm the juvenile judge's decision. . . . We hold that because Jones's rap lyrics constituted a true threat to Arnold, the rap song is not protected by the First Amendment.

Affirmed.

Case 7.6

BOARD OF EDUCATION v. EARLS
122 S. Ct. 2559 (2002)

JUSTICE THOMAS *delivered the opinion of the Court.*

The Student Activities Drug Testing Policy implemented by the Board of Education of Independent School District No. 92 . . . (School District) requires all students who participate in competitive extracurricular activities to submit to drug testing. Because this Policy reasonably serves the School District's important interest in detecting and preventing drug use among its students, we hold that it is constitutional.

The city of Tecumseh . . . is a rural community located approximately 40 miles southeast of Oklahoma City. . . . In the fall of 1998, the School District adopted the Student Activities Drug Testing Policy (Policy), which requires all middle and high school students to consent to drug testing in order to participate in any extracurricular activity. In practice, the Policy has been applied only to competitive extracurricular activities sanctioned by the Oklahoma Secondary Schools Activities Association, such as the Academic Team, Future Farmers of America, Future Homemakers of America, band, choir, pom-pom, cheerleading, and athletics. Under the Policy, students are required to take a drug test before participating in an extracurricular activity, must submit to random drug testing while participating in that activity, and must agree to be tested at any time upon reasonable suspicion. The urinalysis tests are designed to detect only the use of illegal drugs, . . . not medical conditions or the presence of authorized prescription medications.

. . . Respondent Lindsay Earls was a member of the show choir, the marching band, the Academic Team, and the National Honor Society. Respondent Daniel James sought to participate in the Academic Team. Together with their parents, Earls and James brought a 42 U.S.C. § 1983 action against the School District, challenging the Policy both on its face and as applied to their participation in extracurricular activities. They alleged that the Policy violates the Fourth Amendment. . . .

Applying the principles articulated in *Vernonia School Dist. 47J v. Acton,* 515 U.S. 646 (1995), in which we upheld the suspicionless drug testing of school athletes, the United States District Court . . . rejected respondents' claim . . . and granted summary judgment to the School District. . . . . . .

The United States Court of Appeals for the Tenth Circuit reversed, holding that the Policy violated the Fourth Amendment. . . . . . .

. . . Searches by public school officials, such as the collection of urine samples, implicate Fourth Amendment interests. . . . We must therefore review the School District's Policy for "reasonableness," . . .

In the criminal context, reasonableness usually requires a showing of probable cause. . . . . . . The Court has also held that a warrant and finding of probable cause are unnecessary in the public school context. . . . *Vernonia, supra,* at 653. . . .

. . . [R]espondents do not contend that the School District requires probable cause before testing students for drug use. Respondents instead argue that drug testing must be based at least on some level of individualized suspicion. . . . But we have long held that "the Fourth Amendment imposes no irreducible requirement of [individualized] suspicion." . . . "[I]n certain limited circumstances, the Government's need to discover such latent or hidden conditions, or to prevent their development, is sufficiently compelling to justify the intrusion on privacy entailed by conducting such searches without any measure of individualized suspicion." . . .

* * *

In *Vernonia*, this Court held that the suspicionless drug testing of athletes was constitutional. The Court, however, did not simply authorize all school drug testing, but rather conducted a fact-specific balancing of the intrusion on the children's Fourth Amendment rights against the promotion of legitimate governmental interests. . . . Applying the principles of *Vernonia* to the somewhat different facts of this case, we conclude that Tecumseh's Policy is also constitutional.

We first consider the nature of the privacy interest allegedly compromised by the drug testing. . . .

A student's privacy interest is limited in a public school environment where the State is responsible for maintaining discipline, health, and safety. Schoolchildren are routinely required to submit to physical examinations and vaccinations against disease. . . . Securing order in the school environment sometimes requires that students be subjected to greater controls than those appropriate for adults. . . .

Respondents argue that because children participating in nonathletic extracurricular activities are not subject to regular physicals and communal undress, they have a stronger expectation of privacy than the athletes tested in *Vernonia*. . . . This distinction, however, was not essential to our decision in *Vernonia*, which depended primarily upon the school's custodial responsibility and authority.

In any event, students who participate in competitive extracurricular activities voluntarily subject themselves to many of the same intrusions on their privacy as do athletes. Some of these clubs and activities require occasional off-campus travel and communal undress. All of them have their own rules and requirements for participating students that do not apply to the student body as a whole. . . . We therefore conclude that the students affected by this Policy have a limited expectation of privacy.

Next, we consider the character of the intrusion imposed by the Policy. . . . Urination is "an excretory function traditionally shielded by great privacy." . . . But the "degree of intrusion" on one's privacy caused by collecting a urine sample "depends upon the manner in which production of the urine sample is monitored." . . .

Under the Policy, a faculty monitor waits outside the closed restroom stall for the student to produce a sample and must "listen for the normal sounds of urination in order to guard against tampered specimens and to insure an accurate chain of custody." . . . The monitor then pours the sample into two bottles that are sealed and placed into a mailing pouch along with a consent form signed by the student. This procedure is virtually identical to that reviewed in *Vernonia*. . . . Given that we considered the method of collection in *Vernonia* a "negligible" intrusion, . . . the method here is even less problematic.

In addition, the Policy clearly requires that the test results be kept in confidential files . . . and released to school personnel only on a "need to know" basis. Respondents nonetheless contend that the intrusion on students' privacy is significant because the Policy fails to protect effectively against the disclosure of confidential information and, specifically, that the school "has been careless in protecting that information: for example, the Choir teacher looked at students' prescription drug lists and left them where other students could see them." . . . But the choir teacher is someone with a "need to know," because during off-campus trips she needs to know what medications are taken by her students. Even before the Policy was enacted the choir teacher had access to this information. . . . This one example of alleged carelessness hardly increases the character of the intrusion.

Moreover, the test results are not turned over to any law enforcement authority. Nor do the test results here lead to the imposition of discipline or have any academic consequences. . . . Rather, the only consequence of a failed drug test is to limit the student's privilege of participating in extracurricular activities.

After the first positive test, the school contacts the student's parent or guardian for a meeting. The student may continue to participate in the activity if within five days of the meeting the student shows proof of receiving drug counseling and submits to a second drug test in two weeks. For the second positive test, the student is suspended from participation in all extracurricular activities for 14 days, must complete four hours of substance abuse counseling, and must submit to monthly drug tests. Only after a third positive test will the student be suspended from participating in any extracurricular activity for the remainder of the school year. . . .

Given the minimally intrusive nature of the sample collection and the limited uses to which the test results are put, we conclude that the invasion of students' privacy is not significant.

Finally, this Court must consider the nature and immediacy of the government's concerns and the efficacy of the Policy in meeting them. . . . This Court has already articulated in detail the importance of the governmental concern in preventing drug use by schoolchildren. . . . The drug abuse problem among our Nation's youth has hardly abated since *Vernonia* was decided in 1995. In fact, evidence suggests that it has only grown worse. . . . The health and safety risks identified in *Vernonia* apply with equal force to Tecumseh's children. . . .

Additionally, the School District in this case has presented specific evidence of drug use at Tecumseh schools. . . . Teachers testified that they had seen students who appeared to be under the influence of drugs and that they had heard students speaking openly about using drugs. . . . A drug dog found marijuana cigarettes near the school parking lot. Police officers once found drugs or drug paraphernalia in a car driven by a Future Farmers of America member. And the school board president reported that people in the community were calling the board to discuss the "drug situation." . . . We decline to second-guess the finding of the District Court that "[v]iewing the evidence as a whole, it cannot be reasonably disputed that the [School District] was faced with a 'drug problem' when it adopted the Policy." . . .

* * *

Furthermore, this Court has not required a particularized or pervasive drug problem before allowing the government to conduct suspicionless drug testing. . . . Indeed, it would make little sense to require a school district to wait for a substantial portion of its students to begin using drugs before it was allowed to institute a drug testing program designed to deter drug use.

. . . We reject the Court of Appeals' novel test that "any district seeking to impose a random suspicionless drug testing policy as a condition to participation in a school activity must demonstrate that there is some identifiable drug abuse problem among a sufficient number of those subject to the testing, such that testing that group of students will actually redress its drug problem." . . . Among other problems, it would be difficult to administer such a test. As we cannot articulate a threshold level of drug use that would suffice to justify a drug testing program for schoolchildren, we refuse to fashion what would in effect be a constitutional quantum of drug use necessary to show a "drug problem."

* * *

We also reject respondents' argument that drug testing must presumptively be based upon an individualized reasonable suspicion of wrongdoing because such a testing regime would be less intrusive. . . . In this context, the Fourth Amendment does not require a finding of individualized suspicion, . . . and we decline to impose such a requirement on schools attempting to prevent and detect drug use by students. . . . In any case, this Court has repeatedly stated that reasonableness under the Fourth Amendment does not require employing the least intrusive means, because "[t]he logic of such elaborate less-restrictive-alternative arguments could raise insuperable barriers to the exercise of virtually all search-and-seizure powers." *Martinez—Fuerte*, 428 U.S., at 556–557, n. 12. . . .

Finally, we find that testing students who participate in extracurricular activities is a reasonably effective means of addressing the School District's legitimate concerns in preventing, deterring, and detecting drug use. . . .

. . . In upholding the constitutionality of the Policy, we express no opinion as to its wisdom. Rather, we hold only that Tecumseh's Policy is a reasonable means of furthering the School District's important interest in preventing and deterring drug use among its schoolchildren. Accordingly, we reverse the judgment of the Court of Appeals.

It is so ordered.

[4 Justices dissented from the above decision]

Case 7.6 Review Question

1. Under the above decision that school authorities may subject students to suspicionless searches in the interest of student health or safety, are there still constitutional limits to that authority? If so, how would you describe them?

Case 7.7

U.S. v. MIAMI UNIVERSITY
294 F.3d 797 (6th Cir. 2002)

[**Focus Note.** *The U.S. Department of Education sued Miami and Ohio State universities to enjoin the university authorities from releasing student disciplinary records that contained information of criminal activities and punishment, which the university newspaper (referred to in the opinion as* The Chronicle), *demanded. The Department alleged that the release of those records violated the nondisclosure provisions of the Family Educational Rights and Privacy Act (FERPA). The following opinion affirmed the lower court injunction and held (1) that student disciplinary records are "education records" within the contemplation of FERPA and (2) that there is no First Amendment right of the student press to have access to student disciplinary records.]*

KARLI S. FORESTER

* * *

Under a plain language interpretation of the FERPA, student disciplinary records are education records because they directly relate to a student and are kept by that student's university. . . .

The FERPA sanctions the release of certain student disciplinary records in several discrete situations through exemption. The Act does not prohibit disclosure "*to an alleged victim* of any crime of violence . . . or a nonforcible sex offense, the final results of any disciplinary proceeding conducted by the institution against the alleged perpetrator. . . ." . . . (emphasis added). The *public generally* may be informed of "the final results of any disciplinary proceeding conducted by [an] institution against a student who is an alleged perpetrator of any crime of violence . . . or a nonforcible sex offense, if the institution determines . . . that the student committed a violation of the institution's rules or policies with respect to such crime or offense." . . . "[T]he final results of any disciplinary proceeding (i) shall include only the name of the student, the violation committed, and any sanction imposed by the institution on that student; and (ii) may include the name of any other student, such as a victim or witness, only with the written consent of that other student." . . . Next, the disciplinary records of a student posing a significant risk to the safety or well-being of that student, other students, or other members of the school community may be disclosed to individuals having a "legitimate educational interest in the behavior of the student." . . . . Finally, if an institution of higher education determines that a student, under the age of twenty-one, "has committed a disciplinary violation with respect to" the use or possession of alcohol or a controlled substance, then the institution may disclose information regarding such violation to a parent or legal guardian of the student. . . .

In addition to the exemptions discussed above, Congress also provided some exceptions to the "education records" definition. Relevant among those exceptions, the term "education records" does not include "records maintained by a law enforcement unit of the educational agency or institution that were created by that law enforcement unit for the purpose of law enforcement." . . .

* * *

To the extent that the permanent injunction limits access to those documents, *The Chronicle* argues that it constitutes a violation of *The Chronicle's* First Amendment rights. . . .

* * *

"It has generally been held that the First Amendment does not guarantee the press a constitutional right of special access to information not available to the public generally." *Branzburg v. Hayes,* 408 U.S. 665, 684–85 . . . (1972). Moreover, "[t]he Constitution itself is [not] a Freedom of Information Act," permitting the release of government records at the will of the public. . . . "Neither the First Amendment nor the Fourteenth Amendment mandates a right of access to government information or sources of information within the government's control." . . .

* * *

The Chronicle colors certain student disciplinary proceedings as criminal proceedings. . . . University disciplinary proceedings are not criminal proceedings. . . . *The Chronicle* may still request student disciplinary records that do not contain personally identifiable information. . . .

Case 7.8

MISSOURI v. JENKINS
515 U.S. 70 (1995)

> *[**Focus Note.** The following opinion covers one of the longest, most intensive exercises of court desegregation supervision of local and state school officials. The 5–4 division among the justices forecasts continuing controversy over those limits.]*

CHIEF JUSTICE REHNQUIST *delivered the opinion of the Court.*

. . . This case has been before the same United States District Judge since 1977. . . .

After a trial that lasted 7 1/2 months, the District Court determined that the State and the KCMSD [Kansas City, Missouri School District] . . . operated a segregated school system within the KCMSD. . . .

In June 1985, the District Court issued its first remedial order. . . . . . .

. . . First, the District Court ordered that the KCMSD be restored to an AAA classification. . . . . . . Second, it ordered that the number of students per class be reduced so that the student-to-teacher ratio was below the level required for AAA standing. . . . The District Court also ordered programs to expand educational opportunities for all KCMSD students: full-day kindergarten; expanded summer school; before- and after-school tutoring; and an early childhood development program. . . . Finally, the District Court implemented a state-funded "effective schools" program. . . . . . .

. . . The total cost for these . . . programs has exceeded $220 million. . . .

* * *

. . . In November 1986, the District Court approved a comprehensive magnet school and capital improvements plan. . . . . . . Under the . . . plan, every senior high school, every middle school, and one-half of the elementary schools were converted into magnet schools. . . .

In June 1985, the District Court ordered substantial capital improvements. . . . . . . In November 1986, the District Court approved further capital improvements . . . "to . . . attract non-minority students back to the KCMSD." . . .

In September 1987, the District Court adopted . . . KCMSD's long-range capital improvements plan. . . . . . . The plan called for the renovation of approximately 55 schools, the closure of 18 facilities, and the construction of 17 new schools. . . . The District Court rejected what it referred to as the "patch and repair" approach . . . because it "would not achieve suburban comparability. . . ." . . . As of 1990, the District Court had ordered $260 million in capital improvements. . . . Since then, the total cost of capital improvements ordered has soared to over $540 million.

. . . Since that time, however, the District Court has ordered salary assistance to all but three of the approximately 5,000 KCMSD employees. The total cost of this component . . . is over $200 million.

The District Court's desegregation plan has been described as the most ambitious and expensive remedial program in the history of school desegregation. . . . The annual cost per pupil . . . far exceeds that of . . . any school district in Missouri. Nevertheless, the KCMSD, which has pursued a "friendly adversary" relationship with the plaintiffs has continued to propose ever more expensive programs. . . . Not surprisingly, the cost . . . has "far exceeded KCMSD's budget, or its authority to tax." . . . The State . . . has borne the brunt of these costs. The District Court candidly has acknowledged that it has allowed the District planners to dream". . . . . . .

* * *

. . . [W]e granted certiorari to consider the following: (1) whether the District Court exceeded its constitutional authority when it granted salary increases to virtually all instructional and noninstructional employees of the KCMSD, and (2) whether the District Court properly relied upon the fact that student achievement test scores had failed to rise to some unspecified level when it declined to find that the State had achieved partial unitary status as to the quality education programs.

* * *

. . . The ultimate inquiry is "'whether the [constitutional violator] ha[s] complied in good faith with the desegregation decree since it was entered, and whether the vestiges of past discrimination ha[ve] been eliminated to the extent practicable.'" . . . .

* * *

The District Court's remedial plan . . . is not designed solely to redistribute the students within the KCMSD in order to eliminate racially identifiable schools. . . . Instead, its purpose is to attract nonminority students from outside the KCMSD schools. But this interdistrict goal is beyond the scope of the intradistrict violation. . . .

* * *

. . . A district court seeking to remedy an intradistrict violation that has not directly caused significant interdistrict effects . . . exceeds its remedial authority if it orders a remedy with an interdistrict purpose. This conclusion follows directly from Milliken II. . . .

* * *

. . . In this posture, we conclude that the District Court's order of salary increases . . . is simply too far removed from an acceptable implementation of a permissible means to remedy previous legally mandated segregation. . . .

Similar considerations lead us to conclude that the District Court's order requiring the State to continue to fund the quality education programs because student achievement levels were still "at or below national norms at many grade levels" cannot be sustained. . . .

Case 7.9

DEBRA P. BY IRENE P. v. TURLINGTON
730 F.2d 1405 (11th Cir. 1984)

[**Focus Note.** *High school graduation competency tests. Suit challenging Florida's Educational Accountability Act which required students to pass a competency test in order to receive the state high school diploma. The Eleventh Circuit Court of Appeals held that under conditions prevailing in 1984, the racially disproportionate impact of the competency test did not make it discriminatory and unlawful.*]

R. Lanier Anderson III, Circuit Judge.

The district court held that use of the SSAT-II for diploma denials violated the due process and equal protection clauses, Title VI, and the EEOA. . . .

The court enjoined the test's use as a diploma sanction until the 1982–83 school year. . . . . . . The district court found that the SSAT-II's content was valid, which would allow the state to use it as a diploma sanction after 1982. The district court issued the four-year injunction for two reasons. First, the court found that the examination violated the equal protection clause, Title VI, and the EEOA by perpetuating past discrimination against black students who had attended segregated schools for the first four years of their education. . . . Second, the court held that the test's implementation schedule provided insufficient notice, in violation of the due process clause. . . . . . .

On appeal, the former Fifth Circuit Court of Appeals upheld the district court's injunction, but remanded for further findings on two issues. . . .

* * *

On remand, the district court tried the two issues separately. . . . [O]n the first issue, the district court concluded that the state had met its burden of proving . . . that the competency examination is "instructionally valid," *i.e.,* a fair test of that which is taught in Florida's schools. . . .

. . . [O]n the second issue, the court found that although vestiges of past segregation still exist to some extent, and although the test still has a racially discriminatory impact, there is no causal link between the disproportionate failure rate of black students and those present effects of past segregation. . . . The court found, moreover, that even if there were a causal connection, the defendants had carried their burden of showing that the diploma sanction would remedy those effects. . . . The propriety of these findings forms the basis for this appeal. . . .

I. Instructional Validity

* * *

B. Factual Findings

Appellants challenge on several grounds the district court's factual finding that students are afforded an adequate opportunity to learn the SSAT-II skills. . . .

1. The Focus on the 1981–82 School Year
The appellants object that the IOX study . . . is invalid because it evaluated only the 1981–82 school year. . . .

* * *

To the extent that the IOX study relies on an inference that what was taught in 1981–82 was taught as far back as 1971, we acknowledge some concern. . . .

* * *

On the other hand, there was a clearly reasonable inference that the instruction revealed in the 1981–82 survey was substantially the same as the post-Act instruction, *i.e.,* beginning in 1977. . . .

* * *

Florida's remedial efforts are extensive. . . . Students have five chances to pass the SSAT-II between 10th and 12th grades, and if they fail, they are offered remedial help. Students may also elect to remain in school for an additional year on a fulltime or parttime basis to receive, at the state's expense, "special instruction designed to remedy [their] identified deficiencies." . . . If they then pass the SSAT-II, they are awarded their diplomas. . . .

* * *

The results of the student survey are also impressive. Ninety to ninety-nine percent of the students surveyed statewide said they had been taught the test skills. . . . Dr. Popham found this "very powerful evidence" of instructional validity. . . .

The remedial efforts and the student survey . . . persuade us that there was adequate evidence to support the district court's finding of instructional validity, notwithstanding our reservations. . . . We are also persuaded . . . by the SSAT-II pass rate in the Class of 1983. After four of five test administrations, 99.84 percent of the class had passed the communications portion of the test and 97.23 percent had passed the math portion. . . .

* * *

II. "Vestiges" of Past Discrimination

. . . Use of the test as a diploma sanction would be permissible only if the state satisfied the test set forth in *McNeal v. Tate County School District* . . . by demonstrating either (1) that the disproportionate failure of blacks was not caused by the present effects of past intentional segregation, or (2) that the use of the test as a diploma sanction would remedy those effects. . . . . . . [T]he district court concluded that vestiges of past purposeful segregation still exist to some extent in Florida schools. . . . The court also noted the plaintiffs' evidence "that black students are still being suspended more often than white students . . . . that racial stereotypes still persist, and that blacks are being assigned to EMR [educable mentally retarded] classes more readily than whites." . . .

The court also noted the undisputed fact that the SSAT-II failure rate among black students is still disproportionately high. . . . However, the court found . . . that there is no causal link between the present effects of past school segregation and the disproportionate failure rate. . . . The district court found, moreover, that even if there were a causal connection, the state had proven that the test will help remedy those effects. . . .

A. The Finding of No Causal Link

* * *

We think that this was sufficient evidence upon which to base a finding that whatever vestiges of discrimination remain do not cause the disproportionate failure rate among black students. . . .

* * *

B. The Finding That the Diploma Sanction Remedies Vestiges

The district court also found that, even assuming there was a causal link between vestiges and disparate impact, the state had satisfied the second prong of the *McNeal* test by demonstrating that use of the SSAT-II as a diploma sanction would remedy the vestiges of past intentional segregation. . . .

* * *

The remarkable improvement in the SSAT-II pass rate among black students over the last six years demonstrates that use of the SSAT-II as a diploma sanction will be effective in overcoming the effects of past segregation. Appellants argue that the improvement has nothing to do with diploma sanctions. . . . However, we think it likely that the threat of diploma sanction . . . contributed to the improved pass rate, and that actual use of the test . . . will be equally, if not more, effective in helping black students overcome discriminatory vestiges. . . .

* * *

Conclusion

We affirm the district court's findings (1) that students were actually taught test skills, (2) that vestiges of past intentional segregation do not cause the SSAT-II's disproportionate impact on blacks, and (3) that use of the SSAT-II as a diploma sanction will help remedy the vestiges of past segregation. Therefore, the State of Florida may deny diplomas to students (beginning with the Class of 1983) who have not yet passed the SSAT-II.

Affirmed.

Case 7.10

DAVIS v. MONROE COUNTY BOARD OF EDUCATION
119 S. Ct. 1661 (1999)

*[**Focus Note.** Suit by LaShonda, a fifth-grade student, and her parent (Davis) against the school board (Board) and school officials to recover monetary damages under Title IX for failing properly to protect her from sexual harassment by her classmate, G.F., over a period of five months. The lower courts held that Title IX did not provide a private cause of action for student-on-student sexual harassment. The Supreme Court reversed, and settled several Title IX questions on which the lower courts had divided.]*

JUSTICE O'CONNOR *delivered the opinion of the Court.*

. . . We consider here whether a private damage action may lie against the school board in cases of student-on-student harassment. We conclude that it may, but only where the funding recipient acts with deliberate indifference to known acts of harassment in its programs or activities. Moreover, we conclude that such an action will lie only for harassment that is so severe, pervasive, and objectively offensive that it effectively bars the victim's access to an educational opportunity or benefit.

* * *

Petitioner's minor daughter, LaShonda, was allegedly the victim of a prolonged pattern of sexual harassment by one of her fifth-grade classmates at Hubbard Elementary School. . . . According to petitioner's complaint, the harassment began in December 1992, when the classmate, G.F., attempted to touch LaShonda's breasts and genital area and made vulgar statements. . . . . . . Similar conduct allegedly occurred on or about January 4 and January 20, 1993. . . . LaShonda reported each of these incidents to her mother and to her classroom teacher, Diane Fort. . . . Petitioner [parent], in turn, also contacted Fort, who allegedly assured petitioner that the school principal, Bill Querry, had been informed. . . . Petitioner contends that, notwithstanding these reports, no disciplinary action was taken against G.F. . . .

G.F.'s conduct allegedly continued for many months. . . .

* * *

The string of incidents finally ended in mid-May, when G.F. was charged with, and pleaded guilty to, sexual battery for his misconduct. . . . The complaint alleges that LaShonda had suffered during the months of harassment . . . specifically, her previously high grades allegedly dropped . . . and, in April 1993, her father discovered that she had written a suicide note. . . . . . .

* * *

There is no dispute here that the Board is a recipient of federal education funding for Title IX purposes. . . .

* * *

. . . We must determine whether a district's failure to respond to student-on-student harassment in its schools can support a private suit for money damages. . . . This Court has indeed recognized an implied private right of action under Title IX . . . and we have held that money damages are available in such suits, *Franklin v. Gwinnett County Public Schools,* 503 U.S. 60 . . . (1992). . . .

. . . Respondents contend, specifically, that the statute only proscribes misconduct by grant recipients, not third parties. . . .

We agree . . . that a recipient of federal funds may be liable in damages under Title IX only for its own misconduct. . . .

We disagree . . . however, that petitioner seeks to hold the Board liable for G.F.'s actions instead of its own. . . . In *Gebser,* we concluded that a recipient of federal education funds may be liable in damages under Title IX where it is deliberately indifferent to known acts of sexual harassment by a teacher. . . .

Accordingly, we rejected the use of agency principles to impute liability to the district for the misconduct of its teachers. . . . Liability arose, rather, from "an official decision by the recipient not to remedy the violation." *Gebser v. Lago Vista Independent School Dist.,* supra, at 290. By employing the "deliberate indifference" theory . . . we concluded in *Gebser* that recipients could be liable in damages only where their own deliberate indifference effectively "cause[d]" the discrimination, 524 U.S., at 291. . . . . . .

* * *

. . . Deliberate indifference makes sense as a theory of direct liability . . . only where the funding recipient has some control over the alleged harassment. . . .

. . . If a funding recipient does not engage in harassment directly, it may not be liable for damages unless its deliberate indifference "subject[s]" its students to harassment. That is, the deliberate indifference must, at a minimum, "cause [students] to undergo" harassment or "make them liable or vulnerable" to it. . . . Moreover, because the harassment must occur "under" "the operations of" a funding recipient . . . the harassment must take place in a context subject to the school district's control. . . .

. . . The dissent consistently mischaracterizes this standard to require funding recipients to "remedy" peer harassment . . . and to "ensur[e] that . . . students conform their conduct to" certain rules . . . Title IX imposes no such requirements. . . . [T]he recipient must merely respond to known peer harassment in a manner that is not clearly unreasonable. This is not a mere "reasonableness" standard, as the dissent assumes. . . . . . .

* * *

. . . Courts, moreover, must bear in mind that schools are unlike the adult workplace and that children may regularly interact in a manner that would be unacceptable among adults. . . . It is thus understandable that . . . students often engage in insults, banter, teasing, shoving, pushing, and gender-specific conduct that is upsetting to the students subjected to it. Damages are not available for simple acts of teasing and name-calling among school children, however, even where these comments target differences in gender. Rather . . . damages are available only where the behavior is so severe, pervasive, and objectively offensive that it denies its victims the equal access to education that Title IX is designed to protect.

. . . Nor do we contemplate, much less hold, that a mere "decline in grades is enough to survive" a motion to dismiss. . . . The drop-off in LaShonda's grades provides necessary evidence of a potential link . . . but petitioner's ability to state a cognizable claim here depends equally on the alleged persistence and severity of G.F.'s actions. . . . . . .

* * *

On this complaint, we cannot say "beyond doubt that [petitioner] can prove no set of facts in support of [her] claim which would entitle [her] to relief." . . . Accordingly, the judgment of the United States Court of Appeals for the Eleventh Circuit is reversed, and the case is remanded for further proceedings consistent with this opinion. . . .

Case 7.10 Review Questions

1. Why were the involved teachers and supervisors not subject to liability under Title IX?

2. How can a school board protect itself against false oral claims that it was notified or had knowledge of alleged sexual harassment? Would an official announcement of a policy requiring the filing of written harassment complaints with school personnel and a prompt official investigation of such complaints be useful? Does the Chapter 6 discussion of Title VII defenses, from the *Faragher* opinion (Case 6.8) suggest like defenses for Title IX?

3. The Supreme Court limited Title IX liability "only for harassment that is so severe, pervasive, and objectively offensive that it effectively bars the victim's access to an educational opportunity or benefit." Can lower courts disagree in what kinds of student heckling is nonactionable banter rather than "severe," "objectively offensive" conduct that "effectively bars" access to educational opportunity? Can courts buck that question to a jury?

4. How would knowledge or ignorance of a victim's fragile condition affect the prior question?

Case 7.11

ABC SCHOOL v. MR. AND MRS. M
1997 Mass. Super., 97-518, Lexis 43

*[**Focus Note.** Parent/school conflict on control of student medical treatment. Parents delivered to school authorities a "Do Not Resuscitate" ("DNR" Order) on behalf of their child, Minor M, who has severe disabilities. The school brought suit requesting a court order allowing it to refuse to honor the parents' order. The parents requested a court ruling that school refusal to honor the DNR Order would violate their constitutional right to refuse medical treatment.]*

Opinion by: RICHARD F. CONNON

Background

ABC School educates disabled children between the ages of 3 and 22 who reside in member towns and whose educational needs exceed the capabilities of their own public school.

... Minor M is a four-year-old girl who is severely disabled both mentally and physically. At present, Minor M weighs only twenty pounds. ... ... While at ABC School, Minor M receives physical, occupational and speech therapies and vision stimulation activities. She is transported to and from school . . . provided by DEF Schools.

During the past year, Minor M's medical condition deteriorated significantly. In March of 1997, Minor M had an apneic spell, meaning her breathing ceased. The school nurse administered care to Minor M until she was transported to the local hospital via ambulance. Following this incident, Minor M was evaluated by her private physician, Dr. Nedda Hobbs, M.D., in Boston. On April 10, 1997, after consultation with Mr. and Mrs. M, Dr. Hobbs issued a DNR Order which states in relevant part:

> Should Minor M have a cardiorespiratory arrest, she may receive oxygen, suction and stimulation. She should receive rectal valium if she appears to be having a prolonged seizure. Minor M should not receive cardiopulmonary resuscitation, intubation, defibrillation, or cardiac medications. Invasive procedures such as arterial or venous puncture should only be done after approval of her parents. Should Minor M have an apneic spell at school, she should receive oxygen, suction and stimulation. If she responds to this, her parents should be contacted and she can be transported home. If she does not respond, she should be transported by ambulance to the local hospital.

The DNR Order was submitted to ABC School and Mr. and Mrs. M were informed that ABC School would not honor it. . . .

* * *

Prior to Minor M's enrollment at ABC School, Mr. and Mrs. M were notified of the institution's preservation of life policy and Mrs. M stated that no DNR Order was in effect. . . .

Discussion

This case presents an issue of first impression in Massachusetts. . . . Plaintiffs argue that their ethical and professional obligations both as an internal matter and as a matter of statutory duty prohibit them from honoring the DNR Order for Minor M. Minor M's parents argue that the DNR Order was obtained for the benefit of their daughter and that their right to refuse medical treatment on behalf of Minor M is constitutionally protected and must be honored by ABC School. For the following reasons, this court finds that Mr. and Mrs. M have the right to refuse medical treatment on behalf of their daughter and that . . . the plaintiffs' [School's] request for declaratory and injunctive relief is denied. Defendants' [Parents'] request for declaratory relief is allowed.

Plaintiffs argue that case law in Massachusetts establishes that a treating facility cannot be forced to honor a DNR Order if transfer to another facility which would honor that order is available. See *Brophy v. New England Sinai Hospital,* 398 Mass. 417, 497 N.E.2d 626 (1986). The string of cases relied upon by the plaintiffs are distinguishable on a critical point. The cases cited by plaintiffs hold that individual medical personnel and medical institutions cannot be compelled "to take active measures which are contrary to their view of their ethical duty toward their patient." *Brophy,* 398 Mass. at 441.

Unlike those cases which involved medical personnel taking active measures to potentially hasten death, ABC School and its staff are being asked to refrain from giving unwanted and potentially harmful medical treatment to Minor M. The DNR Order does not prohibit all life-saving measures, but rather prohibits the use of cardiopulmonary resuscitation, intubation, defibrillation, and other invasive procedures in the event that Minor M suffers cardiac arrest. Moreover, as the guardians of their minor child, Mr. and Mrs. M have the right to refuse unwanted medical treatment on her behalf. See *Superintendent of Belchertown v. Joseph Saikewicz,* 373 Mass. 728, 370 N.E.2d 417 (1977) (right to refuse medical treatment stems from constitutional right to privacy). . . . This court is not in a position to find that such a refusal is not in the best interests of Minor M. . . .

* * *

ABC School argues that equitable considerations weigh in ABC School's favor because of the undue burden that would be placed on the R.N. in charge of the program who does not have the ability to confer with other medical personnel concerning Minor M. However, the DNR Order at issue is very specific in what is prohibited: cardiopulmonary resuscitation, intubation, defibrillation, and cardiac medication. Based on plaintiffs' argument, it appears that the R.N. at ABC School does not have the capability to conduct intubation or defibrillation and, therefore the only concern is the prohibition of CPR and medication. An order prohibiting CPR and medication does not require consultation with other medical personnel.

Finally, ABC School argues that even if this court refuses to grant the requested injunctive relief, this court should issue a declaratory judgment shielding ABC School personnel from liability in the event that they violate the DNR Order and administer aid pursuant to *G.L.C.* 71, 55A. Section 55A reads in relevant part:

> No collaborative school teacher . . . or other . . . collaborative employee who, in good faith, renders emergency first aid or transportation . . . shall be liable in

a suit for damages as a result of his acts or omissions either for such first aid or as a result of providing such emergency transportation to a place of safety. . . .

. . . [T]his court will not issue a declaratory judgment that any action taken in violation of the DNR Order would be "in good faith." To do so would vitiate the DNR Order and essentially constitute an end-run around this court's denial of the request for injunctive relief.

* * *

Order

. . . The plaintiffs are hereby ORDERED to honor the terms of the Do Not Resuscitate Order for the care and treatment of Minor M pending adjudication of this case on its merits.

Case 7.12

HENDRICK HUDSON DIST. BOARD OF EDUC. v. ROWLEY
458 U.S. 176 (1982)

[*Focus Note. What "special educational services" are mandated by the IDEA to provide the required Free Appropriate Education? What guidelines are provided by the following lead opinion?*]

JUSTICE REHNQUIST *delivered the opinion of the Court.*

This case arose in connection with the education of Amy Rowley, a deaf student. . . . Amy has minimal residual hearing and is an excellent lipreader. . . .

As required by the Act, an IEP was prepared for Amy. . . . The Rowleys agreed with parts of the IEP but insisted that Amy also be provided a qualified sign-language interpreter in all her academic classes. . . . Such an interpreter had been placed in Amy's kindergarten class for a 2-week experimental period, but the interpreter had reported that Amy did not need his services at that time. The school administrators likewise concluded that Amy did not need such an interpreter in her first-grade classroom. . . .

. . . Pursuant to the Act's provision for judicial review, the Rowleys then brought an action . . . claiming that the administrators' denial of the sign-language interpreter constituted a denial of the "free appropriate public education" guaranteed by the Act.

The District Court found that Amy "is a remarkably well adjusted child" who interacts and communicates well with her classmates and has "developed an extraordinary rapport" with her teacher. . . . It also found that "she performs better than the average child in her class and is advancing easily from grade to grade," . . . but "that she understands considerably less of what goes on in class than she could if she were not deaf" and thus "is not learning as much, or performing as well academically, as she would without her handicap,". . . . This disparity between Amy's achievement and her potential led the court to decide that she was not receiving a "free appropriate public education." . . .

* * *

. . . It is beyond dispute that . . . the Act does expressly define free appropriate public education:

> The term, free appropriate public education means *special education* and *related services* which (A) have been provided at public expense, under public supervision and direction, and without charge, (B) meet the standards of the State educational agency, (C) include an appropriate preschool, elementary, or secondary school education in the State involved, and (D) are provided in conformity with the individualized education program required under section 1414(a)(5) of this title. § 1401(18) (Emphasis added).

"Special education," as referred to in this definition, means "specially designed instruction, at no cost to parents or guardians, to meet the unique needs of a handicapped child, including classroom instruction, . . . home instruction, and instruction in hospitals and institutions." § 1401(16). "Related services" are defined as "transportation, and such developmental, corrective, and other supportive services . . . as may be required to assist a handicapped child to benefit from special education." § 1401(17).

. . . Thus, if personalized instruction is being provided with sufficient services to permit the child to benefit from the instruction, and the other items on the definitional checklist are satisfied, the child is receiving a "free appropriate education" as defined by the Act.

Noticeably absent from the language of the statute is any substantive standard prescribing the level of education to be accorded handicapped children. Certainly the language of the statute contains no requirement . . . that States maximize the potential of handicapped children "commensurate with the opportunity provided to other children." . . .

. . . Respondents contend that "the goal of the Act is to provide each handicapped child with an equal educational opportunity." . . . We think, however, that the requirement that a State provide specialized educational services . . . generates no additional requirement that the services so provided be sufficient to maximize each child's potential "commensurate with the opportunity provided other children." . . .

. . . The theme of the Act is "free appropriate public education," a phrase which is too complex to be captured by the word "equal" whether one is speaking of opportunities or services.

The District Court and the Court of Appeals thus erred when they held that the Act requires New York to maximize the potential of each handicapped child commensurate with the opportunity provided nonhandicapped children. Desirable though that goal might be, it is not the standard that Congress imposed upon States which receive funding under the Act. . . .

Implicit in the congressional purpose . . . is the requirement that the education . . . be sufficient to confer some educational benefit upon the handicapped child. . . . The statutory definition of "free appropriate public education," . . . expressly requires the provision of "such . . . supportive services . . . as may be required to assist a handicapped child to *benefit* from special education." § 1401(17). We therefore conclude that the "basic floor of opportunity" provided by the Act consists of access to specialized instruction and related services which are individually designed to provide educational benefit to the handicapped child.

The determination of when handicapped children are receiving sufficient educational benefits to satisfy the requirements of the Act presents a more difficult problem. . . . We do not attempt today to establish any one test for determining the adequacy of educational benefits conferred upon all children covered by the Act. . . .

. . . Insofar as a State is required to provide . . . a "free appropriate public education," we hold that it satisfies this requirement by providing personalized instruction with sufficient support services to permit the child to benefit educationally from that instruction. Such instruction and services must be provided at public expense, must meet the State's educational standards, must approximate the grade levels used in the State's regular education, and must comport with the child's IEP. . . . In addition the IEP . . . should be reasonably calculated to enable the child to achieve passing marks and advance from grade to grade.

* * *

The parties disagree sharply over [other] provisions, petitioners contending that courts are given only limited authority to review for state compliance . . . and no power to review the substance of the state program, and respondents contending that the Act requires courts to exercise de novo review over state educational decisions and policies. . . .

* * *

. . . [A] court's inquiry is twofold. First, has the State complied with the procedures set forth in the Act? And second, is the individualized educational program . . . reasonably calculated to enable the child to receive educational benefits? If these requirements are met, the State has complied with the obligations . . . and the courts can require no more.

In assuring that the requirements of the Act have been met, courts must be careful to avoid imposing their view of preferable educational methods upon the States. . . .

Entrusting a child's education to state and local agencies does not leave the child without protection. . . . As this very case demonstrates, parents and guardians will not lack ardor in seeking to ensure that handicapped children receive all of the benefits to which they are entitled by the Act.

Case 7.13

TAYLOR v. VERMONT DEPARTMENT OF EDUCATION
313 F.3d 768 (2d Cir. 2002)

*[**Focus Note.** Divorced, noncustodial mother sued multiple educational entities and individuals, including the state department of education, school district, and school officials, alleging violations of her rights under IDEA and FERPA for denying her demands for an Independent Educational Evaluation of her child, denial of full access to and correction of her child's educational records, and a due process hearing on those demands. The following opinion addresses the rights of natural parents under the "IDEA" and the "FERPA" statutes in light of state laws governing parental rights. Please note that the court recognized in endnote 9 to the following opinion that other courts took a different position on the right of a noncustodial parent to participate in a child's IEP proceedings.]*

SOTOMAYOR, CIRCUIT JUDGE.

We are presented with the question of who is entitled to exercise the rights afforded to a "parent" under the Individuals with Disabilities Education Act. . . , and the Family Educational Rights and Privacy Act. . . . . . . Pam Taylor alleges that the defendants have violated statutory rights she possesses as the natural mother of a child who suffers from a disability. The United States District Court . . . granted defendants' motion to dismiss plaintiff's action . . . holding that plaintiff, whose legal authority over the child had been curtailed by a state divorce decree, lacked standing to pursue an action under either statute.

. . . Taylor argues that a natural mother is entitled to exercise parental rights under the IDEA and FERPA, and that state law cannot abrogate these federal rights. We decline plaintiff's invitation to federalize the law of domestic relations and hold that the IDEA and FERPA leave intact a state's authority to determine who may make educational decisions on behalf of a child, so long as a state does so in a manner consistent with the federal statutes. We therefore affirm the district court's dismissal of the claims related to plaintiff's requests for an Individual Educational Evaluation and amendment of inaccurate information contained in her daughter's academic files. We also affirm the dismissal of plaintiff's 42 U.S.C. § 1983 claim based on FERPA, . . . Nevertheless, because plaintiff retains some important rights under the divorce decree—specifically the right to reasonable information regarding her daughter's health and progress in school—we vacate the district court's judgment insofar as it dismissed her IDEA claim that she was denied access to her child's educational records. We further hold that plaintiff was not required to exhaust her administrative remedies . . . because it would have been futile for Taylor to pursue her IDEA administrative remedies against the ANSU defendants and because it is improbable that she could have obtained relief from the administrative proceedings. . . .

* * *

. . . Taylor is the natural mother of L.D. . . . Taylor obtained a divorce from L.D.'s father in February 1992. . . . The Vermont family court ultimately revoked the prior custody arrangement and awarded L.D.'s father full custody. The divorce decree entered . . . provides:

> The court allocates all legal rights and physical rights regarding the choice of schooling for the child . . . to the father. Such rights shall include the right to choose the school location, and participate in all parent teacher conferences of decision making with full authority on behalf of the child. . . . [The father] shall have the right to make all decisions regarding the child's health and safety while in his care during the school year.

> The mother shall have a right to reasonable information regarding the child's progress in school and her health and safety. . . . The Court places the parental rights and responsibilities for the child . . . both legal and physical fully with the defendant-father. . . .

This ruling was affirmed by the Vermont Supreme Court.

* * *

. . . On October 31, 1999, Taylor demanded an Independent Educational Evaluation ("IEE"). . . . . . . As L.D.'s father opposed further evaluation, and the team likewise concluded that further evaluation would impact L.D. negatively, Taylor's request was denied. Taylor then filed a Request for a Due Process Hearing. . . . A VDOE hearing officer dismissed the petition on the ground that, as a result of the Addison Family Court's custody order, plaintiff lacked legal standing to pursue any claim under the IDEA.

 In October and December 1999, plaintiff again notified the school that she believed that L.D.'s educational file contained inaccurate information and asked that the file be amended. Specifically, Taylor sought to eliminate any reference to L.D.'s stepmother as the child's "mother" or "parent," among other changes. Weybridge did not respond to Taylor's letters but on February 4, 2000, Taylor received a copy of a letter addressed to L.D.'s father. The letter stated that the school had removed certain letters written by Taylor from L.D.'s files but, pursuant to the father's written request, would not amend the school records further. Taylor's petition for a hearing to challenge the content of L.D.'s records was denied by ACSU. . . .

. . . Although FERPA does not contain an implied direct cause of action, Taylor brought her FERPA action under 42 U.S.C. § 1983.

* * *

Taylor has brought three general types of claims under the IDEA and FERPA. First, she demands that the ACSU defendants perform an Independent Educational Evaluation of L.D. Second, she asks to be given access to all of her daughter's educational records. Third, she seeks to challenge the content of her daughter's education records. . . . She also requests compensatory damages for violations of her rights under the IDEA and FERPA, . . . We address each claim in turn.

* * *

II. Taylor's Standing to Request an Independent Educational Evaluation

It is uncontested that one of the primary purposes of the IDEA is to "to ensure that the rights of children with disabilities and parents . . . including a parent's right to demand an IEE. . . ." Yet the invocation of this general statutory purpose is of little assistance in helping us determine whether Taylor is entitled to exercise parental rights under the statute. Whether Taylor may avail herself of the IDEA's procedural protections . . . depends upon whether Taylor is considered a "parent" within the meaning of the Act. Unfortunately, neither the IDEA nor its federal regulatory scheme are models of clarity.

* * *

. . . [P]rior to 1997 the IDEA did not contain any definition of the term "parent." The statute was amended . . . to include the following provision:
    The term "parent"—

(A)   includes a legal guardian; and
(B)   . . . an individual assigned . . . to be a surrogate parent. . . .

. . . Clearly, legal guardians and educational surrogates are not the only persons entitled to the IDEA's procedural protections. . . . Thus, the statutory language provides us with little assistance. . . .

The Department of Education's current set of regulations implementing the IDEA, effective since 1999, contains a more comprehensive definition of parent: . . . The regulation does not purport to list all those who are granted rights under the statute. In fact . . . it indicates exactly the opposite—that the listed persons may or may not be entitled to exercise parental rights under the statute. . . .

* * *

. . . The regulation does not establish a method for choosing which of the possible parents is entitled to exercise rights under the statute. Given the nature of the statutory scheme, we look to state law to fill this gap. . . . . . .

We acknowledge that the federal regulations are inartfully drafted. . . .

The question of which divorced parent should be allowed to perform parental functions under the [IDEA] is not properly a matter for OSEP to decide. Rather, this is a matter for State or local divorce courts. . . .

* * *

Our conclusion is further reinforced by case law. The only other circuit court decision to have addressed this precise issue has likewise held that the extent of a natural parent's rights under the IDEA must be determined with reference to state law. *See Navin v. Park Ridge Sch. Dist. 64*, 270 F.3d 1147, 1149 (7th Cir. 2001). . . .

> Court FN9. The plaintiff cites to two district court opinions to support her claim that non-custodial natural parents may participate in the IEP process unless there has been an official termination of their parental rights. *See W.T. v. Andalusia City Schs.*, 977 F. Supp. 1437, 1444 (M.D. Ala. 1997). . . ; *Doe v. Anrig*, 651 F. Supp. 424, 429 (D. Mass. 1987). . . . (holding that non-custodial father who had financial responsibility for son's education had right to participate in IEP process). . . . To the extent that these cases hold that natural parents may challenge educational decisions under the IDEA regardless of whether they have legal authority over the child, we find them unpersuasive.

. . . [W]e now look to Taylor's parental rights under Vermont law. Vermont's implementing regulations . . . substantially mirror the federal regulations: . . .

In contrast to the facts of the *Navin* case, here Taylor's parental right to participate in her daughter's education has been revoked by a Vermont family court. Moreover, the father, upon whom Vermont has bestowed this legal authority, has opposed the due process hearing requested by Taylor as against the child's best interests. As Taylor does not have the authority to make educational decisions on behalf of L.D., we agree that she lacks standing to demand a hearing under the IDEA on the appropriateness of defendants' IEP evaluation.

III. Taylor's Record-Access Claims

. . . FERPA commands that a parent must be permitted to review and inspect a child's educational records. . . . The IDEA similarly allows parents access to records collected or maintained pursuant to that statute. . . .

Taylor alleges that the ACSU and ANSU defendants violated these provisions. . . . . . .

A. Taylor's FERPA Claim

Before considering the merits of Taylor's FERPA claim, we must first determine whether Taylor may bring a § 1983 action for an alleged violation of FERPA's record-access provisions. . . . In *Gonzaga University v. Doe,* 536 U.S. 273 . . . (2002), the Court . . . held that the non-disclosure provisions of FERPA . . . do not confer federal rights enforceable through a § 1983 action. . . . [A]pplying the analysis set forth in *Gonzaga,* we conclude that plaintiff does not have the personal right required for a § 1983 claim. . . . Under the implied cause of action doctrine, a court must additionally inquire whether Congress intended to create a private remedy, *see Alexander v. Sandoval,* 532 U.S. 275, 286 . . . (2001), while under our § 1983 analysis, we determine if Congress foreclosed a § 1983 remedy either expressly or impliedly through the creation of a comprehensive administrative enforcement scheme. . . .

* * *

. . . Accordingly, because we find that *Gonzaga* compels the conclusion that FERPA's records-access provisions . . . do not create a personal right enforceable under § 1983 . . .

B. Taylor's IDEA claim

A parent's rights under the IDEA must be determined with reference to the rights she retains under the state custody decree, ... [T]aylor retains important rights . . . under the Vermont custody decree, specifically the right to "reasonable information regarding the child's progress in school and her health and safety." Because the custody decree has not "specifically revoked" her informational access prerogatives, Taylor may pursue her record-access claim under the IDEA.

* * *

The ACSU defendants concede that Taylor is entitled to review L.D.'s educational records. They argue, however, first, that they have provided Taylor with all the records she sought. . . . . . .

* * *

. . . As an initial matter, we agree that Taylor is only entitled to "reasonable" information. "Reasonable" information does not mean every last cover letter, transmittal sheet, or scrap of paper that happens to be contained in L.D.'s files. . . . Nonetheless, we cannot say that, as a matter of law, Taylor's complaint fails to state a violation of her right to "reasonable" information to which she was entitled under the IDEA and the custody decree. . . .

* * *

Similarly, Taylor claims that the ANSU defendants denied her access to all records related to L.D.'s suspected disability, with the result that she was not made aware until nearly a year later that her daughter had been diagnosed with serious emotional and behavioral difficulties. . . . [W]e conclude that it is possible that this could constitute the type of "reasonable information regarding the child's progress in school and her health and safety" contemplated by the custody decree. . . .

It remains to be seen whether any of the withheld documents is a record within the definition of 34 C.F.R. § 300.562, whether any failure to provide Taylor with these records was "reasonable," and whether such records were in fact furnished to Taylor. . . . We therefore hold that the district court should not have granted defendants' motion to dismiss with respect to the IDEA records-access claim, at least without granting Taylor an opportunity to cure any alleged insufficiencies in the pleadings.

* * *

IV. Taylor's Record Amendment Claim

Taylor next alleges that the ACSU defendants deprived her of her right under FERPA . . . to challenge inaccuracies in her daughter's school records. . . . . . . [T]he FERPA implementing regulations specifically address the question of a non-custodial parent's rights under the statute: "An educational agency or institution shall give full rights under the Act to either parent, unless the agency or institution has been provided with evidence that there is a court order, State statute, or legally binding document relating to such matters as divorce, separation, or custody that specifically revokes these rights." 34 C.F.R. § 99.4. In other words, the extent of Taylor's rights under FERPA must be determined with reference to the rights she retained under the decree.

The divorce decree clearly states that all legal rights over education lie with the father. The decision to bring a FERPA hearing to challenge the content of L.D.'s records certainly falls within the authority given to the natural father to make educational determinations on behalf of L.D. Plaintiff counters that her FERPA rights were not "specifically revoke[d]" by the divorce decree. . . . It is not necessary, however, for the custody decree to state explicitly that it revokes "FERPA rights,". . . . It is enough that the court determined that Taylor no longer has authority to make decisions related to the education of her daughter. Taylor's right to seek a hearing to challenge the content of her daughter's academic files has therefore been "specifically revoked" within the meaning of the regulation.

* * *

Conclusion

For the reasons stated above, we affirm the dismissal of all claims against the VDOE. We also affirm the dismissal of the claims against the ANSU and ACSU defendants related to the provision of an IEE and to the contents of L.D.'s records and the FERPA record-access claim. We vacate the magistrate judge's judgment dismissing the plaintiff's IDEA record-access claims against the ANSU and ACSU defendants, and remand for further proceedings consistent with this opinion.

☞ ENDNOTES

1. *Re honor societies:* Dangler v. Yorktown Cent. Schools, 771 F. Supp. 625 (S.D. N.Y. 1991); 777 F. Supp. 1177 (S.D. N.Y. 1991); *accord:* Price v. Young, 580 F. Supp. 1 (E.D. Ark. 1983); Karnstein v. Pewaukee School Board, 557 F. Supp. 565 (E.D. Wis. 1983). For an instance where a court found a "liberty" interest in honorary society membership, *see* Warren v. National Assn. of Sec. School Principals, 375 F. Supp. 1043 (N.D. Tex. 1974). *Cf.* Ector County Ind. School Dist. v. Hopkins, 518 S.W.2d 576 (Tex. 1975). *Re student office:* Bull v. Dardanelle Pub. School Dist., 745 F. Supp. 1455 (E.D. Ark. 1990) (no right to run for student council). *See also* Moore v. Hyche, 761 F. Supp. 112 (N.D. Ala. 1991).

2. *Hearing not required:* Farver v. Board of Educ., 40 F. Supp. 2d 323 (D. Md. 1999) (extracurricular activities); Spring Branch I.S.D. v. Stamos, 695 S.W.2d 556 (Tex. 1985) (exclusion for grade deficiency); Palmer v. Merluzzi, 689 F. Supp. 400 (D. N.J. 1988).
    Hearing required: Duffley v. N.H. Interscholastic Athletic Assn., 446 A.2d 462 (N.H. 1982).

3. Goss v. Lopez, 419 U.S. 565 (1975); *accord:* Baxter v. Round Lake Area Schools, 856 F. Supp. 438 (N.D. Ill. 1994).

4. Montoya v. Sanger Un. School Dist., 502 F. Supp. 209 (E.D. Cal. 1980); Garcia v. Los Angeles County Bd. of Educ., 177 Cal. Reptr. 29 (1981).

5. *Transfers to comparable schools:* Everett v. Marcase, 426 F. Supp. 397 (E.D. Pa. 1977); *but see* Madera v. Board of Educ., 386 F.2d 778 (2d Cir. 1967).
    Transfers to less desirable schools: Mills v. Board of Educ., 348 F. Supp. 866 (D.D. Colo. 1972); Pa. Assn. for Retarded Children v. Cmwlth., 343 F. Supp. 279 (E.D. Pa. 1972).

6. Linwood v. Board of Educ., 462 F.2d, at 770 (7th Cir. 1972).

7. Ingraham v. Wright, 430 U.S. 651 (1997).

8. *Cf.* Board of Curators v. Horowitz, 435 U.S. 78 (1978) (medical school student).

9. Atcitty v. San Juan County School Dist., 967 P.2d 1261 (Utah 1998).

10. LaBrosse v. St. Bernard Parish School Board, 483 So. 2d 1253 (La. App. 1986). *Compare* Rucker v. Colonial School Dist., 517 A.2d 703 (Del. Super. 1976) (4 days' notice of expulsion hearing—held adequate), *with* Vought v. Van Buren Pub. Schools, 306 F. Supp. 1388 (E.D. Mich. 1969) (5 days' notice required).

11. *Closed hearing upheld:* Racine Unified School Dist. v. Thomas, 321 N.W.2d 334, 338 (Wis. 1982) (statutory right); Pierce v. School Comm. of New Bedford, 322 F. Supp. 957 (D. Mass. 1971).
    Closed hearing disapproved: DeJesus v. Penberthey, 334 F. Supp. 70–7 (D. Conn. 1972).

12. People in the interest of K.P., 514 P.2d 1131 (Colo. 1973); Intron v. State Board of Educ., 384 F. Supp. 674 (D. Puerto Rico 1974).

13. Williams v. Board of Educ., 626 S.W.2d 361 (Ark. 1982). *See also* Murray v. W. Baton Rouge School Board, 472 F.2d 438 (5th Cir. 1973); Alex v. Allen, 409 F. Supp. 379 (W.D. Pa. 1976); Fielder v. Board of Educ., 346 F. Supp. at 730 (D. Neb. 1972).

14. *See also* Clairborne v. Beebe School Dist., 687 F. Supp. 1358 (E.D. Ark. 1988) (phrase "prior to"—held vague); Leibner v. Sharbaugh, 429 F. Supp. 744 (D. Va. 1977).

15. Hill v. Rankin County Mississippi Sch. Dist., 843 F. Supp. 1112 (S.D. Miss. 1993); McClain v. Lafayette Cty. Board of Educ., 673 F.2d 106 (5th Cir. 1982) (carrying weapon); Gardenshire v. Chalmers, 326 F. Supp. 1200 (D. Ky. 1971) (carrying firearms).

16. *See, e.g.,* Newsome v. Batavia Local School Dist., 842 F.2d 920 (6th Cir. 1988); Murray v. W. Baton Rouge School Board., 472 F.2d 438 (5th Cir. 1973).

17. *See* Pierce v. School Comm. of New Bedford, 322 F. Supp. 957, at 962 (D. Mass. 1971).

18. Warren v. Nat'l Assn. of Secondary School Principals, 375 F. Supp. 43 (N.D. Tex. 1974).

19. *Cross-examination denied:* Jones v. Board of Trustees, 524 So. 2d 968 (Miss. 1988) (suspension); Texarkana Indep. School Dist. v.

Lewis, 470 S.W.2d at 736 (Tex. 1971) (expulsion), and cases there cited.

Cross-examination and counsel allowed: Stone v. Prosser Cons. School Dist., 971 P.2d 125 (Wash. 1999) (expulsion); Newsome v. Batavia Local School Dist., 842 F.2d 920 (6th Cir. 1988); Casada v. Booneville School Dist. No. 65, 686 F. Supp. 730 (W.D. Ark. 1988).

20. Fielder v. Board of Educ., 346 F. Supp. 722 (D. Neb. 1972). *But see contra:* Jones, note 19, *supra;* Greene v. Moore, 373 F. Supp. 1194 (N.D. Tex. 1974). *Re harmless denial of confrontation:* Paredes by Koppenhoefer v. Curtis, 864 F.2d 426 (6th Cir. 1988).

21. *Hearsay testimony allowed:* Tasby v. Estes, 643 F.2d 1103 (5th Cir. 1981); Boykins v. Fairfield Board of Educ., 492 F.2d 697 (5th Cir. 1974).

    Hearsay testimony not allowed: Fielder v. Board of Educ., 346 F. Supp. 722 (D. Neb. 1972); DeJesus v. Penberthey, 344 F. Supp. 70 (D. Conn. 1972).

22. *School counsel not present:* Texarkana, note 19, *supra. Advisory hearing:* Madera v. Board of Educ., 380 F.2d 778 (2nd Cir. 1967).

23. *Re* Goldwyn, 281 N.Y.S.2d 199 (1967). *Cf.* Givens v. Poe, 346 F. Supp. 202 (W.D. N.C. 1972).

24. *Compare* Mason v. Thetford School Board, 457 A.2d 647, 649 (Vt. 1982) (denying right of appeal), *with cases finding statutory right of appeal:* Ross v. Disare, 500 F. Supp. 928, at 931 (S.D. N.Y. 1977).

25. Racine Unified, note 11, *supra* (board minutes as record of a hearing); Ross, note 24, *supra.*

26. *Compare* Mills v. Board of Educ. 348 F. Supp. 866 (D. D.C. 1972) (record required), *with* S. v. Board of Educ., 97 Cal. Rptr. 422 (1971).

27. Pace v. Dryden Cent. School Dist., 574 N.Y.S.2d 142 (1991).

28. Lovell v. Poway Unified School Dist., 847 F. Supp. 780 (S.D. Cal. 1994); Hill v. Rankin County Mississippi School Dist., 843 F. Supp. 1112 (S.D. Miss. 1993).

29. *See* Annot., *Discipline of Pupil for Non-School Conduct,* 53 A.L.R. 3d 1124 (1973). *Re* drugs and assaults, *see* Rucker v. Colonial School Dist., 517 A.2d 703 (Del. Super. 1976); Fisher v. Burkburnett Indep. School Dist., 419 F. Supp. 1200 (N.D. Tex. 1976).

    Re vandalism, *see* Clinton Mun. Sep. School Dist. v. Byrd, 477 So. 2d 237 (Miss. 1985).

30. Howard v. Clark, 299 N.Y.S.2d 65 (1969); Bunger v. Iowa H.S. Athletic Assn., 197 N.W.2d 555 (Iowa 1972).

31. St. Ann v. Palisi, 495 F.2d 423 (5th Cir. 1974).

32. Slocum v. Holton Board of Educ., 429 N.W. 2d 607 (Mich. 1988) (grade reduction); Jacobs v. School Board of Lee County, 519 So. 2d 1002 (Fla. 1987) (expulsion from honor society); *compare* Board of Educ. v. Ambach, 465 N.Y.S.2d 77 (1983) (overturning expulsion for summertime crime).

33. *Abuse of discretion:* Katzman v. Cumberland Valley School Dist., 479 A.2d 671 (Pa.1984). *Ultra vires:* Hamer v. Board of Educ., 383 N.E.2d 231 (Ill. 1978); Guitirrez v. School Dist. R-1, 585 P.2d 935 (Colo. 1978).

34. Fisher, note 29, *supra;* Dunn v. Tyler Indep. School Dist., 460 F.2d 137 (5th Cir. 1972).

35. *See* J. Dayton, *Corporal Punishment in Public Schools,* 89 Ed. Law Rep. 729, at 730, note 7.

36. Ingraham v. Wright, 430 U.S. 651 (1977) at note 47. *For recent developments, see* Jefferson v. Ysleta Indep. School Dist., 817 F.2d 303(5th Cir. 1987); I. M. Rosenberg, *A Study in Irrationality, Refusal to Grant Substantive Due Process Protection Against Excessive Corporal Punishment in the Public Schools,* 27 Hous. L. Rev. 399 (1990).

37. *See* Doe v. Board of Educ., 18 F. Supp. 2d 954 (N.D. Ill. 1998); D.R. v. Middle Bucks Area Voc-Tech School, 972 F.2d 1364 (3d Cir. 1991); Stoneking v. Bradford Area School Dist., 882 F.2d 720 (3rd Cir. 1989)(Stoneking I); Thelma D. by Delores A. v. Board of Educ., 934 F.2d 929 (8th Cir. 1991); J.O. v. Alton Comm. Unit School Dist., 909 F.2d 267 (7th Cir. 1990); D.T. v. Indep. School Dist. No. 16 of Pawnee County, 894 F.2d 1176 (10th Cir. 1990).

    See also W.Valente, *Liability for Teacher's Sexual Misconduct with Students,* 74 Ed.Law Rep., 1021, at 1022 et seq. (1992); G. Sorenson, *Sexual Abuse in Schools,* 27 Educ. Ad. Q., 460 (1991); W. Valente, *School District and Official*

Liability for Teacher Sexual Abuse of Students, 57 Educ. L. Rep. 645 (1990).

Older cases finding a substantive due process right against shocking corporal punishment: Metzger v. Osbeck, 841 F.2d 518 (3d Cir. 1988); Garcia v. Miera, 817 F.2d 650 (10th Cir. 1987); Webb v. McCullough, 828 F.2d 1151 (6th Cir. 1987); Hall v. Tawney, 621 F.2d 607, 610 (4th Cir. 1980). *Contra:* Fee v. Herndon, 900 F.2d 804 (5th Cir. 1990).

Older cases finding punishment not sufficiently shocking: Brown by Brown v. Johnson, 710 F. Supp. 183 (E.D. Ky. 1989); Wise v. Pea Ridge School Dist., 855 F.2d 560 (8th Cir. 1988) (paddlings that caused severe bruises).

38. Estelle v. Gamble, 429 U.S., at 103–4 (1976); Youngsberg v. Romeo, 457 U.S., at 315–6 (1982); Wood v. Ostrander, 851 F.2d 1212 (9th Cir. 1988).

39. Middle Bucks, note 37, *supra* (no constitutional duty to prevent sexual harassment); Walton v. Alexander, 44 F.3d 1297 (5th Cir. 1995)(no special relationship duty to protect a sexually assaulted deaf student as *voluntarily* resident of state school for the deaf); Maldonado v. Josey, 975 F.2d 727 (10th Cir. 1992); Lefall v. Dallas Ind. School Dist., 975 F.2d 137 (5th Cir. 1992); Carroll K. v. Fayette County Board of Educ., 19 F. Supp. 2d 618 (S.D. W.Va. 1998). *Contra:* The Fifth Circuit decision that the school had a special relationship and constitutional duty to protect 14-year-old student against teacher sexual assault is a distinct minority. Doe v. Taylor Ind. School Dist., 15 F.3d 443 (5th Cir. 1994).

40. *Cf.* Walton v. Alexander, 20 F.3d 1350 (5th Cir. 1994); Pagano v. Massepequa Pub. Schools, 713 F. Supp. 641 (E.D. N.Y. 1989). The Supreme Court has rejected any special relationship duties by public employers to public employees. *See, e.g.,* Collins v. City of Harker Heights, 503 U.S. 115 (1992).

41. Armijo by and through Chavez v. Wagon Mound Public Schools, 159 F.3d 1253 (10th Cir. 1998).

42. Doe v. Pulaski County Special School Dist., 306 F.3d 616 (8th Cir. 2002).

43. Saxe v. State College Area School Dist., 240 F.3d 200 (3d Cir. 2001).

44. *Compare* Sypniewski v. Warren Hills Regional Board of Educ., 307 F.3d 243 (3d Cir. 2002), *with* West v. Derby Un. School Dist., 206 F.3d 1358 (10th Cir. 2000).

45. *Compare* Peterson v. Board of Educ., 370 F. Supp. 1208 (D. Neb. 1973), *with* Jacobs, note 32, *supra;* Bystrom and Burch cases, note 50, *infra.*

46. Boyd County H.S. Gay Straight Alliance v. Bd. of Educ. (No. 03-17-DLB, 4-18-2003).

47. 393 U.S. 503 (1969).

48. West v. Derby Unified School Dist., 23 F. Supp. 2d 1223 (D. Kan. 1998) (school ban on possession of confederate flag symbols at racially tense school—upheld); *accord:* Crosby v. Holsinger, 852 F.2d 801 (4th Cir. 1988) (ban on "Johnny Reb" symbol).

49. Walker-Serrano v. Leonard, 325 F.3d 412 (3d Cir. 2003).

50. *Upholding school control:* Vigil v. School Board, 862 F.2d 1517 (11th Cir. 1989); Bystrom v. Fridley H.S. Indep. School Dist., 822 F.2d 747 (8th Cir. 1987); Seyfried v. Walton, 668 F.2d 214 (3d Cir. 1981).

 Overturning school control: Burch v. Barker, 861 F.2d 1149 (9th Cir. 1988). *See also* Pyle v. So. Hadley School Dist., 861 F. Supp. 157 (D. Mass. 1994), *citing* Chandler v. McMinnville School Dist., 978 F.2d 524 (9th Cir. 1992). Some commentators have argued that *Bethel* should only apply to "school-sponsored" speech, and not to all speech "of pedagogical concern", a view that has not found much support in the case reports.

51. *Disruptive incitement:* Gano v. School Dist. 411, 674 F. Supp. 796 (D. Idaho 1987) (portraying school superiors as drunkards); Scoville v. Board of Educ., 425 F.2d 10 (7th Cir. 1970) (criticism of school policies). *Compare* Hatter v. L.A. City H.S. Dist., 452 F.2d 673 (9th Cir. 1971) (peaceful protest against school dress code).

 Call for a strike and takeover: Williams v. Spencer, 622 F.2d 1206 (4th Cir. 1980); Lake Park Educ. Assn. v. Lake Park H.S. Dist., 526 F. Supp. 719 (N.D. Ill. 1981); Ring v. Reorganized School Dist., 609 S.W.2d 241 (Mo. 1980).

52. Perumal v. Saddleback Valley Unified School Dist., 243 Cal. Rptr. 545 (1988)(yearbooks); Papish v. Board of Curators, Univ. of Mo., 410 U.S. 667 (1973)(college press cases). Nitzberg v.

Park, 525 F.2d 378 (4th Cir. 1975); Jacobs v. Board of School Comm'rs, 490 F.2d 601 (7th Cir. 1973); Shanley v. Northeast Indep. School Dist., 462 F.2d 960 (5th Cir. 1972); Eisner v. Stamford Board of Educ., 440 F.2d 803 (2d Cir. 1971); Riseman v. School Comm. of Quincy, 439 F.2d 148 (1st Cir. 1971).

53. *See, e.g.,* Seyfried v. Walton, 668 F.2d 214 (3d Cir. 1981) (ban on play, *Pippin*) and cases at note 50, *supra*.

54. *Compare, e.g.,* Talley v. Cal., 362 U.S. 60 (1960), *with* Healy v. James, 408 U.S. 169 (1972).

55. *Upholding exclusion of ads:* Planned Parenthood of Southern Nevada v. Clark County School Dist., 941 F.2d 817 (9th Cir. 1991) (family planning); Zucker v. Panitz, 299 F. Supp. 102 (E.D. N.Y. 1969) (partisan political ads).
    Overturning exclusion of ads: San Diego Comm. v. Governing Board, 790 F.2d 1471 (9th Cir. 1986) (antidraft ad); Searcey v. Crim, 642 F. Supp. 313 (N.D. Ga. 1986), *modified on appeal,* Searcey v. Crim, 815 F.2d 1398 (11th Cir. 1987).
    Upholding selective refusal of ad: Katz v. McAulay, 438 F.2d 1058 (2d Cir. 1970); Hernandez v. Hanson, 430 F. Supp. 1154 (D. Neb. 1977). *Overturning selective refusal of ad:* Cintron v. State Board of Educ., 384 F. Supp. 674 (D. Puerto Rico 1974).

56. Texas v. Johnson, 491 U.S. 397 (1989).

57. Sheldon v. Fannin, 221 F. Supp. 766 (Ariz. 1963). *Compare* Caldwell v. Craighead, 432 F.2d 213 (6th Cir. 1970), *with* Frain v. Barron, 307 F. Supp. 27 (E.D. N.Y. 1969).

58. *Unprotected class boycotts and walkouts:* Sapp v. Renpoe, 511 F.2d 172 (5th Cir. 1975); Rhyne v. Childs, 359 F. Supp. 1085 (N.D. Fla. 1973); Tate v. Board of Educ., 453 F.2d 975 (8th Cir. 1972).

59. Hatch v. Goerke, 502 F.2d 1189 (10th Cir. 1974); Richards v. Thursten, 424 F.2d 128 (1st Cir. 1970); Crossen v. Fatsi, 309 F. Supp. 114 (D. Conn. 1970); Bannister v. Paradis, 316 F. Supp. 185 (D. N.H. 1970).

60. Littlefield v. Forney Ind. School Dist., 268 F.3d 275 (5th Cir. 2001).

61. Canady v. Bossier Parish School Board, 250 F.3d 437 (5th Cir. 2002).

62. Dunkerson v. Russell, 502 S.W.2d 64 (Ky. 1973); Murphy v. Pocatello School Dist., 480 P.2d 878 (Idaho 1971); Bannister v. Paradis, 316

F. Supp. 185 (D. N.H. 1970); Wallace v. Ford, 346 F. Supp. 156 (E.D. Ark. 1972). *See also* Graber v. Kniola, 216 N.W.2d 925 (Mich. 1974) (*re* bikini); Fowler v. Williams, 251 S.E.2d 889 (N.C. 1979) (graduation dress requirement—upheld).

63. Jeglin v. San Jacinto Unified School Dist., 827 F. Supp. 1459 (Cal. 1993).

64. Pyle v. So. Hadley School Com., 861 F. Supp. 157 (D. Mass. 1994).

65. Humphries v. Lincoln Parish School Board, 467 So. 2d 870 (La. 1985); Long v. Zopp, 476 F.2d 180 (4th Cir. 1973).

66. *Male hair length restrictions upheld:* Zeller v. Donagel School Dist. Board of Educ., 517 F.2d 600 (3d Cir. 1975); Murray v. W. Baton Rouge Parish School Board., 472 F.2d 438 (5th Cir. 1973); Ferrel v. Dallas Indep. School Dist., 392 F.2d 697 (6th Cir. 1968); Gfell v. Rickelman, 441 F.2d 444 (6th Cir. 1971); Olff v. E. Side H.S. Dist., 445 F.2d 932 (9th Cir. 1971); Hatch v. Goerke, note 59, *supra;* Freeman v. Flake, 448 F.2d 258 (10th Cir. 1971).
    Male hair length restrictions—struck down: Richards, note 59, *supra;* Long v. Zopp, prior note; Holsapple v. Woods, 500 F.2d 49 (7th Cir. 1974); Torvik v. Deborah Comm. Schools, 453 F.2d 779 (8th Cir. 1972).

67. *Upheld:* Board of Trustees of Bastrop Independent School Dist. v. Toungate, 958 S.W.2d 365 (Tex. 1997) (male ponytail ban) and cases there cited; Jones v. W.T. Henning, 721 So. 2d 530 (La. 1998) (male earring ban) and cases there cited; Barber v. Colo. Ind. School Dist., 901 S.W.2d 447 (Tex. 1995).
    But see Breese v. Smith, 502 P.2d 159 (Ala. 1972) (state constitutional violation); Jacobs v. Benedict, 316 N.E.2d 898 (Ohio 1974); Neuhaus v. Federico, 505 P.2d 939 (Or. 1972) (as unauthorized by school statutes).

68. Lawrence v. Garner, 123 S. Ct. 2472 (2003).

69. Harper v. Edgewood Board of Educ., 655 F. Supp. 1353 (S.D. Ohio 1987) (male student wishing to dress as female); Fricke v. Lynch, 491 F. Supp. 381 (D.R.I. 1980) (same-sex date to school prom).

70. *Separatist club bans:* Passel v. Ft. Worth Indep. School Dist., 453 S.W.2d 888 (Tex. 1970). For statute and case authorities in more than 25 states, *see* Robinson v.

Sacramento Unified School Dist., 53 Cal. Rptr. 781, 788–9 (1966).

 Hazing bans: McNaughton v. Circleville Board of Educ., 345 N.E.2d 649 (C.D. Ohio 1974) (belt beatings and rubbing of hot pepper into their faces).

71. Healy v. James, 408 U.S. 169 (1972); *cf.* Eisen v. Regents, Univ. of Cal., 75 Cal. Rptr. 45 (1969).

72. *Consent to search:* Carter v. Raybuck, 742 F.2d 977 (6th Cir. 1984); Jones v. Latexo Indep. School Dist., 449 F. Supp. 223, 236–7 (E.D. Tex. 1980).
 Plain view exception: State v. D.T.W., 425 So. 2d 1383 (Fla. 1983).
 Police search incident to arrest: State v. Kimball, 503 P.2d 176 (Hawaii 1972) (student loitering on school grounds).
 Identification or preservation of lost property: Illinois v. Lafayette, 462 U.S. 640 (1983) (warrantless inventory search by police).

73. *Compare* Interest of Feazell, 360 So. 2d 907 (La. App. 1978) (consent found), *with In re* Scott K. 595 P.2d 105 (Cal. 1979) (consent not found). *See also* Tartar v. Raybuck, 742 F.2d 977 (6th Cir. 1984).

74. For later affirmation, of this opinion, see 323 F.3d 950 (11th Cir. 2003).

75. State v. Whorley, 720 So. 2d 282 (Fla. 1998) (student tip); Coronado v. State, 806 S.W.2d 302 (Tex. 1991); Comm. v. Carey, 554 N.E.2d 1199 (Mass. 1990); Appeal in Pima County Juvenile Action, 733 P.2d 316 (Ariz. 1987); State v. Joseph T., 886 S.E.2d 728 (W. Va. 1985); Martens v. Dist. No. 220, 620 F. Supp. 29 (N.D. Ill. 1985); *In re* State in Interest of G.C., 296 A.2d 102 (N.J. 1972). *But see* Waters v. U.S., 311 A.2d 835 (D.C. Cir. 1973).
 The personal history of the searched student is relevant to the suspicion issue. *Compare In re* Bobby B., 218 Cal. Rptr. 253 (1985) (presence in lavatory during class hour—held sufficient), *with In re* William G., 709 P.2d 1287 (Cal. 1985) (furtive gestures—held insufficient basis for suspicion).

76. Bridgman v. New Trier H.S. Dist., 128 F.3d 146 (7th Cir. 1997).

77. *Cases not requiring probable cause:* Illinois v. Dilworth, 661 N.E.2d 310 (Ill. 1996); Cason v. Cook, 810 F.2d 188 (8th Cir. 1987); Martens v.

Dist. No. 220, 620 F. Supp. 29 (N.D. Ill. 1985).
 Cases requiring probable cause: Picha v. Wilgos, 410 F. Supp. 1214, 1219–21 (N.D. Ill. 1976); People v. Bowers, 356 N.Y.S.2d 432 (1974) (school security officer).
 Decisions that schools could act on evidence produced by a police search: Gordon J. v. Santa Ana Unified School Dist., 208 Cal. Rptr. 657 (1984); Bellnier v. Lund, 438 F. Supp. 437 (N.D. N.Y. 1977); Morale v. Grigel, 422 F. Supp. 988 (D. N.H. 1976).

78. J. Stefkovich, *Strip Searching after Williams: Reactions to the Concern for School Safety,* 93 Ed. Law Rep. 1107 (1994).

79. B.C. v. Plumas Unified School Dist., 192 F.3d 1260 (9th Cir. 1999); Horton v. Goose Creek Indep. School Dist., 690 F.2d 470 (5th Cir. 1982); Burnham v. West, 681 F. Supp. 1160 (E.D. Va. 1987); Zamora v. Pomeroy, 639 F.2d 662 (10th Cir. 1981).

80. B.C. v. Plumas, prior note.

81. *Cases upholding such searches:* Cornfield v. School District No. 230, 991 F.2d 1316, 1321 (7th Cir. 1993); Widener v. Frye, 809 F. Supp. 35 (S.D. Oh. 1992); Williams by Williams v. Ellington, 936 F.2d 881 (6th Cir. 1991).
 Cases disapproving such searches: State ex rel Galford v. Mark Anthony B., 433 S.E.2d 41 (W.Va. 1993); M.M. v. Anker, 607 F.2d 588 (2d Cir. 1979).

82. Rhodes v. Guarricino, 54 F. Supp. 2d 186 (S.D. N.Y. 1999).

83. *See, e.g.,* Flanagan v. Munger, 890 F.2d 1557 (2d Cir. 1989) (discussion of constitutional right of privacy). *But see contra:* A.M. Fed of Govt. Employees v. Dept. of Housing, 118 F.3d 786, 791 (D.C. Cir. 1997), *and* J.P. v. DeSanti, 653 F.2d 1080, 1090–1 (6th Cir. 1981).
 The cases on informational privacy are collected in R. Turkington, *Legacy of the Warren and Brandeis Article: The Emerging Unencumbered Constitutional Right to Informational Privacy,* 10 N. Ill. U. L. Rev. 479, 493–510 (1990); Note, *The Constitutional Protection of Informational Privacy,* 71 B.U.L. Rev. 133, 145–50 (1991).

84. *Re potential state constitutional grounds, see, e.g.,* People v. Stritzinger, 68 P.2d 738 (Cal. 1983).

85. *E.g.,* Merriken v. Cressman, 364 F. Supp. 913, 916 (E.D. Pa. 1973).

86. *See* Report, *School Sex and Drug Survey Angers 6th Graders' Parents,* New York Times, B-6 (May 26, 2000).

87. Pupil Protection Rights Amendment, General Education Provisions Act, Sec. 439, 20 U.S.C.A. Sex. 1232(h); 34 Code of Federal Regulations, Part 98, Sections 98.1–98.5 (7-1-99). On the inapplicability of the federal law to surveys that are not federally funded, *see* Altman v. Bedford Cent. School Dist., 45 F. Supp. 2d 368, 391 (S.D. N.Y. 1999).

88. State law variations are noted in Sargent School Dist. No. RE 33J v. Western Services Inc., 751 P.2d 56 (Colo. 1988); Webster Groves School Dist. v. Pulitzer Pub. Co., 898 F.2d 1371 (8th Cir. 1990) (barring disclosure of information hurtful to child with disability); Young v. Armstrong School Dist., 344 A.2d 738 (Pa. 1975) (citizen entitled to copy names and addresses of school parents to prepare a petition on school proposals); Hendricks v. Board of Trustees, 525 S.W.2d 930 (Tex. 1975) (taxpayer right to copy school district financial records).

89. Fay v. S. Colonie Cent. School Dist., 802 F.2d 21 (2d Cir. 1986), ruled that federal courts deciding FERPA issues should follow state court decisions under state law. *Accord:* P. Edward A. v. Williams, 696 F. Supp. 1432 (C.D. Utah 1988).

90. 20 U.S.C. § 1232(g). *See* Annot, *Validity, Construction and Application of Family Educational Rights and Privacy Act,* 112 A.L.R. Fed 1 (1993).

   The FERPA definition of educational records excludes the following: records of applicants who are not admitted to the school; personal notes of teachers that are not discussed with others; and records of treating physicians and certain law enforcement agencies.

   "Personally identifiable educational records" are those that "would make the reader . . . reasonably certain of the identity of the student." 45 C.F.R. Pt. 99 (1976). But contests can arise as to what is nonpersonal data. Sargent School Dist., note 88, *supra.* Many states have similar laws. *See, e.g.,* Bowie v. Evanston Comm. Cons. School Dist., 522 N.E.2d 669 (Ill. 1988).

   Examples of FERPA exemptions: Release of records under court order; to protect public safety; to a parent of dependent student; certain government officials, and teachers and principals for their work with the student.

   Excepted from student access: Financial records or data of parents, doctor's records, and information on which they validly waived a right of access.

91. FERPA regulations (34 C.F.R., part 99); Page v. Rotterdam-Mohonasen Central School Dist., 441 N.Y.S.2d 323 (1981).

92. Dachs v. Board of Educ., 277 N.Y.S.2d 449 (1967); Fay v. South Colonie Cent. School Dist., 802 F.2d 21 (2d Cir. 1986).

93. Strosnider v. Strosnider, 686 P.2d 981 (Ariz. 1984). *See, generally,* Annot., *Non-custodial Parent Rights re Education of Child,* 36 A.L.R. 3d 1093 (1971) and latest pkt.

94. Pesce v. J. Sterling Morton H.S. Dist. 201, 830 F.2d 789 (7th Cir. 1987).

95. Jaffee v. Redmond, 116 S. Ct. 1923 (1996).

96. Hedlund v. Superior Ct., 34 Cal. 3d 695 (1982); McIntosh v. Milano, 403 A.2d 500 (N.J. 1979); Tarasoff v. Regents of the Univ. of Cal., 551 P.2d 334 (Cal. 1976).

97. *Exclusions disapproved:* Shull v. Columbus Mun. Separate School Dist., 338 F. Supp. 1376 (N.D. Miss. 1972); Ordway v. Hargraves, 323 F. Supp. 1155 (D. Mass. 1971).

   Extracurricular activities exclusions: Beeson v. Kiowa City School Dist., 567 P.2d 801 (Colo. 1977); Bell v. Lone Oak Indep. School Dist., 507 S.W.2d 636 (Tex. 1974). *See* Indiana H.S. Athletic Assn. v. Raike, 329 N.E.2d 66 (Ind. 1975) for a survey of relevant cases.

98. Brands v. Shelton Comm. School, 671 F. Supp. 627 (N.D. Iowa 1987).

99. ABC School v. Mr. and Mrs. M., 1997 Mass. Super., 97–518, Lexis 43.

100. DeBord v. Board of Educ., 126 F.3d 1102 (8th Cir. 1997).

101. Leahy v. Leahy, 858 S.W.2d 221 (Mo. 1993); Von Tersch v. Von Tersch, 455 N.W.2d 130 (Neb. 1990); Connelly v. Connelly, 409 So. 2d 175 (Fl. 1982).

102. Evans v. Buchanan, 555 F.2d 373 (3d Cir. 1977).

103. Sheff v. O'Neill, 678 A.2d 1267 (Conn. 1996).

104. *School closures enjoined:* Fisher v. Lohr, 821 F. Supp. 1342 (D. Ariz. 1993). *School closure permitted as assisting desegregation:* Higgins v. Grand Rapids Board of Educ., 508 F.2d 779, 793–5 (6th Cir. 1974).

105. *See also* Freeman v. Pitts, 112 S. Ct. 1430 (1992); Belk v. Charlotte-Mecklenburg Board of Educ., 233 F.3d 232 (2000).

106. Board of Educ. of Okla. Pub. Schools v. Dowell, 111 S. Ct. 630 (1991).

107. Pasadena City Board of Educ. v. Spangler, 427 U.S. 424 (1976).

108. Anderson v. San Francisco Unified School Dist., 357 F. Supp. 248 (N.D. Cal. 1972); *cf.* Villanueva v. Carere, 85 F.3d 481 (10th Cir. 1996).

109. Grutter v. Bollinger, 123 S. Ct. 2325 (2003); Gratz v. Bollinger, 123 S. Ct. 2411 (2003). *See also* Regents, Univ. of California v. Bakke, 438 U.S. 912 (1978) (voiding fixed racial quota for medical school admissions).

110. *See, e.g.,* Brewer v. West Irondequoit Cent. School Dist., 212 F.3d 738, at 747 (2d Cir. 2000); Hopwood v. State of Texas, 78 F.3d 932 (5th Cir.), *cert denied,* 518 U.S. 1033 (1996); Equal Enrollment Assn. v. Board of Educ., 937 F. Supp. 700 (N.D. Ohio 1996); Tuttle v. Arlington County School Board, 189 F.3d 431 (4th Cir. 1999) (special admissions).

111. Hunter v. Regents of the Univ. of Calif., 190 F.3d 1061 (9th Cir. 1999).

112. *Discriminatory treatment:* Lee v. Washington County Board of Educ., 682 F.2d 894, 895 (11th Cir. 1982). *Segregative site selections:* Lee v. Autanga County Board of Educ., 514 F.2d 646 (5th Cir. 1975). *Segregated attendance zones:* Keyes v. School Dist. No. 1, Denver, 413 U.S. 189 (1973). *Segregative school choice plans:* Green v. County School Board, 391 U.S. 430 (1968).

113. *Cases accepting statistical evidence:* Johnson v. Transportation Agency, 480 U.S. 616 (1987) (Title VII claim); United States v. Midland Indep. School Dist., 519 F.2d 60 (5th Cir. 1975). *Case finding statistics insufficient:* Washington v. Davis, 426 U.S. 229 (1976) (constitutional claim).

114. Monteiro v. Tempe Union H.S.Dist., 158 F.3d 1022 (9th Cir. 1988).

115. Jett v. Dallas Ind. School District, 109 S. Ct. 2702 (1989); Barnes v. Gorman, 122 S. Ct. 2097 (2002).

116. *Tests upheld notwithstanding racially disproportionate results:* Quarles v. Oxford Mun. Separate School Dist., 868 F.2d 750 (5th Cir. 1989); Castaneda by Castaneda v. Pickard, 781 F.2d 456 (5th Cir. 1986); Morales v. Shannon, 516 F.2d 411 (5th Cir. 1975); Parents in Action in Special Educ. v. Hannon, 506 F. Supp. 831 (N.D. Ill. 1980).

   Tests voided as producing racially disproportionate results: Larry P. Riles, 793 F.2d 969 (9th Cir. 1984) (under Title VI and Rehabilitation Act).

   The required severity of adverse racial impact remains unresolved. *See* Morales v. Shannon, this note, *supra.*

117. "Wave of Pupils Lacking English Strains Schools," New York Times, 1 (Aug. 5, 2002).

118. United States v. Texas, 466 F.2d. 519 (5th Cir. 1976).

119. Bilingual education laws were enacted in Alaska, Massachusetts, Michigan, Arizona, Arkansas, California, Colorado, Illinois, Iowa, Maine, New Mexico, New York, Oregon, Pennsylvania, Rhode Island, and Texas, among others. Such laws are subject to continual revision.

120. Castaneda by Castaneda v. Pickard, 648 F.2d 989 (5th Cir. 1981); Aspira v. Board of Educ., 394 F. Supp. 1161 (S.D. N.Y. 1975) (consent decree); Serna v. Portales Mun. Schools, 499 F.2d 1147 (10th Cir. 1975) (under Title VI). Bilingual Educ. Act, as amended. 20 U.S.C. § 880(b).

121. Teresa P. v. Berkeley Unified School Dist., 724 F. Supp. 698 (N.D. Cal. 1989).

122. Otero v. Mesa County Valley School Dist., 408 F. Supp. 162 (D. Colo. 1975); Morales, note 116, *supra.* Note, *Bilingual Education Problems—A Problem of Substantial Numbers,* 77 U. Fordham L. Rev. 561 (1977).

123. G. Valeria v. Davis, 307 F.3d 1036 (9th Cir. 2002); Assn. of Mexican-American Educators v. State of California, 231 F.3d 572 (9th Cir. 2001).

124. United States v. Virginia, 116 S. Ct. 2264 (1996); Mississippi Univ. for Women v. Hogan, 458

U.S. 718 (1982); Garrett v. Board of Educ., 775 F. Supp. 1004 (E.D. Mich. 1991) (boys—only high school enjoined under Title IX).

125. Davis v. Monroe County Bd. of Educ., 119 S. Ct. 1661 (1999). *See also* Kinman v. Omaha Public School Dist., 171 F.3d 607 (8th Cir. 1999); Murrell v. School Dist. No. 1, 186 F.3d 1238 (10th Cir. 1999); Haines v. Metropolitan Gov't of Davidson County, 32 F. Supp. 2d 991 (M.D. Tenn. 1998); H.M. v. Jefferson County Board of Educ., 719 So. 2d 793 (Ala. 1998).

126. Soper v. Hoben, 195 F.3d 845 (6th Cir. 1999).

127. Doe v. Beaumont I.S.D., 8 F. Supp. 2d 596 (E.D. Tex. 1998).

128. Davis v. Monroe County Board of Educ., 119 S. Ct. 1661 (1999). The *Davis* ruling was anticipated by earlier lower court decisions. Murrell v. School Dist. No. 1, 186 F.3d 1239 (10th Cir. 1999); Smith v. Metropolitan School District Perry Township, 128 F.3d 1014 (7th Cir. 1997).

129. Abeyta v. Chama Ind. School Dist., 77 F.3d 1253 (10th Cir. 1996).

130. *See, e.g.,* Doe v. Board of Educ., 18 F. Supp. 2d 954 (N.D. Ill. 1998).

131. *Cf.* Schultzen v. Woodbury Central Comm'y School Dist., 187 F. Supp. 2d 1099 (N.D. Iowa 2002).

132. Alston v. Va. High School League, 176 F.R.D. 220 (W.D. Va. 1997); Roberts v. Colo. State Board of Agric., 998 F.2d 824 (10th Cir. 1993).

133. *Upheld:* Barnett v. Texas Wrestling Assn., 16 F. Supp. 2d 690 (N.S. Tex. 1998); Clark v. Ariz. Interscholastic Assn., 695 F.2d 1126 (9th Cir. 1989); Jones v. Okla. Secondary School Activities Assn., 424 F. Supp. 732 (D. Tenn. 1976). *Disapproved:* Noncomparable softball programs for girls and boys. Israel v. W. Va. Secondary Schools Activities Comm'n, 388 S.E.2d 480 (W. Va. 1989).

134. D. Alston v. Va. High School League, 176 F.R.D. 220 (W. Va. 1997); Roberts v. Colo. State Board of Agric., 998 F.2d 824 (10th Cir. 1993); Hoover v. Meiklejohn, 430 F. Supp. 164 (Colo. 1977) (Soccer). *Re* state laws, *see* Annot., *Application of State Law to Sex Discrimination in Sports,* 66 A.L.R. 3d 1262 (1975) and pkt part.

135. Kleczek v. Rhode Island Int. League, 768 F. Supp. 951 (D. R.I. 1991)(field hockey); Clark, note 133, *supra;* Ruman v. Eskew, 343 N.E.2d 806 (Ind. 1976) (tennis); Bucha v. Ill. High School Assn., 351 F. Supp. 69 (N.D. Ill. 1972) (swimming).

136. Petrie v. Ill. H.S. Assn., 394 N.E.2d 855 (Ill. 1985) (exclusion of boys from girls' volleyball team). *But see* Williams v. School Dist. of Bethlehem, 998 F.2d 168 (3d Cir. 1993) (whether field hockey is a contact sport). Note, *The Application of Title IX to School Athletic Programs,* 68 Cornell L. Rev. 222 (1983).

137. Saint v. Neb. School Activities Assn., 684 F. Supp. 626 (D. Neb. 1988) (requiring girl tryout for boys' high school wrestling team). Force v. Pierce City R-VI School Dist., 570 F. Supp. 1020 (W.D. Mo. 1983); Morris v. Michigan State Board of Educ., 472 F.2d 1207 (6th Cir. 1973) (tennis); Bednar v. Neb. School Activities Assn., 531 F.2d 922 (8th Cir. 1976); Gilpin v. Kansas State High School Activities Assn., 377 F. Supp. 1233 (D. Kan. 1973) (cross-country).

138. Force v. Pierce City, prior note. Darrin v. Gould, 540 P.2d 882 (Wash. 1975) (state ERA ruling); Opinion of the Justices, 371 N.E.2d 426 (Mass. 1977) (state ERA ruling).

139. Miami Univ. Wrestling Club v. Miami Univ., 302 F.3d 608 (6th Cir. 2002); Boulahanis v. Board of Regents, 198 F.3d (7th Cir. 1999); *cf.* Neal v. Board of Trustees of Cal. Univ., 51 Fed. Appx. 736 (9th Cir. 2002) (university reduction of roster spots in male athletics to achieve better balance of male and female athletics—upheld).

140. *See, e.g.,* Pfeiffer v. School Board for Marion Center Area, 917 F.3d 779, 783 (3d Cir. 1990); T. A. Schweitzer, *"A" Students Go to Court: Is Membership in the National Honor Society a Cognizable Legal Right?,* 50 Syracuse L. Rev. 63 (2000).

141. *Compare, e.g.,* Pfeiffer, prior note, at p. 784 (upholding disqualification), *with* cases reversing student disqualification: Wort v. Vierling, No. 82–3169, slip op. (C.D. Ill. Sept. 14, 1984); Chipman v. Grant County School Dist., 30 F. Supp. 2d 975 (E.D. Ky. 1998); Cazares v. Barber, Case No. CIV-90–0128-TUC-ACM, slip op. (D. Ariz. May 31, 1990).

142. 20 U.S.C.A. § 1400.

143. (A) In general—The term "child with a disability" means a child—

    (i)with mental retardation, hearing impairments (including deafness), speech or language impairments, visual impairments (including blindness), serious emotional disturbance (hereinafter referred to as "emotional disturbance"), orthopedic impairments, autism, traumatic brain injury, other health impairments, or specific learning disabilities. . . . (B). . . The term "child with a disability" for a child aged 3 through 9 may, at the discretion of the State and the local educational agency, include a child—

    (i) —experiencing developmental delays, as defined by the State. . . . . . . (Sec. 101 of 1977 Amendments). 20 U.S.C.A. § 1401 *et seq.*

144. Martinez v. School Board of Hillsborough County, 711 F. Supp. 1066 (M.D. Fla. 1989). Such children are also covered by §504.

145. *See, e.g.,* Seeking the Right Equation, ABA Journal (Sept. Issue 2002, at p. 48).

146. Charlie F. v. Board of Educ. of Skokie School Dist. 68, 98 F.3d 989 (7th Cir. 1996); Garro v. State of Conn., 23 F.3d 734, 737 (2d Cir. 1994).

147. Meehan v. Pachogue-Medford School, 25 F. Supp. 2d 129 (E.D.N.Y. 1998)(thwarting delays); Gadsden City Board of Educ. v. B.P., 3 F. Supp. 2d 1299 (N.D. Ala. 1998)(school safety); Weil v. Board of Elementary & Secondary Educ., 931 F.2d 1069 (5th Cir. 1991) (statutory procedures tolled as futile where district lacked necessary placement facility).

148. *See* Ridgewood Board of Educ. V. N.E. for M.E., 172 F.3d 238, 247 (3d Cir. 1999) and authorities there cited.

149. Williams v. Gering Pub. Schools, 463 N.W.2d 799 (Neb. 1990) (year-round program—required); Yaris v. Special School Dist., 728 F.2d 1005 (8th Cir. 1984); Crawford v. Pittman, 708 F.2d 1028 (5th Cir. 1983); Georgia Assn. of Retarded Citizens v. McDaniel, 511 F. Supp. 1263 (N.D. Ga. 1981) (extended school year). *See also* Abrahamson v. Hershman, 701 F.2d 233 (1st Cir. 1983) (round-the-clock training for retarded child).

150. Rettig v. Kansas City School Dist., 720 F.2d, at 466–7.

151. *Re IDEA:* Brookhart v. Ill. State Board of Educ., 697 F.2d 179, 1983 (7th Cir. 1983); Board of Educ. v. Ambach, 458 N.Y.S.2d 680, 684–5 (1982). *Re Section 504:* Southeastern Comm. College v. Davis, 442 U.S. 397, 411–2 (1979).

152. Ojai Unified School Dist. v. Jackson, 4 F.3d 1467 (9th Cir. 1994) (blind student housing 80 miles from parents' residence, held a reimburseable related-service expense).
    Facilities modification for transportation: Dubois v. Connecticut State Board of Educ., 727 F.2d 44 (2nd Cir. 1984); Hurry v. Jones, 734 F.2d 829 (1st Cir. 1984); Hawaii Dept. of Educ. v. Kathryn D., 727 F.2d 809 (9th Cir. 1983).

153. Zobrest v. Catalina Foothills School Dist., 509 U.S. 1 (1993). *See also* Woolcott v. State Board of Educ., 351 N.W.2d 601 (Mich. 1984).

154. Burlington, School Comm'ee, Twn. of Burlington v. Dept. of Educ., 471 U.S. 359 (1985); Anderson v. Thompson, 658 F.2d at pp. 1213–4 (emergency change of placement); Christopher N. v. McDaniel, 569 F. Supp., at p. 294. *Compare:* Marvin H. v. Austin Indep. School Dist., 714 F.2d 1348, 1356 (5th Cir. 1983) and authorities cited there.

155. School Committee, Twn. of Burlington v. Dept. of Educ., 471 U.S. 359 (1985); Florence County School Dist. v. Carter, 114 S. Ct. 361 (1993); Muller v. Comm'ee on Special Educ., 145 F.3d 95 (2d Cir. 1998); Matthew J. v. Massachusetts Dept. of Educ., 989 F. Supp. 380 (D. Ma. 1998).

156. The different tests adopted by the Third, Fifth and Eleventh Circuits on one hand, and the Fourth, Sixth, and Eighth Circuits on the other, are explained in Sacramento City Un. School Dist. v. Rachel H., 14 F.3d 1398, 1403–4 (9th Cir. 1994). A court may require only part-time mainstreaming. Springdale School Dist. v. Grace, 693 F.2d 41, 43 (8th Cir. 1982).
    Compare, e.g., Pinkerton v. Moye, 509 F. Supp. 107, 112–4 (W.D. Pa. 1981), *with* Espino v. Besteiro, next note.

157. *Compare* Pinkerton v. Moye, 509 F. Supp. 107, 112–4 (W.D. Pa. 1981), *with* Espino v. Besteiro, 520 F. Supp. 905 (S.D. Tex. 1981) *rev'd* on other grounds, 708 F.2d 1002 (5th Cir. 1983) (mainstreaming ordered, though it required air conditioning of the classroom).

158. Hartmann v. Loudoun County Board of Educ., 118 F.3d 996 (4th Cir. 1997).

159. Springdale School Dist. v. Grace, 693 F.2d 41, 43 (8th Cir. 1982).

160. The Second, Fifth, Seventh, Eighth, and Ninth Circuit Courts of Appeal held that special education services are not required at private school sites if they are made available elsewhere. KDM v. Reedsport School Dist., 196 F.3d 1046 (9th Cir. 1999); K.R. by M.R. v. Anderson Community School Corp., 125 F.3d 1017 (7th Cir. 1997); Russman v. City of Watervliet, 150 F.3d 219 (2d Cir. 1998); Cefalu v. E. Baton Rouge Parish School Board, 117 F.3d 231 (5th Cir. 1997). The Eighth Circuit held that the 1977 amendments gave no individual right to related services at a private site, but only proportional funding for the same class of students. The Tenth Circuit held that such services are required, but that the district need only pay the average cost of such service in a public school setting. Fowler v. Unified School Dist., 128 F.3d 1431 (10th Cir. 1997); Peter v. Wedl, 155 F.3d 992 (8th Cir. 1998). The Sixth Circuit upheld provision of special services to a child with a disability at a private school. Peck v. Lansing School Dist., 148 F.3d 619 (6th Cir. 1998). *See also* Morton Comm. Unit School Dist., 152 F.3d 583 (7th Cir. 1998).

161. S-1 v. Turlington, 635 F.2d 342, 347 (5th Cir. 1981); Thomas v. Davison Academy, 846 F. Supp. 611 (M.D. Tenn. 1994) (reversing expulsion for conduct attributable to handicap); Kaelin v. Grubbs, 682 F.2d 595 (6th Cir. 1982), and cases cited there.

162. 20 U.S.C. § 1415(k). Under the prior law, the Supreme Court held that a suspension of more than 10 days constituted a change in placement subject to "stay put," and statutory due process procedures. Honig v. Doe, 484 U.S. 305 (1988).

163. *See, e.g.,* Fowler v. Unified School Dist., 128 F.3d 1431 (10th Cir. 1997).

164. Strosnider v. Strosnider, 686 P.2d 981 (Ariz. 1984). *See, generally,* Annot., *Non-custodial Parent Rights re Education of Child,* 36 A.L.R. 3d 1093 (1971) and latest pkt part.

165. Leahy v. Leahy, 858 S.W.2d 221, 226 (Mo. 1993); Von Tersch v. Von Tersch, 455 N.W.2d 130 (Neb. 1990); Connelly v. Connelly, 409 So.2d 175 (Fla. 1982).

166. 457 U.S. 202 210 (1982).

167. Martinez v. Bynum, 461 U.S. 321 (1983).

168. San Antonio Ind. School Dist. v. Rodriguez, 411 U.S. 1 (1973).

169. Abbott v. Burke, 710 A.2d 450 (N.J. 1998); Claremont School District v. Governor, 138 N.H. 183, 635 A.2d 1375 (1993); McDuffy v. Secretary of the Executive Office of Education, 415 Mass. 545, 615 N.E.2d 516 (1993); New Haven v. State Board of Educ., 228 Conn. 699, 638 A.2d 589 (1994). For review of the laws in each state, *see* ACIR, Symposium on the Property Tax, 19 Intergovernmental Perspective 10 (1993); Underwood and Sparkman, *School Finance Litigation,* 14 Harv. J.L. & Pub. Policy, 517 (1991).

CHAPTER 8

The Pyramid of Discrimination Remedies

☞ **CHAPTER OUTLINE**

I. Background Note
II. Remedies for Violation of Constitutional Rights
III. Remedies Under Specific Discrimination Statutes
    A. Federal Aid Statutes
        1. The FERPA Statute
        2. Titles VI and IX
        3. The IDEA Statute
    B. Employment Discrimination Statutes
        1. Title VII
        2. ADA and Rehabilitation Acts
        3. Age Discrimination in Employment Act
    C. Equal Rights Statute (42 U.S.C. § 1981)
IV. Remedies Under 42 U.S.C. § 1983
    A. Requisites for § 1983 Relief
    B. School District Defenses
        1. School District Policy or Custom
        2. Causation by Inaction
        3. Special Relationship Claims
        4. School District Immunity Under § 1983
    C. Individual Defenses
        1. Qualified Personal Immunity

V. Recovery of Attorneys' Fees
VI. Eleventh Amendment Immunity Defenses
    A. Statutes Abrogating Immunity
    B. Statutes Not Abrogating Immunity

CASES

8.1 Gonzaga Univ. v. Doe, 122 S. Ct. 2268 (2002)
8.2 Boulahanis v. Board of Regents, 198 F.3d 633 (7th Cir. 1999)
8.3 Walker v. District of Columbia, 969 F. Supp. 794 (D. D.C. 1997)
8.4 Riddick et al. v. School Board, 238 F.3d 518 (4th Cir. 2000)
8.5 Doe v. Board of Educ., 18 F. Supp. 2d 954 (N.D. Ill. 1998)
8.6 Board of Trustees v. Garrett, 121 S. Ct. 955 (2001)
8.7 Buckhannon Bd. and Care Home, Inc., v. W. Va. Dept. of Health and Human Resources et al., 121 S. Ct. 1835 (2001)

ENDNOTES

BACKGROUND NOTE

This chapter is concerned solely with the questions that arise in suits for monetary damages under the federal laws that were discussed in Chapters 6 and 7. As previously noted, courts may always grant equitable relief (injunctions, affirmative action decrees) independently of other laws, as part of their independent equity powers. They do not, however, have independent powers or jurisdiction to grant money judgments, and there is no federal common law for such remedies. Monetary recoveries must be authorized by Congress. The interpretations by courts of each civil rights statute, as to whether Congress intended it to allow, limit, or bar monetary recoveries, thus become crucial.

While Chapters 6 and 7 indicated in a general way what monetary remedies are directly authorized by each discrimination statute, this chapter more fully explains not only the remedies directly authorized by a particular statute, but the legal consequences where more than one statute applies to the same discriminatory conduct, giving rise to potential monetary claims under more than one law. In addressing such questions, the following discussion necessarily refers to some technical court doctrines. These are not presented to be mastered in technical detail, but to explain how the major federal discrimination laws set limits to the respective rights and defenses of school districts, their officials, schoolteachers, and staff with regard to monetary claims for civil rights injuries.

The following two issues are basic and common to all suits by individuals for monetary damages:

1. Does the sued-upon law expressly or impliedly authorize courts to grant monetary damages to a private party for its violation? A civil rights plaintiff must establish that Congress intended to authorize a money remedy. As seen in past chapters, some discrimination laws do not create such a private right to recover damages, and those that do, do not authorize a claimant to recover *punitive* damages (as distinguished from compensatory or fixed damages) from government entities such as school districts,[1] although a private party may recover punitive damages under certain statutes for malicious or reckless discrimination. [*Bains LLC v. Arco Products Co.*, 220 F. Supp. 2d 1193 (W.D. Wash. 2002)]

2. Where the same conduct raises claims under more than one remedial law, did Congress intend that only one of them govern the claim, i.e., provide the sole and exclusive remedy, so that the relief under one of the statutes "precludes" or "preempts" recovery under another statute? The answer depends, in part, on whether the terms or enforcement scheme of an allegedly exclusive statute convinces a court that Congress intended it to "preempt" or "preclude" other legal relief.[2]

As with all cases, the foregoing questions may be compressed into one practical, three-part question: *Who* can sue *whom* for *what?*

As to *who* can sue, a statute (such as the FERPA educational records law) that is construed to limit its enforcement by a government agency creates no *private* party "right" to sue for money damages. Similarly, if a court construes a statute (such as the ADA) to protect only specified disabilities, persons with unspecified disabilities have no "right" to claim or sue for money damages. Thus, even beneficiaries of a statute may not be persons *who* can sue for relief.

As to *whom can be sued,* some laws (such as Titles VII and IX) subject only school districts and not individuals to liability, while others (such as § 1981 and § 1983) allow suit against individuals as well. Finally, as hereafter noted, the reviewed laws do not allow the same defenses and immunities for school district entitities as for individuals.

Part II of this chapter considers the monetary remedies that are allowed for *constitutional* violations. Part III considers the monetary remedies that are allowed by each of the *statutes* there discussed. Part IV discusses the availability of alternative monetary relief under the special remedial statute, 42 U.S.C. § 1983 (hereafter § 1983). Part V discusses the allowance of attorney fee recoveries under various fee-shifting statutes. Part VI discusses the allowance or denial of immunities from suit which are derived from the Eleventh Amendment to the Constitution.

As hereafter noted, the current case law is not settled on many questions, either because they have not worked their way through the courts for decision, or because different courts in different federal circuits have issued conflicting decisions which have yet to be resolved by the United States Supreme Court.

REMEDIES FOR VIOLATION OF CONSTITUTIONAL RIGHTS

Monetary recovery for constitutional violations is provided by the § 1983 statute. The operational requisites of that law are discussed later on pages 394–95.[3]

REMEDIES UNDER SPECIFIC DISCRIMINATION STATUTES

As noted in Chapter 6, the reach of each civil rights statute turns on two separate questions. First, did the Constitution authorize Congress to enact the statute in question? Second, if so, did Congress intend the pleaded statute to cover the alleged civil rights injury? The authority of Congress to enact civil rights laws is drawn from several Constitutional provisions, each of which confers a different scope of legislative power. For example, the commerce power [Art. I, § 8, Clause 3] relates only to discrimination in activities that affect interstate commerce; while the spending power [Art. I, § 8, Clause 1] relates only to laws that grant and impose conditions on federal aid to the states; while the power to enforce Fourteenth Amendment rights [§ 5 of the Fourteenth Amendment][4] relates only to enforcement of constitutional, and not of statutory, civil rights. See Appendix 1 at the end of this book. These different sources of Congressional legislative power produce different limits on the remedies which Congress may enact for particular civil rights violations.

Federal Aid Statutes

Under these "spending" power laws, Congress imposed conditions that require aid recipients to refrain from specified types of discrimination. Whether Congress intended a particular spending power law to authorize private parties to sue for discrimination violations is often unclear, and has drawn conflicting interpretations from different courts.

The FERPA Statute

The question whether Congress intended the FERPA law to confer a private remedy for its violation was finally settled by the Supreme Court in 2002. In *Gonzaga Univ. v. Doe*, 122 S. Ct. 2268 (2002) (Case 8.1 at the end of this chapter)[5] the Court ruled that FERPA did not create a private right to recover money damages for its violation. While the Court noted that Congress could, under its Spending Power, enact a private remedy for FERPA violation, such an intent would not be found unless the statute authorizes a private remedy by unambiguous language or by a scheme that clearly implies such a private right:

> Where the text and structure of a statute provide no indication that Congress intended to create new individual rights, there is not basis for a private suit: whether under § 1983 or under an implied right of action.

The plaintiff in *Gonzaga* claimed that his university unlawfully disclosed his educational records without his consent in violation of the FERPA statute. Had the student claimed that the unauthorized disclosure of his record violated a *constitutional* right, a § 1983 claim would exist for deprivation of a constitutional right, but no constitutional (privacy) claim to nondisclosure of educational records was or could be there made.

Titles VI and IX

While Titles VI and IX were also enacted under Congress' spending powers, the Supreme Court found that Title IX, unlike the FERPA law, directly and unambiguously created a private suit and remedy for its violation. See the *Davis* case (Case 7.10). It later noted this difference in the *Gonzaga* opinion.

As noted in preceding chapters, Title VI and Title IX do not render a school district automatically liable for every act of discrimination by its employees or supervisors (as might be the case under state law torts doctrine).

Only if that conduct was fostered by an official policy or custom of the aided school district may it be held liable.[6] In order to establish an actionable policy or custom, say for a teacher's sexual abuse of a high school student, the claimant must show that:

> an official of the district who at a minimum has *authority to address* the alleged discrimination and *to institute corrective measures* . . . has *actual knowledge* of discrimination in the recipient's program and *fails adequately to respond*. We think, moreover, that *the response must amount to deliberate indifference* to discrimination. . . . The premise in other words is an official decision by the recipient [district] not to remedy the violation. [*Gebser v. Lago Vista Ind. School Dist.*, 118 S. Ct. 1989, 1999 (1998)] (Emphasis added)

This standard obviously requires more than supervisory negligence, whether in failing to discover an employee's sexually abusive conduct or predatory history, or in failing to adopt the best preventive policies to deter sexual harassment.[7]

Employment Discrimination.   Where a Title VI or Title IX violation involves employment discrimination, it appears that the recovery would be limited to the damages specified by Title VII, discussed below, because Title VII also covers employment discrimination and it provides a comprehensive scheme of enforcement that implies a congressional intent that Title VII remedies be exclusive of any other statutory remedy for the same employment discrimination.

Nonemployment Discrimination.   As settled in the above-discussed *Davis* case, a student could recover damages for sexual harassment under Title IX (and inferentially for racial discrimination under Title VI). Here also, the fact that these Titles directly authorize monetary remedies raises the question whether Congress intended them to *preclude* and preempt alternative suit under § 1983 for the same violation. The courts are still sorting out these preemption issues.[8] Some have expressed a statute's exclusivity by stating that the more general relief provided by § 1983 is "subsumed" in legal relief that is directly authorized elsewhere. The *Boulahanis* opinion (Case 8.2) provides a convenient review of these issues.

Where a statute does not expressly authorize recovery of punitive or penal damages for violations of aid conditions, the Supreme Court ruled that it would be unfair to imply an intent to impose punitive damage liability on federal aid recipients as the law did not give them fair notice that their acceptance of federal funds would expose them to extraordinary monetary penalties.[9] That reasoning would apply equally to violations of Titles VI and IX.

The IDEA Statute

The IDEA law on the education of children with handicaps is unique and not comparable to broader federal spending statutes. Its affirmative educational requirements and provision for different benefits under its different parts have no parallel in other spending statutes.

Equitable Relief. As originally enacted, IDEA provided for *equitable* relief only, including court orders to provide compensatory education and reimbursements to parents for their expenses to obtain IDEA benefits that were due but wrongfully denied their child.[10] Such reimbursements are considered equitable cost recoveries and not legal monetary damages.

Legal Relief. Congress amended the IDEA expressly to authorize a private right to recover monetary damages for IDEA violations by way of a § 1983 suit. See the opinion in *Walker* (Case 8.3); also see *Frazier v. Fairhaven School Committee*, 276 F.3d 52, at 59 (1st Cir. 2002) and authorities there discussed.

Attorneys' Fees. A separate provision of the IDEA authorizes courts to award attorneys' fees to a parent who prevails in a suit for equitable or legal relief. The special requirements for fee recovery under this and other fee-shifting statutes are discussed later in this chapter.

Exhaustion of IDEA Administrative Remedies. A party must exhaust the administrative procedures specified by the IDEA before seeking court relief unless excused for reasons hereafter noted. However, where a party brings a § 1983 suit for IDEA violations in order to recover monetary damages, the federal courts are divided on the need to exhaust IDEA administrative remedies before instituting the § 1983 suit. The courts of three federal ciruits (Third, Sixth, and Ninth Circuits) held that the IDEA exhaustion provisions do not apply to money damage suits, while those of three other circuits (First, Seventh, and Eleventh Circuits) held that the IDEA exhaustion provisions do apply to such actions.[11]

However, even in jurisdictions where exhaustion is required, courts may still exempt a party from the exhaustion requirement on showing that the pursuit of administrative relief would be "futile" or would defeat the law's purposes. For example, exhaustion is not required when (a) the relevant administrative body has refused to afford a timely IDEA hearing or (b) the assigned administrative decision maker is unable to provide an essential remedy, or (c) the official denial of the IDEA benefits is based on a clear error of law.[12] Courts may differ in their judgments whether or not administrative procedures would be futile in particular circumstances. Indeed a court may find that exhaustion is required for one IDEA claim but is excused for a different IDEA claim in the same lawsuit.[13]

When parties bring suit under the ADA and Rehabilitation Act to obtain the same relief that is provided by the IDEA, some courts have held that the peculiar IDEA exhaustion requirements also apply to those claims.[14]

The *Walker* case (Case 8.3) provides a good review of the issues raised by overlapping remedial statutes.

Employment Discrimination Statutes

Title VII

Where conduct concurrently violates Title VII rights and a *constitutional* right, courts have, with limited special exceptions, found that Title VII does not preclude suit under § 1983 for deprivation of the *constitutional* right.[15] But where concurrent statutory (but not a constitutional) claims are based on the same conduct, a majority of courts also agree that Title VII remedies for that conduct are exclusive and that Title VII precludes suit under other statutes, including suits under § 1983.[16] In 1991 Congress amended Title VII to authorize additional recoveries, including punitive damages against *private employers* for *intentional* employment discrimination, but not against state subdivisions, such as school districts.[17]

ADA and Rehabilitation Acts

Different parts of the ADA and the Rehabilitation Act provide different remedies for discrimination in employment on one hand, and for nonemployment discrimination on the other. The standards for *employment discrimination* under these laws are the same as those under Title VII.[18] For *nonemployment discrimination* claims, Congress expressly provided that ADA relief shall be the same as that allowed under Title VI. Therefore, the damage limits set by the Supreme Court for Title VI actions also govern nonemployment discrimination claims under the ADA.

Since Title I of the ADA only applies to employers and § 504 of the Rehabilitation Act only applies to federal aid recipients, those laws subject only school districts and not private parties to liability. Moreover, these laws protect only participants who may benefit from a federally aided school activity. For this reason, a businessman could not sue a city for lost business due to the city's alleged discrimination against his patrons.[19]

The remedies provided by the ADA and Rehabilitation Act are exclusive, and parties may not seek alternative relief for their violation under other statutes.[20]

Age Discrimination in Employment Act

The ADEA directly authorizes private suit for monetary damages by age discrimination victim. The majority of courts have held that ADEA remedies are exclusive and preclude suit for like discrimination under § 1983, but a few courts have taken a different view.[21] The majority rulings are consistent with the interpretive guidelines issued by the Supreme Court in the above-discussed *Gonzaga* case (Case 8.1).

Equal Rights Statute (42 U.S.C. § 1981)

A private suit to recover monetary damages for violation of § 1981 (racial discrimination) that does not involve employment discrimination may be brought under § 1983 against a *school district,* [22] but the circuit courts are divided on the question whether § 1981 authorizes recovery against a *private* party, in addition to government entities for such discrimination.[23]

A § 1981 claim for employment discrimination will probably be held to be preempted by Title VII which covers like employment discrimination. Nonetheless, one court suggested that a § 1981 claimant might try to avoid the Title VII bar simply by not pleading a Title VII claim and pleading only a § 1981 claim.[24] That suggestion seems overly simplistic.

REMEDIES UNDER 42 U.S.C. § 1983

This unique law creates only a form of suit to obtain remedy rights that are created elsewhere. It reads:

> Every *person* who, *under color of* any statute, ordinance, regulation, custom, or usage *of any State* . . . subjects or causes to be subjected, any citizen . . . or other person . . . to the *deprivation of any rights* . . . *secured by the Constitution and laws,* shall be liable to the party injured in an action at law, suit in equity . . . for redress. (Emphasis added) [42 U.S.C. § 1983]

As one court explained:

> [§ 1983]. . . [P]rovides a remedy for the violation of rights created elsewhere. As the Supreme Court made clear . . . § 1983 provides a remedy for actions under color of law which contravene federally protected rights, whether those rights derive from the Constitution or from a federal statute. [*Day v. Wayne County Board of Auditors*, 749 F.2d 1199, 1202 (6th Cir. 1984)]

The current case law points to the following conclusions. A § 1983 suit is generally allowed unless the terms or structure of a right-creating statute indicate an intent, expressed or implied, to deny relief under § 1983.

Section 1983 suits may generally be brought for deprivation of *constitutional* rights, except when the constitutional injury arises from violations of the IDEA, and possibly of § 1981, for which suit must be brought directly under the violated statute. The right to bring a suit under § 1983 for violation of a federal *statutory* right depends on whether the right-creating statute authorized resort to a § 1983 suit. Resort to a § 1983 suit is not allowed (is preempted by) statutory claims under the following substantive rights statutes which provide direct and *exclusive* remedies: Title VI, Title IX, Title VII, the ADA, and the ADEA. Even as so confined, § 1983 litigation remains a very significant source of civil rights litigation, since many civil rights suits allege both constitutional and statutory violations.

Requisites for § 1983 Relief

The key terms of the § 1983 law (italicized in the preceding quote), as construed by the courts, have specialized meanings. For example, as used in § 1983 the word "persons" covers school districts and other state *subdivisions*[25] (except in the rare instances where a school district acts as a direct arm of the state). But "persons" does not include a state government or state officials when acting on behalf of the state.[26] Section 1983 also covers private persons, but only if they acted "under color of" state law. The "color of law" concept is further analyzed in the later section titled "Individual Defenses."

In order to recover against a *school district* or against its school board (which is treated as a suit against the district and not against the members personally[27]), a plaintiff must show a *deprivation* of federal right, that was *caused by* a school district's *policy or custom* and not merely by someone's personal misconduct.[28] But in order to recover against a *private individual*, a plaintiff need only show that the individual's action was taken under "color of law" whether or not that action was linked with an official school district policy or custom, and whether or not he was officially authorized to take the action for which he is sued.[29] The § 1983 law also differentiates between immunity defenses. As later explained, school districts are denied immunity, but individuals are allowed immunity in limited circumstances. The following opinions illustrate these principles.

RIDDICK ET AL., v. SCHOOL BOARD
238 F.3d 518 (4th Cir. 2000)

*[**Focus Note.** Members of a women's high school track team brought a § 1983 suit against the city school board, school officials, and former coach for the coach's secret video recording of them in various stages of undress. Although agreeing that those actions clearly abused the students' privacy rights, the court affirmed dismissal of the suit against the school board. The following opinion points up the proof problems which § 1983 claimants face in trying to establish what individuals may establish a school district policy with respect to alleged misconduct, and what conduct by school supervisors amounts to actionable "deliberate indifference" rather than nonactionable negligence with regard to individual misconduct.]*

KING, CIRCUIT JUDGE:

* * *

In order to properly . . . consider this appeal, it is necessary to understand the applicable legal authorities. . . . First, it is well established that a municipality cannot be held liable simply for employing a tortfeasor. *Monell v. Dept. of Social Services of City of New York*, 436 U.S. 658, 691 . . . (1978). On the other hand, a municipality may be subject to liability . . . if the alleged injury was caused by an identifiable municipal policy or custom. *Board of the County Comm'rs of Bryan County v. Brown*, 520 U.S. 397 . . . (1997). A government policy or custom need not have received formal approval through the municipality's official decisionmaking channels. . . . . . . [T]he "official policy" requirement was "intended to distinguish acts of the municipality from acts of employees . . . , and thereby make clear that municipal liability is limited to action for which the municipality is actually responsible." *Pembaur v. City of Cincinnati*, 475 U.S. 469, 479 . . . (1986).

Of course, not every decision by every municipal official will subject a municipality to section 1983 liability. Rather, "[m]unicipal liability attaches only where the decisionmaker possesses final authority to establish municipal policy with respect to the action ordered." *Pembaur*, 475 U.S. at 481. . . . To qualify as a "final policymaking official," a municipal official must have the responsibility and authority to implement *final* municipal policy with respect to a particular course of action. *Id.* at 482–83, [emphasis added]. . . . . . . Therefore, to impose municipal liability on the Board, the Riddick plaintiffs must identify municipal officials with "final policymaking authority" to implement the alleged policy of "acquiescence" with respect to Crute's conduct.

The question of who possesses final policymaking authority is one of state law. *Pembaur*, 475 U.S. at 483. . . . . . . Pursuant to Va. Code Ann. . . . the Board retains exclusive final authority over matters concerning the discipline of school employees. . . .

Although the Riddick plaintiffs correctly assert that final policymaking authority may be delegated, . . . there was no showing that the Board delegated any such authority in this case. While the superintendent and other school officials have limited authority to investigate complaints against teachers and to implement disciplinary policy, all *final* personnel decisions . . . including decisions to terminate employees—are subject to final review by the Board. When a municipal official's discretionary action "is subject to review by the municipality's authorized policymakers, they have retained the authority to measure the official's conduct for conformance with their policies." *Praprotnik*, 485 U.S. at 127. . . . . . .

Because the Board retained the final "say-so" on personnel matters, Judge Smith correctly concluded that the Board cannot be subjected to municipal liability based on the decisions of the superintendent and principal.

. . . A municipality is not subject to section 1983 liability simply because a claimant is able to identify conduct attributable to the municipality. Rather, "[t]he plaintiff must also demonstrate that, through its *deliberate* conduct, the municipality was the 'moving force' behind the injury alleged." *Bryan County,* 520 U.S. at 404. . . . Accordingly, . . . a claimant must first show that "a municipal decision reflects *deliberate indifference* to the risk that a violation . . . follow the decision." *Id.* at 411. . . . If a section 1983 claimant can demonstrate the requisite degree of culpability, she must then show "a direct causal link between the municipal action and the deprivation of federal rights." *Id.* at 404 . . . .

GERNETZKE v. KENOSHA UNIFIED SCHOOL DISTRICT

274 F.3d 464 (7th Cir. 2001)

* * *

Monell v. Department of Social Services, 436 U.S. 658, 690, 694 (1978), holds that the doctrine of respondeat superior may not be used to fasten liability on a local government in a suit under section 1983. . . .

. . . So the plaintiffs in this case cannot prevail against the **school district** (Bold emphasis added) by showing merely that the superintendent of the district and the principal of their school, acting within the scope of [their] . . . employment and therefore under color of state law. . . . They must show that the district itself, which is to say the officials or official boards that constitute the relevant final decisionmaking authority . . . was directly responsible for the deprivation. *Horwitz v. Board of Education,* 260 F.3d 602, 619 (7th Cir. 2001).

This standard for municipal liability is often referred to as liability for "policy or custom," . . . . It doesn't matter what *form* the action of the responsible authority that injures the plaintiff takes. It might be an ordinance, a regulation, an executive policy, or an executive act (such as firing the plaintiff). The question is whether the promulgator, or the actor, as the case may be—in other words, the decisionmaker—was at the apex of authority for the action in question. An executive official who rather than making policy merely implements legislative policy acts merely as a delegate . . . , and his act is therefore not the act of the municipality itself for purposes of liability under section 1983.

The bearing of delegation . . . turns out to be critical in this case. The final decisionmaking authority of the school district is lodged in the district's school board, but the board has promulgated regulations that delegate the administration of the five high schools . . . to the principal of each school. This delegation, the plaintiffs argue, makes the principal the final decisionmaker. . . . That cannot be right. . . . *Every* public employee, including the policeman on the beat and the teacher in the public school, exercises authority ultimately delegated to him or her by their public employer's supreme governing organs. . . . [A] teacher does not have to consult anyone before flunking a student. That is a perfectly good use of the word "final" in ordinary conversation but it does not fit the cases. . . . . . . School superintendents, principals, and teachers in Wisconsin do not have final authority in this sense, Wis. Stat. § 120.13(b)(1); . . . Delegation is not direction; authorization is not command; permission does not constitute the permittee the final policymaking authority. Only the delegation ("conferral" would be a better term) of final authority makes the "delegate" the final authority. *City of St. Louis v. Praprotnik, supra,* 485 U.S. at 126–27. . . .

It is true that by adopting an employee's action as its own (what is called "ratification"), a public employer becomes the author of the action for purposes of liability under section 1983. . . . The plaintiffs argue that ratification occurred here when after they brought this suit the school board refused to direct the principal of their school to alter his response to their demand. The argument if accepted would convert every public employee's action . . . into the action of the employer. . . . From the plaintiff's standpoint it would be a case of "heads I win, tails you lose." The plaintiff would ask the employer for relief and if the employer granted it would not have to sue, while the employer who refused to grant the relief requested would be punished by being deemed to consent to the application of the doctrine of respondeat superior. *Deliberate* inaction might be convincing evidence of delegation of final decision-making authority, or of ratification, . . . but there is no evidence of that here.

* * *

School District Defenses

The principal defense which school districts raise in § 1983 suits are (1) whether the claimant has shown an actionable official school policy or custom, as distinguished from negligence; and if proven, whether that policy or custom caused the injury to a federal right[30]; and (2) whether a school district is entitled to immunity from suit.

School District Policy or Custom

As noted in the above opinions, school district policy may be created in different ways, i.e., by formal school board resolutions and regulations; or by decisions of individuals who have legal authority to make a *final* policy for the district[31]; whether by affirmative conduct or by passive conduct that amounts to a policy of "deliberate indifference". A court may, in appropriate circumstances, find that deliberate indifference expresses a school policy of permitting an injury to a federal right, even though a policy-making individual did not affirmatively foster the misconduct.

To establish "deliberate indifference" liability, the claimant must show several linked elements, namely, that the threats of injury, were either *known* or reasonably discoverable by the authorized policy maker; that the policy-maker's response amounted to "deliberate indifference", and that such indifference provided an affirmative *causative* link to injuries resulting from the ignored threats.[32] Each of these links involve questions of degree, i.e., the sufficiency of notice of a threat; the inadequate nature or duration of the response, and a sufficient, though not exclusive, causal connection to the threatened harm. In student suits against a school district for sexual assault by others, the finding or denial of deliberate indifference has turned largely on specific case circumstances.[33]

As noted above, policy-making authority may be delegated to school superiors, but not all supervisors are so delegated. A school principal's order to make an unconstitutional student search did not establish a school policy or custom, since his decision merely attempted to carry out a school security policy that itself did not authorize unconstitutional searches. Nor, as above noted, does a teacher's sexually abusive conduct suffice to establish a policy of the school district,[34] unless a person authorized to set school district policy or custom had sufficient notice of it and had a reasonable opportunity to take corrective action and failed to do so. The *Doe* case (Case 8.5) illustrates the burdens of proving these essential elements.

A school practice that is well settled may ripen into a custom that has the same force as a school policy for the purpose of establishing a basis for § 1983 liability, even though the custom was not formally or officially approved as a school policy.[35] Here also courts must decide whether a course of conduct was of a sufficient nature, clarity, and duration to support a finding of a school custom for § 1983 purposes.

Under the foregoing standards, a district was held not liable for a bus driver's assault of student passengers as his action was not taken pursuant to an official policy or custom, nor could supervisor carelessness alone support a finding of an actionable policy or custom.[36] Where a supervisor negligently failed to carry out the district's security policy of screening school entrants for weapons, the district's security policy could not be held to have caused the resultant use of the smuggled weapon.[37]

Causation by Inaction

The required causal link between a school policy and a plaintiff's injury is more difficult to prove in cases where a plaintiff seeks to demonstrate that the injury resulted from inaction, i.e., proving a positive fact from a negative circumstance. The Supreme Court noted that difficulty in its lead case on causation in § 1983 claims:

> Thus our first inquiry . . . is the question whether there is a *direct causal link* between a . . . policy or custom, and the alleged [right] . . . deprivation. The inquiry

is a difficult one; one that has left this Court deeply divided in a series of cases . . . , one that is the principal focus of our decision again today. (Emphasis added) [*City of Canton v. Harris*, 489 U.S. 378 (1989)]

The student suicide case in Chapter 7 (Case 7.1) further illustrates the bounds of deliberate indifference culpability.

Special Relationship Claims

A fairly new theory of school district liability under § 1983 which skirts the need to prove an actionable school policy asserts that by reason of their special relationships with students entrusted to their care, school districts have a duty to protect students in their custody from conduct that infringes their constitutional right to bodily security and safety, and that failure to do so, especially in cases of sexual assault or abuse by school personnel, deprives the student victims of federal rights. The case career of this "special relationship" theory, which arose from mounting instances of school violence, sexual abuse, and student suicides, is explored in Chapter 7, particularly the *Hasenfus* case (Case 7.1), which outlines the current limitations on that theory.

School District Immunity Under § 1983

The Supreme Court has flatly ruled that school districts may not claim any governmental immunity from a § 1983 suit, and further that they may not avail themselves of any immunity defenses which may be allowed to their officers or agents.[38]

Individual Defenses

The personal liability of individuals under § 1983 rests on the independent ground that they acted under "color of law", whether or not their actions express a school policy or custom. The "color of law" foundation may be established in three ways, namely, (1) that the individual purported to be exercising a legal power traditionally exercised by a government entity such as a school district or a state education agency; (2) that there existed a close nexus or relationship between the private actor and the school district or government agency (for example, an off-time policeman, acting as a security guard, uses his police car and police weapon to chase and shoot a robbery suspect); or (3) that the actor had acted under compulsion of the law.[39]

Under the second and third tests, school superiors and schoolteachers act under "color of law" when their acts fall within the zone of their job authority, even if their action contravenes official school policy. The "color of law" test thus makes it possible that identical teacher conduct in different circumstances will be deemed to be under color of law in one set of circumstances, but not in the other set of circumstances. For example, a bus driver could be held personally liable under § 1983 for physical or sexual abuse of students during a school term,[40] while a teacher would not be liable under § 1983 for sexually molesting a student during the summer when the school was in recess.[41] A teacher at one school was not required by her school employment to report child abuse by a teacher at another school, and therefore could not be said to have acted under "color of law" in failing to report that abuse.[42] Nor could a school supervisor who had no authority over an offending employee be found to have acted under "color of law" in ignoring that employee's misconduct and thus could not be held liable under § 1983.[43]

The *Hasenfus* case reported in Chaper 7 (Case 7.1) also added an instructive note on the difference between policy-based school district liability and color-of-law-based personal liability. *Hasenfus* cites a decision of the Tenth Circuit Court which allowed a parent to pursue a § 1983 claim against the school principal and counselor personally, though not against the school district. The plaintiff there alleged that the individuals actively created the risk of a student suicide by exercising their "color of law" authority of sending him home without notifying the parents, which was contrary to school policy, even though that student had earlier threatened to kill himself.[44]

Qualified Personal Immunity

In contrast to the denial of any school district immunity from a § 1983 suit, school superiors and employees have a limited, qualified personal immunity from § 1983 suits if they show that they had *no reason to know* that their conduct interfered with a federal right at the time of their alleged wrongful act or omission.[45] If the asserted federal right was not then *clearly established* in law so that a reasonable person would not have reason to know that his or her conduct deprived a claimant of a federal right, the Supreme Court held that the individual is qualifiedly immune from § 1983 suit and liability.[46]

> We therefore hold that government officials performing discretionary functions generally are shielded from liability for civil damages insofar as their conduct does not violate *clearly established* statutory or constitutional rights of which a reasonable person would have known. . . . Reliance on the objective reasonableness of an official's conduct, as measured by reference to clearly established law, should avoid excessive disruption of government. (Emphasis added) [*Harlow v. Fitzgerald*, 457 U.S. 800, 817–9 (1982)]

The qualified immunity standard of reason to know about an asserted federal right is objective as well as subjective, so that an individual claiming immunity must prove more than personal ignorance or innocent mistake. The courts must ultimately decide when in the continuing development of civil rights law, an asserted federal right becomes "clearly established". This determination, made with the benefit of hindsight, may hold some surprises for legal counsel and the individuals whom they represent.[47]

RECOVERY OF ATTORNEYS' FEES

American law generally requires that all parties to a suit pay their own attorneys' fees. A prevailing party may not therefore recover its fees from the losing party, unless a legislature authorizes that fee recovery. Congress has enacted several fee-shifting laws that supercede the general American rule in specified cases. Such statutes give courts discretion to award or deny attorneys' fees requests,[48] but the Supreme Court has construed the major fee-shifting statute (42 U.S.C. § 1988) as limiting court discretion to award attorneys' fees to prevailing defendants only where the plaintiff's suit is found to be frivolous, and without a reasonable foundation.[49] The Court reasoned that the fee-shifting law was intended to encourage civil rights victims to seek court redress, and that its purpose would be defeated if such victims were deterred from suing out of fear that they might be held liable for the defendant's attorney's fees if their suit failed. Barring a change in the wording of fee-shifting statutes, the Court's reasoning will likely be extended to fee claims under other fee-shifting statutes.

Fee statutes limit recoveries to a "prevailing party". The definition of "prevailing party" becomes crucial where a case is not pursued to a final court judgment. Where plaintiffs after initiating a suit under the ADA obtained their desired relief by an out-of-court settlement without proceeding to a final judgment or entry of a court order approving the settlement, the Supreme Court ruled that they were not a prevailing party within the meaning of the ADA and therefore did not qualify for an award of their attorneys' fees.

> Now that the issue is squarely presented, it behooves us to reconcile the plain language of the statutes with our prior *holdings.* We have only awarded attorney's fees where the plaintiff has received a judgment on the merits, or obtained a court-ordered consent decree—we have not awarded attorney's fees where the plaintiff has secured the reversal of a directed verdict, or acquired a judicial pronouncement that the defendant has violated the Constitution unaccompanied by "judicial relief." [*Buckhannon Board and Care Home v. W. Virginia Dept of Health and Human Resources,* 121 S. Ct. 1835, 1841 (2001)]

The *Buckhannon* decision (Case 8.7) contains a fuller expositoin of the law regarding a prevailing party. Three federal courts of appeal (Second, Third, and Seventh Circuits) adopted the *Buckhannon* analysis in holding that court-ordered or approved relief is a prerequisite for the award of attorneys' fees under the IDEA, while another court (the Ninth Circuit) upheld the award of attorneys' fees to a plaintiff who obtained a favorable settlement though it was not court ordered or approved, on the ground that a judicial officer noted the settlement though he failed to enter it as an official judgment or order.[50] In the Third Circuit case, the court denied a fee award to a student with a handicap who sued to obtain an acceptable IEP, and thereafter obtained an out-of-court settlement following entry of a preliminary injunction and contempt order against the district. It remains to be seen if these readings of the *Buckhannon* decision will prevail in future fee disputes.

ELEVENTH AMENDMENT IMMUNITY DEFENSES

State law immunity doctrines cannot defeat federal law claims by reason of the Supremacy Clause (Article IV) of the Constitution. However, the Eleventh Amendment to the Constitution independently creates state immunities from suits. That Amendment reads:

> The Judicial power of the United States shall not be construed to extend to any suit in law or equity, commenced or prosecuted *against one of the United States by Citizens of another State,* or by Citizens or Subjects of any Foreign State. (Emphasis added)

Although this language refers only to suits against a state by citizens of another state, it has been interpreted to bar citizens from suing their own states.[51] The Amendment also shields state officials from suit for *money damages* when sued in their official capacity, but it does not bar suit *to enjoin* them from engaging in unconstitutional actions.[52] Although school districts and local education agencies are not generally deemed to be "arms of the state" as to be clothed with Eleventh Amendment immunity,[53] the limits of a parent state's Eleventh Amendment immunity is of material import to school districts and their officials. For if a state can be sued as a codefendant in a suit seeking money recovery for federal rights violations, and be stripped of its Eleventh Amendment immunity defense under an exception to Eleventh Amendment coverage, the state will have to share the burdens of defending the suit and of contributing to the payment of any money judgments and awards granted the suing party in that suit.

The major grounds to defeat state Eleventh Amendment immunity are that a state has waived its immunity or that Congress has abrogated the state's Eleventh Amendment immunity for the claim in question. In deciding if either of these exceptions apply, courts must address and answer the following questions:

1. *With respect to a federal aid statute,* did Congress by its enactment *intend* to require a state to waive its immunity from suit as a condition of receiving federal aid?
2. *Under any civil rights law,* did Congress by its enactment *intend* to abrogate the state's Eleventh Amendment immunity from suit?

3. If Congress did by its statutes intend to strip a state of Eleventh Amendment immunity, the court must then decide if Congress had the constitutional authority to require the waiver or abrogation.
4. If the answer to any of the foregoing questions (of intent or legislative authority) is "no," the state retains its Eleventh Amendment immunity.

As seen in the *Gonzaga* case (Case 8.1), Congress may constitutionally require federally aided states to comply with nondiscrimination aid conditions and to *waive* their Eleventh Amendment immunity from suit for violating those aid conditions. State receipt of federal aid is not per se a waiver of its immunity. Congress must have manifested an intent to require state waiver of its immunity in clear and unambiguous language. [*Atascadero State Hospital v. Scanlon*, 473 U.S. 234, 246–7 (1985); *Pace v. Bogalusa*, 325 F.3d 609 (5th Cir. 2003)]

With respect to statutes not extending federal aid, Congress must also express its intent to abrogate state immunity unambiguously, and must have enacted the law under a provision of the Constitution which empowers Congress to abrogate Eleventh Amendment immunity. As explained in the *Garrett* case (Case 8.6) which follows, Congress may not abrogate Eleventh Amendment immunity by laws enacted under the Commerce Clause of the Constitution, but it may abrogate Eleventh Amendment immunity by laws enacted under the Enforcement Clause of the Fourteenth Amendment to protect constitutional rights. In any event, the courts, not Congress, decide whether the necessary constitutional foundation exists to empower Congress to abrogate state immunity.

The following opinion presents an authoritative review of the principles that govern removal of state immunity under the Eleventh Amendment.

BOARD OF TRUSTEES v. GARRETT
121 S. Ct. 955 (2001)

CHIEF JUSTICE REHNQUIST delivered the opinion of the Court.

We decide here whether employees of the State of Alabama may recover money damages by reason of the State's failure to comply with the provisions of Title I of the Americans with Disabilities Act of 1990 (ADA or Act). . . . We hold that such suits are barred by the Eleventh Amendment.

* * *

Garrett and Ash filed separate lawsuits . . . both seeking money damages under the ADA. Petitioners [Defendant State University and its Board] moved for summary judgment, claiming that the ADA exceeds Congress' authority to abrogate the State's Eleventh Amendment immunity. . . .

. . . [T]he District Court agreed with petitioners' position. . . . . . . The Court of Appeals reversed. . . .

We granted certiorari . . . to resolve a split among the Courts of Appeals. . . .

* * *

Although . . . the Amendment applies only to suits against a State by citizens of another State, our cases have extended the Amendment's applicability to suits by citizens against their own States. . . .

We have recognized, however, that Congress may abrogate the States' Eleventh Amendment immunity when it both unequivocally intends to do so and "act[s] pursuant to a valid grant of constitutional authority." . . . The first of these requirements is not in dispute here. . . . The question, then, is whether Congress acted within its constitutional authority by subjecting the States to suits in federal court for money damages under the ADA.

Congress may not, of course, base its abrogation of the States' Eleventh Amendment immunity upon the powers that are conferred by Article I [of the Constitution]. See *Kimel, supra,* at 79, (". . . if the [Age Discrimination in Employment Act of 1967] rests solely on Congress' Article I commerce power, the private petitioners . . . cannot maintain their suits against their state employers"). . . . In *Fitzpatrick v. Bitzer,* 427 U.S. 445, . . . we held that "the Eleventh Amendment, and the principle of state sovereignty which it embodies, are necessarily limited by the enforcement provisions of § 5 of the Fourteenth Amendment." . . . As a result, we concluded, Congress may subject nonconsenting States to suit in federal court when it does so pursuant to a valid exercise of its § 5 power. . . . Section 5 of the Fourteenth Amendment grants Congress the power to enforce the substantive guarantees contained in § 1 [of the Fourteenth Amendment] by enacting "appropriate legislation." . . .

City of Boerne also confirmed, however, . . . that it is the responsibility of this Court, not Congress, to define the substance of constitutional guarantees. . . .

The first step . . . is to identify . . . the scope of the constitutional right at issue. . . .

In *Cleburne v. Cleburne Living Center, Inc.,* . . . (1985), we considered an equal protection challenge to a city ordinance requiring a special use permit for the operation of a group home for the mentally retarded. . . .

. . . "Such a classification cannot run afoul of the Equal Protection Clause if there is a rational relationship between the disparity of treatment and some legitimate governmental purpose." . . .

* * *

Thus, . . . States are not required by the Fourteenth Amendment to make special accommodations for the disabled, so long as their actions toward such individuals are rational. . . .

* * *

. . . [W]e examine whether Congress identified a history and pattern of unconstitutional employment discrimination by the States against the disabled. . . . The legislative record of the ADA, however, simply fails to show that Congress did in fact identify a pattern of irrational state discrimination in employment against the disabled.

* * *

. . . Congressional enactment of the ADA represents its judgment that there should be a "comprehensive national mandate for the elimination of discrimination against individuals with disabilities." . . . Congress is the final authority as to desirable public policy, but in order to authorize private individuals to recover money damages against the States, there must be a pattern of discrimination by the States which violates the Fourteenth Amendment. . . . Those requirements are not met here, and to uphold the Act's application to the States would allow Congress to rewrite the Fourteenth Amendment law laid down by this Court in *Cleburne*. Section 5 does not so broadly enlarge congressional authority. The judgment of the Court of Appeals is therefore

Reversed.

The courts have not fully considered the existence of Eleventh Amendment immunity under each of the statutes discussed in this chapter, but recent cases have arrived at the following results.

Statutes Abrogating Immunity

We consider here the Equal Pay Act, Title VII, Title IX, the IDEA, and § 504 of the Rehabilitation Act.

The Seventh Circuit Court of Appeals held that the *Equal Pay Act* validly abrogated state immunity under Congress' power to enforce Fourteenth Amendment rights (gender-based equal protection).[54] With regard to *Title IX*, it held that Congress could and did condition the grant of federal aid funds on waiver by the recipient states of their Eleventh Amendment immunity from suit for violating *Title XI*, a position also taken by the Fourth and Fifth Circuit courts.[55]

The Seventh, Eighth, and Eleventh Circuit Courts ruled that Congress abrogated state immunity states from suit under Title VII pursuant to its power to enforce equal protection rights under the Fourteenth Amendment.[56]

With regard to the *IDEA* and § 504, the Third Circuit Court ruled, contrary to the Second Circuit, that Congress did effect aided state waiver of Eleventh Amendment immunity from suit under those statutes.[57]

Statutes Not Abrogating Immunity

In the above *Garrett* opinion, the Supreme Court held that Congress did not establish the required constitutional foundation for its attempt to abrogate state Eleventh Amendment immunity under the ADA employment discrimination provisions. However, the Court there declined to rule on congressional authority to abrogate state immunity for violating ADA provisions on disability discrimination in the provision of public services. The lower courts remain divided on that question.[58]

With regard to the ADEA, the Supreme Court ruled that Congress lacked the constitutional power to abrogate state Eleventh Amendment immunity for age discrimination because Congress enacted the ADEA under the Commerce Clause of the Constitution, which Clause does not empower Congress to abrogate Eleventh Amendment immunity. [*Kimel v. Florida Bd. of Regents,* 120 S. Ct. 631 (2000)]

✆ CASES

Case 8.1

GONZAGA UNIV. v. DOE
122 S. Ct. 2268 (2002)

*[**Focus Note.** A student studying for state teacher certification sued his university for monetary damages under § 1983, alleging that the university violated the FERPA law by disclosing to the state certifying agency certain information without the student's consent. In this decision, the Supreme Court endeavored to clarify the confusion among the lower courts on the question whether FERPA created a private right to sue for money damages. The opinion discussed kindred issues under other federal spending statutes. The portion of the Court's opinion on state law tort claims is omitted from the following excerpt.]*

Chief Justice Rehnquist delivered the opinion of the Court.

The question presented is whether a student may sue a private university for damages under 42 U.S.C. § 1983, to enforce provisions of the Family Educational Rights and Privacy Act of 1974 (FERPA or Act). . . . We hold such an action is foreclosed because the relevant provisions of FERPA create no personal rights to enforce. . . .

Respondent John Doe is a former undergraduate in the School of Education at Gonzaga University. . . . . . . Washington [State] at the time required all of its new teachers to obtain an affidavit of good moral character from a dean of their graduating college or university. In October 1993, Roberta League, Gonzaga's "teacher certification specialist," overheard one student tell another that respondent engaged in acts of sexual misconduct against Jane Doe, a female undergraduate. League launched an investigation and contacted the state agency responsible for teacher certification, identifying respondent by name and discussing the allegations against him. Respondent did not learn of the investigation, or that information about him had been disclosed, until March 1994, when he was told by League and others that he would not receive the affidavit required for certification as a Washington schoolteacher.

Respondent then sued Gonzaga and League. . . . He alleged . . . a pendent violation of § 1983 for the release of personal information to an "unauthorized person" in violation of FERPA. A jury found for respondent [plaintiff] on all counts, awarding him $1,155,000, including $150,000 in compensatory damages and $300,000 in punitive damages on the FERPA claim.

* * *

. . . [O]ther . . . courts have divided on the question of FERPA's enforceability under § 1983. The fact that all of these courts have relied on the same set of opinions from this Court suggests that our opinions in this area may not be models of clarity. . . .

* * *

The [FERPA] Act directs the Secretary of Education to enforce this and other of the Act's spending conditions. . . . Respondent contends that this statutory regime confers upon any student enrolled at a covered school . . . a federal right, enforceable in suits for damages under § 1983, not to have "education records" disclosed to unauthorized persons without the student's express written consent.

In *Maine v. Thiboutout*, 448 U.S. 1 . . . (1980), . . . we recognized . . . that § 1983 actions may be brought against state actors to enforce rights created by federal statutes as well as by the Constitution . . . A year later, in *Pennhurst State School and Hospital v. Halderman*, 451 U.S. 1 . . . (1981), we rejected a claim that the Developmentally Disabled Assistance and Bill of Rights Act of 1975 conferred enforceable rights, saying: ". . . [T]he typical remedy for state noncompliance with federally imposed conditions is not a private cause of action for noncompliance but rather action by the Federal Government to terminate funds to the State." . . . *We made clear that unless Congress "speak[s] with a clear voice," and manifests an "unambiguous" intent to confer individual rights, federal funding provisions provide no basis for private enforcement by § 1983.* [Emphasis added]. . . .

Since *Pennhurst*, only twice have we found spending legislation to give rise to enforceable rights. In *Wright v. Roanoke Redevelopment and Housing Authority*, . . . we allowed a § 1983 suit by tenants to recover past overcharges under a rent-ceiling provision of the Public Housing Act. . . . The key to our inquiry was that Congress spoke in terms that "could not be clearer," and conferred entitlements "sufficiently specific and definite to qualify as enforceable rights under *Pennhurst*". . . . Three years later, in *Wilder v. Virginia Hospital Assn.*, we allowed a § 1983 suit brought by health care providers to enforce a reimbursement provision of the Medicaid Act, on the ground that the provision, . . . explicitly conferred specific monetary entitlements upon the plaintiffs. . . .

Our more recent decisions, however, have rejected attempts to infer enforceable rights from [all] Spending Clause statutes. In *Suter v. Artist M.*, 503 U.S. 347 . . . (1992), the Adoption Assistance and Child Welfare Act of 1980 required States receiving funds for adoption assistance to have a "plan" to make "reasonable efforts" to keep children out of foster homes. . . . Since the Act conferred no specific, individually enforceable rights, there was no basis for private enforcement. . . .

* * *

. . . Section 1983 provides a remedy only for the deprivation of "rights, privileges, or immunities secured by the Constitution and laws" of the United States. Accordingly, it is *rights,* not the broader or vaguer "benefits" or "interests," that may be enforced under the authority of that section. . . .

. . . We have recognized, for example, that Title VI of the Civil Rights Act of 1964 and Title IX of the Education Amendments of 1972 create individual rights because those statutes are phrased "with an *unmistakable focus on the benefited class.*" . . .

* * *

. . . ("[A] claim based on a statutory violation is enforceable under § 1983 only when the statute creates 'rights, privileges, or immunities' in the particular plaintiff"). . . . Accordingly, where the text and structure of a statute provide no indication that Congress intends to create new individual rights, there is no basis for a private suit, whether under § 1983 or under an implied right of action.

* * *

With this principle in mind, there is no question that FERPA's nondisclosure provisions fail to confer enforceable rights. To begin with, the provisions entirely lack the sort of "rights-creating" language critical to showing the requisite congressional intent to create new rights. Unlike the individually focused terminology of Titles VI and IX ("no person shall be subjected to discrimination"), FERPA's provisions speak only to the Secretary of Education. . . . . . .

* * *

In sum, if Congress wishes to create new rights enforceable under § 1983, it must do so in clear and unambiguous terms. . . . FERPA's nondisclosure provisions contain no rights-creating language. . . . They therefore create no rights enforceable under § 1983. Accordingly, the judgment of the Supreme Court of Washington is reversed, and the case is remanded for further proceedings not inconsistent with this opinion.
It is so ordered.

Case 8.2

BOULAHANIS v. BOARD OF REGENTS
198 F.3d 633 (7th Cir. 1999)

> *[Focus Note. This suit was brought under the § 1983 statute and charged, among other things, that the university elimination of men's soccer and wrestling teams in order to provide comparable athletic resources to women's teams was based on sex*

and therefore constituted gender and racial discrimination in violation of their con-
stitutional rights to equal protection and their Title IX rights.]

FLAUM, CIRCUIT JUDGE.

* * *

In the fall of 1993, the Gender Equity Committee of Illinois State University undertook a year-long investigation of gender equity and Title IX compliance at the University. The results of this study indicated that enrollment at the University was 45% male and 55% female, while athletic participation was 66% male and 34% female. The study concluded that these numbers did not constitute equitable participation opportunities for women. . . . Under Title IX, Illinois State University is required to "provide equal athletic opportunity" for men and women. . . .

* * *

In order to effectively accommodate the athletic interests of both male and female students, the University had three options under the policy interpretations of Title IX promulgated by the Office of Civil Rights. . . . . . . [T]he University focused on achieving the goal of substantial proportionality. . . .

. . . This resulted in the addition of women's soccer and the elimination of men's soccer and men's wrestling. . . .

The plaintiffs-appellants are former members of the men's soccer and men's wrestling teams. . . .

They contend that the University's decision to eliminate the programs . . . was based on sex, and is therefore a violation of Title IX. They also allege various violations of their constitutional rights. . . . . . .

* * *

Title IX states that "No person . . . shall, on the basis of sex, be excluded from participation in, be denied the benefits of, or be subjected to discrimination under any education program or activity receiving Federal financial assistance." . . . According to the plaintiffs-appellants, because these discriminatory actions would not have been taken "but for" the sex of the participants, the actions violate Title IX. . . . . . .

The plaintiffs-appellants' argument is similar to one this Court has already considered in *Kelley v. Board of Trustees*, 35 F.3d 265 (7th Cir. 1994). The plaintiffs in *Kelley* were members of the men's swimming team at the University of Illinois. . . . Although the men's swimming team . . . was eliminated . . . , the women's swimming program was maintained because of concerns about compliance with Title IX. . . . We rejected that challenge, ...

* * *

As we noted in *Kelley*, the elimination of men's athletic programs is not a violation of Title IX as long as men's participation . . . continues to be "substantially proportionate" to their enrollment . . . . After the elimination of men's soccer and men's wrestling at the University, the athletic participation of men remained within three percentage points of enrollment. . . . Under such circumstances, Illinois State University's actions in eliminating the programs at issue do not constitute a violation of Title IX.

* * *

The plaintiffs-appellants next contend that if Title IX is construed to permit the elimination of men's programs for reasons of sex, then Title IX . . . would violate the Equal Protection Clause. . . .

. . . The elimination of sex-based discrimination in federally-funded educational institutions is an important government objective, and the actions of Illinois State University in eliminating the men's soccer and men's wrestling programs were substantially related to that objective. . . . In light of these conclusions, we repeat our holding in *Kelley* that "[w]hile the effect of Title IX . . . is that institutions will sometimes consider gender when decreasing their athletic offerings, this limited consideration of sex does not violate the Constitution." . . .

The plaintiffs-appellants also brought numerous claims under § 1983 and § 1985(3) of Title 42, arguing that they have a protected property interest in participating in athletics. . . . The district court dismissed these claims under our decision in *Waid v. Merrill Area Public Schools*, 91 F.3d 857 (7th Cir. 1996). In that case, we held that the availability of a Title IX claim preempted claims under § 1983. . . .

1. Sex-Based Discrimination Under Section 1983

* * *

. . . The plaintiffs-appellants contend that because individual claims are not available under Title IX, individual claims must be available under Section 1983. Under this interpretation . . . Title IX preempts only Section 1983 suits against institutions . . . .

. . . [T]he plaintiff-appellants misconstrue the doctrine of preemption. . . . [T]he district court was correct in determining that the availability of that claim preempts the remedies available for sex discrimination under Section 1983.

* * *

Case 8.3

WALKER v. DISTRICT OF COLUMBIA
969 F. Supp. 794 (D. D.C. 1997)

*[**Focus Note.** A student and his guardian sued the District of Columbia and its school superintendent to recover money damages under the § 1983 law, for alleged violations of the Individuals with Disabilities Education Act (IDEA) and of the Rehabilitation Act, by failing to provide special education due the student. In reading the opinion, note how the court arrived at the following conclusions: (1) The IDEA itself does not authorize monetary recovery beyond reimbursement of parents for special education expenses; (2) the § 1983 law provides a monetary remedy for violation of IDEA rights; (3) that plaintiffs must prove facts that establish that the alleged violation arose from a school district custom or practice that would subject it to § 1983 liability; (4) the required proofs to show a school violation of the Rehabilitation Act; and (5) punitive damages, in any case, are not recoverable from a school district.]*

PAUL L. FRIEDMAN, DISTRICT JUDGE.

Phillip Walker is a sixteen year-old student. . . . He complains that for many years he was not given the special education to which he was entitled under the Individuals with Disabilities Education Act ("IDEA"). . . . Specifically, he claims that he was misdiagnosed, that the statutorily-required due process hearings . . . were not held in a timely manner, that his educational evaluations were conducted improperly, and that he was deprived of services related to his special educational needs. On March 26, 1996, a Hearing Officer awarded Phillip a private placement at the Kennedy School and two years of compensatory education and ordered an occupational therapy evaluation and a neurological screening. Plaintiffs sought damages but the Hearing Officer concluded that he lacked authority to award them.

* * *

Defendants maintain (1) that damages are not available for violations of the IDEA; (2) that plaintiffs cannot bring a Section 1983 action based on IDEA violations; (3) that even if plaintiffs could bring a Section 1983 action, they have failed to state a claim because they have not alleged a custom or practice of IDEA violations; and (4) that plaintiffs have failed to state a claim under the Rehabilitation Act.

The Court concludes that damages are not available under the IDEA itself but that plaintiffs can bring a Section 1983 claim for damages to vindicate their rights under the IDEA. The Court further finds that plaintiffs have raised an allegation of a custom or practice of IDEA violations on the part of the District sufficient to survive defendants' motion to dismiss on that basis. Plaintiffs have also alleged a valid Rehabilitation Act claim. Whether the

District of Columbia in fact has a custom or practice of failing to enforce the IDEA or whether the Rehabilitation Act was actually violated in this case are questions of fact not susceptible to summary judgment on this record. This case therefore shall be set for trial.

II. Discussion

A. The IDEA and Section 1983

* * *

Where a school system fails to provide special education or related services, a student is entitled to compensatory education. . . . If a parent pays for educational placements or related services to which a child is later found to be entitled, the school system must reimburse the parent. . . . Reimbursement is considered an equitable remedy, and compensatory damages beyond reimbursement are not provided for by the IDEA. . . . In sum, while Phillip can and has been awarded compensatory education, he cannot obtain money damages under the IDEA . . . .

Plaintiffs maintain, however, that they can obtain compensatory damages under 42 U.S.C. § 1983, as could any civil rights plaintiff. Defendants respond that a Section 1983 cause of action is unavailable because the IDEA establishes a comprehensive remedial scheme that precludes such an action. Defendants' argument, however, ignores the 1986 amendments to the IDEA. . . . Section 1415(f) of the IDEA provides: Nothing in this chapter shall be construed to restrict or limit the rights, procedures, and remedies available under the Constitution, Title V of the Rehabilitation Act of 1973, *or other Federal statutes* protecting the rights of children and youth with disabilities. . . . 20 U.S.C. § 1415(f). (Emphasis added)

Congress added this section to the IDEA in order to overturn the Supreme Court's decision in *Smith v. Robinson,* 468 U.S. 992 . . . (1984), in which the Court held that the IDEA precluded claims under the Rehabilitation Act and the Equal Protection Clause. . . . The Third Circuit has held that with Section 1415(f), Congress intended to permit Section 1983 actions to vindicate rights under the IDEA and that money damages may be awarded under Section 1983 for an IDEA violation. See *W.B. v. Matula,* 67 F.3d at 494–95. The Seventh Circuit also appears to assume . . . that damages are available in Section 1983 actions for IDEA violations. See *Charlie F. v. Bd. of Education of Skokie School District 68,* 98 F.3d 989, 991–93 (7th Cir. 1996). . . . See also *Doe v. Alfred,* 906 F. Supp. 1092, 1098–1100 (S.D. W. Va. 1995). . . . By contrast, the Sixth Circuit has held that damages are not available under Section 1983 because the IDEA does not provide for them directly, see *Crocker v. Tennessee Secondary Sch. Athletic Assoc.,* 980 F.2d 382, 386–87 (6th Cir. 1992), but the Sixth

Circuit in Crocker did not address the legislative history of Section 1415(f). The D.C. Circuit has not addressed the issue of damages in a Section 1983 action brought for alleged violations of the IDEA. The Court is persuaded by the reasoning of the Third Circuit. The plain language of Section 1415(f) indicates that Congress intended to preserve all alternative civil rights remedies, including those available under Section 1983, to vindicate the rights created by the IDEA. . . . Accordingly, plaintiffs may maintain a Section 1983 action here.

As in any Section 1983 action . . . the burden is on the plaintiffs . . . to establish that the District of Columbia has a custom or practice that is the moving force behind the alleged IDEA violations. . . . . . . [P]laintiffs' submissions do not establish that the District of Columbia has or had such a custom or practice. Accordingly, plaintiffs' motion for partial summary judgment must be denied.

B. The Rehabilitation Act

Plaintiffs also allege a violation of Section 504 of the Rehabilitation Act. . . . In the context of children who receive benefits pursuant to the IDEA, the D.C. Circuit has noted that "'in order to show a violation of the Rehabilitation Act, something more than a mere failure to provide the "free and appropriate education" required by the [IDEA] must be shown.'" . . . "[E]ither bad faith or gross misjudgment must be shown before a Section 504 violation can be made out. . . ." . . . Plaintiffs have alleged sufficient facts to raise a genuine dispute over whether District officials exercised gross misjudgment in Phillip's case, a dispute that can only be resolved at trial. . . .

* * *

C. Punitive Damages

Plaintiffs also seek punitive damages but such damages are not available against the District as a matter of law. See *City of Newport v. Fact Concerts*, 453 U.S. 247 . . . (1981). . . . The claim for punitive damages therefore will be dismissed.

III. Conclusion

The Court concludes that if plaintiffs prove their case at trial compensatory damages are available under Section 1983 for violations of the IDEA. Damages are also available under Section 504 of the Rehabilitation Act if plaintiffs prove at trial that the District of Columbia demonstrated bad faith or gross misjudgment in exercising its responsibilities under the IDEA. Punitive damages are not available.

Case 8.4

RIDDICK ET AL. v. SCHOOL BOARD
238 F.3d 518 (4th Cir. 2000)

See case opinion at p. 395, *supra.*

Case 8.4 Review Questions

1. Where state law, unlike the unusual Virginia law in *Riddick*, does not expressly reserve teacher discipline authority exclusively in a school board, the Supreme Court has recognized that policy-making authority may be delegated by a school board to subordinate supervisors. Whether policy-making authority was in fact so delegated will depend essentially on the working relationships that prevail in a given school district. Can you think of some board actions that would effect such a delegation of policy making to the School Superintendent? the School Principal and Vice Principal?

2. Is the difference between actionable "deliberate indifference" and nonactionable "negligence" subject to an objective legal measure, or to a slide-rule appraisal of case facts and circumstances?

Case 8.5

DOE v. BOARD OF EDUC.
18 F. Supp. 2d 954 (N.D. Ill. 1998)

> [**Focus Note.** *High school students sued the school district and district administrators and teachers, alleging numerous violations of constitutional, statutory, and common law rights arising from teacher's sexual activity with them. The portion of the court opinion dealing with the state law claims is reported in Chapter 4 and is not included in the following excerpt.*]

Memorandum Opinion and Order
Gettleman, District Judge.

Plaintiffs . . . brought a six count . . . complaint against defendants Board of Education of Consolidated School District 230 (District) and Arlene See, Daniel Romano, Patrick Vasquez, Charles Cummings, Lisa Otto, Cyndie Skroch and Dr. Timothy Brown. . . .

* * *

Facts

... [A]ll of the parties ... agree that Vasquez, who was an Instructor for the Andrew High School Winter Guard and Marching Band ("Winter Guard"), had a sexual relationship with two of his students. ... The first student, identified as Jane Doe I, was 16 ... when the relationship began. ... Jane Doe I was a member of the Winter Guard. ... Jane Doe II was 15 when her relationship with Vasquez began. ... Jane Doe II was also a member of the Winter Guard. ... ...

Vasquez was originally hired ... in 1985. He was approximately 20 years old at that time. ... He took the 1990 season off. ... He was rehired in Fall 1991, apparently on defendant Romano's [Band Director] recommendation, and remained an instructor until February 14, 1996, when he was arrested as a result of his relationships with [plaintiffs] Jane Doe I and Jane Doe II.

It is also uncontested that plaintiffs, as well as Vasquez, worked hard at keeping the relationships secret. ... Nor, apparently, were they aware that between April 1993 through August 1994 Vasquez had a sexual relationship with Skroch, a teacher-supervisor of the Winter Guard. There is also nothing in the record to demonstrate that any of the individual board members had actual knowledge of the situation.

* * *

Count I

In Count I ... plaintiffs charge the individual defendants with having "promulgated and maintained policies which fostered sexual abuse of minor female high school students ... by Vasquez. ..." The doctrine of respondeat superior cannot be used to impose § 1983 liability on a supervisor for the conduct of a subordinate. ... ... "Personal involvement is a prerequisite for individual liability in a § 1983 action. Supervisors who are simply negligent in failing to detect and prevent subordinate misconduct are not personally involved. Rather, supervisors must know about the conduct and facilitate it ... condone it, or turn a blind eye for fear of what they might see. They must in other words act either knowingly or with deliberate, reckless indifference." ... In the instant case, there is no evidence clearly demonstrating that any of the individual defendants had actual knowledge of the sexual relationships between plaintiffs and Vasquez. ... Therefore, they can be liable only if there are facts to support an inference that they acted with deliberate, reckless indifference, i.e., that they turned a blind eye to the evidence before them.

The facts regarding what each of the individual defendants knew are hotly contested. ... At most, the record reveals that: (1) the individual defendants were aware of rumors about Vasquez and plaintiffs ... (2) defendants knew that plaintiffs were helping Vasquez chart Winter Guard programs at his house after school hours; (3) Skroch and Otto discussed their own personal, sexual and marital lives with Winter Guard members; and (4) Skroch was having sexual relations with Vasquez. There is also testimony ... that

Skroch was aware of the situation between Vasquez and plaintiffs. This testimony was denied by Skroch. In addition, all of the individual defendants knew that Vasquez had married a former student shortly after her graduation.

Although there is no direct evidence establishing that any of the individual defendants had actual knowledge of Vasquez's relationships with plaintiffs, the evidence set forth above, if true, could lead a reasonable jury to conclude that some or all of the individual defendants had enough knowledge to suspect some improper activity and did nothing about it. Because the extent of that knowledge is in dispute and material to any claim that "they turned a blind eye" to Vasquez's abuse of plaintiffs, summary judgment for either party on Count I is inappropriate and denied.

The individual defendants also argue that they are entitled to the defense of qualified immunity. Under this defense, "government officials performing discretionary functions are shielded from liability for civil damages in so far as their conduct does not violate clearly established statutory or constitutional rights of which a reasonable person would have known." *Harlow v. Fitzgerald*, 457 U.S. 800, 818 . . . (1982). . . .

There is no dispute that plaintiffs had a clearly established constitutional right to be free from Vasquez's sexual abuse. Defendants argue, however, that under existing case law . . . they can be liable . . . only if they had actual notice of Vasquez's unconstitutional acts and then demonstrated deliberate indifference to those acts. . . . . . .

As noted above, however, the record regarding what each individual defendant knew about plaintiffs' relationships with Vasquez, and when he/she knew it, is replete with disputed facts. . . . [T]he court is persuaded that there is enough evidence in the record for a reasonable jury to decide that some or all of the individual defendants were aware of or "turned a blind eye" to Vasquez's unconstitutional conduct. . . . Because a material question of fact remains in dispute, defendants are not entitled to summary judgment . . . based on the defense of qualified immunity.

Count II
In Count II, plaintiffs allege that the District violated § 1983 by acquiescing and/or ratifying the actions or inactions of the individual defendants, resulting in policies, customs and/or practices that facilitated Vasquez's abuse of plaintiffs. . . .

* * *

In the instant case, plaintiffs' claim . . . is based predominately on the District's decision to rehire Vasquez knowing that he had recently divorced his first wife and married Amy, a former Winter Guard member and recent graduate with whom he may have had physical contact while she was a student. Plaintiffs . . . argue that this single decision by the District constitutes a policy. . . .

Recently, in *Board of County Commissioners of Bryan County, Okl. v. Brown*, 520 U.S. 397 . . . (1997), the Supreme Court examined the issue of whether a municipality can be liable under § 1983 for a single hiring decision. In *Brown,* an arrestee brought a § 1983 action against the county, the county sheriff, and a reserve deputy seeking to recover for injuries sustained while being forcibly removed from an automobile after it was stopped. . . . The deputy, who was the son of the sheriff's nephew, had a record of driving infractions and had pleaded guilty to various driving-related and other misdemeanors including assault and battery, resisting arrest, and public drunkenness. The jury found in favor of the plaintiff, and the appellate court affirmed, based on the sheriff's decision to hire the deputy. The Supreme Court reversed, holding that the county was not liable for the sheriff's isolated decision to hire the deputy without adequate screening because the plaintiff had not demonstrated that the sheriff's decision reflected a "conscious disregard for a high risk that [the deputy] would use excessive force in violation of [the plaintiff's] federally protected right." 117 S. Ct. at 1394.

* * *

A finding of culpability simply cannot depend on the mere probability that any officer inadequately screened will inflict any constitutional injury. Rather it must depend on the finding that *this officer* was highly likely to inflict the *particular injury* suffered by the plaintiff. . . . . . .

. . . [T]here is evidence in the record to suggest that the District decided to rehire Vasquez with some knowledge that he may have engaged in an extramarital sexual relationship with a student (Amy). If plaintiffs can prove that to be true, Vasquez would have been violating Amy's constitutional rights. From that, a jury could conclude that a decision to ignore Vasquez's relationship with Amy would reflect more than just an indifference to Vasquez's record, but a deliberate indifference to plaintiff's constitutional rights, and that it was highly likely that Vasquez would do the same thing with other students that he had done with Amy. . . . Accordingly, the District's motion for summary judgment on Count II is denied.

* * *

Conclusion

For the reasons set forth above, plaintiffs' motion for partial summary judgment is denied. Defendants' motion for summary judgment is denied as to Counts I and II. . . .

Case 8.6

BOARD OF TRUSTEES v. GARRETT
121 S. Ct. 955 (2001)

See case opinion at p. 404, *supra.*

Case 8.7

BUCKHANNON BOARD AND CARE HOME, INC. v. W. VA. DEPT. OF HEALTH AND HUMAN RESOURCES ET AL.

121 S. Ct. 1835 (2001)

> [**Focus Note.** *After receiving court orders to close their residential care facilities for alleged violations of state laws, the operators brought suit to overturn the state law as violating federal law. The West Virginia legislature thereafter amended the law to eliminate the challenged state law provisions and the operators then requested but were denied attorney's fees as a prevailing party under the fee-shifting provisions of the ADA and FHAA. They appealed to the Supreme Court which issued the following opinion.]*

CHIEF JUSTICE REHNQUIST *delivered the opinion of the Court.*

Numerous federal statutes allow courts to award attorney's fees and costs to the "prevailing party." The question presented here is whether this term includes a party that has failed to secure a judgment on the merits or a court-ordered consent decree, but has nonetheless achieved the desired result because the lawsuit brought about a voluntary change in the defendant's conduct. We hold that it does not.

Petitioners requested attorney's fees under the FHAA, [fair housing law] ("[T]he court, in its discretion, may allow the prevailing party . . . a reasonable attorney's fee and costs"), and ADA [disability act], . . . ("[T]he court . . . , in its discretion, may allow the prevailing party . . . a reasonable attorney's fee, including litigation expenses, and costs"). Petitioners argued that they were entitled to attorney's fees under the "catalyst theory," which posits that a plaintiff is a "prevailing party" if it achieves the desired result because the lawsuit brought about a voluntary change in the defendant's conduct. Although most Courts of Appeals recognize the "catalyst theory," the Court of Appeals for the Fourth Circuit rejected it in *S-1 and S-2 v. State Bd. of Ed. of N. C.,* 21 F.3d 49, 51 (C.A.4 1994) (en banc). . . .

To resolve the disagreement amongst the Courts of Appeals, we granted certiorari. . . .

In the United States, parties are ordinarily required to bear their own attorney's fees. . . . Under this "American Rule," we follow "a general practice of not awarding fees to a prevailing party absent explicit statutory authority." Congress, however, has authorized the award of attorney's fees to the "prevailing party" in numerous statutes in addition to those at issue here, such as the Civil Rights Act of 1964, 78 Stat. 259, 42 U.S.C. § 2000e-5(k), . . . and the Civil Rights Attorney's Fees Awards Act of 1976, 42 U.S.C. § 1988.

In designating those parties eligible for an award of litigation costs, Congress employed the term "prevailing party," a legal term of art. . . . This view that a "prevailing party" is one who has been awarded some relief by the court can be distilled from our prior cases.

In *Hanrahan v. Hampton*, 446 U.S. 754, 758, . . . (1980) . . . , we reviewed the legislative history of § 1988 and found that "Congress intended to permit the interim award of counsel fees only when a party has prevailed on the merits of at least some of his claims. Our . . . [r]espect for ordinary language requires that a plaintiff receive at least some relief on the merits of his claim before he can be said to prevail." . . .

In addition to judgments on the merits, we have held that settlement agreements enforced through a consent decree may serve as the basis for an award of attorney's fees. . . . These decisions, taken together, establish that enforceable judgments on the merits and court-ordered consent decrees create the "material alteration of the legal relationship of the parties" necessary to permit an award of attorney's fees.

We think, however, the "catalyst theory" falls on the other side of the line from these examples. It allows an award where there is no judicially sanctioned change in the legal relationship of the parties. . . . A defendant's voluntary change in conduct, although perhaps accomplishing what the plaintiff sought to achieve by the lawsuit, lacks the necessary judicial *imprimatur* on the change. Our precedents thus counsel against holding that the term "prevailing party" authorizes an award of attorney's fees *without* a corresponding alteration in the legal relationship of the parties.

. . . We have only awarded attorney's fees where the plaintiff has received a judgment on the merits, or obtained a court-ordered consent decree—we have not awarded attorney's fees where the plaintiff has secured the reversal of a directed verdict, or acquired a judicial pronouncement that the defendant has violated the Constitution unaccompanied by "*judicial* relief." Never have we awarded attorney's fees for a nonjudicial "alteration of actual circumstances." . . .

Petitioners nonetheless argue that the legislative history of the Civil Rights Attorney's Fees Awards Act supports a broad reading of "prevailing party" which includes the "catalyst theory." . . .

. . . We think the legislative history cited by petitioners is at best ambiguous. . . . Particularly in view of the "American Rule" that attorney's fees will not be awarded absent "explicit statutory authority," such legislative history is clearly insufficient. . . .

* * *

Given the clear meaning of "prevailing party" in the fee-shifting statutes, we need not determine which way these various policy arguments cut.

. . . For the reasons stated above, we hold that the "catalyst theory" is not a permissible basis for the award of attorney's fees under the FHAA, 42 U.S.C. § 3613(c)(2), and ADA, 42 U.S.C. § 12205.

⟨⟩ ENDNOTES

1. City of Newport v. Fact Concerts, 453 U.S. 247 (1981)(§ 1983 claim); Barnes v. Gorman, 122 S. Ct. 2097 (2002)(Title VI claim); Schultzen v. Woodbury Central Comm'y School Dist., 187 F. Supp. 2d 1099 (2002)(Title IX claim).

2. *See, e.g.*, Middlesex County Sewerage Authority v. National Sea Clammers Assn., 453 U.S. 13 (1981); Maine v. Thibotout, 448 U.S. 1 (1980). While the terms *preemption* and *preclusion* have technically different implications in legal parlance, they are used interchangeably here to express their common results.

3. *See, e.g.*, Bryant v. City of Blackfoot, 48 P.2d 636(Idaho 2002), citing the numerous federal authorities to this effect.

4. Jett v. Dallas Ind. School Dist., 109 S. Ct. 2702 (1989).

5. To like effect, *see* Frazier v. Fairhaven School Committee, 276 F.3d 52, 67 (1st Cir. 2002).

6. Smith v. Metropolitan School Dist., 128 F.3d 1014 (7th Cir. 1997); Doe v. Claiborne County, 103 F.3d 495 (6th Cir. 1996).

7. Doe v. Beaumont I.S.D., 8 F. Supp. 2d 596 (E.D. Tex. 1998).

8. Boulahanis v. Bd. of Regents, 198 F.3d 633 (7th Cir. 1999); Waid v. Merrill Area Pub. Schools, 91 F.3d 857 (7th Cir. 1996); Canty v. Old Rochester Reg'l School District, 54 F. Supp. 2d 66 (D. Mass. 1999); Seneway v. Canon McMillan School Dist., 969 F. Supp. 325 (W.D. Pa. 1997); Mann v. Univ. of Cincinatti, 864 F. Supp. 44 (S.D. Ohio 1994). *Contra*: Carroll K. v. Fayette County Board of Educ., 19 F. Supp. 2d 618 (S.D. W. Va. 1998). *Re* preemption of constitutional claim by ADEA, *see* Ford V. City of Oakwood, Ga., 905 F. Supp. 1063 (N.D. Ga. 1995).

9. Barnes, note 1, *supra*.

10. Hall v. Knott County Board of Education, 941 F.2d 402, 407 (6th Cir. 1991); Town of Burlington School Committee v. Department of Education, 471 U.S. 359, 369 (1985).

11. *Exhaustion not required*: W. B. v. Matula, 67 F.3d 484, 495–96 (3d Cir. 1995); Covington v. Knox County Sch. System, 205 F.3d 912, 917 (6th Cir.

2000); Witte v. Clark County Sch. Dist., 197 F.3d 1271, 1275 (9th Cir. 1999).
   Exhaustion required: Frazier v. Fairhaven School Committee, 276 F.3d 52, 60 (1st Cir. 2002); Charlie F. v. Board of Educ., 98 F.3d 989, 991(7th Cir. 1996); N.B. v. Alachua County School Bd., 84 F.3d 1376, 1379 (11th Cir. 1996).

12. *See, e.g.*, McAdams v. Board of Educ., Rocky Point Un. Free School District, 216 F. Supp. 2d 86 (E.D. N.Y. 2002) and authorities there cited.

13. *E.g.*, Vultaggio v. Board of Educ., 216 F. Supp. 2d 96 (E.D. N.Y. 2002).

14. McAdams, note 12, *supra*.

15. The Second, Third, Fourth, Fifth, Sixth, Seventh, Tenth, and Eleventh Circuits directly or by dicta found no preemption by Title VII of § 1983 suits for *constitutional* violations. *See* Thigpen v. Bibb County, 223 F.3d 1231 (11th Cir. 2000); W. B. v. Matula, note 11, *supra*, and following endnote for similar cases from the 2d, 4th, 5th, 6th, 7th, and 10th federal circuits. *See also* Madon v. Laconia School Dist., 952 F. Supp. 44 (D. N.H 1996) from the First Circuit.

16. Gibson v. Kickman, 2 F. Supp. 2d 1481 (M.D. Ga. 1998); Duello v. Board of Regents, 487 N.W.2d 56 (Wis. 1998). *Re* preclusion of § 1983 relief for a pure Title VII statutory claim: *e.g.*, Poulson v. Davis, 895 F.2d 705, 710 (10th Cir. 1990); Day v. Wayne County Bd. of Auditors, 749 F.2d 1199, 1204 (6th Cir. 1989); Lakoski, 66 F.3d 751, 755 [citing Irby v. Sullivan, 737 F.2d 1418 1428 (5th Cir. 1984)]; Walker v. City of Little Rock, 787 F.2d 1223 (8th Cir. 1986).

17. Kolstad v. Am. Dental Assn., 527 U.S. 526 (1990).

18. Cons. Rail Corp. v. Darrone, 465 U.S. 624 (1984).

19. Discovery House Inc. v. Indianapolis, 319 F.3d 277 (7th Cir. 2003).

20. Bryant, note 3, *supra*; Arocho v. Dept. of Labor, 218 F. Supp. 2d 145 (D. Puerto Rico 2002) and authorities there collected.

21. *Majority view:* Arocho v. Dept. of Labor, prior note; Ford v. City of Oakwood, 905 F. Supp. 1063 (N.D. Ga. 1995); LaFleur v. Texas Dept. of

Health, 126 F.3d 758 (5th Cir. 1977). The case law is summarized in Bond v. Board of Educ. of the City of New York, 1999 WL 151702 (E.D. N.Y. 1999).

The district courts of the Second Circuit are split. *Compare* Reed v. Town of Branford, 949 F. Supp. 87, 90 (D. Conn. 1996) (no ADEA preclusion of § 1983 claim), *with* Gregor v. Dewinski, 911 F. Supp. 643, 651 (W.D. N.Y. 1996) (ADEA provides the exclusive remedy).

22. Jett v. Dallas Ind. School District, 109 S. Ct. 2702 (1984).

23. *Suit against individual:* Allowed in the Second and Sixth Circuits, and in lower courts of the Eleventh Circuit. Disallowed in the Third and Eight Circuits. The conflicting authorities are noted in Chapman v. Higbee Co., 319 F.3d 825 (6th Cir. 2003); Lightner v. Town of Ariton, Alabama, 902 F. Supp. 1489 (M.D. Ala. 1995).

24. Lightner, prior note.

25. Goss v. Lopez, 419 U.S. 565(1975); Ballantine v. Virgin Is. Port Authority, 955 F. Supp. 480 (D. Virgin Is. 1997). *Cf.* Daddow v. Carlsbad Mun. School Dist., 898 P.2d 1235 (N.M. 1995).

26. *See, e.g.,* Hockaday v. Texas Dept. of Crim. Justice, 914 F. Supp. 1439 (S.D. Tex. 1996).

27. Brandon v. Holt, 469 U.S. 464 (1985).

28. Smith v. Metropolitan School Dist., 128 F.3d 1014 (7th Cir. 1997); Doe v. Claiborne County, 103 F.3d 495 (6th Cir. 1996).

29. Busek v. State, 785 P.2d 855 (Wyo. 1990); Tower v. Glover 467 U.S. 914 (1984).

30. Doe v. Beaumont I.S.D., note 7, *supra*; Doe v. Board of Educ., 18 F. Supp. 2d 954 (N.D. Ill. 1998); Ware v. Unified School Dist., 902 F.2d 815, 819 (10th Cir. 1990).

31. St. Louis v. Praprotnik, 485 U.S. 112 (1988); Hall v. Marion School Dist. No. 2, 31 F.3d 183 (4th Cir. 1994).

32. City of Canton v. Harris, 489 U.S. 378 (1989).

33. *Compare* Doe, note 28, *supra* (insufficient allegations), *with* Murrell v. School Dist. 1, Denver, Colorado, 186 F.3d 1238 (10th Cir. 1999) (sufficient allegations). Doe, v. Board of Educ. note 30, *supra*.

34. Williams v. Ellington, 936 F.2d 881 (6th Cir. 1991)(school principal order for an unconstitutional student search was not sufficient to prove a school policy to authorize that search); Doe v. Beaumont I.S.D., note 7, *supra*.

35. *See* Monell v. Dept. of Social Services, 436 U.S. 658 (1978). Williams v. Ellington, 936 F.2d 881 (6th Cir. 1991).

36. R.L.R. v. Prague Pub. School Dist., 838 F. Supp. 1526 (W.D. Okla. 1993); Jones v. Board of Educ., 854 P.2d 1386 (Colo. App. 1993); Daniels v. Williams, 474 U.S. 327 (1986).

37. Johnson v. Dallas Ind. School Dist., 38 F.3d 198 (5th Cir. 1994).

38. Owen v. City of Independence, 445 U.S. 622 (1980); Stoddard v. School Dist., 590 F.2d 829 (10th Cir. 1979); Craig v. Columbus City Schools, 760 F. Supp. 128 (S.D. Ohio 1991).

39. *See* Chapman v. Higbee, 319 F.3d 825, 833–836 (6th Cir. 2003).

40. Jane Doe v. Special School Dist., 682 F. Supp. 451 (E.D. Mo. 1988).

41. D.T. v. Ind. School Dist., 894 F.2d 1176 (10th Cir. 1990).

42. Doe v. Raines County Ind. School Dist., 66 F.3d 1402 (5th Cir. 1995).

43. Harrington v. Lauer, 893 F. Supp. 352 (D. N.J. 1995).

44. *See* Armijo by and through Chavez v. Wagon Mound Public Schools, 159 F.3d 1253 (10th Cir. 1998).

45. Seneway v. Canon Mcmillan School District, 969 F. Supp. 325 (W.D. Pa. 1997); Ford v. City of Oakwood, Ga., 905 F. Supp. 1063 (N.D. Ga. 1995).

46. *See also* W.B. v. Matula, 67 F.3rd 484, 499 (3d Cir. 1995) [quoting Harlow v. Fitzgerald, 457 U.S. 800 (1982)]; Doe v. Taylor Ind. School Dist., 15 F.3d 433 (5th Cir. 1994).

47. *See, e.g.,* Flores v. Morgan Hill Un. School Dist., 324 F.3d 1130 (9th Cir. 2003)(finding a clearly established right).

48. *E.g.,* The Civil Rights Attorneys Fees Award Statute, 42 U.S.C. § 1988 (for actions brought

under §§ 1981, 1983, Titles VI, VII, and IX); The Handicapped Children's Protective Act of 1986, 20 U.S.C. § 1415; the Civil Rights Act of 1991 (for actions under § 504 and ADA). *See* New York City Fire Dept. v. Civil Service Commission, 490 F.2d 387, 390 (2d Cir. 1973); Poulson v. Davis, 895 F.2d 705 (10th Cir. 1990). These and other authorities are reviewed in detail in the Keller v. Prince Georges County Dept. of Soc. Services, 827 F.2d 952 (4th Cir. 1987); Annot., *Civil Rights Act—Attorneys Fees,* 16 A.L.R. Fed 621 (1973) and pkt. part.

49. Christiansburg Garment Co. v. EEOC, 434 U.S. 412 (1978); Oldring v. School Board of DuVal County, 567 So. 2d 519 (Fla. 1990) (denying fees to defending board); Dahlem v. Board of Educ., 901 F.2d 1508 (10th Cir. 1990) (court discretion to deny fees).

50. *Compare* John T. v. Delaware County, 318 F.3d 545 (3d Cir. 2003); Union of Needleworkers Indus. and Textile Employees v. Immigration and Naturalization Service, 336 F.3d 200 (2d Cir. 2003), T.D. v. LaGrange School District, 349 F. 3d 469 (7th Cir. 2003), *with* Richard S. v. Dept. of Developmental Services, 317 F.3d 1080 (9th Cir. 2003).

51. Kimel v. Fla. Board of Regents, 528 U.S. 62, 72, 73 (2000).

52. Ex parte Young, 209 U.S. 123 (1908); Gibson v. Arkansas Dept. of Corrections, 265 F.3d 718 (8th Cir. 2001); C.H. ex rel. Z.H. v. Oliva, 226 F.3d 198, 201 (3d Cir. 2000).

53. Board of Trustees v. Garrett, 121 S. Ct. 955, 965 (2000); Eason v. Clark County School Dist., 303 F.3d 1137 (9th Cir. 2002) (ADA claim).

54. Cherry v. U. Wis. System Bd. of Regents, 265 F.3d 541 (7th Cir. 2001).

55. *Ibid.;* Pederson v. Lousiana State U., 213 F.3d 858 (5th Cir. 2000); Litman v. Georgetown U., 186 F.3d 544 (4th Cir. 1999).

56. Nanda v. Bd. of Trustees, U. of Illinois, 303 F.3d 817 (7th Cir. 2002); Okruhlik v. U. of Arkansas, 255 F.3d 615 (8th Cir. 2001); Downing v. Board of Trustees, 321 F.3d 1017 (11th Cir. 2003).

57. Koslow v. Pennsylvania, 302 F.3d 161 (3d Cir. 2002); A.W. v. Jersey City Public Schools, 341 F.3d 234 (3d Cir. 2003). *But see contra*: Garcia v. S.U.N.Y. Health Sciences Ctr., 280 F.3d 70 (2d Cir. 2001).

58. *See* authorities collected in Vives v. Fajardo, 218 F. Supp. 2d 124, 127 (D. Puerto Rico 2002). *Minority circuits:* Kiman v. United States, 311 F.3d 439 (1st Cir. 2002); Garcia v. SUNY Health Sci. Center, 280 F.3d 70 (2d Cir. 2001); Popovitch v. Cuyahoga County Court, *en banc,* 276 F.3d 808 (6th Cir. 2002).

CHAPTER 9

Private Education: Alternatives to Public Schools

∽ **CHAPTER OUTLINE**
I.   Background Note
II. Private Schools: State Regulation and Services
     A. Constitutional Constraints on State Regulation
     B. State Approval Requirements
     C. Teacher Rights and Duties
         1. Individual Contracts
         2. Collectively Bargained Contracts
     D. Student Rights and Duties
         1. Contract Rights
         2. Student Discipline
     E. Civil Rights: Teachers and Students
         1. Note on Civil Rights in Private Schools
         2. Race and Ethnic Discrimination
         3. Gender Discrimination
         4. Disability Discrimination
         5. Age Discrimination
         6. Religious Considerations
         7. State Antidiscrimination Laws
     F. Government Aids to Education in Private Schools
         1. Aid Directed to Religious Schools
         2. Aid Directed to Students and Parents
         3. School Transportation
         4. Instructional Materials and Equipment
         5. Remedial Services
         6. Tuition Assistance and Tax Relief
         7. Aid Directed to Nonreligious Schools
III. Charter Schools
     A. Background Note
     B. Creation and Legal Status
         1. Charter Grant, Renewal, and Revocation

    C.   Operational Requirements
        1.   Student Admissions
        2.   Teacher Qualifications
        3.   Curriculum Requirements
    D.   Funding of Charter Schools

IV.   Home Schooling
    A.   State Regulation
    B.   Participation in Public School Activities

V.   Tort Liability in Nonpublic Schools
    A.   Topical Tort Situations
        1.   Premises Liability
        2.   Duties of Supervision
        3.   Affirmative Defenses
        4.   First Aid
        5.   Defamation Liability
        6.   Educational Malpractice
    B.   Immunity Defenses and Dollar Recovery Limits

CASES

9.1   Catholic High School Assn. of Archdiocese of New York v. Culvert, 753 F.2d 1161 (2nd Cir. 1985)
9.2   Geraci v. St. Xavier High School, 3 Ohio Op. 3d 146 (1978)
9.3   Agostini v. Felton, 521 U.S. 203 (1997)
9.4   Mitchell v. Helms, 530 U.S. 793 (2000)
9.5   Zelman v. Simmons-Harris, 122 S. Ct. 2460 (2002)
9.6   Hooks v. Clark County School District, 228 F.3d 1036 (9th Cir. 2000)

ENDNOTES

BACKGROUND NOTE

The major alternative forms of education outside traditional public schools, namely, private schools, home schooling, and charter schools are in many respects unique in their legal and administrative structure and in the degree of control to which they are subject by the state laws. While some laws commonly apply to all three forms of schooling, most states have enacted separate statutes to cover each class of private education, and have adopted different schemes of regulation for each of them. For this reason, each of three dominant forms of private education are considered separately in Parts II, III, and IV of this chapter. Dual enrollment or share-time classes or activities of these students in public schools were discussed generally in Chapter 3 and also raise questions which are currently working their way through the courts.

Administrators of nonpublic education and of public authorities who provide them with law-mandated services and regulate their activities must all have a working knowledge of their respective rights and obligations in order to avoid unnecessary frictions and conflicts.

PRIVATE SCHOOLS: STATE REGULATION AND SERVICES

Private schools, the dominant alternative to public education, may be defined as schools that are privately operated and supported primarily by other than public funds, though they are subject to government regulation and oversight.

Private schools predated the creation, regulation, and operation of public schools by the states. States did not attempt substantial direct regulation of such schools until the twentieth century. That regulation continues to develop with ongoing changes in the laws regarding the scope of state regulation.

Constitutional Constraints on State Regulation

As explained in past chapters, the First and Fourteenth Amendments apply only to *state action* so that the constitutional constraints that operate against state agencies such as public schools do not govern the purely private actions of private schools. For this reason, the *constitutional* rights of public school teachers and students (such as due process, equal protection of the laws, freedom of speech, association, and religion, and freedom from unreasonable search) do not attach to private school teachers, employees, and students, *unless* the challenged private school action is so bracketed or intertwined with government action as to take on the color of state action. See, for example, the discussion of state action requisites in the *Geraci* opinion (Case 9.2) at the end of the chapter.

The facts that states regulate private schools and provide some forms of public aid to those schools do not alone create a state action foundation to invest individuals with constitutional rights against private schools.[1] An example of a sufficient state–private connection to constitute state action by a private school appeared where a private school joined and was subject to a statewide interscholastic athletic association which served both public and private schools.[2]

The failure to recognize the different constitutional status of public and nonpublic schools underlies many misunderstandings about the bounds of state authority to regulate private schools and their patrons. Public school administrators and state educational agencies are bound, as state actors, to observe the constitutional rights of private school patrons or operators, on one hand, but private schools are not bound to accord constitutional rights to those parties in engaging in their private action. Thus, state attempts to require all parents to send their children to public schools and federal laws prohibiting the use of foreign languages in private schools were struck down as infringing fundamental constitutional liberties of the parents.[3] Those rulings involved nonsectarian as well as church-related schools and are founded on unenumerated fundamental liberties of private school operators rather than on freedom of religion, as is commonly thought. Nevertheless, the Supreme Court has made clear that states may constitutionally regulate private schools to ensure adequate education for and the health and safety of their students, so long as the state regulations reasonably serve secular public interests, and do not impinge on the protected civil rights of regulated parties.[4]

The Chapter 3 review of the First Amendment religion clauses (Establishment and Free Exercise) will not be repeated here except with reference to their unique applications to religiously affiliated schools and school groups. As discussed in Chapter 3, courts have refused to extend the exemption of Amish children from state compulsory education beyond eighth grade (*Wisconsin v. Yoder*) under the Free Exercise Clause, to religious objections that do not outweigh the state's strong interest in assuring minimal child education. State prosecutions of parents who violate compulsory education laws raise different questions, because in criminal proceedings the presumption of innocence requires the state to prove beyond a reasonable doubt that parents intended to violate the law. In civil enforcement proceedings, many courts held that parents who do not enroll their children in a qualified school program are *prima facie* guilty unless they prove that they are entitled to exemption from the law.[5] Where public authorities seek the ultimate sanction of terminating parental custodial rights to their children, courts may require the state to prove their unfitness by "clear and convincing" evidence and that the drastic remedy serves the child's best interests.[6]

Private schools and their patrons have no constitutional exemption from laws that protect public health, safety, and welfare. Unless such laws implicate a specific constitutional liberty, all schools must comply with them. Prominent examples of binding regulations include laws regarding Social Security obligations, unemployment compensation, workers' compensation, minimum wages, and pension regulations.[7] Nevertheless, many state legislatures have, as a matter of legislative policy, elected to regulate private school operations more loosely than public schools.

The major area of private school disputes under the religion clauses relates to the validity of federal and state laws that provide financial aid to religious schools. That topic is reviewed in the later section titled "Government Aids to Education in Private Schools."

State Approval Requirements

State approval or licensure requirements for nondenominational and church-related schools, private academies, schools for exceptional children, and residential schools vary considerably from state to state.[8] The following report indicates that diversity:

> Acceptable ways of meeting the schooling requirement vary widely among states. Some states require certification of teachers and schools, some only approval and some only minimal evidence that schooling takes place.... Some states, such as Alaska, Arizona, Georgia and Ohio give state and local school officials wide discretionary authority to excuse a child from the compulsory attendance requirement.... Some states have consciously deregulated their private schools...." [P. Lines, *Private Education Alternatives and State Regulation*, pp. 3–4 (Education Commission of the States, March 1982)]

Courts have generally rejected private school objections that state regulations are unconstitutionally vague, or violate religious liberty, or are discriminatory or interfere with parental rights, or personal rights of contract, association, and privacy.[9] Parties raising such challenges have the heavy burden of proving either that the state regulations are unreasonable, or in the case of a religious liberty claim, that the state has not proven an overriding state interest in assuring minimal adequate child education. Parties may seek exemption from only certain parts of an otherwise valid state requirement.[10]

Where an attendance law refers only to a "school," courts have to decide whether that word includes nontraditional programs such as home instruction.[11] The importance of state approval standards is illustrated by the *Hooks* case (Case 9.6), which is discussed later.

Where state approval requirements are contested, courts have developed two divergent approaches. In one, courts consider whether the state is limited to setting "output" standards that ensure adequate educational achievement. In the other approach, courts consider whether the state may set "input" standards of educational resources that are "equivalent" or "comparable" to those of public schools. The courts in a majority of states have upheld laws that specify input approval standards, including requirements that private school instructors be state approved or certified, and that the covered schools meet prescribed curriculum requirements.[12] In a few states, courts struck down state requirements that private schools provide equivalent or substantially comparable resources and programs as public schools, on the grounds that those requirements were not necessary to achieve proper state educational goals and that they infringed religious freedom.[13] The broader objection that state approval standards are too vague to provide fair notice and due process ultimately depends on the specific language of the challenged law or regulation. State standards were found vague in Georgia, Pennsylvania, and Wisconsin, and upheld as not vague in most other states, including Illinois, Maine, Idaho, Iowa, and New York.[14]

Administrative decisions under otherwise valid laws may still be contested on the administrative law grounds that were reviewed in Chapter 2, namely, that the specific decision is not authorized in law (*ultra vires*), or rests on an erroneous view of the law, or involves an arbitrary abuse of the administrator's discretion. Thus a state board's attempt to supervise private schools where the statute only authorized it to approve the school's instructional program was overturned as *ultra vires*.[15]

Private schools are subject to state and local land use laws and building regulations which reasonably relate to public health, safety, or welfare and which are nondiscriminatory.[16] Zoning regulations that exclude private schools from the entire municipality have been overturned as unreasonable, as has the imposition of oppressive use conditions, such as the requirement that a private school be located on at least 50 acres of land.[17] Schools may be lawfully excluded from selected residential areas, but where only private schools were so excluded, a majority of cases voided the law, though some courts upheld them on the narrow ground that public schools as state entities are exempt from local zoning regulation, or that the burdens created by private schools in residential areas are different from those created by public schools.[18]

The cases are divided on the validity of different zoning restrictions for different kinds of schools (i.e., nursery and elementary schools, profit and nonprofit schools) as being discriminatory or reasonable.[19] A few states and localities expressly prohibit different zoning treatment of public and nonpublic schools. As with all administrative decisions, zoning decisions may also be challenged as *ultra vires* or as an abuse of discretion.[20]

Zoning disputes often turn on court interpretation of the contested meaning of key terms in the law:

> [T]he zoning ordinance issue in this case reduces to whether Washington Christian Academy is "church" use . . . sufficient to bring it within the excepted prior use. The church maintains that since the school is an integral and inseparable part of their religious faith, the use for church and school are one and the same. The City views the uses as separable. [*City of Sumner v. First Baptist Church*, 639 P.2d 1358, 1365 (Wash. 1982)]

The zoning classification of mixed-purpose institutions, e.g., those that provide education services, temporary housing, and therapeutic treatment, varies with the use standards of individual laws. Such institutions were excluded from school zones in New York as being more like treatment centers than private schools, while courts in Massachusetts and New Jersey ruled that a rehabilitative and educational center retained the status of a school for zoning purposes.[21]

Private school properties are subject to the eminent domain power of states to take private property for public uses, but as in all condemnations, the government must pay the school owner just compensation for the taken property.[22]

Teacher Rights and Duties

The employment rights and obligations of private school teachers and employees are largely determined by the law governing their individual and collectively bargained contracts, and by employment statutes that govern private as well as public employers, such as the Title VII statute discussed in Chapter 6.

Individual Contracts

In law, a contract is a *legally enforceable* agreement, hence, not all agreements are contracts. The chief area of contract concern for private school teachers is their terms of employment, particularly rights against contract termination before the expiration of an individual or union bargained contract. Such a termination in violation of contract agreements amounts to a contract breach by the school that entitles the discharged employee to recover lost contract salary.[23] Conversely, a *material* breach of contract terms by a teacher would release the employer school from its contract obligations and justify termination without further pay.[24] Private school contracts are not standardized by law, as are public school contracts, particularly with reference to crucial terms regarding retention and tenure. Since private school contracts are often peculiar to the educational mission of a particular school, court interpretations of private school contracts are necessarily more individualized than public school contracts. Even so, some basic standards of contract law apply universally, such as the principle that contract terms will be interpreted to reflect the fair expectations of the parties when entering into their contract. Courts may, therefore, derive contract obligations that are within the fair expectation of the parties, even though those obligations are not expressly specified in the contract form. Private school contracts increasingly refer to and incorporate obligations specified in other school documents, such as school handbooks and regulations, or union agreements in order to clarify contract obligations. Courts may further imply contract duties from the parties' past course of dealings, the nature of the school, and the position in question, but they will not imply an obligation that contradicts express contract terms.[25] Some contracts, particularly those of religiously affiliated schools, may contain a stipulation that teachers are subject to discharge for publicly contradicting, by word or action, the moral teachings of the school and affiliated denomination. Where no such duty is stipulated, courts have taken different positions on such duties. One case overturned the discharge of a Catholic school teacher for marrying a Catholic priest contrary to church law, because the school documents failed to specify that employee observance of church law was a condition of continued employment,[26] whereas other cases upheld nonrenewal or dismissal of Catholic teachers who remarried contrary to precepts of the Catholic church,[27] or who intentionally concealed material facts regarding their marriage that did not comport with the teaching of the sponsoring church.[28] Courts will not question the accuracy or validity of a school's asserted religious precepts since such investigation would entangle the government with religion in violation of the religion clauses of the First Amendment. The implication of a contract duty not to undermine a school's value goals may also be made in contracts of nonreligious private schools.[29]

Collectively Bargained Contracts

Collective bargaining between private schools and teacher associations or unions is mandated by law in some, but not all, states.[30] When a state labor relations statute is challenged as not controlling religiously affiliated schools, courts must first decide whether the involved labor statute requires private schools to engage in collective bargaining, and if so, whether such a requirement violates constitutional rights. To answer the first question, courts will look to the terms and intent of the invoked labor statute. As to the second question, the Supreme Court has not squarely ruled on the constitutionality of state-mandated collective bargaining by religion-affiliated schools, under either the National Labor Relations Act (NLRA) or under a state law. In the only case to reach the Supreme Court on the constitutional question, *NLRB v. Catholic Bishop,* 440 U.S. 490 (1979), the Court avoided a constitutional ruling by deciding that Congress did not intend the NLRA to apply to *religious* elementary and secondary private schools. The First Circuit Court of Appeals later held that the NLRA does apply to a nonreligious day care.[31] The courts of New Jersey and New York have held that the NLRA does not preempt or displace state labor laws,[32] and, along with Minnesota, have upheld the constitutionality of their state bargaining laws as applied to religious schools, on the ground that the challenged laws require bargaining only on secular and not religious aspects of school employment.[33] Some legal commentators and one circuit court have questioned whether state labor boards can neutrally decide whether a particular labor issue is only a secular or only a religious matter, or both.[34] Until higher federal courts rule otherwise, private school administrators and their employees will be governed by the laws of their home state. The validity of state regulation of religious school labor relations, while technically open to challenge in many states, has become moot because religious schools have elected not to challenge them, and instead to accede to state labor jurisdiction.

Where the validity of a state labor law is not contested, courts must still resolve the slippery question whether a particular state labor board decision is validly confined to secular aspects of a school's employment or unconstitutionally intrudes into matters of religion. The *Culvert* case, which appears at the end of this chapter as Case 9.1, directly addressed this problem.

The rights of private school teachers and employees under equal opportunity statutes are discussed in a later section.

Student Rights and Duties

As with teachers and employees, the law of contracts is the dominant source of student and parent rights in their dealing with private schools. Their rights under equal opportunity statutes are discussed in a later section.

Contract Rights

The express and implied terms of the contract of admission to a private school primarily define and govern the rights of admitted students and their parents. Student enrollment generally connotes agreement to abide by the documents of admission, and terms that are fairly incorporated or implied from the school's catalogs, regulations, handbooks, and generally understood customs.[35] The importance of such terms is evident in disputes over tuition obligations, school release of academic records, and the legality of school disciplinary actions. The *Geraci* case, which appears at the end of this chapter as Case 9.2, illustrates these points.

Courts enforce contract stipulations on tuition obligations unless they are found to be unconscionable or against public policy. Courts have enforced agreements that call for full tuition payment without refund, notwithstanding later parental decision not to enroll or to withdraw a child from the school, or student failure or inability to complete the covered semester.[36] Nor can parents claim tuition refund when the student is dismissed for violating valid school rules, or when a student is withdrawn upon school request for reasons which are specified in the admissions contract.[37] A parent's failure to pay agreed charges in breach of a contract relieves the school of any further obligations, including any duty to prepare or provide the student's academic records, but a court may find grounds in particular circumstances to imply a school obligation to release grade records for satisfactorily completed courses.[38] Where a school breaches an implied contract duty, that breach precludes recovery of unpaid tuition. For instance, where a vocational school failed to maintain educational records required for student licensure to practice the skills taught by the school, the school could not recover unpaid tuition.[39]

Courts will not second-guess academic decisions or the school's educational performances, but if they find that a school acted in bad faith, they can treat such action as a contract breach.[40]

Student Discipline

Contracts are often unclear on the limits of student discipline and punishment. Although courts are not inclined to question school conduct standards or to overturn student punishments,[41] they are likely to overturn disciplinary procedures or severe punishments that are patently unfair on the ground that those actions exceed the fair contract expectations of the parties.[42] Disciplinary sanctions for conduct that is "immoral" or "detrimental" to the school or its honor code are generally considered to be within the fair understanding of the parties. Though the contract terms on such sanctions might be somewhat vague, they are not subject to constitutional objection because, as previously noted, private schools are not engaged in "state action" as to be subject to constitutional prohibitions.[43]

Where a private school educates children with handicaps and receives payment for such service under the IDEA and Rehabilitation Act, they must comply with the limits which those laws set for the discipline of students with handicaps. See the discussion of those laws in Chapter 7. For example, schools may not employ disciplinary measures that will deprive a child with a disability of the educational services required by those laws. Most private schools receive *some* financial assistance from the federal Commissioner of Education and must, therefore, comply with the Family Education Rights and Privacy Act of 1974 (FERPA), also discussed in Chapter 7. In addition, private schools must comply with state laws that require them to maintain and provide state agencies with specified records and reports, such as those dealing with student health, attendance, testing, and graduation.

A school's duty to maintain confidentiality of student information will depend on the information in question. Subject to these limitations, a court might imply a contract obligation that student information be kept confidential. That possibility should incline administrators to keep student information confidential wherever practicable.

Civil Rights: Teachers and Students

In addition to their affirmative contract duties, private schools must also refrain from conduct that violates the rights of their employees, students, and parent patrons that are created by antidiscrimination statutes whose terms extend to private actors as well as to government actors. The discussion of those statutes in Chapters 6, 7, and 8 provides the essential references for their application to private schools.

Note on Civil Rights in Private Schools

The general state action limit of constitutional protections renders the following question of particular import: In what circumstances will private school activity be sufficiently bracketed with or intertwined with government action as to make private school activity equivalent to "state action"?

As shown by the *Geraci* case (Case 9.2), it takes much more than a government–school contact or contract to create state action. A classic illustration of private school state action appeared in the case of Girard College, a private primary and secondary school that was created by the Will of Stephen Girard, which limited admissions to the school to "white male orphans". Because that Will required the state and city to enact enabling laws, to make public contributions for constructing the school, and to manage it by a city Board of Trustees, the courts found the school was engaged in "state action" and accordingly could not constitutionally deny admission to African-American students based on their race.[44] The Girard College case does not outlaw private discrimination, or prohibit privately created racial restrictions, but it does prohibit extensive private–state involvement in racial discrimination.[45]

While the government may not interfere with a purely private decision to discriminate, it may refuse to extend public benefits to private parties who do discriminate. The Supreme Court noted this distinction in holding that federal tax exemptions could be denied to a private university that prohibited interracial dating by its students.[46]

Absent a state action nexus, private schools may *constitutionally* engage in religious discrimination, though, as reported in Chapter 3, public schools may not do so. In like vein, a state may not constitutionally or under Title VII impose on religious institutions an *absolute* duty to provide religious accommodation for all its employees in circumstances where that accomodation interferes with basic religious tenets of the employer.[47]

Unlike the Constitution, some discrimination statutes do cover private schools. For example, under the Act of 1866 (42 U.S.C. § 1981) a court could enjoin a private school from refusing admission to African-American applicants, solely on the basis of race, once the school had publicly invited members of the public to seek a contract of admission for their children.[48] The statutes discussed in this section have been reviewed at length in the past three chapters. The information there presented provides the essential background for this chapter, and need not be repeated here.

Race and Ethnic Discrimination

The Title VII law that prohibits race-based employment discrimination applies to private employers with a minimum number of 15 employees, but that law exempts religiously based employment decisions by religion-related schools. The Supreme Court held that the religious exemption did not constitute aid to religion and, accordingly, did not violate the Establishment Clause.[49] However, church affiliation alone is not automatic grounds for the Title VII exemption. To qualify for the religious exemption, a private school employer must establish not only that the school has a religious character, but that the challenged employment decision or position in question involves a bona fide religious need of the employer school.[50]

A qualified religious school could lawfully adopt work terms and conditions that are essential to its religious mission even though such terms and conditions exclude persons who fall within the group protections of Title VII. For example, a religious school may hire only members of its faith to teach religion courses. It may, without violating Title VII, discharge a teacher for public conduct that is contrary to the school's religious tenets, though such conduct does not violate public laws.[51]

The Title VI law that prohibits racial or ethnic discrimination in federally aided programs applies to federally aided private schools, and does not exempt religious schools. Since a private school is free to decline federal aid conditions that are contrary to its religious tenets, there is no basis for the school to complain that the law interferes with its practice of religion.

Gender Discrimination

Subject to the Title VII exception for religiously based employment decisions, private schools may not lawfully enage in gender-based employment discrimination.

The application of the Equal Pay Act (EPA) to church-related schools is not fully settled. Several courts interpreted the EPA as not covering church-related schools.[52] Each school must, therefore, check whether the courts governing its territory have addressed that question, until such future time as the Supreme Court shall have considered and decided it.

Title IX also prohibits gender discrimination by private employers. Like Title VI, it applies only to federally aided private school programs; it does not provide for a religious exemption. Private schools are free to decline federal aid conditions that are contrary to its religious tenets and, hence, may not complain that the aid conditions interfere with their religious freedom. A religious school may, however, defend a challenged employment decision as based on business need or a bona fide employment qualification with respect to religiously sensitive positions.

Disability Discrimination

Private schools are not required to admit students with disabilities or accept referrals by a school district or other state agency of children under the Individuals with Disabilities Education Act (IDEA). However, those that do so are subject to the conditions and regulations imposed by the IDEA. Private schools that receive government funds for educating students with disabilities must comply with the funding conditions. A private school that employs state-funded teachers must comply with the state-set salary for those teachers, and must observe expense limits and conditions that are set by the grantor government.[53] A school that accepts a child with a disability without an official referral thus assumes the risk that the school district or agency charged with that Act's administration may decline to pay for its services.[54]

The Americans with Disabilities Act (ADA) and Title I of the Rehabilitation Act oblige private school employers not to discriminate against teachers or other employees whose disabilities are covered by those laws. As explained in Chapter 6, the ADA does not require employers to hire or retain employees whose disabilities render them incapable of performing "essential functions" of their job. The extent to which religious schools may claim that employment decisions for religiously sensitive positions are based on the candidate's inability to perform an "essential job function" rather than on a disability has not been fully explored by the courts.

Age Discrimination

Private schools are also bound by the provisions of the Age Discrimination in Employment Act (ADEA),[55] but the federal courts are not in agreement on the question whether the ADEA could be constitutionally applied to church-related schools. The Second and Third Circuits found no such constitutional barrier, but lower courts in other circuits held that the religion clauses of the Constitution prohibit application of the ADEA to religious schools.[56]

Religious Considerations

Where a church-sponsored school defended its dismissal of teachers on the grounds that the teachers breached their employment contract not to violate church law, but the teacher alleged that the discharge was based on the teacher's age, the court ruled that trial must be held to decide whether the school dismissal was motivated by age or by religious concerns. The court further noted that the issue of motivation did not require an inquiry into the validity of asserted church doctrine.[57] Any claim of religious need will fail if the employee proves that the claim of religious need is unfounded, but is a pretext for age discrimination.[58]

State Antidiscrimination Laws

State antidiscrimination laws often parallel federal laws,[59] but many prohibit forms of private discrimination that are not prohibited or remedied by the federal laws. State-to-state law variations require parties to check the law of the governing state.

Government Aids to Education in Private Schools

Nonpublic education is predominantly financed privately by student tuition, fees, and private contributions. Private schools are free to adopt their own fiscal policies for privately generated funds, but they must either comply with government-imposed conditions for receipt of government funds, or decline them. The major disputes on government financial assistance involve challenges under provisions of state constitutions and under the First Amendment religion clauses.

Challenges under state constitutions have fared differently depending on the wording, history, and interpretation of each state's constitution. Some forms of state aid to private schools that were held valid under the national Constitution were overturned in some states as barred by the state constitution. Some instances of these state variations will be noted in the following discussion of aid topics under the national Constitution.

The tortuous Supreme Court interpretations of the First Amendment religion clauses were noted in Chapter 3 with regard to public school religion disputes. That history is even more ragged with respect to government assistance to religiously affiliated schools. Under the latest Supreme Court decisions, the validity of government aid to religiously affiliated schools depends in part on the level of education that is aided and in part on the form of the challenged aid program. The Court had distinguished between aid to religiously affiliated colleges and religiously affiliated primary and secondary schools, uniformly allowing direct government aid to church-related colleges and their students, while striking down direct grants and subsidies to religious schools.[60] The Sixth Circuit Court of Appeals recently upheld a law that authorized government authorities to issue tax-exempt bonds to raise funds to finance (by way of loans) the construction of educational buildings of private schools, including admittedly religious private schools. Citing the Supreme Court decision in the *Agostini* case (Case 9.3), which is discussed below, the court upheld the law as religiously neutral and valid under the Establishment Clause.[61]

The Supreme Court Justices remain sharply divided on various forms of government aid to religious schools. The Court, by close 5–4 votes, recently overruled several of its prior school aid decisions and rejected the constitutional tests espoused by the overruled cases. The latest decisions place greater emphasis on government "neutrality" as a touchstone of constitutionality and expound that "neutrality" standard much differently than do the dissenting Justices.

In *Agostini*, however, we brought some clarity to our case law, by overruling two anomalous precedents . . . and by consolidating some of our previously disparate considerations under a revised test. Whereas in *Lemon* we had considered whether a statute (1) has a secular purpose, (2) has a primary effect of advancing or inhibiting religion, or (3) creates an excessive entanglement between government and religion, . . . in *Agostini* we modified *Lemon* for purposes of evaluating aid to schools. . . . . . . We then set out revised criteria for determining the effect of a statute: . . . [See *Mitchell*, Case 9.4, infra]

In *Agostini*, the [Supreme] Court recognized that '[i]nteraction between church and state is inevitable.' 521 U.S. @ 233. . . . Thus the '[e]ntanglement must be 'excessive' before it runs afoul of the Establishment Clause'. [*Johnson v. Econ. Development of Cty. of Oakland*, 241 F.3d 501, 515 (6th Cir. 2001)]

Even as so delimited, the wavering force of the slippery *Lemon* case[62] will continue to fuel debate within the Court.

The latest Supreme Court decisions (*Agostini, Mitchell,* and *Zelman*—Cases 9.3, 9.4, and 9.5, respectively) present the current state of the constitutional law on various forms of government aid.

Aid Directed to Religious Schools

Direct government grants to church-related private schools for building maintenance in poverty areas and for instructional expenses in secular courses were overturned as unconstitutional, while comparable direct government subsidies to church-related orphanages or protectories have withstood like challenges.[63] With regard to grants of federal *surplus* property, the Supreme Court has held that the challenger lacked "standing" to mount a First Amendment challenge since congressional disposition of surplus government property did not involve tax revenue or current taxes which affect taxpayers.[64]

State reimbursement of church school expenses to conduct state-mandated student achievement tests and to report the results to the state was first voided as an unconstitutional aid to religion, but later upheld if the tests were prepared and scored by state employees, and finally upheld even if the tests were scored as well as conducted by parochial school teachers.[65]

The Constitution *permits,* it does not *require,* state governments to grant any benefits to private schools. State tax exemptions for private schools are provided as a matter of legislative policy, not constitutional compulsion, and such allowances have withstood constitutional challenge that they impermissibly aid religion.[66]

Aid Directed to Students and Parents

Some government benefits for students or parents are provided through school channels (such as student lunch programs, transportation, job training, and instructional materials) while others are delivered directly to students or parents (such as remedial services, tuition grants, and tax deductions). Some of these aid forms, such as lunch programs and job training programs, have not been seriously challenged by test litigation, while others are perennially litigated and appealed to the Supreme Court. The best guidance as to each form of aid is best gathered from case lines that deal with a specific form of government aid.

School Transportation

In *Everson v. Board of Education* [330 U.S. 1 (1947)] the Supreme Court upheld publicly provided student transportation to church-related schools as a child-benefit welfare measure. The Court later overturned state-funded field trip transportation for such students on the ground that the presence of religious school teachers on such trips risked giving support to a school's religious teaching.[67] That reasoning was undercut by the recent Supreme Court decisions in *Agostini* (Case 9.3) and in *Zobrest v. Catalina Foothills School Dist.* [509 U.S. 1 (1993)], which are discussed below. Both cases held that the Establishment Clause does not prohibit publicly paid special educational services inside a parochial school classroom.

The federal Constitution *permits,* but does not *require,* states to provide school transportation to church schools. State denial of school transportation to nonpublic schoolchildren does not deny them equal protection of the law or penalize their free exercise of religion.[68]

Different state courts have taken conflicting positions on private school busing under their respective state constitutions. In a majority of states the courts upheld state provision of nonpublic school transportation as valid under their state constitutions, but the courts of a significant minority of states have overturned the practice as a violation of their state constitutions.[69]

Where busing is allowed, parents may not demand transportation beyond the limits authorized by state law. Where a state law authorized interdistrict transportation for both public and nonpublic school students, the law was sustained even though nonpublic school students made much greater use of interdistrict transportation.[70] However, where the law permits interdistrict transportation only for nonpublic school students, the state courts have divided on the validity of that arrangement.[71]

Where a statute expressly mandates (rather than merely permits) private school transportation, state administrators have no discretion to deny it.[72] Neither may they ignore statutory restrictions and provide parochial school busing beyond the limits set by statute.[73] Discriminatory application of an otherwise valid busing law, e.g., by denying transportation services based on enrollment levels in public or private schools, may also be enjoined.

Some courts have allowed the busing agency to furnish parents funds to obtain substitute transportation, in lieu of direct busing services, so long as the fare payment is reasonable and less than the district's cost of directly providing that service.[74] Administrative decisions on transportation arrangements are always subject to challenge for abuse of discretion, but parents must make timely application for school transportation or be foreclosed from complaining.[75]

Instructional Materials and Equipment

State loans of secular textbooks to nonpublic schoolchildren have been upheld under the federal Constitution,[76] and under the state constitutions of New York, Ohio, and Pennsylvania. Such loans were held unconstitutional under the state constitutions of California, Kentucky, Massachusetts, Michigan, Missouri, Nebraska, Oregon, and South Dakota.[77]

The Supreme Court initially differentiated government loans of books from loans of other instructional materials and equipment, but it later reversed that position and upheld the state loan of instructional materials and computers to religiously affiliated schools for student use, although the materials and computers were placed in the custody of those schools. See the *Mitchell* decisions (Case 9.4). *Mitchell* removed a major fiscal barrier to wiring all primary and secondary schools for computer education.

Remedial Services

The constitutionality of government provision of "auxiliary services" to students of church-related schools is best understood against the following case history. After invalidating the use of federal funds for on-site remedial services (e.g., therapeutic counseling) by public school specialists to students inside a church school, the Justices split three ways to develop the decision which also nullified laws that provided for *remedial instruction* by public school teachers *inside* parochial schools, while distinguishing classroom and nonclassroom sites for such services.[78] The Court recently reversed these holdings and upheld education-related services *inside* parochial schools in the following instances:

- Provision of a sign-language interpreter inside a parochial school classroom under the IDEA. [*Zobrest v. Catalina Foothills School Dist.* [509 U.S. 1 (1993)]
- Provision of *remedial instruction* to disadvantaged children inside parochial schools by publicly employed professionals under Title I of the federal education aid statute. [*Agostini* (Case 9.3)]
- Loan of computers and instructional materials for student use inside religious school. [*Mitchell* (Case 9.4)]
- Grant of tuition vouchers to low-income parents for use in parochial, private, or public schools. [*Zelman* (Case 9.5)]

Tuition Assistance and Tax Relief

State grants of tuition assistance or reimbursement to parents for private school tuition, sometimes involving the use of state vouchers, have taken different forms. Such programs usually limit the number of parents who are eligible to receive that assistance, either to a flat amount, or to a percentage of tuition, or to persons below a poverty income line, or to parents of children enrolled in distressed, poorly performing public schools. There are many proposed formulas for tuition assistance programs, but most of them are driven more by policy considerations than by constitutional doctrine.

In 1973, the Supreme Court held that partial state reimbursement of tuition costs at religious schools was an unconstitutional aid to the religious mission of those schools.[79] Several states thereafter enacted broader laws that covered all parents, on the theory that a program of general assistance could pass constitutional muster, regardless of the parents' choice of schools. The high court of Wisconsin upheld that state's law which authorized state tuition grants to students of low-income families, for use in public or nonsectarian private schools.[80] A similar Florida tuition voucher law is currently pending court decision under the state constitution.[81] In the above-mentioned *Zelman* case (Case 9.5) the Supreme Court upheld the Ohio law that authorized tuition grants to low-income parents for use in public or private schools, including religious schools.

A variant on tuition grant aid appeared in Maine and Vermont laws that granted tuition and tax relief benefits to parents of students enrolled in non-sectarian private schools where their local school districts did not operate a public school, but not to similarly resident parents whose children were enrolled in a religious school. Those laws were held to be constitutional against the challenge that they denied parochial school parents the equal protection of the law and infringed their free exercise of religion. The Supreme Court declined petitions to review those challenges.[82]

Tuition tax credits and deductions for educational expenses are available on a limited basis in three states. Like vouchers, they raise policy as well as constitutional objections by opponents of such aid. In 1975, the Supreme Court overturned a New York tax relief provision as an indirect form of subsidy for church school tuition, but it later sustained a Minnesota tax deduction law that allowed all parents a state income tax deduction for educational expenses, though church school parents gained the most benefit from that law.[83] The Court concluded that because the Minnesota law benefits were available to all parents and not just private school parents, its prior New York ruling was not controlling:

> [T]his case is vitally different from the scheme struck down in *Nyquist.* There, public assistance amounting to tuition grants, was provided only to parents of children in *nonpublic* schools. [Moreover] we intimated that "public assistance (e.g., scholarships) made available generally without regard to the sectarian–nonsectarian or public–nonpublic nature of the institution benefitted," might not offend the Establishment Clause. We think the tax deduction adopted by Minnesota is more similar to this latter type of program than it is to the arrangement struck down in *Nyquist.* [*Mueller v. Allen*, 463 U.S. 388, 397, 398 (1983)]

The Arizona Supreme Court recently upheld that state's law which provided a tax credit up to $500 for taxpayer contributions to organizations that provide tuition support to private schools, including church-related schools.[84] The thesis that governments could constitutionally employ tax policy to lessen parental financial burdens of educating children in sectarian as well as other schools continues to be debated.

Where federal aid laws survive federal constitutional challenge, but state officials are prohibited by their state constitution from distributing the federal aid to religious or other private schools or their patrons, Congress enacted "bypass" provisions to authorize federal agencies to withhold from the state the funds allocable to religious schools or their patrons and to deliver them through nonstate sources.[85]

Some states have avoided being bypassed by interpreting their state constitution as applying only to state funds and not to federal funds. State officials and courts may also avoid the foregoing problem as to nonreligious private schools by interpreting the federal educational aids as serving a public, not a private, purpose that accords with their state constitution.

Aid Directed to Nonreligious Schools

The only serious constitutional barrier to government aid to nonreligious private schools is found in some states where educational aid to any private school is considered a private, not public, purpose and therefore barred by the state constitution. As noted above, if state authorities feel compelled not to participate in distribution of federal funds to private schools, the state may not accept the federal aid, and a federal agency will "bypass" state offices and deliver the federal funds or services directly to the private school.

CHARTER SCHOOLS

Background Note

Charter schools are nonsectarian schools that are created under a state law by a "charter," which establishes their structure and mode of operation. They are not subject to many regulations that govern traditional public schools, but they are accountable to the public authorities in greater degree than traditional private schools. The data here presented on the creation, status, and operation of charter schools has been drawn principally from the following recent studies, which, for convenience are later cited by the short reference that follows their listing.

Charter Schools, The Center for Educational Reform, 1001 Connecticut Ave. NW, Washington D.C. 10036 (website: www.edreform.com) (March 2003) (hereafter cited as the *Center Study*)

Charter School Laws, A. Cotherman, Wisconsin Center for Education Research (website: www.wcer.wisc.edu) (2000) (hereafter cited as *Cotherman*)

Annotation: *Validity, Construction and Application of Statutes or Regulations Governing Charter Schools*, 78 A.L.R. 5th 533 (2000) (hereafter cited as *Annotation—Charter Schools*)

The Charter School Challenge, 162, 163, B.C. Hassel, Brookings Institution Press, Washington, D.C. (1999) (hereafter cited as *Hassel*)

A Comparison of Charter School Legislation, U.S. Dept. Of Education (1998) (hereafter cited as *Dept. of Education*)

Charter Schools, National Education Association (May 1996) (hereafter cited as *NEA Study*)

FIGURE 9.1   Charter Schools in Operation, by State, Fall 2003

State	Number	State	Number
Alaska	15	Mississippi	1
Arizona	464	Nevada	13
California	428	New Jersey	56
Colorado	93	New Mexico	28
Connecticut	16	New York	38
Delaware	11	North Carolina	93
District of Columbia	39	Ohio	131
Florida	227	Oklahoma	10
Georgia	35	Oregon	25
Hawaii	25	Pennsylvania	91
Idaho	13	Rhode Island	8
Illinois	29	South Carolina	13
Indiana	10	Texas	221
Kansas	30	Utah	1
Louisiana	20	Virginia	8
Massachusetts	46	Wisconsin	130
Michigan	196	Wyoming	1
Minnesota	87	Total	2,695

Source: Data from the Center for Education Reform, "Charter School Highlights and Statistics," published on the Center's website: http://edreform.com.

The *Center Study, supra,* reports that, as of the 2002–2003 School Year, there were 2,695 charter schools which served more than 684,000 students in 36 states and the District of Columbia (Figure 9.1). These figures reveal the burgeoning creation of charter schools, since the 1,129 charter schools that were reported as of the 1998–1999 school year.

The substantial differences in state charter laws prevent any reliable summary of the legal developments and practice found in each state. This overview indicates the range of terms found in state charter statutes. Readers who desire specific information on charter school operations in a particular state may refer to the above-listed studies.

Some charter schools are highly specialized and dedicated to serving a narrow class of students, such as "at-risk" or "special needs" children.[86] Some of them mimic special-purpose academies in their organization, curriculum, and teaching methods. In some states, they may be treated as new school districts, or as public schools operating within an existing district, or as private, nonprofit corporations.[87]

The commonly espoused goal of charter school laws is to improve student achievements by enabling private associations to establish schools that are free to experiment with and adopt new educational reforms and initiatives, curricula, and instructional methods. An ancillary purpose is to provide a competetive stimulus for public schools to improve their performance. State legislatures have not pursued any common vision of charter schools. The state-to-state charter law variations reveal a pervasive underlying tension between the legislative desire to encourage independent charter school initiatives, on one hand, and a legislative determination to retain official control over their creation and operation, often by public school administrators. The reservation of a high degree of state and local school district control has raised the criticism that the charter laws raise barriers to charter school growth:

> For charter schools to have a positive impact on public education as a whole, policymakers will need to go back to the drawing boards of charter school legislation. . . . And regulators will need to retool systems of oversight to ensure accountability while minimizing the administrative burdens. . . . They [charter schools] have surprised many by surviving . . . despite philosophical opposition. . . . . . . Perhaps despite the host of political and operational challenges they face, charter schools will surprise skeptics yet again. [*Hassel, supra,* at 162, 163]

The level of support provided by individual states ranges broadly from strong support to nominal or weak support. Under its standard of "strong" and "weak" laws, namely, those which encourage the growth of charter schools, both in number and independence, versus those which provide few incentives for such growth, the *Center Study* lists 20 states with strong to medium strength laws, and 20 states with "weak" laws.[88]

A charter school may be described as "a public school established under a contract between public authorities and a private organization or a group of private schools." [*Annotation—Charter Schools, supra*] As such, it remains a state-sponsored school whose status and operation are closely tied to and dependent on the state-granted charter, state funding, and state administrative oversight and enforcement of the state charter. Charter schools are, therefore, more like public schools than private schools, and are sometimes even referred to as Community Schools. They are not to be confused with Magnet Schools and other "schools within schools" which are part of the official structure of a public school district. These legal shadings were recently noted by the Supreme Court:

> That undertaking includes programs governing community and magnet schools. Community schools are funded under state law but are run by their own school boards, not by local school districts. These schools enjoy academic independence to hire their own teachers and

to determine their own curriculum. They can have no religious affiliation and are required [under Ohio law] to accept students by lottery. During the 1999–2000 school year, there were 10 start-up community schools in the Cleveland City School District with more than 1,900 students enrolled. . . .

Magnet schools are public schools operated by a local school board that emphasize a particular subject area, teaching method, or service to students. For each student enrolled in a magnet school, the school district receives $7,746, . . . the same amount received per student enrolled at a traditional public school. [*Zelman v. Simmons-Harris*, 122 S. Ct. 2460, at 2464, 2465 (2000)]

The courts have, with narrow, limited exception, upheld the constitutional validity of charter school laws, and of challenged official actions under those laws. Such challenges have included claims that charter school laws violate the national and state constitutions because they are unconstitutionally vague, or discriminatory, or aid religion, or violate state constitutional provisions that prohibit the use of public monies for private purposes, or do not meet the state constitution requirement that the state provide an efficient public education. [*Annotation—Charter Schools, supra*]

Creation and Legal Status

In order to commence operations, charter school sponsors must receive a state charter. The "charter" establishing each such school is like a contract between a charter school and the public agency or authority which is empowered by the charter statute to grant the charter to an individual school. The charter outlines the school's mission, programs, and performance obligations, including the school's educational methods, organization, management, students to be educated, instructional requisites, and required student achievement. Charter obligations may include criteria on admissions, testing, teacher qualifications, and student transportation. These criteria may differ significantly from standards that govern traditional public schools. Many statutes expressly require active participation by teachers, staff, parents, and/or local community groups in the creation and administration of charter schools. The elemental characteristics of charter schools vary with the terms of their charters:

> [I]t appears that in ten states charter schools organized by a district are considered part of that local school district. In four states charter schools are considered independent public schools, and in 14 states they are organized as nonprofit entities. Wisconsin law seems to provide the most options. There, a charter school may be under the authority of the local school board; the local board may contract with an outside entity to govern and operate the school; or schools not sponsored by a local board may become independent entities—as they are in Milwaukee, for example. Michigan is unique in that charter schools are corporate

entities subject to leadership and general supervision of the state board. It is not clear in the law whether charter schools can sue and be sued, nor what liability the granting agencies bear. [*Cotherman, supra*]

Charter Grant, Renewal, and Revocation

The eligibility of parties seeking to obtain a charter and the procedures and standards governing charter approvals also vary with each charter law. Some states allow an existing public school, nonprofit organization, group of teachers, or parents to apply for a charter, while others limit applications to existing public schools and to new nonsectarian schools. A few permit an existing private school to convert to a charter school, provided the charter school is nonsectarian. A law may even require the local school district to receive the charter and to then contract with third parties to operate the chartered school within the district.

In some states, charter approval may be made by any one of several entities, including a community college or a state university. Where an existing private school seeks to convert to a charter school, the law may require that a specified percentage of the teachers, employees, parents, or members of the local community participate in the discussions leading to a proposed conversion. In some instances, public hearings are required as part of the charter application and grant process. The right to appeal administrative denials of charters or charter renewals to higher tribunals is granted in some states, but not in others.

In most states, the term or length of a charter grant is limited by law, usually three to five years, with an opportunity to obtain successive charter renewals. Some statutes specify the grounds for revoking a charter or for denying its renewal, such as the school's failure to meet achievement standards.

Operational Requirements

Charter school requirements of student admissions, teacher qualifications, curriculum, and other operatonal requirements also vary with the terms of each charter law and the granted charter.

Student Admissions

A state charter may require charter schools to admit all students, subject only to restrictions based on the grade levels, curriculum offering, or student residence, or it may require charter schools to have a specified makeup of minority racial and ethnic groups that reflect the general population mix of the school's served area.

The charter may authorize competitive admissions, or allow significant options for alternative admissions practices. For example, the law of some states allows a charter school to serve specified *special education* or *"at-risk" students,* or to require charter schools to serve a specified percentage of at-risk students. Louisiana went further to require that the percentage of "at-risk" students in charter school equal or exceed the percentage of such students in the local district. Whether these arrangements would also support gender-based admissions has yet to be tested as gender discrimination at special-purpose charter schools. As reported in Chapter 7, a lower court has overturned as unconstitutional, single-sex public schools and rejected the argument that single-sex education would benefit at-risk students in distressed urban schools. Whether that decision will be followed to prohibit single-sex charter schools or distinguished to permit such schools remains an open question.

Teacher Qualifications

The above-cited *Cotherman* study reports that state laws for teacher credentials in charter schools are checkered. More than two-thirds of states require charter school teachers to have the same credentials as public school teachers. Other states allow waiver of certification requirements or, as in Wisconsin, provide for a special charter school teacher license, or even authorize the board of an approved charter school to set teacher employment criteria.

Curriculum Requirements

The law of individual states is equally varied on charter school curriculum requirements. Some states impose minimum curricular requisites, others exempt charter schools from state or local curriculum or textbook controls; and some authorize elective curricula alongside state prescribed minimums.

Funding of Charter Schools

Charter school funding is primarily private. Whether they receive public financial assistance depends in part on state legislative policy, and in part on their official classification as primarily more kindred to public education than to private education. The validity of public financial assistance would depend on the form, purpose, and effect of that assistance, as discussed earlier in this chapter.

The federal government's Public Charter Schools Program provides grants to the states to fund start-up costs of new charter schools.

HOME SCHOOLING

State Regulation

Home schooling has grown even more dramatically than charter schools in recent decades. There are currently more children being home schooled than are attending charter schools. The reported home school population of half a million students represents an almost one-third increase from the home school population in 1991. [*See* Gardner and McFarland, *Legal Precedents and Strategies Shaping Home Schooled Students' Participation in Public School Sports,* 11 J. Legal Aspects of Sport 25 (2001), 27]

The three top reasons given by parents for home-schooling are (1) ability to give a child a better education at home; (2) religious reasons; and (3) a poor school learning environment. Government regulation of home schooling has been light, but is expected to grow with the growth of home schooling.

All states and the District of Columbia now allow home schooling in some form to satisfy the state's compulsory education laws, but their home schooling laws and regulations do not follow a general pattern. Some states require that home education be "equivalent" or "comparable" to public education; others require "regular and thorough" instruction; others provide limited exemptions for home education; and still others treat home education much as they do private schools. The diverse approaches to home schooling are indicated in the studies listed above and in the endnotes.[89] These studies reveal that the majority of states require explicit home schooler compliance with state regulations in order to satisfy the state compulsory education laws. These approval standards vary greatly with respect to teacher eligibility, required curriculum and instructional time, progress reports, student achievement, state standardized testing, and even of home visits by local school supervisors. A minority of states allow home schooling without imposing very detailed approval requirements. These requirements have been generally upheld as reasonable and constitutional, though a minority of cases have found that some details of regulatory provisions were unreasonable.[90] There is also disuniformity in the strictness with which public officials administer and enforce home schooling regulations.

The *Hooks* case (Case 9.6 at the end of this chapter) illustrates how state approval standards must be adjusted where federal laws mandate special services, in that case for a home-schooled child with a handicap, under the IDEA.

Different states use different "input" (teacher training or qualification, prescribed curriculum, instructional time) and "output" standards to measure student achievement. A court upheld the West Virginia statute that made children ineligible for further home schooling if their standardized test scores fell below the 40th percentile, without improvement after remedial home schooling.[91]

Home education laws and regulations have been challenged on constitutional grounds. Challenges that rely *solely* on asserted parental rights fail almost universally, as the state interest in assuring adequate home education overrides parental claims to control a child's education.[92] Constitutional claims that home education laws are impermissibly vague have also failed in most cases.[93] Where challenges to state requirements rest upon a claim of religious liberty under the Free Exercise Clause, the courts have been more divided. Two recent cases illustrate that division. In Michigan, the court held that an otherwise valid requirement of state certification of home education teachers could not be constitutionally applied to parents whose religious convictions prohibited the use of certified teachers. It concluded that the state's demand of a teaching certificate was not so essential to achieving its educational purpose as to justify the restraint on religious conscience. But courts in Iowa and the Fourth federal circuit rejected that reasoning and found that the state's interest in mandating certified teachers was "compelling" and therefore sufficient to outweigh the religious objections.[94] Similar divisions on the religious issue are found in other states. The foregoing jurisdictional variations are summarized and discussed in the endnotes.

Participation in Public School Activities

Home school advocates have increasingly turned their attention to gaining access for home-schooled children to public school extracurricular programs, such as interscholastic sports, music programs, and school bands. For a variety of educational, administrative, and fiscal reasons, public school authorities and interscholastic associations have resisted the demand that home-schooled children be allowed to participate in noncurricular public school activities. Cases to test the legality of their refusal have become increasingly common. While the case law is still fairly new and incomplete, it usually centers on the usual issues of what the Constitution and relevant federal and state statutes allow or require.

For constitutional purposes, Interscholastic Athletic Associations are considered "state actors" because their activities are so closely "intertwined" with public school operations.[95] Where state law has not established positive rights to participate in public school activities, the assertion of a federal constitutional right of access under the Due Process, Equal Protection, and Free Exercise of Religion Clauses has met with only limited success. Most courts found that, for Due Process purposes, students do not have any constitutional liberty to participate in public school athletic activities, and may not, accordingly, claim any Due Process right to participation.[96] With respect to the Equal Protection Clause, the majority of courts likewise found that student interest in extracurricular activities does not involve a fundamental right, so that any decision to exclude home-schooled students from public school activities would not violate equal protection so long as the exclusion had a rational basis. Most cases held restriction of public school activities to public school students to be rational, but a few minority courts have arrived at a contrary decision. The courts have generally rejected the claim that exclusion of religiously based home-schooled students violates their free exercise of religion because home-schooled students and their parents who choose not to attend public school suffered no religious coercion in making that choice.[97]

The extent to which state constitutions may provide a right of home-schooled students to "opt into" public school programs has not been tested in most states and will depend on the peculiar provisions of each state's laws. While such a right was found under the state constitution of New Hampshire,[98] it is doubtful that the constitutions of most states will be held to provide greater participation rights for home-schooled children than does the federal constitution.

Enabling state legislation holds more promise for parents who wish to enroll their home-schooled children in public school programs. Under the press of home school associations, more than a dozen states have enacted statutes that give nonpublic school students, including home schoolers, a right or opportunity to participate in public school activities, either generally or under specified conditions.[99] A voluntary "open door" policy adopted by a public school board or school superintendent raises the additional objection that their actions are *ultra vires* and not authorized by law. These issues have not triggered many suits for court clarification.[100] Given the diverse laws and ongoing legislative proposals to expand access of home-schooled children to public school activities, the residents of each state must check the current law of their home state.

Student access to federally aided extracurricular programs of public schools would depend on the specifics of federal law and the circumstances in which the programs are administered. See, for example, the discussion in Chapter 7 of the rights of nonpublic schoolchildren under the federal IDEA, Title XI, and IX laws. While those laws will not cover many public school activities, they will have significant impact where they do apply.

TORT LIABILITY IN NONPUBLIC SCHOOLS

The general principles of tort liability that were reviewed in Chapter 4 apply as well to private schools, but the immunity or other defenses of private schools are not coextensive with those of public schools.

Topical Tort Situations

Premises Liability

As noted in Chapter 4, schools are liable to invitees (students, staff, and visitors on school business) for injuries caused by hazardous conditions of buildings, equipment, and grounds if those conditions could have been prevented by reasonable inspection and maintenance. That duty extends only to the physical areas to which students or other persons are invited.

With respect to noninvitees, such as *licensees* who enter the premises lawfully but without invitation, or *trespassers* who enter the premises unlawfully, the school's duty of care is more limited. As to licensees the only school duty is to warn them of known latent dangers and to refrain from intentionally harming them. As to trespassers, a school generally owes no duty of care or prior warning, except where their exposure to particular harm is known to school authorities. A special rule applies to child licensees or trespassers in states that have adopted the *attractive nuisance* doctrine—under which schools are liable for injuries arising from dangerous property conditions that are reasonably known to attract unwitting children to them.[101] The determination whether a condition of school property constitutes an attractive nuisance is a pivotal issue in such cases.

Liability for negligence or lack of due care is ascertained by the foreseeability of a risk of harm from particular conditions and by the presence or absence of a reasonable opportunity to ascertain and prevent that harm.[102] The lack-of-notice defense does not apply, however, where the school affirmatively created the dangerous condition (e.g., by using glass panels rather than thick plate glass in a school door).[103] Issues of foreseeability and timely notice of danger are often left to jury determination. Examples of conditions for which private schools may be held liable in negligence include slippery floors, unstable equipment or furnishings, defective elevators, inadequate lighting in walkways and parking lots, and unsafe machinery, ramps, and fire extinguishers.[104] Known increases of school-site assaults creates the duty to minimize such conduct by reasonable security and protection measures, and failure to take such measures has rendered schools liable for injuries suffered from such assaults.[105]

Duties of Supervision

Under the doctrine of *respondeat superior,* the school is liable for the negligence or tortious misconduct of its agents and employees when they are acting within the scope of their employment or authority. Vicarious liability may extend to conduct of unpaid aides who work under the direction of school staff.[106] A school would, therefore, be liable for negligent bus operation along the driver's assigned route, but not liable for negligence of its bus driver after he left his assigned route for his own purposes. "Scope of employment" issues are not always so clear. Where a school medical doctor caused injury in the negligent exercise of his medical judgment, a court held that the school was not liable since it had no control over that judgment.[107] The duty to provide reasonable supervision includes a duty of prudent care in selecting individuals who are entrusted with supervisory duties. Schools may be liable for negligent hiring of incompetent persons who cause injuries,[108] but they are not insurers of continuing competence of all employees, e.g., where future lapses of previously competent employees are not reasonably foreseeable.

The duty of supervision was well stated in the following case that involved a second grader whose holiday costume was ignited by a nearby candle:

> Negligent supervision . . . involves a breach of a duty defendant owes plaintiff which causes plaintiff to suffer damages. . . . To recover, plaintiff need not show that the very injury resulting from defendant's negligence was foreseeable, but merely that a reasonable person could have foreseen that injuries of the type suffered would be likely to occur under the circumstances. . . . . . . The defendant is not an insurer of plaintiff's safety . . . nor is defendant required to maintain a constant vigil over each member of the class by keeping every student within eyesight. . . . The duty of defendant . . . was merely to exercise reasonable or ordinary care in the supervision of plaintiff. . . . The exercise of ordinary care where children are involved, however, requires more vigilance and caution than might the exercise of ordinary care where adults are concerned. . . . This is particularly true when a potentially dangerous condition exists and the supervisor is or should be aware of it. [*Smith v. Archbishop of St. Louis*, 632 S.W.2d 516, 521, 522 (Mo. 1982)]

Courts and juries must consider all relevant circumstances in determining issues of negligence and proximate cause, including such factors as (1) the nature of the activity, (2) the age and past conduct history of the students, and (3) the practicability and probable effect of general or special supervision. A jury readily found negligence for lack of supervision where a young child fell from a schoolyard merry-go-round,[109] but another court dismissed a tort suit for an unsupervised child who fell from monkey bars in the schoolyard. Still another court refused to dismiss suit for a child's fall from a four-foot railing in the schoolyard.[110] Courts often leave these and other fact-bound questions to jury determination, and they seldom overrule jury findings since so much depends on the assessment of specific circumstances.

Tort claimants have the burden of proving negligence and proximate cause, i.e., that a supervisor should have foreseen the risk of harm, and that the lack of supervision caused the harm. This burden is difficult in unexplained accidents, such as where a young student with mental retardation was drowned in a pond on a 50-acre rural campus. The court held that because the child had been at the school for some weeks and had often walked near the pond, there was no indication of any risk and consequent need to provide more direct supervision against the child falling or jumping into the pond.[111] Discharge of a firearm by a student in the presence of a supervising teacher was ground for finding negligent supervision.[112] Circumstantial evidence of negligent supervision may support tort recovery. Where a private nursery school student was found by her mother at the end of the school day to have suffered a brain concussion and the school failed to explain what had occurred,[113] the court applied the doctrine of *res ipsa loquitur,* meaning "the thing speaks for itself," to uphold tort liability.

Because school personnel cannot observe every movement of every child at all times, reasonable *general supervision* rather than *special, direct supervision,* of students is all that is required in most cases. Knowledge of special danger, however, triggers more stringent duties of special supervision.

General supervision is required in situations where students are engaged in activities which are not usually dangerous. Specific supervision is required when activities are unusually dangerous or the supervisor is instructing an activity with which students are not familiar.[114]

Reasonable general supervision is sufficient in most cases. Schools are not liable for unforeseeable student violations of school rules, for instance, where students cycled across school grounds in violation of regularly enforced school rules.[115] Similarly, a student who returned to school before he was directed to do so could not recover for injuries sustained while playing on a snow-covered bush.[116] Recovery was also denied students placed on disciplinary assignment (to pull weeds) who instead decided to play football and were thereby injured.[117] However, a school may be held liable for schoolyard injuries where school superiors had notice of, but made no effort to prevent, injurious student activities, such as playing "crack the whip" or throwing pebbles at each other.[118] Courts repeatedly stress that schools are not liable for unavoidable accidents. A child spectator at a school baseball game who was struck by a bat that slipped from the batter's hands had no claim in tort.[119] While courts recognize a supervisory duty of coaches to provide safe athletic equipment, the cases on the extent of care in inspecting and fitting such equipment are not consistent.[120] The Chapter 4 discussion of student injuries during a teacher's temporary absence from class is equally pertinent here. Such cases present the two familiar issues, whether the supervisor's absence was itself reasonable or negligent; and if negligent, whether that absence was a proximate cause of the student injury, i.e., whether the supervisor's presence could have prevented the injury. A teacher's 25-minute absence from class rendered the school liable for a classroom assault, but a teacher who left her class to seek help to stop a fight was not deemed negligent.[121] Thus absence of a teacher or supervisor from a class does not automatically render the school liable.[122] Negligence from lack of supervision is more readily found where students are permitted to engage in risky activities with other students. A jury could find actionable negligence for injury from a hurled discus during schoolyard discus-throwing practice.[123] But a private high school was held to have no duty to supervise nonhazardous after-school activities.[124] The duty of special (direct) supervision clearly attaches where a student is affirmatively directed by a school superior to perform a potentially dangerous task. But where the need for such supervision is unclear, courts may let the jury decide whether the circumstances required general or special supervision.

Private schools are duty bound to supervise school-sponsored activities. Where a school superior authorized an off-duty employee to transport a student to a field trip, the school was held liable for the driver's negligence.[125]

Affirmative Defenses

As explained in Chapter 4, an injured party may be totally or partially barred from recovering for another's tort under the doctrines of contributory negligence or assumption of risk. The burden of proving these defenses lies with the defending school or teacher. Findings of contributory negligence and assumption of risk depend on inferences to be drawn from widely varying circumstances. A high school freshman who was permitted to work in a chemistry lab without supervision could not recover for injuries arising from his unauthorized attempt to concoct gunpowder.[126] Juries were also permitted to find a student contributorily negligent where the student attempted to board a school vehicle by stepping on the side wheel before it started up,[127] and even where an adolescent student climbed a tree to gather pecans on instructor's order, but negligently put his weight on a shaky branch.[128] The legislatures and courts in a majority of states have modified the defenses of contributory negligence and assumption of risk to permit partial recovery based on the degree of the victim's contributory or comparative negligence. A private school may thus be liable for injuries in the proportion that *its* negligence contributed to the injury.[129]

First Aid

A duty to render reasonable first aid assistance to students only arises when the need is apparent. The duty to render first aid is limited and does not require an individual to venture a diagnosis, treatment, or procedure that requires special training, such as CPR, if the assisting party lacks the training to provide it.[130] However, when teachers volunteer medical assistance to students, they will be held liable for injuries caused by their well-intentioned but negligent actions.[131]

Defamation Liability

The Chapter 4 discussion of liability for defamation pertains equally to private schools and their employees.

Educational Malpractice

For the reasons explained in Chapter 4, courts have refused to recognize a general tort duty that schools provide adequate educational results for their students. Courts normally find that private school enrollment contracts do not create a special duty to ensure adequate educational results.[132] In the absence of a clear and specific undertaking to the contrary, courts only require schools to make reasonable, good-faith instructional efforts.[133]

Immunity Defenses and Dollar Recovery Limits

At common law, nonprofit private schools were treated as charitable organizations and were accorded immunity from tort liability as charities. This *entity* immunity of private school does not confer *personal* immunity on the staff of such schools. While personal tort immunity did not exist at common law, such immunity may be created by legislation. See for example, the *Soper* case, which is discussed in the immunity section of Chapter 4.

Charitable immunity is not coextensive with the governmental immunity that may be accorded public schools. But, like governmental immunity, charitable immunity has also been abrogated or delimited in many states by court decision or by superceding legislation.

Immunity defenses will vary with the law in each state.[134] For example, Illinois law immunizes public and private schools and their teachers from liability for negligence, but not for willful, reckless, or wanton misconduct.[135] Many states deny immunity for injuries caused by nuisances or defective conditions of school property.[136] In some states, the law grants tort immunity for conduct that involves the performance of educational functions but denies such immunity for conduct arising out of activities that are deemed "proprietary" or commercial in nature.

Aside from immunity from liability, state legislatures may also limit the amount of damages a tort victim may recover against a liable party by fixing limits on recoverable tort damages, either in terms of fixed dollar amounts or in terms of reductions of recoveries to the extent that a school is covered by liability insurance.[137] These recovery caps have been largely sustained against constitutional attack. Even so, the best shield against tort losses is prevention and minimization of tort hazards in school property and activities.

❧ C A S E S

Case 9.1

CATHOLIC HIGH SCHOOL ASSN. OF ARCHDIOCESE OF NEW YORK v. CULVERT
753 F.2d 1161 (2nd Cir. 1985)

> [**Focus Note**. *This decision considered the two principal questions regarding state power to regulate the labor relations of religious schools, namely, whether state labor relations laws are preempted and superceded by the National Labor Relations Act (NLRA); and whether the states are barred from such regulation by the religion clauses of the First Amendment. The following opinion opened a split between the Second and Seventh Circuit Courts of Appeals.*]

CARDAMONE, CIRCUIT JUDGE.

. . . The issue in this case is whether the Religion Clauses of the First Amendment, . . . prohibit the New York State Labor Relations Board from exercising jurisdiction over the labor relations between parochial schools and their lay teachers. This "difficult and sensitive" question, expressly left open by the Supreme Court in *NLRB v. Catholic Bishop*, 440 U.S. 490 . . . is one of first impression in this Circuit. . . .

The New York State Labor Relations Board (State Board or Board) administers the New York State Labor Relations Act (SLRA or Act). As originally enacted in 1937 the Act's provisions did not apply to employees of charitable, educational or religious associations and corporations. In 1968 the Act was amended to bring these employees within its scope. . . . The parties agree that the schools are "church-operated". . . . The faculty of the Association is composed of both lay and religious teachers, all of whom are directly involved in the transmission of religious values to the students. . . . The by-laws of the Union specifically exclude religious faculty, and each of the agreements was expressly limited to nonreligious issues. . . .

In 1980 . . . the Union filed unfair labor practice charges against the Association for the first time. . . . None of these charges raised a religious issue. . . . . . . As a result of its investigation the Board issued a formal complaint. The Association immediately brought an action seeking a declaratory judgment and injunctive relief against the State Board. It challenged the State Board's assertion of jurisdiction, alleging that it violates the Religion Clauses of the First Amendment and that jurisdiction by the Board over lay teachers in church-operated schools is preempted by the National Labor Relations Act. . . . The virtually identical issue was presented but left unresolved in *Catholic Bishop.* There a closely-divided Supreme Court held that the National Labor Relations Board (NLRB) lacked jurisdiction over lay teachers because Congress had not affirmatively indicated that it intended them to be covered by the National Labor Relations Act (NLRA).

. . . Judge Lasker [district court below] . . . held that application of the Act to lay teachers violated the Establishment Clause because it "threatens to produce excessive entanglement between church and state." . . . He specifically limited his holding to lay teachers, as opposed to other church employees . . . and found it unnecessary to rule on the Association's free exercise claim. . . .

The district court also held that limitations in the collective bargaining agreement would not cure the conflict with the Establishment Clause. . . . Finally, Judge Lasker held that the NLRA does not preempt the State Board from asserting jurisdiction over parochial schools. . . .

* * *

We turn first to the Association's argument that the State's assertion of jurisdiction violates the Establishment Clause. The Supreme Court has made it clear . . . that "total separation is not possible in an absolute sense, [for s]ome relationship between government and religious organizations is inevitable." *Lemon v. Kurtzman,* 403 U.S. 602, 614 . . . (1971). It explained that "the line of separation, far from being a 'wall,' is a blurred, indistinct, and variable barrier depending upon all the circumstances of a particular relationship." . . . The Court has often found it useful to use the familiar three-pronged test in determining whether there has been a violation of the Establishment Clause.

* * *

. . . The parties do not dispute that the Act has a secular purpose and that its primary effect is not to advance or inhibit religion. Nonetheless, the district court found that assertion of jurisdiction under the Act violates the Establishment Clause because it threatens to produce an excessive administrative entanglement of government with religion.

. . . First, it found that there was an "imminent possibility" that the Association would be required to bargain with lay teachers on religious subjects. Second, it found that . . . the State Board might have to determine whether an asserted religious reason was a valid part of church doctrine. . . .

. . . The State Board's relationship with the religious schools . . . does not involve the degree of "surveillance" necessary to find excessive administrative entanglement. In the three key Supreme Court cases addressing excessive administrative entanglement . . . states attempted to provide aid to support certain secular aspects of classroom instruction in parochial schools. In these three cases the Supreme Court held that the aid resulted in excessive administrative entanglement, finding that the restrictions imposed would inevitably require "comprehensive, discriminating, and continuing state surveillance." . . . This is quite unlike the situation here where the State Board's supervision over the collective bargaining process is neither comprehensive nor continuing.

. . . A "church-operated" school believing itself aggrieved by such an [Labor Board] order may refuse to comply and raise a First Amendment defense when and if the Board seeks judicial enforcement of its order.

The Association relies, as did the Seventh Circuit in *Catholic Bishop*, on a passage from an article on collective bargaining in colleges and universities. . . .

* * *

We decline to follow the Seventh Circuit down this slippery slope. . . .

The second ground for the district court's finding of excessive administrative entanglement was that the State Board's jurisdiction would require it to determine the validity of asserted religious motives as part of church doctrine. . . .

In the present case it is not the inquiry into whether a belief is sincerely held by an individual that is at issue. Rather, it is the possibility of recurrent questioning of whether a particular church actually holds a particular belief. . . . One of the primary purposes of the Establishment Clause was to avoid just this result. Thus, the First Amendment prohibits the State Board from inquiring into an asserted religious motive to determine whether it is pretextual.

The question remains whether this limitation of the State Board's powers should preclude it from asserting jurisdiction. We think not. . . . It is still free to determine, using a dual motive analysis, whether the religious motive was in fact the cause of the discharge. . . . Other circuits have made a similar accommodation by permitting the EEOC to assert jurisdiction but precluding it from determining whether an asserted reason is pretextual. See, e.g., *EEOC v. Mississippi College*, 626 F.2d at 485.

. . . We agree with the Seventh Circuit that in cases involving lay faculty the Board should not be allowed to find a violation simply because anti-union animus motivated a discharge "in part." Nonetheless, we adopt the accommodation that the Seventh Circuit rejected. . . . Were the Board allowed to apply an "in part" test in addressing an asserted religious motive, an order based on such a finding would violate the First Amendment. . . . To avoid this unconstitutional result, the Board therefore may order reinstatement of a lay teacher at a parochial school only if he or she would not have been fired otherwise for asserted religious reasons.

* * *

For basically the same reasons, we reach the same result with respect to the Association's Free Exercise claim. The Association, quoting the Seventh Circuit . . . first argues that "the very threshold act of certification of the union necessarily alters and impinges upon the religious character of all parochial schools." . . . Support for such an absolute view is found neither in case law nor the history of the First Amendment. . . .

. . . The burden the state imposes on the Association's exercise of its religious beliefs must be weighed against the State's interests in enforcing the

Act. We must consider whether: . . . (2) the State action burdened the religious exercise; and (3) the State interest was sufficiently compelling to override the constitutional right of free exercise of religion. See *Wisconsin v. Yoder,* 406 U.S. 205. . . .

We first turn to whether the claims presented here are religious and not secular. . . . Many matters that pertain to private schools are already subject to governmental regulation. The Association must meet state requirements for fire inspections, building and zoning regulations and compulsory school attendance laws, all of which regulate the conduct of the Association's schools. . . .

* * *

The Association does not contend that collective bargaining is contrary to the beliefs of the Catholic Church. . . .

. . . To find that an enactment violates the right to free exercise of religious beliefs, "it is necessary . . . for one to show the coercive effect of the enactment as it operates against him in the practice of his religion." *School District v. Schempp,* 374 U.S. 203, 223. . . . The injury must be "a demonstrable reality," not merely a speculative possibility . . . and compliance with the regulation must be directly contrary to claimant's religious beliefs. . . . For the reasons discussed [above] . . . and because of the restrictions we have placed on the Board's power, these claims do not burden freedom of religious exercise.

But a lingering question remains as to whether State Board jurisdiction may impermissibly chill free exercise rights; whether " . . . [t]o minimize friction . . . prudence will ultimately dictate that the bishop tailor his conduct and decisions to 'steer far wider of the unlawful zone' of impermissible conduct." 559 F.2d at 1124. . . .

It is necessary, then, to decide whether this indirect and incidental burden on religion is justified by a compelling state interest. . . . Here a compelling state interest exists. State labor laws are essential to the preservation of industrial peace and a sound economic order. . . . . . . Thus, even if the exercise of Board jurisdiction has an indirect and incidental effect on employment decisions in parochial schools involving religious issues, this minimal intrusion is justified by the State's compelling interest in collective bargaining.

The judgment appealed from insofar as it held there was no preemption by the National Labor Relations Act is affirmed. . . . Insofar as the judgment granted summary judgment . . . in favor of the plaintiff Association upon a finding of a First Amendment violation, it is reversed. . . .

GEORGE C. PRATT, CIRCUIT JUDGE, *dissenting.*

Although I agree with the majority opinion on the preemption issue, I dissent on the constitutional issue for the reasons set forth in Judge Lasker's opinion below . . . and in the seventh circuit's opinion in *Catholic Bishop v. NLRB,* 559 F.2d 1112 (7th Cir. 1977). . . .

Case 9.1 Review Questions

1. Do you find the Second or the Seventh Circuit Court decision on the constitutional issues more persuasive?

2. What constitutional limits does the above decision place on state labor boards in dealing with religious school labor relations?

3. As the above opinion notes, prior to its amendment, the New York labor statute excluded religious school employees from its coverage. Does the original law suggest that the state legislature wished to avoid the constitutional question or only to exclude religious schools as a matter of policy?

4. The above opinion contained the following important footnote:

   "2. If *Catholic Bishop* had held that teachers are within the jurisdiction granted by the NLRA but are not "employees" within the meaning of that Act, the State Board would be plainly preempted from exercising jurisdiction. . . . In this case, the State Board has validly asserted jurisdiction because Congress did not indicate that the NLRB had jurisdiction."

   Does this mean Congress can still preempt the state labor law by revising the NLRA to give exclusive jurisdiction to the NLRB?

Case 9.2

GERACI v. ST. XAVIER HIGH SCHOOL
3 Ohio Op. 3d 146 (1978)

[**Focus Note**. *Competing claims of contract breach by expelled parochial school student and his parochial school. The following opinion also explores the limits to which private schools may be deemed to be engaged in "state action" as to be subject to constitutional constraints.*]

BETTMAN, J.

. . . This appeal raises basically two issues. First, whether appellants' constitutional right to due process has application to the conduct of disciplinary proceedings by a private school. Secondly, whether appellees' handling of Mark's expulsion was arbitrary and unreasonable and therefore a breach of appellants' contract of enrollment.

* * *

The due process requirements of the Fourteenth Amendment are only applicable to situations involving state action. . . .

Where . . . the enterprise in question is regulated by the state, state action will be found if there is "a sufficiently close nexus between the State and the challenged action of the regulated entity so that the action of the latter may be fairly treated as that of the State itself." . . . This mode of analysis would here focus on the specific action of expulsion from St. Xavier. The state regulation of St. Xavier is relatively minimal. Our attention has been directed to nothing indicating state involvement in St. Xavier's disciplinary process. . . .

Even without state involvement in the disciplinary proceedings, state action may still be found if the state is so entwined with the administration and operation of the school that a "symbiotic relationship" has developed. . . .

St. Xavier is approved by the state as a high school. It files annual reports with the state dealing with its curriculum, class loads, number of teachers, etc. The teachers at St. Xavier all have state certificates of qualification. The state provides, on loan, certain standard textbooks and furnishes transportation to students. The school is exempted from state taxation. However, other than ascertaining that the school meets minimum state standards for a high school, the state exercises no control over the school whatsoever. This is certainly not the sort of pervasive state involvement required for a finding of a symbiotic state action. . . .

Our conclusion that there is no state action in the disciplinary proceedings of a private high school such as St. Xavier is supported by *Wisch v. Sanford School, Inc.,* 420 F. Supp. 1310 (D.C. Del. 1976); *Bright v. Isenbarger,* 314 F. Supp. 1382 (N.D. Ind. 1970); and a long line of federal cases involving private universities. The assignment is, accordingly, overruled.

Appellants' assignments of error . . . maintain that the trial court erred in finding that the contract between the parties was breached by Mark's conduct. . . .

Mr. Geraci had paid Mark's tuition for his junior year and made the required deposit toward the senior year tuition. The parties are in agreement that this gave rise to a contract that St. Xavier would continue to provide education to Mark so long as he met its academic and disciplinary standards. They are further in agreement that the catalogue, describing St. Xavier High School's academic program and its standards and requirements constituted a part of the terms and conditions of such contract. The catalogue . . . provides in pertinent parts:

> By the act of registering at St. Xavier High School, a student and his parents (or guardians) understand and agree to pursue the educational objectives and practices as stated in this catalogue and to observe the disciplinary code of the school. . . .

Disciplinary Norms

The St. Xavier norms of conduct are predicated on two premises: first, that every student has the right to certain situations (such as the protection of his personal property, the physical integrity of the facilities, an atmosphere conducive to personal growth and development) and, second, that every student has the duty to preserve these rights for others. . . . Since no list of norms can cover every situation, the administration presumes that common sense, mature judgment, and Christian charity are the guides by which every St. Xavier student should measure his actions.

The assistant principal is in charge of all matters of discipline. . . .

Expulsion

The following offenses are grounds for expulsion:

1. conduct detrimental to the reputation of the school. . . .
8. immorality in talk or action.

. . . The evidence before the trial court was as follows. On the final day of the school year Tom McKenna, a student at Moeller High School, entered St. Xavier High School, went to the classroom where Mark Geraci and his classmates were taking a final test and threw a meringue pie in the face of Mr. Downie, the teacher. Pandemonium ensued. . . . By Mark's own testimony, several weeks before he and some fellow students had decided it would be a "funny prank" to get McKenna to "pie" Mr. Downie. . . . The original plan was that Mark would collect $50.00 from the group to pay McKenna. He did not, however, collect any money. Nevertheless, the evening preceding the last day of school . . . McKenna asked "whatever happened about the pie throwing." Geraci told him he had not collected any money and McKenna said "he might come over and do it anyway." Mark made no response to this statement. On McKenna's inquiry Geraci told him the room number of the class where Mr. Downie would be teaching and, on further inquiry, which door of the building to enter. At McKenna's request, Geraci called another Moeller student to arrange for transportation for McKenna.

The very recital of the above facts makes abundantly clear that Geraci aided and abetted McKenna's throwing of the pie in the face of his teacher, Mr. Downie, an act patently "immoral," "detrimental to the reputation of the school" and violative of Geraci's acknowledged duty to exercise "common sense, mature judgment, and Christian charity." The trial court's finding that Geraci's acts constituted a breach of the contract with St. Xavier is, therefore, fully supported by the evidence.

Although . . . a private school's disciplinary proceedings are not controlled by the due process clause, and accordingly such schools have broad discretion in making rules and setting up procedures for their enforcement, nevertheless, under its broad equitable powers a court will intervene where such discretion is abused or the proceedings do not comport with fundamental fairness. . . .

The record shows that Mr. Meyer, the Assistant Principal . . . called Mark to his office several hours after the event. At that time Mark, though protesting that he did not really expect McKenna to go through with it, admitted substantially all the elements of his involvement. . . . Meyer forthwith advised him that he was expelled. The transcript further shows that before this decision was finalized Mr. Meyer, Mr. Trainor, the Principal, and Father Borgmann, President of St. Xavier, all discussed and considered the matter; that Meyer discussed it with Mr. Geraci; that Trainor discussed it with Mr. Geraci and that Father Borgmann discussed it with both father and son. The testimony as to these discussions shows an appreciation and consideration by appellees of Mark's previously unblemished disciplinary record and his academic excellence. . . . On the basis of the record we cannot say that appellees abused their discretion nor that the procedures were unfair.

The trial court did not err in holding that Mark's expulsion was just, proper, and in accordance with the contract between the parties and did not constitute an abuse of discretion. . . .

The judgment of the trial court must accordingly be affirmed.

Case 9.3

AGOSTINI v. FELTON
521 U.S. 203 (1997)

[**Focus Note**. *Twelve years after deciding that the New York City Board of Education could not constitutionally send public school teachers into parochial schools to provide remedial education to disadvantaged children, the Supreme Court overruled that decision by the following opinion, which explains its new approach to measure constitutional limits on government aids to church-related education.*]

Justice O'Connor delivered the opinion of the Court

In *Aguilar v. Felton*, 473 U.S. 402 . . . (1985), this Court held that the Establishment Clause of the First Amendment barred the city of New York from sending public school teachers into parochial schools to provide remedial education to disadvantaged children. . . . . . . Petitioners maintain that *Aguilar* cannot be squared with our intervening Establishment Clause jurisprudence. . . . We agree with petitioners that *Aguilar* is not consistent with our subsequent Establishment Clause decisions and further conclude that, on the facts presented here, petitioners are entitled . . . to relief [lifting of the injunction against allowing public school teachers from providing remedial services inside a parochial school]. . . .

In 1965, Congress enacted Title I of the Elementary and Secondary Education Act of 1965 . . . to "provid[e] full educational opportunity to every child regardless of economic background." . . . Toward that end, Title I channels federal funds, through the States, to "local educational agencies" (LEA's). . . . Title I funds must be made available to all eligible children, regardless of whether they attend public schools . . . and the services provided to children attending private schools must be "equitable in comparison to services and other benefits for public school children." . . .

. . . The Title I services themselves must be "secular, neutral, and non-ideological," § 6321(a)(2), and must "supplement, and in no case supplant, the level of services" already provided by the private school. . . .

Petitioner Board of Education . . . (Board), an LEA . . . has grappled ever since with how to provide Title I services. . . . . . . Recognizing that more than 90% of the private schools within the Board's jurisdiction are sectarian . . . the Board initially arranged to transport children to public schools for after-school Title I instruction. But this enterprise was largely unsuccessful. Attendance was poor, teachers and children were tired, and parents were concerned for the safety of their children. . . . The Board then moved the after-school instruction onto private school campuses, as Congress had contemplated when it enacted Title I. . . .

After this program also yielded mixed results, the Board implemented the plan we evaluated in *Aguilar v. Felton.* . . . . . . Assignments to private schools were made on a voluntary basis and without regard to the religious affiliation of the employee or the wishes of the private school. . . . . . . Before any public employee could provide Title I instruction at a private school, she would be given a detailed set of written and oral instructions. . . . Specifically, employees would be told that (i) they were employees of the Board and accountable only to their public school supervisors; (ii) they had exclusive responsibility for selecting students for the Title I program and could teach only those children who met the eligibility criteria for Title I; (iii) their materials and equipment would be used only in the Title I program; (iv) they could not engage in team-teaching or other cooperative instructional activities with private school teachers; and (v) they could not introduce any religious matter into their teaching or become involved in any way with the religious activities of the private schools. . . . All religious symbols were to be removed from classrooms used for Title I services. . . . The rules acknowledged that it might be necessary for Title I teachers to consult with a student's regular classroom teacher to assess the student's particular needs and progress, but admonished instructors to limit those consultations to mutual professional concerns regarding the student's education. . . . To ensure compliance . . . a publicly employed field supervisor was to attempt to make at least one unannounced visit to each teacher's classroom every month. . . . In 1978 . . . taxpayers . . . sued the Board claiming that the Board's Title I program violated the Establishment Clause. . . . . . . The District Court granted summary judgment for the Board, but the Court of Appeals for the Second Circuit reversed. While noting that the Board's Title I program had "done so much good and little, if any, detectable harm," . . . the

Court of Appeals nevertheless held that *Meek v. Pittenger*, 421 U.S. 349 . . . (1975), and *Wolman v. Walter*, 433 U.S. 229 . . . (1977), compelled it to declare the program unconstitutional. In a 5–4 decision, this Court affirmed on the ground that the Board's Title I program necessitated an "excessive entanglement of church and state in the administration of [Title I] benefits." [*Aguilar*] 473 U.S., at 414. . . . . . . On remand, the District Court permanently enjoined the Board "from using public funds for any plan or program under [Title I] to the extent that it . . . permits public school teachers and guidance counselors to provide teaching and counseling services on the premises of sectarian schools. . . .

* * *

In order to evaluate whether *Aguilar* has been eroded by our subsequent Establishment Clause cases, it is necessary to understand the rationale upon which *Aguilar,* as well as its companion case, *School Dist. of Grand Rapids v. Ball,* 473 U.S. 373 . . . (1985), rested.

In Ball, the Court evaluated two programs. . . . The district's Shared Time program . . . provided remedial and "enrichment" classes, at public expense, to students attending nonpublic schools. The classes were taught during regular school hours by publicly employed teachers, using materials purchased with public funds, on the premises of nonpublic schools. The Shared Time courses were in subjects designed to supplement the "core curriculum" of the nonpublic schools. . . .

. . . The Court acknowledged that the Shared Time program served a purely secular purpose. . . . . . . Nevertheless, it ultimately concluded that the program had the impermissible effect of advancing religion. . . .

* * *

Distilled to essentials, the Court's conclusion that the Shared Time program in *Ball* had the impermissible effect of advancing religion rested on three assumptions: (i) any public employee who works on the premises of a religious school is presumed to inculcate religion in her work; (ii) the presence of public employees on private school premises creates a symbolic union between church and state; and (iii) any and all public aid that directly aids the educational function of religious schools impermissibly finances religious indoctrination, even if the aid reaches such schools as a consequence of private decisionmaking. Additionally, in *Aguilar* there was a fourth assumption: that New York City's Title I program necessitated an excessive government entanglement with religion because public employees who teach on the premises of religious schools must be closely monitored to ensure that they do not inculcate religion.

Our more recent cases have undermined the assumptions upon which *Ball* and *Aguilar* relied. To be sure, the general principles we use . . . have not changed. . . . For example, we continue to ask whether the government acted with the purpose of advancing or inhibiting religion. . . . . . . Likewise, we continue to explore whether the aid has the "effect" of advancing or inhibiting religion. What has changed since we decided *Ball* and *Aguilar* is our understanding of the criteria used to assess whether aid to religion has an impermissible effect.

. . . First, we have abandoned the presumption erected in *Meek* and *Ball* that the placement of public employees on parochial school grounds inevitably results in the impermissible effect of state-sponsored indoctrination or constitutes a symbolic union between government and religion. In *Zobrest v. Catalina Foothills School Dist.*, 509 U.S. 1 (1993), we examined whether the IDEA . . . was constitutional as applied to a deaf student who sought to bring his state-employed sign-language interpreter with him to his Roman Catholic high school. We held that this was permissible, expressly disavowing the notion that "the Establishment Clause [laid] down [an] absolute bar to the placing of a public employee in a sectarian school." . . . We refused to presume that a publicly employed interpreter would be pressured by the pervasively sectarian surroundings to inculcate religion. . . . In the absence of evidence to the contrary, we assumed instead that the interpreter would dutifully discharge her responsibilities as a full-time public employee. . . . . . . *Zobrest* also implicitly repudiated another assumption on which *Ball* and *Aguilar* turned: that the presence of a public employee on private school property creates an impermissible "symbolic link" between government and religion. . . .

Second, we have departed from the rule relied on in *Ball* that all government aid that directly aids the educational function of religious schools is invalid. In *Witters v. Washington Dept. of Servs. for Blind*, 474 U.S. 481 . . . (1986), we held that the Establishment Clause did not bar a State from issuing a vocational tuition grant to a blind person who wished to use the grant to attend a Christian college and become a pastor, missionary, or youth director. . . . The grants were disbursed directly to students, who then used the money to pay for tuition at the educational institution of their choice. . . . The same logic applied in *Zobrest* . . . because the IDEA's neutral eligibility criteria ensured that the interpreter's presence in a sectarian school was a "result of the private decision of individual parents" and "[could] not be attributed to state decisionmaking." 509 U.S., at 10. . . . . . . *Zobrest* and *Witters* make clear that, under current law, the Shared Time program in *Ball* and New York City's Title I program in *Aguilar* will not, as a matter of law, be deemed to have the effect of advancing religion through indoctrination. . . . Certainly, no evidence has ever shown that any New York City Title I instructor teaching on parochial school premises attempted to inculcate religion in students. . . .

. . . We do not see any perceptible (let alone dispositive) difference in the degree of symbolic union between a student receiving remedial instruction in a classroom on his sectarian school's campus and one receiving instruction in a van parked just at the school's curbside. To draw this line based solely on the location of the public employee is neither "sensible" nor "sound," and the Court in *Zobrest* rejected it. . . . In all relevant respects, the provision of instructional services under Title I is indistinguishable from the provision of sign-language interpreters under the IDEA. . . .

* * *

. . . A number of our Establishment Clause cases have found that the criteria used for identifying beneficiaries are relevant in a second respect. . . . Specifically, the criteria might themselves have the effect of advancing religion by creating a financial incentive to undertake religious indoctrination. . . . This incentive is not present, however, where the aid is allocated on the basis of neutral, secular criteria that neither favor nor disfavor religion, and is made available to both religious and secular beneficiaries on a nondiscriminatory basis. . . .

. . . [W]e have sustained programs that provided aid to all eligible children regardless of where they attended school. See, e.g., *Everson v. Board of Ed. of Ewing,* 330 U.S. 1 . . . (1947) (sustaining local ordinance authorizing all parents to deduct from their state tax returns the costs of transporting their children to school on public buses); *Board of Ed. of Central School Dist. No. 1 v. Allen,* 392 U.S. 236 . . . (1968) (sustaining New York law loaning secular textbooks to all children); *Mueller v. Allen,* 463 U.S. 388 . . . (1983) (sustaining Minnesota statute allowing all parents to deduct actual costs of tuition, textbooks, and transportation from state tax returns); *Witters,* 474 U.S., at 487–488 . . . (sustaining Washington law granting all eligible blind persons vocational assistance); *Zobrest,* 509 U.S., at 10 (sustaining section of IDEA providing all disabled children with necessary aid).

* * *

We now turn to *Aguilar*'s conclusion that New York City's Title I program resulted in an excessive entanglement between church and state. . . .

Not all entanglements, of course, have the effect of advancing or inhibiting religion. Interaction between church and state is inevitable . . . and we have always tolerated some level of involvement between the two. Entanglement must be "excessive" before it runs afoul of the Establishment Clause. . . . As discussed previously, the Court's finding of "excessive" entanglement in *Aguilar* rested on three grounds: (i) the program would require "pervasive monitoring by public authorities" to ensure that Title I employees did not inculcate religion; (ii) the program required "administrative cooperation" between the Board and parochial schools; and (iii) the program might increase the dangers of "political divisiveness." 473 U.S., at 413–414. . . . Under our current understanding of the Establishment Clause, the last two considerations are insufficient by themselves to create an "excessive" entanglement. . . . Since we have abandoned the assumption that properly instructed public employees will fail to discharge their duties faithfully, we must also discard the assumption that pervasive monitoring of Title I teachers is required. . . . Moreover, we have not found excessive entanglement in cases in which States imposed far more onerous burdens on religious institutions than the monitoring system at issue here. . . .

* * *

To summarize, New York City's Title I program does not run afoul of any of three primary criteria we currently use to evaluate whether government aid has the effect of advancing religion: it does not result in governmental indoctrination; define its recipients by reference to religion; or create an excessive entanglement. We therefore hold that a federally funded program providing supplemental, remedial instruction to disadvantaged children on a neutral basis is not invalid under the Establishment Clause when such instruction is given on the premises of sectarian schools by government employees pursuant to a program containing safeguards such as those present here. The same considerations . . . require us to conclude that this carefully constrained program also cannot reasonably be viewed as an endorsement of religion. . . . Accordingly, we must acknowledge that *Aguilar,* as well as the portion of *Ball* addressing Grand Rapids' Shared Time program, are no longer good law.

* * *

For these reasons, we reverse the judgment of the Court of Appeals and remand to the District Court with instructions to vacate its September 26, 1985 order.

Case 9.3 Review Question

1. Is the *Lemon* test affected by Agostini?

Case 9.4

MITCHELL v. HELMS
530 U.S. 793 (2000)

> [*Focus Note. After 15 years of litigation on the constitutionality of a Louisiana law that authorized state loans of instructional materials and computer equipment for student use in religious schools, the Supreme Court Justices split three ways on the proper standards to determine what constitutes an establishment of religion under the Establishment Clause. The following portions of the plurality, concurring and dissenting opinions invite further debate.]*

> JUSTICE THOMAS . . . *delivered an opinion, in which the CHIEF JUSTICE, JUSTICE SCALIA, and JUSTICE KENNEDY join.*

As part of a longstanding school aid program known as Chapter 2, the Federal Government distributes funds to state and local governmental agencies, which in turn lend educational materials and equipment to public and private schools, with the enrollment of each participating school determining the amount of aid that it receives. The question is whether Chapter 2, as applied in Jefferson Parish, Louisiana, is a law respecting an establishment of religion, because many of the private schools receiving Chapter 2 aid . . . are religiously affiliated. . . .

I

A

Chapter 2 of the Education Consolidation and Improvement Act of 1981 . . . has its origins in the Elementary and Secondary Education Act of 1965 (ESEA) . . . and is a close cousin of the provision of the ESEA that we recently considered in *Agostini v. Felton,* 521 U.S. 203 . . . (1997). Like the provision at issue in *Agostini,* Chapter 2 channels federal funds to local educational agencies (LEA's), which are usually public school districts, via state educational agencies (SEA's), to implement programs to assist children in elementary and secondary schools. Among other things, Chapter 2 provides aid "for the acquisition and use of instructional and educational materials, including library services and materials (including media materials), assessments, reference materials, computer software and hardware for instructional use, and other curricular materials." 20 U.S.C. § 7351(b)(2).

LEA's and SEA's must offer assistance to both public and private schools (although any private school must be nonprofit). . . . . . .

Several restrictions apply to aid to private schools. Most significantly, the "services, materials, and equipment" provided to private schools must be "secular, neutral, and nonideological." . . . In addition, private schools may not acquire control of Chapter 2 funds or title to Chapter 2 materials, equipment, or property. . . . A private school receives the materials and equipment . . . by submitting to the LEA an application detailing which items the school seeks and how it will use them; the LEA, if it approves the application, purchases those items from the school's allocation of funds, and then lends them to that school.

. . . [P]rivate schools have primarily used their allocations for nonrecurring expenses, usually materials and equipment. . . . Among the materials and equipment provided have been library books, computers, and computer software, and also slide and movie projectors, overhead projectors, television sets, tape recorders, VCR's, projection screens, laboratory equipment, maps, globes, filmstrips, slides, and cassette recordings.

* * *

In 1990 . . . Chief Judge Heebe of the District Court . . . granted summary judgment in favor of respondents. . . . He held that Chapter 2 violated the Establishment Clause because . . . the program had the primary effect of advancing religion. . . .

Two years later, Chief Judge Heebe having retired, Judge Livaudais received the case. . . . [H]e reversed the decision of former Chief Judge Heebe and upheld Chapter 2. . . . . . .

* * *

. . . The Fifth Circuit acknowledged that *Agostini* . . . had rejected a premise of *Meek*, but that court nevertheless concluded that *Agostini* had neither directly overruled *Meek* and *Wolman* nor rejected their distinction between textbooks and other in-kind aid. The Fifth Circuit therefore concluded that *Meek* and *Wolman* controlled, and thus it held Chapter 2 unconstitutional. . . .

* * *

In *Agostini*, however, we brought some clarity to our case law, by overruling two anomalous precedents. . . . Whereas in *Lemon* we had considered whether a statute (1) has a secular purpose, (2) has a primary effect of advancing or inhibiting religion, or (3) creates an excessive entanglement between government and religion . . . in *Agostini* we modified *Lemon* for purposes of evaluating aid to schools and examined only the first and second factors. . . . . . .

In this case, our inquiry . . . is a narrow one. Because respondents do not challenge the District Court's holding that Chapter 2 has a secular purpose, and because the Fifth Circuit also did not question that holding . . . we will consider only Chapter 2's effect. Further . . . we will consider only the first two *Agostini* criteria, since neither respondents nor the Fifth Circuit has questioned the District Court's holding . . . that Chapter 2 does not create an excessive entanglement. Considering Chapter 2 . . . we conclude that it neither results in religious indoctrination by the government nor defines its recipients by reference to religion. We therefore hold that Chapter 2 is not a "law respecting an establishment of religion." In so holding, we acknowledge what both the Ninth and Fifth Circuits saw was inescapable—*Meek* and *Wolman* are anomalies in our case law. We therefore conclude that they are no longer good law.

* * *

. . . To put the point differently, if the government, seeking to further some legitimate secular purpose, offers aid on the same terms, without regard to religion, to all who adequately further that purpose, . . . then it is fair to say that any aid going to a religious recipient only has the effect of furthering that secular purpose. . . .

. . . As a way of assuring neutrality, we have repeatedly considered whether any governmental aid that goes to a religious institution does so "only as a result of the genuinely independent and private choices of individuals." *Agostini, supra,* at 226. . . . . . .

The principles of neutrality and private choice, . . . were prominent not only in *Agostini* . . . but also in *Zobrest, Witters,* and *Mueller.* The heart of our reasoning in *Zobrest,* upholding governmental provision of a sign-language interpreter to a deaf student at his Catholic high school, was as follows:

> "The service at issue in this case is part of a general government program that distributes benefits neutrally to any child qualifying as 'disabled' under the [statute], without regard to the 'sectarian–nonsectarian, or public–nonpublic nature' of the school the child attends. By according parents freedom to select a school of their choice, the statute ensures that a government-paid interpreter will be present in a sectarian school only as a result of the private decision of individual parents. In other words, because the [statute] creates no financial incentive for parents to choose a sectarian school, an interpreter's presence there cannot be attributed to state decisionmaking." 509 U.S., at 10, 113 S.Ct. 2462.

. . . *Witters* and *Mueller* employed similar reasoning. . . .

* * *

Agostini's second primary criterion for determining the effect of governmental aid is closely related to the first. The second criterion requires a court to consider whether an aid program "define[s] its recipients by reference to religion." 521 U.S., at 234. . . .

* * *

Respondents inexplicably make no effort to address Chapter 2 under the *Agostini* test. Instead, . . . they offer two rules. . . . They argue first, and chiefly, that "direct, nonincidental" aid to the primary educational mission of religious schools is always impermissible. Second, they argue that provision to religious schools of aid that is divertible to religious use is similarly impermissible. Respondents' arguments are inconsistent with our more recent case law, in particular *Agostini* and *Zobrest,* and we therefore reject them.

* * *

As *Agostini* explained, the same reasoning was at work in *Zobrest,* where we allowed the government-funded interpreter to provide assistance at a Catholic school, "even though she would be a mouthpiece for religious instruction," because the interpreter was provided according to neutral eligibility criteria and private choice. . . .

* * *

Of course, we have seen "special Establishment Clause dangers," . . . when money is given to religious schools or entities directly rather than . . . indirectly. . . . But direct payments of money are not at issue in this case. . . .

2

Respondents also contend that the Establishment Clause requires that aid to religious schools not be impermissibly religious in nature or be divertible to religious use. We agree with the first part of this argument but not the second. Respondents' "no divertibility" rule is inconsistent with our more recent case law and is unworkable. . . .

* * *

Justice O'CONNOR acknowledges that the Court in *Zobrest* and *Witters* approved programs that involved actual diversion. . . . The dissent likewise does not deny that *Witters* involved actual diversion. . . . The dissent does claim that the aid in *Zobrest* "was not considered divertible," . . . . . .

* * *

In *Agostini* itself, we approved the provision of public employees to teach secular remedial classes in private schools partly because we concluded that there was no reason to suspect that indoctrinating content would be part of such governmental aid. . . . . . . [W]e refused to presume that the public teachers would "'inject religious content'" into their classes . . . especially given certain safeguards that existed. . . .

* * *

A concern for divertibility, as opposed to improper content, is misplaced . . . also because it is boundless—enveloping all aid, no matter how trivial—and thus has only the most attenuated (if any) link to any realistic concern for preventing an "establishment of religion." . . . . . .

* * *

The dissent resurrects the concern for political divisiveness that once occupied the Court but that post-*Aguilar* cases have rightly disregarded. . . . . . .

* * *

There are numerous reasons to formally dispense with this factor. . . . Although our case law has consistently mentioned it even in recent years, we have not struck down an aid program in reliance on this factor since 1985, in *Aguilar* and *Ball*. *Agostini* of course overruled *Aguilar* in full and *Ball* in part, ...

. . . If a program offers permissible aid to the religious (including the pervasively sectarian), the areligious, and the irreligious, it is a mystery which view of religion the government has established. . . . . . . Finally, hostility to aid to pervasively sectarian schools has a shameful pedigree that we do not hesitate to disavow. . . . Although the dissent professes concern for "the implied exclusion of the less favored" . . . the exclusion of pervasively sectarian schools from government-aid programs is just that. . . . . . . In short, nothing in the Establishment Clause requires the exclusion of pervasively sectarian schools from otherwise permissible aid programs, and other doctrines of this Court bar it. This doctrine, born of bigotry, should be buried now.

Applying the two relevant *Agostini* criteria, we see no basis for concluding that Jefferson Parish's Chapter 2 program "has the effect of advancing religion." . . . Chapter 2 aid also, like the aid in *Agostini, Zobrest,* and *Witters,* reaches participating schools only "as a consequence of private decisionmaking." . . . It is the students and their parents—not the government—who, through their choice of school, determine who receives Chapter 2 funds. The aid follows the child.

. . . Nor, . . . is it of constitutional significance that the schools themselves, rather than the students, are the bailees of the Chapter 2 aid. The ultimate beneficiaries . . . are the student . . . and this is so regardless of whether individual students lug computers to school each day or, as Jefferson Parish has more sensibly provided, the schools receive the computers. . . . . . .

Finally, Chapter 2 satisfies the first *Agostini* criterion because it does not provide to religious schools aid that has an impermissible content. The statute explicitly bars anything of the sort. . . . . . .

* * *

The District Court found that prescreening by the LEA coordinator of requested library books was sufficient to prevent statutory violations. . . . . . .

. . . Accordingly, we hold that Chapter 2 is not a law respecting an establishment of religion. To the extent that *Meek* and *Wolman* conflict with this holding, we overrule them. . . .

The judgment of the Fifth Circuit is reversed.

It is so ordered.

Concurring Opinion

JUSTICE O'CONNOR, with whom JUSTICE BREYER joins, concurring in the judgment.

. . . To the extent our decisions in *Meek v. Pittenger* . . . and *Wolman v. Walter* . . . are inconsistent with the Court's judgment today, I agree that those decisions should be overruled. I therefore concur in the judgment.

I

I write separately because, in my view, the plurality announces a rule of unprecedented breadth for the evaluation of Establishment Clause challenges. . . . Reduced to its essentials, the plurality's rule states that government aid to religious schools does not have the effect of advancing religion so long as the aid is offered on a neutral basis and the aid is secular in content. The plurality also rejects the distinction between direct and indirect aid, and holds that the actual diversion of secular aid by a religious school to the advancement of its religious mission is permissible. . . . [T]wo specific aspects of the opinion compel me to write separately. First, the plurality's treatment of neutrality comes close to assigning that factor singular importance in the future adjudication of Establishment Clause challenges to government school-aid programs. Second, the plurality's approval of actual diversion of government aid to religious indoctrination is in tension with our precedents and, in any event, unnecessary to decide the instant case.

* * *

I agree with Justice SOUTER that the plurality, by taking such a stance, appears to take evenhandedness neutrality and in practical terms promote it to a single and sufficient test for the establishment constitutionality of school aid. . . .

I do not quarrel with the plurality's recognition that neutrality is an important reason for upholding government-aid programs against Establishment Clause challenges. . . . Nevertheless, we have never held that a government-aid program passes constitutional muster solely because of the neutral criteria it employs as a basis for distributing aid. . . .

* * *

. . . Like Justice SOUTER, I do not believe that we should treat a per-capita-aid program the same as the true private-choice programs considered in *Witters* and *Zobrest*. . . .

Second, I believe the distinction between a per-capita school-aid program and a true private-choice program is significant for purposes of endorsement. . . . That the amount of aid received by the school is based on the school's enrollment does not separate the government from the endorsement of the religious message. . . . To be sure, the plurality does not actually hold that its theory extends to direct money payments. . . . That omission, however, is of little comfort. . . . [T]he plurality opinion foreshadows the approval of direct monetary subsidies to religious organizations, even when they use the money to advance their religious objectives. . . .

* * *

I would reject respondents' proposed divertibility rule. . . .

* * *

. . . [I]f the mere ability of a teacher to devise a religious lesson involving the secular aid in question suffices to hold the provision of that aid unconstitutional, it is difficult to discern any limiting principle to the divertibility rule. . . . It does not follow, however, that we should treat as constitutionally suspect any form of secular aid that might conceivably be diverted to a religious use. . . . . . .

* * *

. . . I would adhere to the rule that we have applied in the context of textbook lending programs: To establish a First Amendment violation, plaintiffs must prove that the aid in question actually is, or has been, used for religious purposes. . . .

* * *

. . . I see no constitutional need for pervasive monitoring under the Chapter 2 program.

The safeguards employed by the program are constitutionally sufficient. . . .

* * *

. . . Accordingly, I concur in the judgment.

Justice Souter, with whom Justice Stevens and Justice Ginsburg join, dissenting.

* * *

. . . It is beyond question that the plurality's notion of evenhandedness neutrality . . . would be the end of the principle of no aid to the schools' religious mission. . . . My concern with these arguments goes not so much to their details as it does to the fact that the plurality's choice to employ imputations of bigotry and irreligion as terms in the Court's debate makes one point clear: that in rejecting the principle of no aid to a school's religious mission the plurality is attacking the most fundamental assumption underlying the Establishment Clause, that government can in fact operate with neutrality in its relation to religion. I believe that it can, and so respectfully dissent.

Case 9.4 Review Questions

1. Why did the concurring and dissenting Justices reject the view of the plurality opinion that government "neutrality" is all that the Establishment Clause requires?

2. What would the concurring Justices require beyond the neutrality standard of the plurality opinion?

Case 9.5

ZELMAN v. SIMMONS-HARRIS
122 S. Ct. 2460 (2002)

> [**Focus Note.** *Constitutional challenge to a state pilot program limited to distressed urban school district (Cleveland) to provide sliding scale tuition grants to low-income parents, based on their poverty level, for use at a state-approved public or private (secular or parochial) school. The Court by 5–4 vote held that the program was neutral with respect to religion and therefore did not violate the Establishment Clause. The following opinion sets the latest Court statement of Establishment Clause jurisprudence, with four Justices disagreeing with that jurisprudence.]*

CHIEF JUSTICE REHNQUIST delivered the opinion of the Court.

The State of Ohio has established a pilot program designed to provide educational choices to families with children who reside in the Cleveland City School District. The question presented is whether this program offends the Establishment Clause of the United States Constitution. We hold that it does not.

There are more than 75,000 children enrolled in the Cleveland City School District. The majority of these children are from low-income and minority families. Few of these families enjoy the means to send their children to any school other than an inner-city public school. For more than a generation, however, Cleveland's public schools have been among the worst performing public schools in the Nation. In 1995, a Federal District Court . . . placed the entire Cleveland school district under state control. Shortly thereafter, the state auditor found that Cleveland's public schools were in the midst of a "crisis that is perhaps unprecedented in the history of American education." The district had failed to meet any of the 18 state standards for minimal acceptable performance. Only 1 in 10 ninth graders could pass a basic proficiency examination. . . . More than two-thirds of high school students either dropped or failed out before graduation. Of those students who managed to reach their senior year, one of every four still failed to graduate. Of those students who did graduate, few could read, write, or compute at levels comparable to their counterparts in other cities.

It is against this backdrop that Ohio enacted, among other initiatives, its Pilot Project Scholarship Program. . . . The program provides financial assistance to families in any Ohio school district that is or has been "under federal court order requiring supervision and operational management of the district by the state superintendent." § 3313.975(A). Cleveland is the only Ohio school district to fall within that category.

The program provides two basic kinds of assistance to parents of children in a covered district. First, the program provides tuition aid for students in kindergarten through third grade, expanding each year through eighth grade, to attend a participating public or private school of their parent's choosing. Second, the program provides tutorial aid for students who choose to remain enrolled in public school.

. . . Any private school, whether religious or nonreligious, may participate in the program and accept program students so long as the school is located within the boundaries of a covered district and meets statewide educational standards. Participating private schools must agree not to discriminate on the basis of race, religion, or ethnic background. . . . . . .

Tuition aid is distributed to parents according to financial need. Families with incomes below 200% of the poverty line are given priority. . . . For these lowest-income families, participating private schools may not charge a parental co-payment greater than $250. For all other families, the program pays 75% of tuition costs, with no co-payment cap. . . . Where tuition aid is spent depends solely upon where parents . . . choose to enroll their child. If parents choose a private school, checks are made payable to the parents who then endorse the checks over to the chosen school.

* * *

. . . In the 1999–2000 school year, 56 private schools participated in the program, 46 (or 82%) of which had a religious affiliation. None of the public schools in districts adjacent to Cleveland have elected to participate. More than 3,700 students participated in the scholarship program, most of whom (96%) enrolled in religiously affiliated schools. Sixty percent of these students were from families at or below the poverty line. . . .

* * *

In July 1999, respondents filed this action . . . to enjoin the reenacted program on the ground that it violated the Establishment Clause of the United States Constitution. . . . . . . In December 2000, a divided panel of the Court of Appeals affirmed the judgment of the District Court, finding that the program had the "primary effect" of advancing religion in violation of the Establishment Clause. . . . We granted certiorari . . . and now reverse the Court of Appeals.

The Establishment Clause of the First Amendment, applied to the States through the Fourteenth Amendment, prevents a State from enacting laws that have the "purpose" or "effect" of advancing or inhibiting religion. *Agostini v. Felton,* 521 U.S. 203 (1997). . . . There is no dispute that the program challenged here was enacted for the valid secular purpose. . . . Thus, the question presented is whether the Ohio program nonetheless has the forbidden "effect" of advancing or inhibiting religion.

To answer that question, our decisions have drawn a consistent distinction between government programs that provide aid directly to religious schools, *Mitchell v. Helms,* 530 U.S. 793 (2000) (plurality opinion); *id.,* at 841–844 (O'CONNOR, J., concurring in judgment); *Agostini, supra,* at

225–227, and programs of true private choice, in which government aid reaches religious schools only as a result of the genuine and independent choices of private individuals, *Mueller v. Allen,* 463 U.S. 388 (1983); *Witters v. Washington Dept. of Servs. for Blind,* 474 U.S. 481 (1986); *Zobrest v. Catalina Foothills School Dist.,* 509 U.S. 1, 113 S. Ct. 2462. While our jurisprudence with respect to the constitutionality of direct aid programs has "changed significantly" over the past two decades, our jurisprudence with respect to true private choice programs has remained consistent and unbroken. Three times we have confronted Establishment Clause challenges to neutral government programs that provide aid directly to a broad class of individuals, who, in turn, direct the aid to religious schools or institutions of their own choosing. Three times we have rejected such challenges.

In *Mueller,* we rejected an Establishment Clause challenge to a Minnesota program authorizing tax deductions for various educational expenses, including private school tuition costs, even though the great majority of the program's beneficiaries (96%) were parents of children in religious schools. . . .

* * *

That the program was one of true private choice, with no evidence that the State deliberately skewed incentives toward religious schools, was sufficient for the program to survive scrutiny under the Establishment Clause.

In *Witters,* we used identical reasoning to reject an Establishment Clause challenge to a vocational scholarship program that provided tuition aid to a student studying at a religious institution to become a pastor. . . .

Five Members of the Court, in separate opinions, emphasized the general rule from *Mueller* that the amount of government aid channeled to religious institutions by individual aid recipients was not relevant to the constitutional inquiry. 474 U.S., at 490–491. . . .

Finally, in *Zobrest,* we applied *Mueller* and *Witters* to reject an Establishment Clause challenge to a federal program that permitted sign-language interpreters to assist deaf children enrolled in religious schools. . . . Looking once again to the challenged program as a whole, we observed that the program "distributes benefits neutrally to any child qualifying as 'disabled.'" . . . Its "primary beneficiaries," we said, were "disabled children, not sectarian schools."

We further observed that "[b]y according parents freedom to select a school of their choice, the statute ensures that a government-paid interpreter will be present in a sectarian school only as a result of the private decision of individual parents." . . . Our focus again was on neutrality and the principle of private choice, not on the number of program beneficiaries attending religious schools. *Id.,* at 10–11. . . .

Mueller, Witters, and *Zobrest* thus make clear that where a government aid program is neutral with respect to religion, and provides assistance directly to a broad class of citizens who, in turn, direct government aid to religious schools wholly as a result of their own genuine and independent private choice, the program is not readily subject to challenge under the Establishment Clause. . . . The incidental advancement of a religious mission, or the perceived endorsement of a religious message, is reasonably attributable to the individual recipient, not to the government, whose role ends with the disbursement of benefits. . . .

It is precisely for these reasons that we have never found a program of true private choice to offend the Establishment Clause.

We believe that the program challenged here is a program of true private choice, consistent with *Mueller, Witters,* and *Zobrest,* and thus constitutional. . . .

* * *

Respondents suggest that even without a financial incentive for parents to choose a religious school, the program creates a "public perception that the State is endorsing religious practices and beliefs." . . . Any objective observer familiar with the full history and context of the Ohio program would reasonably view it as one aspect of a broader undertaking to assist poor children in failed schools, not as an endorsement of religious schooling in general.

* * *

Justice SOUTER speculates that because more private religious schools currently participate in the program, the program itself must somehow discourage the participation of private nonreligious schools. But Cleveland's preponderance of religiously affiliated private schools certainly did not arise as a result of the program; it is a phenomenon common to many American cities. See U.S. Dept. of Ed., National Center for Education Statistics, Private School Universe Survey: 1999–2000, pp. 2–4 (NCES 2001–330, 2001) (hereinafter Private School Universe Survey). . . . To attribute constitutional significance to this figure, moreover, would lead to the absurd result that a neutral school-choice program might be permissible in some parts of Ohio, such as Columbus, where a lower percentage of private schools are religious schools, . . . but not in inner-city Cleveland . . . where the preponderance of religious schools happens to be greater. . . .

Likewise, an identical private choice program might be constitutional in some States, such as Maine or Utah . . . but not in other States, such as Nebraska or Kansas, where over 90% of private schools are religious schools. . . .

Respondents and Justice SOUTER claim that even if we do not focus on the number of participating schools that are religious schools, we should attach constitutional significance to the fact that 96% of scholarship recipients have enrolled in religious schools. . . . We need not consider this argument in detail, since it was flatly rejected in *Mueller,* where we found it irrelevant that 96% of parents taking deductions for tuition expenses paid tuition at religious schools. . . . The constitutionality of a neutral educational aid program simply does not turn on whether and why, in a particular area, at a particular time, most private schools are run by religious organizations, or most recipients choose to use the aid at a religious school. . . .

* * *

Respondents finally claim that we should look to *Committee for Public Ed. & Religious Liberty v. Nyquist*, 413 U.S. 756, to decide these cases. We disagree for two reasons. First, the program in *Nyquist* was quite different from the program challenged here. *Nyquist* involved a New York program that gave a package of benefits exclusively to private schools and the parents of private school enrollees. . . . It similarly provided tuition reimbursements designed explicitly to "offe[r] . . . an incentive to parents to send their children to sectarian schools." Indeed, the program flatly prohibited the participation of any public school, or parent of any public school enrollee. . . . Ohio's program shares none of these features.

. . . To the extent the scope of *Nyquist* has remained an open question in light of these later decisions, we now hold that *Nyquist* does not govern neutral educational assistance programs that, like the program here, offer aid directly to a broad class of individual recipients defined without regard to religion.

. . . In keeping with an unbroken line of decisions rejecting challenges to similar programs, we hold that the program does not offend the Establishment Clause.

The judgment of the Court of Appeals is reversed.

[JUSTICES STEVENS, GINSBURG, BREYER and SOUTER dissented]

Case 9.6

HOOKS v. CLARK COUNTY SCHOOL DISTRICT
228 F.3d 1036 (9th Cir. 2000)

*[**Focus Note.** Following the school district's refusal to provide requested speech therapy services to their home-schooled child, the parents sued the school district and its superintendent, alleging that they violated the Individuals with Disabilities Education Act (IDEA) and the Fourteenth Amendment. The following opinion addressed the question whether states have discretion to determine whether home education qualifies as a "private school," for IDEA purposes.]*

GOODWIN, CIRCUIT JUDGE:

. . . Their case presents novel issues regarding (1) the interpretation of the Individuals with Disabilities Education Act ("IDEA") and (2) the constitutionality of denying benefits to home-educated children. We hold that, pursuant to the IDEA, States have discretion in determining whether home education constitutes an IDEA-qualifying "private school." Further, the challenged regulatory scheme does not unconstitutionally offend equal protection principles or infringe on the parents' liberty interest in guiding their child's education.

. . . Christopher was deemed to be medically eligible for speech therapy services. The Hooks family requested subsidized services, even though there has been no claim that home education is necessary to treat his disability, and even though Christopher was not enrolled in any school within the school district. The school district, in accordance with its policy, opted not to provide the services. . . .

By letter in March 1997, the school district explained that the school district's Policy . . . provides that, in accordance with Nevada law, students who receive the home-education exemption "do not have access to instruction and/or ancillary services with the public schools." . . . The school district suggested that the parents either (1) seek an exception from the Board of Trustees, or (2) enroll Christopher in the school district, where he would have an individualized education plan tailored to his needs. The Hooks family chose neither option.

The IDEA and accompanying regulations provide for special services for three categories of children: (1) students in public schools; (2) children placed in private schools by a public agency; and (3) children placed unilaterally in private schools by their parents. *See* 20 U.S.C. § 1412(1) (1994). . . . This scheme comports with the current version of the IDEA, as amended in 1997. . . . Nothing in the language of the IDEA provides services for children who are not enrolled in school, however "school" is defined.

The Hooks family argues that Christopher is a child of the third category, i.e., a child placed unilaterally in private school by his parents, and thus that he qualifies for services. The regulations in effect at the time of Christopher's request provide that where "parents choose to place the child in a private school or facility," 34 C.F.R. § 300.403(a) (1996), provision shall be made for "special education and related services of [such a] *private school child* [ ]," 34 C.F.R. § 300.452 (1996), "[t]o the extent consistent with their number and location in the State." *Id.* (emphasis added). The amended, current version of the IDEA regarding "private elementary and secondary schools" reads in similar fashion. *See* 20 U.S.C. § 1412(10)(A)(i) (2000). . . .

The question we confront is whether Christopher qualifies as a "private school child," i.e., a child placed in a "private school or facility." Neither the IDEA nor the regulations defines or explains what constitutes a "private school."

* * *

The school district contends, and the district court held, that state law controls the definition of "private school" under the IDEA, and that therefore Christopher does not qualify, because exempted home education does not qualify as a "private school" in Nevada. "Private schools," under pre–1999 Nevada law, "means private elementary and secondary educational institutions. *The term does not include a home in which instruction is provided to a child excused from compulsory attendance pursuant to NRS 392.070.*" NRS 394.103 (1997) (emphasis added). Thus, Christopher does not qualify as a "private school" child under Nevada law, and thereby does not qualify for ancillary services under the school district's policy.

The Hooks family does not dispute the school district's interpretation of Nevada law. . . . Rather, the appellants contend that Nevada's definition, and by extension the school district's policy, violates the IDEA. . . .

Instead, we hold that the IDEA leaves discretion to the States to determine that home education that is exempted from the State's compulsory attendance requirement does not constitute an IDEA-qualifying "private school or facility." In holding that this matter is left to the States, we affirm the district court.

* * *

. . . The Due Process Clause of the Fourteenth Amendment does protect the "liberty of parents and guardians to direct the upbringing and education of children under their control." . . .

* * *

Courts outside our Circuit have applied the *Pierce* parental liberty to a right of parents to educate their children at home, and these courts have held that any such right is subject to reasonable regulation. . . . As these cases suggest, identifying a general parental right is far different than concluding that it has been infringed.

* * *

We locate no infringement here. The school district's policy does not prohibit the Hooks family's desired educational option—indeed, Christopher currently and legally receives his education at home. The school district's policy, in accordance with pre–1999 Nevada law, merely requires that certain benefits attached to school attendance be in fact attached to "school" attendance.

A recent case in the Tenth Circuit concerned a similar issue. In *Swanson v. Guthrie Independent School Dist. I-L,* 135 F.3d 694, 699–700 (10th Cir. 1998), our sister Circuit held that a school district's refusal to allow a home-educated child to attend classes part-time did not infringe on the parents' right to direct their child's education. The *Swanson* court held that parents had no constitutional right "to send their children to public school on a part-time basis, and to pick and choose which courses their children will take from the public school." *Id.* at 700. As in *Swanson,* the Hooks family does not have the right to "pick and choose" the services offered by the school district. . . .

* * *

Under the circumstances of this case, attaching receipt of IDEA services to institutional school attendance, and fulfillment of the according regulatory requirements, constitutes "reasonable government regulation" that does not offend our Constitution. . . . Put differently, even if the parents have a constitutional right to educate Christopher at home, they do not have a constitutional right to state-funded speech therapy services. . . .

* * *

Nevada and its school districts have a legitimate interest in promoting educational environments that fulfill those qualifications that the State deems important. Limiting IDEA services to qualified "private schools" reasonably advances that interest by steering scarce educational resources toward those qualified educational environments. . . . State discretion under the IDEA to define "private schools" also has a rational basis. . . .

Conclusion

We hold that, pursuant to the IDEA, States have discretion to determine whether home education constitutes an IDEA-qualifying educational environment. We also hold that the school district's policy of limiting IDEA funds to institutional schools does not unconstitutionally offend equal protection principles or infringe on the parents' liberty interest in guiding their child's education. We remand to district court so that it may dispose of this case in accord with this opinion and with new Nevada law.

Case 9.6 Review Question

1. Was the question of eligibility for IDEA a question of state law or federal law? If the latter, could the court have construed the federal law right of the student independently of the state's definition of a "school"?

ENDNOTES

1. Rendell-Baker v. Kohn, 457 U.S. 830 (1982); Huff v. Notre Dame High School, 456 F. Supp. 1145 (D. Conn. 1978).

2. Brentwood Academy v. Tenn. Secondary School Athletic Assn., 531 U.S. 288 (2001).

3. Pierce v. Society of Sisters; Pierce v. Hill Military Academy, both reported at 268 U.S. 510 (1925); Meyer v. Nebraska, 262 U.S. 390 (1923); Farrington v. Tokushige, 273 U.S. 284 (1927).

4. Ibid. *See also* State v. Vietto, 247 S.E.2d 298 (N.C. 1978); Scoma v. Chicago Board of Educ., 391 F. Supp. 452 (N.D. Ill. 1974).

5. State v. Shaver, 294 N.W.2d 883 (N.D. 1980).

6. Santosky v. Kremer, 450 U.S. 993 (1982).

7. *Minimum wage coverage:* Donovan v. Shenandoah Baptist Church, 573 F. Supp. 320 (W.D. Va. 1983); *cf.* Tony and Susan Alamo Found. v. Secretary of Labor, 105 S. Ct. 1953 (1985). *Workers' compensation coverage:* Victory Baptist Temple v. Industrial Comm'n, 442 N.E.2d 819 (Ohio 1982). Larson, *Workmen's Compensation Law*, V, 1C, §§ 50.40–.44(a) (1983). *Social Security coverage:* United States v. Lee, 455 U.S. 252 (1982). *Unemployment compensation coverage and exemptions: see, e.g.,* St. Martin's Evangelical Lutheran Church and Northwestern Lutheran Academy v. South Dakota, 451 U.S. 772 (1981); California v. Grace Brethren Church, 457 U.S. 393, 403 (1982).

8. Annotations *Validity of State or Local Regulations Requiring Private Schools to Report Attendance, etc.,* 8 A.L.R. 5th 875 (1992); *Validity of State Regulation of Curriculum and Instruction in Private and Parochial Schools,* 18 A.L.R. 4th 649 (1982); *State Regulation of Private Religious Schools,* 25 Ariz. L. Rev. 123 (1983); Grigg v. Comm., 297 S.E.2d 799 (Va. 1982) and cases there cited; DelConte v. State, 308 S.E.2d 898, 901–2 (N.C. 1983) (legislative differentiation between church-related and nonsectarian private schools).

9. Ibid.; Annotations: *Validity, Construction and Application of Statutes or Regulations Governing Charter Schools,* 78 A.L.R. 5th 533 (2000); *Home Schooling,* 70 A.L.R. 5th 169 (1999); *Re alleged rights of contract, association and privacy, see* Tollefson v. Roman Catholic Bishop, 268 Cal. Rptr. 550 (1990); Atty. General v. Bailey, 436 N.E.2d 139 (Mass. 1982); State v. McDonough, 448 A.2d 977, 979 (Me. 1983). *Re discrimination claim, see* Bailey, *supra;* State v. Edgington, 663 P.2d 74 (N.M. 1983); State v. Bowman, 653 P.2d 254 (Or. 1982).

10. *See* Fellowship Baptist Church v. Benton, 815 F.2d 485 (8th Cir. 1987); State v. Calvary Academy, 348 N.W.2d 898 (Neb. 1984); State v. Andrews, 651 P.2d 473 (Hawaii 1982); Jernigan v. State, 412 So. 2d 1242, 1246 (Ala. 1982).

11. Lines & Bray, *What Is a School?* 16 West Ed. L. Rep. 371 (1984). See also DelConte and Grigg cases, note 8, *supra.*

12. Annotations, notes 8, 9, *supra. Certification:* People v. DeJonge, 470 N.W.2d 433 (Mich. 1991); Fellowship Baptist Church, note 10, *supra. Curriculum requirements:* State v. Shaver, 294 N.W.2d 883 (N.D. 1980).

13. State of Ohio v. Whisner, 351 N.E.2d 750 (Ohio 1976); Kentucky State Board of Elementary & Secondary Educ. v. Rudasill, 589 S.W.2d 877 (Ky. 1979); State of North Carolina v. Columbus Christian Academy, Sup. Ct., Div. No. 78 CUS 1678 (N.C. 1978).

14. *Cases sustaining vagueness objections:* Jefferson v. O'Donnell, 702 F. Supp. 516 (M.D. Pa. 1988); State v. Popanz, 332 N.W.2d 750 (Wis. 1983) (term "private school"—held impermissibly vague); Roemhild v. State, 308 S.E.2d 154 (Ga. 1983).
   Cases rejecting vagueness challenges: Bangor Baptist Church v. State, 549 F. Supp. 1208 (D. Me. 1982) ("equivalent" education—held not vague); State v. Moorehead , 308 N.W.2d 60 (Iowa 1981) ("equivalent instruction" and "certified teacher"—held not vague). Annotation: *Home Schooling,* 70 A.L.R. 5th 169, 243 et seq. (1999).

15. Santa Fe Comm. School v. New Mexico State Board of Educ., 581 P.2d 272 (N.M. 1977).

16. Seward Chapel, Inc. v. City of Seward, 655 P.2d 1293, 1297–8 (Alaska 1982); Johnson & Wales College v. DiPrete, 448 A.2d 1271, 1279

(R.I. 1982); Lakewood, Ohio Congregation of Jehovah's Witnesses Inc. v. City of Lakewood, 699 F.2d 303, 305 (6th Cir. 1983).

17. *Total exclusion:* Brookville v. Paulgene Realty Corp., 180 N.E.2d 905 (N.Y. 1960); Roman Catholic Welfare Corp. v. Piedmont, 289 P.2d 438 (Cal. 1955).
    Oppressive requirements: Westbury Hebrew Congregation Inc. v. Downer, 302 N.Y.S.2d 923 (1969).

18. *Exclusion permitted:* Roman Catholic Diocese v. Ho-Ho-Kus, 220 A.2d 97 (N.J. 1966). *Disparate exclusion voided:* Diocese of Rochester v. Planning Board, 136 N.E.2d 827 (N.Y. 1956); Phillips v. Homewood, 50 So. 2d 267 (Ala. 1951). *Disparate exclusion sustained:* Tustin Heights Assn. v. Board of Supervisors, 339 P.2d 914 (Cal. 1954); State v. Sinar, 65 N.W.2d 43 (Wis. 1954).

19. *Compare* Three L. Corp. v. Board of Adjustment, 288 A.2d 312 (N.J. 1972) (held valid), *with* Chicago v. Sachs, 115 N.E.2d 762 (Ill. 1953).

20. Johnson & Wales College v. DiPrete, 448 A.2d 1271, 1280–2 (R.I. 1982); Saddle River Country Day School v. Saddle River, 144 A.2d 425, *aff'd per curiam,* 150 A.2d 34 (N.J. 1959).

21. *Compare* Brandt v. Zoning Board of Appeals of New Castle, 393 N.Y.S.2d 264 (1977), *with* Harbor Schools v. Board of Appeals of Haverhill, 366 N.E.2d 764, 767–9 (Mass. 1977); Areba School Corp. v. Mayor and Council of Twp. of Randolph, 376 A.2d 1273 (N.J. 1977).

22. *See* Annotations, *Measure of Damages or Compensation—Property Owned or Used by Educational, Religious or Charitable Organizations,* 29 A.L.R. 5th 36 (1995); 80 A.L.R. 3d 833 (1977).

23. Dunn v. Bessie F. Heirn School, Inc., 209 So. 2d 538 (La. 1968).

24. Story v. San Rafaele Military Academy, 3 Cal. Rptr. 847 (1960).

25. Tollefson v. Roman Catholic Bishop, 268 Cal. Rptr. 550 (Cal. App. 1990) (contract provision precluded finding of contrary implied duty); Mullan v. Bishop of the Diocese, 540 So. 2d 174 (Fla. App. 1989) (termination without hearing—reversed).

26. Wiethoff v. St. Veronica's School, 210 N.W.2d 108 (Mich. 1973).

27. Little v. Wuerl, 929 F.2d 944 (3d Cir. 1991); Little v. St. Mary Magdalen Parish, 739 F. Supp. 1003 (W.D. Pa. 1990); Bishop Carrol High School v. Unemployment Compensation Board of Review, 557 A.2d 1141 (Pa. Cmwlth. 1989). *But see* St. Pius X Parish v. Murray, 557 A.2d 1214 (R.I. 1989).

28. Bischoff v. Brothers of Sacred Heart, 416 So. 2d 348 (La. 1982) (intentional concealment of remarriage contrary to teaching of sponsoring church); Ostrolenk v. Louise S. McGhee School, 402 So. 2d 237 (La. 1981) (failure to disclose discharge by another private school).

29. Martin v. Coral Gables Academy, 369 So. 2d 255 (La. 1979) (discharge for opposing school's disciplinary policy).

30. *Compare, e.g.,* Assn. of Catholic Teachers v. Pennsylvania Labor Relations Board, 692 A.2d 1039 (Pa. 1997); *cf.* Central Catholic Educ. Assn. v. Archdiocese of Portland, 891 P.2d 1318 (Or. App. 1995) (state statutory exemption premised on existence of federal NLRA jurisdiction), *with* New York State Emp. Relations Board v. Christ the King Regional High School, 90 N.Y.2d 244 (1997); So. Jersey Catholic School Teachers Assn. v. St. Teresa of the Infant Jesus Church Elementary School, 675 A.2d 1155 (N.J. Super. 1996).

31. Edward Street Daycare Center, Inc. v. NLRB, 189 F.3d 40 (1st Cir. 1999).

32. New York State Emp. Relations Board v. Christ the King Regional High School, 90 N.Y.2d 244 (1997); So. Jersey Catholic School Teachers Assn. v. St. Teresa of the Infant Jesus Church Elementary School, 675 A.2d 1155 (N.J. Super. 1996). The New Jersey court relied on the state constitution as creating a compelling state interest in compulsory bargaining as the ground to subordinate the church school's federal constitutional claim.

33. So. Jersey Catholic Sch. Teachers Org. v. St. Teresa of the Infant Jesus Church Elem'y School, 696 A.2d 709 (N.J. 1997); Catholic H.S. Assn. of the Archdiocese of New York v. Culvert, 753 F.2d 1161 (2d Cir. 1985); Hill-Murray Fed. of Teachers v. Hill-Murray High School, 487 N.W.2d 857 (Minn. 1992).

34. *Compare, e.g.,* University of Great Falls v. N.L.R.B., 278 F.3d 1335 (D.C. Cir. 2002), at 1341–43; Universidad Central de Bayamon v. Natl. Labor Relations Board, 793 F.2d 383 (1st Cir. 1986), at 402 (equally divided court); Catholic Bishop of Chicago v. N.L.R.B., 559 F.2d 1112 (7th Cir. 1958) at 1124. D. Laycock, *Towards a General Theory of the Religion Clauses,* 81 Colum. L.Rev. 1373 (1981); C. Esbeck, *The Establishment Clause as a Structural Restraint on Governmental Power,* 84 Iowa L. Rev. 1 (1998).

35. Annotations: *Liability of Private School or Educational Institution for Breach of Contract Arising from Provision of Deficient Educational Instruction,* 46 A.L.R. 5th 581, 597 (2002); *Liability of Private School or Educational Institution for Breach of Contract Arising from Expulsion or Suspension of Student,* 47 A.L.R. 5th 1 (1997) at note 30 and related text.

36. *Change of mind:* Moyse v. Runnels School, Inc., 457 So. 2d 767 (La. App. 1984). *Failure to complete:* St. Margaret's-McTernan v. Thompson, 617 A.2d 449 (Conn. App. 1993); Lake Ridge Academy v. Carney, 613 N.E.2d 183 (Ohio 1993); Princeton Montessori Society, Inc. v. Leff, 591 A.2d 685 (N.J. Super. 1991); Leo Found'n., Inc. v. Kiernan, 240 A.2d 218 (Conn. 1967). *But see* King v. Dramatic Arts, 102 Misc. 2d 1111 (N.Y. 1980) (contract permitting student dismissal without justification while retaining tuition—voided as unconscionable).

37. Thomas Jefferson School Inc. v. Kapros, 728 S.W.2d 315 (Mo. App. 1987) (discharge for misconduct); Wentworth Military Academy v. Marshall, 283 S.W.2d 868 (Ark. 1955) (withdrawal on school request).

38. Girardier v. Webster College, 563 F.2d 1267 (8th Cir. 1977) (no obligation to release student records); McKee v. Southfield School, 613 So. 2d 659 (La. App. 1993) (implied obligation to release records).

39. Sciortino v. Leech, 242 So. 2d 269 (La. 1971).

40. *Rejection of claim of deficient instruction:* Paladino v. Adelphia Univ., 454 N.Y.S.2d 246 (1980); Cencor, Inc. v. Tolman, 868 P.2d 396 (Colo. 1994); Annotation, *Private Schools— Deficient Educational Instruction,* note 35, supra. *Compare,* Village Comm. School v. Adler, 478 N.Y.S.2d 546 (1984) (misrepresentation counterclaim to suit for tuition).

41. *Expulsion upheld:* Allen v. Casper, 622 N.E.2d 367 (Ohio 1993); Hutcheson v. Grace Lutheran School, 517 N.Y.S.2d 760 (1987); Bloch v. Hillel Torah N. Sub. Day School, 426 N.E.2d 976 (Ill. 1981). *Compare* Aronson v. N. Park College, 418 N.E.2d 776 (Ill. 1981) (damages recovered for wrongful expulsion).

42. Fiedler v. Marumsco Christian School, 631 F.2d 1144 (4th Cir. 1980) (reinstatement of student expelled for interracial dating).

43. Blaine v. Savannah Country Day School, 491 S.E.2d 446 (Ga. App. 1997) (upheld expulsion of high school senior prior to graduation for violation of academic honor code).

44. Pa. v. Brown, 270 F. Supp. 782 (E.D. Pa. 1967), *aff'd* 392 F.2d 120 (3rd Cir. 1968).

45. Evans v. Abney, 396 U.S. 435 (1970).

46. Bob Jones University v. United States, 461 U.S. 574 (1983).

47. Estate of Thornton v. Caldor, 472 U.S. 703 (1985).

48. Runyon v. McCrary, 427 U.S. 160 (1976).

49. Corp. of Presiding Bishop v. Amos, 483 U.S. 327 (1987).

50. EEOC v. Kamehameha Schools/Bishop Estate, 990 F.2d 458 (9th Cir. 1993) (exemption denied). *See also* Dolter v. Ahlert High School, 483 F. Supp. 266 (N.D. Iowa 1980); Pime v. Loyola Univ. of Chicago, 585 F. Supp. 435 (N.D. Ill. 1984).

51. Little v. Wuerl, 929 F.2d 944 (3d Cir. 1991); Little v. St. Mary Magdalen Parish, 739 F. Supp. 1003 (W.D. Pa. 1990).

52. Horner v. Mary Inst., 613 F.2d 706, 713 (8th Cir. 1980). On case divisions regarding application of the Equal Pay Act, *compare* Russell v. Belmont College, 554 F. Supp. 667 (M.D. Tenn. 1982), *with* Ritter v. Mt. St. Mary's College, 495 F. Supp. 724 (D. Md. 1980).

53. Organization to Assure Services v. Ambach, 434 N.E.2d 1330 (N.Y. 1982).

54. Newport-Mesa Unified School Dist. v. Hubert, 183 Cal. Rptr. 334 (1982).

55. Sacred Heart School Board v. Industry Review Comm'n, 460 N.W.2d 430 (Wis. 1990).

56. *Held not exempt:* DeMarco v. Holy Cross High School, 4 F.3d 166 (2d Cir. 1993); *cf.* Geary v.

Visitation of the Blessed Virgin Mary Parish School, 7 F.3d 324 (3d Cir. 1993).
Held exempt: Powell v. Stafford, 859 F. Supp. 1343 (D. Colo. 1994); Cochran v. St. Louis Prep. Seminary, 717 F. Supp. 1413 (E.D. Mo. 1989).

57. Basinger v. Pilarczyk, 707 N.E.2d 1149 (Ohio Ct. App. 1997).

58. Sacred Heart School Board v. L.I.R.C., 460 N.W.2d 430 (Wis. App. 1990).

59. *E.g.*, VanScoyk v. St. Mary's Assumption Parochial School, 580 P.2d 1315 (Kans. 1978) (state antidiscrimination exemption for religious preferences).

60. *Higher education grants and loans—upheld:* Tilton v. Richardson, 403 U.S. 672 (1971); Hunt v. McNair, 413 U.S. 736 (1973); Americans United for Separation of Church and State v. Blanton, 434 U.S. 803 (1977); Roemer v. Md. Pub. Works Board, 426 U.S. 734 (1976). See also Steele v. Ind. Development Board, 301 F.3d 401 (6th Cir. 2002)(city bonds issued to finance construction of pervasively religious college).
Elementary school and tuition aids—struck down: Comm. for Public Educ. and Religious Liberty v. Nyquist, 413 U.S. 756 (1973); Lemon v. Kurtzman, 403 U.S. 602 (1971); Sloan v. Lemon, 413 U.S. 825 (1973).

61. Johnson v. Economic Development of Cty. of Oakland, 241 F.3d 501 (6th Cir. 2001).

62. Lemon, note 60, *supra.*

63. Nyquist, note 60, *supra* (facilities maintenance expenses); Lemon, note 60, *supra* (instructional expense reimbursement to the school). *Cf.* Cmwlth. v. School Comm. of Springfield, 417 N.E.2d 408 (Mass. 1981) (state purchase of special educational services—upheld).

64. Valley Forge Christian College v. Americans United for Separation of Church and State, 454 U.S. 464 (1982).

65. Wolman v. Walter, 433 U.S. 229 (1977); Comm. for Public Educ. v. Regan, 444 U.S. 646 (1980).

66. *Cf.* Walz v. Tax Comm'n, 397 U.S. 664, 674 (1970) (tax exemption for churches—upheld); Summit United Methodist Church v. Kinney, 7 Ohio St. 3d 13 (1983) (church educational unit

not entitled to property tax exemption when part of building rented for use as a child care center); Board of Appraisal Review v. Protestant Episcopal Church Council, 676 S.W.2d 616 (Tex. 1984) (85 acres of 392-acre tract, held "reasonably necessary" to operate a school for purposes of the tax statute).

67. Wolman v. Walter, 433 U.S. 229 (1977).

68. Luetkemeyer v. Kaufmann, 364 F. Supp. 376 (W.D. Mo.); *aff'd* 419 U.S. 888 (1974).

69. *States upholding parochial school busing:* Bowker v. Baker, 167 P.2d 256 (Cal. 1946); Snyder v. Town of Newtown, 161 A.2d 770 (Conn. 1960); Board of Educ. v. Bakalis, 299 N.E.2d 737 (Ill. 1973); Neal v. Fiscal Court, 986 S.W.2d 907 (Ky. 1999); Board of Educ. of Baltimore County v. Wheat, 199 A. 628 (Md. 1938); Bloom v. School Comm., 379 N.E.2d 578 (Mass. 1978); Alexander v. Bartlett, 165 N.W.2d 445 (Mich. 1968); Americans United, Inc., as Protestants v. Indep. School Dist., No. 622, 179 N.W.2d 146 (Minn. 1970); W. Morris Regional Board of Educ. v. Sills, 279A.2d 609 (N.J. 1971); Board of Educ. of Central School Dist. No. 1 v. Allen, 228 N.E.2d 791 (N.Y. 1967); Honohan v. Holt, 244 N.E.2d 537 (Ohio 1968); Springfield School Dist. v. Dept. of Educ., 397 A.2d 1154 (Pa. 1979); Members of Jamestown School Comm. v. Schmidt, 405 A.2d 16 (R.I. 1979); Janasiewicz v. Board of Educ., 299 S.E.2d 34 (W. Va. 1982); O'Connell v. Kniskern, 484 F. Supp. 896, 899 (E.D. Wis. 1980).
States invalidating parochial school busing: Matthews v. Quinton, 362 P.2d 932 (Alaska 1961); Opinion of the Justices, 216 A.2d 668 (Del. 1966); Spears v. Honda, 449 P.2d 130 (Hawaii 1968); Epeldi v. Engelking, 488 P.2d 860 (Idaho 1971); Mallory v. Barrera, 544 S.W.2d 556 (Mo. 1976); Board of Educ. v. Antone, 384 P.2d 911 (Okla. 1963); Visser v. Nooksack Valley School Dist., No. 506, 207 P.2d 198 (Wash. 1949). *See* Annot., *Private Schools—Public Aid—Bus Service*, 41 A.L.R. 3d 344 (1972) and latest pkt part. State busing variations are noted in Janasiewicz v. Board of Educ., 299 S.E.2d 34, 37, 38 (W. Va. 1982).

70. Members of the Jamestown School Comm. v. Schmidt, 669 F.2d 1 (1st Cir. 1983); Springfield School Dist. v. Pennsylvania Dept. of Educ., 397 A.2d 1154, *appeal dismissed sub nom.*, School Dist. of Pittsburgh v. Pennsylvania Dept. of Educ., 443 U.S. 901 (1979).

71. Members of Jamestown School Comm. v. Schmidt, 699 F.2d 1 (1st Cir. 1983); Springfield School Dist. v. Pa. Dept. of Education, 397 A.2d 1154, *appeal dismisssed sub nom.* School Dist. of Pittsburgh v. Pa. Dept. of Education, 443 U.S. 901 (1979).

72. O'Connell v. Kniskern, 484 F. Supp. 896 (E.D. Wis. 1980).

73. Young v. Board of Educ., 246 N.W.2d 230 (Wis. 1976).

74. St. John Vianney School v. Board of Educ., 336 N.W.2d 387 (Wis. 1983) (cost of mass transit—upheld); Janasiewicz v. Board of Educ., 299 S.E.2d , 37–8 (W. Va. 1982) (monetary stipends in lieu of transportation—upheld).

75. Deutsch v. Teel, 400 F. Supp. 598, 600 (E.D. Wis. 1975) (refusal to transport child to school that lay 400 feet beyond the district boundary, overturned as abuse of discretion). Board of Educ., Hauppauge Union Free School Dist. v. Ambach, 462 N.Y.S.2d 294 (1983) (parent failure to make timely request).

76. Board of Educ. v. Allen, 392 U.S. 236 (1968).

77. California Teachers Assn. v. Riles, 172 Cal. Rptr. 300 (1981); Fannin v. Williams, 655 S.W.2d 480 (Ky. 1983); Bloom v. School Comm., 379 N.E.2d 578 (Mass. 1978); McDonald v. School Board of Yankton, 246 N.W.2d 93 (S.D. 1976); Paste v. Tussey, 512 S.W.2d 97 (Mo. 1974); Gaffney v. St. Dept. of Educ., 220 N.W.2d 550 (Neb. 1974); *in re* Advisory Opinion, 228 N.W.2d 772 (Mich. 1975); Dickman v. School Dist. No. 62C, 366 P.2d 533 (Or. 1961).

78. Aguilar v. Felton, 473 U.S. 402 (1985); School Dist. of the City of Grand Rapids v. Ball, 473 U.S. 373 (1985); *Compare, e.g.,* Wolman v. Walter, 433 U.S. 229 (1977), *with* Meek v. Pittinger, 421 U.S. 349 (1985).

79. Sloan v. Lemon, 413 U.S. 825 (1973). *Compare* Americans United for the Separation of Church and State v. Blanton, 434 U.S. 803 (1977) (upholding state scholarship subsidies to students in church-related colleges).

80. Jackson v. Benson, 578 N.W.2d 602 (Wis. 1998), *cert. denied,* 119 S. Ct. 466 (1998).

81. Bush v. Holmes, 767 So.2d 668 (Fla. 2000), rev'g Holmes v. Bush, 2d Judicial Circuit, Florida, CV 99–3370 (March 14, 2000).

82. Strout v. Albanese, 178 F.3d 57 (1st Cir. 1999), *cert. denied,* 120 S. Ct. 329 (1999); Bagley v. Raymond School Dept., 728 A.2d 127 (Me. 1999), *cert denied,* 120 S. Ct. 364 (1999); Chittenden Town School Dist. v. Dept. of Educ., 738 A.2d 539 (Vt. 1999), *cert. denied, sub nom.* Andrews v. Vermont Dept. of Educ., 120 S. Ct. 626 (1999).

In February 2004, the Supreme Court ruled that while a state could constitutionally *grant* tuition to a student studying for the ministry theology under the Establishment Clause, it could also constitutionally deny such a tuition grant without violating the Establishment or Free Exercise Clauses. Locke v. Davey, 124 S. Ct. 1307 (2004).

83. Comm. for Public Educ. and Religious Liberty v. Nyquist, 413 U.S. 756 (1973)(voiding tax relief measure); Mueller v. Allen, 463 U.S. 388 (1983)(upholding tax relief measure).

84. Kotterman v. Killian, 972 P.2d 606 (Ariz. 1999).

85. Wheeler v. Barrera, 417 U.S., at 402 (1974).

86. *E.g.,* in California, Michigan, Minnesota, Colorado, and Massachusetts. *NEA Study, supra.*

87. *See, e.g.,* NEA, *Charter Schools* (update of May 1996), and *Hassel, supra.*

88. *States with strong laws*: California, Colorado, Delaware, District of Columbia, Florida, Indiana, Massachusetts, Michigan, Minnesota, Missouri, New Jersey, New Mexico, New York, North Carolina, Ohio, Oregon, Pennsylvania, Texas, Wisconsin.

States with weak laws: Alaska, Arkansas, Connecticut, Georgia, Hawaii, Idaho, Illinois, Iowa, Kansas, Louisiana, Mississippi, Nevada, New Hampshire, Oklahoma, Rhode Island, South Carolina, Tennessee, Utah, Virginia, Wyoming.

89. State authorities are collected in Annotation, *Home Schooling* 70 A.L.R. 5th 169 (1999) (hereafter cited as *Annotation*); C. Bjorklun, *Home Schooling in the United States: A Statutory Analysis* (1989); C. J. Klicka, *The Right to Home School* 161 (1995); Gordon, William MacGuire, *The Law of Home Schooling* (1994); *Legal Precedents and Strategies Shaping Home Schooled Students' Participation in Public School Sports*, 11 J. Legal Aspects of Sport 25 (2001); J. McMullen, Behind Closed Doors: Should

States Regulate Homeschooling? 54 South Carolina Law Review 75 (2002).

90. Ibid. *See, e.g.,* State v. McDonough, 468 A.2d 977 (Me. 1983) (teacher training, facilities—upheld); Blount v. Dept. of Educational Services, 551 A.2d 1377 (Me. 1988) (curriculum requirements—upheld). *But see contra,* Brunelle v. Lyon Pub. Schools, 702 N.E.2D 1182 (Mass. 1998) (home-visit inspection—voided as unnecessary to serve state purpose, hence unreasonable.)

91. Null v. Board of Educ., 815 F. Supp. 937 (S.D. W.Va. 1993).

92. *E.g.,* People v. Bennett, 501 N.W.2d 106 (Mich. 1993); Murphy v. State of Arkansas, 852 F.2d 1039 (8th Cir. 1988).

93. *See, e.g.,* State v. Popanz, 332 N.W.2d 750 (Wis. 1983); State v. Newstrom, 371 N.W.2d 525 (Minn. 1985); Fellowship Baptist Church v. Benton, 815 F.2d 485 (8th Cir. 1987); Roemhild v. State, 308 S.E.2d 154 (Ga. 1983); Brunelle v. Lyon Pub. Schools, 702 N.E.2d 1182 (Mass. 1998).

   Re certification for home education: State v. Moorehead, 308 N.W.2d 60 (Iowa 1981); Jeffery v. O'Donnell, 702 F. Supp. 516 (M.D. Pa. 1988).

94. *Compare, e.g.,* Duro v. District Attorney, 712 F.2d 96 (4th Cir. 1983); State v. Riviera, 497 N.W.2d 878 (Iowa 1993) (rejecting religious objection defense), *with* People v. DeJonge, 501 N.W.2d 127 (Mich. 1993) (upholding religious objection).

95. *Cf.* Brentwood Academy v. Tenn. Sec'y School Athletic Assn., 531 U.S. 288 (2001).

96. *See, e.g.,* Palmer v. Merluzzi, 868 F.2d 90 (3d Cir. 1989); McFarlin v. Newport Spec. School Dist., 980 F.2d 1208 (8th Cir. 1992).

97. *Re Due Process, see* prior note; McNatt v. Frazier Sch. Dist., 1995 WL 568380 (W.D. Pa. 1995); Bradstreet v. Sobol, 630 N.Y.S.2d 486 (1995). *Contra*: Boyd v. Board of Directors of the McGhee School District No. 17, 612 F. Supp. 86, 93 (D. Ark. 1985) (exceptional student athlete with potential for college scholarship held to have a property interest protected by the Due Process clause).

   Re Free Exercise, see, e.g., Thomas v. Allegany Bd. of Educ., 443 A.2d 622 (Md. App. 1998).

   Re Equal Protection, see, e.g., Schaill v. Tippecanoe County Sch. Corp., 864 F.2d 1309(7th Cir. 1988). *But see* Davis v. Massachusetts Interscholastic Athletic Ass'n, No. CA942887, 1995 WL 808968 (Mass. Super. Jan. 18, 1995) (Interscholastic Association rule—held not rational).

   See, generally, Gardner and McFarland, *Students Participation in Public School Sports,* 11 J. Legal Aspects of Sport 25 (2001); Note, *Access Denied: Prohibiting Homeschooled Students from Participating in Public-School Athletics and Activities,* 16 Ga. State. U. Law Rev. 823 (2000); Article, Home Schooled Children, Gaining Limited Access to Public Schools, 28 J.L. Education, 25 (1999).

98. Duffley v. New Hampshire Interscholastic Athletic Ass'n, 446 A.2d 462 (N.H. 1982).

99. See Annotations and Articles cited in note 68, *supra;* Brockett, Home School Kids in Public School Activities, 61 Ed. Dig. 67 (1995) citing of relevant state statutes. *Cf.* Snyder v. Charlotte Pub. Sch. Dist., 365 N.W.2d 151 (1984); Travis City Sch. Dist. v. Attorney General, 185 N.W.2D 9 (1971).

100. See article, Students Schooled at Home Welcome, the Phila. Inquirer (Main Line ed., 10–19–99) at p. RE–6.

101. Yeske v. Aron Old Farm Schools, 470 A.2d 705 (Conn. 1984) (child trespasser injured by a cable); Saul v. Roman Catholic Church, 402 P.2d 48 (N.M. 1965) (child fall into school site excavation). *But see contra,* Siver v. Atlantic Union College, 154 N.E.2d 360 (Mass. 1958).

102. Velez v. Our Lady of Victory Church, 486 N.Y.S.2d 302 (1985).

103. Wilkinson v. Hartford Acc. & Ind. Co., 411 So. 2d 22 (La. 1982).

104. Garofoli v. Salesianum School, Inc., 208 A.2d 308 (De. 1965); case authorities in 68 Am. Jur. 2d § 324.

105. Kim v. State, 616 P.2d 1376 (Hawaii 1980) (duty to prevent criminal assault by students); James v. Charlotte-Mecklenburg Board of Educ., 300 S.E.2d 21, 24 (N.C. 1983).

106. Annotation, *Liability of Charitable Organization for Tort of Unpaid Volunteer,* 82 A.L.R. 3d 1213 (1978).

107. Cramer v. Hoffman, 390 F.2d 19 (2d Cir. 1968).

108. For a discussion of administrative negligence in hiring school personnel, *see* J. v. Victory Tabernacle Baptist Church, 372 S.E.2d 391 (Va. 1988).

109. Roman Catholic Church v. Keenan, 243 P.2d 455 (Ariz. 1952).

110. Hillman v. Greater Miami Hebrew Academy, 72 So. 2d 668 (Fla. 1954) (case dismissed); Mlynarski v. St. Rita's Congregation, 142 N.W.2d 207 (1966) (trial granted).

111. Hunter v. Evergreen Presbyterian Vocational School, 338 So. 2d 164 (La. 1976).

112. Noland v. Colorado School of Trades, Inc., 386 P.2d 358 (Colo. 1963).

113. Fowler v. Seaton, 394 P.2d 697 (Cal. 1964).

114. *See* Note, *School Liability for Athletic Injuries,* 21 Washburn L.J. 315, 321, note 52.

115. Selleck v. Insurance Co. of North America, 182 So. 2d 547 (La. 1966).

116. Shanahan v. St. James' Roman Catholic Church, 223 N.Y.S.2d 519 (1960).

117. Martin v. Roman Catholic Archbishop, 322 P.2d 31 (Cal. 1958).

118. Bernesak v. Catholic Bishop, 409 N.E.2d 287 (Ill. 1980); Sheehan v. St. Peter's Catholic School, 188 N.W.2d 868 (Minn. 1971). *See also* Titus v. Lindberg, 228 A.2d 65 (N.J. 1967).

119. Benedetto v. Travelers Insurance Co., 172 So. 2d 354 (La. 1965).

120. *Compare* Everett v. School Dist., 380 N.E.2d 653 (Mass. 1978) (liability for use of defective hockey helmets), *with* Brackman v. Adrian, 472 S.W.2d 735 (Tenn. 1971) (no liability for coach's failure to require catcher's mask in softball game).

121. *Compare* Christofides v. Hellenic Eastern Orthodox Christian Church, 227 N.Y.S.2d 946 (1962), *with* Kim v. State, 616 P.2d 1376 (Hawaii 1980).

122. Townsend by Benevente, 339 F.2d 421 (9th Cir. 1964) (student struck by nut thrown by another student during noon recess).

123. Marques v. Riverside Military Academy, 73 S.E.2d 574 (Ga. 1952).

124. *See* Martin v. Roman Catholic Archbishop, 322 P.2d 31 (Cal. 1958).

125. Sharpe v. Quality Educ. Inc., 296 S.E.2d 661 (N.C. 1982); Brokaw v. Black-Foxe Military Inst., 231 P.2d 816 (Cal. 1951).

126. Moore v. Order Minor Conventuals, 267 F.2d 296 (4th Cir. 1959).

127. Beardsell v. Tilton School, 200 A. 783 (N.H. 1938).

128. Bryant v. Thunderbird Academy, 439 P.2d 818 (Ariz. 1968).

129. Faber v. Roelofs, 212 N.W.2d 856 (Minn. 1973).

130. Applebaum v. Nemon, 678 S.W.2d 533 (Tex. 1984) (no duty to provide CPR). *See* Stineman v. Fontbonne College, 664 F.2d 1082 (8th Cir. 1981), and the authorities there cited from other states.

131. Guerrieri v. Tyson, 24 A.2d 468 (Pa. 1942); *cf.* Benhart v. Rockford Dark Dist., 578 N.E.2D 600 (Ill. 1991).

132. Helm v. Professional Children's School, 431 N.Y.S.2d 246 (1980).

133. Pietro v. St. Joseph's School, N.Y. Sup. Ct., Suffolk County (1979), reported at 48 U.S. Law Week 2229.

134. For varied treatment of private school charitable immunity, *see* Annots.: *Tort Immunity—Nongovernmental Charities,* 25 A.L.R. 4th 517 (1983); *Tort Immunity—Private Schools,* 38 A.L.R. 3d 480 (1971). States that abrogated private school tort immunity, in whole or in part, include Arizona, California, District of Columbia, Idaho, Illinois, Indiana, Iowa, Kansas, Kentucky, Louisiana, Massachusetts, Minnesota, Missouri, New Jersey, New York, Ohio, Oklahoma, Pennsylvania, Rhode Island, South Carolina, Texas, Utah, Vermont, Washington, and Wisconsin. Some states substituted limited or partial immunity, including Arkansas, Connecticut, Colorado, Maryland, Nebraska, Nevada, Tennessee, and Virginia.

135. Bernesak v. Catholic Bishop, 409 N.E.2d 287 (Ill. 1980); Merrill v. Catholic Bishop of Chicago, 290 N.E.2d 259 (Ill. 1972).

136. Love v. Nashville A. and Normal Inst., 243 S.W.304 (Tenn. 1922). *See also* discussion of nuisances in Chapter 4.

137. On statutory waiver of immunity to amount of liability insurance, *see, e.g.,* Maine Rev. Stat. Ann. title. 14, § 158 (1980). *Cf.* Stiff v. Eastern Ill. Area of Spec. Educ., 621 N.E.2d 218 (Ill. 1993).

Selected Provisions— Constitution of the United States*

We the people of the United States, in Order to form a more perfect Union, establish Justice, insure domestic Tranquility, provide for the common defence, promote the general Welfare, and secure the Blessings of Liberty to ourselves and our Posterity, do ordain and establish this Constitution for the United States of America.

Article I

* * *

Section 8. [1] **The Congress shall have Power to** lay and collect Taxes, Duties, Imposts and Excises, to pay the Debts and provide for the common Defence and general Welfare of the United States; . . .

* * *

[3] **To Regulate Commerce** with foreign Nations, and among the several States, and with the Indian Tribes; . . .

* * *

[18] To make all Laws which shall be necessary and proper for carrying into Execution the foregoing Powers, . . .

* * *

Section 10. [1] **No State shall** . . . pass any . . . Law impairing the Obligation of Contracts. . . .

* * *

Article III

Section 1. **The judicial Power of the United States, shall be** vested in one supreme Court, and in such inferior Courts as the Congress may from time to time

---

*The words printed in bold type indicate the key sources of constitutional doctrines that prominently apply to school cases.

ordain and establish. The Judges, both of the supreme and inferior Courts, shall hold their Offices during good Behaviour . . . .

Section 2. [1] **The judicial Power shall extend to all Cases**, in Law and Equity, arising under this Constitution, the Laws of the United States and Treaties made, or which shall be made, under their Authority; . . . to Controversies to which the United States shall be a party;—to Controversies between two or more States;— between a State and Citizens of another State;—between Citizens of different States; . . . and between a State, or the Citizens thereof, and foreign States, Citizens or Subjects. . . .

* * *

Article VI

* * *

This Constitution, and the Laws of the United States which shall be made in Pursuance thereof; and all Treaties made, or which shall be made, under the Authority of the United States, **shall be the supreme Law of the Land; and the judges in every State shall be bound thereby,** any Thing in the Constitution or Laws of any State to the Contrary notwithstanding.

* * *

Amendment I [1791]

Congress shall make no law respecting an establishment of religion, or prohibiting the free exercise thereof; or abridging the freedom of speech, or of the press; or the right of the people peaceably to assemble, and to petition the Government for a redress of grievances.

* * *

Amendment IV [1791]

The right of the people to be secure in their persons, houses, papers, and effects, **against unreasonable searches** and seizures, shall not be violated, and no Warrants shall issue, but upon probable cause, supported by Oath or affirmation, and particularly describing the place to be searched, and the persons or things to be seized.

Amendment V [1791]

No person shall be . . . compelled in any criminal case to be a witness against himself, nor **be deprived of life, liberty, or property, without due process of law; nor shall private property be taken for public use, without just compensation.**

Amendment VIII [1791]

Excessive bail shall not be required, . . . nor cruel and unusual punishments inflicted.

Amendment IX [1791]

The enumeration in the Constitution, of certain rights, shall not be construed to deny or disparage others retained by the people.

Amendment X [1791]

The powers not delegated to the United States by the Constitution, nor prohibited by it to the States, are reserved to the States respectively, or to the people.

Amendment XI [1798]

The Judicial power of the United States shall not be construed to extend to any suit in law or equity, commenced or prosecuted against one of the United States by Citizens of another State, or by Citizens or Subjects of any Foreign State.

Amendment XIII [1865]

Section 1. **Neither slavery nor involuntary servitude,** except as a punishment for crime whereof the party shall have been duly convicted, **shall exist within the United States,** or any place subject to their jurisdiction.

Section 2. Congress shall have power to enforce this article by appropriate legislation.

Amendment XIV [1868]

Section 1. All persons born or naturalized in the United States, and subject to the jurisdiction thereof, are citizens of the United States and of the State wherein they reside. No State shall make or enforce any law which shall abridge the privileges or immunities of citizens of the United States; **nor shall any State deprive any person of life, liberty, or property, without due process of law; nor deny to any person within its jurisdiction the equal protection of the laws**.

* * *

Section 5. **The Congress shall have the power to enforce this article, by appropriate legislation.**

Principal Federal Laws Affecting Equal Opportunity in Education[*]

Summary List

Post–Civil War Statutes

42 U.S.C. § 1981—Civil Rights Acts of 1866, 1870

42 U.S.C. § 1983—Civil Rights Acts of 1871

42 U.S.C. § 1985—Civil Rights Acts of 1866, 1870

Modern Era Statutes

Title VI, Civil Rights Act of 1964 (42 U.S.C. § 2000(d))

Title VII, Civil Rights Act of 1964 (VI-42 U.S.C. § 2000(e))

Title IX, Education Amendments of 1972 (20 U.S.C. § 1681)

Equal Pay Act of 1964 (29 U.S.C. § 206(d))

Age Discrimination in Employment Act (29 U.S.C. § 621)

Equal Education Opportunities Act (29 U.S.C. § 1703)

Rehabilitation Act of 1973 (§ 504) (29 U.S.C. § 794)

Individuals with Disabilities Education Act (formerly Education of the Handicapped Act) (20 U.S.C. § 1401)

Americans with Disabilities Act (42 U.S.C. § 12101)

Civil Rights Restoration Act of 1991

Core Requirements—Reconstruction Era Statutes, 42 U.S.C. §§ 1981–1988 (as amended to date)

42 U.S.C. **§ 1981 All persons** . . . shall have the **same right** . . . to make and enforce contracts, . . . and to the full and equal benefit of all laws and proceedings for the security of persons and property **as is enjoyed by white citizens**. . . .

---

[*]The words printed in bold type indicate the key requirements for protection by the cited statute.

42 U.S.C. **§ 1983 Every person who,** under color of any statute, ordinance, regulations, custom or usage of any State . . . **subjects** . . . **any** . . . **person** . . . to the **deprivation of any rights** . . . **secured by the Constitution and laws,** shall be liable to the party injured. . . .

42 U.S.C. **§§ 1985 and 1986** [provides in part that any persons **conspiring to deprive** *"any person* or class of persons of the **equal protection of the laws,** shall be liable to the party so injured. . . ."]

42 U.S.C. **§ 1988** [authorizes recovery of attorney fees by a prevailing party in the following suits]

In any . . . proceeding to enforce a provision of sections 1981, 1982, 1983, 1985, and 1986 of this title, Title IX of Public Law 92-318, or Title VI of the Civil Rights Act of 1964, the court . . . **may allow the prevailing party** . . . **a reasonable attorney's fee as part of the costs.**

Core Requirements—Modern Era Statutes

Title VII—1964 Civil Rights Act. It shall be an unlawful employment practice **for an employer**—(1) . . . [to] discriminate against any individual with respect to his compensation, terms, conditions, or privileges of employment **because of** such individual's **race, color, religion, sex, or national origin** . . . [with exemptions for seniority or merit systems, good faith employment qualifications, and religiously based decisions by religious educational institutions or associations].

Equal Pay Act (EPA). No employer shall discriminate . . . between employees **on the basis of sex by paying wages** . . . at a rate less than the rate in which he pays wages to employees of the opposite sex . . . **for equal work** . . . which requires **equal skill, effort, and responsibility** . . . [with exception for seniority-based pay differentials].

Title VI—1964 Civil Rights Act. No person . . . shall, on the ground of **race, color, or national origin** . . . **be denied the benefits of, or be subjected to discrimination under any program or activity receiving federal financial assistance.** . . .

Title IX—Education Amendments of 1972, § 901. (A) **No person** . . . shall on the basis of sex . . . **be denied the benefits of, or be subjected to discrimination under any education program or activity receiving federal financial assistance.** . . .

Americans with Disabilities Act (ADA). No covered entity shall **discriminate against a qualified individual with a disability** [as defined in the Act] **because of the disability** . . . in regard to [work opportunity, terms, conditions and privileges, in language largely parallel to Title VII, above].

Age Discrimination in Employment Act (ADEA). [Prohibits employment discrimination **because of an individual's age,** with exception for bona-fide employment qualifications.]

Rehabilitation Act (§ 504). No otherwise qualified handicapped individual . . . shall solely by reason of his handicap [as defined by the Act], be denied the benefit of, or be subjected to discrimination under **any program or activity receiving federal financial assistance.**

Individuals with Disabilities Education Act (IDEA). [Requires that any state recipient of federal aid provide a **free appropriate public education** to all children with covered handicaps, and comply with the Act's procedures and requirements to assure that education.]

Select Table of Cases

This table lists significant cases that have affected prior law, either by overruling, limiting, or extending the law to new situations or by raising conflicts of law between different federal Courts of Appeal where the Supreme Court has not as yet settled those conflicts.

Part I lists decisions, mostly from the United States Supreme Court and federal Courts of Appeal. Supreme Court cases which did not appear in past editions or which were not there highlighted are indicated by a double asterisk (**). New lower court decisions are preceded by a single asterisk. Part I cases are generally referenced to the text page number where they appear.

Part II lists other significant decisions, including some which address novel questions not previously adjudicated. Part II cases are generally referenced to their chapter endnote number and, in some cases, to the page where they appear. Decisions by the United States Supreme Court in Part II are listed in bold type.

Part I: Decisions of Major Impact in School Law

*ABC School v. Mr. and Mrs. M., ch. 7, p. 363
Adler v. Duval County School Board, ch. 3, pp. 75, 95
Agostini v. Felton, ch. 3, p. 66; ch. 9, p. 465
Aguilar v. Felton, ch. 9, n. 78
** Alexander v. Sandoval, ch. 6, n. 92; ch. 7, p. 318
Aubrey v. School Board of Lafayette Parish, ch. 6, p. 254
Auerbach v. Board of Education, ch. 6, p. 270
Ayala v. Philadelphia Board of Public Education, ch. 4, p. 142

Bethel School District No. 403 v. Fraser, ch. 7, p. 336

Bibby v. Phila. Coca Cola Bottling Co., ch. 6, p. 264
**Board of Education v. Earls, ch. 7, p. 348
Board of Educ. v. Pico, ch. 2, p. 51
Board of Educ. of Westside Community Schools v. Mergens, ch. 3, p. 69
**Board of Trustees v. Garrett, ch. 8, pp. 408, 419
*Boulahanis v. Board of Regents, ch. 8, p. 410
Brown v. Hot, Sexy and Safer Productions, Inc., ch. 3, p. 101
**Buckhannon Bd. and Care Home v. West Va. Dept. of Health and Human Resources, ch. 8, pp. 402, 420

Capital Square Review Board v. Pinette, ch. 3, p. 67
Cardiff v. Bismark Public School Dist., ch. 2, p. 54
Catholic H. S. Assn., Archdiocese of New York v. Culvert, ch. 9, p. 458
Cedar Rapids Community School Dist. v. Garrett, ch. 7, p. 326
**Chevron U.S.A. v. Echazabal, ch. 6, p. 230
City of Canton v. Harris, ch. 8, pp. 399–400
Committee for Public Education and Religious Liberty v. Nyquist, ch. 9, p. 403
Connick v. Myers, ch. 6, p. 203
Conover v. Board of Education of Nebo School District, ch. 1, p. 33
Curtis v. Oklahoma City Public Schools Board of Education, ch. 6, p. 240

Davis v. Monroe County Board of Educ., ch. 7, p. 360
Dawson v. East Side Union High School District, ch. 1, p. 29
Debra P. by Irene P. v. Turlington, ch. 7, p. 357
**Desert Palace, ch. 6, n. 120
*Doe v. Board of Educ., ch. 4, n. 109 ; ch. 8, p. 416
*Downs v. Los Angeles Un. School Dist., ch. 6, p. 244

Everson v. Board of Education, ch. 3, p. 66, ch. 9, p. 440

**Faragher v. City of Boca Raton, ch. 6, p. 263

**Gebser v. Lago Vista Ind. School Dist., ch. 7, pp. 319, 320; ch. 8, p. 391
**General Dynamics Land Systems Inc. v. Cline, ch. 6, n. 166
  Geraci v. St. Xavier High School, ch. 9, p. 462
  *Gernetzke v. Kenosha Un. School Dist., ch. 3, n. 28; ch. 8, p. 397
**Gonzaga Univ. v. Doe, ch. 8, p. 408
  Gonzales v. McEuen, ch. 7, p. 341
**Good News Club v. Milford Central School, ch. 3, p. 85
  Goss v. Lopez, ch. 6, p. 196; ch. 7, p. 287
  Grant v. Lake Oswego School District No. 7, ch. 4, p. 138
**Gratz v. Bollinger, ch. 7, n. 109
**Gruttinger v. Bollinger, ch. 7, n. 109

  *Hasenfus v. LaJeunesse, ch. 7, p. 233
  Hazelwood School District v. Kuhlmeier, ch. 7, p. 368
  Hoffman Plastics Compounds Inc. v. N.L.R.B., ch. 6, n. 169
  *Hooks v. Clark County School District, ch. 9, p. 482
  Hudson District Board of Educ. v. Rowley, ch. 7, p. 366

  *Jones v. State, ch. 7, p. 344

  *Kolstad v. Am. Dental Assn., ch. 8, n. 17
**Kyllo v. United States, ch. 6, n. 81; ch. 7, p. 306

  Lacks v. Ferguson Reorganized School District R-2, ch. 6, pp. 206, 248
  Lamb's Chapel v. Center Moriches Union Free School District, ch. 3, p. 70
**Lawrence v. Garner, ch. 5, p. 176; ch. 7, n. 68
  Lee v. Weisman, ch. 3, p. 98
  Lemon v. Kurtzman, ch. 3, p. 66; ch. 9, p. 439

  Mathews v. Eldridge, ch. 6, p. 147
  Milliken v. Bradley (Milliken I), ch. 7, p. 313
  Missouri v. Jenkins, ch. 7, p. 355

  Mitchell v. Helms, ch. 3, p. 66, ch. 9, p. 440
  Mueller v. Allen, ch. 9, n. 83

  National Labor Relations Board v. The Catholic Bishop of Chicago, ch. 9, p. 433
**Newdow v. U.S. Congress et al., ch. 3, p. 73
  New Jersey v. T.L.O., ch. 7, p. 302

  O'Connor v. Ortega, ch. 6, pp. 209, 251
**Oncale v. Sundowners Offshore Services Inc., ch. 6, p. 263
**Owasso Ind. School Dist., ch. 7, p. 310

  Pickering v. Board of Education, ch. 6, pp. 203, 204
  Plyler v. Doe, ch. 7, p. 166
  Poole v. Little Valley Central School District, ch. 5, p. 178

  *Riddick v. School Board, ch. 8, p. 416

  Salmon v. Dade County School Bd., ch. 6, p. 267
  Santa Fe Ind. School District v. Jane Doe, ch. 3, pp. 73, 91
  *Schroeder v. Hamilton School District, ch. 6, p. 258
  *Soper v. Hoben, ch. 4, p. 140
  Sutton v. United Air Lines, Inc., ch. 6, n. 143

  Taxman v. Board of Education, ch. 6, p. 256
  *Taylor v. Vermont Department of Education, ch. 7, p. 369
  Tinker v. Des Moines Ind. School Dist., ch. 7, p. 296
**Toyota Mfg. v. Williams, ch. 6, p. 229

  *U.S. v. Miami University, ch. 7, p. 353

  Vernonia School Dist. v. Acton, ch. 6, n. 83; ch. 7, p. 302

  *Walker v. District of Columbia, ch. 8, p. 413

**Zelman v. Simmons-Harris, ch. 9, p. 478
  Zobrest v. Catalina Foothills School District, ch. 9, p. 441

Part II: Significant Decisions in School Law

ABC League v. Mo. State High School Activities Association, ch. 2, n. 34

A.W. v. Jersey City Public Schools, ch. 8, n. 57

Abbott v. Burke, ch. 7, n. 168

Abood v. Detroit Board of Education, ch. 5, n. 91

Alfonso v. Fernandez, ch. 3, n. 50

Allegheny County v. Greater Pittsburgh American Civil Liberties Union, ch. 3, n. 25

Alston v. Virginia High School League, ch. 7, n. 132

Ambach v. Norwick, ch. 5, n. 15

American Civil Liberties Union v. Schundler, ch. 3, n. 26

Apicella v. Valley Forge Mil. Academy, ch. 4, n. 16

Arcadia School Dist. v. State Dept. of Educ., ch. 2, n. 61

Arkansas Activities Assn. v. Meyer, ch. 2, n. 38

Armijo by and through Chavez v. Wagon Mound Pub. Schools, ch. 7, n. 41; ch. 8, n. 44

Association of Catholic Teachers v. Pennsylvania Labor Relations Board, ch. 9, n. 30

Austin Ind. Sch. Dis. v. U.S., ch. 7, n. 154

B.C. v. Plumas, ch. 7, n. 79

Bacus v. Palo Verde Un. School Dist., ch. 3, nn. 6, 16

Bagley v. Raymond School Dept., ch. 9, n. 82

Bailey v. Truby, ch. 2, n. 39

Baldi v. Mt. Sinai School Dist., ch. 4, n. 133

Barth v. Board of Educ., ch. 4, n. 5

Basinger v. Pilarczyk, ch. 9, n. 57

Baumann v. West High School, ch. 3, n. 21

Bell v. New Jersey, ch. 3, n. 10

Bischoff v. Brothers of Sacred Heart, ch. 9, n. 28

Blaine v. Savannah Country Day School, ch. 9, n. 43

Board of Curators, Univ. of Missouri v. Horowitz, ch. 7, n. 8

Board of Educ. v. Allen, ch. 9, n. 76

Board of Educ., Hauppauge Union Free School District v. Ambach, ch. 9, n. 75

Board of Educ. of Jefferson County School Dist. v. Wilder, ch. 6, n. 56

Board of Educ. of Kiryas Joel Village School Dist. v. Grumet, ch. 3, n. 2

Board of Educ. of Oklahoma Public Schools v. Dowell, ch. 7, n. 106

Board of Trustees of Bastrop Ind. School Dist. v. Toungate, ch. 7, n. 67

Bob Jones University v. United States, ch. 9, n. 46

Bond v. Board of Educ. of the City of New York, ch. 8, n. 21

Boring v. The Buncombe County Board of Educ., ch. 6, n. 57

Bown v. Gwinnett County School Dist., ch. 3, n. 15

Brands v. Sheldon Comm'y School Dist., ch. 2, n. 36; ch. 7, n. 98

Branti v. Finkel, ch. 6, n. 71

Brantley v. Surles, ch. 6, n. 72

Brewer v. W. Irondequoit Central School District, ch. 7, n. 10

Bronx Household of Faith v. Community School Dist., ch. 3, n. 16

Brookhart v. Ill. State Board of Educ., ch. 2, n. 45

Brooks v. Logan, ch. 4, nn. 100, 125

Brown v. Board of Education (Brown II), ch. 8, p. 314

Brown v. Gilmore ch. 3, n. 15

Bryant v. City of Blackfoot, ch. 8, n. 3

Buckner v. School Board, ch. 5, n. 53

Burlington School Comm. v. Dept. of Education, ch. 7, n. 154

Bush v. Holmes, ch. 9, n. 81

Cantwell v. Connecticut, ch. 3, p. 64

Carter v. Raybuck, ch. 7, n. 72

Cathe v. Doddridge County Board of Education, ch. 1, n. 2

Catlin by Catlin v. Sobol, ch. 2, n. 43

Cefalu v. E. Baton Rouge Parish School Board, ch. 7, n. 160

Chicago Teachers Union v. Hudson, ch. 5, n. 91

Chipman v. Grant County School Dist., ch. 8, n. 39

Chittenden Town School Dist. v. Dept. of Education, ch. 9, n. 82

Christiansburg Garment Co. v. EEOC, ch. 8, n. 49

City of Madison Joint School District No. 8 v. Wisconsin, ch. 5, n. 93

Clayton v. Place, ch. 3, n. 36

Cleveland Board of Education v. Loudermill, ch. 6, n. 14

Clever v. Cherry Hill Twp. Bd. of Educ, ch. 3, n. 37

Cole v. Cleveland Bd. of Educ., ch. 3, n. 19

Cole v. Richardson, ch. 5, n. 16

Coleman v. Reed, ch. 6, n. 13

Committee for Public Education v. Regan, ch. 9, n. 65

Connel v. Higginbotham, ch. 5, n. 16

Corp. of Presiding Bishop v. Amos, ch. 9, n. 49

Covington v. Knox County Sch. System, ch. 8, n. 11

Crane v. Indian H. S. Athletic Assn., ch. 2, n. 35

Crim v. Board of Education, ch. 6, n. 9

Curtis v. School Committee, ch. 3, n. 5

D.R. v. Middle Bucks Area Vo-Tech School, ch. 7, n. 37

Dangler v. Yorktown Cent. Schools, ch. 7, n. 1

Daniels v. Williams, ch. 8, n. 36

Davis v. E. Baton Rouge Par. School Board, ch. 6, n. 36

DeBord v. Board of Educ, ch. 3, n. 15

DeShaney v. Winnebago County Department of Social Services, ch. 8, p. 293

Doe v. Beaumont I.S.D., ch. 8, n. 7

Doe v. Beaumont School District, ch. 3, n. 17

Doe v. DeKalb County School Dist. ch. 6, p. 231

Doe v. Duncanville Ind. School Dist., ch. 3, n. 17

Doe v. Pulaski, ch. 7, n. 42

Doe v. Taylor Ind. School Dist., ch. 8, n. 46

Dudley v. Augusta School Dept., ch. 6, n. 4

Duello v. Board of Regents, ch. 8, n. 16

Duffley v. N.H. Interscholastic Athletic Assn., ch. 7, n. 2

Durant v. Ind. School Dist., ch. 5, n. 41

E.E.O.C. v. Community Unity School District, ch. 6, n. 164

Edwards v. Aguillard, ch. 3, n. 42

Engel v. Vitale, ch. 3, n. 65

Epperson v. Arkansas, ch. 3, n. 41

Erie v. Tompkins, ch. 1, n. 39

Evans v. Buchanan, ch. 7, n. 102

Fairbairn v. Board of Educ., ch. 6, n. 96

Fellowship Baptist Church v. Benton, ch. 9, n. 10

Ferguson v. City of Phoenix, ch. 6, n. 139

Fiedler v. Marumsco Baptist Church, ch. 9, n. 42

Flast v. Cohen, ch. 1, n. 40

Florence County School District v. Carter, ch. 7, n. 155

Fogarty v. Boles, ch. 6, n. 55

Fowler v. Unified School District, ch. 6, n. 127; ch. 7, n. 163

Franklin v. Gwinnett County Public Schools, ch. 7, p. 320

Frazier v. Fairhaven School Committee, ch. 8, n. 5

Freeman v. Flake, ch. 7, n. 66

Freeman v. Pitts, ch. 7, n. 105

Garcia v. S.U.N.Y. Health Sciences Ctr., ch. 8, n. 57

Garufi v. School Board, ch. 4, n. 50

Georgia Association of Retarded Citizens v. McDaniel, ch. 7, n. 149

Gilbert v. Homar, ch. 6, n. 19

Girardier v. Webster College, ch. 9, n. 38

Givhan v. Western Line Consol. School District, ch. 5, n. 23, ch. 6, n. 43

H.M. v. Jefferson County Board of Education, ch. 6, n. 132; ch. 7, n. 125

Haines v. Metropolitan Government of Davidson County, ch. 6, n. 32; ch. 7, n. 125

Harlow v. Fitzgerald, ch. 8, p. 401

Hartman v. Loudoun County Bd. of Educ., ch. 7, n. 158

Healy v. James, ch. 7, n. 71

Hearn v. Board of Public Education, ch. 6, n. 86

Heilbig v. City of New York, ch. 4, n. 109

Herndon v. Chapel Hill Carbora City Board of Educ, ch. 2, n. 28

Hill v. Safford Unified School District, ch. 4, n. 49

Hills v. Scottsdale, ch. 3, n. 5

Hopwood v. State of Texas, ch. 7, n. 110

Horton v. Goose Creek Independent School District, ch. 7, n. 79

Hortonville Joint School District No. 1 v. Hortonville Educ. Assn., ch. 5, n. 118; ch. 6, n. 21

Immediato v. Rye Neck School Dist., ch. 2, n. 28

Ingraham v. Wright, ch. 4, p. 121; ch. 7, n. 7

Jackson v. Benson, ch. 9, n. 80

Jacobsen v. Tillman, ch. 6, n. 150

Jacobson v. Comm. of Massachusetts, ch. 2, n. 16

Jett v. Dallas Ind. Sch. Dist., ch. 7, n. 115; ch. 8, n. 4

Johnson v. Dallas Independent School District, ch. 8, n. 37

Johnson v. Transportation Agency, ch. 6, n. 99

John T. v. Delaware County, ch. 8, n. 50

Jones v. Board of Trustees, ch. 7, n. 9

Jones v. Latexo Independent School District, ch. 2, n. 44, ch. 7, n. 72

KDM v. Reedsport School District, ch. 7, n. 160

K.R. by M.R. v. Anderson Community School Corp., ch. 7, n. 160

Kadrmas v. Dickinson Public Schools, ch. 2, n. 51

Katruska v. Dept. of Education, ch. 6, n. 25

Keyes v. School District No. 1, Denver, ch. 7, n. 112

Khuans v. School District, ch. 6, n. 48

Kim v. State, ch. 9, n. 105

Kimel v. Florida Board of Regents, ch. 8, n. 51

Kincel v. Supt. of Marion County Schools, ch. 1, n. 41

Kindred v. Northome/Ind. School Dist., ch. 6, n. 112

King v. Board of Educ., ch. 5, n. 33

Kinman v. Omaha Public School District, ch. 6, n. 132; ch. 7, n. 125

Knox County Educ. Assn. v. Knox County Bd. of Educ., ch. 6, n. 82

Koenick v. Felton, ch. 3, n. 34

Koslow v. Pennsylvania, ch. 8, n. 57

Kotterman v. Killian, ch. 9, n. 84

Lake Ridge Academy v. Carney, ch. 9. n. 36
Lancaster v. Ind. School Dist., ch. 6, n. 6
Lanner v. Wimmer, ch. 3, n. 9
Larry P. v. Riles, ch. 7, n. 116
Lau v. Nichols, ch. 7, pp. 317–318
Lehnert v. Ferris Faculty Association, ch. 5, n. 76
Little v. Wuerle, ch. 9, n. 51
Loder v. Glendale, ch. 6, n. 82
Los Angeles v. Manhart, ch. 6, nn. 113, 162
Lybrook v. Members of Framingham Mun. School
    Board, ch. 6, n. 41
Lynch v. Donnelly, ch. 3, n. 22

Martinez v. Bynum, ch. 2, n. 10; ch. 7, n. 167
Martinez v. School Board, ch. 2, n. 17
Massachusetts Board of Retirement v. Murgia, ch. 6,
    n. 154
Matthews v. Eldridge, ch. 6, p. 197
Maynard v. Board of Education, ch. 4, nn. 47, 105
McCollum v. Board of Education, ch. 3, n. 39
McMackins v. Elk Grove Un. School Dist., ch. 6,
    n. 53
Meehan v Pachogue-Medored School, ch. 7, n. 147
Meek v. Pittenger, ch. 9, n. 78
Mendoza v. Borden, Inc., ch. 6, n. 116
Mercer v. Michigan State Board of Education, ch. 2,
    n. 29
Merriken v. Cressman, ch. 7, n. 85
Metzl v. Leininger, ch. 3, n. 34
**Middlesex County Sewerage Auth'y v. National
    Sea Clammers Assn.**, ch. 8, n. 2
Monell v. Department of Social Services, ch. 8,
    n. 35
Mississippi Univ. for Women v. Hogan, ch. 7, n. 124
Monteiro v. Tempe Un. H.S. District, ch. 7, n. 114
Morales v. Shannon, ch. 7, n. 116
Morton v. Community Unit School District, ch. 7,
    n. 160
**Mt. Healthy City School Dist. Board of Educ. v.
    Doyle**, ch. 4, n. 11; ch. 5, n. 49
Murphy v. United Parcel Service, ch. 6, n. 144
Murrell v. School District No.1, ch. 6, n. 132
Mustafa v. Clark County School District, ch. 6, n. 11
Myer v. Nebraska, ch. 9, n. 3

New York State Employee Rel'ns Bd. v. Christ the
    King Regional H.S., ch. 9, n. 30
Niederhuber v. Camden County Vocational
    Technical School District Board of Education,
    ch. 3, n. 32; ch. 6, n. 170
Null v. Board of Education, ch. 9, n. 91

Owen v. City of Independence, ch. 8, n. 38

Pace v. Bogalusa City Sch. Board, ch. 8, p. 404
Packer v. Board of Education of the Town of
    Thomason, ch. 1, n. 11
Parents United for Better Schools v. School District
    of Philadelphia, ch. 3, n. 50
Pasadena City Board of Education v. Spangler,
    ch. 7, n. 107
Patchogue-Medford Congress of Teachers v. Board
    of Education, ch. 6, n. 84
Peck v. Lansing School District, ch. 7, n. 160
Peck v. Upshur County Board of Trusts, ch. 3, n. 4
Perry v. Sindermann, ch. 6, n. 10
**Perry Education Assn. v. Perry Local Educators
    Assn.**, ch. 5, n. 93
Pfeiffer v. School Board, ch. 7, n. 140
Phair v. Montgomery County Public Schools, ch. 6,
    n. 158
Pierce v. Society of Sisters, ch. 9, n. 3
Price Waterhouse v. Hopkins, ch. 6, nn. 117, 119

Rankin v. McPherson, ch. 6, n. 46
Reeves v. Sanderson Plumbing, ch. 6, n. 156
Regents of University of California v. Bakke,
    ch. 7, n. 109
Rendell-Baker v. Kohn, ch. 9, n. 1
Rhodes v. Guarricino, ch. 7, n. 82
Ridgewood Board of Educ. v. N.E. for M.E., ch. 7,
    n. 148
Riles, Larry P., ch. 7, n. 116
Rodriguez v. Inglewood Un. School Dist., ch. 4, n. 5
Roemer v. Md. Pub. Works Board, ch. 9, n. 60
Romer v. Evans, ch. 6, n. 48
Roth v. Board of Regents, ch. 5, n. 57
Runyon v. McCrary, ch. 9, n. 48
Russman v. City of Watervliet, ch. 7, n. 160
Russo v. Central School Dist., ch. 3, n. 57
Rutan v. Republican Party of Illinois, ch. 6, n. 71

**San Antonio Independent School District v.
    Rodriguez**, ch. 7, n. 168
Sanchez v. Denver Public Schools, ch. 6, n. 156
Santosky v. Kremer, ch. 2, n. 8; ch. 9, n. 6
Saratoga Bible Training Inst. v. Schuylerville, ch. 3,
    n. 7
Schaill by Kross v. Tippecanoe County School
    Corp., ch. 6, n. 84
School Board of Nassau County v. Arline, ch. 6,
    n. 147
School District of Abington Twp. v. Schempp,
    ch. 3, n. 11
Sease v. School Dist. of Phila., ch. 3, n. 21
Seyfried v. Walton, ch. 7, n. 53
Sheff v. O'Neill, ch. 7, n. 103
Simonetti v. School District of Phila., ch. 4, n. 63

Sleesman v. State Board of Educ., ch. 2, n. 12

Sloan v. Lemon, ch. 9, n. 60

Smith v. Archbishop of St. Louis, ch. 9, p. 454

Smith v. Metropolitan School District of Perry Twp, ch. 6, n. 130

Smith v. Midland Brake, Inc., ch. 6, n. 153

So. Jersey Catholic School Teachers Assn. v. St. Teresa Church Elementary School, ch. 9, n. 33

Stansberry v. Argensbright, ch. 5, n. 170

State of Florida v. Whorley, ch. 7, n. 75

State of Ohio v. Whisner, ch. 9, n. 13

State v. Moorehead, ch. 9, n. 93

Stirer v. Bethlehem Area School Dist., ch. 2, n. 28

Stone v. Graham, ch. 3, n. 23

Strasburger v. Board of Educ., ch. 6, n. 34

Strout v. Albanese, ch. 9, n. 82

Sugarman v. Dougall, ch. 5, n. 15

Sullivan v. River Valley School Dist., ch. 6, n. 148

Swann v. Charlotte-Mecklenburg Board of Education, ch. 8, n. 314

Taylor v. White, ch. 6, nn. 121, 124

Textile Employees v. Immigration and Naturalization Service, ch. 8, n. 50

Thigpen v. Bibb County, ch. 6, n. 3; ch. 8, n. 15

Thomas Jefferson School Ins. v. Kapros, ch. 9, n. 37

Torcaso v. Watkins, ch. 3, n. 43

Travis v. Oswego-Apalachian School Dist., ch. 3, n. 8

Tuttle v. Arlington County School Board, ch. 7, n. 110

United States v. Virginia, ch 6, n. 3; ch. 7, n. 319

U.S.Trust Co. v. New Jersey, ch. 1, n. 20

Valley Forge Christian College v. Americans United for Separation of Church and State, ch. 9, n. 64

Virgil v. School Board, ch. 2, n. 3; ch. 7, n. 50

W.B. v. Matula, ch. 8, nn. 11, 15, 46

Wagenblast v. Odessa School Dist., ch. 4, n. 14

Walcott v. Lindenhurst Un. Free School Dist., ch. 4, n. 11

Walz v. Tax Commission, ch. 9, n. 66

Washington v. Davis, ch. 7, n. 113

West v. Derby Un. School Dist., ch. 7, n. 48

West Virginia Bd. of Educ. v. Barnette, ch. 3, p. 69

Wheeler v. Barrera, ch. 3, n. 10; ch. 9, n. 85

Whelan v. Roe, ch. 6, n. 88

Wisconsin v. Yoder, ch. 2, p. 40

Wolman v. Walter, ch. 9, n. 65

Wyke v. Polk County School Bd., ch. 4, n. 6

Zorach v. Clauson, ch. 3, p. 66

∞ GLOSSARY

This glossary lists legal terms that are commonly used to describe particular legal principles and proceedings. The first part lists phrases from Latin, Old French, and Early English which are still used in the law. The second part lists words and phrases that have peculiar legal meaning and usage.

Legal Phrases Drawn from Latin and French

Ab initio. From the beginning.

Ad valorem. To the value. The value basis of property for property tax purposes.

Amicus curiae. Friend of the court. Refers to a party who is permitted to file a brief and arguments with a court, though the "amicus" is not a party to the case.

Arguendo. For the sake of argument, assuming a contested fact for the purpose of analyzing the argument without admitting the truth of that fact.

Assumpsit. Literally, he or she undertook (promised). A form of lawsuit claiming breach of contract.

Bona fide. In good faith. Refers to action taken innocently and without notice of legal error or of other party rights.

Caveat. Beware. A warning to guard against a contingency or risk.

Certiorari. A petition to have a case certified for review by a higher court.

De facto. A situation arising from situational facts, but not required by law. A contrast to a *de jure* situation.

De jure. A situation derived from law; i.e., as founded in written laws or official action.

De minimis. A matter of minimal importance; insufficient to command judicial attention or relief.

De novo. Fresh proceeding anew, without reference to prior legal findings or proceedings.

Dicta. Court side remarks in a case opinion which are not deemed essential to the decision and therefore not legally binding.

Ejusdem generis. Of the same kind or class. A rule of statutory construction to read general words as limited to the kinds of matters that are specified in examples which follow those words.

En banc. By the full bench; a hearing and decision by all of the judges of a particular court rather than the usual decision by a smaller number of judges of the same court.

Et alii (et al.). And others.

Et sequentes (et seq.). And the following. Usually refers to pages that follow a referenced page of a case opinion.

Ex officio. The public official status that confers a right of the office holder to act in a particular proceeding.

Ex parte. Action by only one of potentially opposed parties, usually in a proceeding brought without notice to or participation by the adverse party.

Ex rel. Out of relation. Refers to proceeding instigated by or in the name of an official who brings an action on behalf of a private individual.

Ibidem (ibid.). In the same place. To cite a prior citation without repeating it.

Idem (id.). The very same. To cite a prior citation without repeating it.

In loco parentis. In the place of the parent.

In pari materia. On like subject matter.

In re. In the matter of; regarding.

Inclusio unius est exclusio alterius. A rule of construction to include only mentioned subjects and to exclude other matters.

Infra or Below. Refers to a later text or endnote.

Inter alia. Among other things.

Ipse dixit. The thing (or person) speaks for itself.

Ipso facto. By reason of the stated fact.

Mandamus. Literally, we command. A form of suit and court order to compel an official to perform a ministerial duty imposed by law.

Ministerial. A legal duty that does not allow for the use of official discretion to avoid it.

Modus operandi. The mode or method of operation.

Non obstante verdicto (N.O.V.). Notwithstanding the verdict. A judgment N.O.V. is one that overturns a jury verdict as being unsupported by fact or law.

Non sequitur (non seq.). It does not follow. A logical fallacy.

Nunc pro tunc. Now for then. A present ruling that applies to a past event.

Per curiam. By the court; usually an unsigned judicial opinion of the entire court.

Per se. By or of itself; not requiring further support.

Prima facie. At first impression. A sufficient case presentation which will stand unless defeated by a proven defense or rebuttal evidence.

Quantum meruit. The value of received goods or services, as the basis to award damages in order to avoid unjust enrichment.

Quasi. Nearly but not truly the same in law.

Ratio decidendi. The rationale or reason for a judicial decision.

Res ipsa loquitur. The thing speaks for itself. A legal rule to infer a conclusion from the nature of the subject matter.

Res judicata. Adjudicated matter that forecloses the litigating parties from relitigating the same claim.

Respondeat superior. Let the master answer [for the acts of his servant]. The basis for holding employers liable for the negligence of their employees.

Scienter. Knowledge (of operative facts).

Sine die. Without a fixed day. An indefinite adjournment without setting a future time for resumption of proceedings.

Stare decisis. Let the past decision stand. The basis of making case precedents binding on like later cases.

Sua sponte. Of one's own motion.

Subpoena. Court order to appear at a designated time and place.

Supra. Above, referring to preceding text or cases.

Ultra vires. An act beyond (in excess of) official authority, and therefore without legal effect.

Vel non. Or not.

Volenti non fit injuria. A volunteer may not claim injury, e.g., harm from the course of a gratuitous, volunteered action.

English Terminology Having Special Meaning in the Law

Abandonment. Knowing relinquishment of one's legal right to property or legal position.

Abatement. Reduction, suspension, or termination of a legal obligation or proceeding.

Abridge. To shorten. In constitutional law, to interfere with.

Abuse of discretion. Capricious exercise of administrative judgment or authority. A basis for reversal by a court.

Action (at law). A lawsuit.

Affidavit. A written declaration under oath.

Affirmative action. Intentional preference, usually of a disadvantaged person or minority group.

Agency shop. Situations in which nonunion employees are by law required to pay service fees to the union representative.

Appearance. A party's entry to a legal proceeding.

Appellant. A party who appeals a decision to a higher court.

Appellee. A party against whom an appeal is taken.

Arbitrator. A person chosen to resolve a dispute under rules of legal arbitration.

Assault. An offer or threat to inflict physical harm.

Assignment. A transfer.

Battery. Unlawful physical contact with the person of another.

Bond. A written promise containing guarantees or security to perform an obligation or debt.

Brief. Written argument presented by lawyers to a court.

Cause of action. A legal ground to institute a lawsuit and to obtain a legal remedy.

Class action. A suit brought by one or more claimants on behalf of a large class of individuals who allegedly share the same legal claim.

Cohabitation. A state of living together, often referring to extramarital relations.

Color of law. Under the appearance or aegis of legal authority.

Common law. Law developed by courts through their own case decisions, independently of written laws.

Complainant. See *plaintiff.*

Complaint. The written pleading of a claimant (plaintiff) setting forth the facts to support a legal claim.

Consideration. In contract law, the bargained-for value given in exchange for another's promise.

Contempt of court. Conduct that disobeys or interferes with a court order or proceeding.

Contract. A legally enforceable promise or set of promises.

Corporation. A fictional entity or party that is created by statute.

Counterclaim. A demand by a sued party (defendant) against the suing party (plaintiff).

Covenant. An agreement or promise.

Damages. Monetary compensation to redress a legal injury.

Defendant. The party against whom a legal proceeding is brought.

Delegation. The transfer of authority or power.

Demurrer. Objection that a pleading states no valid legal claim.

Deposition. Written testimony taken under oath at a location away from a formal court trial.

Directory. A legal instruction that is not obligatory (mandatory).

Discretion. The use of personal judgment and choice.

Duress. Unlawful coercion.

Emancipation. Legal release from a control status, such as a married child's freedom from parental control.

Eminent domain. The sovereign power of government to take private property for public use.

Enjoin. An order that a party forbear from or take specific action.

Estoppel. Doctrine that precludes a party from asserting or denying a fact or promise, regardless of its truth.

Excise. A tax on a privilege to engage in a specified transaction (e.g., to buy jewelry).

Executory. An incomplete transaction or interest.

Expunge. Delete completely, as from a court record.

Felony. A class of serious crime, as distinguished from lesser *petty* or *misdemeanor* offenses.

Fornication. Sexual intercourse between unmarried persons.

Forum. The court or place where an action is taken.

Grievance. A claim of injury. In collective bargaining a procedure to resolve disputes.

Holding. The precise limits of a court's decision.

Hung jury. A jury whose members cannot agree on a verdict.

Immunity. Exemption from legal obligations or liability, based on special status conferred by law.

Implied. Inferred; not expressed in language.

Infancy. The age below that of legal majority.

Invitee. A visitor by invitation, as distinguished from a trespasser.

Judgment. The final court disposition in a legal proceeding.

Jurisdiction. The lawful authority to manage or decide particular activities or disputes.

Latent defect. A defect not reasonably ascertainable by normal prudent observation.

Libel. An unprivileged defamatory publication.

Licensee. In tort law, a party permitted, but not invited, to enter school property.

Mandate. A legal command.

Ministerial. A directed, mechanical act that does not involve the addressee's choice or discretion.

Minority. Not of legal age.

Misdemeanor. See *felony.*

Mitigation of damages. Duty of an injured person to minimize losses caused by another's legal wrong.

Motion. A request for a court ruling.

Opinion. A court's report and explanation of its decision.

Petitioner. Party seeking relief by a trial or appeals court.

Plagiarism. Use and presentation of another's work, as one's own product.

Plaintiff. The party who brings a lawsuit.

Police power. The inherent power of government to promote public welfare.

Privilege. An advantage accorded by law to a particular class of persons.

Probative. Having evidentiary value.

Quorum. The required number of participants for a legally binding action or meeting.

Remand. A return of a case for further proceedings, usually from a higher to a lower legal tribunal.

Respondent. The party answering to a petition.

Restitution. The restoration of value received, in kind or money, to rectify a wrong to another party.

Review. Court reconsideration of a decision by a lower administrative agency or a lower court.

Slander. Defamation by oral communication, as distinguished from defamation by a writing (*libel*).

Syllabus. An abridged statement; of a court's decision which often precedes the full court opinion.

Tender. An offer.

Trespass. An unlawful interference with another's person or property; also a form of action to recover damages for such interference.

Unilateral. Action taken by one party only.

Venue. A place selected for a legal trial or proceeding.

Verdict. A jury finding.

Vested. Complete and fixed; not contingent.

Vicarious. In tort law, derivation of a right or obligation from the actions of an agent. See, e.g., *respondeat superior.*

Void. Without any legal force.

Voidable. Capable of being declared void under certain circumstances.

Waiver. A voluntary and knowing surrender of particular rights or immunities.

Writ. Official court order commanding a response from the addressee.

Zoning. Legislative restrictions on locality, uses, and construction of particular classes of real property.

A

Abandonment, teacher, 170
Abuse of discretion, 22, 23
Academic freedom, 205–7, 248–51
Academic penalties, 47–48, 288, 292
Academic standards, 48
Accommodation. *See* Disabilities; Religion
Administrative law, 10–15
    administrative structure of public
        education, 12–15
    judicial review of administrative decisions,
        19–23
    local school boards, 13–15
    local school districts, 13
    regional agencies, 13
    state-level agencies, 12
Admission standards
    age, 43
    charter schools, 448
    citizenship, 235, 329
    immunization and health requirements, 42
    residence, 42
Advertising in schools, 29–33, 298
Affirmative action. *See* Discrimination
Affirmative defenses, 118–20, 139, 456–57. *See*
    also Immunity under Section 1983
Age discrimination, 232–34, 270–72, 393,
    407, 438
AIDS, 43
Aliens. *See* Discrimination
Americans with Disabilities Act (ADA). *See*
    Discrimination
    remedies, 393
    state immunity, 404–6, 407
Amish children. *See* Attendance
Antidiscrimination laws, 7, 212–15. *See* Civil
    Rights—Statutes

Appearance regulations, 82, 207, 299
Arbitration. *See* Labor relations
Art, religious, 76
Associational rights, 46, 207, 300
Assumption of risk. *See* Torts
Athletics, 47, 127
Attendance, 40, 68, 429
Attorneys' fees, 320, 402–3, 420–21
Attractive nuisances, 123, 133–34, 457
Autonomy (decisional privacy), 212, 311,
    363–66

B

Bargainable matters. *See* Labor relations
Bargaining units. *See* Labor relations
Bible, the
    reading in public schools, 72–76, 85–90
    secular teaching of, 79
Bilingual education, 281 *n.* 177, 317,
    382 *n.* 119
Boards of education. *See* School boards; School
    districts
Bodily security, 292–93, 333–36, 400, 416–19
Body searches. *See* Searches
Books. *See* Textbooks and reading materials;
    Religion
Busing. *See* Transportation

C

Canine searches, 307
Case law, 15–27. *See also* Courts
    citations to, 25–27
Certification, teacher, 156–58
Charter schools, 444–49
    creation and legal status, 447–48
    funding, 449
    operational requirements, 448–49

Children with disabilities, 228–32, 324–29, 363–75
  home schooled children, 328, 482–85
  private school children, 328, 385 *n.* 160, 435, 437
  related services, 326, 366–69
  remedies for, 392–93, 413–15
  separated parents, 329, 369–75
Church institutions
  church uses of public school property, 83–84
  public school uses of churches, 83
Civil rights. *See* Discrimination
Civil Rights—Statutes. *See also* Discrimination
  Act of 1866 (42 U.S.C. Sec. 1981), 216–17, 394
  Age Discrimination in Employment Act (ACEA), 232–34, 393
  Americans with Disabilities Act (ADA), 228–29, 393
  Civil Rights Act of 1871 (42 U.S.C. Sec. 1983), 394–95
  Civil Rights Act of 1964 (Title VI), 390–92
  Civil Rights Act of 1999, 224
  Education Amendments of 1972 (Title IX), 225–26, 319–21, 390–92
  Equal Pay Act (EPA), 224–25
  Individuals with Disabilities Education Act (IDEA), 392
  Rehabilitation Act (Sec. 504), 228–29, 393
  Title VII, 215–16, 218–25, 313, 393
Classroom supervision. *See* Torts
Clubs and organizations, student, 46, 300–301
Collective bargaining. *See* Labor relations
"Color of law," under Section 1983 statute, 395, 400–401
Common law, 19
Comparable worth, 319–23, 410–12
Comparative negligence. *See* Torts
Compulsory attendance laws, 40, 429
Confidentiality. *See* Privacy rights
Conflicts of interest, 159, 180 *n.* 18
Constitution—United States, 7–8. *See also* First Amendment; Fourteenth Amendment; Fourth Amendment; Procedural due process; Substantive due process
  impairment of contracts, 13

  legislative authority under, 389–90
  in private schools, 428–30, 435–36
Constitutional rights, 9–10. *See* Discrimination; Due process; Freedom of speech; Religion; Searches
Constitutions, state, 7
  in private schools, 439, 444
Contracts
  private school students, 434–35, 462–65
  private school teachers, 432–34
  public school teachers. *See* Labor relations; Teachers
Contributory negligence. *See* Torts
Corporal punishment, 121–22, 288, 292
Counsel, right to, 199, 290
Courts, 15–16
  access to courts, 19–21
  federal Circuit Courts of Appeal, 17, 18, 25–26
  federal District Courts, 17, 26
  judicial review by, 19–23
  structure and jurisdiction, 16–19
"Creation science," 79
Crime, school, 5–6, 41, 125, 129–30, 140–42. *See also* Drug abuse; Drug testing
Critical speech. *See* Freedom of speech
Cross-examination, 199, 289–90
Curriculum, 44–45
  curriculum-related speech, 205–7, 248–51
  religious issues, 79–81

D

Decertification of teachers, 158. *See also* Teachers
De facto/de jure discrimination, 213
Defamation, 130–31, 456
Delegation doctrines, 11–12
Deliberate indifference liability, 398–400, 416–19
Demotions, 161–62
Desegregation, 313–16, 355–57
Directory/mandatory statutes, 22
Disabilities, 228–32, 324–29, 363–75
Discharge for cause. *See* Teachers, discharge of
Discipline. *See also* Procedural due process
  academic penalties, 47–48, 288, 292
  children with disabilities, 328–29

corporal punishment, 121–22, 288, 292
  in private schools, 435, 462–65
  suspension/expulsion, 287
Discretionary/ministerial functions, 12, 134–36
Discrimination. *See also* Civil Rights—Statutes;
    Private schools
  students
    alien children, 329
    disabilities. *See* Children with disabilities
    gender discrimination, 319–23, 410–12
    homosexual discrimination, 323
    language barriers, 317, 328 *n.* 19
    racial discrimination, 313–17, 355–57
    remedies for, 318
    testing and placement disparities, 316,
      357[60]
  teachers and other employees
    age, 232–34
    aliens, 235
    disabilities, 228–32
    gender discrimination, 217, 223, 224, 228,
      263–67
    language barriers, 236–37
    racial discrimination, 215–17, 256–58
Dispute resolution. *See* Labor relations
Dollar recovery caps, 137, 457
Dress codes, 82, 207, 299–300
Drug abuse, 6
  discharge for, 175
  out of school, 291–92
Drug testing, 210–11, 254–55, 307, 348–53
Dual enrollment, 83
Due process. *See* Procedural due process;
    Substantive due process
Duty of care requirement, 117
Duty to protect, 293, 333–36, 400

E
Educational malpractice, 131, 456
Employment discrimination. *See*
    Discrimination
Employment rights and duties. *See*
    Teachers
English-only requirements, 236–37, 317–18
Equal Access Act, 71, 296

Equal Education Opportunities Act (EEOA), 317
Equal Employment Opportunity Commission
    (EEOC), 236
Equal Pay Act (EPA), 224–25, 406, 437
Equal Protection Clause, 213–14
Equal Rights Statute (42 U.S.C. Sec. 1981),
    216–17, 394
Equitable relief, 19, 285, 312, 392
Equity law, 19
Establishment Clause, 64, 65–68. *See also*
    Religion *and related headings*
Evaluations and ratings. *See* Teachers
Evidence, right to present and confront, 199,
    289–90
Evolution, teaching of, 79
Exhaustion of administrative remedies,
    20–21, 392
Expressed powers, 11
Expulsion, 286
Extracurricular activities, 46–47
  drug testing, 348–53
  home schoolers, 451–52

F
Family Educational Rights and Privacy Act of
    1974 (FERPA), 309–11, 353–54, 369–70,
    372–75, 381 *n.* 90, 390, 408–10, 435
FAPE (free appropriate public education),
    325–26, 366–69
Federal aid statutes, 8–9
Federal courts. *See* Courts
Federal government, legal interests of, 7–8
Federal law, supremacy, 8, 72
Fees and charges, public schools, 49, 54–58
FERPA. *See* Family Educational Rights and
    Privacy Act of 1974
"Fighting words," 294
First aid, 129, 456
First Amendment, 64–69, 235, 429. *See also*
    Freedom of speech; Religion *and related
    headings*
Flag salutes, 41, 72–73, 82, 201, 299
Forum doctrines, 202
Fourteenth Amendment, 64, 104–5, 194–95,
    213–14. *See also* Procedural due process

Fourth Amendment, 208–11, 251–55, 301. *See also* Searches

Free appropriate public education (FAPE), 325–26, 366–69

Freedom of religion. *See* Religion *and related headings*

Freedom of speech. *See also* Religion
  in general, 68–69, 200–208, 293–301
  advertisements, 298–99
  associational freedom, 46, 207–8, 300–301
  book selection and removal, 45–46, 51–54
  classes of protected speech, 202–5
  critical speech, 298
  curriculum-related speech, 205–7, 248–51
  defamation, 131
  free speech zones, 202
  government speech, 202–3, 244–48
  harassing speech, 295–96
  offensive speech, 295–96, 336–38
  pedagogical concern speech, 296–98, 336–41
  personal concern speech, 203–5, 296–98
  political speech, 205, 298
  public concern speech, 203–5, 242–43
  public forum doctrines, 202
  student press, plays, and literature, 248–51, 298, 338–41
  symbolic expression, 207, 299–300
  time, place, and manner regulation, 202, 296
  unprotected speech, 201–2, 294–95, 344–48

Free Exercise Clause, 64, 65, 68, 235, 429. *See also* Religion *and related headings*

G

Gender. *See* Discrimination

Governmental immunity, 132–36, 141–42, 143–44
  discretionary *vs.* ministerial functions, 134–36
  Eleventh Amendment immunity, 237–38, 403–7
  nuisance exceptions, 133–34

Grading, 47–48
  peer grading, 310

Graduation ceremonies, 73–74, 75, 95–101

Graduation requirements, 45, 48, 357–60

Grievance disputes, 168–69. *See also* Labor relations

H

Hair styles, student, 300

Harassment
  racial, 316
  sexual, 219

Harmless error, 22

Health
  admission requirements, 42–43
  in employment, 158–59

Hearing record, 199–200, 270–90

HIV, 43

Holiday commemorations, 76–77

Home schooling, 328, 450–52, 482–85

Homeless Assistance Act of 1987, 42

Homicides, 129–30

Homosexual discrimination, 223–24, 226–28, 258–67, 323–24

Homosexuality, discharge for, 176–77

Hostile work environment. *See* Harassment

I

IDEA. *See* Individuals with Disabilities Education Act

Immunity under Section 1983, 400–402. *See also* Torts

Immunizations, 42–43, 82

Impartial tribunals, 198–99, 289, 341–44

Implied duties, 160

Implied powers, 11

In loco parentis privilege, 121

Incapacity, 174

Incompetence, 174

Indemnification statutes, 136

Individuals with Disabilities Education Act (IDEA), 291, 324–29
  Eleventh Amendment immunity defense, 407
  in home schooling, 328, 482–85
  in private schools, 328, 435, 437
  related services, 326, 366–69
  remedies, 392–93, 413–15

separated parents, 329, 369–75
Informational picketing, 169
Informational privacy, 211–12, 308–11, 353–54, 381 *n.* 90
  private schools, 435
  of separated parents, 310, 369–70, 372–75
Injunctions, 19
Instructional materials and equipment, 441–42, 470–77. *See also* Textbooks and reading materials
Insubordination, 174
Interdistrict racial segregation, 313–14
Interest disputes. *See* Labor relations
Interest groups, 4–5, 6–9
Interscholastic athletic associations, 47, 451
Invitees. *See* Torts

J
Judicial review of administrative decisions, 19–23
Jurisdiction, defined, 9
Just cause dismissals, 173–77

L
Laboratories. *See* Torts
Labor relations
  arbitration, 168–69, 178–79, 186 *n.* 109
  bargainable matters, 166–68, 184 *n.* 87
  bargaining units, 165–66, 183 *n.* 74
  dispute resolution, 168–70, 178–79, 186 *n.* 109
  interest disputes, 168
  management rights, 166–67
  mandatory bargaining, 166–67
  permissive bargaining, 166–67
  in private schools, 433–34, 458–61
Legal and equitable relief, 19, 285, 312
Legal citations, 23–27
Legal interests of participants, 6–9. *See* Standing to sue
Legislative delegation of authority, 11–12
Liability, 452–57
Libel. *See* Defamation
Liberty interests, 104–5, 195–96, 286
Libraries, 45–46, 51–54
Licensees, 123, 453

Linguistically disadvantaged minorities, 236–37, 317–18, 382 *n.* 119
Local school boards and districts. *See* School boards; School districts
Loyalty oaths, 159

M
Mainstreaming, 326–27
Malpractice, educational, 131, 456
Management rights. *See* Labor relations
Mandatory bargaining. *See* Labor relations
Mandatory statutes, 22
Mediation, 168
Medical care
  decisional privacy, 311–12, 363–66
  of disabled students, 326
  examinations, 210–11
Meditation, 72–76. *See also* Religion
Meetings, school board, 14–15, 33–35, 37 *n.* 35
Ministerial *vs.* discretionary functions, 134–36
Mixed-motive decisions, 201, 224

N
National Honor Society, 322
National Labor Relations Act (NLRA), 235, 433, 458–61. *See also* Labor relations
Native American children, 41
Negligence. *See* Torts
Negligent supervision. *See* Torts
Nepotism. *See* Conflicts of interest
Newspapers, school, 298, 338–41
Notice and hearing, right to, 197–98, 287–89
Notice of claim statutes. *See* Torts
Nuisances. *See* Torts

O
Off-campus activities, supervision of, 129
Offensive speech, 295–96, 336–38
Open meeting laws, 15, 37 *n.* 35
Order of release and recall, 172

P
Parents, 8, 310, 329, 369–75
Parochial schools. *See* Religious schools

Personal immunity. *See* Torts
Personal searches. *See* Searches
Physical education, 127, 138–40
Placement, 47–48
    mainstreaming, 326–27
    racial disparities, 316–17
Plays, 248–51, 298
Pledge of Allegiance, 41, 72–73, 82, 201, 299
Policy or custom. *See* Section 1983 actions
Political speech. *See* Freedom of speech
Poverty groups, 330
Prayer. *See* Religion
Pregnancy Discrimination Act, 219
Pregnant students, 311, 322
Prior restraints, 201
Privacy rights, 103–5. *See also* Informational
        privacy; Searches
Private schools, 428–44. *See also* Charter
        schools
    civil rights laws coverage, 435–38
    constitutional coverage, 428–30, 435–36, 462–63
    contracts, 462–65
    disabled students, 328, 385 *n.* 160, 435, 437
    government aid to, 438–44
        instructional materials, 441–42, 470–77
        remedial services, 442, 465–70
        tuition assistance, 442–43, 478–82
    state approval requirements, 430–32
    student rights and duties, 434–35, 462–65
    teacher rights and duties, 432–34, 458–61
    tort liability, 452–57
Privileged conduct, 119, 121–22
Procedural due process, 105
    athletics, 47
    as to employees, 195–200; students, 286–91,
        341–44
    hearing notice, record and appeal, 197–200,
        287–90
    impartial tribunal, 198–99, 289, 341–44
    prehearing terminations and suspensions, 198
    in private schools, 462–63
    protected interests, 195–96, 286
    right to counsel, 199, 290
    right to present and confront evidence, 199,
        289–90

statutory procedures, 291
Profanity, 177, 248–51
Professional employees. *See* Teachers
Promotion, 47–48
Property interests, 163, 164, 196, 243, 286
Property searches, 209–10, 251–54, 308
Proprietary functions, 134
Protection, duty of, 293, 333–36, 400
Proximate cause. *See* Torts
Public education, legal structure, 12–15
Public forum doctrines, 202
Public records, 15, 33–35
Public schools. *See also* Religion
    church uses of property, 83–84
    community uses of facilities, 69–71, 85–90
    constitutional provisions on religion, 64–69,
        71–72
    curriculum, 44–45, 79–81
    desegregation, 313–16, 355–57
    dress codes, 82, 207, 299–300
    extracurricular activities, 46–47, 49, 451–52
    fees and charges, 49, 54–58
    graduation ceremonies, 73–74, 75, 95–101
    home schoolers, 451–52
    immunizations, 42–43, 82
    religion-related courses and programs,
        79–81
    school assignments, 43
    services to church-school students, 82–83
    sports events, 72–73, 91–94
    textbooks and reading materials,
        45–46, 81
    transportation, 48–49, 61 *n.* 50
    use of church property by, 83
Punishment. *See* Discipline
Punitive damages, 388, 391
Pupil Protection Rights Amendment, 309

Q
Questionnaires, student, 308–9
Quorum, 14

R
Racial and ethnic discrimination. *See also*
    Discrimination

in private schools, 436–37
Ratification, 22–23
Rational treatment, right to, 291–92
Records. *See also* Family Educational Rights
    and Privacy Act of 1974 (FERPA)
    employee records, privacy, 211–12
    noncustodial parent rights, 310, 369–70,
        372–75
    private school records, 435
    public records, 15, 33–35
    student records, 309–11, 353–54, 390, 408–10
Reductions in force (RIF), 171–72
Regional education agencies, 13
Regulations, citations to, 24–25
Rehabilitation Act of 1973, 228, 324, 393, 407,
    413–15
    private schools, 435, 438
Related services, to disabled students, 326,
    366–69
Religion. *See also* Public schools
    compulsory attendance laws, 40–41, 429
    definition of, 110 *n.* 1
    dress codes, 82
    graduation ceremonies, 73–74, 75, 95–101
    holiday commemorations, 76–77
    immunizations, 42–43, 82
    prayer, meditation, and Bible reading, 72–76
    religious discrimination, 78, 235–36
    religious Freedom Restoration Act of 1993, 68
    school excusals, 77–78
    sex education, 79–81, 101–7
    sports events, 72–73, 91–94
    state law constraints, 71–72
Religious schools
    government aid to religious schools, 439–43
      instructional materials, 441–42, 470–77
      remedial services, 442, 465–70
      tuition assistance, 442–43, 478–82
    teacher contracts in, 433–34, 458–61
Remedies. *See also* Section 1983 actions
    attorneys' fees, 392, 402–3, 420–21
    for: constitutional violations, 389;
        discrimination, 388–90
    employment discrimination statutes, 391, 393
    Equal Rights Statute, 394

    equitable *vs.* legal relief, 19, 285, 312
    federal aid statutes, 226, 390–93, 410–15
    informational privacy, 390, 408–10
    wrongful discharge, 177
Representation disputes. *See* Labor Relations
Residency
    admission to school, 42
    employment eligibility, 158
Resignation, 170–71
Respondeat superior, 120–21, 453

S
Safe school acts, 6, 36 *n.* 1
Safety, child, 5–6, 41
School assignments
    staff, 159–60
    students, 43
School boards, 13–15
    meetings, 14–15, 33–35, 37 *n.* 35
School districts, 13
    immunity, 132–36, 141–42, 143–44
    policy or custom of, 396–99
    vicarious liability, 120–21
School grounds, supervision of, 125–26
School newspapers, 298, 338–41
School searches. *See* Searches
School-sponsored speech, 296–97, 336–41
Searches, 208–11
    body searches, 210–11, 254–55, 302–7, 348–53
    property searches, 209–10, 251–54, 308
    school searches, 208–9, 301–7
Section 504. *See* Rehabilitation Act of 1973
Section 1981 (Equal Rights Statute), 217, 394
Section 1983 actions, 389, 394–98, 414–15,
    416–19
    defenses, 398–402
Segregation, interdistrict, 313–14
Self-defense, corporal punishment, 122
Seniority, 172
Sex discrimination, 217, 223, 224, 228, 263–67,
    319–23, 410–12
Sex education, 45, 79–81, 101–7
Sexual abuse, 292, 320, 391, 416–19
    discharge for, 176
    tort liability for, 134–35, 140–42

Sexual harassment, 217, 223, 224, 228, 263–67, 319–23, 410–12
Sexual misconduct, discharge for, 176–77
Sexual orientation. *See* Homosexual discrimination
Shared time programs, 83
Shop facilities, supervision of, 127–28
Slander. *See* Defamation
Sovereign immunity, 132. *See also* Torts
Spatial privacy. *See* Searches
Special education. *See* Individuals with Disabilities Education Act (IDEA)
Special relationship theory, 293, 400
Spending power, 389–90
Standards, academic, 48
Standing to sue, 7–9, 20
Stare decisis, 19
State action, 47, 213
    in private schools, 428–29, 435–36, 462–63
State courts, 17, 19
State laws, 10, 24–25. *See also* Employment rights and duties
State-level education agencies, 12
States, legal interests of, 7
Statutes of limitations, 137
Statutory law, 10
Strict scrutiny, 213
Strikes, 168, 169–70
Strip searches, 302–6, 307
Students. *See also* Children with disabilities; Discipline; Discrimination; Freedom of speech; Private Schools; Procedural due process; Religion; Searches; Torts
Subject matter jurisdiction, 16
Substantive due process, 64, 103–4, 243
    right to bodily security, 292–93, 333–36, 400, 416–19
    right to rational treatment, 291–92
Suicides, student, 129–30, 135–36, 293, 333–36
Supervision. *See* Torts
Supremacy Clause, 8, 72
Supreme Court, United States, 17, 25, 64–65
Suspect classifications, 213–14
Suspension and termination. *See* Discipline; Teachers

T
Tax relief for private schools, 442–43
Teachers. *See also* Discrimination; Freedom of speech; Procedural due process
  discharge of
    for cause—generally, 173–77
    dishonesty, 175
    immorality, 175–77
    incapacity, 174
    incompetence, 174
    insubordination, 174
    reductions in force, 171–72
    unprofessional conduct, 174–75
    wrongful discharge, remedies, 177–79
  employment rights and duties
    certification and decertification, 156–58
    citizenship, 159, 234–35
    conflicts of interest, 159, 180 *n.* 18
    demotions, 160–61
    health, 158–59
    implied duties, 160
    nonrenewal of contracts, 162–63
    private schools, 432–34
    residence, 158
    resignation and abandonment, 170–71
  rights of privacy, 208–12, 251–55
Tenure, 163–65, 172
Territorial jurisdiction, 16
Testing, racial disparities in, 316–17, 357–60
Textbooks and reading materials, 45–46, 51–58
Threats, 294–95, 344–48
Title VI. *See* Civil Rights—Statutes
Title VII. *See* Civil Rights—Statutes
    Eleventh Amendment defense, 407
    mixed-motive decisions, 224
Title IX. *See* Civil Rights—Statutes
    remedies, 226, 390–91, 410–12
Torts
    affirmative defenses, 118–20, 139, 456–57
    assumption of risk, 119, 456
    causation, 118, 129–30, 399–400
    charitable immunity, 456–57
    comparative negligence, 119–20
    contributory negligence, 119–20, 121, 139, 456
    corporal punishment, 121–22, 288

defamation, 130–31, 456
dollar caps, 137, 457
duty of care
duty to supervise, 140–42
  educational malpractice, 131, 456
  general principles, 116–21
  immunity, 132–36, 141–44, 456–57
  invitees, 123, 453
  negligent supervision, 124–30, 140–42,
      453–56
    athletics and physical education, 127,
        138–40
    classrooms and corridors, 126–27
    laboratory and shop facilities, 127–28
    notice of claim statutes, 136–37
    nuisances, 123, 133–34, 457
    off-campus activities, 129
    premises liability, 123–24, 452–53
    privileged conduct, 119, 121–22
    school grounds, 125–26
    student suicides, 129–30, 135–36
    student transportation, 128
  in private schools, 452–57
  proximate cause, 118, 129–30, 399–400
  release and waivers of tort claims, 120
    statutes of limitations, 137
    vicarious liability, 120–21, 453

Transfers, staff, 161–62
Transportation
  private schools, 440–41
  public schools, 48–49, 61 *n.* 50
Trespassers, 123–24, 453
Tuition aid, 434, 442–43, 478–82

U
Ultra vires actions, 11
Unions. *See* Labor relations
Unprofessional conduct, discharge for,
    174–75

V
Viewpoint neutrality, 203
Violence, 5–6, 125, 129–30, 140–42
  threats of, 294–95, 344–48
Vouchers, 442–43, 478–82
Vulgar language, 177, 248–51

W
Wage discrimination, 224–25, 406, 437
Weapons in schools, 6
Witnesses, 199, 289–90

Z
Zoning regulations, 431–32